Communication Networks for Manufacturing

Juan R. Pimentel
GMI Engineering & Management Institute
Flint, Michigan

Prentice Hall, Englewood Cliffs, New Jersey 07632

Library of Congress Cataloging-in-Publication Data

PIMENTEL, JUAN R.
   Communication networks for manufacturing / Juan R. Pimentel.
     p. cm.
   Bibliography: p.
   Includes index.
   ISBN 0-13-154402-0
    1. Computer integrated manufacturing systems. 2. Local area
networks (Computer networks) 3. Manufacturing Automation Protocol.
   I. Title.
TS155.6.P56 1989
670.42'7—dc 19
                                                                    88-27533
                                                                             CIP

Editorial/production supervision
and interior design: *Jean Lapidus*
Cover design: *Wanda Lubelska Design*
Manufacturing buyer: *Ray Sintel*

© 1990 by Prentice-Hall, Inc.
A Division of Simon & Schuster
Englewood Cliffs, New Jersey 07632

This book can be made available to businesses
and organizations at a special discount when
ordered in large quantities. For more information
contact:

Prentice-Hall, Inc.
Special Sales and Markets
College Division
Englewood Cliffs, N.J. 07632

All rights reserved. No part of this book may be
reproduced, in any form or by any means,
without permission in writing from the publisher.

Printed in the United States of America

10 9 8 7 6 5 4 3 2 1

ISBN 0-13-154402-0

PRENTICE-HALL INTERNATIONAL (UK) LIMITED, *London*
PRENTICE-HALL OF AUSTRALIA PTY. LIMITED, *Sydney*
PRENTICE-HALL CANADA INC., *Toronto*
PRENTICE-HALL HISPANOAMERICANA, S.A., *Mexico*
PRENTICE-HALL OF INDIA PRIVATE LIMITED, *New Delhi*
PRENTICE-HALL OF JAPAN, INC., *Tokyo*
SIMON & SCHUSTER ASIA PTE. LTD., *Singapore*
EDITORA PRENTICE-HALL DO BRASIL, LTDA., *Rio de Janeiro*

To my wife, Melissa,

my parents, Ricardo and Consuelo,

and to the memory of my grandparents

Contents

Foreword   *xv*

Preface   *xvii*

Acknowledgments   *xx*

1   Introduction to Local Area Networks   *1*

    1.1   History of Computer Networks   1

    1.2   Elements of Computer Communication Networks   4

    1.3   Network Classification   6

         1.3.1   Message Transfer-Based Classification, 6
         1.3.2   Distance-Based Classification, 11

    1.4   Local Area Networks   12

         1.4.1   LAN Topologies, 13

    1.5   Local Area Network Applications   16

         1.5.1   Automated Manufacturing Applications, 18

    1.6   The OSI Reference Model   19

1.7 Outline of the Rest of the Book   23

Summary   24

Problems   25

PART 1   27

2 Background for the OSI Lower Layers   27

2.1 Signal Transmission   27

2.2 Signals   29

2.2.1 Fourier Series and Fourier Transforms, 32

2.3 Transmission Channel   43

2.3.1 Transmission Lines, 44 / 2.3.2 Channel Characterization, 52 / 2.3.3 Noise, 55 / 2.3.4 Optical Fibers, 57

2.4 Introduction to the OSI Reference Model   64

2.5 The Elements of the OSI Architecture   66

2.5.1 Systems, Communication Requirements, and Functions, 66 / 2.5.2 Layers and Entities, 67 / 2.5.3 Services and Service Access Points, 68 / 2.5.4 Functions and Protocols, 69 / 2.5.5 Naming, 69 / 2.5.6 Issues Common to All Layers, 70

2.6 Virtual Circuits and Datagrams   71

2.6.1 Virtual Circuits or Connection-Oriented Communications, 71 / 2.6.2 Datagrams or Connectionless Communications, 73

2.7 The Seven-Layer OSI Reference Model   75

2.8 OSI Services and Protocols   76

2.8.1 The Concept of Service, 76 / 2.8.2 Layers, 77 / 2.8.3 Protocols, 77 / 2.8.4 Interfaces, 78 / 2.8.5 Information Units, 79

2.9 OSI Service Conventions   79

2.10 OSI Model Extensions   83

Summary   83

Problems   85

3 The Physical Layer   88

3.1 Functions of the Physical Layer   88

3.2 Digital Transmission   90

3.3   Data Encoding   92

    3.3.1   On-Off Signaling, 94   /   3.3.2   Polar Signaling, 95   /
    3.3.3   Bipolar Signaling, 96   /   3.3.4   Duobinary Signaling, 97   /
    3.3.5   Manchester (Split-Phase) Signaling, 97

3.4   Intersymbol Interference   100

    3.4.1   Nyquist's First Criterion for Zero ISI, 101   /
    3.4.2   Nyquist's Second Criterion for ISI, 102

3.5   Scrambling   104

3.6   Baseband Communications   106

3.7   Wideband (Broadband) Communications   109

    3.7.1   Time Division Multiplexing (TDM), 109   /
    3.7.2   Frequency Division Multiplexing (FDM), 112   /
    3.7.3   Broadband Communication Components, 115

3.8   Modulation   119

    3.8.1   Pulse Wave Modulation, 119   /   3.8.2   Continuous Wave Modulation, 119

3.9   Performance of Digital Modulation Systems   120

    3.9.1   Bandwidth Efficiency, 120   /   3.9.2   Bit Error Rate (BER), 125

3.10   IEEE 802.4 Physical Layer   128

    3.10.1   Services, 128   /   3.10.2   Physical Layer Description, 128

3.11   IEEE 802.3 Physical Layer   131

3.12   MAP Physical Layer   134

    3.12.1   TOP Physical Layer, 135

Summary   135

Problems   137

4   *The Data Link Layer*   *139*

4.1   Data Link Layer Functions   140

4.2   Synchronization at the Data Link Layer   140

    4.2.1   Protocol Classification, 143

4.3   Asynchronous Protocols   143

    4.3.1   Error Control, 143   /   4.3.2   Echo Checking, 143   /
    4.3.3   Flow Control (X-on/X-off), 144

4.4   Synchronous Protocols   144

    4.4.1   Error Control, 144   /   4.4.2   Sequence Numbers, 149   /
    4.4.3   Flow Control, 150

4.5   Link Connection Management   150

4.6   Medium Access Control   151

4.7   Classification of Access Schemes   156

    4.7.1   Communication Phase-Based Classification, 156   /
    4.7.2   Channel Assignment-Based Classification, 160

4.8   Token Bus   161

4.9   Random Access Schemes   171

    4.9.1   The ALOHA Random Access Scheme, 172   /   4.9.2   Slotted ALOHA, 172   /   4.9.3   Carrier Sense Multiple Access (CSMA), 173   /   4.9.4   Carrier Sense Multiple Access with Collision Detection (CSMA/CD), 177   /   4.9.5   Deterministic CSMA/CD, 180

4.10   Token Ring Protocol   183

    4.10.1   IEEE 802.5 Token Ring Protocol, 184

4.11   Error Detection and Correction Codes   187

4.12   IEEE 802.2 Logical Link Control (LLC)   196

    4.12.1   Services Provided by the LLC Sublayer, 197   /
    4.12.2   LLC Protocol Operation, 199   /   4.12.3   Classes of LLC, 201

4.13   IEEE 802.4 Medium Access Control (MAC) Sublayer   202

4.14   IEEE 802.3 Medium Access Control (MAC) Sublayer   203

4.15   MAP Data Link Layer   204

    4.15.1   Logical Link Control (LLC) Sublayer, 205   /
    4.15.2   Medium Access Control (MAC) Sublayer, 206   /
    4.15.3   TOP Data Link Layer, 207

Summary   207

Problems   209

5   The Network Layer   *211*

5.1   Network Layer Functions   211

5.2   Naming, Addressing, and Routing   214

    5.2.1   Classification of Routing Algorithms, 216

5.3 Fixed Routing Schemes 219

5.4 Dynamic Routing Schemes 221

5.5 Network Congestion 223

    5.5.1 Flow Control Techniques, 224 / 5.5.2 Routing Techniques, 229

5.6 Deadlocks 230

5.7 Network Interconnection 233

5.8 The ISO Network Layer Standard Protocol 239

    5.8.1 The OSI Network Service, 239 / 5.8.2 ISO Network Layer Architecture, 242

5.9 MAP Network Layer 244

    5.9.1 TOP Network Layer, 246

Summary 246

Problems 248

6 *The Transport Layer* **250**

6.1 Transport Layer Functions 250

    6.1.1 Transport Layer Services, 252

6.2 A Transport Layer Model 254

    6.2.1 Use of Network Services, 256

6.3 Transport Layer Protocol Issues 258

    6.3.1 Addressing, 258 / 6.3.2 Multiplexing, 259 / 6.3.3 Flow and Error Control, 260 / 6.3.4 Information Units, 263 / 6.3.5 Protocol Operation, 264 / 6.3.6 Protocol Specification, 265

6.4 ISO Transport Layer 265

    6.4.1 Class 4 Transport Services, 268 / 6.4.2 Class 4 Transport Protocol, 271

6.5 MAP Transport Layer 276

    6.5.1 TOP Transport Layer, 277

Summary 277

Problems 278

PART 2 — 280

7 Background for the OSI Upper Layers — 280

7.1 Introduction to Operating Systems   280

    7.1.1 Generation of Operating Systems, 281 / 7.1.2 Processes or Tasks, 282

7.2 Process Concepts   283

    7.2.1 Process States, 285 / 7.2.2 Operations on Processes, 286 / 7.2.3 Critical Sections and Mutual Exclusion, 287

7.3 Scheduling Techniques   290

    7.3.1 Scheduling Criteria, 291 / 7.3.2 Priorities, 292

7.4 Introduction to Distributed Systems   294

    7.4.1 Closely Coupled and Loosely Coupled Distributed Systems, 296 / 7.4.2 Synchronization, 297 / 7.4.3 Solutions to the Synchronization Problem, 301

Summary   305

Problems   306

8 The Session Layer — 309

8.1 Session Layer Functions   309

8.2 Distributed Systems Issues   312

8.3 Session Protocol Issues   314

    8.3.1 Data Transfer, 314 / 8.3.2 Dialog Management, 315 / 8.3.3 Process Synchronization, 315

8.4 The ISO Session Layer   318

    8.4.1 ISO Session Layer Functional Units, 319 / 8.4.2 ISO Session Services, 321

8.5 MAP Session Layer   325

    8.5.1 TOP Session Layer, 326

Summary   327

Problems   328

9 The Presentation Layer — 329

9.1 Presentation Layer Functions   329

    9.1.1 Data Transformation Purposes, 330

9.2 Message Compression   331

9.2.1 *End User Encoding, 332* / 9.2.2 *Source Encoding, 333* / 9.2.3 *Fixed Length Encoding, 337* / 9.2.4 *Variable Length Encoding, 339*

9.3 Data Encryption   341

9.3.1 *Uses of Encryption, 342* / 9.3.2 *Key-Based Encryption, 343* / 9.3.3 *Data Encryption Standard (DES), 343* / 9.3.4 *Public Key Encryption, 343*

9.4 ISO Presentation Layer Protocol   345

9.4.1 *Overview of the ISO Presentation Services, 348*

9.5 MAP Presentation Layer   352

9.5.1 *TOP Presentation Layer, 352*

Summary   352

Problems   353

10 The Application Layer   356

10.1 Application Layer Functions   357

10.2 Application Layer Concepts   358

10.3 Association Control Service Element (ACSE)   363

10.3.1 *Overview of the Service Definition, 365*

10.4 The Manufacturing Message Specification   367

10.4.1 *A Multiple Robot Assembly System, 368* / 10.4.2 *Application Layer Functionality, 370* / 10.4.3 *Variable Access, 370* / 10.4.4 *Message Passing, 373* / 10.4.5 *Resource Sharing, 373* / 10.4.6 *Program Management, 378* / 10.4.7 *Event Management, 379* / 10.4.8 *Other Services, 381* / 10.4.9 *An Object Oriented View of MMS, 381*

10.5 File Transfer Access and Management   383

10.5.1 *File Systems, 384* / 10.5.2 *The Filestore Concept, 387* / 10.5.3 *Overview of the FTAM Services, 393*

10.6 Distributed Databases   395

10.6.1 *Review of Databases, 398* / 10.6.2 *Distributed Database Organization, 406* / 10.6.3 *Distributed Database Design, 409* / 10.6.4 *A Remote Database Access Standard, 411*

10.7 MAP Application Layer 413

Summary 414

Problems 415

PART 3 418

11 Introduction to Automated Manufacturing 418

11.1 What Is Automated Manufacturing? 419

11.2 Production Planning and Control 420

11.3 Elements of Automated Manufacturing Systems 421

11.4 Organization of Manufacturing Systems 426

11.5 Models for Automated Manufacturing Systems 431

11.5.1 Cell Control System Types, 437

11.6 Characteristics of Automated Manufacturing Systems 440

11.7 Design Considerations for Computer Controlled Systems 441

Summary 445

Problems 446

12 Network and Protocol Implementation 447

12.1 Characteristics of Hardware and Software Implementations 448

12.2 Design Considerations 449

12.3 Detailed Example: An ISO Session Layer Implementation 452

12.4 Design Optimization 457

12.5 Integrated Circuit Components 460

12.6 Board Level 467

12.7 Box Level: Intel's 310 Development Station 469

12.8 Software Components 470

12.9 MAPNET 472

Summary 479

Problems 480

13 LAN Design and Performance — 482

- 13.1 Performance-Based Network Design 483
- 13.2 User Classification 484
- 13.3 Network Performance Evaluation 487

    13.3.1 Analytical Models, 487 / 13.3.2 Simulation, 490 / 13.3.3 Measuremens, 491

- 13.4 Applications of LAN Performance Evaluation 491

    13.4.1 Performance Evaluation of MAP's Physical and Data Link Layers, 491

- 13.5 Performance Metrics 492

    13.5.1 Control Service Metrics, 493 / 13.5.2 Transmission Service Metrics, 494 / 13.5.3 Applications, 495

- 13.6 Queueing Theory Fundamentals 495

    13.6.1 Queueing Systems, 497 / 13.6.2 Little's Law, 498 / 13.6.3 Main Queueing Results (M/M/1 and M/G/1), 499

- 13.7 Token Bus Performance Analysis 502

    13.7.1 Average Cycle Time (T_c) Calculation, 503 / 13.7.2 Exhaustive, Gated, and Limited Service Types, 505

- 13.8 Performance of Random Access Protocols 505

    13.8.1 ALOHA, 506 / 13.8.2 Slotted ALOHA, 507 / 13.8.3 Carrier Sense Multiple Access (CSMA), 508 / 13.8.4 Carrier Sense Multiple Access with Collision Detection (CSMA/CD), 511

- 13.9 Network Performance 511

    13.9.1 MAC Sublayer Modeling, 512 / 13.9.2 Transport Layer Modeling, 514

Summary 515

Problems 517

14 Manufacturing Applications — 519

- 14.1 Networks in Manufacturing 519
- 14.2 Computer Networks and Hierarchical Control 525
- 14.3 The Network Design Problem 528
- 14.4 The Problem Solution 531

14.5   Sensor Level Network   532

14.6   Machine Level Network   542

14.7   Cell Level Network   546

14.8   Case Study: GMT400 System Architecture   548

14.9   Case Study: The Factory of the Future Project   552

Summary   558

Problems   560

Appendix A: ADA   **561**

Appendix B: Who's Who in Standards   **568**

Appendix C: MAP and TOP Architectures   **571**

Appendix D: ASN.1 with MMS Examples   **576**

References   **585**

Index   **593**

Foreword

MAP and TOP moved significantly toward becoming the data communications touchstone for the world when their 3.0 versions were demonstrated at the Enterprise Networking Event at Baltimore, Maryland, in June 1988. These data communications specifications, based on international standards, will undoubtedly be an essential element for computer and intelligent device based automation well into the twenty-first century.

Standards have impacted many areas over the years from automobiles to electricity to telephony. But what makes the MAP and TOP effort unique is the influence of *users* to establish the direction for development of standards based products that they would use.

In 1980, General Motors, among others, recognized the significant need for computer communication standards and decided to do something about it. A small group of engineers from seven GM divisions formed the MAP Task Force to pursue the International Organization for Standardization (ISO)–Open Systems Interconnection (OSI) seven-layer communication model. Shortly after, in 1982, a small GM staff group was formed to act as the nucleus of the worldwide effort which was to emerge. I was privileged to head that group. I firmly believed in the potential for "users" to help make standardized computer communications occur. So did others. Most didn't share my optimism about when it would occur, but I guess missionary zeal is a powerful tool.

Soon, in early 1984, the MAP Users Group (with the Society of Manufacturing Engineers as Secretariat) was formed. Then the first successful demonstration of MAP occurred at the 1984 National Computer Conference (with the capable help of the National Bureau of Standards and the Industrial Technology Institute of Ann Arbor, Michigan). Seven vendors participated in a GMsponsored booth. At Autofact '85, 21 vendors helped demonstrate MAP and TOP version 2.1. Shortly after, many companies began to implement MAP products. In 1986 the Technical and Office Protocol (TOP) Users Group was formed under the sponsorship of Boeing, and the effort became known as MAP/TOP. At about the same time it became an international Users Group. Today a World Federation of MAP/TOP users Groups exists which represents thousands of users. Other large organizations such as the Corporation for Open Systems and the European ESPRIT–SPAG–CCT have joined the movement. All these efforts are helping to move dozens of countries toward implementation of MAP/TOP version 3.0, the first practical OSI network.

However, a major impediment to succeeding in the utilization of MAP and TOP has been the delay in development of educational programs. Users and vendors must not only understand communication technology but they must know how to intelligently use this capability to install successful factory and office automation systems. There has been a remarkable lack of comprehensive training programs, college courses and understandable books to help gain this capability. Communication networks for manufacturing helps to close that gap.

After careful review by myself and others, I believe this book meets the criteria to become one of the best textbooks and references about MAP/TOP and its use in practical automation. It is very well written and is especially comprehensive and practical. And to my knowledge it is the first book to address communication and manufacturing network applications, the all-important link to what benefits MAP (and TOP) really provide.

I highly recommend this book as required reading to everyone (because ultimately this technology will permeate the world). This book provides an accurate portrayal of what MAP is (and isn't) and will be a valuable addition to anyone's repertoire. Dr. Pimentel has been closely involved with the MAP development and has had a close interaction with the MAP development team for several years. Thus, he is uniquely qualified to write about MAP and TOP. Several of Dr. Pimentel's former students have also participated in the development of MAP while others have been actively involved in designing MAP-based manufacturing systems at GM.

Michael Kaminski
Manager, Communications/MAP

Preface

Recently, there has been much interest in interconnecting computers and intelligent devices of various kinds. By intelligent devices we mean any device with some form of intelligence capable of sending or receiving information to or from other computers or intelligent devices. Examples of intelligent devices include personal computers, laser printers, file servers, some data terminals, and digital telephones. The emphasis in this book, however, is to consider devices used as components of modern manufacturing systems such as vision systems, robots, graphic stations, programmable logic controllers, numerically controlled machines, and others.

The reasons for the interest in multidevice interconnection are twofold: First, all intelligent devices of interest have some kind of embedded processor or computer whose prices are plummeting at unbelievable rates; second, applications such as manufacturing can benefit immensely from an interconnected system of main elements. The latter reason forms the foundation of modern manufacturing concepts such as computer integrated manufacturing (CIM).

There are several types of networks in existence. Probably the two best known are telecommunication and office automation. However, the class of networks considered in this book is relatively new and belongs to the class of manufacturing networks, which indicates that the networks are suitable for applications involving automated manufacturing. Although this is not a book on the Manufacturing Automation Protocol (MAP) and the Technical and Office Protocol (TOP), the MAP and TOP network architectures are used throughout the book as the primary examples for explaining the main concepts.

In the beginning, the interconnection of computers and intelligent devices was done in an ad hoc manner. Vendors had their own methods for interconnecting their devices. The problems that this situation posed were numerous, with perhaps the major one being the incompatibility of multivendor equipment.

There are two key elements to the solution of this problem. The first is to view a network as a collection of several layers with each layer performing well-defined communication functions, and the second is to have a few well-recognized standards applicable to each layer. By using the same communication standards, the problem of incompatibility of multivendor equipment can be solved. This book presents the fundamentals of multilayered networks suitable for manufacturing and introduces the concepts behind the most important standards in use or under development for each of the layers.

Accordingly, the objectives of this book are as follows:

- to provide the fundamentals of local area networks (LAN) suitable for manufacturing;
- to provide a brief introduction to automated manufacturing concepts;
- to present and discuss network applications in manufacturing; and
- to present and analyze the MAP and TOP network architectures through the use of examples and discussions throughout the book.

The reference model for computer communications developed by the International Organization for Standardization (ISO) is used as the framework within which all network material is presented. The reference model is also known as the open system interconnection (OSI) model and the rationale for its development is discussed in Chapter 1. The seven-layer ISO reference model is analyzed layer-by-layer along with appropriate international standards suitable for automated manufacturing.

The book is organized into three parts, each covering a major aspect of manufacturing networks. Part I deals with transmission systems, whose main function is the transfer of messages from a source to a destination station in a reliable manner, regardless of their location, the actual transmission method, or how the information transferred is to be used. Part II deals with the communication support provided by the network on behalf of end applications. Part II includes Chapters 7 through 10, which deal with a background chapter, the session, presentation, and application layers, respectively. Finally, Part III deals with the application of local area networks in automated manufacturing. Chapter 11 provides an introduction to automated manufacturing, and Chapter 12 covers the hardware and software implementation of network protocols. Issues regarding protocol and network performance are covered in Chapter 13, whereas LAN architectures for automated manufacturing are covered in Chapter 14.

Currently, writing anything about OSI protocols is difficult, since many of the concepts are still evolving. To minimize the chance that this book will be obsolete soon after publication, the book concentrates on the major concepts rather than the details of the protocols. Thus, the reader should not approach this book looking for protocol details, but rather for finding explanations for the principles used in the protocol standards.

This book is intended to be a textbook for advanced undergraduates or beginning graduate students in courses dealing with computer networks and/or automated manufacturing; and also as a reference book for practicing engineers. As a text, the book contains a synthesis of theoretical principles with careful explanations, examples, problems, and questions at the end of each chapter. Discussions of actual systems and up-to-date practical applications should be of interest to practicing engineers. Three types of courses can be offered based on this book: computer networks with emphasis on the lower layers, computer networks with emphasis on the upper layers, and communication aspects of automated manufacturing. The book can also be used for appropriate training seminars on related areas.

A great deal of effort has been placed on making the book self-contained. With the exception of Chapter 13, the only prerequisites are a course on computer organization (including hardware aspects) and another course on a structured high-level language such as Pascal or PL/I. Of course, equivalent practical experience is also appropriate. The prerequisite for understanding Chapter 13 is a course on probabilities including random processes. Although not prerequisites, the following background can be beneficial for understanding some portions of the book: digital communications, automatic controls, operating systems, and additional programming courses.

The following notation has been used to make the book more readable. Words in boldface indicate a definition or an important explanation regarding a concept or a term. One or more words in italics are used to indicate that the words should be treated collectively as a noun. No effort should be made to explain the meaning of individual words belonging to a group of words in italics. Words in italics are previously defined or are assumed to be part of the reader's background. In program segments, boldface is used for ADA's reserved words, whereas italics are used to indicate variable names, types, etc.

Flint, Michigan   *Juan R. Pimentel*

Acknowledgments

Many people and institutions have contributed to make this book a reality. I would like to thank M. Kaminsky from the General Motors Corporation for facilitating partial funding for undertaking this project. GMI Engineering & Management Institute provided adequate support and facilities for writing the book. I would like to thank B. Lichty and F. Cribbins from GMI for their support. Many individuals from the Advanced Engineering Staff of General Motors provided invaluable support. The individuals are too numerous to mention. In particular, I would like to thank G. Workman, P. Amanrath, R. Peterson, V. Narayanan, and H. W. Chen. The following individuals from other GM divisions also provided valuable information: S. Dana, R. Keil, and C. Groff. I have also benefited from discussions with the following individuals: J. Daigle, A. Weaver, K. Mills, P. D. Fisher, A. Jayasumana, H. K. Muralidhar, J. D. Decotignie, L. Ciminiera, S. Dillon and K. Watson. I would also like to thank my students at GMI who suffered by studying from early drafts of the book and for contributing with comments, ideas, examples, etc. In particular, the following students provided invaluable assistance: B. Mellish, B. Gornick, K. Domino, B. Seidle, and M. Huber. Special thanks go to A. DeLellis and J. Drummond for helping with my diction, and also to my brother Edgar for searching the literature to find appropriate information for the book.

Last but not least, I'd like to thank my wife Melissa for her help typing the manuscript and also for her patience, encouragement, and understanding during the long hours spent in front of the word processor, and my two young daughters, Cristina and Brittany. Cristina kept small children from entering Daddy's office, and Brittany somehow managed to miss the computer keyboard in her wanderings through the office.

1

Introduction to Local Area Networks

In this chapter we begin our study of *networks for manufacturing* by reviewing some history of computer networks. Essential network concepts and definitions are provided when discussing network elements followed by a classification of networks. We next concentrate on additional definitions, characteristics, and applications of local area networks. A telephone analogy with which most of us are familiar is then used to briefly introduce the OSI reference model in Section 1.6. A more detailed and formal introduction is given in Chapter 2. This chapter concludes with an outline of the remainder of the book.

Although several types of networks will be used in automated manufacturing, it is expected that local area networks will be the most common ones. Hence, the primary objective of this book is to study how local area networks are used in automated manufacturing applications.

1.1 HISTORY OF COMPUTER NETWORKS

One of the earliest computer communication network projects began in 1969 under the sponsorship of the Advanced Research Projects Agency (ARPA). The initial goal of the ARPA network (ARPANET) was to interconnect research centers supported by the ARPA community to achieve two objectives: to develop and test computer communication techniques, and to obtain the benefits of resource sharing for the ARPA community (Roberts et al., 1973). Initially, there were about 20 candidate centers, each with different computers, models, and operating systems. A sample of the various computer systems were IBM 360/65, PDP10, Univac 1108, Burroughs 6500, and the Illiac.

There were two established technologies that had an effect on computer networks prior to the development of the ARPANET: *time-sharing systems*[1] and *common carrier systems* (i.e., the telephone network). The ARPANET took advantage of these already established technologies by assuming that all centers had time-sharing facilities, and by incorporating the common carrier systems as components of the new communication network. The idea was to emulate a time-sharing dialog using the telephone network rather than the usual point-to-point direct connection between a terminal and a computer which was common in a time-sharing system.

A major difficulty was encountered because of the inadequacy of the telephone network for the communication task. There were three main problems: First, the telephone network introduced excessive errors in the transmission; second, a particular circuit could fail (i.e., it could break) causing a system failure; and third, the telephone network introduced excessive response time. What was needed was a message service whereby any computer could send a message to another computer and be sure it would be delivered promptly and correctly. As in a time-sharing interaction, it was also desired that each interactive dialog between two computers would have messages flowing back and forth.

To overcome the preceding three problems, the ARPANET introduced the following schemes: error detection and retransmissions, two physically separate paths to route each message to compensate for circuit failures, and the requirement that the end to end propagation delay be less than 0.5 sec. to achieve short response times. Three possible communication methods were considered: fully interconnected *point-to-point* leased lines, *line-switched* (dial-up) service, and *message switched* (store and forward service). The message switched method was chosen because of greater flexibility, higher effective bandwidth, and lower cost than the other two methods.

The message switched system introduced nodes at appropriate places in the network. Every node in the network has a switch or *store and forward* center, with few connections to other nodes; messages are thus routed from node to node until reaching their destination. The switching centers were based on small general-purpose computers called *Interface Message Processors* (IMP) for routing messages, for checking errors in the transmissions, and for providing asynchronous communications to main (Host) computers. The topology of the ARPANET is shown in Figure 1.1.

Parallel to the development of ARPANET, a similar development was taking place at the Univerity of Hawaii in the late 1960s, the ALOHA system. The goal of the ALOHA system was to provide another alternative for network system design, and to determine those situations in which radio communications are preferable to conventional wire communications (i.e., leased lines or dial-up telephone connections). In the beginning, computer communication systems made widespread use of wire communications. This is because dial-up telephones and leased lines were (and still are) widely available transmission systems using an existing and well-developed technology.

As developed initially, the ALOHA system is depicted in Figure 1.2. (Abramson, 1973). Two channels were assigned for data communication, one from the IMP to the remote stations and the other for data from the stations to the IMP. Message transmission from the central computer (host) to the consoles was straightforward, since the transmitter could be controlled to send messages ordered in a queue according to any given priority scheme. Messages from the remote stations to the IMP were not capable of being multiplexed in such a direct manner because the remote stations transmitted asynchronously.

Instead, a random access method was employed; one based on the assumption that the system

---

[1] Time-sharing systems are discussed in Section 7.1.

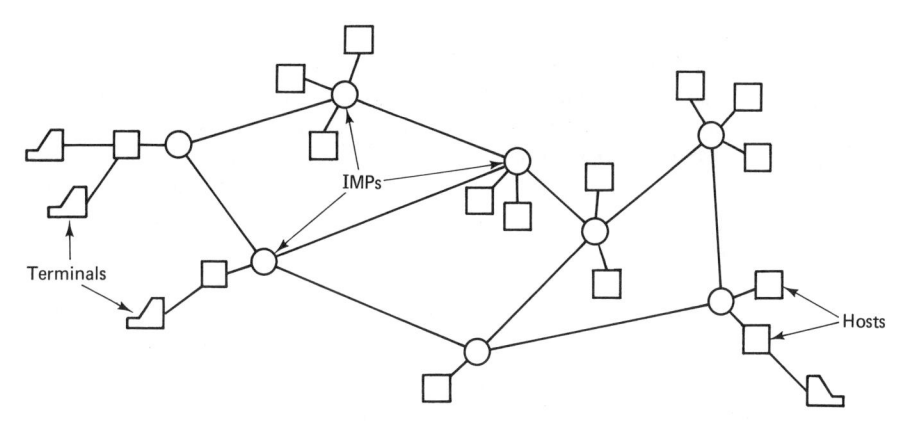

Figure 1.1 ARPANET Topology. Interface message processors (IMPs) are network nodes.

could detect errors in the message transmission. Nearly all errors were caused by interference with a message transmitted by another station. Stations transmitted to the central computer in a completely unsynchronized (from one station to another) manner. If a message was received without error, it was acknowledged by the IMP. After transmitting a packet the transmitting station waited a given amount of time for an acknowledgment; if none was received, the message was retransmitted automatically. The process was repeated until a successful transmission and acknowledgment occurred or three unsuccessful transmissions had been attempted. The ALOHA system was rather inefficient in its channel use. As shown in Section 13.8, the maximum utilization of the channel was only about 18 percent, whereas the slotted ALOHA which was later developed increased the channel utilization to about 37 percent.

Both the ARPANET and the ALOHA systems were developed to interconnect computers located far away from each other (long haul networks). Subsequent network development laid the foundation for the following network types: terrestrial, satellite, packet radio, and local (Kleinrock, 1982).

As noted earlier, the ARPANET belongs to the class of terrestrial networks. These networks

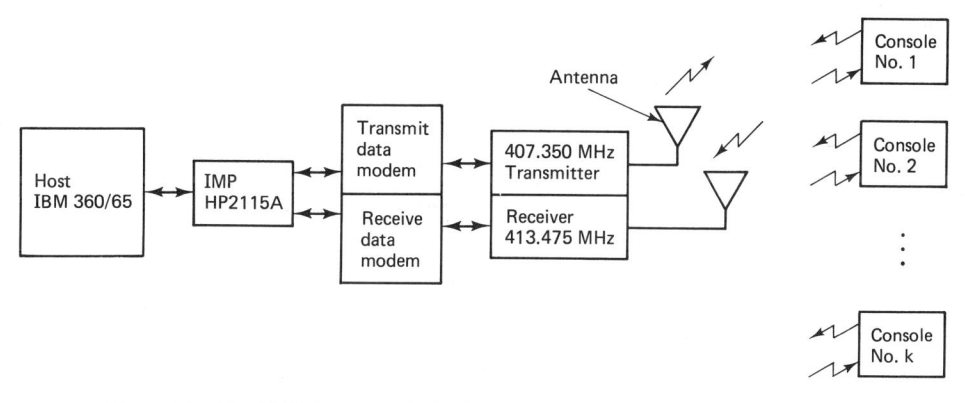

Figure 1.2 The ALOHA system. Transmitter and receiver frequencies are 407.350 MHz and 413.475 MHz respectively.

Sec. 1.1   History of Computer Networks

typically use wires for the interconnection of computers which could be dispersed in a wide geographical area. **Satellite networks** use free space and a satellite as the communication medium with a number of earth stations distributed over a large geographical region attempting to use the common medium. The satellite simply sends back to earth all that it receives, thus covering a large portion of the earth. **Packet radio networks** communicate via radio channels with communicating stations located in a relatively small geographical area (on the order of a few tens of kilometers). Local networks typically provide communication among devices within a building or within a collection of buildings.

The ALOHA system mentioned earlier led to the development of the carrier sense multiple access (CSMA) and carrier sense multiple access with collision detection (CSMA/CD) networks which are discussed in Section 4.9. Based on the experience provided by ARPANET and the ALOHA systems, research institutions as well as computer and data processing companies began experimenting with other communication techniques. The result was a proliferation of a number of schemes used for interconnecting computers. Among the most important communication systems developed were the System Network Architecture (SNA) by IBM, DECnet by DEC, and ETHERNET by Xerox.

A very difficult situation has resulted from the proliferation of different network interconnection techniques, protocols, and interfaces, that of network incompatibility. It is generally very difficult for two computers to communicate with one another if they are made by different manufacturers.

Latest developments in computer networks concentrate in three areas: *technology*, *standards*, and *internetworking*. Technological advances aim at designing very large scale integration (VLSI) circuits that implement one or several protocols in one single chip, using new communication media (e.g., fiber optics), designing better and faster interfaces with the communication medium, and other hardware developments. Chapter 12 is devoted entirely to technological advances in implementing network protocols.

Developments in communication protocol standards aim at solving the network incompatibility problem. Network and computer manufacturers, along with professional and user organizations, are working together to establish a common (standard) communication framework. Examples in the United States of this multiorganization effort are the Manufacturing Automation Protocol (MAP) and the Technical and Office Protocol (TOP), being developed by General Motors and Boeing with the cooperation of many other organizations. In Europe, a similar development known as the Computer Network for Manufacturing Applications (CNMA) project is taking place. MAP is a set of protocol *standards* which enables communication among computers and other *intelligent devices* interconnected by a LAN in *manufacturing environments*. Features of the MAP network architecture are used throughout this book to illustrate the main concepts.

Internetworking consists of interconnecting several networks to form a **catanet,** just as several computers are interconnected to form a network. For example, several local area networks can be interconnected by means of a satellite network. Section 5.8 discusses internetworking in detail.

1.2 ELEMENTS OF COMPUTER COMMUNICATION NETWORKS

Much interest has been placed on interconnecting many computers into a network. One reason for this interest is that it is cost-effective to provide users with their own computer instead of having the users bring their work to a single computer located centrally. Other reasons include the sharing of expensive resources (e.g., laser printers, backup storage, and complex programs), electronic mail, the development of distributed processing, sharing of databases, and others. Currently, much of the interest in computer networks is due to their importance in supporting automation in the office, laboratory, and factory environments. In this book, the term computer is used broadly when referring to a mainframe computer, minicomputer, or microcomputer.

A **computer communication network** is a system of interconnected computers and other devices capable of exchanging information. A generic network component (i.e., computer or device) is referred to as a network station or simply as a **station.** A station belonging to a network is capable of communicating with any other station in the same network. In other words, the network is supportive of *full connectivity*.

Some authors include data terminals, digital telephones, or video equipment as stations when defining a network. The criterion that we use to determine if a certain device can be a network station is that the device should have enough intelligence or be programmed to engage in a communication transaction in an autonomous fashion without the assistance of humans. For example, in a manufacturing environment an industrial robot can be considered a network station if it has the capability to receive and send messages to other stations autonomously. Accordingly, *intelligent devices* or *programmable devices* can be network stations.

In order for two stations (i.e., a sender and a receiver) to communicate with one another there must be a medium or transmission facility over which the transmission signals can flow. Transmission facilities sometimes place restrictions on the number and type of signals that can be transmitted. For example, twisted pair wires cannot support communications requiring very high data rates. If transmission facilities are to be general purpose, some communication devices are required to interface network stations with transmission facilities. However, two stations with a physical path between them (using a transmission facility) and with compatible communication devices (i.e., network interfaces) are not guaranteed to be able to communicate with each other. To begin with, both stations must be *ready* and *agree* to exchange information prior to any communication. Even after two stations are ready and have agreed to communicate, one station may tend to send data much faster than what the receiver station is able to handle. Thus, a set of rules or protocol is needed if successful communication is to take place.

A **transmission facility** is a general term used to describe any facility that carries data signals from one location to another. In general, transmission facilities include repeaters, modulators, amplifiers, filters, medium interfaces, and physical media. They can involve just one transmission medium or a combination of transmission media. Some examples of transmission media include twisted pair wires, coaxial cables, optical fibers, and free space (for electromagnetic wave signals). Some transmission facilities can be supplied by certain companies. For example, GTE Telenet and Tymnet are transmission facilities for computer communications available to users located in a wide geographical area.

Communication devices are used to interface network stations with transmission facilities. The interface function is varied because it depends on the nature of the stations, the transmission facility, and the protocols used. Typical interface functions are multiplexing, data encoding, modulation, data buffering, and switching. Accordingly, typical communication devices are multiplexers, encoders, modulators, concentrators, and switches. Depending upon variations in the preceding details, communication devices are referred to as **network interface units** (NIUs) or **bus interface units** (BIUs).

Communication protocols are essential to ensure efficient, correct, and smooth transfer of information among network stations. A few of the questions that protocols address are the following. How do stations begin and end a communication dialog? How does one keep a fast station from clobbering a slow station? How does a station get access to a shared communication medium? How do stations exchange messages? How do stations deal with transmission errors?

1.3 NETWORK CLASSIFICATION

Several criteria can be used to classify computer networks. Our approach in selecting suitable criteria is a practical and simple one. A criterion should not be based on many specific details but rather on major network characteristics. Two criteria are useful for a general network classification. One criterion is based on the distance between any two stations and the other is based on the method used for message transfer. Some authors consider other criteria, such as the multiplexing technique used, locality of network control, medium access control technique, and so on, for classifying networks. The disadvantage with this latter set of criteria is that one needs to be familiar with the preceding concepts for understanding the network classification. Chou (1983) gives a taxonomy for network classification based on 18 criteria.

1.3.1 Message Transfer-Based Classification

According to the method used for message transfer, there are the following network types (Chou, 1983): *broadcast*, *relaying*, and *switching* networks. The broadcast type uses a **direct** communication scheme whereas relaying and switching networks use an **indirect** communication scheme. *Direct* communications involve only two stations, the sender and the receiver; whereas *indirect* communications involve at least one intermediate station in addition to the sender and receiver.

In a **broadcast network,** several stations share a common communication channel. Messages are transmitted from a source station to a destination station via the shared communication channel without going through an intermediate station. Broadcast networks are very important since most local area networks are of this type. A major problem occurs involving multiple message interference when at least two stations attempt to send messages via the shared channel at about the same time. Thus, there must be some way to regulate access to the common medium so that stations do not interfere with one another. This problem is referred to as the **medium access control** problem. Several solutions are presented in Chapter 3. Figure 1.3 shows the major broadcast network topologies.

A **relaying network** has stations that interface with the communication medium forming a closed loop or ring. The path between a source station and a destination station may include intermediate stations. A message is relayed from one station to another until it reaches the destination. The only topology for relaying networks is a ring, as shown in Figure 1.4. The key to understanding

Bus
(a)

Satellite
(b)

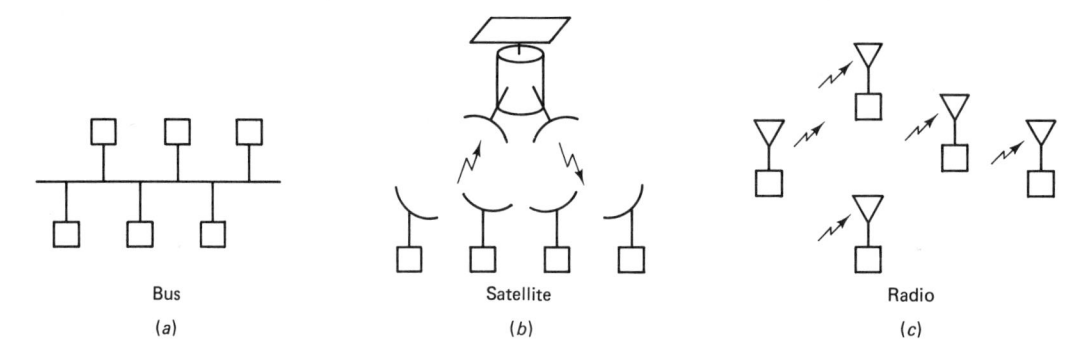

Radio
(c)

Figure 1.3 Topologies for broadcast networks: (a) Bus; (b) Satellite; (c) Radio.

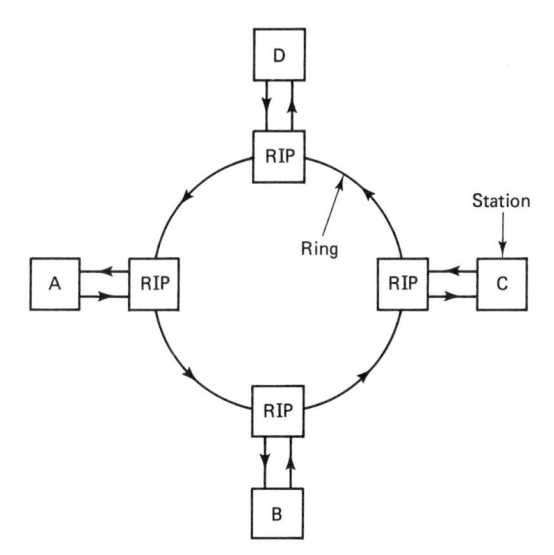

Figure 1.4 Relaying network topology. The station's interface with the ring is called ring interface processor (RIP).

relaying networks involves understanding how the station interfaces with the communication medium. The interface, called *Ring Interface Processor* (RIP), is typically a shift register such as the one depicted in Figure 1.5. Data traffic circulates around the ring as a continuous bit stream from one RIP to the next. If a message entering a RIP is not addressed to its corresponding station, the message is relayed immediately to the next RIP through the shift register. Perhaps the best example of a *relaying network* is the IBM token ring network, which is based on the token passing protocol.

When transmission of a message from one station to another involves intermediate stations which perform a switching function, the corresponding network is referred to as a **switching network.** Switching can be performed by using either circuit or store-and-forward switches. **Circuit switching** requires that all segments of the path from the source station to the destination station be available before the message transmission can be started. The principle is shown in Figure 1.6. If station A wants to send a message to station B, first a physical connection A-B must be established. Connection establishment simply means making appropriate physical connections[2] so that A and B are physically connected.

In a **store-and-forward switching** network, messages or packets are routed at each station so that eventually they will reach their destination stations. Stations performing the routing function are also called **switching nodes.** As the name implies, entire messages are stored temporarily by the switching stations before they are forwarded. The ARPANET is a store-and-forward packet switching network. Store-and-forward networks are also called **point-to-point** networks. Figure 1.7 shows the main store-and-forward topologies (Tanenbaum, 1988).

Propagation and message transmission delays. As discussed in detail in Chapter 13, performance is a very important aspect of local area networks. Performance analysis involves, among other things, calculating the time required by a message for traveling along a transmission medium and calculating the time needed to send a given number of bits once transmission has started. The elapsed time from when a leading (or trailing) bit is transmitted (i.e., put on the

---

[2] In the past, the connections were made by flipping switches to appropriate positions, and hence the name. Currently, solid state switches are used.

Sec. 1.3 Network Classification

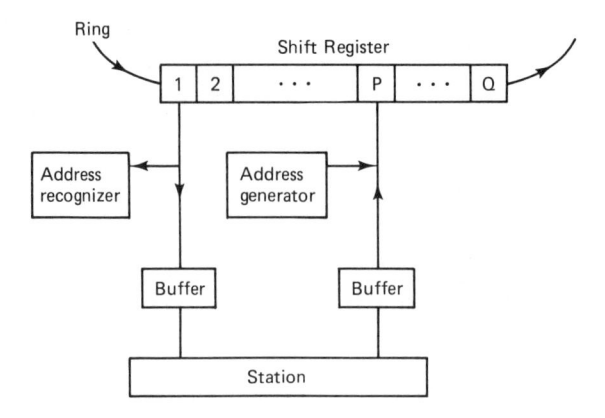

Figure 1.5 Example of a ring interface processor (RIP).

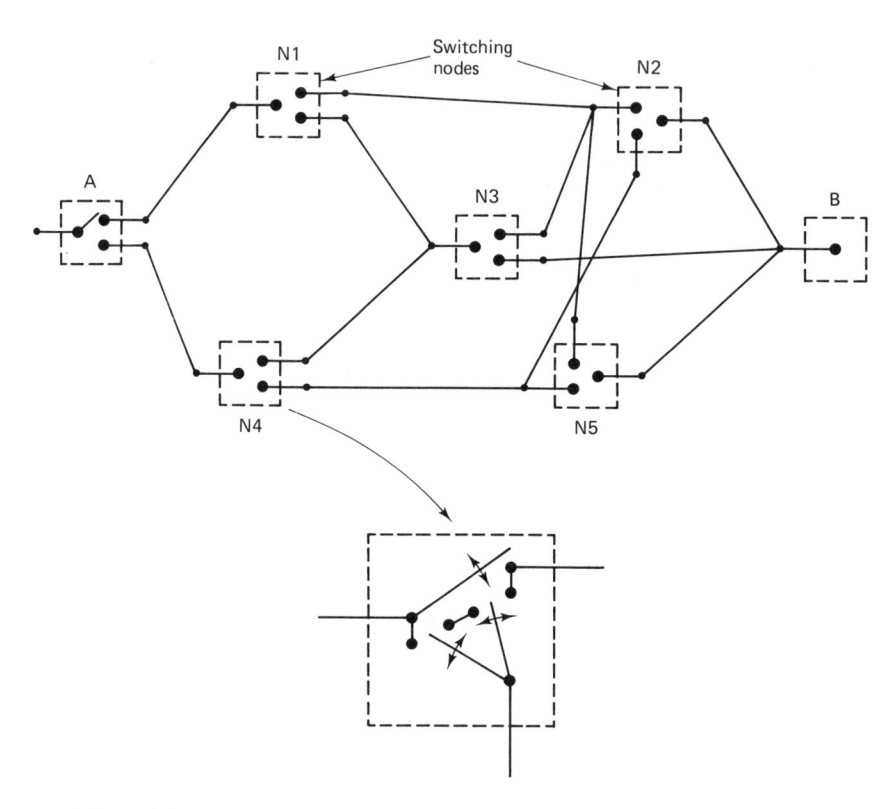

Figure 1.6 An example of a circuit switching network. Actual implementations use solid-state switches.

medium) by the sender until the same bit arrives at a receiver is referred to as the **propagation delay.** The factors influencing the *propagation delay* are the medium length L between sender and receiver, the speed v at which the energy[3] carrying the information travels on the medium, and

---
[3] The energy can be electrical, optical, or electromagnetic.

8   Introduction to Local Area Networks   Chap. 1

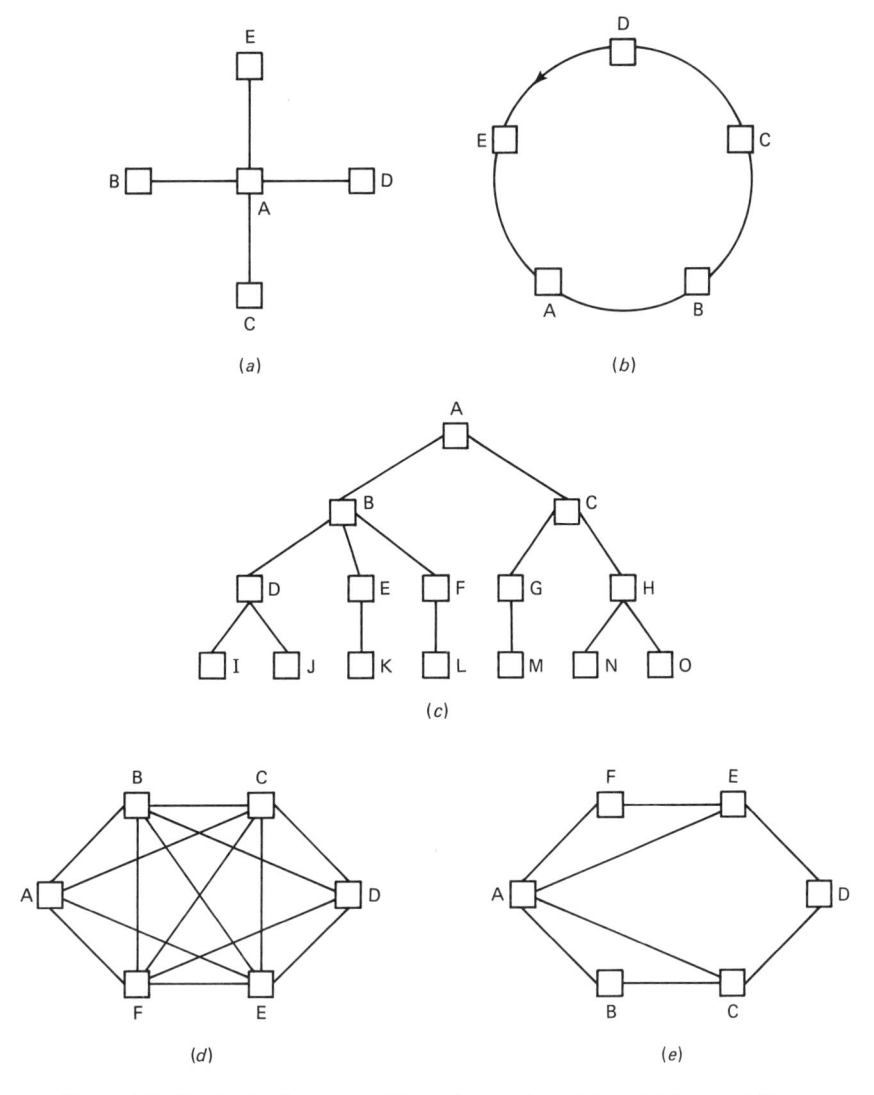

Figure 1.7 Topologies for store-and-forward networks: (a) Star; (b) Loop; (c) Tree; (d) Complete interconnection; (e) Partal interconnection.

other factors, depending upon whether the network is broadcast, relaying, or switching. Typical values for v are $v = c = 3 \times 10^8$ m/s (speed of light) for optical fibers and free space media, and $v = 0.85 \times c$ for wires and coaxial cable media.

For broadcast and circuit-switched networks the propagation delay is given by

$$Tp = L/v \qquad (1.1)$$

For relaying and store-and-forward networks the propagation delay depends on the actual configuration of the *ring interface processor* and the switching nodes, respectively. Since messages are

Sec. 1.3 Network Classification

temporarily stored before they are forwarded, the propagation delay involved in *store-and-forward* networks is usually greater than that of *circuit switching* networks.

The elapsed time from when the first bit of a message is transmitted until the last bit of the same message is transmitted by the sender is called the **message transmission delay.** There are only two factors influencing *message transmission delays*: data rate R (bit/sec),[4] and message length X (bits). **Data rate** is the speed at which individual bits are put into the medium by a sender transmitter. The receiver station has no choice but to receive data at the same rate. Regardless of the method used for message transfer, message transmission delay is simply

$$Tm = X/R \qquad (1.2)$$

Example

Consider the ring shown in Figure 1.4 with a fiber optic medium and a data rate R = 100 Mbps. The medium length between any two consecutive stations is 0.5 Km. The ring interface processor is that of Figure 1.5, where the shift register length Q = 64 bits and bits are inserted into the ring at the 33th bit position (i.e., P = 33). Calculate the bit propagation delay between stations A and C.

Solution The bit propagation delay has two components: the first one a function of the medium length, and the second a function of the delay in the shift registers denoted respectively by T1 and T2. Thus, Tp = T1 + T2. Since the total distance between stations A and C is L = 1 Km, the delay due to medium length is

$$T1 = 1000 \text{m}/3 \times 10^8 \text{ m/sec} = 3.33 \ \mu \text{ sec}$$

The shift register delays at stations A, B, and C are respectively 32, 64, and 1 bit. Thus, the delay T2 due to the shift registers is

$$T2 = (32 + 64 + 1)\text{bit}/100 \times 10^6 \text{ bit/sec} = 0.97 \ \mu \text{ sec}$$

Finally, Tp = 4.30 μ sec

Another measure of network performance is that of message delay. As discussed in Chapter 13, message delay is a variable that can be defined in several contexts. For the purposes of this chapter we define **message delay** (Dm) as the elapsed time from when the first bit of a message is placed on the medium by a source station until the last bit of the message reaches the network interface of the destination station. Clearly,

$$Dm = Tp + Tm \qquad (1.3)$$

Example

Calculate the message delay associated with source and destination stations separated by 1 Km on a coaxial cable configured in a bus topology. Assume a message size of 1024 bytes and a data rate R = 10 M bps.

Solution Since the bus topology is broadcast and the medium is a coaxial cable, the propagation delay is Tp = L/v, where L = 1 Km and v = 0.85 × 3 × 10^8 m/sec. Thus Tp = 3.92 μ sec. The message transmission delay is Tm = X/R where X = 8192 bits, thus Tm = 819.2 μ sec. Finally, the message delay Dm = Tp + Tm = 823.12 μ sec.

The *message delay* defined earlier assumes that the channel has been acquired and thus it does not take into account the delay associated with channel access. As will be discussed qualitatively

---

[4] The accronym bps is often used to denote bit/sec.

in Chapter 4 and quantitatively in Chapter 13, channel access delay is an important measure of network performance. Communication control responsibilities (e.g., channel access control, ring access, switching) for broadcast, relaying, and switching networks can either be spread equally among all stations or can be centrally controlled. The corresponding schemes are called decentralized (distributed) and centralized communication control. **Centralized schemes** are based on a master-slave or primary-secondary relationship among stations. **Decentralized** schemes on the other hand assume no special relationship among stations. We will emphasize decentralized medium access control schemes in Chapter 4, presenting several classifications.

1.3.2 Distance-Based Classification

According to the distance between stations, we have the following network types.

Closely coupled networks. Closely coupled networks, also referred to as **multiprocessor networks,** have stations located very close to one another. The interstation distance is on the order of magnitude of a few centimeters. Typically, the stations are located in one single board which plugs into the host computer motherboard. Communication between stations is done in parallel (e.g., 16 bits at a time) because the internal computer buses are used for the communication. In fact, a multiprocessor is the only network that provides parallel communication between stations. Because of cost considerations and other factors, the other network types discussed below provide serial communication between stations. Multiprocessor networks find applications in systems requiring high performance (e.g., high sampling rates, large processing bandwidth, and high accuracy). An example of a multiprocessor network is one used in a robot controller. Many industrial robots have six independent movements (i.e., degrees of freedom) for the manipulator. Typically, a microcomputer is used to control each independent movement, with another microcomputer used for overall coordination and communications. Thus, the robot controller is typically a multiprocessor network consisting of seven microcomputers which together cooperate to control the robot movements.

Presently, the interconnection and communication mechanisms for multiprocessor networks are designed in an ad hoc manner. Each manufacturer has its own method for interconnecting its processors. Fortunately, some standards are beginning to appear and others are on the drawing tables (e.g., IEEE 488, VME, Multibus II, and others). A good discussion, of multiprocessor networks is given by Enslow (1974).

Local area networks (LAN). As already noted, local area networks constitute the main subject of this book, and a more complete introduction is given in Section 1.4. Local area networks are characterized by an interstation distance in the order of magnitude of a few kilometers. Typically, a LAN is owned by one single organization such as a hospital, a university, a manufacturing plant, or an office. In addition, the network geographical coverage extends only to cover the owner's premises. The communication between stations is done serially (i.e., one bit at a time) to decrease interconnection costs. The three most important LAN applications support the development of automation in the office, the laboratory, and the factory. By using a LAN in an office environment, a manager can review and edit a financial document created at another terminal by a secretary. When the document is finalized, the secretary can print the document on a laser printer available through the network.

Metropolitan area network (MAN). Local and metropolitan area networks are similar. The key difference lies in their intended application. Whereas a LAN typically supports communication in a single company or privately owned office, a MAN is intended to be a facility to cover an entire city (i.e., a utility). Thus, a MAN enables communications between stations belonging to different parties. The interstation distance for metropolitan area networks ranges from a few meters to tens of Km. A feature of MAN applications is the support of communications among devices located in different premises.

For example, a financial investor living in one of the suburbs of Washington DC could use a personal computer connected to a MAN to obtain crucial investing information maintained by a computer firm located near the White House. Klessig (1986) provides an overview of metropolitan area networks.

Long haul network (LHN). The interstation distance for long haul networks is in the order of magnitude of hundreds or thousands of Km. Their main application is in the interconnection of computers located in different cities, different states, and even different countries. Two professors located at different universities as far apart as Harvard and UCLA can write portions of a book and send them to one another for review using a long haul network. The ARPANET considered earlier in this chapter belongs to this class.

1.4 LOCAL AREA NETWORKS

Recently, there has been much interest in local area networks. In fact, some computer industry sectors declared the year 1985 as the year of the LAN. As noted in the introduction, there are numerous reasons for the interest in computer networks and, in particular, in local area networks. Perhaps the most significant reasons involve resource sharing, dissemination of information, distributed processing, and last, but certainly not least, the possibility of automating the office, laboratory, and factory environments.

Since we are interested primarily in local area networks, this section provides a more detailed introduction to the subject than that given in the previous section. We next discuss general LAN issues such as characteristics, topologies, and applications without going into the technical details which are left for the remainder of the book.

Local area networks exhibit the following characteristics:

Intracompany, Privately Owned, Not Subject to Regulation by the Federal Communications Commission (FCC). A local area network is typically used within an organization (e.g., company, plant, campus, office) and is owned by that organization. Traditional local connections using the telephone system, as well as other public data networks, are not generally considered local area networks. Although network manufacturers may need FCC approval for their designs, installing a LAN does not typically require FCC approval, since most of the radiated energy is contained in the user's premise.

Structured. The constituent elements of a LAN (i.e., computers and other intelligent devices) are configured as an integrated system involving communication media, medium interfaces (NIUs and BIUs), and communication software. All network stations have appropriate medium interfaces and communication software for enabling them to communicate. The medium interfaces and communication software are highly structured using specific rules, formats, protocols, and interfaces. Structured communications is best explained in terms of the OSI reference model and the OSI architecture. Both are discussed in Chapter 2.

Limited in Geographical Scope. Network stations can be located on the same or on different floors of the same building, or in different buildings of a campus or compound. The maximum distance between two communicating stations in a LAN environment depends on a number of parameters which, in turn, depend on, among other things, specific network configurations. Thus, there is no simple formula for calculating how far two stations can be from one another and still be able to communicate; however, typical maximum distances range from a few hundred meters to a few Km.

Supportive of Full Connectivity. A station in a LAN environment is able to communicate with any other station either directly (e.g., using a broadcast channel) or indirectly (e.g., using a store-and-forward station).

Fast with High Data Rates. Typical data rates for local area networks range from a few hundred of K bps to several hundred of M bps,[5] which are faster than those used in long haul networks. Long haul networks such as the ARPANET are generally used for comparison purposes because they were the first to be developed; however, when compared with multiprocessor networks, LAN rates are typically slower.

Reliable with Low Error Rates. The combination of transmission medium, signaling techniques, and modulation techniques used in local area networks translates into a communication channel with low bit error rates (BER). Typical BER associated with the most used modulation techniques is given in Section 3.9.

1.4.1 LAN Topologies

As noted earlier, LANs are highly structured. One aspect of a LAN structure is its topology, with the most common ones being the tree, bus, ring, and the star (depicted in Figure 1.8). Some topologies have certain advantages over others. The following criteria are useful for comparing different LAN topologies.

Initial Medium Installation Cost. Given a certain number of stations, what is the initial medium cost of installing a network? Some topologies require longer cabling for interconnecting the same number of stations.

Medium Expansion Cost. What is the additional medium (i.e., cable) cost involved in adding a new station to an already existent network?

Network Interface Expansion Cost. What is the additional interface (i.e., NIU or BIU) cost involved in adding a new station to the network? We assume that the network interface cost for stations performing a routing function such as station A in Figure 1.8(a) is higher than the interface cost for stations such as D, E, and F in Figure 1.8(a).

Communication Bottleneck. The network interface or the channel could limit the rate of information transfer. For example, a channel with low data rate can slow down communications. On the other hand, if the network interface for station A in Figure 1.8(a) is slow, it can be the bottleneck for communications between the left and right sides of the tree.

---

[5] The abbreviations K = 1000, M = 1000,000, bps = bit/sec are used throughout this book. When referring to memory sizes, K = 1024.

(a) Tree

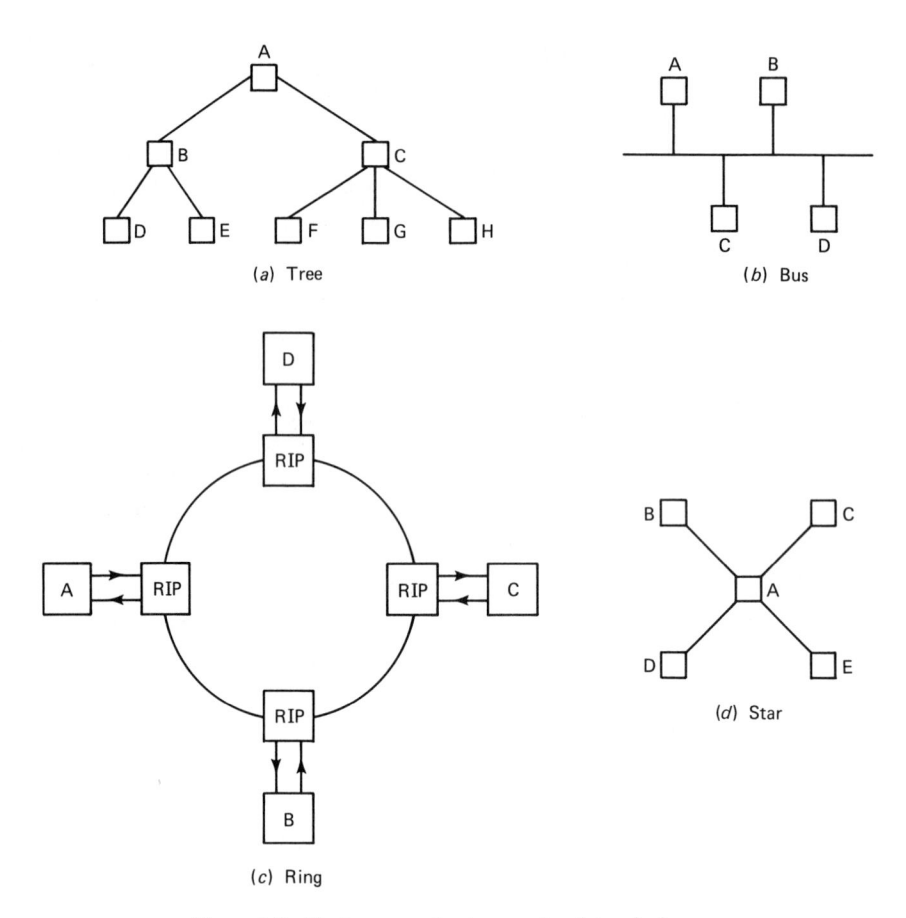

(b) Bus

(c) Ring

(d) Star

Figure 1.8 Most common local area network topologies.

Routing Complexity. Routing complexity is related to the complexity introduced by the topology in routing a message from a source to a destination station. For example, the bus topology is the simplest one, since there is no routing involved.

Delay. Contribution to the message delay due to the network topology. In general, if intermediate stations are involved in the communications (e.g., store-and-forward), message delays are longer than communications involving the source and destination stations directy (e.g., broadcast).

Effect of Station Failure on Network. What is the effect of a station failure on the communication capabilities of the other network stations? For example, if station A in Figure 1.8(d) fails, then does the entire network fail?

The bus topology. The bus topology is one of the most popular topologies in local area networks because it enjoys several advantages, such as

1. low initial medium installation cost,
2. low medium expansion cost,

3. low network interface expansion cost,
4. simple routing,
5. low delay, and
6. high reliability when some stations fail.

However, all these advantages do not come without the following disadvantages:

1. The medium constitutes a single point of failure,
2. high data rates are required to avoid the medium being a communication bottleneck, and
3. schemes for accessing the shared channel are required.

Two of the most important LAN networks using the bus topology are Ethernet and MAP.

LAN transmission media. Our presentation of transmission media in this chapter is very brief. A more detailed presentation is provided in Chapter 2. The transmission media are the physical facilities used to interconnect network stations. Local area networks use serial communications, which involves using only one transmission medium rather than the multiple lines required by multiprocessor networks. The most common transmission media are:

Twisted Pair Wires. A pair of wires that are twisted together as shown in Figure 1.9(a) is known as a **twisted pair line.** One wire carries the signal and the other serves as the ground

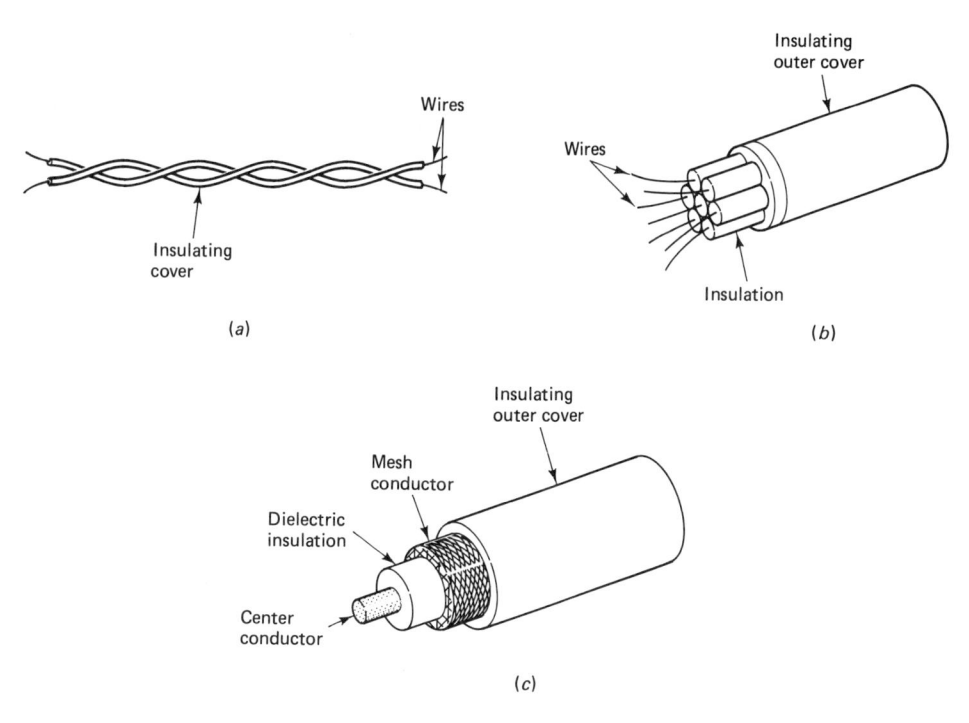

Figure 1.9 Common local area network transmission media: (a) Twisted pair; (b) Multicore wires; (c) Coaxial cable.

Sec. 1.4   Local Area Networks

reference. Since both, the signal wire and the ground reference wire are in close proximity, they both pick up about the same signal interference, and thus its effect on the difference signal is reduced. Enclosing several wires within the same insulating outer cover as shown in Figure 1.9(b) also helps with signal interference. Twisted pair wires are the least expensive, supporting lower data rates than the other media. Many current LAN implementations, most notably in office applications, use twisted pair wires. For example, one version of the IBM token ring network uses twisted pair wires. Typical data rates range from 300 bps to 1 M bps.

Coaxial Cable. A coaxial cable consists of a center conductor wire surrounded by dielectric insulation and a mesh conductor, and finally covered with an outer insulator. The center conductor carries the signal whereas the mesh conductor serves as the ground reference. Because of its geometry, as depicted in Figure 1.9(c), the mesh conductor effectively shields the signal from external interference.

Coaxial cables are manufactured differently, depending upon the type of signal to travel on the cable. If the signal is not modulated before transmission, baseband coaxial cables can be used. If modulation is used, broadband coaxial cables are required. The modulation process enables the utilization of different channels on the same cable. Each channel can be designated for voice, video, or data transmission, and the cable can carry all three types of information simultaneously. Typical data rates supported by coaxial cables range from 1 M bps to 50 M bps. Ethernet and MAP both use coaxial cables as their physical medium. The modulation process is discussed in Section 3.8.

Optical Fibers. A fiber optic cable consists of a thin central core of glass or plastic with good reflective properties. A signal-encoded lightbeam is introduced onto the fiber by a laser or light emitting diode (LED), and is transmitted along the fiber by reflection against the core. For LAN applications, the optical fiber medium is not yet as well developed as the coaxial cable, but it appears very promising in the near future. This promise is because of its high bandwidth and low noise immunity. Currently, optical fibers support data rates up to a few hundred M bps. Twisted pair wires, coaxial cables, and optical fibers are discussed in more detail in Section 2.3.

1.5 LOCAL AREA NETWORK APPLICATIONS

Local area networks are being used in a wide variety of applications that include office automation, laboratory automation, factory automation, personal computers, and computer room networks. The following characteristics are useful in describing the use of networks in the various applications:

- response time,
- volume of data,
- environment,
- communication type,
- number and type of devices, and
- type of device processing.

Response time is the elapsed time from when a user issues a transaction to when the transaction is completed. Response time is mostly due to delays involved in performing protocol functions. Each transaction involves the transmission of a certain volume of data between the communicating devices. **Volume of data** can be characterized by message sizes. The **environment** identifies the factors and conditions influencing the operation of the communication system. For example, some networks operate in clean, temperature regulated environments, whereas others do not. The different possibilities for communication among different entities (i.e., device-to-device or human-to-device) define the **communication type.** Finally, the amount and type of operations to be performed on the data define the **type of device processing.** For example, some applications may involve *transactions* requiring extensive data processing operations.

We next discuss the characteristics listed previously, which are associated with office automation, personal computer, and computer room networks.

Office automation networks. Networks for **office automation** enhance productivity by interconnecting information systems to support managers, secretaries, and other office personnel. Transactions in an office environment are characterized by the following components: audio, video, screen reports, printed reports, query reports, access to databases, and electronic mail (Chorafas, 1984). Thus, networks for office automation must support the preceding transaction types. Personal computer networks are applicable for most office automation applications.

Desired response time for office networks depends on what a person can tolerate. Typical values of response time are from a few seconds to a few minutes. The volume of data is low and the environment is mechanically (i.e., free of dust, grease, etc.) and electrically clean. The communication type is mostly interactive, involving a human and a device. The number of devices is relatively low and includes word processors, personal computers, file servers, letter quality printers, and document readers. The operations are relatively simple, consisting mostly of text operations.

We use the term laboratory in a very broad sense to include different application fields (e.g., medicine, engineering, and astronomy). A laboratory environment is typically characterized by the following functions: data collection, data processing, data interpretation, and data display. Response time in a laboratory environment depends on the nature of data processing done. For example, a computer aided design (CAD) station could take a few hours to complete a complex design. Volume of data ranges from a few bytes to several M bytes. A laboratory environment is typically clean. The communication type involves human interaction. Device types are numerous, including microcomputers, heart monitors, engine dynamometers, computer aided design stations, and radiotelescopes. The type of processing is typically complex, involving scientific calculations such as evaluating the Discrete Fourier Transform (DFT) of the data collected and performing image processing calculations.

Personal computer networks. *Personal computer networks* are a recent development prompted by the seemingly ever-decreasing price of personal computers. This application is somewhat similar to that of office automation, except that a personal computer network is intended for more generic applications such as language compilers, file servers, plotting packages, etc. Examples of personal computer networks include PC network (IBM), and Appletalk (APPLE).

Computer room networks. A **computer room network** interconnects high performance computers located close to one another. The maximum distance between any two computers is limited to just a few meters. The key characteristic of this type of network application is increased performance. Consequently, a computer room network has very low response time, high volume on data, a clean environment, mixed communication type, (i.e., human-to-machine and machine-to-machine), a small number of homogeneous devices, and large processing requirements.

The preceding applications are fairly well established. There is, however, an emerging application in the area of automated manufacturing under active development. It is as revolutionary as the development of the assembly line at the beginning of this century.

1.5.1 Automated Manufacturing Applications

In the beginning of computer networks, the major reasons for interconnecting several computers to form a network were resource sharing and remote communications. Current network developments, however, are mostly driven by automation. The trend is to have automated offices, automated laboratories, and automated manufacturing facilities. In manufacturing, automation has been identified as a key factor for improving productivity. Manufacturing enterprises all around the world face stiff competition, and they are forced to use advanced automation techniques to remain competitive.

There is now very little disagreement that computer networks play a crucial role in significantly advancing the state of the art in automated manufacturing. Networks allow the design and operation of a manufacturing facility in which all operations are mostly automated.

Four areas are crucial to significantly advancing the state of the art in automated manufacturing: all digital-based controllers, hierarchical control methodology, standard programming languages for manufacturing, and standards for communication networks to support automated manufacturing. This book addresses the last area. Traditionally, networks have been used to increase the processing power of computers (i.e., multiprocessing), electronic mail, sharing expensive resources (e.g., laser printers, expensive programs), file transfer, and others. However, most of these applications support an office or a laboratory environment. Recently there has been much interest in applying networks in a manufacturing environment.

There are two key elements that distinguish networks for manufacturing from other networks. First, manufacturing devices (e.g., robots) that traditionally have not been interconnected into a network need now be interconnected with other network elements including other robots. Second, the network must have enough functionality and capabilities for supporting the intended manufacturing application. By intended application, we refer to the functions of modern manufacturing systems such as a production planning and control system.

Thus, designing a good manufacturing network requires not only an understanding of manufacturing devices such as robots, machine conveyors, and vision systems, but also manufacturing applications.

As discussed in Chapter 11, automated manufacturing systems are heavily dependent upon computer systems and computer networks. Extensive use of hardware and software components is used for performing the various automated manufacturing functions. Software components are typically arranged into modules, also referred to as *application processes* or, simply, *processes*. Because the constituent elements of a manufacturing facility are scattered throughout the entire plant and interconnected by a computer network, the system is termed a *distributed system*.

A major feature of networks for manufacturing is their support of distributed systems. More specifically, in an automated manufacturing environment, distributed systems involve communication and synchronization among the various application processes responsible for automation. For example, a manufacturing network must be able to provide a mechanism for communication and synchronization among several robots working together in an assembly operation. Typically, one process may control the operation of one or more robots. Together, the several processes cooperate in performing the function of automated assembly. Distributed systems are introduced in Chapter

7. Chapter 11 provides an introduction to automated manufacturing and Chapter 14 discusses networks suitable for supporting automated manufacturing.

1.6 THE OSI REFERENCE MODEL

Most computer networks are organized in a structured fashion using the (Open System Interconnection) OSI reference model. This section provides a brief overview of the OSI reference model, with a more comprehensive treatment given in Chapter 2. Because of the importance of the OSI reference model, this book is organized accordingly with a chapter devoted entirely to each layer.

Communication between computers is somewhat similar to communication between persons when using the telephone system. However, care must be used in comparing these two communication systems, because in the telephone system case many functions are provided by the telephone system in a transparent way. For example, when talking to another person in another state, users need not worry about the actual circuit path to be used in the communications, since it is transparent to the user.

Another source of difficulty in the comparison is that there are other communication functions performed by persons, which are taken for granted but are, nevertheless, necessary for successful communication. For example, sometimes we get a noisy connection, making it very difficult to hear the conversation. What people normally do is hang up and try again, until a good connection is obtained. Other times, we do not hear a word or sentence very clearly and we request retransmission by asking, *would you say that again*? or something similar. The latter illustrates an error control scheme used by the user of the telephone system services.

A computer network is a very complex system because of the many different functions that it must perform in order to provide services in a transparent fashion. To illustrate the complexity associated with computer networks, an analogy with the familiar telephone network is useful.

Let us suppose that you want to call your friend who lives in another state. To begin with, we have two intelligent, highly adaptable people who want to communicate. There are many communication aspects that we usually take for granted in telephone conversations. First, we have the issue of naming and addressing. You have your friend's telephone number and proceed to dial. If someone other than your friend answers, you need to name the person with whom you wish to talk. Thus, it is not only necessary that you have the telephone number (similar to an address in computer communications) but also the name of the person (similar to a process) to whom you wish to speak. Assuming that your friend is on the other end now, both use implicit rules for deciding when to start or stop talking (a synchronization function), both speak at a pace which is comfortable for the other person to understand (a flow control function), and both speak the same language. However, our ears can tolerate some errors in the transmission, while computers cannot.

The telephone system relies on the intelligence of human beings for ensuring communications involving complex situations. For example, assume that your friend went on a two-week vacation, and upon his return he calls you and asks that you tell him what happened on the favorite TV program that you both watch. Assuming that the task of informing him what happened on TV for two weeks takes several hours, you decide to do this in several telephone conversations. In each call, you identify the last portion of the story already communicated (an example of using synchronization marks in long messages) and tell him an additional portion of the story. Synchronization marks are useful in situations when you get interrupted in the middle of a message portion and you decide to go back to the last mark and continue from there.

Even when all the preceding problems are resolved, it does not mean that two persons can communicate about an application. One person may want to talk about brain surgery (i.e., the application) but the person at the other side may be a radio astronomer who knows nothing about the application.

In a communication system involving machines rather than humans, we cannot make such assumptions. To begin with, machines are far less intelligent[6] than humans, implying that we must take a great many precautions to handle all kinds of contingencies. First, there is the need to address another network station and identify (i.e., name) a process for exchanging information. The machines must synchronize their dialog so that they know when to start or stop transmitting. One machine may send data to the other machine much faster than the receiving machine is able to receive it correctly. Thus, some form of flow control is required. When errors occur in the transmission, the machines must use some kind of error control.

Machines do not always speak the same language. For example, some machines use different codes for representing the English alphabet and numbers, thus requiring data transformation functions. When large messages are exchanged, the use of synchronization marks are advantageous. Lastly, even when all of these problems are resolved, the communicating processes must understand messages in the context of an application.

In the design of a computer network, one has to ensure that any two communicating machines perform a variety of communication functions similar to the ones just considered. Some of these functions are:

- Application support: The communication network should support application processes exchanging messages about specific applications. The application determines the semantics of communication.

- Data encoding and transformation: This function is useful for saving communication bandwidth and when the machines do not use the same data representation.

- Communication management: Since communication functions are complex, some management is required for efficient operation.

- Synchronization: The machines must synchronize their communication so that they know when to start or stop a message transmission. Other types of synchronization also exist, but they are not discussed here.

- Reliable message transfer: The services of the communication system must be reliable and transparent to the user.

- Routing: In the presence of several messages paths between source and destination, the transmission system must find appropriate routes.

- Flow control: A sender must send messages at a pace so that the receiver is not swamped with data.

- Error control: A communication channel is not perfect and errors will occur from time to time. A communication system for a computer network must include some error control mechanism for dealing with errors.

---

[6] This is so, in spite of developments in artificial intelligence.

- Medium interface: A network station must interface with the communication medium using appropriate protocols and interfaces.

When faced with the preceding problem, the International Organization for Standardization (ISO) used the *divide and conquer* principle. This principle states that a very complex system should be partitioned into its constituent subsystems, and that the subsystems in turn be partitioned into smaller subsubsystems until the smallest subsystems are manageable. The partition of communication functions that the ISO developed is known as the Open System Interconnection (OSI) reference model.

Basically, the OSI reference model partitions the overall communication functions into seven groups. The communication functions are organized hierarchically, and each group of functions constitutes a **layer** of communication functions, as illustrated in Figure 1.10. A brief explanation of the functions of each layer follows.

The application layer. The application layer is one of the most important layers of the ISO reference model because it provides the necessary communication support to end applications. The application layer interfaces with application processes which, together, perform a function such as the manufacture of a part using several robots. The application layer must provide mechanisms for process communication and synchronization specifically geared for end applications. Thus, one can expect several versions of the application layer depending upon the application itself. Some examples for application layer protocols include a file transfer protocol, a teletext and videotext protocol, and a special protocol for machines used in automated manufacturing (e.g., robots). The application layer is discussed in detail in Chapter 10, where we concentrate on the ISO standard protocol for file transfer and the Manufacturing Message Specification (MMS) used in the MAP network.

The presentation layer. Often, communicating machines use different codes to represent their data (e.g., ASCII and EBCDIC). In other cases, some functions are performed sufficiently often to warrant their inclusion in one of the layers. Examples of such a function are message compression and data encryption. Most signals (e.g., audio and video) contain much redundant information. In other words, there is a high degree of correlation between two consecutive signal values that are to be transported by the communication system. By removing the redundancy, a reduction on the bandwidth that is required to transmit the signal is also obtained. For example, by using image bandwidth compression techniques, the bandwidth required to transmit a video signal

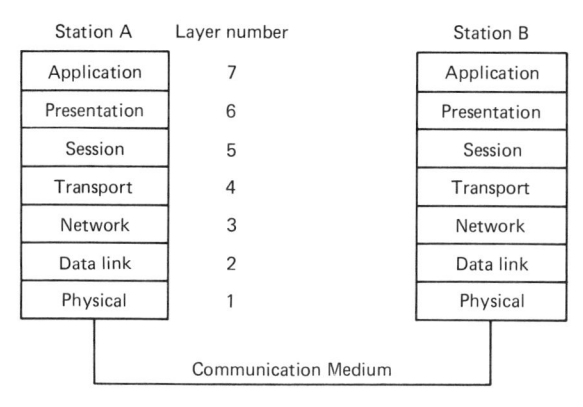

Station A	Layer number	Station B
Application	7	Application
Presentation	6	Presentation
Session	5	Session
Transport	4	Transport
Network	3	Network
Data link	2	Data link
Physical	1	Physical
Communication Medium		

Figure 1.10 OSI reference model for a communication system.

can be reduced from a standard 6 MHz down to 0.5 MHz. The presentation layer deals with transformations of the data as it moves from the application layer to the session layer or vice versa. Its primary function is context negotiation. As detailed in Chapter 9, there are three fundamental reasons why data transformations are desirable: message security, message compression, and data compatibility.

The session layer. The key difference between the session and transport layers is that the session layer is process-oriented, whereas the transport layer is station-oriented. That is, the transport layer is responsible for reliable message transmission between two stations, regardless of the identity of the processes residing at each station. The session layer, on the other hand, is responsible for reliable message transmission between two processes, regardless of the identity of the station containing the processes.[7]

Processes communicating using the session layer are analogous to people communicating through assistants who, in turn, use the telephone system. Station to station communication is analogous to the assistants communicating directly via the telephone system. The purpose of the session layer is to provide the necessary means for cooperating processes to organize and synchronize their dialog and to manage their data exchange. The session layer is discussed in Chapter 8.

The transport layer. The main function of the transport layer is to accept data from the session layer, split it up into smaller pieces, if need be, pass these to the network layer, and ensure that the pieces arrive correctly and reliably at the other end. The transport layer provides end-to-end communication in an error-free and reliable fashion. It hides from the upper layers (i.e., session, presentation, and application) the details of operation of the lower layers (i.e., physical, data link, and network). Other functions of the transport layer include multiplexing several transport connections into one network connection or, vice versa, flow control, and error control.

The network layer. Routing messages through several possible paths is a major function of the network layer. Additional functions include resolving message congestion and performing message segmentation. In some networks (e.g., switching networks) there is more than one path between a source station and the destination station. The routing function consists of finding a path over which messages can be sent.

Routing can be complex, provided that there are many paths to choose from. For broadcast networks there is only one path (i.e., the common communication channel) so routing is not necessary. However, the interconnection of several networks requires several paths for secure internetwork communications, thus requiring routing.

The data link layer. The physical communication channel provided for data transmission is usually unreliable (i.e., prone to error). The main function of the data link layer is to take an unreliable channel and make it appear as a reliable one to the network layer (or the layers above the data link layer). Other functions include flow control, connection establishment, link management, and medium access control.

The physical layer. Finally, the physical layer handles the transmission of a long string of bits (as provided by the data link layer) by using a communication medium. To do this,

---

[7] It is assumed that some form of directory containing a process-station mapping is available.

the physical layer performs a variety of functions designed to optimize the usage of the communication medium. Functions performed by the physical layer include data encoding, signal modulation, and connector specification. The communication medium, along with the functions performed by the physical layer, appear as a binary communication channel to the data link layer.

1.7 OUTLINE OF THE REST OF THE BOOK

Modern industrial automation systems involve an integrated system of computers, communications, controls, and other manufacturing subsystems. Thus, the subject of manufacturing networks is interdisciplinary in nature. It involves transmission systems, communication systems, computer hardware and software, computer networks, and control systems. It crosses the boundaries of electrical engineering, manufacturing engineering, computer engineering, computer science, and industrial engineering. Therefore, it is practically impossible to cover each area in great detail.

The approach taken in this book is based on presenting a synthesis of the fundamental principles and major results with no rigorous proof. Whenever possible, intuitive developments and explanations are provided. Numerous references are provided for those readers desiring to pursue more detailed coverage of specific topics.

Because of the crucial role played by the ISO reference model in local area networks, this book is organized around each layer of the model, with chapters 3 through 6 covering the lower layers, and chapters 8 through 10 covering the upper layers. With the exception of the introductory chapter, the book is divided into three parts, with Part I dealing with the lower layers, Part II dealing with the upper layers, and Part III dealing with network applications in manufacturing.

Part I begins with Chapter 2, which provides sufficient background to understand the lower layers. The background covered in Chapter 2 includes signal transmission, a more detailed introduction to the OSI reference model, and the OSI architecture. The rationale for providing the material on signal transmission is twofold: first, there are few books on networks that also cover signal transmission; and second, it is important to emphasize the fundamental principles used in developing the concepts associated with local area networks. Some of the literature on networks contains inaccurate terms, descriptions, and definitions concerning signal transmission. It is expected that the reader will gain additional insight after reading the material in the first portion of Chapter 2 dealing with signal transmission.

Whereas the lower layers deal primarily with *data transmission* mechanisms, the upper layers deal mostly with *data processing* aspects of communications. Thus, the nature of the communication functions changes radically as one moves from the transport layer to the session layer. In the upper layers the concern is no longer how to transport a message from one station to another in an error-free and reliable fashion. Rather, the concern is in providing appropriate communication support for end user application processes. Recently, there has been much interest in designing *distributed systems*. Much of the functionality of distributed systems belongs to the upper layers of the OSI reference model. Accordingly, we provide an introduction to *processes* and *distributed systems* in Chapter 7, the introductory chapter of Part II. The concept of a process is intimately tied to that of an *operating system*; thus we discuss both concepts in Chapter 7. Two additional reasons for including operating system concepts are that operating systems not only play an important role in the implementation of communication protocols but also are required to understand *distributed operating systems* concepts.

Chapters 11 through 14 constitute Part III of the book, dealing with automated manufacturing and features of networks for manufacturing, including protocol implementation and network performance. A definition as well as the elements, characteristics, and organization of *automated manufacturing systems* is provided in Chapter 11. Since an automated manufacturing system is very complex, we narrow our scope and concentrate on *production planning and control* and more specifically on *cell level control systems*, which involve unique networking requirements. Chapter 12 deals with hardware and software implementation of communication prototcols, whereas Chapter 13 addresses LAN performance and emphasizes the application of LAN performance evaluation to LAN design. Finally, Chapter 14 identifies the following network levels as appropriate for supporting automated manufacturing: sensor level, machine level, cell level, shop level, and factory level networks.

Two case studies featuring the use of the MAP network are also provided at the end of Chapter 14. These describe the *GMT 400 project* and the Saginaw *Factory of the Future*. Both projects are under active development by the General Motors Corporation in Pontiac and Saginaw, Michigan respectively. Four appendices are also included, which provide an overview of some aspects of the ADA language, who is who in standards, MAP architectures, and an overview of the abstract syntax notation (ASN.1) with MMS examples. We do not imply that ADA is the language of choice for automated manufacturing, but rather, that it is an appropriate language for accurately describing design concepts.

SUMMARY

In this chapter we have presented a brief history, the elements, and a classification of computer networks while concentrating on local area networks, their characteristics, and applications. The OSI reference model was introduced by means of a telephone analogy. The chapter concluded with an outline of the rest of the book.

Two of the earliest computer networks, developed during the late 1960s, were the ARPANET and the ALOHA system. Much of what is known today is the result of these pioneer networks. Subsequent developments laid the foundation for terrestial, satellite, packet radio, and local networks. Latest developments concentrate on issues related to technology, standards, and internetworking.

A computer communication network is a system of interconnected computers and other devices capable of exchanging information. There are three main elements in any computer communication network: transmission facilities, communication devices, and communication protocols. Of particular importance are communication protocols, which deal with issues such as keeping a fast station from overwhelming a slow station.

According to the method used for message transfer, networks are classified as broadcast, relaying, and switching networks. According to the distance between stations, networks are classified as closely coupled (multiprocessor), local area, metropolitan area, and long haul networks.

Recently, there has been much interest in local area networks because of their applications involving not only resource sharing, dissemination of information, and distributed processing, but because of the possibility of automating the office, laboratory, and factory environments. The most common LAN topologies are the tree, bus, ring, and star, with the bus topology enjoying widespread use. The most common media used in LANs are twisted pair wires, coaxial cable, and optical fibers.

Traditional local area network applications include office automation, laboratory automation, personal computer, and computer room networks. Another LAN application under active development is in the area of automated manufacturing. LANs allow the design and operation of a manufacturing facility in which all operations are highly automated.

The OSI reference model is used as the framework in which all network material is presented. The model partitions a communication system into seven layers: application, presentation, session, transport, network, data link, and physical.

Bibiliographic Notes

Many books and articles provide a good introduction to LANs. In particular, the reader is referred to Clark et al. (1978), Cypser (1978), Davies (1973), Dixon et al. (1983), Halsall (1988), Tanenbaum (1989), Chou (1983), Schwartz (1987), Stallings (1987), Meijer et al. (1982), and Franta et al. (1981). Most books deal with telecommunications networks concentrating on the lower layers of the OSI reference model. In contrast, this book deals with all seven layers while concentrating on networks for a specific application: that of automated manufacturing.

It is very difficult to list all available literature in a certain subject; thus, we apologize to the authors of fine contributions which are not listed in the bibliography.

PROBLEMS

1. What were the two established technologies just prior to the development of the ARPANET and ALOHA networks?
2. State the main reasons why communications in local area networks, metropolitan area networks and long haul networks are serial rather than parallel.
3. What is the main difference between circuit switching and packet switching?
4. For a complete interconnection network topology with N stations, find a formula giving the number of required point-to-point physical transmission links.
5. Consider a message with M bits going from station A to station C in each of the topologies of Figures 1.7(b) and 1.8(c) which are the loop and ring topologies respectively. Is the message delay in the loop topology greater than that of the ring topology? Assume that both networks have the same data rate and the same distance between stations A and C.
6. Consider the ring shown in Figure 1.4 with a fiber optic medium and a data rate $R = 100$ Mbps. The medium length between any two consecutive stations is 0.5 Km. The ring interface processor is that of Figure 1.5 where the shift register length $Q = 64$ bits and bits are inserted into the ring at the 33th bit position (i.e., $P = 33$). Calculate the message delay for a 1 K byte message, as measured from when the first bit of the message is placed on the medium by station A until the last bit of the message reaches station C.
7. Using the criteria for evaluating LAN topologies discussed in section 1.4, evaluate the tree, ring, and star topologies.
8. List typical devices interconnected by networks in
    (a) an office environment.
    (b) a laboratory environment.
    (c) a factory environment.
9. Take a specific application that you are familiar with and analyze it in terms of the system characteristics identified in section 1.5.
10. When providing an overview of the OSI reference model in section 1.6, a telephone analogy was used to illustrate some concepts. In the telephone analogy assume that a house has several

telephone extensions using the same phone number. Further assume that when the phone rings, two persons answer at the same time thus making their speech unintelligible. Find an analogous situation when two computers communicate via a communication network.

11. At a data rate of 5 M bps and a propagation velocity of 2c/3, how many meters of cable is a 1 bit delay in a token ring interface equivalent to?

12. Provide a network classification from the viewpoint of distance between stations. List a few characteristics and applications for each category.

PART 1

2

Background for the OSI Lower Layers

The OSI lower layers basically deal with data transmission in a reliable manner. Data transmission includes signal transmission over a transmission channel, and protocol mechanisms for message exchange. Accordingly, this chapter is intended to provide sufficient background in signal transmission and the OSI reference model for understanding modern communication networks. **Signal transmission** is the study of how signals propagate when going from a transmitter to a receiver in a communication system. Although signals exist in many forms, we concentrate on electrical signals.[1] Understanding how signals propagate provides an insight into some fundamental concepts of data transmission in communication networks such as bandwidth, channel, medium, modulation, frequency division multiplexing (FDM), time division multiplexing (TDM), signal contention, signal collision, and power and voltage levels. Understanding the OSI reference model is of course crucial to the understanding of the layered structure of modern computer networks, and is discussed in this chapter.

2.1 SIGNAL TRANSMISSION

We begin by discussing a general block diagram of a communication system. Regardless of the application, all communication systems have three major subsystems: transmitter, channel, and

---

[1] An exception is optical signals, when discussing optical fibers in Section 2.3.

receiver, as depicted in Figure 2.1. The transmitter performs some signal processing on the input signal so that the transmitted signal can be sent over the communication channel. The channel coexists in a physical medium, such as wire or air, over which signals travel. At the other end, the receiver attempts to restore the input signal from the received signal.

In this book we are interested in electrical communications (i.e., sending and receiving electrical signals). However, most signals of interest are nonelectrical. Examples of nonelectrical signals include temperature, pressure, speech, position, velocity, and others. Thus, a mechanism is needed to convert nonelectrical signals into electrical signals in the form of a current or voltage before they are transmitted over a communication system. Electrical currents or voltages are referred to as electrical signals or simply as signals. The mechanism that performs the conversion is known as the **transducer.** A transmission system ultimately is concerned with sending and receiving signals. Signals are converted into electrical signals because it is more efficient to transmit signals as voltages or currents instead of transmitting signals in their original form.

Example

Figure 2.2 shows the communication system used to transmit tremor and earthquake signals from several sites to a central location, with the sites typically located a few Km away from the center. A system such as this can be used for a variety of geological studies such as earthquake epicenter location, oil exploration, earthquake prediction, and others. The source is constituted by the multilayer structure of the earth. An earthquake or tremor is caused by wave-like displacements in some of the earth's layers. Thus, the input signal is composed of manifestations of wave-like displacements such as its amplitude, phase, shape, etc. The input transducer is an accelerometer which converts earth displacements into a voltage signal (input signal). The transmitter performs some signal processing operations on the input signal in order to transmit it as electromagnetic radiation (transmitted signal) over the air (channel). The signal received is the signal picked up by the receiver's antenna. It is then processed by the receiver to recover the output signal, which resembles the input signal. Depending upon the intended application, the output transducer can take several forms. If the application requires the registration of the output signal in a graph, then the output transducer is a plotter. On the other hand, if the application requires the signal to be stored for later processing, then the output transducer can be a magnetic tape.

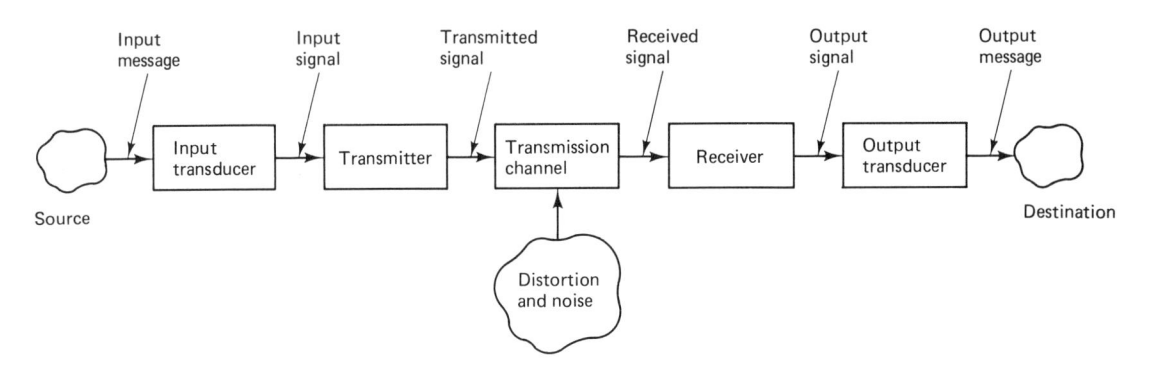

Figure 2.1 Model for a transmission system.

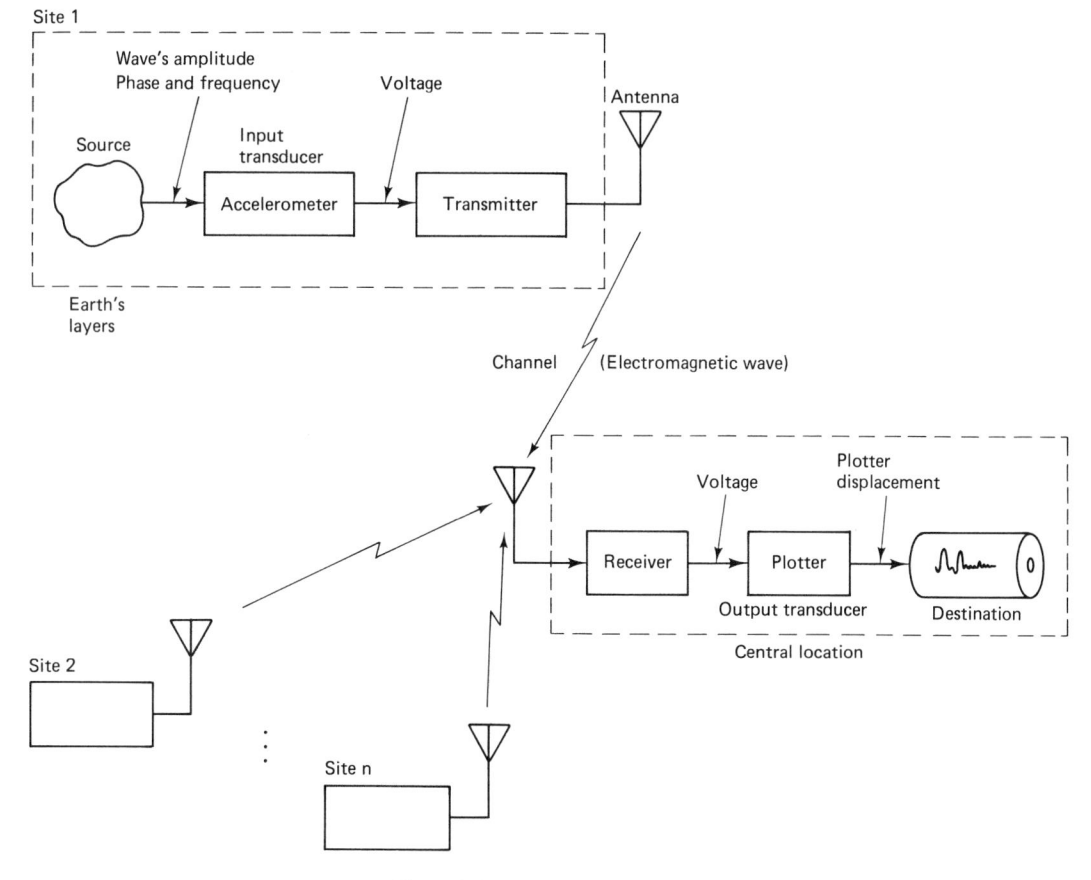

Figure 2.2 A geological telemetry system.

2.2 SIGNALS

The main objective of this section is to provide a fairly rigorous definition of *signal bandwidth*. Characterizing signal bandwidth requirements is important for sizing network resources such as the number of channels required and their bandwidth.[2] The definition of signal bandwidth is based on the concept of energy, power, and power spectral density. This section begins with an analysis of signal propagation using Fourier series and transforms, convolution, correlation, and autocorrelation.

Understanding the concept of a signal is crucial in transmission systems, because signals are used to represent the messages to be transmitted. Thus, voice, video, computer data, and other messages are represented by appropriate signals before transmission. Signals can be characterized in terms of time (i.e., a time domain representation) or in terms of frequency (i.e., a frequency domain representation). The reason that both representations are useful is that some signal processing

---

[2] Medium bandwidth and channel bandwidth are defined in subsection 2.3.2.

operations required for communication are easier to visualize and perform if one representation is chosen over the other. For example, distortion introduced by amplifiers is easily seen if one observes the frequency domain representation of the amplifier's input and output signals. And by contrast it is easier to see how a signal's amplitude varies in the time domain.

A graphical or mathematical description of a signal as we observe it throughout time is referred to as a **time domain representation.** An alternative way to describe a signal is in terms of its frequency components or tones. For example, a signal that corresponds to a single musical tone can be represented as two numbers: its magnitude and frequency. A graphical or mathematical description of a signal in terms of the frequencies that comprise it is referred to as a **frequency domain representation.** In describing a signal graphically or mathematically, time will be denoted as t and frequency as f. Thus, it will be obvious from the graph or mathematical equation whether we are dealing with a time domain or frequency domain representation.

Signal propagation through linear systems. When signals travel from a source to a destination, they usually go through several devices (e.g., transducers, amplifiers, filters, transmission medium, etc.) which are generally classified as linear or nonlinear. Linear models for devices are important because they are more simple than nonlinear device models, they provide a good approximation for practical cases, and they can be used for comparison purposes with nonlinear devices.

A system performing an operation F is linear if for all signals $f_1, f_2, \ldots$ and for all constants $c_1, c_2, \ldots$ the following holds

$$F[c_1.f_1 + c_2.f_2 + \ldots] = c_1.F[f_1] + c_2.F[f_2] + \ldots \tag{2.1}$$

where F is an operator on the signals $f_1, f_2, \ldots$. The symbology F[f] should not be interpreted as the product of two functions F and f. Rather, the interpretation should be thought of as the function F being defined in terms of another function f. Some authors classify functions such as F as functionals. Equation 2.1 defines a property of linear systems also referred to as the **superposition principle.** This principle states that an operator applied to the sum of weighted signals is equal to the weighted sum of the operator applied to each signal individually, as interpreted from Equation 2.1.

Example

Consider a system consisting of an amplifier with gain A. Every signal f appearing at the input of the amplifier appears at its output as Af. The operator F is then defined as $F[f] = Af$. If we have the following input $c_1.f_1 + c_2.f_2$, then the amplifier's output is

$$F[c_1.f_1 + c_2.f_2] = A(c_1.f_1 + c_2.f_2)$$
$$= c_1(Af_1) + c_2(Af_2)$$
$$= c_1 F[f_1] + c_2 F[f_2]$$

Since the amplifier satisfies the superposition principle (i.e., Equation 2.1), it is linear.

Example

Consider an amplifier with a voltage gain which is proportional to the input signal and given by $G_v = Af$. Thus, every signal f appearing at the input of the amplifier appears at the output as

$$Af(f) = Af^2$$

The operator F is then defined as $F[f] = Af^2$. To see if the system is linear, we must see if the principle of superposition holds.

$$\begin{aligned}
F[c_1.f_1 + c_2.f_2] &= A(c_1.f_1 + c_2.f_2)^2 \\
&= A(c_1^2.f_1^2 + 2c_1.f_1.c_2.f_2 + c_2^2.f_2^2) \\
&= c_1^2(Af_1^2) + c_2^2(Af_2^2) + 2A(c_1.f_1)(c_2.f_2) \\
&= c_1^2 F[f_1] + c_2^2 F[f_2] + 2A(c_1.f_1)(c_2.f_2) \\
&\neq c_1.F[f_1] + c_2 F[f_2]
\end{aligned}$$

Since Equation 2.1 does not hold, the system is nonlinear.

The graphical interpretation of a linear system is depicted in Figure 2.3. In general, one can think of $F[f]=g$ as the operation to be performed on f to yield g. Both f and g can be functions defined in the time or frequency domains. For example, the relation defining the derivative of a time domain function $g(t) = df(t)/dt$ defines $F[f(t)]$ as $df(t)/dt$. The following is an example of an operator performed on a frequency domain function.

Example

The use of sinusoidal signals in communication systems is pervasive. An interesting operator on sinusoidal signals is the following

$$F[\cos \omega t] = A(\omega) \cos(\omega t + \theta(\omega)) \qquad (2.2)$$

where $A(\omega)$ is referred to as the amplitude characteristic and $\theta(\omega)$ as the phase characteristic of the operator F. Thus, the operator takes every frequency component of $\cos(\omega t)$ and multiplies it by $A(\omega)$, and the phase of $\cos(\omega t)$ is increased by the amount $\theta(\omega)$. This operator is useful for realistic channels, as discussed in Section 2.3.

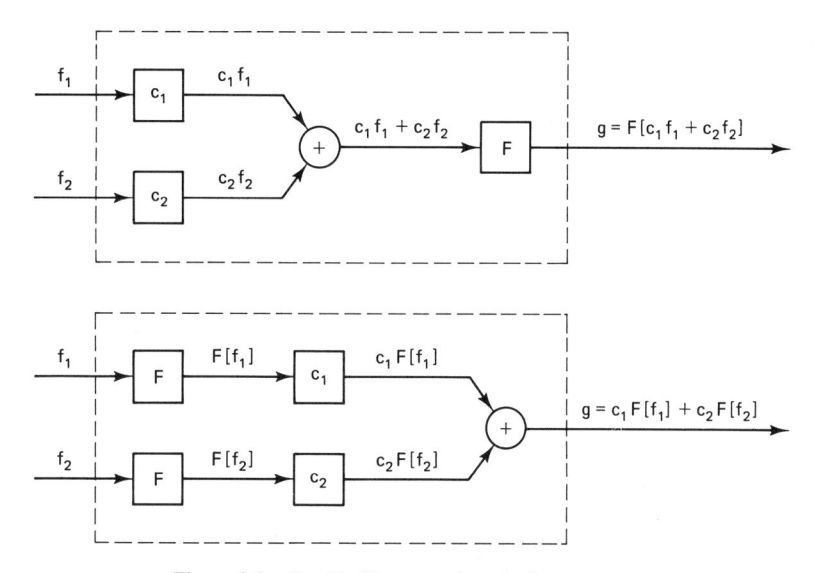

Figure 2.3 Graphical interpretation of a linear system.

Sec. 2.2   Signals

2.2.1 Fourier Series and Fourier Transforms

The Fourier series and the Fourier transform are mathematical tools that allow one to obtain a frequency domain representation from a time domain representation. The Fourier series is useful for signals that repeat themselves after a certain interval (i.e., periodic signals). The Fourier transform is a generalization of the Fourier series and is useful for any signal regardless of whether it repeats itself.

As mentioned previously, signals can be periodic or nonperiodic. Periodic signals repeat themselves after a fixed interval T_o known as the **period** of the signal. Any periodic signal f(t) can be defined by

$$f(t) = f(t+T_o) \; ; \; T_o \neq 0 \tag{2.3}$$

where T_o is the smallest value satisfying Equation 2.3.

Representation of periodic signals. The Fourier series is widely used for representing periodic signals. Basically, the Fourier series allows the representation of any periodic function f(t) as the sum of an infinite number of weighted sine and cosine terms. That is, if f(t) is periodic with period T_o, then one can write f(t) as

$$f(t) = a_o + \sum_{n=1}^{\infty} (a_n \cos 2\pi n f_o t + b_n \sin 2\pi n f_o t) \tag{2.4}$$

where the weighting factors a_o, a_n, and b_n are given by

$$a_o = \frac{1}{T_o} \int_{t_o}^{t_o+T_o} f(t) dt \tag{2.5}$$

$$a_n = \frac{2}{T_o} \int_{t_o}^{t_o+T_o} f(t) \cos 2\pi n f_o t \, dt \tag{2.6}$$

$$b_n = \frac{2}{T_o} \int_{t_o}^{t_o+T_o} f(t) \sin 2\pi n f_o t \, dt \tag{2.7}$$

and

$$f_o = \frac{1}{T_o} \tag{2.8}$$

The frequency f_o is known as the **fundamental frequency** and the frequency nf_o is the **nth harmonic frequency.**

Example

Consider a periodic signal f(t) applied to a linear system performing an operation F given by $F[\cos \omega t] = A(\omega) \cos(\omega t + \theta(\omega))$. Write an expression for the system output g(t).

Solution Since the input signal f(t) is periodic, it can be expanded as a Fourier series such as Equation 2.2. For every input term $\cos 2\pi n f_o t$, the corresponding output term is $A(2\pi n f_o) \cos(2\pi n f_o t + \theta(2\pi n f_o))$. Using the principle of superposition, the system output g(t) is given by

$$g(t) = A(0) a_o + \sum_{n=1}^{\infty} [A(2\pi nf_o) a_n \cos(2\pi nf_o t + \theta(2\pi nf_o))$$
$$+ A(2\pi nf_o) b_n \sin(2\pi nf_o t + \theta(2\pi nf_o))]$$

Another version of the Fourier series which is useful for certain situations is the exponential Fourier series. In this case, the signal is represented as the weighted sum of an infinite number of complex exponential terms as

$$f(t) = \sum_{n=-\infty}^{\infty} F_n e^{j2\pi nf_o t} \qquad (2.9)$$

where the weight F_n is given by

$$F_n = \frac{1}{T_o} \int_{t_o}^{t_o+T_o} f(t) e^{-j2\pi nf_o t} dt \qquad (2.10)$$

Unlike a_n and b_n in Equation 2.4, which are always real numbers, F_n is in general a complex number. However, both representations are equivalent.

Let us consider once again the operator F defined as $F[\cos \omega t] = A(\omega) \cos(\omega t + \theta(\omega))$. Since $\cos \omega t = \text{Re}\{e^{j\omega t}\}$ where Re stands for the real part of the expression in brackets, and $j^2 = -1$, we can generalize the definition of the operator F in the following manner:

$$F[\cos \omega t] = A(\omega) \cos(\omega t + \theta(\omega))$$
$$\text{Re}\{F[e^{j\omega t}]\} = \text{Re}\{A(\omega) e^{j\omega t + j\theta(\omega)}\}$$

or

$$F[e^{j\omega t}] = A(\omega) e^{j\theta(\omega)} e^{j\omega t}$$

The previous result can be generalized in the following way:

$$F[G(\omega)] = A(\omega) e^{j\theta(\omega)} G(\omega) = H(\omega)G(\omega) \qquad (2.11)$$

The term $H(\omega) = A(\omega) e^{j\theta(\omega)}$ is also referred to as the system *transfer function* or *operator's characteristic*.

Example

Find the trigonometric and exponential Fourier series for the signal shown in Figure 2.4.

Solution From the figure, $T_o = 1/2$, $f_o = 2$, and

$$a_o = 2 \int_0^{1/2} e^{-t} dt = 0.79$$

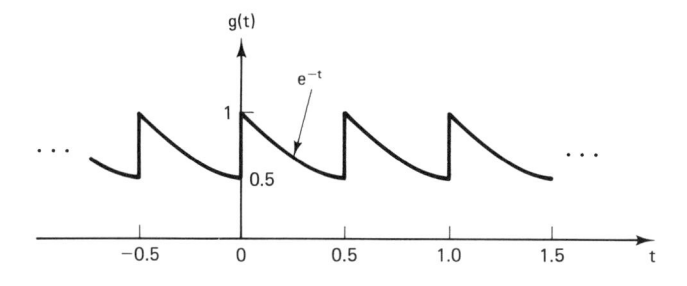

Figure 2.4 A periodic signal.

$$a_n = 4 \int_0^{1/2} e^{-t} \cos 4\pi nt\, dt = 0.79 \left(\frac{2}{1+16\pi^2 n^2}\right)$$

$$b_n = 4 \int_0^{1/2} e^{-t} \sin 4\pi nt\, dt = 0.79 \left(\frac{8\pi n}{1+16\pi^2 n^2}\right)$$

Therefore, the trigonometric Fourier series is given by

$$f(t) = 0.79 + \sum_{n=1}^{\infty} \frac{0.79}{(1+16\pi^2 n^2)} (2\cos 4\pi nt + 8\pi n \sin 4\pi nt)$$

Likewise, the coefficients of the exponential Fourier series is given by

$$F_n = 2 \int_0^{1/2} e^{-t} e^{-j4\pi nt}\, dt$$

$$= 2 \int_0^{1/2} e^{-(1+j4\pi n)t}\, dt$$

$$= \frac{0.79}{1+j4\pi n}$$

Therefore, the exponential Fourier series is given by

$$f(t) = \sum_{n=-\infty}^{\infty} F_n e^{j2\pi n f_o t}$$

$$= 0.79 \sum_{n=-\infty}^{\infty} \frac{1}{(1+j4\pi n)} e^{j2\pi n f_o t}$$

Since F_n is a complex number, its magnitude $|F_n|$ is given by

$$|F_n| = \frac{0.79}{(1+16\pi^2 n^2)^{1/2}}$$

and the phase θ_n of F_n is

$$\theta_n = -\tan^{-1}(4\pi n)$$

The magnitude $|F_n|$ and phase θ_n of F_n are plotted in Figure 2.5.

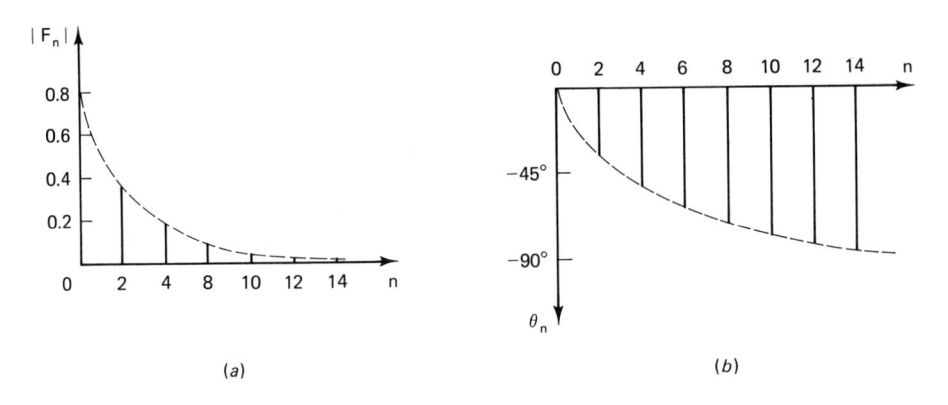

Figure 2.5 Discrete frequency spectrum of a periodic signal: (a) Magnitude spectrum; (b) Phase spectrum.

Because sinusoids and exponentials are related by Euler's formula

$$e^{\pm j\omega t} = \cos \omega t \pm j \sin \omega t \qquad (2.12)$$

the coefficients of the trigonometric and exponential Fourier series are related by

$$F_o = a_o \qquad (2.13)$$

$$F_n = 1/2 \, (a_n - j \, b_n) \text{ for } n \geq 1 \qquad (2.14)$$

$$F_{-n} = 1/2 \, (a_n + j \, b_n) \text{ for } n \geq 1 \qquad (2.15)$$

The Fourier series is an important tool in communications because it allows one to calculate the bandwidth of periodic signals. In addition, the Fourier series helps one to simplify the analysis of complicated waveforms by decomposing them into more elementary signals (i.e., sinusoids). Another major advantage of using the Fourier series is that, for most signals encountered in the real world, the Fourier coefficients F_n (or equivalently a_n and b_n) decay in size very rapidly as n increases. Thus, it is possible to retain only a few terms from the infinite series and still obtain a very good approximation.

Example

For the periodic signal shown in Figure 2.6, find the nth harmonic frequency such that the amplitude of the harmonics of f(t) beyond the nth one are negligible.

Solution Using the complex Fourier series (Equation 2.9) we have

$$f(t) = \sum_{n=-\infty}^{\infty} F_n \, e^{jn\omega_o t}, \; \omega_o = 2\pi f_o$$

where

$$F_n = \frac{1}{T_o} \int_{t_o}^{t_o + T_o} f(t) \, e^{-jn\omega_o t} dt$$

From Figure 2.5, $T_o = 1$, $\omega_o = 2\pi/T_o = 2\pi$, and choosing $t_o = -0.5$; thus

$$F_n = \frac{1}{1} \int_{-0.5}^{0.5} f(t) \, e^{-jn\omega_o t} \, dt$$

$$= \int_{-0.5}^{0.5} e^{-jn\omega_o t} dt = \left. \frac{e^{-jn\omega_o t}}{-jn\omega_o} \right|_{-0.25}^{0.25}$$

$$= \sin\pi n / \pi n$$

Therefore, the nth harmonic decreases by the factor $1/n$. The amplitude of the harmonics for $n > 10$ is less than 0.1 times the amplitude of the first harmonic. The signal can be approximated by retaining only the first 10 harmonics of the complex Fourier series.

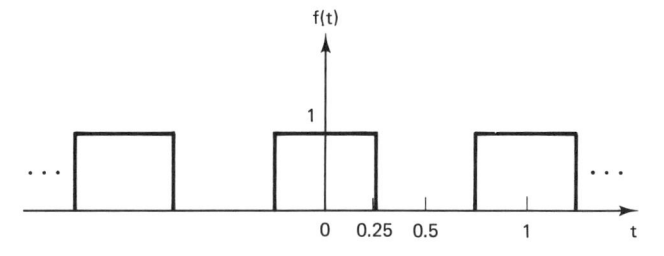

Figure 2.6 A pulse train periodic signal.

Representation of nonperiodic signals. Just as the complex Fourier series allows the representation of periodic signals as the weighted sum of exponentials, the Fourier transform allows the representation of nonperiodic signals as the integral of a weighted exponential:

$$f(t) = \frac{1}{2\pi} \int_{-\infty}^{\infty} F(\omega) e^{j\omega t} d\omega, \ \omega = 2\pi f \quad (2.16)$$

where

$$F(\omega) = \int_{-\infty}^{\infty} f(t) e^{-j\omega t} dt \quad (2.17)$$

$F(\omega)$ is referred to as the Fourier Transform of $f(t)$. Conversely, $f(t)$ is the inverse Fourier transform of $F(\omega)$. The operator F is sometimes used to denote a Fourier transformation. Thus, $F(\omega) = F[f(t)]$.

If $f(t)$ is applied to a system with transfer function $H(\omega) = A(\omega)e^{j\theta(\omega)}$, then the system output $G(\omega)$ is

$$G(\omega) = H(\omega) F(\omega) \quad (2.18)$$

and, therefore, the output signal $g(t)$ is given by

$$g(t) = \frac{1}{2\pi} \int_{-\infty}^{\infty} F(\omega) A(\omega) e^{j\theta(\omega)} e^{j\omega t} d\omega \quad (2.19)$$

where

$$G(\omega) = \int_{-\infty}^{\infty} g(t) e^{-j\omega t} dt \quad (2.20)$$

Operators taking functions as inputs and providing other functions as outputs are useful in transmission systems. Operators are used to represent practical transmission devices such as filters, amplifiers, equalizers, cable segments, and others.

Example

A low pass filter can be characterized by an operator F having the following characteristic:

$$H(\omega) = \begin{cases} 1 & \text{for } |\omega| < \omega_o \\ 0 & \text{otherwise} \end{cases}$$

The effect of the filter on an input signal is shown in Figure 2.7.

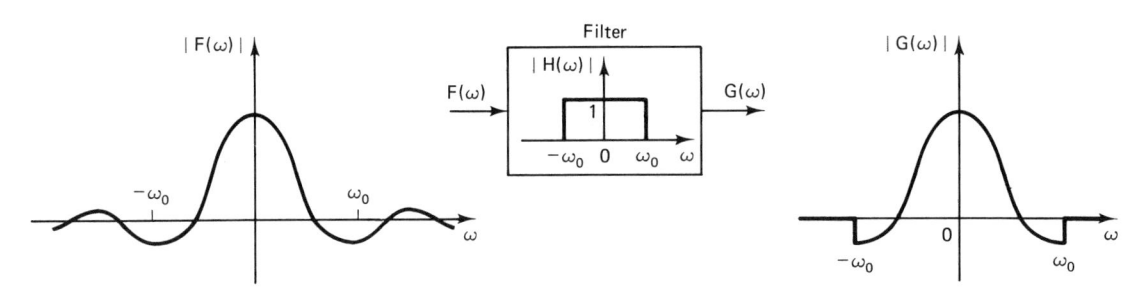

Figure 2.7 Effect of a filter on a signal's spectrum.

Example

Find the Fourier transform of the function f(t) defined as follows:

$$f(t) = \begin{cases} e^{-t} & \text{for } t \geq 0 \\ 0 & \text{for } t < 0 \end{cases}$$

Note that this function is exactly the same function as in Figure 2.4 for $0 \leq t \leq 0.5$.

Solution

$$F(\omega) = \int_{-\infty}^{\infty} f(t) e^{-j\omega t} dt = \int_{0}^{\infty} e^{-t} e^{-j\omega t} dt$$

$$= \int_{0}^{\infty} e^{[-(1+j\omega)t]} dt = -\frac{e^{[-(1+j\omega)t]}}{1+j\omega} \bigg|_{0}^{\infty}$$

$$F(\omega) = \frac{1}{1+j\omega}$$

Thus,

$$|F(\omega)| = \frac{1}{(1+\omega^2)^{1/2}} \quad \text{and} \quad \theta(\omega) = -\tan^{-1}(\omega)$$

The magnitude $|F(\omega)|$ and phase $\theta(\omega)$ of $F(\omega)$ are plotted in Figure 2.8.

In some of the preceding examples, a signal f(t) was given as a time domain representation, and we found the coefficients for the Fourier series if the signal is periodic, or the Fourier transform of f(t) if the signal is not periodic. The values of a_o, a_n, and b_n or equivalently F_n for n = 0, 1, 2, . . . define the **frequency domain representation** for f(t). Likewise, the values of $F(\omega)$ for $-\infty < \omega < \infty$ define the frequency domain representation for f(t). Figure 2.5 depicts a plot of $|F_n|$, the magnitude of F_n and θ_n, and the phase of F_n versus n. The corresponding plots for $|F(\omega)|$ and $\theta(\omega)$ versus ω are shown in Figure 2.8. Equations or plots for F_n and $F(\omega)$ are referred to as the **discrete frequency spectrum** and **continuous frequency spectrum** of f(t), respectively. The energy

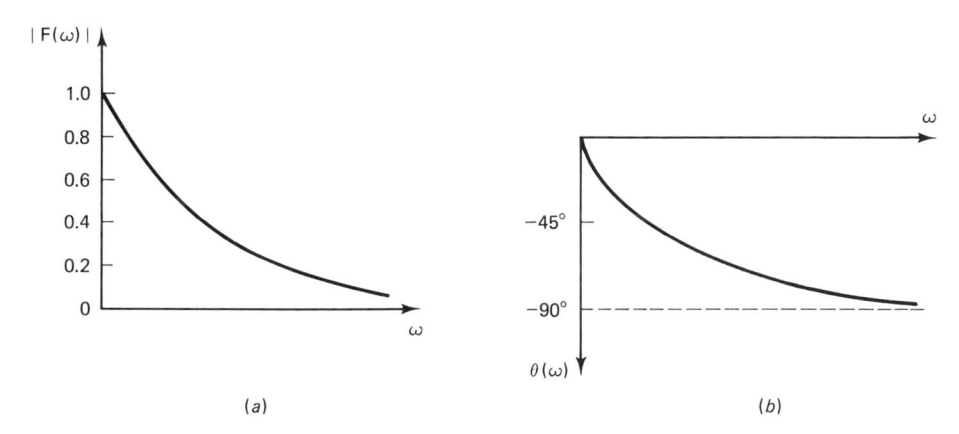

Figure 2.8 Frequency spectrum of an aperiodic signal: (a) Magnitude spectrum; (b) Phase spectrum.

Sec. 2.2   Signals

and power of a signal can be expressed in terms of its frequency spectrum; thus the importance of a signal's spectrum. The advantages of the Fourier transform are similar to those of the Fourier series, with the difference that the Fourier transform is generally used for nonperiodic signals.

Energy, power. The concepts of energy and power are not only useful for understanding the concept of bandwidth, but also practical for performing design calculations. The following are important applications of the concepts of energy and power.

Determination of Signal Levels. Once the topology of a communication network is defined, the next step in the design procedure involves determining appropriate signal levels throughout the entire network. The signal levels are typically measured in terms of voltage, or power. If the signal level at one point of a network is too low, the network interface of a receiver is unable to decode the signals. Thus, having appropriate signal levels is essential for correct operation of the network.

Budget Calculations. Transmitters in a local area network deliver a certain amount of power, which is distributed over the entire network. Sometimes it is desirable to redistribute power in the network using special devices discussed in Chapter 3.

Determination of Signal Bandwidth. If we look at power in the frequency domain we can see how power is distributed as a function of frequency. Signal bandwidth is a measure of the concentration of signal power in a region of the frequency spectrum. Signal bandwidth is defined at the end of this section in terms of energy and power concepts.

Signal to Noise Ratio (SNR) Calculation. As discussed in subsection 2.3.3, noise is a major contributor to signal degradation. The effect of noise in a transmission system is measured by the ratio of signal power to noise power, which is referred to as the signal to noise ratio (SNR).

We begin by defining the functions of *convolution*, *crosscorrelation*, and *autocorrelation*, which are useful for energy and power calculations in the frequency domains.

The convolution of two signals $f_1(t)$ and $f_2(t)$ is another signal $f(t)$ given by

$$f(t) = \int_{-\infty}^{\infty} f_1(x) f_2(t-x) dx \qquad (2.21)$$

The convolution operation is usually represented by the following shorthand notation:

$$f(t) = f_1(t) * f_2(t) \qquad (2.22)$$

The cross correlation function of two signals $f_1(t)$ and $f_2(t)$ is another signal $\psi_{f_1 f_2}(\tau)$ given by

$$\psi_{f_1 f_2}(\tau) = \int_{-\infty}^{\infty} f_1(t) f_2(t + \tau) dt \qquad (2.23)$$

From equations 2.21 and 2.23 it can be seen that the definitions of convolution and cross correlation are somewhat similar. However, most mathematical properties are expressed in terms of the convolution operation. The cross correlation function can be expressed in terms of a convolution by letting $t = -x$ in Equation 2.23.

Thus,

$$\psi_{f_1 f_2}(\tau) = \int_{-\infty}^{\infty} f_1(-x) f_2(-x + \tau) dx \qquad (2.24)$$

$$= f_1(-\tau) * f_2(\tau) \qquad (2.25)$$

If $f_1(t) = f_2(t)$, the cross correlation function is called the **autocorrelation function.** Thus, if $f_1 = f_2 = f$

$$\psi_f(\tau) = f(-\tau) * f(\tau) \tag{2.26}$$

Taking the Fourier transform on both sides of equations (2.25) and (2.26) and using the time-convolution property we obtain

$$F[\psi_{f_1 f_2}(\tau)] = F_1(-\omega) F_2(\omega)$$
$$F[\psi_f(\tau)] = F(-\omega) F(\omega) = |F(\omega)|^2 \tag{2.27}$$

The **energy** E_g of a signal is defined as the integral of the signal squared. That is,

$$E_g = \int_{-\infty}^{\infty} g^2(t) dt \tag{2.28}$$

Example

For the following exponential signal

$$g(t) = \begin{cases} b\, e^{-at}, & t > 0 \\ 0, & \text{otherwise} \end{cases}$$

calculate the signal energy E_g.

Solution From Equation 2.28,

$$E_g = \int_0^\infty b^2 e^{-2at} dt = b^2 \left. \frac{e^{-2at}}{-2a} \right|_0^\infty$$
$$= b^2/2a$$

The result is finite for $a > 0$ (i.e., negative exponential). For $a < 0$, the reader can verify easily that E_g is not finite.

An important property, known as Parseval's Theorem, allows the calculation of E_g in terms of the Fourier transform of $g(t)$ rather than in terms of $g(t)$ itself.

The Parseval's theorem states that

$$E_g = \frac{1}{2\pi} \int_{-\infty}^{\infty} |G(\omega)|^2 d\omega \tag{2.29}$$

As depicted in Figure 2.9, the interpretation of Equation 2.29 is that the energy of a signal can be obtained by adding the infinitesimal energy components $|G(\omega)|^2 \Delta f$ over all frequencies. Thus, the term $|G(\omega)|^2$ has an energy density interpretation, and it is called the **energy spectral density** $\Psi_g(\omega)$ of $g(t)$.

Therefore

$$\Psi_g(\omega) = |G(\omega)|^2 \tag{2.30}$$

Equation 2.29 can thus be rewritten as

$$E_g = \frac{1}{2\pi} \int_{-\infty}^{\infty} \Psi_g(\omega) d\omega \tag{2.31}$$

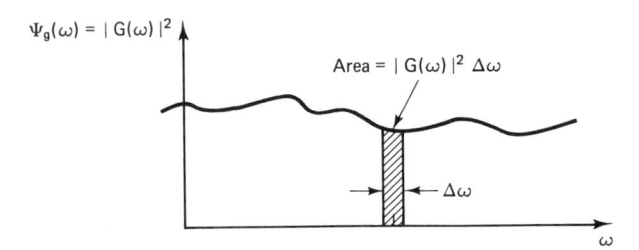

$\Psi_g(\omega) = |G(\omega)|^2$

Area = $|G(\omega)|^2 \Delta\omega$

$\Delta\omega$

ω

Energy of g(t) = $\dfrac{1}{2\pi}$ [area under $\Psi_g(\omega)$]

Figure 2.9 A signal's energy as a function of the energy spectral density.

$$E_g = \int_{-\infty}^{\infty} \Psi_g(f)\, df \qquad (2.32)$$

Bandlimited Signals. If a signal g(t) has a Fourier transform which is zero outside a finite interval, i.e.,

$$G(\omega) = 0 \quad \text{for} \quad |\omega| \geq 2B \qquad (2.33)$$

then g(t) is a **bandlimited signal.** Likewise, a function g(f) is **time-limited** if

$$g(t) = 0 \quad \text{for} \quad |t| > T/2 \quad \text{and} \quad E_g < \infty \qquad (2.34)$$

The energy E_g of a bandlimited signal is finite, since

$$E_g = \int_{-\infty}^{\infty} g^2(t)\, dt = \int_{-B}^{B} |G(f)|^2 df < \infty$$

Example

Find the energy spectral density of a signal p(t) given by

$$p(t) = g(t) \cos \omega_o t$$

where g(t) is a baseband signal bandlimited to B Hz.

Solution The energy spectral density is

$$\Psi_p(\omega) = |P(\omega)|^2 \qquad (2.34a)$$

where

$$P(\omega) = F[p(t)] \qquad (2.34b)$$

$$P(\omega) = \dfrac{1}{2}[G(\omega + \omega_o) + G(\omega - \omega_o)] \qquad (2.34c)$$

Replacing Equation 2.34c in Equation 2.34a, one obtains

$$\Psi_p(\omega) = \dfrac{1}{4}[|G(\omega + \omega_0)|^2 + |G(\omega - \omega_0)|^2] \qquad (2.34d)$$

$$= \dfrac{1}{4}[\Psi_p(\omega + \omega_0) + \Psi_p(\omega - \omega_0)] \qquad (2.34e)$$

In Equation 2.34d the cross product terms do not appear, because $G(\omega + \omega_o)$ and $G(\omega - \omega_o)$ are nonoverlapping for bandlimited signals with $B < (\omega_o/2\pi)$ Hz, as depicted in Figure 2.10.

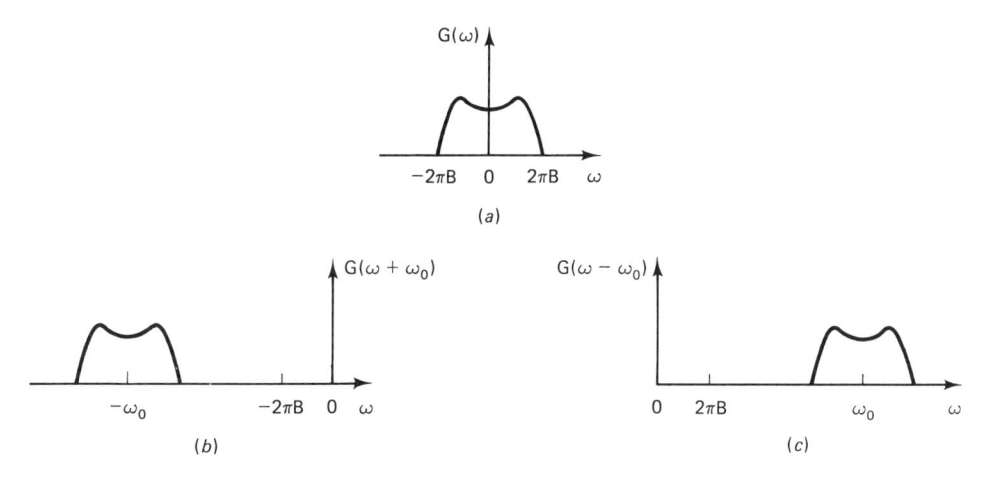

Figure 2.10 (a) Spectrum of a bandlimited signal g(t); (b), (c) Plots of $G(\omega+\omega_0)$ and $G(\omega-\omega_0)$ for $|\omega_0| > 2\pi B$.

Power spectral density. As noted earlier, there are many signals of interest (e.g., periodic signals) for which the signal energy is not finite. In such situations, another variable, P_g, closely related to energy, is used and it is given by

$$P_g = \lim_{T \to \infty} \frac{1}{T} \int_{-T/2}^{T/2} g^2(t)dt \qquad (2.35)$$

P_g is referred to as the average power of the signal g(t). P_g can be interpreted as the average power dissipated in a 1 ohm resistor when a voltage g(t) is applied across it. When Equation 2.35 is used in the context of electrical currents, it should be divided by the resistor value.

Example

A coaxial cable delivers the voltage v(t) = 14.1 sin t (mV)[3], to a resistive load R = 75 ohms. Calculate the power of the signal v(t).

Solution The current is i(t) = v(t)/R = (14.1 sin t)/75 (mA), and the instantaneous power is p(t) = v(t) i(t) = v(t)^2/75. The average power is then

$$P_v = \lim_{T \to \infty} \frac{1}{T} \int_{-T/2}^{T/2} \frac{v^2(t)dt}{75}$$

Since $v^2(t) = (14.1)^2 \sin^2 t = (14.1)^2 [1 - \cos 2t]/2$, the average of the cos 2t term is zero, and

$$P_v = (14.1)^2 / 2 \times 75 = 1.32 \; \mu W$$

---

[3] The notations m = 10^{-3}, μ = 10^{-6}, n = 10^{-9}, and p = 10^{-12} are used throughout this book. Also note that V = volt, W = watt, and A = ampere. Another useful notation for representing voltage and power values is that of decibels defined in terms of the magnitude of the voltage or power values relative to some reference values (e.g., 1 mV or 1 mW). A voltage value v expressed in dBmV is 20 log(v/1 mV) and a power value p expressed in dBmW is 10 log(p/1 mW). Naturally, any other unit (e.g., 1 μv or 1μw) can be used as the reference value with the corresponding decibel units being dBμV and dBμW respectively.

Using Parseval's Theorem in Equation 2.35, one obtains

$$P_g = \frac{1}{2\pi} \int_{-\infty}^{\infty} \lim_{T \to \infty} \frac{|G(\omega)|^2}{T} d\omega \tag{2.36}$$

Proceeding in a similar manner as in the signal energy calculation, we define the power spectral density $S_g(\omega)$ as

$$S_g(\omega) = \lim_{T \to \infty} \frac{|G(\omega)|^2}{T} \tag{2.37}$$

Thus,

$$P_g = \frac{1}{2\pi} \int_{-\infty}^{\infty} S_g(\omega) d\omega = \frac{1}{\pi} \int_{0}^{\infty} S_g(\omega) d\omega \tag{2.38}$$

For the special case of periodic signals, the signal power P_g can be written as

$$P_g = \frac{1}{T} \int_{-T/2}^{T/2} g^2(t) \, dt \tag{2.39}$$

The corresponding Parseval's theorem is

$$P_g = \sum_{n=-\infty}^{\infty} |G_n|^2 \tag{2.40}$$

Signals for which E_g is finite are referred to as **energy signals,** and signals for which P_g is finite are referred to as **power signals.**

The cross correlation of power signals $s_{g_1 g_2}(\tau)$ is defined as

$$s_{g_1 g_2}(\tau) = \lim_{T \to \infty} \frac{1}{T} \int_{-T/2}^{T/2} g_1(t) g_2(t+\tau) dt \tag{2.41}$$

Likewise, autocorrelation function $s_g(t)$ is given by

$$s_g(\tau) = \lim_{T \to \infty} \frac{1}{T} \int_{-T/2}^{T/2} g(t) g(t+\tau) dt \tag{2.42}$$

It can be shown that

$$F[s_g(\tau)] = \lim_{T \to \infty} \frac{|G(\omega)|^2}{T} = S_g(\omega) \tag{2.43}$$

From Equation 2.42, it can be seen that

$$P_g = s_g(0) \tag{2.44}$$

Equation 2.43 defines a very important property, stating that the power spectral density $S_g(\omega)$ can be obtained by taking the Fourier transform of the auto correlation function $s_g(\tau)$.

Most power signals have power spectral densities $S_g(\omega)$, which have nonzero values for $0 \leq \omega < \infty$. However, the power P_g is usually concentrated at frequencies below a certain frequency

B[4]. The range of frequencies within which all or most of the energy or power of a signal is concentrated is referred to as the **signal bandwidth.** For example, B can be defined as the frequency for which 95 percent of the power P_g is contributed by frequencies below B (in Hz). In terms of Equation 2.38, this is equivalent to

$$0.95\, P_g \geq \frac{1}{2\pi} \int_{-2\pi B}^{2\pi B} S_g(\omega)d\omega \tag{2.45}$$

For a certain percentage of P_g, the frequency B that results from Equation 2.45 is the *bandwidth of the signal* g(t). Usually, signals that have little power above B are made bandlimited by passing the signal through a low pass filter, thus, removing power above B Hz.

2.3 TRANSMISSION CHANNEL

As depicted in Figure 2.1, the transmission channel is an essential component of any communication system including local area networks. In this section we discuss the three most used channel types in local area networks: pair wires, coaxial cables, and optical fibers. The first two types of channels are special cases of transmission lines, and thus they are treated together. Signal propagation in optical fibers is based on light propagation rather than voltage (or current) propagation, as is the case for pair wires and coaxial cables. However, both electrical signals and light are special cases of *electromagnetic waves*; thus some of the discussion includes electromagnetic waves.

A major component of a transmission channel is the medium over which a signal propagates from a transmitter to a receiver. The medium for a telephone communication system can be a pair of wires, whereas the medium for a television communication system can be a combination of free air and coaxial cable. There is a subtle difference between a channel and a medium; indeed some authors use them interchangeably.[5] A **communication channel** accepts *input symbols* at its transmitter side and delivers *output symbols* at its receiver side. In addition to the transmission medium, a channel involves appropriate amplifiers, data encoders, filters, modulators, etc.

Ideally, the channel should reproduce a signal at the receiver which is identical to that sent by the transmitter. However, all channels introduce some impairments, which makes it difficult, sometimes nearly impossible, to recover the original signal that was sent at the transmitter. For example, as signals travel through channels they experience loss of signal strength. This is known as **attenuation.**

Transmission media can be bounded or unbounded, depending upon whether the transmitted signal is radiated by means of an antenna. Bounded media do not require the use of antennas at the transmitter side. The transmitter places the signal directly on the bounded medium, which is physically connected to the receiver. Examples of bounded media include pair-wires, coaxial cable, waveguides, and optical fibers. Antennas are required in order to radiate signals into an unbounded medium. The medium is unbounded, in that no effort is made to contain the radiation in a bounded area or volume. The signal is radiated in several directions, depending on the *directivity*[6] of the

---

[4] It is assumed that the signal is not modulated.

[5] A channel can be viewed as the logical subdivision of the signal transmission capacity of a medium. For example, a coaxial cable (i.e., the medium) carrying TV signals is typically divided into channels of 6 MHz each.

[6] Directivity is a figure of merit of an antenna which measures the spatial distribution of radiated energy.

antenna. An antenna that radiates energy equally in all directions is *omnidirectional*; otherwise it is directional. Any receiver located in the path of the radiation is able to detect the transmitted signal. Examples of unbounded media include air, water, earth, and free space.

As noted, electrical signals belong to the family of electromagnetic waves. For example, radio, TV, and computer communication signals are all forms of electromagnetic energy. What characterizes one signal from another is its frequency f or wavelength, λ which are related by

$$v = \lambda f \qquad (2.50)$$

where v is the speed of the electromagnetic wave. For example, if the electromagnetic wave is light traveling in free space as the medium, then v = c, referred to as the speed of light, which is approximately 3×10^8 m/sec.

Depending upon the frequency spectrum of a transmitted signal, certain media are more appropriate than others for the transmission of that signal. For example, pair-wires are generally used for the transmission of bandlimited signals whose cutoff frequency B is relatively low (up to a few Mhz)[7], because the resistance and radiation of the wire increase at higher frequencies. Figure 2.11 shows the electromagnetic spectrum divided into several regions, along with appropriate media used and typical applications.

As noted, we are mostly interested in *bounded media* in the form of *transmission lines* and *optical fibers*. In the remainder of this section, a brief summary of transmission lines is presented only as it relates to signal transmission. Another important type of bounded media is the optical fiber, which is also treated briefly.

2.3.1 Transmission Lines

In this subsection we are interested primarily in signal power relationships and medium attenuation associated with transmission lines, which are fundamental for defining the important concept of medium bandwidth. We begin with the equations governing current and voltage relationships in a transmission line, followed by the concepts of characteristic impedance, propagation velocity, and attenuation. Medium bandwidth is defined at the end of this subsection.

A transmission line such as a pair-wire or coaxial cable can be thought of as a distributed electrical circuit, as shown in Figure 2.12. Several types of transmission lines are shown in Figure 2.13, along with the generated electric and magnetic fields caused when current flows through the line. The instantaneous voltage v(x,t) and current i(x,t) can be thought of changing as one moves in one direction or the opposite direction in the transmission line. Because of the distributed nature of the transmission line, the equations governing v(x,t) and i(x,t) are partial differential equations given by

$$\frac{\partial v}{\partial x} = -\left(Ri + L\frac{\partial i}{\partial t}\right) \qquad (2.51)$$

$$\frac{\partial i}{\partial x} = -\left(Gv + C\frac{\partial v}{\partial t}\right) \qquad (2.52)$$

where R, L, G, and C are the resistance, inductance, conductance, and capacitance per unit length, respectively. The units for R, L, G, and C are Ω/m (ohm/meter), H/m (henry/meter), ℧/m (mho/meter), and F/m (farad/meter) respectively.

---

[7] The exact value of B depends on the length of the transmission medium.

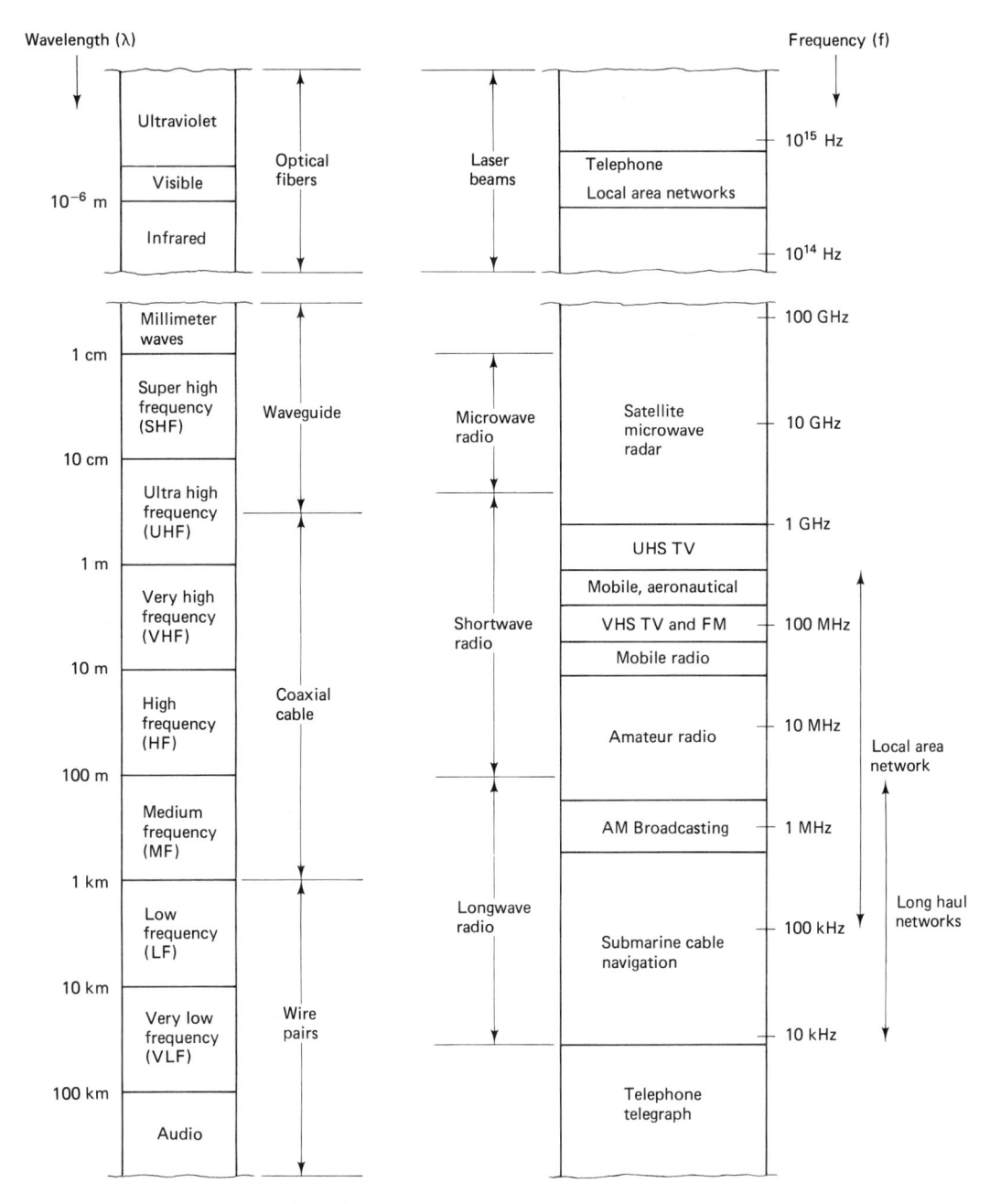

Figure 2.11 The electromagnetic spectrum and some applications.

Sec. 2.3 Transmission Channel

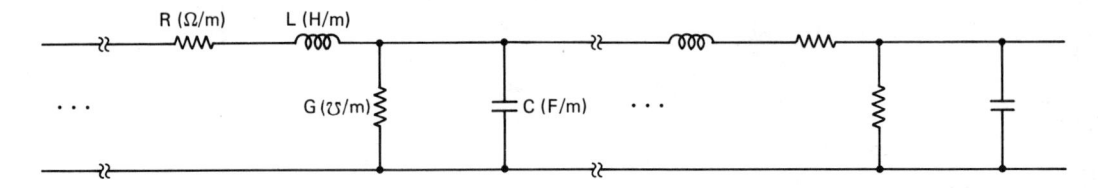

Figure 2.12 A transmission line model and its distributed parameters.

Many of the important properties of transmission lines can be obtained if one assumes that the signals v and i are sinusoids; thus

$$v(x,t) = \text{Re}\{V(x)\,e^{j\omega t}\} = V(x)\cos\omega t \tag{2.53}$$

$$i(x,t) = \text{Re}\{I(x)\,e^{j\omega t}\} = I(x)\cos\omega t \tag{2.54}$$

Under these assumptions, the equivalent differential equations for the transmission line are

$$\frac{dV}{dx} = -(R + j\omega L)I \tag{2.55}$$

$$\frac{dI}{dx} = -(G + j\omega C)V \tag{2.56}$$

(a) Open two-wire line

(b) Shielded pair

(c) Coaxial cable

- - - - Electric field

———— Magnetic field

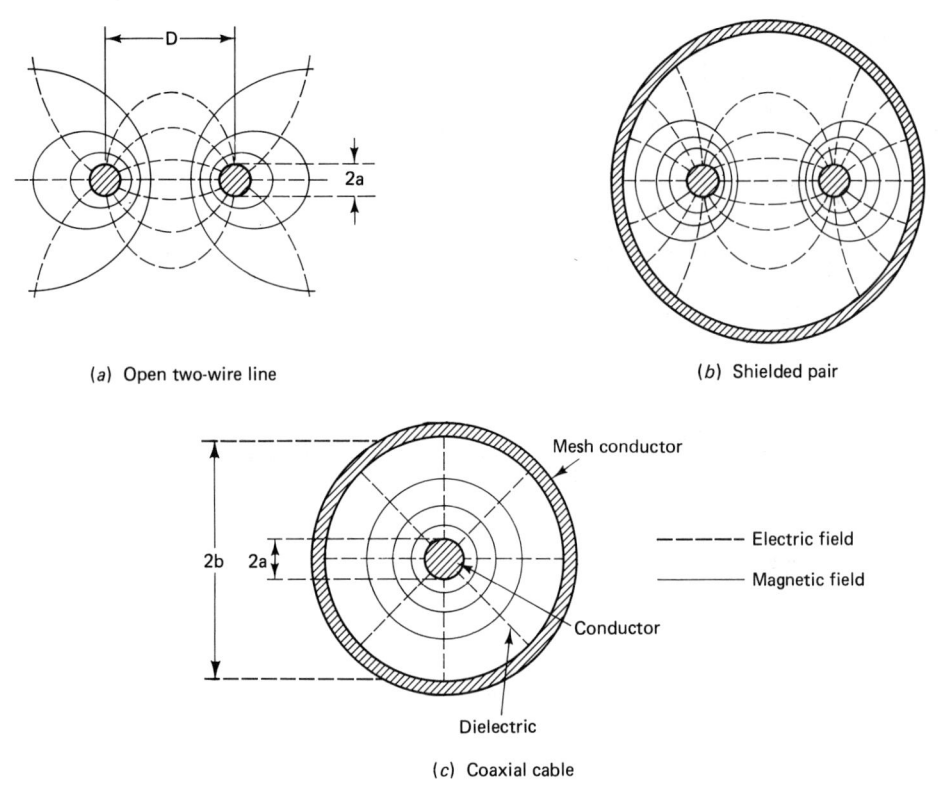

Figure 2.13 Electric and magnetic fields on three types of transmission lines.

46   Background for the OSI Lower Layers   Chap. 2

whose solution is

$$V(x) = A_1 e^{-\gamma x} + A_2 e^{\gamma x} \tag{2.57}$$

$$I(x) = \frac{1}{Z_o}[A_1 e^{-\gamma x} - A_2 e^{\gamma x}] \tag{2.58}$$

where

$$\gamma = \sqrt{(R + j\omega L)(G + j\omega C)} \tag{2.59}$$

and

$$Z_o = \sqrt{\frac{R + j\omega L}{G + j\omega C}} \tag{2.60}$$

The parameters A_1 and A_2 depend on initial conditions. γ is referred to as the *propagation constant*. In general, γ is a complex number of the form $\gamma = \alpha + j\beta$ where α is the *attenuation constant* and β is the *phase constant*. Z_o is referred to as the **characteristic impedance** of the transmission line. The characteristic impedance Z_o is one of the most important parameters of high frequency transmission lines (e.g., coaxial cable).

Transmission lines are used in transmission systems such as the one shown in Figure 2.14. Z_l could represent the impedance of the receiver and Z_t could represent the impedance of the transmitter. An important characteristic of transmission lines is that when a signal arrives at the load Z_l, part of the signal is absorbed by Z_l and part of the signal is reflected. Once reflected, that part of the signal travels back to the transmitter.

Reflected signals cause interference problems with signals sent by the transmitter, and methods exist to overcome these problems as described next. The parameters that characterize the reflection are:

$$k = \frac{\text{voltage reflection}}{\text{coefficient}} = \left(\frac{A_2 e^{\gamma l}}{A_1 e^{-\gamma l}}\right) = \frac{Z_l - Z_o}{Z_l + Z_o} \tag{2.61}$$

$$\frac{\text{current reflection}}{\text{coefficient}} = -\left(\frac{A_2 e^{\gamma l}}{A_1 e^{-\gamma l}}\right) = \frac{Z_o - Z_l}{Z_o + Z_l} \tag{2.62}$$

When $R \ll \omega L$ and $G \ll \omega C$, the transmission line is referred to as **loss-free line.** Loss-free transmission lines are obtained when the values of R and G are negligible or when working at very high frequencies so that the inequalities above are satisfied. For loss-free lines:

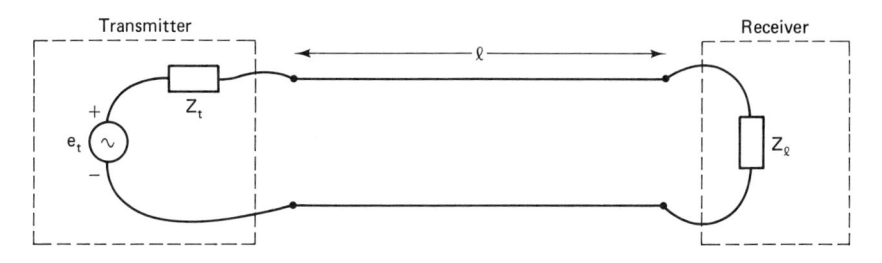

Figure 2.14 A transmission line in a transmission system.

$$Z_o = \sqrt{L/C} \tag{2.63}$$

$$\gamma = j\omega \sqrt{LC} \tag{2.64}$$

An important practical situation in transmission lines occurs when there are no reflections. From Equation 2.61 it can be seen that if the line is terminated in its characteristic impedance (i.e., $Z_l = Z_o$) then there is no reflection. Although unpractical, another way to avoid reflections is to have a line with infinite length (i.e., a very long line). These two equivalent cases are illustrated in Figure 2.15. For this situation, the expressions for V and I become

$$V = V_s e^{-\gamma x} = V_s e^{-\alpha x} e^{-j\beta x} \tag{2.65}$$

and

$$I = \frac{V_s}{Z_o} e^{-\alpha x} e^{-j\beta x} \tag{2.66}$$

A line terminated in its characteristic impedance is referred to as a **correctly terminated** or a nonresonant line. On a line so terminated, energy flows from the transmitter and gets absorbed by the receiver with no reflection. This solves the problem of a reflected signal interfering with a transmitted signal.

Equation 2.65 is equivalent to

$$v(x,t) = \sqrt{2} \, V_s \, e^{-\alpha x} \cos(\omega t - \beta x) \tag{2.67}$$

Thus, the amplitude of $v(x,t)$ is attenuated by the factor $e^{-\alpha x}$ and its phase is decreased by βx. The phase lag is caused by the finite time required for the wave to travel the distance x at a velocity

$$v = \omega/\beta \tag{2.68}$$

The parameter v is referred to as the **propagation velocity.**

Example

Consider a correctly terminated transmission line of length l meters as shown in Figure 2.16. Calculate the ratio of the average power at the input of the line and the average power at the output of the line.

Solution Let us assign a coordinate system so that $x = 0$ at the input of the line and $x = l$ at the output of it. The voltage and current at the input of the line are then given by

$$v(0,t) = \sqrt{2} \, V_s \cos \omega t$$

$$i(0,t) = \sqrt{2} \, (V_s/Z_o) \cos \omega t$$

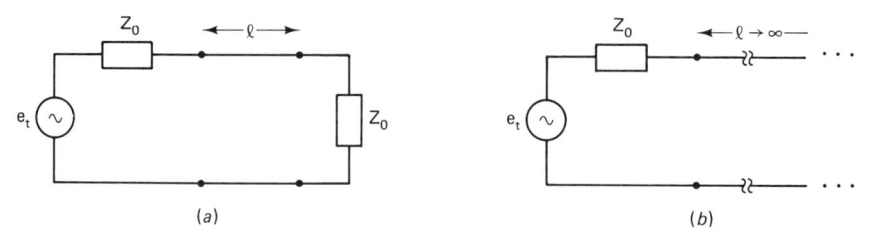

Figure 2.15 Transmission lines with no reflections.

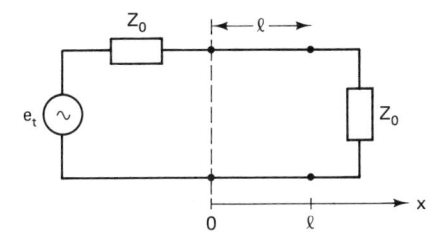

Figure 2.16 A correctly terminated line.

Thus, the input power is

$$p(0,t) = 2\,(V_s^2/Z_o)\cos^2\omega t$$

whose average value is $P_1 = V_s^2/Z_o$.

Likewise, at the output of the line we have

$$v(l,t) = \sqrt{2}\,V_s\,e^{-\alpha l}\cos(\omega t - \beta l)$$

$$i(l,t) = \sqrt{2}\,\frac{V_s}{Z_o}\,e^{-\alpha l}\cos(\omega t - \beta l)$$

The output power is then

$$p(l,t) = 2\,\frac{V_s^2}{Z_o}\,e^{-2\alpha l}\cos^2(\omega t - \beta l)$$

whose average value is $P_2 = (V_s^2/Z_o)\,e^{-2\alpha l}$

Thus, the ratio of average output power to average input power is

$$P_2/P_1 = e^{-2\alpha l} \qquad (2.69)$$

which depends only on the attenuation constant and the cable length.

The previous example shows that, for a correctly terminated transmission line, the line can be modeled by a linear system with transfer function $H(\omega) = e^{-\alpha l}$ and $\theta(\omega) = -\beta(\omega)l$. A correctly terminated line has several advantages, with perhaps the two most important being that, first, voltages and currents get absorbed by the load and are not reflected, and second, maximum power transfer to the load is achieved. This is why in community antenna television (CATV) systems and networks based on coaxial cable technology, it is important that all cable segments are correctly terminated.

For a loss-free line, from Equation 2.59, $\beta = \omega\sqrt{LC}$, thus

$$v = 1/\sqrt{LC} \qquad (2.70)$$

Equations 2.59 and 2.60 are generally difficult to work with because of the square root operator. The following approximations are often used for most practical cases. For lines with good insulation $G \ll \omega C$ and Z_o can be written more simply as

$$Z_o \approx \sqrt{\frac{L}{C}}\sqrt{1 - j\frac{R}{\omega L}} \qquad (2.71)$$

Likewise, as the frequency increases, $\omega L \gg R$ and $\omega C \gg G$. Under these conditions, γ can be expanded by the binomial theorem and retain only the first two terms. The result is

Sec. 2.3 Transmission Channel

$$\gamma \approx \frac{R}{2}\sqrt{\frac{C}{L}} + \frac{G}{2}\sqrt{\frac{L}{C}} + j\omega\sqrt{LC} \qquad (2.72)$$

For high frequencies, $Z_o \approx \sqrt{L/C}$, thus

$$\alpha \approx \frac{R}{2Z_o} + \frac{G}{2}Z_o \qquad (2.73)$$

and

$$\beta \approx \omega\sqrt{LC} \qquad (2.74)$$

The constants of parallel-wire lines. The previous section showed that the most important parameters of a transmission line, namely Z_o, α, and β are expressed in terms of R,G,L, and C, which are referred to as the **constants of the transmission line.**

For the parallel-wire transmission line shown in Figure 2.13(a), when the wire radius a is much smaller than the spacing between wires D, we have

$$C = \frac{27.77 \, (Er)}{\ln(D/a)} \qquad \text{pico farad/meter} \qquad (2.75)$$

$$Z_o = \frac{120}{\sqrt{Er}} \ln(D/a) \qquad \text{ohms} \qquad (2.76)$$

where Er is the relative dielectric constant and ln is the natural logarithm operator. For a copper conductor, where the wire radius a is in centimeters

$$R = 8.34 \times 10^{-6} \sqrt{f}/a \qquad \text{ohms/meter} \qquad (2.77)$$

where f is the frequency of operation in Hz.

The constants of coaxial lines. Consider the coaxial line as depicted in Figure 2.13(c) with outer radius b and inner radius a. For high enough frequencies so that $\omega L \gg R$ and $\omega C \gg G$, the line constants are

$$C = \frac{55.55 \, (Er)}{\ln(b/a)} \qquad \text{pico farad/meter} \qquad (2.78)$$

$$Z_o = \frac{60}{\sqrt{Er}} \ln(b/a) \qquad \text{ohms} \qquad (2.79)$$

Assuming copper conductors with radii given in centimeters

$$R = 4.2 \times 10^{-6} \sqrt{f} \left(\frac{1}{a} + \frac{1}{b}\right) \qquad \text{ohms/meter} \qquad (2.80)$$

Example

Assume a coaxial cable with solid polyethylene dielectric with relative constant Er = 2.26 and radius ratio b/a = 3.59. Calculate the characteristic impedance Z_o.

Solution Direct application of Equation 2.79 yields

$$Z_o = 60 \ln (3.59) / \sqrt{2.26}$$
$$= 51.01 \text{ ohms}$$

If we use air as a dielectric with Er = 1, the characteristic impedance Z_o = 76.68 ohms.

Example

For the coaxial cable in the previous example with Er = 2.26, calculate the propagation velocity v.

Solution Since $Z_o = \sqrt{L/C}$, from Equation 2.70,

$$v = 1 / Z_o C$$

From Equation 2.78

$$C = 55.55 \text{ Er} / \ln (b/a) = 98.23 \text{ pF/m}$$

Therefore,

$$v = 1 / 51.01 \times 98.23 \text{ pF/m} = 1.922 \times 10^8 \text{ m/sec}$$

It is sometimes convenient to express v as a percentage of the speed of light c; thus v% = 100 v/c = 66.52%. Thus, the signal travels on this particular coaxial cable at about 2/3 of the speed of light.

Example

Cable attenuation is an important parameter used for network design. The coaxial cable attenuation constant given by Equation 2.73 can be approximated by $\alpha \approx R / 2 Z_o$. Using Equations 2.80 and 2.69, find an expression for the cable attenuation A per length of cable defined as

$$A = \frac{10 \log (P2/P1)}{L} \quad \text{in (dB/Km)} \tag{2.80a}$$

where L is the cable length in Km, and P_2 and P_1 are average output and input power respectively.

Solution Using Equation 2.80, we have

$$\alpha = \frac{4.2 \times 10^{-6}}{2 Z_o} \sqrt{f} \left(\frac{1}{a} + \frac{1}{b} \right) \quad \text{meter}^{-1} \tag{2.80b}$$

From Equation 2.69,

$$A = 10 \log (e^{-2\alpha l})/L \tag{2.80c}$$
$$= -20\alpha l \log(e) / L$$

Since l is the cable length in meters, l/L = 1000; thus

$$A = -20000\alpha \log(e) \quad \text{(dB/Km)} \tag{2.80d}$$
$$= -8685.8\alpha \quad \text{(dB/Km)}$$

The preceding example shows that the attenuation of a line is proportional to the square root of the frequency f, and is inversely proportional to the conductor dimensions (i.e., a and b in Figure

2.13). Since the other constants of a line (i.e., C, Z_o) are dependent on the ratio b/a, doubling the size of a line reduces its attenuation by one-half while leaving the other constants unaltered.

Medium bandwidth. We are now in a position to define medium bandwidth. It is clear from equations 2.69 and 2.80 or 2.77 that the cable attenuation (P_2/P_1) is proportional to the square root of the frequency f. In other words, as f increases, less power is delivered at the receiver side of a transmission system. If f is very high, practically no power is delivered to the receiver. The frequency f_{bw} for which the delivered power P_2 is half of the transmitted power P_1 is known as the *medium bandwidth*. Thus, medium bandwidth indicates the ability of a medium to deliver most of the signal power up to a certain frequency. The relationship between signal bandwidth and medium bandwidth is simple; a signal can be transmitted on a certain medium only if the signal bandwidth is less than the medium bandwidth.

2.3.2 Channel Characterization

Channel definition. In many cases, the entire medium bandwidth is not used by just one signal because of the following reasons: First, some signals have bandwidths which are much lower than the medium bandwidth. Second, even if several signals are combined into a new one having longer bandwidth, digital technology is not so well advanced to work at very high speeds. Lastly, some frequency ranges are susceptible to noise and interference and are avoided altogether. Instead, the overall medium bandwidth is typically divided into a number of segments, called **channels,** of arbitrary size. **Channel bandwidth** is the portion of medium bandwidth assigned to that channel. For example, coaxial cables are typically divided into a number of channels each having 6 MHz of bandwidth.

Channel model. In addition to channel bandwidth, we are also interested in a model that could aid in studying the effect of a channel on signal propagation. One of the most simple and useful channel models is to view it as a linear system. A linear system is characterized by a single function $H(\omega)$, known as the system transfer function. Figure 2.17 depicts a channel modeled as a linear system where the input signal g(t) is the transmitted signal and the output signal r(t) is the received signal. The basic relationship between the input spectrum $G(\omega)$ and the output spectrum $R(\omega)$ is

$$R(\omega) = H(\omega) \, G(\omega) \tag{2.81}$$

In general,

$$G(\omega) = |G(\omega)| \, e^{j\theta_g(\omega)} \text{ and } H(\omega) = |H(\omega)| e^{j\theta_h(\omega)}$$

thus,

$$R(\omega) = G(\omega) \, H(\omega) = |G(\omega)||H(\omega)|e^{j(\theta_g(\omega) + \theta_h(\omega))} \tag{2.82}$$

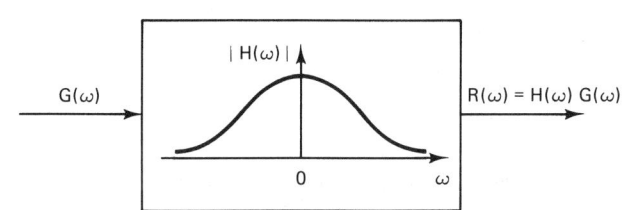

Figure 2.17 A linear system representing a channel.

Therefore, the effect of the channel is to multiply the magnitude of the input spectrum $G(\omega)$ by the amount $|H(\omega)|$ at every frequency, and to add $\theta_h(\omega)$ to the input phase spectrum $\theta_g(\omega)$. Because *attenuation constants* are nonnegligible, channels with $|H(\omega)| = 1$ and $\theta_h(\omega) = 0$ are impossible to obtain in practice. The next best thing to do is to be willing to tolerate some delay in the transmission. Channels that allow the input and output signals to have identical waveshapes and the output to be delayed an amount t_d of time are called *distortionless channels*. Thus, for a distortionless channel we have

$$r(t) = k\, g(t - t_d) \tag{2.83}$$

Because we are assuming that the input and output signals have identical waveshapes, this implies

$$|H(\omega)| = k \tag{2.84}$$

If the output signal $r(t)$ is always delayed an amount t_d, then for $r(t) = \cos \omega(t - t_d) = \cos(\omega t - \omega t_d)$ this implies that the output phase is always lagged by ωt_d. Hence,

$$\theta_h(\omega) = e^{-\omega t_d} \tag{2.84a}$$

The reasoning for obtaining $H(\omega)$ and $\theta_h(\omega)$ can be supported analytically by taking the Fourier transform on both sides of Equation 2.83, yielding

$$R(\omega) = k\, G(\omega)\, e^{-j\omega t_d} \tag{2.85}$$

$$= G(\omega)\, H(\omega)$$

from which Equations (2.84) and (2.84a) follow.

Example

A certain transmission medium is modeled as an RC circuit, as shown in Figure 2.18. a) Determine the transfer function $H(\omega)$ and sketch its magnitude $H(\omega)$ and phase $\theta_h(\omega)$. For distortionless transmission through this channel, b) what is the condition to be met by the bandwidth of $g(t)$? c) What is the transmission delay? d) Find $r(t)$ when $g(t) = 5\cos 1000t$. Assume that $R = 75\,\Omega$ and $C = 30$ pF.

Solution For the circuit shown

$$H(\omega) = \frac{1/j\omega C}{R + (1/j\omega C)} = \frac{1}{1 + j\omega RC} = \frac{a}{a + j\omega}$$

where

$$a = 1/RC = 1/75 \times 30 \times 10^{-12} = 444.44 \times 10^6$$

a) The magnitude of $H(\omega)$ is given by $|H(\omega)| = \dfrac{a}{(a^2 + \omega^2)^{1/2}}$

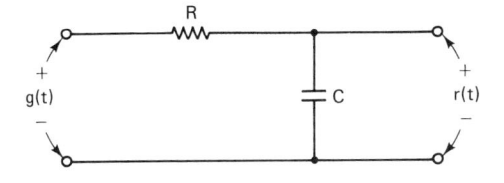

Figure 2.18 An RC circuit model for a transmission medium.

The phase of H(ω) is given by

$$\theta_h(\omega) = -\tan^{-1}(\omega/a)$$

Note that the transfer function is similar to the frequency domain function plotted in Figure 2.8. Thus, the magnitude and phase shift of the channel are similar to those of Figure 2.8. b) From Figure 2.8 and the expression for H(ω), one can see that for $\omega \ll a$, the magnitude and phase characteristics are practically ideal. Thus, for a low pass signal of bandwidth B $\ll a/2$ the transmission is practially distortionless. c) The transmission delay t_d is the negative slope of the phase characteristic. For $\omega \ll a$, $\theta_h(\omega) = -\omega/a$, and $t_d = 1/a = 2.25$ nano seconds. d) For the input g(t) = 5 cos 1000t, because $\omega = 1000 \ll 4.44 \times 10^8$, the transmission is practically distortionless, hence,

$$r(t) = \cos(1000(t - 2.25 \times 10^{-9}))$$

Distortionless channels for bandpass signals. The general expression for a bandpass signal is

$$g_{bp}(t) = g_c(t) \cos \omega_o t + g_s(t) \sin \omega_o t \qquad (2.86)$$

If a bandpass signal is to be transmitted with no distortion over a channel, then the conditions for distortionless transmission are

a) $\qquad |H(\omega)| = k \qquad \text{for } |\omega - \omega_o| < 2B \qquad (2.87)$

b) $\qquad \dfrac{d\theta_h}{d\omega} = t_g \qquad \text{a constant for } |\omega - \omega_o| < 2B \qquad (2.88)$

For a proof of the preceding conditions see Lathi (1983). The corresponding received signal is

$$r_{bp}(t) = k[g_c(t-t_g) \cos \omega_o(t-t_p) + g_s(t-t_g) \sin \omega_o(t-t_p)] \qquad (2.89)$$

where

$$t_p = -\frac{\theta_h(\omega_o)}{\omega_o} \qquad (2.90)$$

t_g and t_p are known as the **group delay** and **phase delay**, respectively.

Effect of channels on spectral densities. Let g(t) and r(t) be the input and output signals of a channel characterized with a transfer function H(ω); then

$$R(\omega) = H(\omega) G(\omega)$$

The energy spectral density of the input and output are related by

$$\Psi_r(\omega) = |R(\omega)|^2 \qquad (2.91)$$

$$= |H(\omega) G(\omega)|^2 = |H(\omega)|^2 \Psi_g(\omega) \qquad (2.92)$$

Likewise, the power spectral densities are related by

$$S_r(\omega) = |H(\omega)|^2 S_g(\omega) \qquad (2.93)$$

Thus, the effect of a channel on either the energy or power spectral density of the input signal is to multiply them by the square of the magnitude of the channel transfer function to obtain the corresponding output energy or power spectral density.

Signal distortion over a channel. When signals travel over a channel they are subject to a number of impairments. There are several sources of impairment such as linear distortion, channel nonlinearities, and multipath effects. Linear distortion is the most simple one to consider. Distortion occurs because the channel attenuation is not constant at different frequencies and the phase shift is not linear with frequency. Thus, a channel introduces linear distortion when

$$|H(\omega)| \neq k \tag{2.94}$$

and

$$\theta_h(\omega) \neq -\omega t_d \tag{2.95}$$

2.3.3 Noise

As signals travel from a source to their destination they get contaminated by unwanted signals referred to as **noise.** Noise sources can be varied. Noise signals introduced or gathered by a channel are of the following types: thermal noise, crosstalk noise, and impulse noise. **Thermal noise** is caused by the random movements of electrons in electrical conductors. **Crosstalk noise** is caused by unwanted signals coming from adjacent channels on the same transmission medium or other media in close physical proximity. **Impulse noise** is caused by signal (e.g., voltage) spikes originated by equipment located close to the cable. An example of equipment generating impulse noise are *welding machines*, going on and off.

In the remainder of this section we concentrate on thermal noise, because in some cases crosstalk and impulse noise can be avoided or reduced. For example, in a medium where there are neither other channels nor other media in close proximity, there is no crosstalk noise. Impulse noise can be reduced by appropriate shielding or choosing appropriate media. One advantage of optical fibers is that impulse noise is practically eliminated.

Thermal noise. Thermal noise is caused by the random movements of electrons in electrical conductors. The random movement of electrons produces a random current which, over a long period of time, averages to zero. This is because as many electrons on the average move in one direction as another. In the 1920s J. B. Johnson found experimentally, and H. Nyquist verified theoretically, that the mean squared value of voltage fluctuations across a resistor due to thermal noise is given by

$$E[v^2] = 4kTRB \tag{2.96}$$

where T is the temperature in degrees Kelvin °K, R is the resistance value in Ohms, k is the Boltzmann constant equal to 1.38×10^{-23} J/°K, B is any arbitrary bandwidth in Hz, and E is the expected value operator (i.e., the mean).[8] Equation 2.96 implies that noise is white (i.e., it does not change with frequency). For white noise, $E[v^2]$ is usually written as NB, where N/2 is the voltage noise spectral density in volts^2/Hz. From Equation 2.96 the voltage thermal-noise spectral density is thus given by

---

[8] See Stark and Woods (1986) for a review of probabilities.

$$VSD = N/2 = E[v^2]/2B = 2kTR \qquad (2.97)$$

Example

Calculate the amount of thermal voltage noise generated by a coaxial cable with 75 ohms of characteristic impedance, operating at 20 °C (68 °F) on a channel of 6 M Hz bandwith. This bandwidth is the standard bandwidth used by the CATV industry, and the resulting noise is referred to as the *noise floor*.

Solution From Equation 2.96,

$$E[v^2] = 4kTRB$$

for $T = 20 + 273 = 293$ °K, and $R = 75\ \Omega$

$$E[v^2] = 4 \times 1.38 \times 10^{-23}\ (J/°K) \times 293(°K) \times 75\ \Omega\ B$$

$$E[v^2] = 121.3 \times 10^{-20} \times B$$

The root mean square (rms) value is then

$$\sqrt{E[v^2]} = 11 \times 10^{-10}\ \sqrt{B}\ \text{volts (rms)}$$

The equivalent circuit of the cable segment with the thermal noise appearing as a voltage source is depicted in Figure 2.16. For a line terminated in its characteristic impedance, the voltage delivered to any load is half of that generated. Thus, the thermal noise appearing at any device or coupled to any circuit is

$$v = 5.5 \times 10^{-7}\ \sqrt{B}\ \text{mV (rms)} \qquad (2.98)$$

Expressing the voltage in units of dBmV, we have

$$v\ \text{dBmV} = 20 \log (v/1mV)$$

$$= 20 \log 5.5 - 140 \log 10 + 10 \log B \qquad (2.99)$$

$$= -125.19 + 10 \log B \quad \text{in dBmV.}$$

For $B = 6$ M Hz, the noise floor voltage is then

$$v\ \text{dBmV} = -57.40\ \text{dBmV} \qquad (2.100)$$

Thermal noise can also be expressed in terms of power. The maximum power available obtained under matched conditions is called the *available power*. From Figure 2.16, the available power in a bandwidth of B Hz is

$$P = E[v^2]/4R = kTB = NB \qquad (2.101)$$

The corresponding power spectral density (PSD) in watts/Hz is given by

$$PSD = N/2 = kT/2 \qquad (2.101a)$$

The expression for thermal noise given in Equation 2.96 is actually an approximation for frequencies satisfying $f \ll kT/h$, where k is the Boltzmann constant and h is the Planck constant equal to 6.6257×10^{-34} J-sec. At room temperature, $kT/h = 6.1 \times 10^{12}$ Hz, the general expression for the voltage thermal noise spectral density is given by

$$VSD = E[v^2]/2B = 2(hf/2 + hf/(\exp(hf/kT) - 1)))\ R \qquad (2.102)$$

which corresponds to a power spectral density of

$$PSD = (hf/2 + hf/(\exp(hf/kT) - 1)))/2 \tag{2.103}$$

The importance of equations 2.102 and 2.103 is that for optical fibers which operate in the infrared and optical frequencies ($f \approx 10^{14}$ Hz) the term hf/2, which is negligible for transmission lines, starts playing a dominant role.

Example

Random noise with spectral density given by (N/2) is passed through an ideal low pass filter of bandwidth B Hz. Calculate the noise power N_o of the output.

Solution:

$$N_o = 2 \int_0^B S_n(\omega) \, df = 2 \left(\frac{N}{2}\right) B = NB \tag{2.103a}$$

Signal to noise ratio. An important parameter which is useful for performance analysis of transmission systems is the ratio of signal power S_o to noise power N_o, referred to as the **signal to noise ratio** (SNR). Thus, if a signal (plus its noise) is passed through a low pass filter of bandwidth B Hz, then, using Equation 2.103a,

$$SNR = \frac{S_o}{N_o} = \frac{S_o}{NB} \tag{2.104}$$

For digital communications, if a signal is transmitted at a rate of R bits/sec, then

$$SNR = \frac{E_b R}{N_o} \tag{2.105}$$

where E_b is the **energy per bit.** Another parameter of interest is the ratio of E_b to noise power spectral density N. From equations 2.104 and 2.105, the ratio is given by

$$\frac{E_b}{N} = \frac{S_o}{R\,N} \quad \text{(Watt/bps)} \tag{2.106a}$$

$$= SNR \times B/R \tag{2.106b}$$

2.3.4 Optical fibers

An optical fiber is another transmission medium which can be used instead of twisted pair or coaxial cables in local area network and other communication systems. Figure 2.20(a) shows some applications of optical fiber transmission systems (Nakagami and others, 1988). When compared with twisted pair and coaxial cables, optical fibers offer the following advantages:

Lower Attenuation. Optical fibers exhibit low loss over a large range of frequencies, typically 1 dB/Km.

Better Noise Immunity. Optical fibers are immune to electromagnetic interference (EMI), which enables them, for instance, to be installed along power lines without suffering interference.

More Bandwidth Available. Typical medium bandwidths are 1 G Hz for multimode fibers and 10 G Hz for single mode fibers spanning distances over 1 Km.

Small Size and Corresponding Low Weight. Typical cable diameters range from 1 to 2 mm with plastic coating.

Elements of an optical fiber transmission link. An optical fiber transmission link is composed of the same major elements as any other communication link, which include a transmitter, the medium, and a receiver, as depicted in Figure 2.19. The transmitter is composed of a drive circuit for conditioning the input electrical signal and a light source acting as a transducer to convert electrical power into optical power. Semiconductor light-emitting diodes (LED) and laser diodes (LD) are suitable light sources. One or several optical fibers are typically enclosed in a cable offering mechanical and enviromental protection. The photodetector performs the inverse function to that of the light source (i.e., converting optical power into electrical power). Semiconductors PIN[9] and avalanche photodiodes (APD) are the principal photodetectors used in a fiber optical link. Since the power of the electrical signal at the output of the photodetector is very small, an amplifier is required. The signal restorer block attempts to shape the amplifier's output signal so that it looks like the transmitted signal.

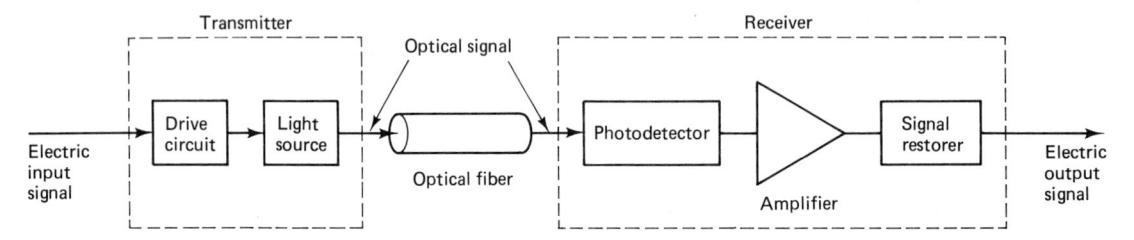

Figure 2.19 Elements of an optical fiber-based transmission system.

One of the most important elements in an optical fiber link is the cabled optical fiber. In addition to protecting the optical fiber during installation and operation, the cable may contain copper wires for powering repeaters, which are needed for amplifying and reshaping the signals when the link spans long distances. As with copper cables, the installation of optical fiber cables can be aerial, in ducts, undersea, or buried directly in the ground.

After an optical signal has been launched into the fiber, it will become progressively attenuated and distorted with increasing distance because of scattering, absorption, and dispersion mechanisms in the fiber. As noted earlier, one of the principal advantages of optical fiber technology is its low attenuation. However, attenuation varies at different optical wavelengths. In the early 1970s, the lowest attenuation was about 4 dB/Km at around 900 nm wavelength. In the mid-1970s, the lowest attenuation was reduced to about 0.5 dB/Km at around 1500 nm wavelength. In the early 1980s, attenuation values as low as 0.3 dB/Km were achieved in the 1100 to 1600 nm region. Current research and development on new fiber optic materials for use in the 3 to 5 nm wavelength band indicates that attenuation values of less than 0.01 dB/Km can be obtained (Keiser, 1983). Hatfield et al (1988), discuss optical fiber-based LANs for manufacturing. Optical fiber as LAN media for Ethernet and MAP networks are discussed by Thompson, (1987) and Bergman, (1987) respectively.

Structure of an optical fiber. An optical fiber is a circular solid core with refraction index n_1 surrounded by a cladding with refraction index $n_2 < n_1$ and a buffer coating encapsulating

---

[9] PIN is a special semiconductor photodiode.

the fiber, as shown in Figure 2.20(b). The fiber confines electromagnetic energy in the form of light within its surfaces and guides the light in a direction parallel to its axis. The core and surrounding cladding is also referred to as a **dielectric waveguide.** In low and medium-loss fibers, the core material is generally glass surrounded by either glass or plastic cladding. Higher-loss plastic core fibers with plastic cladding are also widely used.

Variations in the material composition of the core give rise to the two commonly used fiber types shown in Figure 2.21. When the refractive index of the core is uniform throughout and undergoes an abrupt change (i.e., a step) at the cladding boundary, the fiber type is referred to as a **step-index fiber.** Also, when the core refractive index varies as a function of the radial distance from the center of the fiber, the type is a **graded-index fiber.** Regardless of its type (i.e., step-index or graded-index) a fiber can sustain one (single mode) or many (multimode) modes of prop-

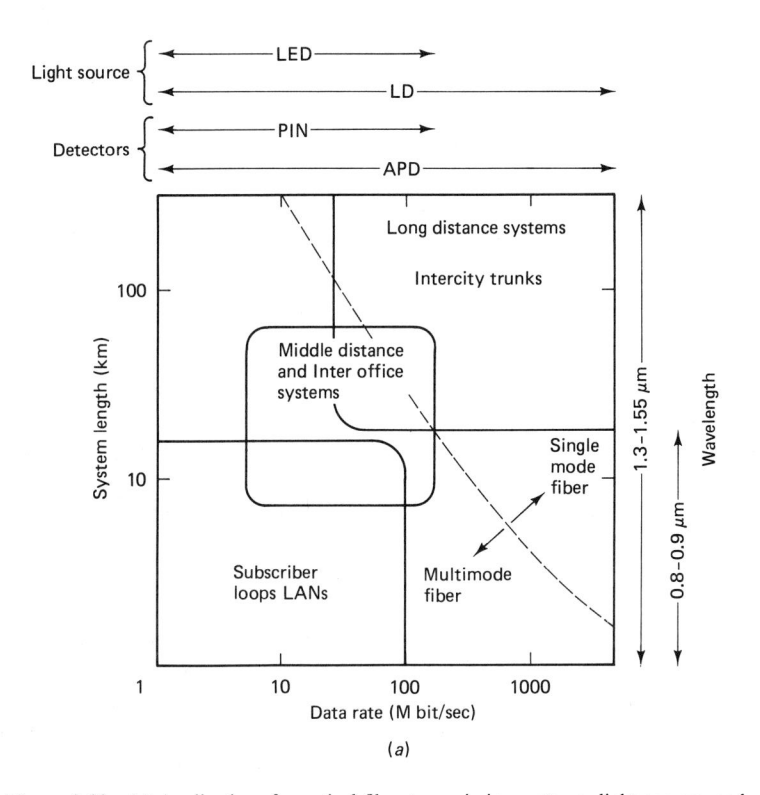

Figure 2.20 (a) Applications for optical fiber transmission systems, light sources, and detectors.

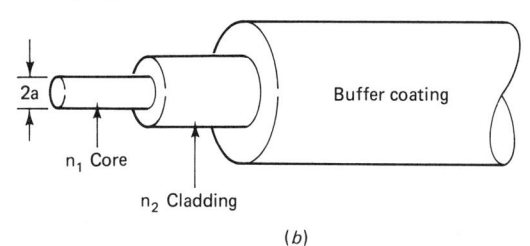

Figure 2.20 (b) Structure of an optical fiber.

Sec. 2.3 Transmission Channel

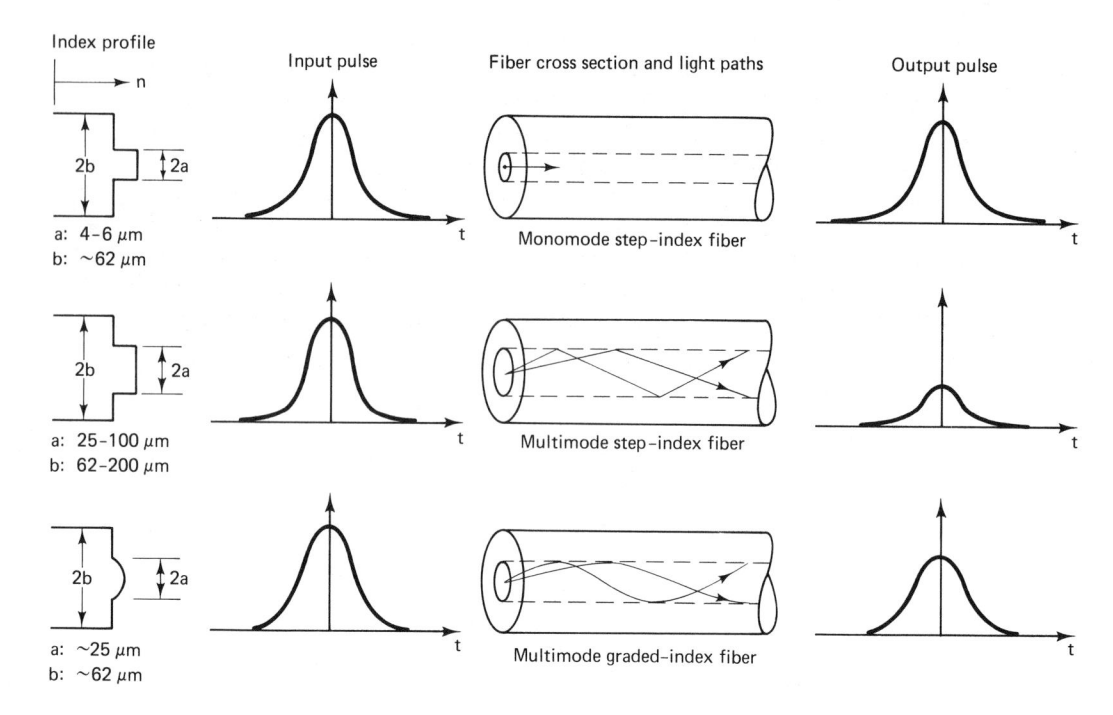

Figure 2.21 Types of optical fibers.

agation. Multimode fibers offer several advantages when compared to single-mode fibers. First, the larger core radii of multimode fibers make it easier to launch optical power into the fiber and facilitate the interconnection of similar fibers. Another advantage is that light can be launched into a multimode fiber using a light-emitting-diode (LED) source, whereas single-mode fibers must be excited with laser diodes. Although LEDs have less optical output power than laser diodes, they are easier to make, are less expensive, require less complex circuitry, and have longer lifetimes than laser diodes, thus making then more desirable in many applications.

A disadvantage of multimode fibers is that they suffer from intermodal dispersion. When an optical pulse is launched into a fiber, the optical power is distributed over all (or most) of the modes of the fiber. Each of the modes propagating in a multimode fiber travels at a slighty different velocity, thus arriving at the fiber end at different times. The effect known as **intermodal dispersion,** is that the pulse is spread out in time as it travels along the fiber. *Intermodal dispersion* can be reduced by using graded-index fibers, thus allowing larger bandwidths. Even higher bandwidths are possible in single mode fibers, since intermodal effects are not present.

Step-index fibers. In a step-index fiber, the refractive indices of the core n_1 and its cladding n_2 can be written as

$$n_2 = n_1 (1 - D) \qquad (2.107)$$

where D is called the **core cladding index difference,** or simply the **index difference.** Since the core refractive index is larger than the cladding index, light propagates along the fiber through internal reflection at the core-cladding interface.

As depicted in Figure 2.22, depending upon n_1 and n_2, light rays can be refracted or reflected at the core-cladding boundary. Using Snell's law, the minimum angle θ_{min} that supports total internal reflection is

$$\sin(\phi_{min}) = n_2/n_1 \qquad (2.108)$$

Rays striking the core-cladding boundary at angles less than ϕ_{min} are refracted and lost in the cladding. The condition in Equation 2.108 is related to the maximum entrance angle θ_o,max through the relationship

$$n \sin \theta_o, \text{max} = n_1 \sin \theta_c = [n_1^2 - n_2^2]^{1/2} \qquad (2.109)$$

where θ_c is the critical angle. Thus, those rays having entrance angles θ_o less than θ_o,max are totally reflected at the core-cladding interface. The term NA $= n \sin \theta_o$,max is related to the maximum acceptance angle and is known as the **numerical aperture** of the step-index fiber. For multimode fibers, the number of modes entering the fiber is approximately given by

$$M = 2(\pi a/\lambda)^2 (n_1^2 - n_2^2) \qquad (2.110)$$

Signal attenuation A (or fiber loss) is defined as the ratio of the optical output power P_{out} from a fiber of length L to the optical input power P_{in}

$$A = \frac{P_{in}/P_{out}}{L} \qquad (2.111)$$

Usually, A is expressed in dB/Km as

$$A \text{ (dB/Km)} = \frac{10 \log(P_{in}/P_{out})}{L} \text{ (dB/Km)} \qquad (2.112)$$

Electrical signals are transmitted as light rays through a modulation process. Figure 2.23 shows how a signal s(t) is used to modulate directly an optical source about a bias current point I_B. With no signal input the optical power output is P_t. When the signal s(t) is applied, the optical output power P(t) is

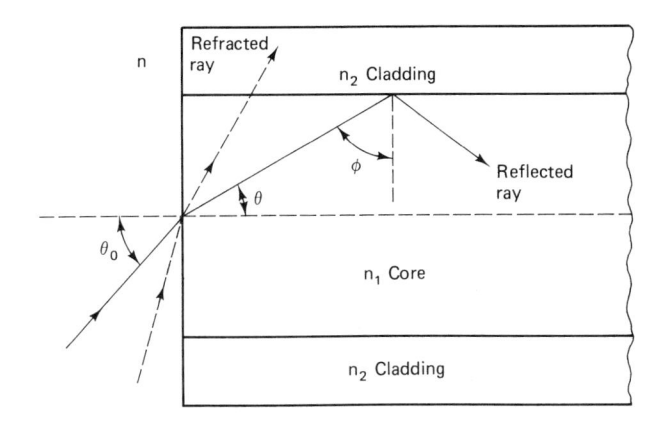

$$P(t) = P_t[1 + m s(t)] \qquad (2.113)$$

Figure 2.22 Refracted and reflected rays in an ideal step-index optical waveguide.

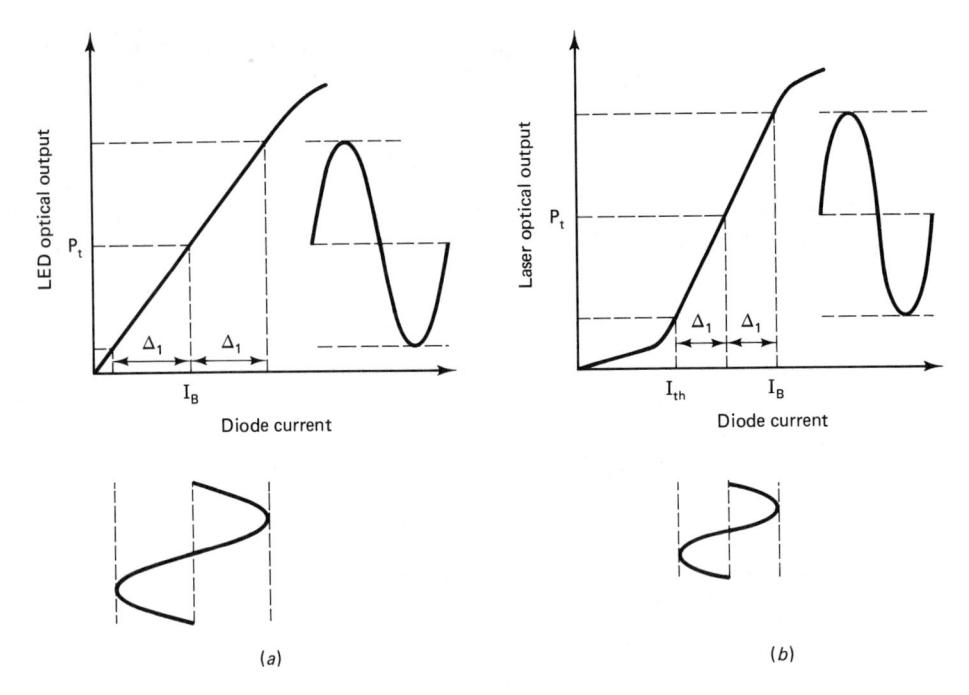

Figure 2.23 Bias point and amplitude modulation range for analog applications of: (a) LED's; and (b) LASER diodes.

where m is called the **modulation index** and is given by

$$m = \Delta I / I'B \tag{2.114}$$

where $I'B = I_B$ for LEDs and $I'B = I_B - I_{th}$ for laser diodes. I_{th} is the threshold current above which optical power is sustained in laser diodes.

A important parameter that characterizes photodetectors is the **responsivity R,** defined by the photocurrent generated per unit optical power. Responsivity is given by

$$R = I_p / P_o \quad (\mu A / \mu W) \tag{2.115a}$$

$$= \eta q / h\nu \tag{2.115b}$$

where η is an equivalent photodetector parameter called the **quantum efficiency,** q is the electron charge, and $h\nu$ is the *photon energy*. Typical values for responsivities are 0.65 $\mu A / \mu W$ for silicon at 800 nm and 0.45 $\mu A / \mu W$ for germanium at 0.3 μm. For avalanche photodiodes (APD), the responsiveness is given by

$$R_{APD} = \frac{\eta q}{h\nu} M \tag{2.116}$$

where M is the *current multiplication factor* associated with avalanche photodiodes.

Photodetector noise. As noted earlier, the signal to noise ratio SNR is an important measure of the channel performance. For optical fiber links, the SNR depends on the fiber parameters and on the photodetector and amplifier characteristics. The signal to noise ratio at the output of an optical receiver is defined by

$$\text{SNR} = \frac{\text{Signal power from photocurrent}}{\text{Photodetector noise power} + \text{amplifier noise power}}$$

Noise contributions at the receiver include photodetector noise resulting from the statistical nature of the photon-to-electron conversion process and thermal noise associated with amplifier circuitry.

Figure 2.24, which shows a model for a photodetector receiver and its equivalent circuit, can help in examining the different noise sources. Let us calculate the SNR for an avalanche photodiode with an average photocurrent I_p^2 and a signal component $i_p(t)$. The mean square signal current $\langle i_s^2 \rangle$ is

$$\langle i_s^2 \rangle = \langle i_p^2(t) \rangle M^2 \quad (2.117)$$

The **quantum** or **shot noise** component is

$$\langle i_Q^2 \rangle = 2q\, I_p\, B\, M^2\, F(M) \quad (2.118)$$

where $F(M)$ is a noise figure associated with the random nature of the avalanche process. A reasonable approximation for $F(M)$ is $F(M) = M^x$, where $0 \leq x \leq 1$ depends on the material.

The **bulk dark current** i_{DB} is given by

$$\langle i_{DB}^2 \rangle = 2q\, I_D\, M^2\, F(M)\, B \quad (2.119)$$

where I_D is the primary (unmultiplied) detector bulk dark current.

The surface dark current is

$$\langle i_{DS}^2 \rangle = 2q\, I_L\, B \quad (2.120)$$

where I_L is the surface leakage current.

Since the dark current and the signal currents are uncorrelated, the total noise current $\langle i_N^2 \rangle$ is

$$\langle i_N^2 \rangle = \langle i_Q^2 \rangle + \langle i_{DB}^2 \rangle + \langle i_{DS}^2 \rangle \quad (2.121a)$$

$$= 2q(I_p + I_D)\, M^2\, F(M)\, B + 2q\, I_L\, B \quad (2.121b)$$

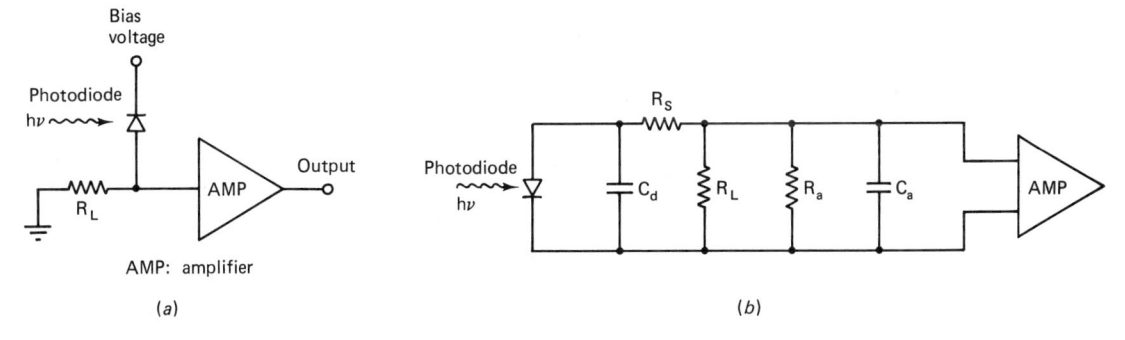

Figure 2.24 (a) Simplified model of a photodetector receiver; and (b) Its equivalent circuit.

The last noise contribution corresponds to that of the thermal noise associated with the photodetector load resistor R_L, which is given by

$$(i_T^2) = \frac{4kTB}{R_L} \qquad (2.122)$$

where k is the Boltzmann's constant and T is the absolute temperature. Substituting equations 2.122, 2.121b, and 2.117 into the SNR definition, we obtain

$$SNR = \frac{(i_p^2) M^2}{2q(I_p + I_D) M^2 F(M) B + 2q I_L B + 4kTB/R_L} \qquad (2.123)$$

2.4 INTRODUCTION TO THE OSI REFERENCE MODEL

History of the OSI reference model. In 1978, the International Organization for Standardization (ISO) Technical Committee 97 on Information Processing recognized the urgent need for standards development for networks of heterogeneous systems, and thus created a new subcommittee number 16 (SC16) for **Open Systems Interconnection.** The term **open** emphasizes that by conforming to OSI standards, a system is open to communication with any other system obeying the same standard anywhere in the world. It was then clear that the commercial systems would not wait for SC16 to develop communication standards nor for the research community to address the most outstanding issues. If there was to be a consistent set of international standards, OSI would have to lead rather than follow commercial development, and make use of the most recent research work when available. The size and nature of the task required the work to be divided among several working groups, each developing standards with close overall coordination.

During the first few meetings of SC16, which started in March 1978, a consensus was reached on a basic layered architecture which would satisfy requirements of the OSI and which could be extended later to meet additional requirements. SC16 decided to give the highest priority to the development of a standard Model and Architecture, which would constitute the framework for the development of standard protocols.

Within 18 months of discussions, SC16 completed the development of the *Reference Model* of Open Systems Interconnection, which was submitted to TC97 along with recommendations to start a number of projects for developing an initial set of standard protocols for OSI. These recommendations were adopted by TC97 at the end of 1979 as the basis for development of standards for Open System Interconnection within the ISO. The OSI Reference Model was also recognized by the CCITT[10] Rapporteur's Group on *Public Data Network Services*. At this time, SC16 began development of standard OSI Protocols for the upper four layers (i.e., transport, session, presentation, and application).

In late 1980, SC16 recommended that the Reference Model be forwarded as a Draft Proposal (DP) for an International Standard. After two rounds of comments, the Reference Model was promoted to a Draft International Standard (DIS) status in the Spring of 1982. Comments on the DIS were processed late in 1982, and the Basic Reference Model became an International Standard (ISO 7498) in the Spring of 1983.

After the OSI reference model was developed, SC16 faced a fairly unusual problem, that of

---

[10] The International Telegraph and Telephone Consultative Committee.

developing a set of standards which emerging products could use before the commercial practices were in place and while some of the more fundamental research issues remained unsolved. Standard committees usually take sets of commercial practices, and the current research results when applicable, and specify the procedures into a single standard that can be utilized by commercial products. Although the problem was not completely solved, SC16 found a way to cope with the problem in such a way as to maximize flexibility and to minimize the impact of new technologies or new implementation techniques.

Layered architecture. As noted in Chapter 1, the approach adopted by SC16 was to use a *layered architecture* to break up the overall task into manageable pieces. The OSI reference model is a framework for coordinating the development of OSI standards. In OSI, the problem is approached in a top-down fashion, with general requirements at the highest level, proceeding to more and more refined descriptions at lower levels. In OSI terms, three levels of abstraction are explicitly recognized: the *architecture*, the *service* specifications, and the *protocol* specifications.

At the highest level of abstraction, we have the *OSI architecture*. The term **architecture** should be defined precisely, since it has been used to describe everything from a framework for development, to a particular form of organization, to hardware. The OSI architecture is covered in detail in Section 2.5.

The OSI reference model defines objects that are used to describe an open system, relations among the objects, and constraints on the objects and relations. Specifications for the lower levels of abstraction may define other relations for their purposes, but these must be consistent with those defined in the reference model.

ISO 7498, the document which describes the OSI architecture, defines the objects, relations, and constraints, and also defines a seven-layer model for interprocess communication constructed from these objects, relations, and constraints. The seven-layer model is used as a framework for coordinating the development of layer standards by OSI committees, as well as for the development of standards built on top of OSI.

The *OSI Service* respresents the next lower level of abstraction for defining the services provided by each layer in a detailed fashion. A **service specification** defines the facilities provided to the service user independent of the mechanisms used to accomplish the service. It also defines an abstract interface for the layer, in that it defines the primitives that a user of the layer may request regardless of how the interface is implemented.

Finally, the *OSI Protocol* represents the lowest level of abstraction in the OSI reference model. Each **protocol** defines precisely what control information is to be sent and what procedures are to be used to interpret this control information. The protocol specifications represent a very detailed set of rules and formats for implementations conforming to OSI standards.

The architecture, services, and protocols define, in increasing level of detail, the **OSI environment.** There are many services and protocols that satisfy the functions required by the reference model. This is the reason why many vendors claim that their products are OSI compatible. There are fewer protocols that satisfy both the reference model and the OSI services specifications Thus, a protocol specification *constrains* implementations sufficiently to allow open systems to communicate, but still allows flexibility in implementation.

Although products can satisfy the architectural constraints imposed by the reference model, they may not be able to communicate with one another unless they also conform to the OSI services and protocols. Thus, conforming to the OSI reference model is a necessary condition but not sufficient for communication among OSI systems. The statement that **this product conforms to the OSI**

Reference Model does not imply the ability to interwork with other products which might make the same claim. Likewise, products can satisfy the service specifications of all network layers and still not be able to communicate with one another unless they conform to the same protocol. The OSI reference model cannot be implemented, and it does not represent a preferred implementation approach. It is a model only for describing the concepts for coordinating the parallel development of interprocess communication standards.

In the remaining sections of this chapter we discuss the elements of the OSI architecture, virtual circuits and datagrams, the seven-layer OSI reference model, and the OSI services and protocols.

2.5 THE ELEMENTS OF THE OSI ARCHITECTURE

The basic OSI reference model (ISO 7498), is divided into two major sections. The first section describes the elements of the architecture, and the second section describes the services, functions, and protocols of each layer.

The architectural elements constitute the building blocks that are used to construct the seven-layer model. The major elements of the OSI Architecture are: layers, entities, services, protocols, virtual circuits, and datagrams. Before discussing the elements in detail, we review general concepts associated with systems, communication requirements, and communication functions, which were introduced briefly in Chapter 1.

2.5.1 Systems, Communication Requirements, and Functions

The OSI reference model is an abstract description of interprocess communication with processes residing in different systems. In the OSI reference model, communication takes place between application processes running in distinct systems. A **system** is considered to be one or more autonomous computers (e.g., a multiprocessor system) and their associated software, peripherals, and users that are capable of information processing and/or transfer. Although OSI techniques could be used to standardize the internal organization of a system, that is not the intent of OSI standardization.

Successful communication between systems involves certain requirements to be met by the communication system. The requirements were briefly identified in Chapter 1, and typically involve:

- an interface with the physical medium used,
- a mechanism for dealing with errors,
- a transparent and reliable message delivery mechanism,
- synchronization between the communication processes, and
- a mechanism for resolving syntax and encoding differences between the communicating systems.

Accordingly, appropriate communication functions must be provided to meet the communication requirements. They are as follows:

- medium interface,
- error control,

- error recovery,
- process synchronization, and
- data transformation and encoder negotiation.

Having reviewed the general concepts associated with systems, communication requirements, and communication functions, we are now in a position to discuss the OSI architecture constituent elements.

2.5.2 Layers and Entities

As noted in Chapter 1, the nature of communication functions can be very complex. The fundamental principle used by OSI in dealing with the complex nature of communication functions is the subdivision of communication functions into several layers, as depicted in Figure 2.25. Thus, we view layering as a structuring technique for logically decomposing a system into independent, smaller subsystems. Each individual subsystem is in turn viewed as being logically composed of a succession of smaller subsystems, each subsystem corresponding to the intersection of the system with a layer. In other words, a layer is viewed as being locally composed of subsystems of the same rank in each of the interconnected stations.

In OSI terms, anything that is used to provide layer functions is referred to as an **entity.** For this reason, the term *entity* is often unclear. Although used extensively in the OSI literature, we avoid using the term *entity* in subsequent chapters of this book, and instead use more specific terms such as *process*. Each subsystem can be viewed as being composed of one or several entities. A layer, therefore, comprises many entities distributed among interconnected systems. Entities in the same layer but located in different stations are called **peer entities** (i.e., peer processes).

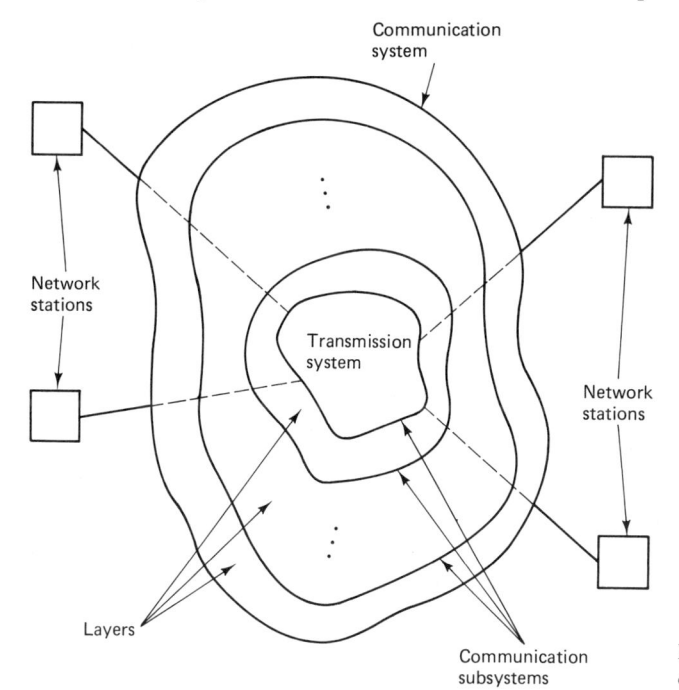

Figure 2.25 Subdivision of communication functions into layers.

Sec. 2.5   The Elements of the OSI Architecture

For simplicity, any layer is referred to as the (N)-layer,[11] while its next lower and next higher are referred to as the (N-1)-layer and the (N + 1)-layer, respectively. The same notation is used to designate all concepts relating to layers. For example, entities in the (N)-layer are termed (N)-entities, as illustrated in Figure 2.26.

The basic idea of layering is that each layer adds value to the functions provided by the lower layers in such a way that the highest layer (i.e., the application layer) is offered the full set of functions needed to support distributed applications. Layering thus divides the overall communication functions into smaller function groups, with each function group constituting a layer.

2.5.3 Services and Service Access Points

The functions performed by a layer are made available to the layer immediately above as a set of *services*. Thus, we can think of a **service** as the functional capability of the (N)-layer which is

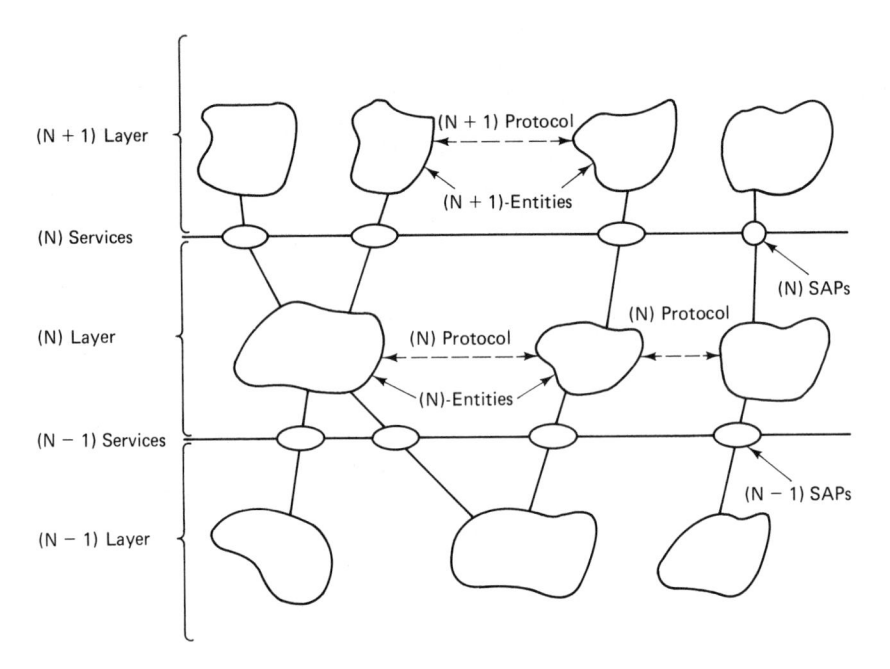

Figure 2.26 Layers, entities, services, and protocols.

provided to the (N + 1)-entities. There are other communication functions performed by a layer that are not made available to the layer immediately above; thus they are not services.

An advantage of layering is that it allows layers to be independent from one another by defining services to be provided by a layer to the next higher layer. Services provided to a layer are independent of how they are performed by the lower layer. This permits changes to be made in the way a layer or a set of layers operates, provided they still offer the same service to the next higher layer. This technique is similar to the one used in structured programming, where only the functions performed by a module, rather than the details of the module, are known by its users.

---

[11] When referring to specific layers, we use a nomenclature such as layer 2 or layer 3.

(N)-entities distributed among the interconnected systems work collectively to provide the (N)-service to (N + 1)-entities, as illustrated in Figure 2.26. Thus, the (N)-entities add value to the (N − 1) service they get from the (N − 1)-layer and offer this value-added service (i.e., the (N)-service) to the (N + 1)-entities.

Services are offered to higher layer entities at **service access points** (SAPs), which represent logical interfaces between the entities at adjacent layers. An (N + 1)-entity communicates with an (N)-entity in the same system through an (N)-SAP. An (N)-SAP can be served by only (N)-entity and used by only one (N + 1)-entity. However, an entity can serve several SAPs; likewise, an entity can use several SAPs. The former is called **upward multiplexing,** whereas the latter is called **downward multiplexing.**

2.5.4 Functions and Protocols

We can think of a protocol function as being part of the activity of an entity. Flow control, error control, message sequencing, and encoder negotiation are all examples of protocol functions. Cooperation among peer entities is governed by one or more protocols. A **protocol** is the set of rules and formats which govern the communication between peer entities performing protocol functions in different systems (i.e., computer stations). In particular, communication between the local entities (e.g., for sharing resources) is not visible from outside the system and thus is not covered by the OSI Architecture.

2.5.5 Naming

Successful communication requires that objects within a layer or at the boundary between adjacent layers be uniquely identified. For example, in order to establish a connection between two SAPs, one must be able to identify them uniquely. The OSI architecture defines identifiers for entities, SAPs, and connections as well as relations between these identifiers, as discussed following.

Each (N)-entity is identified with a global title, which is unique and identifies the same (N)-entity anywhere in the network. Within more limited domains, an (N)-entity can be identified with a local title, which uniquely identifies the (N)-entity only in that domain. For instance, within the domain corresponding to the (N)-layer, (N)-entities are identified with (N)-global titles, which are unique within the (N)-layer. Likewise, as shown in Figure 2.27, each SAP is identified by an address which uniquely locates the SAP at the boundary between adjacent layers.

Bindings between entities and the SAPs they use are defined in a directory which maps the global titles of entities and the addresses through which they can be reached. In particular, a binding between addresses at adjacent layers is performed by a mapping function. In addition to the simple one-to-one mapping, mapping may be hierarchical, with the (N)-address being made of an (N − 1)-address and an (N)-suffix. Mapping information may also be located in a table and accessed by table lookup.

Two types of names can be distinguished: *physical* and *logical*, also referred to as *primitive* and *descriptive*, respectively (Day, 1983). **Physical names** represent objects in a unique way and are assigned by some domain administrator. Examples of *physical names* include phone numbers, social security numbers, etc. The problem with physical names is that it is usually very difficult for humans to remember them. For example, we know our friends as John, David, etc., rather than by social security numbers. *Logical names* are alternative naming schemes, which map to physical names by interpretation. In the preceding example, John and David are logical names.

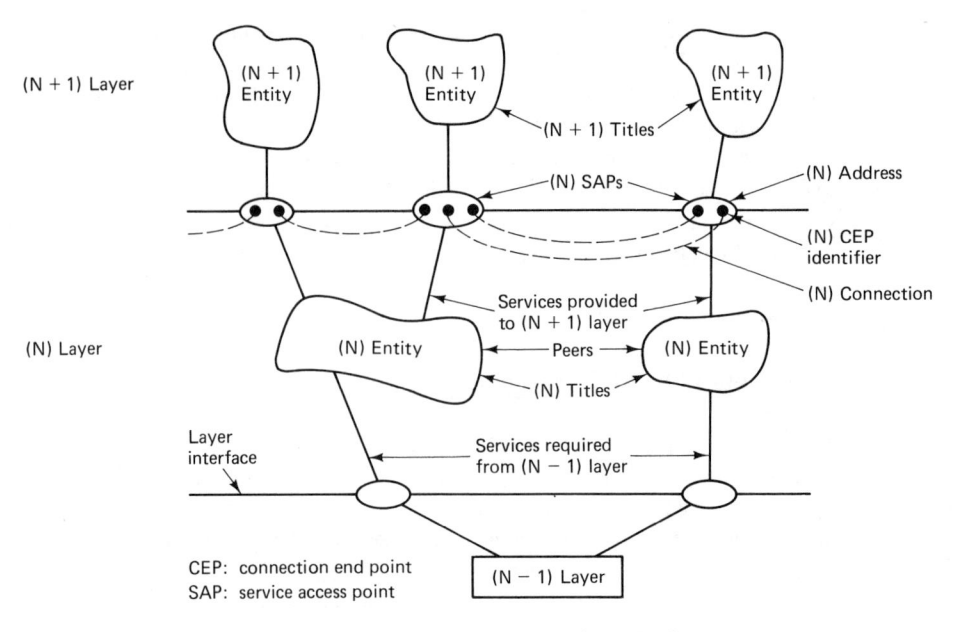

Figure 2.27 Connections and connection end points.

2.5.6 Issues Common to All Layers

Some protocol functions are so general that they could be described without reference to a particular layer. These include connection establishment, multiplexing, flow control, and error control.

A common service offered by all layers consists of providing associations between peer SAPs which can be used in particular to transfer data (as well as for other purposes such as to synchronize service users). More precisely, in the context of Figure 2.27, the (N)-layer offers (N)-connections between (N)-SAPs as part of the (N)-services. The most common type of connection is the point-to-point connection involving just two entities, but there are also multi-endpoint connections, which correspond to multiple associations between entities (e.g., broadcast or multicast communications).

Connections at a layer can be established in terms of connections at a lower layer in three different ways:

(a) one-to-one correspondence, where each (N)-connection is built on one (N − 1)-connection,

(b) multiplexing, where several (N)-connections are multiplexed on one single (N − 1)-connection, and

(c) splitting, where one single (N)-connection is built on top of several (N − 1)-connections, and the traffic on the (N)-connection is divided between the various (N − 1)-connections.

Two forms of flow control are recognized by the reference model: a peer flow control, which regulates the flow of (N)-protocol-data-units between peer entities, and interface flow control, which regulates the flow of information units across an interface.

A variety of error control functions are recognized by the model, including acknowledgment, error detection, and error notification mechanisms. The model also describes a reset function to allow recovery from a loss of synchronization between communicating (N)-entities. Although a number of algorithms and formulas can be used to detect and/or correct errors, the reference model does not specify one in particular. Section 3.10 discusses some codes for error control applicable at the data link layer.

2.6 VIRTUAL CIRCUITS AND DATAGRAMS

Perhaps the two most widely used communication systems are the telephone system and the mail system. Although the main function is the same (i.e., exchange of information) these two communication methods constitute two basic ways in which information can be exchanged. In fact, so basic are these types of communication that computer communication has developed techniques similar to those of the telephone system and the mail system, called **virtual circuits** and **datagrams,** respectively. Another term used to describe virtual circuits is **connection-oriented,** and for datagrams it is **connectionless-oriented** communication.

The OSI reference model currently supports connection-oriented communication as well as connectionless. In connection-oriented communications, the $(N - 1)$-service requires that an $(N - 1)$-connection be established between $(N - 1)$-SAPs before any communication between (N)-entities can take place. When the (N)-entities no longer need to communicate, the $(N - 1)$-connection can be released. This connection mode covers traditional teleprocessing applications. For newer applications, a **connectionless** mode is currently being developed within ISO as a complement to the connection mode. Connection-oriented and connectionless communications differ in many respects, as discussed subsequently.

2.6.1 Virtual Circuits or Connection-Oriented Communications

As noted earlier, *connection-oriented communications* is modeled after the telephone system, in that one can distinguish three distinct phases: *connection establishment*, *data transfer*, and *connection release*. The connection establishment phase is analogous to dialing a number; data transfer is analogous to the actual conversation; and connection release is analogous to hanging up. In OSI terms, a connection is a dynamic association established between two or more service access points (SAPs) to control the transfer of data between them. The ability to establish connections and to transfer data using them is provided by a connection-mode service. Since there are SAPs at each layer of the reference model, we identify connections with each OSI layer.

Characteristics of a connection. Connection mode communication has the following characteristics (Chapin, 1983):

1. Clearly Distinguishable Lifetime: As noted, like telephone conversations, connection mode interactions proceed through three distinct phases:

connection establishment,
data transfer, and
connection release.

Figure 2.28 depicts the sequence of operations associated with connection mode interactions. The three-phase lifetime of a connection may be spread out over a long period, involving many separate

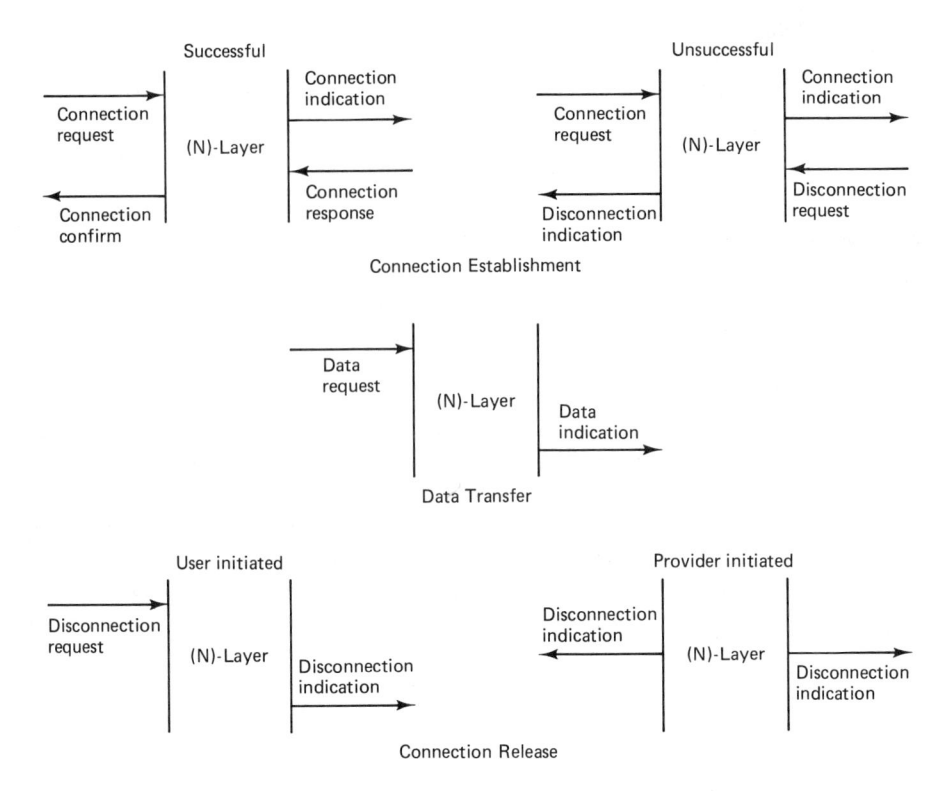

Figure 2.28 Connection-oriented interactions.

exchanges over the connection. The connection may be established at the beginning of a transaction, with the transaction lasting for several hours. At the end of the transaction, the connection is released.

When an (N + 1)-entity requests the establishment of an (N)-connection from a local (N)-SAP to a remote (N)-SAP, the address of the latter (N)-SAP is required. When the (N)-connection is established, both the (N + 1)-entity and the (N)-entity will use the (N)-CEP identifier to designate the (N)-connection, as shown in Figure 2.27.

(N)-connections may be established and released dynamically on top of (N − 1)-connections. In some cases, the (N)-connection may be established simultaneously with its supporting (N − 1)-connection, provided that the (N − 1)-connection establishment service permits (N)-entities to exchange the information necessary to establish the (N)-connection.

2. *Three-Party Agreement.* When a connection is successfully established, an implicit three-party agreement is reached and maintained among the two service users (i.e., local and remote) and the service provider. To begin with, the parties agree on their mutual willingness to exchange information; the agreement is maintained for as long as the connections exist.

3. *Negotiation and Renegotiation.* Connection-oriented communication involves the use of many parameters and options, indicating the characteristics of the connection such as quality of service, message priority, and others. No connection is established and no data are exchanged unless all parameters and options are agreed upon by the communicating service users. An incoming connection request can be rejected if it references parameters or options that are unacceptable to the receiver. Likewise, a receiver may suggest parameter values or options to be renegotiated with the sender.

Since certain resources must be allocated when a connection is established, the negotiation process may cause the request to establish a connection to be rejected because of insufficient resources. The negotiation process may also take into account the following: security, accounting, and identity verification. Furthermore, when more than one protocol is available at a particular layer, the negotiation process may select an appropriate protocol best suited to the current circumstances.

4. Connection Identifiers. Once a connection is established, requests to transfer data over the connection refer to a connection identifier rather than to the addresses of the communicating users. The connection identifier is a significant shorthand reference established by service providers that uniquely identifies an established connection during its lifetime. Using connection identifiers reduces the overhead associated with the resolution and transmission of user addresses. Typically, protocol entities at the responding station establish the connection identifier and respond to the requesting protocol entity as parameter values in protocol data units.

5. Data Unit Relationship. Data units transferred on a connection are related to one another simply by virtue of being transferred in the context of the connection. The data unit relationship implies some form of error control to guarantee the integrity of the data. Error control involves detecting, and recovering from *out of sequence*, missing and duplicated data units. In addition, the data unit relationship maintained by the connection facilitates the use of flow control.

2.6.2 Datagrams or Connectionless Communications

Connectionless communication is analogous to the use of the mail system. In the mail system, when two parties want to communicate, one of them writes the letter, drops it in the post office, and hopes that the letter arrives at its destination. Likewise, in connectionless communications, one of the parties assembles a message, gives it to the transmission system, and prays that the message arrives at its destination. Perhaps the major difference between connection-oriented and connectionless communication is that in connectionless communication, data units are independent and unrelated to one another, while data unit interdependence characterizes connection-oriented communication. The following analogy from the mail system can be used to illustrate this. Three letters addressed to the same person arriving to the mail system in a certain order will not necessarily arrive to their destination in the same order.

Connectionless communication is the transmission of independent, unrelated data units between service users without the need of a connection. The ability to transfer data without establishing, maintaining, and releasing a connection is provided by a **connectionless service** at a certain layer.

Characteristics of connectionless communications. Connectionless communications have the following characteristics:

1. Two-Party Agreement. Unlike connection-oriented communications, which require a three-party agreement, connectionless communications require only a two-party agreement that between the user and the service provider. There is an a priori agreement between peer service users which consists, at least, of their prior knowledge of each other. One aspect of the two-party agreement involves no service support concerning the mutual willingness of the service users to engage in a connectionless communication or to accept a particular data unit.

2. Single-Access Service. The **single access service** required to initiate the transmission of a data unit is the most visible characteristic of connectionless communications. All of the information required to deliver the data unit such as destination address, quality of service, options, and others is delivered to the service provider, along with the data, in a single service primitive, that is unrelated to other service primitives. Further, once the service primitives operation has taken place, no subsequent communication occurs between the service user and provider regarding the current state of or future disposition of the particular data unit.

Although not as flexible as the three-party agreement, the two-party agreement maintains considerable flexibility for allowing a service user to specify parameter values and options such as transfer rate, acceptable error rate, and so on every time the service is invoked.

3. No Negotiation. Users of connectionless services assume an a priori association between them. Other protocols at higher layers can provide interpretation of information exchanged. The connectionless service, however, is not a participant of any agreements reached this way, and does not provide any support for them other than acting as a passive conveyor of data. This is why connectionless protocols are more simple than connection-oriented protocols.

4. Data Unit Independence. As far as the service provider is concerned, a data unit transmitted by a connectionless service is completely unrelated to any other data unit. The data unit independence does not imply that implementations of connectionless services must ensure that data units are unrelated. Rather, the implication is that the service provider does not provide any functions to logically relate service data units while providing a connectionless service.

There are several implications regarding data unit independence, with perhaps the two most important being lack of flow control and error control. Since there is no explicit relationship between consecutive data units, they cannot be numbered to provide flow control procedures. Likewise, a series of data units, handed one after another to a connectionless service for delivery to the same destination, will not necessarily be delivered to the destination in the same order. The lack of a numbering scheme for data units makes it difficult to provide error control procedures.

Although a connectionless service does not guarantee that frames will be delivered in sequence to the destination, there is a good chance that the data units will be delivered in sequence, because of the following reasons:

a. Network management may indicate that there is a high probability that frames will be delivered in sequence in a given situation.

b. The characteristics of the underlying protocol may indicate that there is a high probability that frames will be delivered in sequence if certain services are used.

5. Self-Contained Data Units. Data units in a connectionless service are independent from one another, and they are also entirely self-contained. Unlike the connection-oriented case, all of the addressing and other information needed by the service provider in delivering a data unit to its destination must be included with each message. The advantage is that the scheme is more robust, since a successful transmission does not depend on other data units for carrying parameters or characteristics associated with the data transfer. However, the disadvantage is that the extra information associated with each message represents additional overhead.

2.7 THE SEVEN-LAYER OSI REFERENCE MODEL

In the previous section, the basic elements of the OSI reference model were developed. These serve as the building blocks for constructing the model of interprocess communication. In OSI, interprocess communication is subdivided into seven independent layers, as already depicted in Figure 1.8, and which are described following.

Application layer. As the highest layer of the OSI model, the application layer does not provide services to any other layer. Rather, the services of the application layer are provided to the applications themselves. Thus, the primary concern of the application layer is the communication support of the end user applications. As discussed in detail in Chapter 10, part of application processes resides in the application layer. In particular, those aspects of the application process concerned with interprocess communication, called *application entities*, are within the OSI environment. ISO Subcommittee 16 (SC16) is developing generic Application Service Elements for providing common procedures for constructing application protocols and for accessing the services of OSI. ISO is also developing application protocols of general interest such as file transfer, access and management (FTAM), virtual terminal, and job transfer and manipulation services, as well as OSI application and system management protocols. However, the bulk of application protocols are being defined by the user of OSI. The common Application Service is the only means by which users of OSI access OSI services.

Presentation layer. The primary purpose of the presentation layer is to provide independence to application processes from differences in data representation (i.e., syntax). The presentation layer protocol allows the user to select a *presentation context*. In essence, a presentation context is a data structure containing the internal data representation as used by the source station and as the data representation to be understood by the source and destination stations during communication. Prior to exchanging data, a sender and receiver negotiate an agreed upon presentation context.

The presentation context may be specific to an application such as a library protocol or virtual terminal, to a type of hardware such as a particular machine representation, or to some standard or canonical representation. Thus, a user of OSI wanting to develop an OSI application protocol defines an application protocol using the relevant parts of the common application service elements, and a presentation context which defines the presentation of the data to be transferred. The OSI user may use an existing context or define his or her own.

Session layer. The primary purpose of the session layer is to provide the mechanisms for organizing, structuring, and managing the communications between application processes. The mechanisms provided in the session layer allow for two-way simultaneous and two-way alternate operation, the establishment of major and minor synchronization points, and the definition of special tokens for structuring data exchanges. In essence, the session layer provides the structure for controlling and managing the communication process.

Transport layer. The transport layer provides transparent and reliable transfer of data between end systems, thus relieving the upper layers from any concern regarding the functions of the network, data link, and physical layers. In some cases, the transport/network layer boundary represents the traditional boundary between the carrier and the customer. From this point of view, the transport layer optimizes use of network services and provides any additional service over that supplied by the network layer service.

Network layer. The network layer provides independence from the data transmission technology and independence from relaying and routing considerations. The network layer hides from the upper layers all the peculiarities of the transmission system. For example, the transport layer needs to be concerned only with the quality of service and its cost, not with whether optical fibers, packet switching, satellites, or local area networks are being used. The network layer also handles relaying and routing data through as many concatenated networks as necessary while maintaining the quality of service parameters requested by the transport layer. As discussed in Chapter 5, the ISO network layer protocol consists of the following sublayers:

- Subnetwork Access Facility (SNACF)
- Subnetwork Dependent Convergence Facility (SNDCF)
- Subnetwork Independent Convergence Facility (SNICF)
- Routing and Relaying

Data link layer. The data link layer basically provides transparent and reliable transfer of data between adjacent stations which are physically connected by a transmission medium. The transparent aspect of data transfer typically involves providing flow control, and the reliable aspect involves detecting and possibly correcting errors which may occur in the transmission. Typical data link protocols include HDLC for point-to-point and multipoint communications and IEEE 802 standards for local area networks.

Physical layer. The physical layer deals mostly with transmission technology in order to send bit patterns between two stations which are attached by a transmission medium. A major aspect of the physical layer is the provision of the required interface with the physical medium. The interface typically includes functions such as modulation, filtering, data encoding, and other mechanical and procedural rules.

2.8 OSI SERVICES AND PROTOCOLS

The concepts of *services* and *protocols* are fundamental to understanding the OSI reference model. Many protocol standards are published with separate sections on *service definitions* and *protocol specifications*. Because of their importance, we concentrate in this section on services and protocols. For completeness, the concepts of layer, interfaces, and information units are discussed again in the context of services and protocols.

2.8.1 The Concept of Service

As noted a number of times, the OSI reference model divides the overall communication by defining a series of layers, with each layer performing specific functions. Each boundary from one layer to another represents a demarcation between groups of functions; these functions are given visibility by different aspects of the protocol rules. The term **service** represents a boundary between functions. Protocols layers are normally viewed vertically, with the most user-oriented functions at the top and successively more specific, technology-dependent functions at the bottom.

Together, the communication system components above the service boundary making use of the service are called **service users.** Likewise, the system components below the boundary responsible for providing the service are called the **service providers.** As depicted in Figure 2.29, service users and service providers interact at service access points. A **protocol service** provides to the *service users* a set of communication capabilities regardless of the detailed way in which they are realized. As we will see in Chapter 12, a *service provider* can be designed as a set of asynchronous, cooperating processes. Thus, when designing the service provider, the *protocol service* constitutes one of the major design considerations.

As noted, the *service provider* may be realized as a set of cooperating processes. Since services must be provided at each network station, *service providers* can be thought of as being distributed across the network. However, the way in which the distribution takes place is not of concern to the *service user*. The user may view the service provider as a distributed abstract machine whose operation provides the specified service.

2.8.2 Layers

The service concept of OSI involves two peer users interacting with a service provider. The service provider may provide services based on services at another layer. A *layer* can be viewed as a set of service units which provide services to the next higher layer, and it does so by making use of the services of the layer immediately below. The service units constituting a layer can be provided by interacting processes which cooperate to provide the service.

A user of services provided by layer N works entirely in terms of that service, and is not even aware of services performed by layers (N-1), (N-2), etc. Similarly, the definition of services provided by layer N is not related to the number of layers which exists above layer N.

2.8.3 Protocols

Distributed communication services implies cooperation between peer communicating entities. A set of rules is required in order for successful communication to take place. The set of rules and formats governing communication between communicating entities located at the same layer in two different stations is referred to as a **communication protocol.** For example, a layer N protocol defines how a protocol entity at layer N in one station exchanges data or supervisory information with a protocol entity at the same layer in another station. The protocol defines the format of the information exchanged and any actions to be performed on receipt of the information.

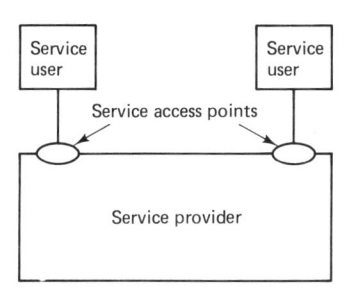

Figure 2.29 The service model.

Syntax and *procedures* are two important components associated with protocols. Protocol syntax and procedures define ways in which a layer provides services to a higher layer by making use of the service of a lower layer. Whereas the syntax component identifies the composition (i.e., the format) of the units of data exchanged, the procedure components define the rules for using the data units exchanged.

Example

> Many communication protocols use check bits for error detection and retransmission. The syntax component of the protocol defines the location of the check bits in the context of the overall data unit. The protocol component specifies what to do in case the check bits indicate errors in the transmission. Some protocols do not send an acknowledgment; others send a negative acknowledgment.

The majority of the protocol rules are often concerned with the use of a supporting data transfer service, but a complete protocol must specify an interpretation of all possible events in the supporting service, including such actions as connection establishment and error reporting, where appropriate.

Properties of higher layer services can be derived from the protocol rules and the properties of lower services. Given a level of service, there may be many different protocols supporting it. The protocol model for the OSI is illustrated in Figure 2.30.

As noted earlier, one of the main objectives of the layering approach is to define a set of functions and services regardless of the detailed way each layer provides the functions and services. Thus, for a given set of functions and services, there are many possible protocols which provide those functions and services.

2.8.4 Interfaces

The **interface** between two layers defines the means by which one layer makes use of the services provided by a lower layer. It defines the rules and formats for exchanging information across the boundary between adjacent layers within the same station. The interface may be specified in terms of its mechanical, electrical, timing, or software characteristics. Thus, the interface may be physical or logical. The interaction of adjacent protocol entities gives rise to certain events at the interface. Associated with events at the interface are certain protocol actions which are carried out by protocol services.

OSI standardization is not concerned with interfaces; the standards only concern communication entities located at different stations. However, there are other areas of standardization, such

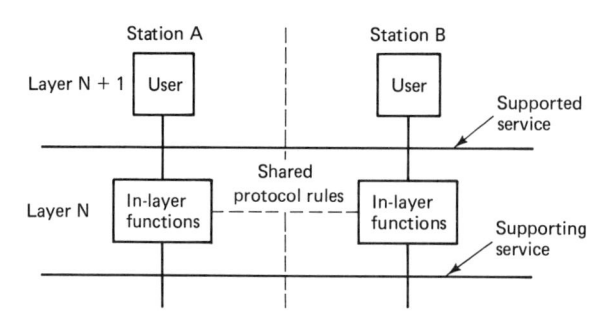

Figure 2.30 The protocol model.

as the definition of programming or control languages, which are directly concerned with interfaces, and so their relation to protocol standards is of considerable interest. The interface concept is depicted in Figure 2.31.

Just as there could exist alternate protocols providing the same service, so there can be many interfaces supporting a level of service. Actual interfaces are computer system-dependent and are left to the implementor of the OSI standards. Some theoretical models exist for relating SAP, services, and interfaces (Garcia-Tomas, et al, 1987).

2.8.5 Information Units

Protocol entities located at different stations communicate with one another by exchanging units of information with fixed or variable length. The information units are called **protocol data units** (PDU) and corrrespond to messages, packets, frames, etc., depending upon the layer at which they are exchanged.

Protocols are only concerned with logical communications. Messages actually move vertically through various interfaces until reaching the physical medium at the source station, then go up through the various interfaces at the destination station until reaching their destination. In order to transfer a layer (N+1) PDU according to the layer (N+1) protocol, the layer (N+1) must pass the PDU across the layer N interface to the layer N. The unit of information passed across the interface using the services of layer N is called a layer N **service data unit** (SDU).

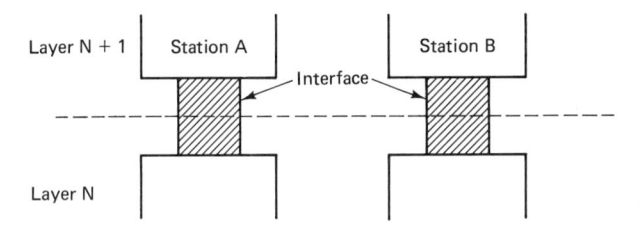

Figure 2.31 The interface model.

In addition to the layer N *service data unit*, the layer N *protocol data unit* may contain additional control information indicating the type of service required, the address or name of the receiver, a time-out period for which the (N+1) layer will wait for a reply, an indication that no reply is expected, or a priority level for delivery of the information. Thus, a PDU is composed of two major parts: a *service data unit* and a *protocol control information*, as depicted in Figure 2.32.

Layer N sees a layer (N+1) PDU as a unit of user information which must be transported. In general, it will add its own envelope of control information consisting of a header and possibly a trailer, which makes the layer N PDU. The layer (N+1) PDU is completely transparent to layer N, which may process it in some way to form a layer N PDU. The composition of user information as it moves from the application layer to the physical medium is depicted in Figure 2.33.

2.9 OSI SERVICE CONVENTIONS

In order to provide uniformity in the service and protocol specifications, a single set of conventions has been established by the individual service and protocol standards. The set of conventions constitutes an addendum to the ISO reference model known as *OSI Service Conventions*.

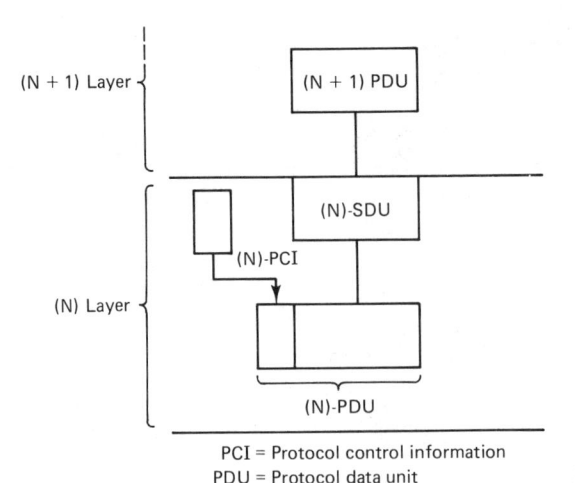

Figure 2.32 Logical relationship between data units in adjacent layers.

PCI = Protocol control information
PDU = Protocol data unit
SDU = Service data unit

The service conventions define a service model incorporating the roles of the service user and service provider. The model introduces the concept of a *service primitive* as an abstract, implementation-independent element of the interaction between the service user and the service provider. Four types of service primitive are defined, corresponding to the major stages in an exchange between the service users and the service provider. However, services do not necessarily involve all types of service primitives. The primitive types are:

request a primitive issued by a service user to a service provider for invoking some action (i.e., a procedure);

indication a primitive issued by a service provider to a service user either for invoking some action or for indicating that an action has been invoked by the peer service user;

response a primitive issued by a service user to a service provider for indicating the completion of some action previously invoked by an indication;

confirmation a primitive issued by a service provider to a service user for completing some action previously invoked by a request.

As noted earlier, the preceding primitive types are issued either by service users or service providers at *service access points*.

Certain dialog patterns occur repeatedly in the definition of the services offered by a certain layer. The dialog patterns can be used to characterize the services into types. The following service types occur most frequently:

Unconfirmed Service: a service element in which a *request* from a service user leads to an *indication* to the corresponding user with no further primitives involved;

Confirmed Service: a service element in which a *request* from one service user leads to an *indication* to the corresponding user. The latter then issues a *response*, which finally leads to a *confirmation* delivered to the originating service user.

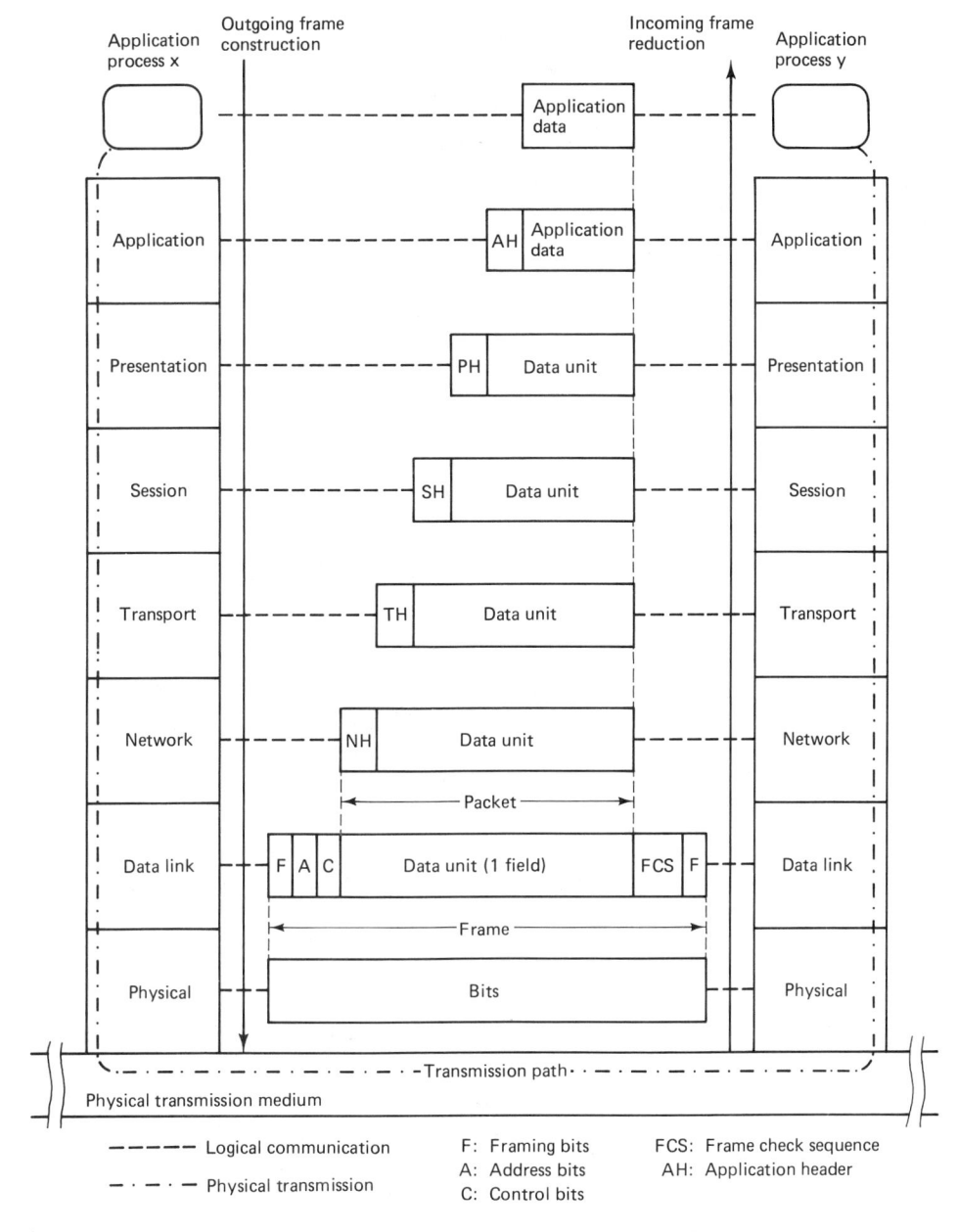

Figure 2.33 Information units at different layers of the ISO reference model.

Thus, whereas an unconfirmed service involves only two primitive types (i.e., a request and an indication), a confirmed service involves four primitive types: request, indication, response, and confirmation. Service primitives typically occur only in certain sequences, as depicted in Figure 2.34(a) and 2.34(b) for the unconfirmed and confirmed services, respectively.

Although the primitive sequences involved in certain services are helpful in understanding

Sec. 2.9   OSI Service Conventions

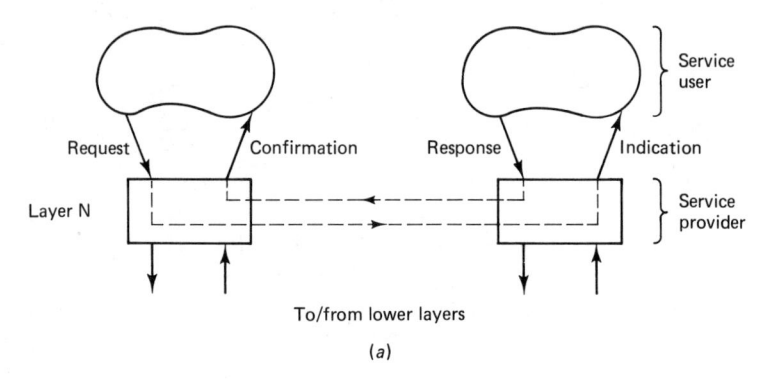

Figure 2.34 (a) Confirmed service primitives at layer N.

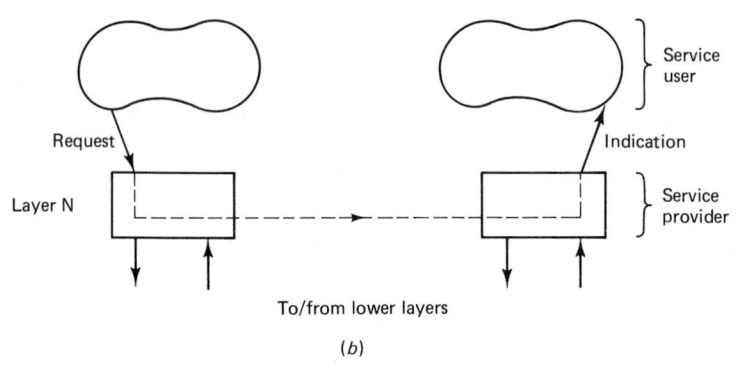

Figure 2.34 (b) Unconfirmed primitives at layer N.

the relationship among primitives, service users, and service providers; the sequences do not provide information regarding the relative occurrence of primitives (i.e., a time sequence).

The time sequence in which related service primitives can occur is illustrated in Figure 2.35, where the diagram is partitioned by two vertical lines into three sections, with the central section representing the service provider and the adjacent sections representing the two service users. The vertical axis represents time increasing downwards. Service users and providers interact when certain events happen. Issuance of request primitives and delivery of request primitives (i.e., indication) are examples of events.

The relative sequence of primitives is indicated by the vertical location of associated events. Arrows are used to indicate where the primitives are generated and where they are directed. For

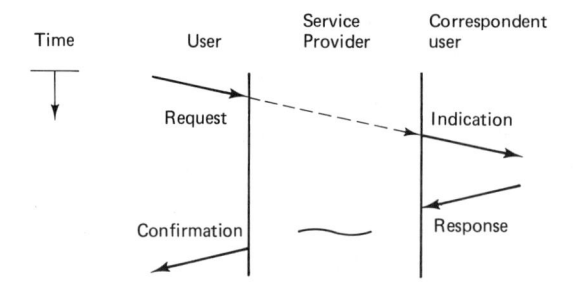

Figure 2.35 Definition of a time sequence diagram.

82 Background for the OSI Lower Layers   Chap. 2

example, an arrow directed toward the service provider originates from a service user. Necessary sequence relations between the two service access points are emphasized by a horizontal dashed arrow between the lines. Such sequencing may require synchronization or a causal relationship between the primitives. In the absence of an arrow, no specific sequence is implied between points in time on the two lines. Where the layout of the diagram might otherwise suggest a spurious sequence, a tilde (˜) is inserted between the lines to emphasize asynchrony. An example of the asynchronous relationship between response and confirmation is the delivery of a confirmation before the response is issued. In this case, the confirmation simply indicates that an indication was issued rather than that a response has been received.

2.10 OSI MODEL EXTENSIONS

So far, the emphasis has been on a simple service involving two users and the corresponding protocols to support the required services. Models considered thus far represent services or protocols supporting connection-oriented or connectionless services. However, the models are not sufficiently powerful to handle more complex situations arising in sophisticated network applications, such as distributed processing. Thus, extensions to the model are required. Some extensions are outlined briefly following.

The first extension involves the interconnection of several networks, which requires the introduction of a new kind of entity called a **relay** entity. This allows communications between two stations, one on each side of the relay entity. Currently, the ISO network layer standard has incorporated some of the model extensions, described with the network layer internal architecture in Chapter 5. The specification of a relay entity is, in effect, the specification of the interrelation of events in the two services. Since the relay provider links two different service providers, it can be considered as the dual of the simple service provider linking two users.

Another extension involves a service user communicating with multiple peers simultaneously. As noted earlier, one example involves broadcast communications, while another involves identifying a number of peers individually.

The final extension involves models for evaluating the performance of network services, such as quality of service, message priority, and others in the context of connection-oriented and connectionless services.

SUMMARY

In this chapter, we have provided sufficient background on signal transmission and the OSI reference model in order to obtain a good understanding of LANs and their applications. The main signal transmission topics discussed were: signals, transmission lines (i.e., wires and coaxial cables), channels, noise, and optical fibers. The main OSI topics discussed were: architecture, communication functions, layers, services, protocols, the seven-layer model, and service conventions.

Signal Transmission

All communication systems have three major subsystems: transmitter, channel, and receiver. Signals are used to represent messages to be transmitted in a transmission system. Signal representation in terms of the frequency domain is useful when modeling systems such as the channel of a communication system. The concepts of energy and power are crucial for defining signal and channel bandwidth.

Media can be bounded or unbounded. Unbounded media make use of antennas to radiate energy in many directions. The most frequent uses of bounded media are transmission lines and optical fibers. Transmission lines are distributed electrical circuits where the voltage and current travel in both directions of the line.

The major impairments introduced by a channel are attenuation, noise, and distortion. Thermal noise is caused by the random movement of electrons in a conductor. Distortion is due to the nonlinear nature of the devices that make up the channel (e.g., amplifiers). The ratio of *signal power* to *noise power* is useful for performance analysis of communication systems, and is referred to as the *signal to noise ratio*. Another ratio of interest is the ratio of energy per bit to noise spectral density.

Optical fibers are an alternative medium used when low attenuation, good noise immunity, and large channel bandwidth are desired. An optical fiber is a circular solid core with a certain refraction index surrounded by a cladding with a higher refraction index.

OSI Reference Model

The International Organization for Standardization developed a layered model for organizing the overall communication functions into seven layers called the application, presentation, session, transport, network, data link, and physical layers. The major elements of the OSI reference model include layers, services, protocols, interfaces, and information units.

A layer is a subdivision of communication functions providing services to the layer above by making use of the services of the layer below. The functions performed by a layer are made available to the layer immediately above it as a set of services. Protocols are the rules and formats used by communicating entities. The flow of information between layers is defined by an interface. Information can be exchanged on a connection-oriented or connectionless basis.

The communication system components above the service boundary making use of the service are called *service users*, whereas the components below the boundary responsible for providing the service are called the *service providers*. A *service primitive* is an abstract, implementation-independent element of the interaction between the service user and the service provider. Whether communication is connection-oriented or connectionless, multiple endpoint or single endpoint, a basic characteristic of the communication type is the definition of the services it provides. Services involve a relationship between the **service user,** the **peer service user,** and the **service provider.**

Certain dialog patterns occur repeatedly in the definition of the services offered by a certain layer, with the following service types occurring most frequently: unconfirmed service and confirmed service. Although the current set of OSI standards defines *protocol services* involving one *service provider* and two *service users* engaged in a dialog, recent refinements to the reference model introduce other communication concepts. Two of these are the multiple endpoint connection and broadcast communications.

Bibliographic Notes

Although much information exists on transmission systems, it is not discussed in a computer communication context. In particular, the books by Lathi (1983), Ziemer and Tranter (1985), Carlson (1975), Johnson (1950), Cooper (1984), Bylanski and Ingram (1976), and Metzger and Vabre (1969) are recommended. Optical fibers are covered in the books by Keiser (1983) and Baker (1986). Information on the OSI reference model is just starting to appear. In particular, the books by Stallings (1985 and 1987), Schwartz (1987), Hammond and O'Reilly (1986), Halsall (1988), Sloman and Kramer (1987), and Tanenbaum (1988) provide various levels of discussion on the reference model. The December 1983 issue of the proceedings of the IEEE is devoted entirely to OSI concepts. In this issue, the papers by Linnington, Day and Zimmerman, and Chapin cover introductory material. In addition, other journals and periodicals cover a great deal of OSI literature. A sample includes the *Journal of Telecommunication Networks*, *Computer Networks and ISDN Systems*, and the *ACM Computer Communications Review*. However, the most accurate description of the OSI reference model is the standard ISO 7498 which contains four parts: basic reference model, security architecture, naming and addressing, and management framework. In addition, there is an addendum covering *connectionless data transmission*.

PROBLEMS

Signal Transmission

1. Identify the major components of a communication system. State the role played by each component.
2. An Amplifier used in typical coaxial cable media have the following transfer characteristic $E_{out} = 10\, E_{in} + 5E_{in}^2$. Is this amplifier a linear device?
3. Is the following signal $f(t) = (\sin 2t + \sin 4t)$ periodic? If so, find the period T of the signal.
4. Find the trigonometric and exponential Fourier series for the signal in Figure P2.1.

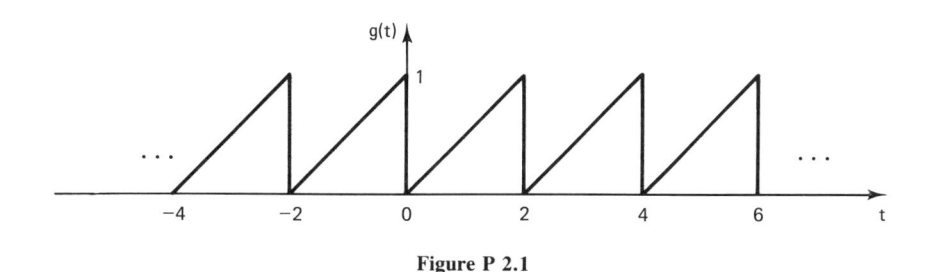

Figure P 2.1

5. Find the Fourier transform of the function f(t) defined as follows:

$$f(t) = \begin{cases} \cos t & \text{for } |t| < \tfrac{1}{2} \\ 0 & \text{otherwise} \end{cases}$$

6. Find the corresponding signals g(t) whose Fourier transforms are shown in Figure P2.2

|G(ω)| graphs with rectangles from -2 to 2, amplitude 1; θ_g(ω) phase plots

(a)

(b)

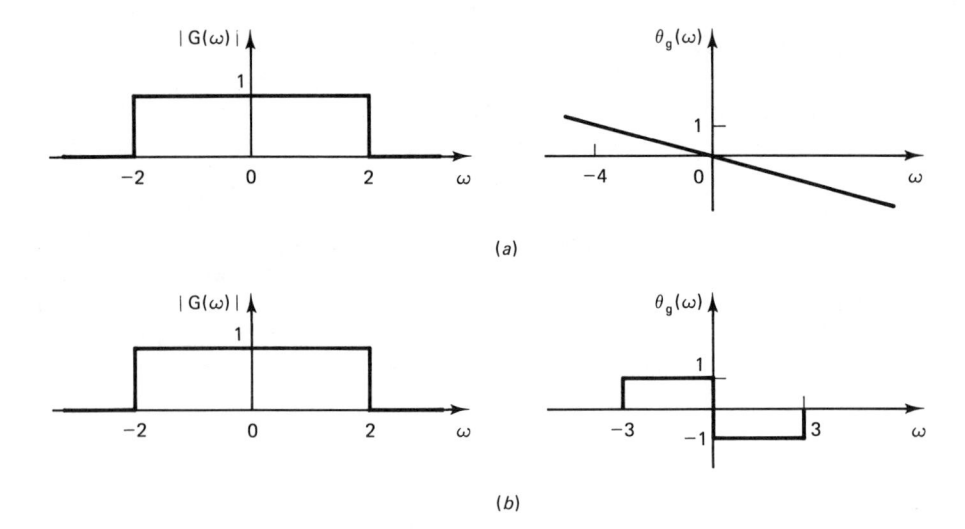

Figure P 2.2

7. Most signals of interest are not bandlimited. Because of noise considerations and other factors a signal g(t) is made bandlimited by passing it through an ideal lowpass filter with bandwidth B. The output $g_1(t)$ of the filter is an approximation of g(t). For the signal

$$g(t) = \begin{cases} \exp(-t) & \text{for } t > 0 \\ 0 & \text{otherwise} \end{cases}$$

   (a) Sketch the spectra $|G(\omega)|$ and $|G_1(\omega)|$.
   (b) Sketch the spectrum $|E(\omega)|$ of the error signal $e(t) = g(t) - g_1(t)$.
   (c) Find the energy of e(t) in terms of B.
   (d) Find the bandwidth of the signal g(t). Use the following criterion for determining the bandwidth: (Energy of e(t)) < 0.01 (Energy of g(t)).

8. What determines the bandwidth of a signal?

9. Calculate the characteristic impedance Z_o, for a copper wire pair with D = 4 mm, and d = 1 mm.

10. The IEEE 802.3 physical layer specification specifies a coaxial cable with a = 2.17 mm, and b = 6.15 mm. Calculate the cable's characteristic impedance Z_o assuming copper wires and E_r = 2.26.

11. For the cable in problem 9, plot the attentuation A (in dB/Km) versus frequency from 10 M Hz to 10 G Hz. Use a logarithmic scale for A as well as the frequency f. The corresponding plot is referred to as the attenuation curves for coaxial cables.

12. Assuming a = 2.17 mm, b = 6.15 mm, Er = 2.26, and a medium length L = 1 Km, calculate the medium bandwidth for (a) a pair of wires (b) a coaxial cable. Also, for each case, plot the medium bandwidth versus L.

13. A TV signal requires 6 M Hz of channel bandwidth for its transmission. Can a TV signal be transmitted over a pair of wires of length 1 Km and with a = 2.17 mm and D = 6.15 mm.

14. Consider an optical fiber with an avalanche photodiode receiver having the following parameters: dark current I_D = 1 nA, leakage current I_L = 1 nA, quantum efficiency η = 0.85, avalanche gain M = 100, excess noise factor F with x = 0.5, load resistor R_L = 100,000 ohms, and bandwidth B = 10 kHz. Suppose a sinusoidally varying 850-nm signal having a modulation index m = 0.85 falls on the photodiode which is at room temperature (T = 300 °K). To compare the contributions from the various noise terms to the signal-to-noise ratio for this particular set of parameters, plot the following terms in decibels (i.e., 10 log SNR) as a function

of the average received optical power P_o. Let P_o range from -70 to 0 dB mW, that is, from 0.1 nW to 1.0 mW:

(a) $(SNR)_Q = [i_s^2] / (i_Q^2)$

(b) $(SNR)_{DB} = [i_s^2] / (i_{DB}^2)$

(c) $(SNR)_{DS} = [i_s^2] / (i_{DS}^2)$

(d) $(SNR)_T = [i_s^2] / (i_T^2)$

What happens to these curves if either the load resistor, the gain, the dark current, or the bandwidth is changed?

15. Consider an avalanche photodiode with the parameters: $I_L = 1$ nA, $I_D = 1$ nA, $\eta = 0.85$, excess noise factor F with $x = 0.5$, $R_L = 10{,}000$ ohms, and $B = 1$ kHz. Consider a sinusoidally varying 850-nm signal, which has a modulation index $m = 0.85$ and average power level $P_o = -50$ dB mW, to fall on the detector at room temperature. Plot the signal-to-noise ratio as a function of M for gains ranging from 20 to 100. At what value of M does the maximum signal-to-noise ratio occur?

16. The thermal voltage noise generated by a coaxial cable with $Z_o = 75$ ohms, and at 68 °F was shown by Equation (2.98) to be $v = 5.5 \times 10^{-7} \sqrt{B}$ mV. Since the power in a correctly terminated line is $p = v^2 / Z_o$, calculate the thermal power noise expressed in dB mW for a) $B = 4$ M Hz, and b) $B = 6$ M Hz.

17. In some of the literature on computer networks, use is made of the term *computer network bandwidth*. Does this term make sense? If so provide your interpretation.

Open System Interconnection (OSI)

18. (a) What is the aim of the ISO reference model for Open System Interconnection?
    (b) Produce a sketch showing the constituent layers which make up the reference model outlining the main functions of each layer.
    (c) Briefly describe the user service categories associated with each layer and how the detailed operation of the underlying layers is transparent to the higher layers.

19. (a) What is a communication network protocol?
    (b) Why are communication network protocols needed?

20. (a) What does it mean for a network product to be *compatible* with the ISO reference model?
    (b) Are two ISO compatible network products guaranteed to communicate with one another?

21. What protocol functions are common to most layers?

22. How do connection oriented communications differ from connectionless communications?

23. Explain the similarities and differences between the *three party agreement* of connection oriented and the *two party agreement* of connectionless communications.

24. Data units are related in connection oriented communications whereas they are independent in connectionless communications. Explore the consequences of this basic difference.

25. (a) What is a service primitive?
    (b) Provide a brief explanation of the four basic primitive types.
    (c) Explain the similarities and differences between *unconfirmed services* and *confirmed services*.

3

The Physical Layer

As noted in Chapter 1, this book is organized around the OSI reference model. We begin our study of the OSI layers by moving bottom up, starting with the physical layer and moving toward the application layer. An advantage of the bottom-up approach of studying the OSI layers is that by covering the lower layers first, the functionality needed by the upper layers is already understood. Although not part of the OSI reference model, the transmission medium, which was discussed in Chapter 2, could be thought of being *layer 0*.

This chapter addresses the lowest layer of the OSI reference model. The chapter's objectives are to address the functions of the physical layer, its organization, and the most common techniques used to incorporate such functions in a local area network environment. The physical layer used in the MAP and TOP networks is used to illustrate the chapter concepts.

3.1 FUNCTIONS OF THE PHYSICAL LAYER

In the previous chapter, we saw that the transmission medium imposes several limitations on the signals to be transmitted. The major limitations are summarized next. The finite bandwidth of a channel produces two limitations: First, it limits the number of signals that can travel simultaneously over the channel. Second, the spreading effect of one bit over its neighbor (intersymbol interference) contributes to errors. A limitation of transmission lines used as the transmission medium is that signals are reflected upon reaching the end of their travel and are combined with incoming signals, thus contributing to errors. A limitation encountered with optical fibers is that of *intermodal dispersion*. In addition, as signals travel longer on the communication channel they experience three major problems: first, noise continues to be accumulated along the way; second, attenuation increases; and third, the phase lag also increases.

Engineering and economic aspects of communication systems also dictate some requirements that influence the design of the physical layer. To prevent ground loops it is convenient to avoid dc (direct current) coupling between the stations and the physical medium. A danger that exists in networks that are dc coupled is that the ground potential (i.e., voltages) of one network end (perhaps located in a different building) can rise relative to the other end, producing a large amount of current on the medium. The high current will burn anything that is encountered in its path, including computers, robots, etc. Fortunately, some encoding techniques (e.g. Manchester Encoding) allows ac (alternating current) coupling, thus solving this problem.

When required, techniques are available for increasing the number of signals that can be sent over a given channel bandwidth. The electrical resistance of transmission lines produces power dissipation that increases as the magnitudes of voltages and currents get larger. On the other hand, decreasing the magnitude of these signals makes it difficult to distinguish them from noise. Thus, there is a trade-off between these two extremes. The state of the art of the technology currently used limits the data rate at which bits can be sent over the medium. Technology also determines the type of interface connection between stations and the medium.

The physical layer performs functions that overcome many of the preceeding limitations of the medium in an effective way, from the viewpoint of engineering and economics. The number of signals that can be sent simultaneously over the medium can be increased by the use of time division multiplexing (TDM) or frequency division multiplexing (FDM). Intersymbol interference can be reduced using special pulse shapes other than rectangular. Reflected signals on transmission lines can be avoided by using cable interfaces with input impedance equal to Zo, the line's characteristic impedance. The physical layer attempts to minimize the effects of noise and attenuation by the use of repeaters. Encoding schemes avoid dc coupling and maximize bandwidth efficiency. Other functions of the physical layer include determination of voltage levels, data rate, and type of connectors compatible with the medium used.

Thus, the physical layer functions can be summarized as follows: performing data encoding and decoding operations; if broadband communications is used, performing modulation and demodulation functions; providing medium interface for the transmitter and receiver; rejecting noise from other channels by means of filters; providing a channel with a desired bandwidth and low error rate performance; generating control signals for proper operation of the data link layer (e.g. collision and bad signal detection); and defining the physical connections to the medium.

Figure 3.1 depicts a model for the physical layer, incorporating the functions just listed for baseband and broadband communications. A baseband system does not include the modulator and demodulator blocks.

Regarding Figure 3.1, the data link layer provides the physical layer with a group of bits to be transmitted. The physical layer first encodes the bits into a set of *symbol codes*. The advantages of encoding include improving bandwidth efficiency, reducing transmission errors, the possibility of ac coupling to the medium, and others. If broadband transmission is used, the set of symbol codes is used for modulating a carrier, which shifts the frequency spectrum of the signal into a specific channel of the many available in the medium. In either case, whether modulation is used or not, the corresponding signal is coupled to the medium using the medium interface.

Likewise, the signal waveform traveling on the medium is interfaced with the receiver by

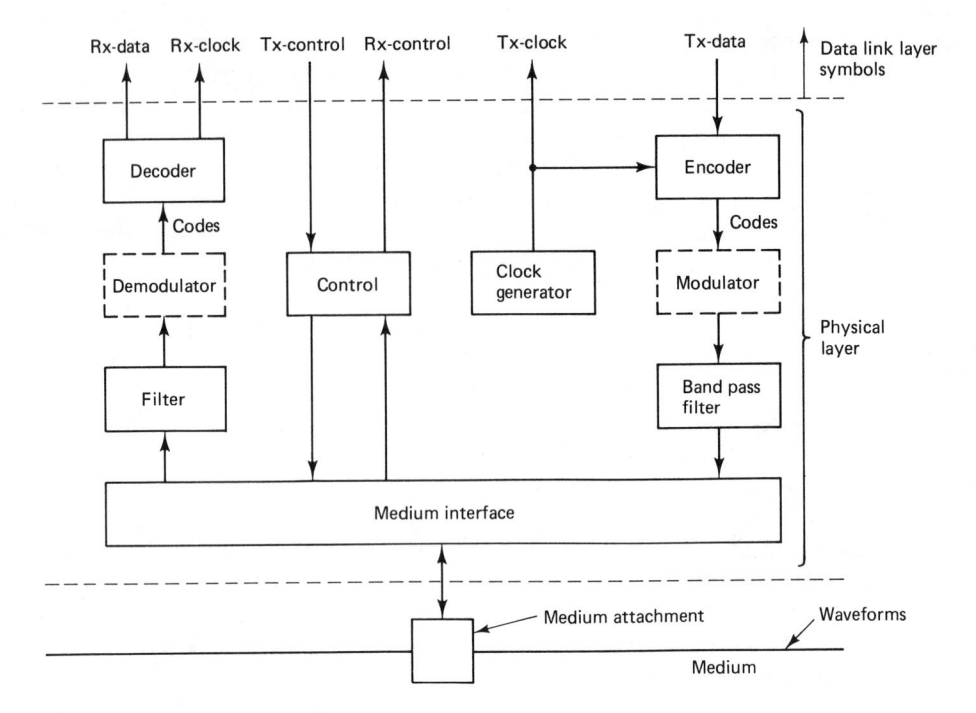

Figure 3.1 A physical layer model. Modulator and Demodulator blocks are for broadband communications. The solid blocks represent a baseband system.

means of the medium interface. The filter is intended to eliminate noise from frequency bands other than the one used by the signal. For a broadband system, the demodulator performs an inverse function to that of the modulator. The decoder restores the original transmitted bits out of the demodulated symbol codes.

In the remainder of this chapter, we discuss the most common techniques used for performing the functions of a LAN's physical layer. A natural approach to follow for studying how the physical layer performs its functions is to look at the different methods available for signal transmission.

3.2 DIGITAL TRANSMISSION

Basically, a digital message is an ordered sequence of symbols drawn from an alphabet of finite size M. For example, for binary communications, $M = 2$ and the alphabet consists of the digits 0 and 1. The two most important parameters that characterize a digital communication system are the signaling rate and the bit error probability.[1] The rate at which bits are sent over the channel is referred to as the signaling rate, also known as **data rate.** The bit error probability is the probability that a 0 is received when a 1 is transmitted or that a 1 is received when a 0 is transmitted.

---

[1] Also known as bit error rate (BER).

Maximum Data Rate

If the channel bandwidth were infinite, one could transmit pulses at any rate because all frequency components are passed through the channel undistorted. However, all channels have a finite bandwidth, and this poses a limitation on the maximum data rate. H. Nyquist investigated this problem as early as 1924 and found that the maximum data rate that can be achieved over a channel with bandwidth B is

$$\text{Max. data rate} = 2 B \log_2 M \quad \text{bits/sec} \tag{3.1}$$

where M is the number of levels (symbols) in the digital waveform. For example, a coaxial cable is usually divided into many channels, each with a bandwidth of B = 6 MHz. Thus, each channel can support binary (M = 2) data rates up to 12 M bit/sec.

Nyquist's result gives a very conservative estimate of the maximum data rate, since it neglects the *effect of noise*. Shannon extended Nyquist's result to include the effect of additive white Gaussian noise.[2] Shannon's important result states that, through proper data encoding, the maximum data rate that can be achieved by transmitting a signal with a *signal to noise ratio* SNR over a channel with bandwidth B is

$$\text{Max. data Rate} = C = B \log_2 (1 + \text{SNR}) \tag{3.2}$$

C is also referred to as the channel capacity.

Example

Video signals require a SNR of about 50 dB for excellent transmission. Assuming that an appropriate modulation scheme is found which provides a SNR = 50 dB, calculate the maximum data rate that can be achieved over a channel with 6M Hz bandwidth.

Solution The signal to noise ratio expressed in decibels (dB) is SNR (dB) = 10 log SNR from which SNR = 10^5. By direct application of Equation 3.2, we get

$$C = 6 \text{ M Hz} \log_2 (1 + 10^5) \approx 6 \times 10^6 \log_2 (10^5)$$

$$C = 30 \times 10^6 \times \log_2 10 = 99.6 \text{ M bit/sec}.$$

Let us analyze Equation 3.2 in a bit more detailed fashion. For a SNR = 0, C = 0, confirming our expectation that when no signal is sent, the information rate is 0. When the SNR increases, C also increases. It appears that by increasing the SNR one could achieve any desired data rate C over a channel with finite bandwidth. However, because of physical constraints, it is not possible to have an arbitrarily large value for SNR. One of the major limiting factors for achieving large values of SNR is thermal noise. In fact, at room temperature (assumed to be 68 °F) the noise power on a CATV system (with 75 ohm characteristic impedance and 4M Hz channel bandwidth) is −108 dB mW.[3] When amplifying a signal, noise is also amplified. Thus, it is not possible to increase the maximum data rate by amplifying the signal.

Two important implications of Shannon's result deserve further discussion. The first implication is that it is possible to exchange channel bandwidth B and *signal to noise ratio* to achieve

---

[2] White noise means that the noise frequency components extend over all frequencies. Gaussian noise means that the probability distribution of noise is Gaussian or normal.

[3] See Equation 2.98.

error-free communication at a given data rate. This can be illustrated by considering the previous example where the same data rate of 99.6 M bit/sec can be achieved if the bandwidth is increased to 10 M Hz and the SNR is decreased to 30 dB, because 99.6 M bit/sec = $10 \times 10^6 \log_2 (1 + 10^3)$. In general, the exchange of bandwidth for SNR can be derived from Equation 3.2, assuming SNR $\gg$ 1, yielding

$$SNR_1 = (SNR_2)^{B2/B1} \qquad (3.3)$$

The second implication of Shannon's result is that through proper coding it is possible (at least in theory) to achieve error-free transmission at a data rate C given by Equation 3.2, even in the presence of noise. The key observation is that noise can be overcome through the proper use of data encoding. However, Shannon's result does not indicate how to achieve the maximum data rate. Practical data encoders achieve data rates much lower than that given by Equation 3.2. Suitable encoders for local area networks are addressed in Section 3.3.

Example

For the MAP network, the IEEE 802.4 specification for a broadband system sets a maximum value for SNR as 10^5 (50 dB) over a channel with a bandwidth of 12 MHz. Thus, according to Shannon's result, if the ideal encoding technique is used, the maximum data rate is

$$C = 12 \times 10^6 \log_2 (1 + 10^5) \text{ bits/sec}$$
$$= 199.2 \text{ M bits/sec.}$$

It is interesting to compare the previous channel capacity C of 199.2 Mbit/sec with the actual data rate of 10 Mbits/sec on a 12 MHz channel specified as one of the options by the IEEE 802.4 standard. The 10 Mbits/sec data rate is achieved using a duobinary encoding technique (in combination with a AM/PSK modulator) discussed in the next section.

Using Equation 2.105, C can be written as

$$C = B \log_2 \left(1 + \frac{E_b C}{NB}\right) \qquad (3.4)$$

Here E_b is the energy per bit and $N/2$ is the noise power spectral density in Watt/H_z.

3.3 DATA ENCODING

As noted earlier, the physical layer receives a sequence of bits from the data link layer to be sent over the physical medium. Since we are assuming that the physical medium can propagate only electrical signals,[4] there must be a way of representing bits as electrical signals. Techniques for representing bits as electrical signals for transmission on a physical medium are known as **signaling techniques** or **data encoding** techniques. In addition to performing the encoding functions, data encoders provide compensation for the following impairments: probability of error, finite bandwidth, and the presence of noise. The following criteria are useful when selecting an appropriate encoding scheme (Lathi, 1983):

---

[4] Our discussion does not change if signals other than electric are used (e.g., optical).

1. Adequate timing content. Digital communications require a clock signal at the receiver which is synchronized to that of the transmitter in order to properly decode the received signal. Some encoding techniques (e.g., Manchester) are capable of combining data and clock information in one signal.

2. Noise efficiency. Given a fixed bandwidth and transmitted power, some encoders maximize their immunity to channel noise.

3. Error detection and correction capability. Some encoders allow the user to detect and even correct bit errors. The error detection and correction capability is an added benefit of data encoders and should not be confused with explicit error detection and correction codes normally used at the data link layer, such as Hamming codes and cyclic redundancy checks (CRCs).

4. Favorable power spectral density. One of the main functions of data encoding is to match the spectrum of the signals to be transmitted to the medium frequency response or channel bandwidth.

Two aspects are important in order to have favorable power spectral density. The first aspect involves having no dc components and the second involves concentrating most of the energy of the transmitted signal in a certain channel bandwidth. The degree of energy concentration is measured in terms of bandwidth efficiency, which is measured in Hz per bit/sec.

5. Data transparency. The system should be able to correctly transmit a digital signal regardless of the pattern of 1s and 0s.

The selection of appropriate encoding techniques depends on the environment in which the network operates and on other factors which are somewhat application dependent.

Example

A certain local area network has its stations located very close to one other (e.g., less than 50 m). Assume that the network operates in a noisy environment. Identify the main encoder requirements.

Solution Because of the need to perform bit synchronization, we require that the encoding technique have adequate timing content. Since the network operates in a noisy environment, it would be advantageous to have an encoding technique with good noise efficiency. Since the stations are located relatively close to each other, it is not imperative that they are ac coupled. Furthermore, it is not indicated that the network medium is used as a backbone for communications involving the use of other channels. Thus, having a favorable spectral density is not a requirement. Any encoding and modulation scheme, regardless of its efficiency, can be used since no other channel is used. Therefore for this example, the main data encoding requirements are:

1. adequate timing content, and
2. noise efficiency.

Typically, error detection and correction capability and data transparency are performed at the data link layer. Thus, they are not major requirements for data encoders unless they are additional benefits.

We next analyze data encoding methods in terms of the *encoding rules* and in terms of the *frequency spectrum* of the encoded signals. The encoding rule is of course used by the transmitter that generates the waveforms out of the data bits and for the receiver to properly decode the data.

The encoding rule is also useful for analyzing whether the encoder has adequate timing content, appropriate error detection and correction capability, and data transparency. The frequency spectrum of the encoded signal is useful for analyzing whether the encoder has adquate timing content, noise efficiency, and favorable power spectral density.

When discussing the various data encoding techniques, we make use of a general expression for the power spectral density of a signal encoded by any encoder. The power spectral density of the encoded signal is given by Lathi (1983):

$$S_y(\omega) = |P(\omega)|^2 S_x(\omega) \tag{3.5}$$

where $P(\omega)$ is the Fourier transform of the pulse waveform $p(t)$ used for data transmission and $S_x(\omega)$ is the power spectral density of an impulse train that defines the location and amplitude of the pulses $p(t)$. $S_x(\omega)$ depends on the data (i.e., bit pattern) and the encoding rule. Together, the pulse shape and the location and amplitude of the pulses (as given by the encoder rule) determine the encoded waveform. The simplest pulse $p(t)$ has a rectangular shape. For a halfwidth rectangular pulse shown in Figure 3.2

$$p(t) = \pi\left(\frac{t}{T_o/2}\right) = \pi\left(\frac{2t}{T_o}\right) \tag{3.6}$$

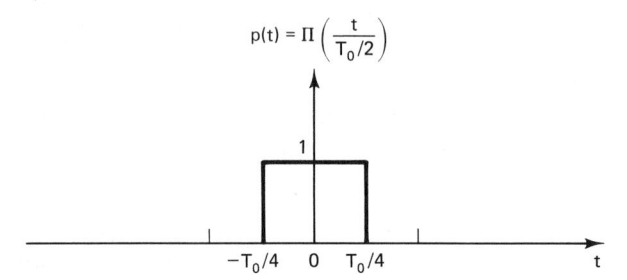

Figure 3.2 Halfwidth rectangular pulse.

whose Fourier Transform is[5]

$$P(\omega) = \frac{T_o}{2} \operatorname{sinc} \frac{\omega T_o}{4\pi} \tag{3.7}$$

the power spectral density of the encoded signal is

$$S_y(\omega) = \frac{T_o^2}{4} \operatorname{sinc}^2 \frac{\omega T_o}{4\pi} S_x(\omega) \tag{3.8}$$

Equation 3.8 is a general result applicable to any encoding rule. We now proceed to treat each encoder separately and we make use of Equation 3.8 directly or in a modified version.

3.3.1 On-Off Signaling

A version of this scheme is the return to zero (RZ) scheme. The rule can be summarized as follows: A **1** is encoded as the halfwidth rectangular pulse $p(t)$ and a **0** is encoded as no pulse. For example, the data stream 0110010 is encoded as the pulse waveform shown in Figure 3.3.

[5] The notation $\pi(t/T_o)$ simply means a rectangular pulse centered at t = o and having a width equal to T_o (see Figure 3.2). Also, the notation $\operatorname{sinc}(x) = \sin(\pi x)/\pi x$.

[Figure 3.3 shows RZ encoding of 0110010 with pulses of width T_o]

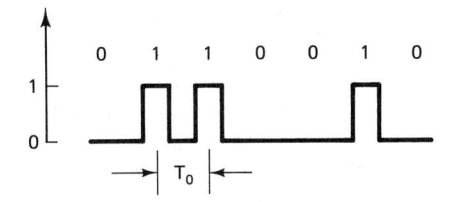

Figure 3.3 Return to zero (RZ) encoding of 0110010.

The power spectral density of the encoded signal is

$$S_y(\omega) = \frac{T_o}{16} \text{sinc}^2 \frac{\omega T_o}{4\pi} \left[1 + \frac{2\pi}{T_o} \sum_{n=-\infty}^{\infty} \delta\left(\omega - \frac{2\pi n}{T_o}\right) \right] \quad (3.9)$$

where $\delta(\omega)$ is the *impulse delta function* in the frequency domain. The plot of $S_y(f)$ versus f is depicted in Figure 3.4, where $f = \omega/2\pi$.

Because most of the energy is located at frequencies for which $|f| < 2 f_o$, the essential bandwidth is $2f_o$ where f_o is the clock frequency. The advantage of on-off signaling is that it is simple to generate using electronic circuitry. However, it has a number of disadvantages. First, for a given transmitted power, it is less immune to noise interference than the polar scheme. Second, as shown in Figure 3.4, it has a nonzero power spectral density at dc (f = 0). This is inconvenient, because it prevents the user from using ac coupling during transmission. Thirdly, the transmission bandwidth requirements are larger than other encoding schemes. Fourthly, on-off signaling has no error detection or correction capability, and lastly, it is not transparent.

Another version of on-off signaling is the nonreturn to zero (NRZ) scheme, which is obtained using the same encoding rules, with the difference that p(t) is the full width rectangular pulse given by $p(t) = \pi (t/T_o)$.

3.3.2 Polar Signaling

In polar signaling a **1** is transmitted by a pulse p(t) and a **0** is transmitted by $-p(t)$. The power spectral density of the encoded pulse is

$$S_y(\omega) = \frac{T_o}{4} \text{sinc}^2 \frac{\omega T_o}{4\pi} \quad (3.10)$$

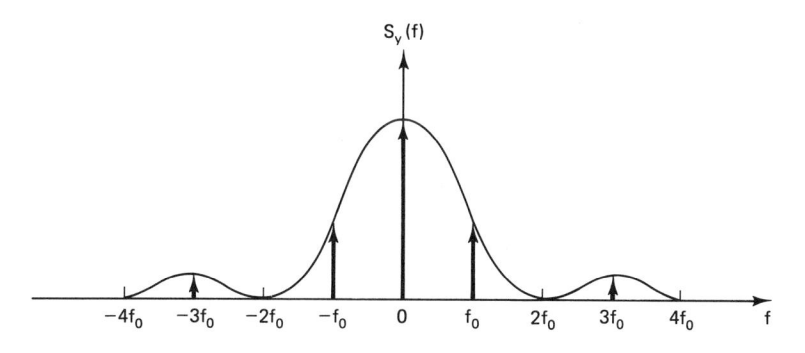

Figure 3.4 Power spectral density of on-off and polar signals.

Sec. 3.3 Data Encoding

The spectrum of a polar encoded signal is identical to the continuous component of the on-off signal. From transmitted power considerations, polar encoding is more efficient than *on-off* encoding when comparing their noise immunity capabilities. This is because noise immunity depends on the difference of amplitudes representing **1** and **0**. Thus, for the same noise immunity if *on-off* encoding uses pulse amplitudes 2 and 0, polar encoding need only use pulse amplitude 1 and −1, which require less power.

An advantage of polar encoding is that it is transparent. This is because a long sequence of **0**s or **1**s is transmitted as a square waveform which can be decoded faithfully. However, it suffers from all the other disadvantages of on-off encoding. Since there is no discrete clock frequency component in a polar signal, timing extraction cannot be done by filtering the clock signal. Fortunately, the rectified polar signal contains a periodic signal at the clock frequency that can be used for timing extraction.

3.3.3 Bipolar Signaling

Under this scheme, a **1** is encoded either as p(t) of − p(t), depending upon whether the previous pulse was − p(t) or p(t), respectively. A **0** is encoded as no pulse. The power spectral density of the encoded pulse is

$$S_y(\omega) = \frac{T_o}{4} \text{sinc}^2 \frac{\omega T_o}{4\pi} \sin^2 \frac{\omega T_o}{2} \qquad (3.11)$$

From the spectrum of the bipolar encoded signal, shown in Figure 3.5, we see that the signal bandwidth is approximately f_o, which is half of that of on-off encoding. The advantages of bipolar encoding are that its spectrum is not excessive, and it has a single error detection capability. This is because a single detection error will cause a bipolar violation of the alternating pulse rule, which can be easily detected. The disadvantages are that it requires twice as much power as compared to polar encoding, and it is not transparent.

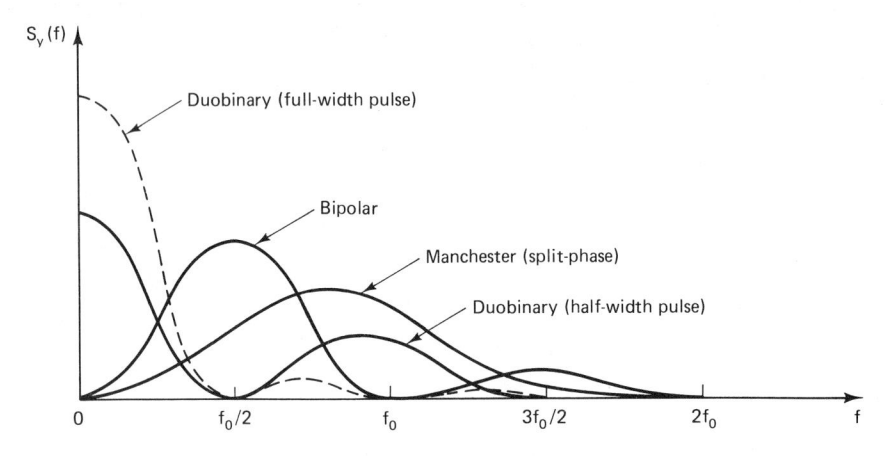

Figure 3.5 Power spectral densities of several encoding schemes.

3.3.4 Duobinary Signaling

This encoder is similar to bipolar signaling. A **0** is transmitted by no pulse, and a **1** is transmitted by a pulse p(t) or − p(t), depending upon the polarity of the previous pulse and the number of **0**s between them. Two **1**s that have an even number of **0**s between them are encoded by the same pulse. Two **1**s that have an odd number of **0**s between them are encoded by opposite pulses. For a full-width rectangular pulse, the power spectral density (PSD) of the encoded signal, shown in Figure 3.5 is given by

$$S_y(\omega) = \frac{T_o}{4} \operatorname{sinc}^2 \frac{\omega T_o}{4\pi} \cos^2 \frac{\omega T_o}{2} \qquad (3.12)$$

From the PSD we can see that the essential bandwidth is about $f_o/2$. It can be noticed that there is appreciable power at frequencies above $f_o/2$. However, by appropriately choosing the shape of p(t) (i.e., other than the rectangular shape) it is possible to achieve negligible PSD at frequencies above $f_o/2$. The advantages of duobinary encoding are: timing can be extracted by rectifying the signal, it has error detection capability, and the signal bandwidth is about $f_o/2$. The disadvantages are that it requires twice as much power as compared to polar encoding, and it has a nonzero PSD at f = 0. However, a modified duobinary encoding version exists that gets rid of the latter disadvantage.

The duobinary encoding technique is particularly attractive for local area networks requiring the use of many channels (e.g., for voice, video, and data) because it requires only a channel bandwidth of $f_o/2$; thus, it is very efficient from the bandwidth standpoint. The power disadvantage of the duobinary encoding technique is easily solved, since power is not really a problem for terrestrial networks.[6] The IEEE 802.4 (and hence the MAP network) specification specifies a duobinary encoding, referred to as *Class 1 partial response coding*, to be used with appropriate modulation yielding a *bandwidth efficiency* of 1.2 Hz per bit/sec at a data rate of 10 M bps.

3.3.5 Manchester (Split-Phase) Signaling

So far, we have been considering signaling schemes having the same pulse shape (i.e., rectangular). For encoders with rectangular pulses, the power spectral density of the encoded signal is actually controlled by changing the position, amplitudes, and polarities of the pulses (i.e., $S_x(\omega)$). As noted earlier, one of the most important criteria in any signaling scheme is the dc power level, i.e., the value of $S_y(\omega)$ at $\omega = 0$. For practical purposes, it is desirable to have $S_y(0) = 0$, because this allows the use of ac coupling between a network's station and the medium. The advantages of ac coupling include the provision of electrical isolation as well as the avoidance of power dissipation. It is possible to force $S_y(0) = 0$ by having $P(0) = 0$. Since

$$P(\omega) = \int_{-\infty}^{\infty} p(t)\, e^{-j\omega t}\, dt \qquad (3.13)$$

P(0) is simply the area under p(t). Thus, any pulse waveform with area equal to zero will give $S_y(0) = 0$. Manchester encoding uses a pulse p(t) shown in Figure 3.6. A **1** is encoded as p(t) and a **0** is encoded as −p(t). Although the pulses are different, Manchester encoding use the same rules

---

[6] It would be, however, for satellite networks.

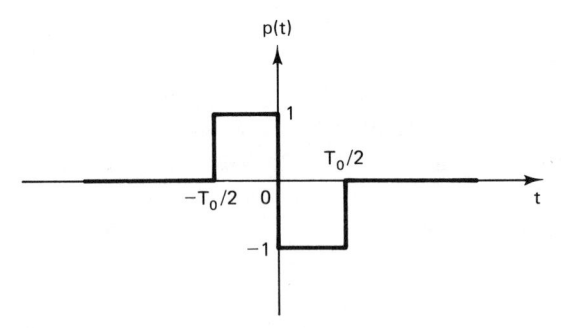

Figure 3.6 Pulse $p(t)$ used in Manchester (split-phase) encoding.

as polar coding. Thus, Manchester is also a polar encoding technique. The power spectral density of the encoded signal is

$$S_y(\omega) = T_o \, \text{sinc}^2 \frac{\omega T_o}{4\pi} \sin^2 \frac{\omega T_o}{4} \tag{3.14}$$

whose spectrum is shown in Figure 3.5. Perhaps the best example of a local area network using Manchester encoding is Ethernet.[7]

Example

The bit sequence 010001101011 is to be encoded separately, using each of the encoding techniques discussed previously. Sketch the pulse waveforms at the output of each encoder.

Solution Using the encoding rules for each technique, we obtain the waveforms shown in Figure 3.7.

Example

Consider four transmission systems corresponding to the following environments:

1. satellite networks,
2. local area networks (LAN),
3. computer room networks (CRN), and
4. instrumentation/consumer electronics.

Although category 4 is not a network, consumer electronics (e.g., digital recording, compact disk) uses data encoding techniques to represent digital data into magnetic media, which is equivalent to a transmission medium.

The following table shows some major system characteristics in terms of the channel bandwidth (BW) required, signal power required, type of physical medium, whether a common clock

---

[7] Ethernet uses a random channel access technique known as CSMA/CD, to be discussed in Section 4.9. The access technique specified by IEEE 802.3 is similar to that of Ethernet.

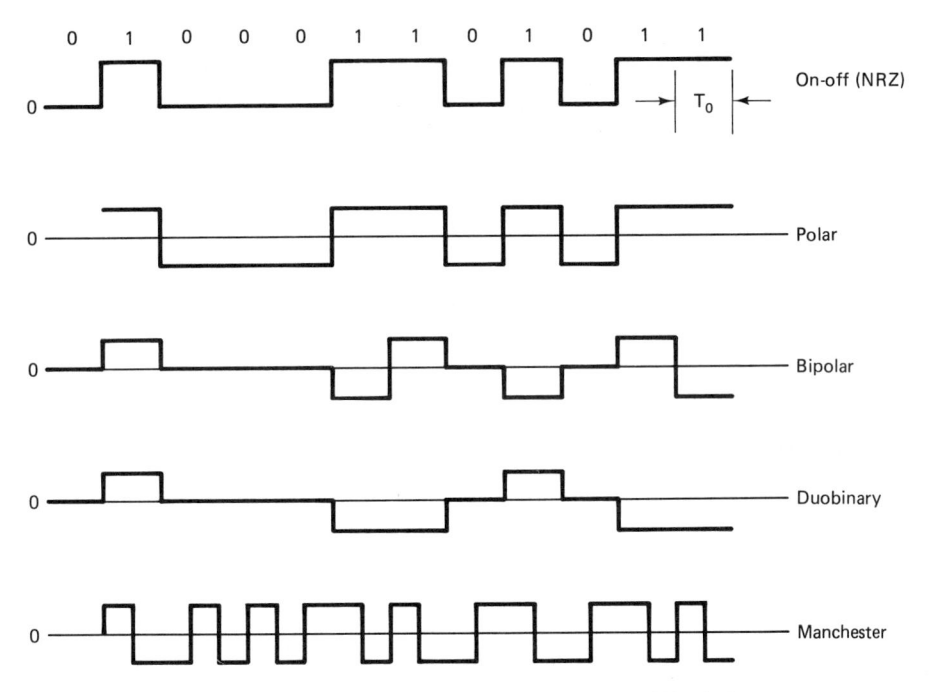

Figure 3.7 Encoded waveforms for the bit sequence 010001101011.

is used, and typical SNR required. Recommend appropriate encoding techniques to be used with each of the four transmission systems. Include at least two reasons to support the decision.

System	Channel BW	Signal power	Physical medium	Common clock	SNR
Satellite	a	very small	unbounded	no	small
LAN	a b	medium	bounded	no	medium to small
CRN	b	medium to large	bounded	no	large to medium
Digital recording	b	medium to large	bounded	yes	large to medium

a: finite (i.e., limited) bandwidth.
b: infinite (i.e., unlimited) bandwidth.

Solution There are several encoding rules that are appropriate for each of the systems; the following table is a possible set.

Sec. 3.3 Data Encoding

System	Encoding technique	Reasons
Satellite	Polar	Efficient in terms of power; contains timing information
LAN a	Duobinary	Efficient in terms of bandwidth, timing
b	Manchester	DC null, timing
CRN	Manchester	Timing, no BW restrictions
Digital recording	NRZ, RZ	No timing required, no power restrictions

3.4 INTERSYMBOL INTERFERENCE

One of the major difficulties that arises in digital communications is that messages are usually represented by rectangular pulses that require infinite channel bandwidth for undistorted transmission. Rectangular pulses injected at one end of a communication channel appear at the other end as pulses which decay gradually to zero, as shown in Figure 3.8. The gradual decay of rectangular pulses causes problems with neighboring pulses is known as intersymbol interference (ISI). For example, Figure 3.9(a) shows a sequence of rectangular pulses at the transmitter end of a transmission system. The corresponding sequence of pulses at the receiving end of the system is shown in Figure 3.9(b). From these figures, it is clear that ISI causes problems with the correct detection of the transmitted pulses.

Two well-known techniques for solving the intersymbol interference problem are based on the first and second Nyquist criteria for zero ISI.

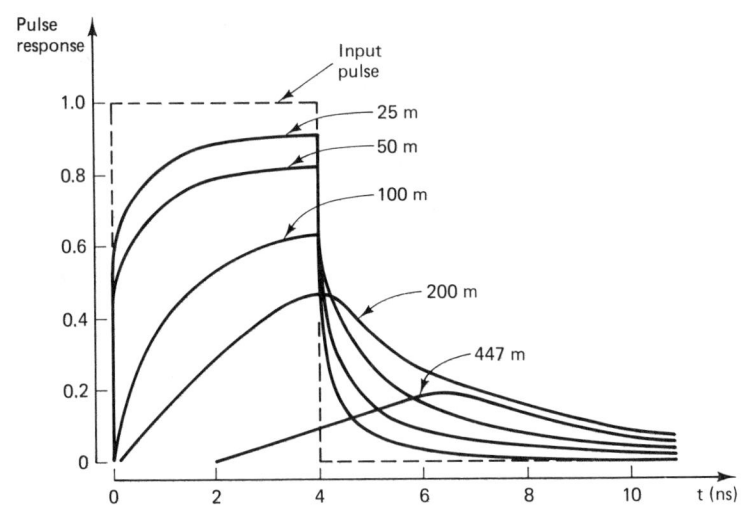

Figure 3.8 Signal response of a coaxial cable to a rectangular pulse. Values in meters indicate distance between transmitter and receiver.

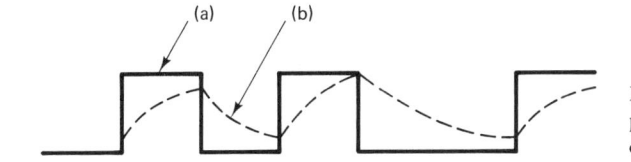

Figure 3.9 (a) Sequence of rectangular pulses at the transmitting end. (b) Sequence of received pulses at the receiving end.

3.4.1 Nyquist's First Criterion for Zero ISI

The first Nyquist criterion states two conditions that the pulse p(t) must satisfy in order to avoid ISI. First, p(t) must have a nonzero amplitude at its origin, and second, p(t) must be zero at t = ± nT$_o$ where T$_o$ is the separation between successive transmitted pulses. Thus, the conditions are

$$p(0) \neq 0 \qquad (3.15)$$

$$p(\pm n T_o) = 0 \qquad (3.16)$$

Many pulses exist which satisfy the preceding criteria. A well-known pulse often used is the *raised cosine pulse*, shown in Figure 3.10, which has the following power spectrum

$$P(\omega) = \cos^2 \frac{\omega}{4f_o} \pi \left(\frac{\omega}{4\pi f_o} \right) \qquad (3.17)$$

and the following impulse response

$$p(t) = f_o \frac{\cos(\pi f_o t)}{1 - 4 f_o^2 t^2} \text{sinc}(f_o t) \qquad (3.18)$$

Example

The sequence 101100 is encoded using an NRZ on-off encoder with pulses satisfying the Nyquist first criterion for ISI. Since the pulse is bandlimited, it will travel through a medium having sufficient bandwidth with little distortion. The received signal is shown in Figure 3.11. Clearly, the effect of neighboring pulses has been cancelled, because at the sampling instants their effect is zero.

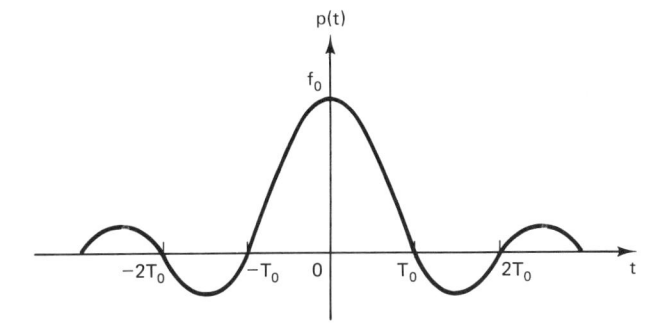

Figure 3.10 Raised cosine pulse satisfying Nyquist's first criterion for zero ISI.

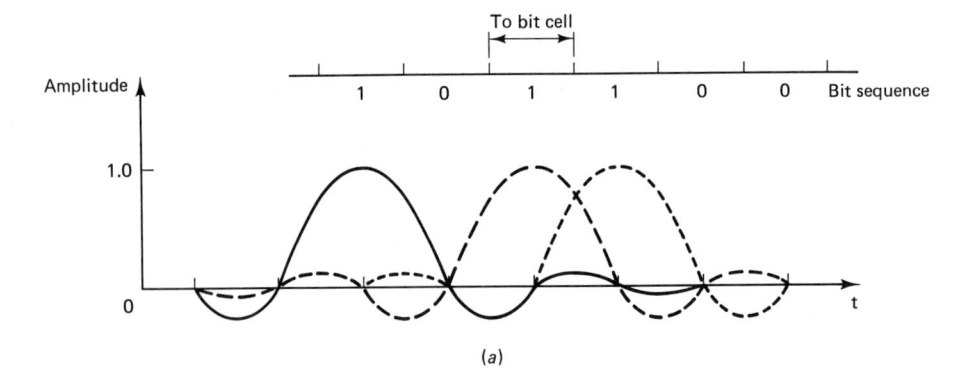

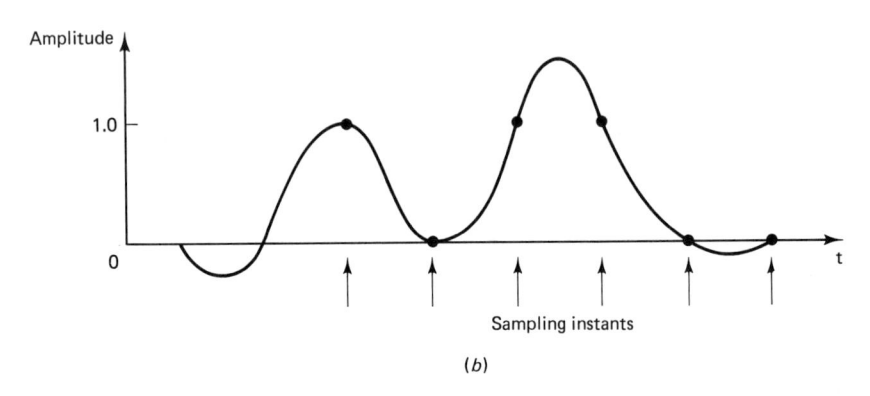

Figure 3.11 Encoding of the sequence 101100 using Nyquist's first criterion for ISI: (a) Constituent pulses using NRZ encoding; (b) Receiver's output.

3.4.2 Nyquist's Second Criterion for ISI

The second Nyquist criterion also states two conditions for p(t):

$$p\left(\pm \frac{T_o}{2}\right) = c \qquad (3.19)$$

and

$$p\left(\pm \frac{nT_o}{2}\right) = 0 \qquad n = 3, 5, 7, \ldots \qquad (3.20)$$

For pulses bandlimited to $f_o/2$ Hz, the only pulse p(t) satisfying the preceding properties is shown in Figure 3.12 and given by

$$p(t) = \frac{2 f_o \cos(\pi f_o t)}{\pi(1 - 4 f_o^2 t^2)} \qquad (3.21)$$

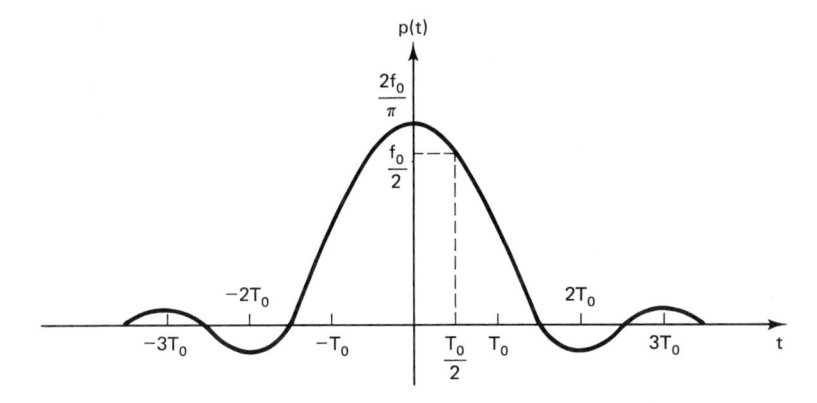

Figure 3.12 Pulse satisfying Nyquist's second criterion for zero ISI.

Example

To illustrate the application of Nyquist's second criterion for ISI, assume the same sequence 101100 of the previous example. A **1** is transmitted by p(t) and a **0** is transmitted by −p(t). We note that

$$p(\pm T_o/2) = f_o/2 \qquad (3.22)$$

and

$$p(\pm nT_o/2) = 0; \quad n = 3,5,7,\ldots \qquad (3.23)$$

When a **1** is followed by a **0**, we have p(t) followed by −p(t). Alternatively, when a **0** is followed by a **1**, we have −p(t) followed by p(t). Thus, by sampling at the midpoint of the two pulses we obtain zero, as shown in Figure 3.13. Likewise, if two **1**s or two **0**s are transmitted together, the sampled values are f_o and $-f_o$, respectively. The following table shows all the possibilities to be used in the decoding process.

Bit sequence	Sampled value
0 0	$-f_o$
0 1	0
1 0	0
1 1	f_o

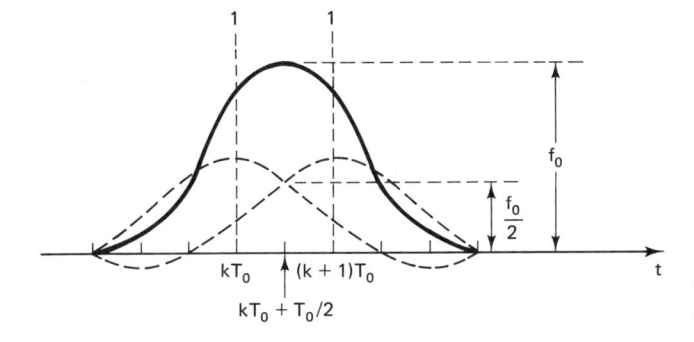

Figure 3.13 Sampling a midpoint of two pulses.

Sec. 3.4   Intersymbol Interference

Applying the encoding and sampling process described previously to the sequence 1011001, we obtain the waveform of Figure 3.14. We can see that the interference from neighboring pulses (with the exception of the immediate neighbor) has been eliminated. As shown in the preceding table, interference with immediate neighbors is explicitly taken into account in the decoding process.

The IEEE 802.4 specification uses the pulse waveform of Equation 3.21 to eliminate intersymbol interference.

3.5 SCRAMBLING

Having a long sequence of **1**s or **0**s produces two negative effects: The first one is that some encoding techniques (e.g., NRZ) cannot provide accurate clock information, because the encoded signal does not make a transition as long as the data bits do not change. The second negative effect is that the frequency spectrum of modulated signals has more frequency components than the situation where the average number of **1**s is about the same as the average number of **0**s in the sequence. Thus, for these two reasons it is convenient to remove long sequences of **1**s or **0**s from the data.

The process of removing long strings of **1**s of **0**s so as to make the data more random is referred to as **scrambling**. A scrambler typically consists of a feedback shift register, as shown in Figure 3.15. The scrambler output can be written as

$$y(n) = x(n) + y(n-3) + y(n-5) \quad \text{Modulo 2} \quad (3.24)$$

Taking the Z transform on both sides of Equation 3.24, where the Z transform is defined as $Z[y(n-k)] = z^{-k} Z[y(n)] = z^{-k} Y(z)$, we obtain

$$Y(z) = X(z) + (z^{-N} z^{-(N+M)}) Y(z) \quad \text{Modulo 2} \quad (3.25)$$

$$= X(z) + F(z) Y(z) \quad \text{Modulo 2} \quad (3.26)$$

from which

$$Y(z) = \frac{1}{1 - F(z)} X(z) \quad \text{Modulo 2} \quad (3.27)$$

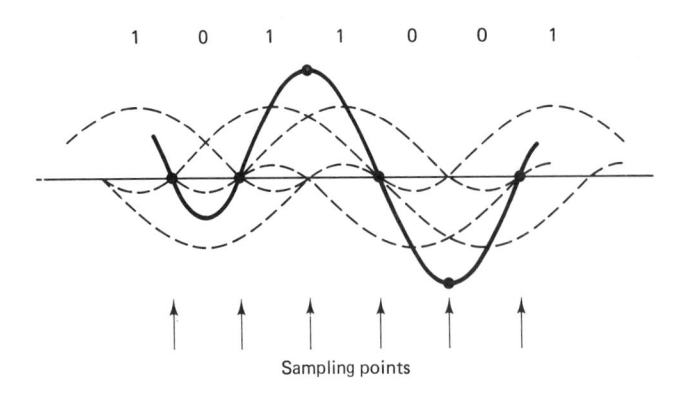

$$= (1 - F(z) + F^2(z) - F^3(z) + \ldots) X(z) \quad \text{Modulo 2} \quad (3.28)$$

Figure 3.14 Encoding of the sequence 1011001 using Nyquist's second criterion for ISI.

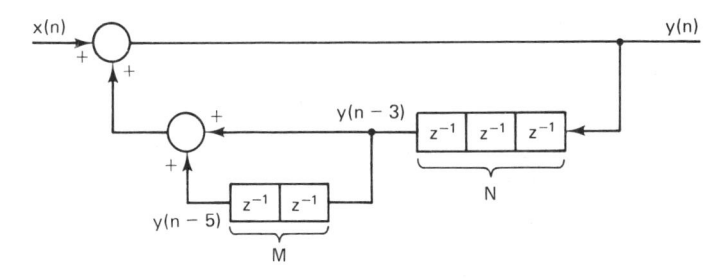

[Figure: Scrambler's block diagram showing x(n) input, y(n) output, with delay elements z⁻¹ forming N=3 and M=2 taps, with y(n−3) and y(n−5) feedback]

Figure 3.15 Scrambler's block diagram.

The modulo 2 qualifier in the previous equations is used to indicate that all the operations are performed using modulo 2 arithmetic, obeying the following addition and substraction rules.

0 + 0 = 0
0 + 1 = 1
1 + 0 = 1
1 + 1 = 0
0 − 0 = 0
0 − 1 = 1
1 − 0 = 1
1 − 1 = 0

Modulo 2 arithmetic is another way to express the logical *exclusive-or* operation. As can be seen from the preceding list, using modulo 2 arithmetic, a binary number added to itself is always 0. Thus, in general $nG(z) = 0$ for n any even number. Furthermore, by analyzing the substraction table, the reader can realize that the addition and substraction operations are identical using modulo 2 arithmetic.

Example

The data sequence 101010100000111 is fed to a scrambler with N = 3 and M = 2. Find the scrambler output y(n), assuming the initial content of the registers to be zero.

Solution The input sequence corresponds to x(n) for $0 \leq n \leq 14$ where the leftmost bit corresponds to x(0) and the rightmost bit to x(14). From Equation 3.28,

$$Y(z) = (1 - F(z) + F^2(z) - \ldots) X(z)$$

where

$$F(z) = z^{-N} + z^{-(N+M)} = z^{-3} + z^{-5}$$

Thus,

$$F^2(z) = (z^{-3} + z^{-5})^2 = z^{-6} + 2z^{-8} + z^{-10} = z^{-6} + z^{-10}$$

$$F^3(z) = (z^{-6} + z^{-10})(z^{-3} + z^{-5}) = z^{-9} + z^{-11} + z^{-13} + z^{-15}$$

and so on. Hence,

$$Y(z) = (1 + z^{-3} + z^{-5} + z^{-6} + z^{-9} + z^{-10} + z^{-11} + z^{-13} + z^{15} + \ldots) X(z)$$

Using the identity $z^{-k} X(z) \leftrightarrow x(n-k)$, the previous equation is equivalent to

$$y(n) = x(n) + x(n-3) + x(n-5) + x(n-6) + x(n-9)$$
$$+ x(n-10) + x(n-11) + x(n-13) + x(n-15) + \ldots$$

Because $x(n-k)$ is simply the sequence $x(n)$ delayed by k bits, the various terms in the preceding equation correspond to the following sequences:

$$x(n) = 1010\ 1010\ 0000\ 111$$
$$x(n-3) = 0001\ 0101\ 0100\ 0001$$
$$x(n-5) = 0000\ 0101\ 0101\ 0000$$
$$x(n-6) = 0000\ 0010\ 1010\ 1000$$
$$x(n-9) = 0000\ 0000\ 0101\ 0101$$
$$x(n-10) = 0000\ 0000\ 0010\ 1010$$
$$x(n-11) = 0000\ 0000\ 0001\ 0101$$
$$x(n-12) = 0000\ 0000\ 0000\ 1010$$
$$x(n-13) = 0000\ 0000\ 0000\ 0101$$
$$x(n-15) = 0000\ 0000\ 0000\ 0001$$
$$y(n) = 1011\ 1000\ 1101\ 001$$

Notice, in the preceding example, that either any periodic string or the same string has been removed from the original sequence. For instance, the initial string 10101010 has been made more randomized. Likewise, the string 00000 has also been made more randomized. Of course, the receiver has to perform exactly the inverse operation (descrambler) to recover the original sequence.

3.6 BASEBAND COMMUNICATIONS

Depending upon whether signals are modulated before transmission, there are two types of communication systems: wideband (broadband) and baseband communications. When signal transmission is achieved without the resort to modulation, we refer to **baseband** communications. Whenever any type of modulation is used, communication is of the **broadband** type. The term **carrierband** is often used when referring to a broadband system where only one channel is used. Like baseband, *carrierband* uses only one channel. However, unlike baseband, carrierband utilizes modulation. Perhaps the best example of a baseband system is an Ethernet[8]-based network. The MAP architecture includes both a broadband and carrierband system, called the *full MAP architecture*[9] and the *enhanced performance architecture* (EPA). We first examine baseband communications for two reasons: First, it is simpler than broadband communications; and second, it can be used as a reference for comparisons with broadband systems and also for performance studies.

In baseband communications, the signal is transmitted directly without any modulation. The

---

[8] Several manufacturers, including DEC, have announced Ethernet networks as a broadband system.
[9] It is also expected to have a full MAP architecture on a carrierband system.

signal at the output of the transmitter is sent through the channel to its destination. Baseband communication is used for both forms of signal transmission: analog and digital. However, most baseband communication systems for local area networks are digital.

So far, we have been considering issues which are applicable to both baseband and broadband systems. Sections 3.7, 3.8, and 3.9 discuss issues only applicable to broadband systems. All other issues discussed in this chapter could be applied in a baseband or broadband context. Although channel impairments, such as noise and attenuation, can be discussed in the context of baseband or broadband systems, we discuss them next before discussing issues which are specific to broadband systems only.

Additive Noise

Figure 3.16 shows a transmission system model with a medium of length L (Km) in which the effect of noise is additive. At the receiver, the signal is amplified with an amplifier with voltage gain A, and it is passed through a filter with bandwidth equal to B Hz to limit excess noise. The noise power at the filter output is

$$N_o = A^2 N B \qquad (3.29)$$

where N/2 is the noise power spectral density in (Watt/Hz); and the signal output is

$$S_o = A^2 S_r \qquad (3.30)$$

where S_r is the received power equal to S_i/L_1 and

$$L_1 = 10^{-A_t L} \qquad (3.30a)$$

where A_t is the attenuation loss in dB/Km.

Thus, the signal to noise ratio is

$$\frac{S_o}{N_o} = \frac{S_r}{NB} = \frac{S_i}{L_1 NB} \qquad (3.31)$$

which is the same equation as Equation 2.104.

Repeater Systems

Equation 3.31 shows that the signal to noise ratio deteriorates as the length of the medium increases. One way to achieve a desirable value for (S_o/N_o) is by the use of repeaters. Repeaters can be amplifiers or regenerative devices. Figure 3.17 depicts the block diagram for a channel with several repeaters.

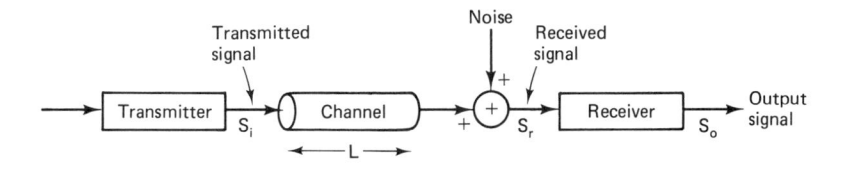

Figure 3.16 A communication system with additive noise.

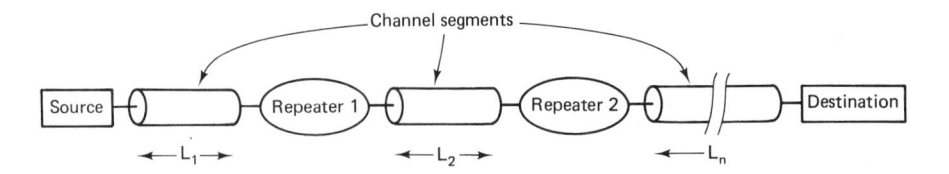

Figure 3.17 A communication channel with several repeaters.

Assuming that each repeater system is designed with just enough gain to overcome the loss of the previous segment, then (Carlson, 1975),

$$\frac{S_o}{N_o} = \frac{1}{M} \cdot \frac{S_1}{N_1} \quad (3.32)$$

where (S_1/N_1) is the signal to noise ratio at the output of the first repeater, and M is the number of segments. Equation 3.32 shows that the introduction of repeaters decreases the signal to noise ratio. However, this is better than the alternative given by Equation 3.31, where the *signal to noise ratio* can decrease even more because of the large value of L (as the next example shows).

Example

A signal is to be transmitted 40 Km using a transmission medium whose attenuation loss is $A_t = -3$ dB/Km. The noise power spectral density $N = 0.2 \times 10^{-18.7}$ and B = 5 KHz. a) Find the value of S_i (in watts) required to get $(S_o/N_o) = 50$ dB. b) Repeat the calculation for S_i when there is a repeater at the halfway point.

Solution From Equations 3.31 and 3.32,

$$\frac{S_o}{N_o} = \frac{S_i}{M L_1 N B}$$

From which,

$$S_i = M \cdot L_1 \cdot N \cdot B \cdot \frac{S_o}{N_o}$$

$$(S_i) \text{ dB} = 10 \log M + (L_1)\text{dB} + 10\log (N B) + (S_o/N_o)\text{dB}$$

$$= 10 \log M + (L_1)\text{dB} - 157 \text{ dBW} + 50 \text{ dB}$$

a) For this case, M = 1, and L = 40 Km. Thus, using Equation 3.30a,

$$(S_i)\text{dB} = 0 + 3 \text{ (dB/Km)} \times 40 \text{ Km} - 107 \text{ dB W} = 13 \text{ dB W}$$

and

$$S_i = 10^{1.3} \text{ Watts} = 20 \text{ Watts}$$

b) For this case there are two segments thus, M = 2, and L = 20 Km. Thus,

$$(S_i)\text{dB} = 10 \log 2 + 3 \text{ (dB/Km)} \times 20 \text{ Km} - 107 \text{ dB W}$$

$$= -44 \text{ dB}$$

and

$$S_i = 10^{-4.4} \text{ Watts} = 40 \, \mu \text{ Watts}$$

Therefore, the difference in the required power is appreciable by simply putting a repeater at the halfway point.

3.7 WIDEBAND (BROADBAND) COMMUNICATIONS

So far, we have been dealing with baseband transmission systems which do not use modulation. Most of the energy in baseband systems is concentrated at low frequencies (i.e., near f = 0). However, there are situations in which it is desirable to shift the energy that normally lies at low frequencies to other regions of the frequency spectrum. Some of the advantages of modulation are: radiation efficiency, noise and interference reduction, frequency assignment capability, multiplex capability, and optimum use of transmission devices and equipment (Carlson, 1975).

When air or free space are used as the transmission medium, energy is radiated by the transmitter, using antennas. For efficient radiation, antenna sizes must be of the order of magnitude of $\lambda/10$, where λ is the wavelength of the signal. For electromagnetic waves, $\lambda = c/f$, where c is the speed of light and f is the frequency of the wave to be radiated. For example, voice signals are bandlimited to about 3 KHz. Thus, the minimum wavelength for radiating the signal into air (or free space) is $\lambda_{min} = 3 \times 10^8$ m/s$/3 \times 10^3$ Hz $= 10^5$ m $= 100$ Km. Thus, to radiate voice signals without the use of modulation, we need antennas of about 10 Km in size, which are difficult and uneconomical to construct.

Modulation allows a trade-off of bandwidth for noise and interference reduction. In order to achieve the desired level of noise and interference reduction, sometimes it is necessary to provide a channel bandwidth larger than the bandwidth of the original baseband signal.

Because of the widespread use of broadband communications, it has been convenient to regulate and assign certain portions of the frequency spectrum referred to as channels. The use of modulation allows the efficient and practical use of any channel in the frequency spectrum.

Example

In Community Antenna Television (CATV) systems, the entire coaxial cable bandwidth is divided into channels of 6 M Hz each. Figure 3.18 shows the channels designations[10] with their frequency assignments assuming a cable bandwidth of 300 M Hz.

Multiplexing allows several signals to share the same physical medium. Although multiplexing can be used at any layer of the OSI reference model, in this section we discuss multiplexing as it relates to the physical layer. Multiplexing can be performed in the time domain as well as in the frequency domain. The former is referred to as *time division multiplexing* (TDM) and the latter as *frequency division multiplexing* (FDM). We next discuss the fundamental principles of each of the multiplexing schemes.

3.7.1 Time Division Multiplexing (TDM)

In time division multiplexing, a physical medium is time-shared among a number of signals. Time is divided into **time slots,** or simply **slots,** with each signal utilizing the medium for the duration

---

[10] There are two other frequency assignments which assume a cable bandwidth of 400 M Hz, referred to as *incremental* and *harmonic* frequency assignments (Cooper, 1984).

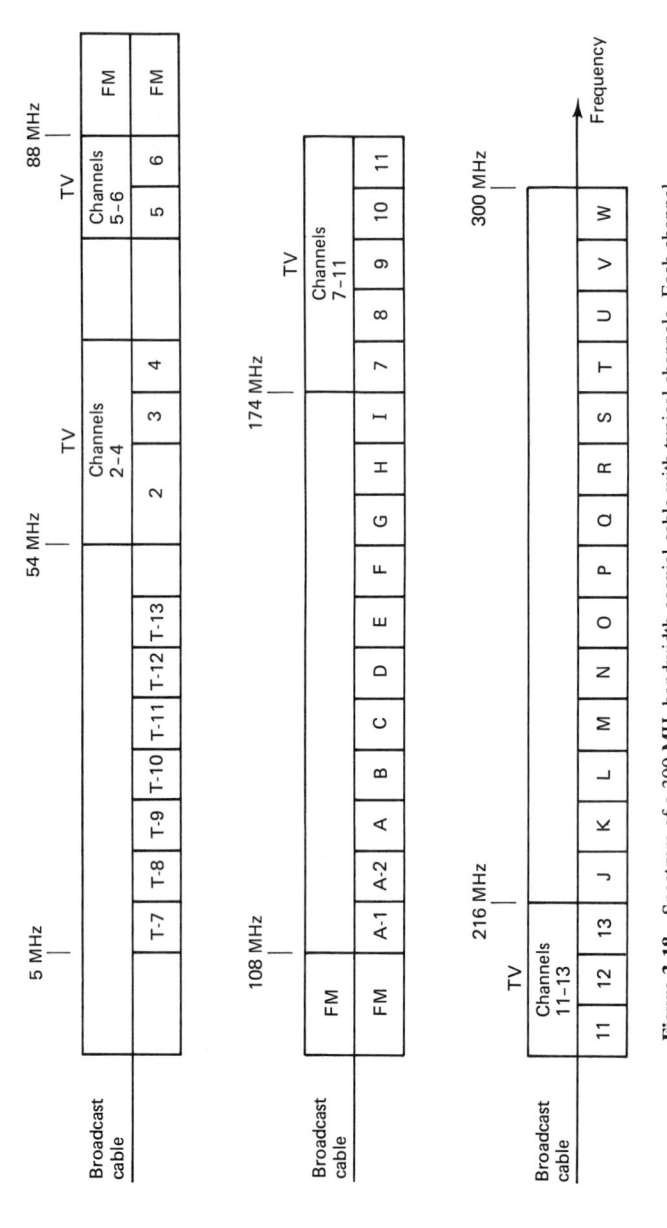

Figure 3.18 Spectrum of a 300 MHz bandwidth coaxial cable with typical channels. Each channel is 6 MHz wide.

of a slot during one cycle. After all signals have used their *slots*, the cycle repeats as illustrated in Figure 3.19. The signals can be analog or digital. For computer networks TDM is primarily digital; thus, we concentrate on *digital multiplexing*. The signals to be multiplexed may come from data encoders.

When the time slots are preassigned to the signals, the multiplexing scheme is **synchronous.**

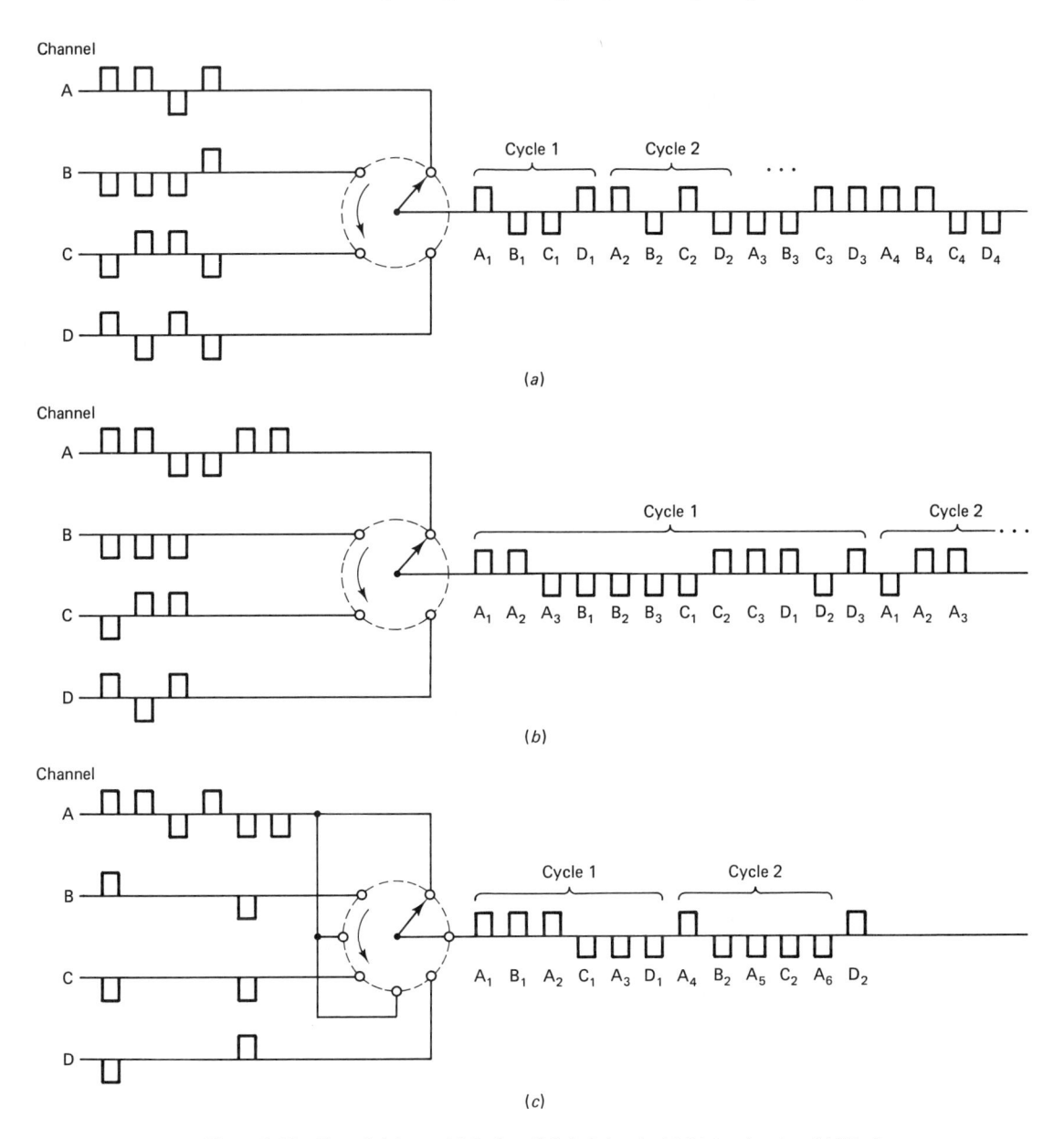

Figure 3.19 Time division multiplexing of digital signals: (a) Bit interleaving; (b) Word interleaving; (c) Multiplexing channels at different rates.

Sec. 3.7 Wideband (Broadband) Communications

When the slots are assigned on demand, the multiplexing scheme is **asynchronous.** We limit our discussion to synchronous time division multiplexing, because it is mostly applicable at the physical layer. Asynchronous time division multiplexing is discussed in the context of channel access mechanisms at the data link layer in Section 4.6.

Depending upon the transmission rates of the signals to be multiplexed, two cases are noted. The first case involves multiplexing signals which have the same data rate. As depicted in Figure 3.19(a) and 3.19(b), multiplexing can be done on a bit by bit basis, also known as **digit interleaving,** or on a word by word basis known as **word interleaving.** In the example corresponding to Figure 3.19(b) each word has three bits. The second case involves multiplexing signals having different rates. In this case, the signals with higher bit rates are allocated proportionally more slots within each cycle. Figure 3.19(c) shows the multiplexing of four signals consisting of three signals B, C, and D with identical rate R and another signal A with rate 3R.

At the receiver, the incoming bit string must be divided and individual bits corresponding to the various signals must be separated. For this purpose, the receiver must not only identify each frame[11] but also each bit within the frame. Thus, the receiver must be able to perform *frame* and *bit synchronization*, which is typically accomplished by adding framing and synchronization bits to the data. Collectively, bits other than data bits (e.g., synchronization bits) are called **control bits.**

Example

A very good example for illustrating the principle of synchronous TDM is the T1 carrier system, which is used extensively for carrying voice signals digitally. A T1 system consists of 24 analog voice signals multiplexed into one channel. Since the signals to be multiplexed are voice, results from signal processing theory (Nyquist theorem) indicate that they must be sampled at a rate greater or equal than 8 K Hz[12] in order to convert the analog signal to a digital one. The T1 system utilizes a sampling rate of precisely 8 K Hz (125 μsec/sample). Furthermore, each sample of the voice signal is converted into an 8-bit digital pattern, as depicted in Figure 3.20, with 7 bits for data and an additional bit for *bit synchronization*. The technique for sampling an analog signal and converting each sample into a digital word is called **pulse code modulation** (PCM). A frame consists of $24 \times 8 = 192$ bits plus an additional bit for *frame synchronization*, yielding a total of 193 bits per frame (i.e., 193 bits per 125 μsec), thus giving a data rate of 1.544 M bps.

3.7.2 Frequency Division Multiplexing (FDM)

As noted, multiplexing allows transmission of several signals on the same channel or medium. Whereas in TDM several signals share time on the channel, in frequency division multiplexing several signals share the bandwidth of the medium. Obviously, in order for this scheme to work, the medium bandwidth must be greater than the bandwidth of the individual signals to be multiplexed.[13] Each signal is modulated by a different carrier frequency. The various carriers are adequately separated to avoid overlap among the spectrum of the modulated signals, as shown in Figure 3.21. Each signal may be modulated differently (e.g., amplitude modulation, frequency modulation, phase modulation, etc). The modulated signal spectrum is separated by a small *guard band* to avoid

---

[11] A frame is defined here as the group of bits in a cycle.

[12] The assumption is that the bandwidth of voice signals is 4 K Hz.

[13] That is, unless techniques for signal bandwidth reduction are used.

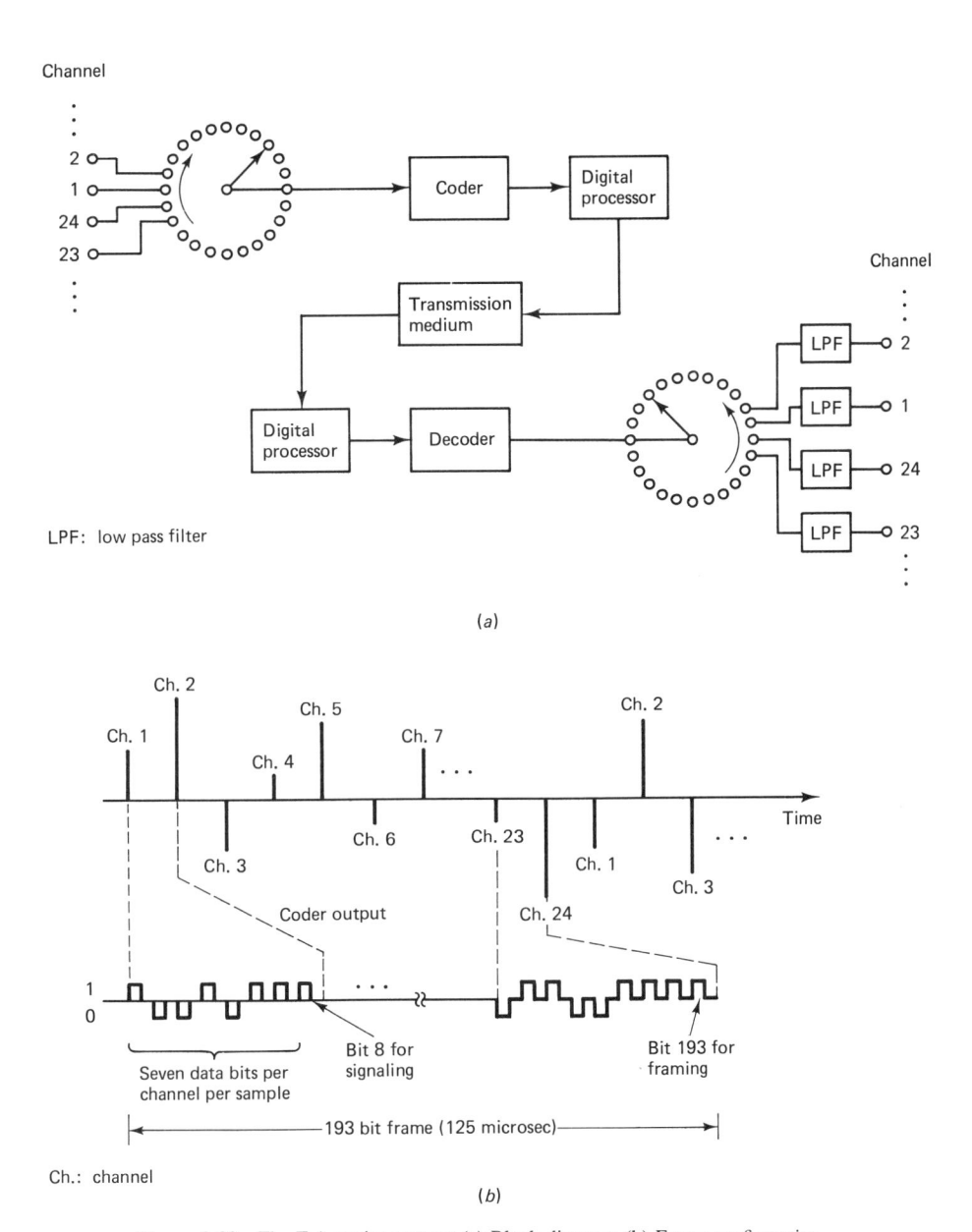

Figure 3.20 The T-1 carrier system: (a) Block diagram; (b) Frame configuration.

interference (e.g., cross-talk noise) and facilitate signal separation at the receiver. The modulated signals are added yielding a *composite signal* having a bandwidth greater than the sum of the bandwidths of each multiplexed signal. The receiver uses a bandpass filter for separating each modulated signal. Each modulated signal is in turn individually demodulated to recover the original baseband signals.

Sec. 3.7 Wideband (Broadband) Communications 113

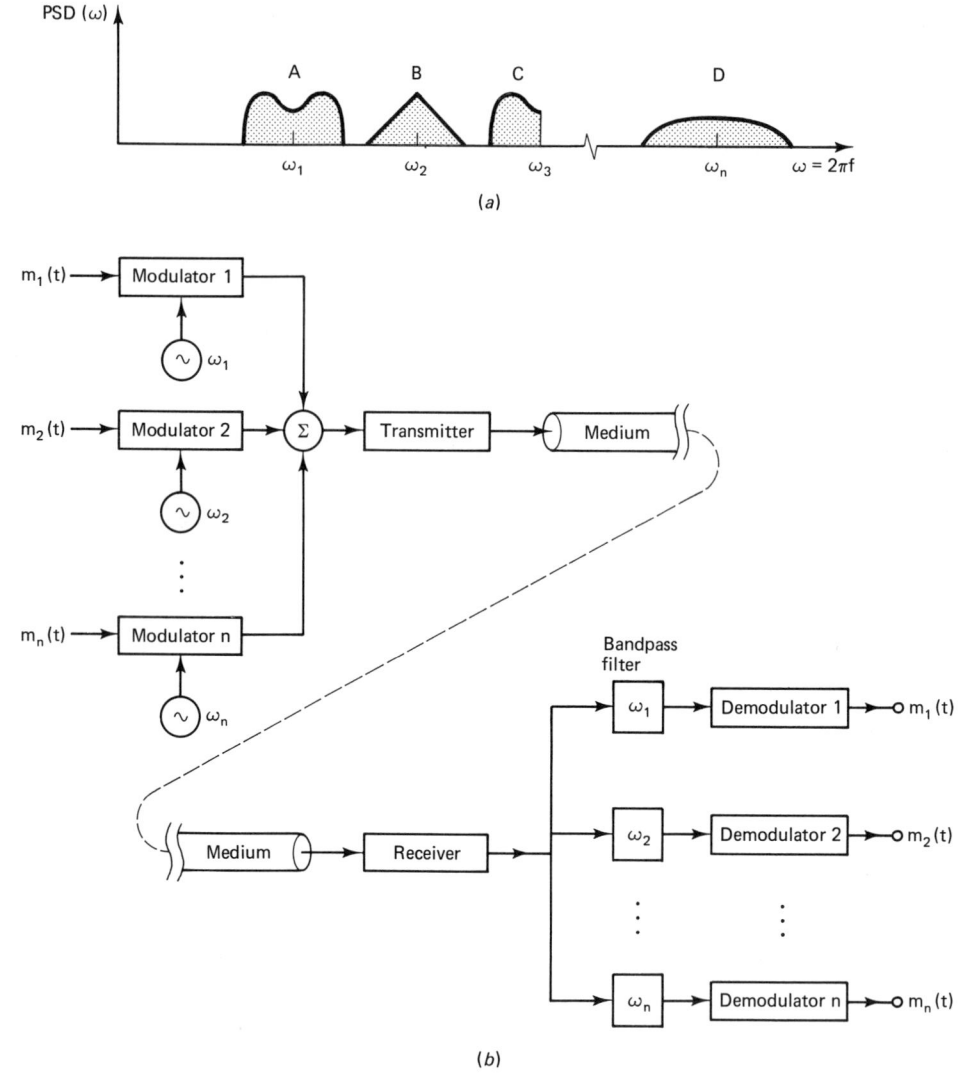

Figure 3.21 Frequency division multiplexing (FDM): (a) Channels A, B, C, and D on the frequency spectrum; (b) FDM-based transmission system.

Example

One of the main advantages of optical fibers is their large bandwidth, which may be as high as several G Hz. Assume an optical fiber with a bandwidth of 4 G Hz for the transmission of voice signals each with a signal bandwidth of 4 K Hz. Calculate the maximum number of voice signals that can be multiplexed on the optical fiber.

Solution Since each voice signal requires 4 K Hz of channel bandwidth, and assuming that a guard band of 0 Hz is used, the maximum number of voice signals that can be multiplexed is 4 G Hz/ 4K Hz = 1,000,000 voice signals. In practice, it is very difficult to achieve this limit because of overhead bits (e.g., synchronization) and the electronics required to achieve extremely high data rates.

3.7.3 Broadband Communication Components

In addition to the transmission medium itself (i.e., twisted pair wires, coaxial cable, optical fibers) several devices are necessary to carry out the transmission functions and overcome impairments introduced by the medium. Obviously, the nature of the specific devices depend on the medium and the nature of signal processing operations performed by the physical layer. We next discuss devices used for broadband communications using coaxial cables due to their widespread utilization. Most signals traveling on coaxial cables using broadband communications are analog in nature. Thus, we will concentrate on devices for analog signals, with the major ones being amplifiers, couplers, splitters, taps, attenuators, and repeaters.

Amplifiers. Amplifiers are often required because of attenuation. When signals travel long distances on coaxial cables, they experience considerable attenuation. Inserting amplifiers restore signals to desired levels. Ideal amplifiers can be characterized by just one parameter, its voltage gain G_v (or power gain G_p), which is constant for all frequencies. The ideal amplifier multiplies the voltage signal V_i at its input side by the voltage gain G_v to obtain the voltage signal V_o at its output side, thus $V_o = G_v V_i$. For example, an ideal amplifier with a gain of 100 (i.e., 40 dB) will provide 1 volt (60 dBmV) at its output side whenever a 10 mV (20 dBmV) is applied at its input side, regardless of the signal frequency.

Practical amplifiers however, exhibit several impairments. First, the voltage (or power) gain depends on frequency; i.e., $G_v = G_v(f)$. In general, G_v decreases as f increases. Thus, amplifiers have a finite range over which they provide useful amplification. The behavior of $G_v(f)$ in terms of frequency is referred to as the *frequency response* of the amplifier gain. A typical frequency response of an amplifier used in broadband communications is shown in Figure 3.22. The **amplifier's bandwidth** is defined as the range of frequencies over which the power gain is at least one-half the maximum gain in the same range of frequencies. In terms of the amplifier voltage gain, the *bandwidth* is defined as the range of frequencies over which the voltage gain is at least 0.701 of the maximum voltage gain. For example, the amplifier with frequency response shown in Figure 3.22 has a bandwidth of 6 MHz.

Another source of impairment is due to a certain amount of noise generated by the amplifier, which is combined with the incoming signal to produce the output signal. Figure 3.23 depicts an amplifier with power gain G_p, input signal power S_i, and input noise power N_i. Let S_o and N_o

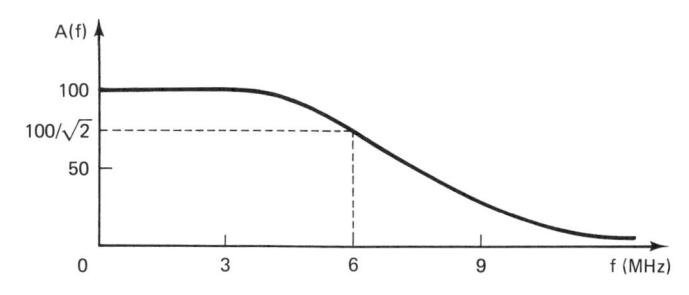

Figure 3.22 Typical frequency response of an amplifier.

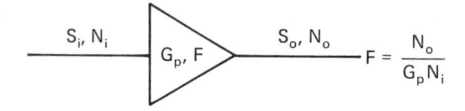

Figure 3.23 Noise figure F of an amplifier.

represent the signal and noise power at the amplifier's output. If the amplifier is noise-free, then the input and output signals are simply related by the power gain $S_o = G_p S_i$, and $N_o = G_p N_i$. Therefore,

$$SNR_o = S_o/N_o = S_i/N_i = SNR_i \qquad (3.33)$$

Thus, in a noise-free amplifier, the *signal to noise ratio* at the input and output sides are the same.

For noisy amplifiers, however, the output noise power is greater than the input noise power (i.e., $N_o > G_p N_i$) so that in general

$$SNR_o = S_o/N_o \leq S_i/N_i = SNR_i \qquad (3.34)$$

The input and output SNR are related by the **noise figure** F in the following way:

$$F = SNR_i/SNR_o = \frac{S_i/N_i}{S_o/N_o} = \frac{S_i/N_i}{G_p S_i/N_o} = \frac{N_o}{G_p N_i} \qquad (3.35)$$

The *noise figure* concept is also applicable to any device that is capable of generating internal noise. Other devices in broadband coaxial cable communications generating noise are filters, cable segments, attenuators, etc.

Example

Equation 3.35 provides a technique for calculating the noise figure of an amplifier with power gain G_p by measuring the input and output power noise N_i and N_o respectively. Figure 3.23 provides a setup for such measurement. Assume that the following data is collected: $G_p = 40$ dB, $N_i = -108$ dBm, $N_o = -58$ dBm. Calculate the amplifier's noise figure F.

Solution   Taking logarithms on both sides of Equation 3.35, we obtain

$$F \text{ dB} = N_o \text{ dBm} - G_p \text{ dB} - N_i \text{ dBm}$$
$$= -58 \text{ dBm} - 40 \text{ dB} - (-108 \text{ dBm})$$
$$= 10 \text{ dB}$$

Attenuators.   In some situations, it is necessary to reduce signal levels prior to performing certain signal processing operations. For example, amplitudes of input signals to frequency converters and mixers must be in a specified amplitude range. If actual signal levels are larger than specified, they must be attenuated. Devices that reduce signal levels are known as **attenuators.** Sometimes attenuators are housed inside amplifier cases for greater flexibility. Attenuators are characterized by their *attenuator factor* (similar to the amplifier's gain).

Couplers, splitters, and taps.   Couplers, splitters, and taps are used for dividing power from one input line into several output lines. They also perform the function of redirecting the power from one of several output lines to the input line. This concept is illustrated in Figure 3.24, where the arrows pointing in both directions indicate that the power could flow in either direction.

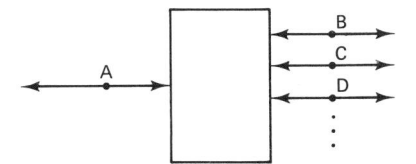

Figure 3.24 A general block diagram for couplers, splitters, and taps.

Splitters divide power equally well into two or more outputs. Figure 3.25 shows a two-way splitter. If splitters were ideal devices (i.e., no power loss in the splitting process) then they would divide power equally in both directions with half the power going in each direction. Thus, the insertion loss[14] in each direction is 10 log 2 = 3 dB. Practical splitters, however, exhibit some power loss in the splitting process, thus making the insertion loss greater than the minimum value of 3 db. For the splitter in Figure 3.25 with a insertion loss of 3 dB, if a signal of 20 dBmV is applied at point A, then the signals at point B and C have the same rms value of 17 dBmV each. A splitter attenuates a signal traveling in the reverse direction as well. Thus, a signal of 17 dBmV at B traveling to the left will reach point A with a value of 14 dBmV.[15]

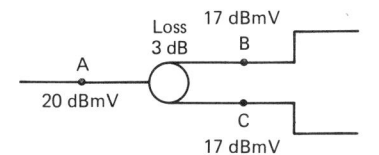

Figure 3.25 Two-way splitter. Signals traveling from A to B or C experience a loss of 3 dB.

Directional couplers are functionally identical to splitters. They differ in that power is not divided equally well into the several outputs. Usually, couplers are used to divert a small amount of power from long *trunk cables* to small cable segments called *drop cables*, which are connected to network stations. Thus, it is required that most of the power going into the coupler continues on the trunk cable. Therefore, the insertion loss is usually very small. Because the power being diverted into the branch cable is small, the corresponding loss, referred to as *tap loss*, is high. Figure 3.26 shows the schematic diagram of a directional coupler with 1.5 dB of insertion loss and 13 dB of tap loss. A 20 dBmV signal at point A traveling from left to right will produce a signal at B of 18.5 dBmV and another at C of 7 dBmV. The reason couplers are designed with large tap losses is that it is assumed that network stations will be located close to point C.

As noted in Section 2.3.1, it is important that all loads to the coaxial cable have an impedance of Z_o ohms (i.e., the characteristic impedance of the cable) in order to avoid reflections on the cable. An additional function of directional couplers is impedance matching so that reflections are kept to a minimum.

The combination of couplers and splitters, as shown in Figure 3.27, are referred to as **taps** (or multitaps). Taps are the final devices used to configure station outlets by means of small drop cables.

---

[14] Insertion loss is used to describe the effect of inserting a device on the medium. Insertion loss denotes the effect of the insertion effect and is given by insertion loss (dB) = 20 log (V_2/V_1) where V_1 and V_2 are voltages on the load side with and without the device respectively.

[15] C must refrain from sending a different signal towards the splitter at the same time that B is doing so, otherwise signal contention occurs.

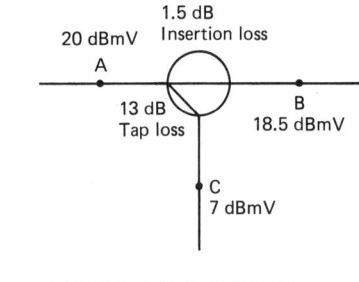

Figure 3.26 Schematic diagram of a directional coupler with a tap loss of 13 dB and an insertion loss of 1.5 dB.

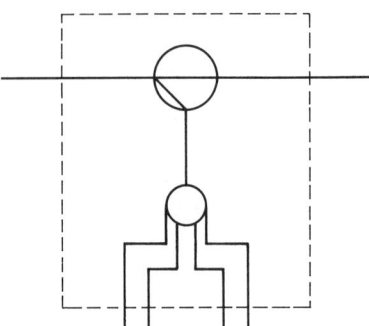

Figure 3.27 Schematic diagram for a multitap.

Head end. Head end are devices used in broadband systems to provide the desired geographical network coverage using a single cable. The need for a head end device can be understood by understanding how amplifiers work. Networks are designed to cover a geographical area determined at the network design stage. Often, because of cable attenuation and insertion losses in other devices, amplifiers are needed to restore signal levels to appropriate values. Here is where the major problem takes place. Amplifiers amplify signals in their frequency spectrum in one direction only. Thus, as long as communication takes place between two stations in one direction only,[16] with the source located on one side of the cable and the destination located on the other side of the cable, then communication could take place without the need of a head end. However, the previous condition is too restrictive and unpractical. For example, if the source and destination stations exchange roles (i.e., the source becomes the destination and vice versa) they cannot communicate, because the amplifiers would need to amplify in the opposite direction. Thus, we need a better solution.

Clearly, we need the capability of providing amplification in the other direction as well. Since amplifiers work in one direction on a channel basis, we can invoke the FDM principle to allow signal propagation (and amplification) in one direction at one channel centered in frequency f_1, and signal propagation on the opposite direction in another channel centered at frequency f_2. Consequently, a device is needed to provide the frequency conversion from f_1 to f_2 (or vice versa, depending on the assignment). Such device is known as the **head end.** The head end's main function is to provide frequency translation on incoming signals centered at f_1 to outgoing signals centered at f_2. When we refer to signals at a certain frequency f, of course we mean signals having a certain bandwidth B being modulated by a sinusoidal carrier at frequency f.

As signals get amplified by many stages, noise keeps being accumulated and the *signal to noise ratio* deteriorates. Thus, amplifiers alone cannot provide a solution to the signal degradation

---

[16] Broadcast Television works in this fashion.

problem for large distances. What we need is a mechanism that decodes the symbols and regenerates them fresh (i.e., noise has been eliminated). Certain types of head ends include a remodulation function, which helps to combat noise.

3.8 MODULATION

Many different modulation schemes are currently used in communication systems. For our purposes, we will deal only with modulation techniques suitable for digital communications, since they are used with communication networks. Readers interested in a complete discussion of modulation should consult the many textbooks available for communication systems. Modulation techniques for digital communications can be classified into *pulse* and *continuous wave modulation*. The process of encoding information into a pulse carrier is referred to as pulse modulation. Continuous wave modulation uses a continuous wave, such as a sinusoid, as the carrier.

3.8.1. Pulse Wave Modulation

As noted, pulse wave modulation encodes information in a train of pulses by varying its amplitude, width, and relative position. Accordingly, we have the following pulse wave modulation schemes: PAM, PWM, and PPM.

If the information is conveyed in the amplitude of the pulse carrier, we have **pulse amplitude modulation** (PAM). When the information is conveyed in the width of the pulse carrier, the process is known as **pulse width modulation** (PWM). Finally, when the information is conveyed in the position of the pulse carrier, the process is referred to as **pulse position modulation** (PPM). When the pulses of a PAM system are encoded using a binary scheme, the resulting process is referred to as pulse code modulation (PCM), as described in Section 3.7.1. With the exception of PCM, pulse modulation is not widely used in computer communications. For this reason, it will not be expanded further.

3.8.2 Continuous Wave Modulation

Modulation involves shifting the spectrum of a signal to a frequency range that is compatible with the transmission medium. Figure 3.28 shows a block diagram of a modulator where the input signal modifies some characteristic (e.g., amplitude, phase, or frequency) of a sinusoidal *carrier* signal $\sin(\omega_c t)$ to produce an output signal. The input and output signals of the modulator are referred to as the **modulating** and **modulated** signals, respectively. Only three parameters could be changed in a sinusoidal carrier: its amplitude, its frequency, or its phase. Accordingly, three major modulation

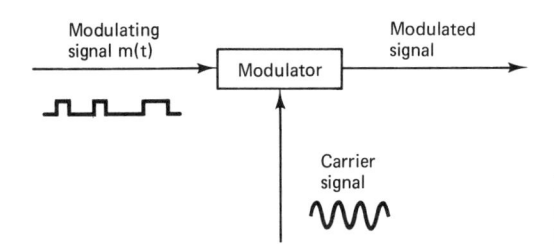

Figure 3.28 Modulation process. An input signal modulates a carrier signal to produce a modulated signal.

schemes exist in which a modulating signal modifies in the amplitude, frequency, or the phase of a sinusoidal carrier.

In **amplitude shift keying** (ASK), the amplitude of the sinusoidal carrier is varied in accordance with the signal m(t). If the frequency of the sinusoidal carrier is varied in accordance with the signal m(t), the modulation process is referred to as **frequency shift keying** (FSK). **Phase shift keying** (PSK) involves the variation of the phase of the sinusoidal carrier according to m(t).

Figure 3.29 depicts three modulated signals obtained when ASK, FSK, and PSK modulators are used to modulate a binary signal m(t). For local area networks, the most common modulation schemes are PSK and FSK, because of their efficiency in terms of *bit error rate* and simplicity of implementation. In the next section we evaluate the relative merits of each modulation scheme. The comparison is useful, because some modulation schemes are more advantageous than others for certain network environments.

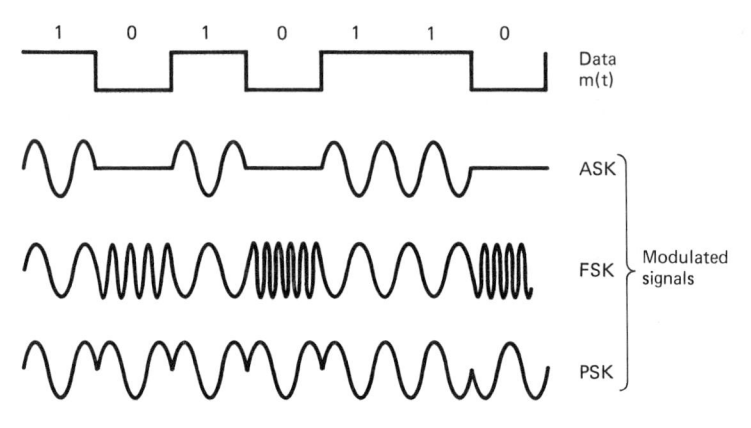

Figure 3.29 ASK, FSK, and PSK modulated signals.

3.9 PERFORMANCE OF DIGITAL MODULATION SYSTEMS

Two measures are generally used to characterize the performance of modulation techniques. The measures are the **bandwidth efficiency** (BWE) and the **bit error probability,** also referred to as the **bit error rate** (BER).

3.9.1 Bandwidth Efficiency

The ratio R/W is referred to as the **bandwidth efficiency** of any digital modulation technique, where R is the data rate in bit/sec and W is the channel bandwidth in Hz required to support transmission at that data rate. Given a fixed data rate R, different modulation techniques require different bandwidths. The bandwidth requirement W for any modulation technique can be evaluated from the power spectral density of the modulated signals. The approach used for evaluating the bandwidth requirements for ASK, FSK, and PSK modulation techniques consists of plotting the *power spectral density* (PSD) of the modulated signals and calculating W based on a certain criterion.[17] As discussed

---

[17] We find the modulated signal PSD theoretically.

in Section 2.2, the criterion often used is that most of the power of the signal lies within a frequency band of length W. In general, the PDS of digital modulated signals extend over to infinity (i.e., they are not bandlimited). However, most of the power lies at low frequencies, and the modulated signals can be approximated by signals bandlimited to B Hz. Under these conditions, W = B.

There is, however, an experimental approach to obtain W, which consists in physically building a modulator and using a special instrument called *spectrum analyzer*. The spectrum analyzer basically provides a picture of the power spectral density. The required channel bandwidth can be estimated visually using the usual criterion that most of the power is concentrated within W.

Amplitude shift keying (ASK). As noted earlier, in ASK the modulated signal has only two amplitudes corresponding to the values the binary signal m(t). As depicted in Figure 3.29, the two amplitude values are typically 0 and the amplitude value of the carrier signal. In what follows, we are interested in deriving an expression for the PSD of the ASK modulated signal. The required channel bandwidth to transmit an ASK modulated signal can then be obtained from the PSD.

The theoretical approach used for obtaining the PSD of the modulated signal follows that used by Proakis (1983). Since the effect of the carrier signal $\sin(\omega_c t)$ is simply shifting the frequency spectrum an amount ω_c, (or f_c if another frequency scale is used), we concentrate on the baseband (i.e., unmodulated) signal u(t). The time domain representation of an unmodulated ASK signal is

$$u(t) = \sum_{n=0}^{\infty} I_n \, g(t - nT) \tag{3.36}$$

where $\{I_n\}$ is a sequence of binary symbols appearing at the input of the modulator at a rate R bits/sec. The signal g(t) is a pulse, such as the rectangular or a raised cosine pulse, and T = 1/R is the bit duration or bit cell.

The power spectrum density of u(t) is given by

$$S_u(f) = \frac{1}{T} |G(f)|^2 \, S_x(f) \tag{3.37}$$

where G(f) is the Fourier transform of g(t), and $S_x(f)$ denotes the PSD of the information sequence $\{I_n\}$, defined as

$$S_x(f) = \sum_{m=-\infty}^{\infty} s_{xx}(m) \, e^{-j2\pi f m T} \tag{3.38}$$

For the case in which the information symbols in the sequence are mutually uncorrelated, the autocorrelation function $s_{xx}(m)$ can be expressed as

$$s_{xx}(m) = \begin{cases} \sigma_i^2 + \mu_i^2 & m = 0 \\ \mu_i^2 & m \neq 0 \end{cases} \tag{3.39}$$

where μ_i and σ_i^2 are the mean and variance of an information symbol. Replacing Equation 3.39 in Equation 3.38, one obtains

$$S_x(f) = \sigma_i^2 + \frac{\mu_i^2}{T} \sum_{m=-\infty}^{\infty} \delta\left(f - \frac{m}{T}\right) \tag{3.40}$$

Finally, using Equation 3.37,

$$S_u(f) = \frac{\sigma_i^2}{T}|G(f)|^2 + \frac{\mu_i^2}{T^2} \sum_{m=-\infty}^{\infty} \left|G\left(\frac{m}{T}\right)\right|^2 \delta\left(f - \frac{m}{T}\right) \quad (3.41)$$

The PSD $S_{ask}(f)$ of an ASK modulated signal is simply $S_u(f)$ shifted an amount f_c, as depicted in Figure 3.30.

Phase shift keying (PSK). The time domain representation of an equivalent baseband PSK signal is

$$u(t) = \sum_{n=0}^{\infty} I_n\, g(t - nT) \quad (3.42)$$

where $I_n = e^{j\Theta_n}$ and $\Theta_n = 2\pi(n-1)/M$, n = 1, 2, ..., M and M is the number of phases.

Because the expressions for the unmodulated signal u(t) are the same for ASK and PSK, the power spectral density of PSK modulated signals is also given by Equation 3.37. In this case,

$$\mu_i = E[I_n]$$

$$= \frac{1}{2}[e^{j0} + e^{j\pi}] = 0; \text{ i.e., two phases only.}$$

$$\sigma_i^2 = E[I_n^2] - (E[I_n])^2 = E[I_n^2]$$

$$= \frac{1}{2}(1 + e^{j2\pi}) = 1$$

Thus,

$$S_u(f) = \frac{1}{T}|G(f)|^2 \quad (3.43)$$

The PSD of a PSK modulated signal is depicted in Figure 3.31.

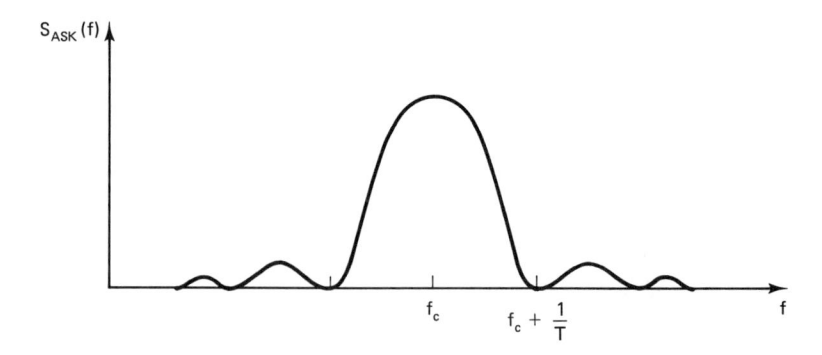

Figure 3.30 Power spectral density of an ASK modulated signal.

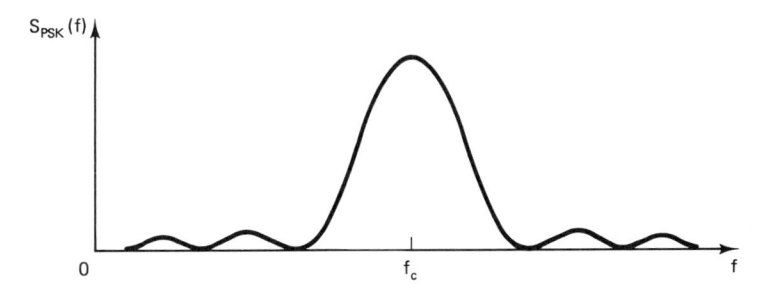

Figure 3.31 Power spectral density of a PSK modulated signal.

Frequency shift keying (FSK). In frequency shift keying modulation, the carrier frequency is shifted by an amount $f_n = (\Delta f/2) I_n$, $I_n = \pm 1, \pm 3, \ldots, \pm(M-1)$ where M is the number of frequencies. The change from one frequency to another, say from f_{c1} to f_{c2}, can be accomplished by having M different oscillators tuned to the desired frequency and selecting one of the M frequencies according to the bit sequence to be transmitted. The time domain representation of an equivalent baseband FSK signal is

$$u(t) = \sum_{n=0}^{\infty} e^{j \pi \Delta f\, I_n t} g(t - nT) \qquad (3.44)$$

A major difficulty with having different oscillators is the relatively large spectral sidelobes that result because of the sudden change from one frequency f_{c1} to another f_{c2}. This difficulty can be avoided by using a single oscillator and allowing the frequency to change gradually from one frequency to another. FSK modulation schemes that allow the frequency to change gradually are referred to as **phase continuous FSK**. FSK modulation schemes that allow the different frequencies to be integral multiples of 1/T are referred to as **phase coherent FSK**. The terms phase continuous or phase coherent are not related to phase modulation. The information is still modulated as changes in frequency, and the term phase in this context simply means the way in which frequency is changed.

Phase-continuous FSK. We present the results for the case M = 2. The equivalent baseband waveform u(t) is given by

$$u(t) = \exp\{j[2\pi f_d \int_0^t d(x)dx + \phi]\} \qquad (3.45)$$

where

$$d(t) = \sum_{n=0}^{\infty} I_n\, g(t - nT) \qquad (3.46)$$

and f_d is called the peak frequency deviation and ϕ is the initial phase of the carrier.

If g(t) is a rectangular pulse,

$$u(t) = e^{j\phi} \sum_{n=0}^{\infty} \exp[j2\pi f_d(\alpha_n T + (t-nT)I_n)]\, g(t-nT) \qquad (3.47)$$

where

Sec. 3.9 Performance of Digital Modulation Systems

$$\alpha_n = \sum_{k=0}^{n-1} I_k \tag{3.48}$$

The power spectral density is given by

$$S_u(f) = \frac{T}{4}\left[\frac{1}{2}\sum_{n=1}^{2} A_n^2(f) + \frac{1}{2}\sum_{n=1}^{2}\sum_{m=1}^{2} B_{nm}(f)A_n(f)A_m(f)\right] \tag{3.49}$$

with

$$A_n(f) = \text{sinc}\{\pi T[f - (2n-3)f_d]\} \tag{3.50}$$

$$B_{nm}(f) = \frac{\cos(2\pi fT - \alpha_{nm}) - \psi \cos\alpha_{nm}}{1 + \psi^2 - 2\psi \cos 2\pi fT} \tag{3.51}$$

$$\alpha_{nm} = 2\pi f_d T(m+n-3) \tag{3.52}$$

$$\psi = \cos 2\pi f_d T \tag{3.53}$$

The PSD of a phase-continuous FSK modulated signal is depicted in Figure 3.32.

From the power spectral density plots shown in Figures 3.30, 3.31, and 3.32, we can estimate the bandwidth W required by each of the modulation schemes. For ASK and PSK, W can be approximated by

$$W = (1 + r)R \tag{3.54}$$

where R is data rate, and r is the roll-off factor of a pulse shaping filter used prior to modulation, typically $0 \le r \le 1$. For FSK modulation, W can be approximated by

$$W = 2\Delta F + (1 + r)R \tag{3.55}$$

where $\Delta F = f_2 - fc = fc - f_1$ is the offset of the modulated frequencies from the carrier frequency.

Example

The IEEE 802.4 standard specifies phase-continuous FSK as one of the modulation schemes with R = 1 M bit/sec, f_1 = 3.75 M Hz ± 80 K Hz, f_2 = 6.25 M Hz ± 80 K Hz and Manchester encoding. Estimate the required bandwidth W.

Solution Let us assume f_1 = 3.75 M Hz and f_2 = 6.25 M Hz, thus $2\Delta F = f_2 - f_1$ = 2.5 M Hz. Manchester encoding does not use a shaping pulse; thus r = 1. From Equation 3.55,

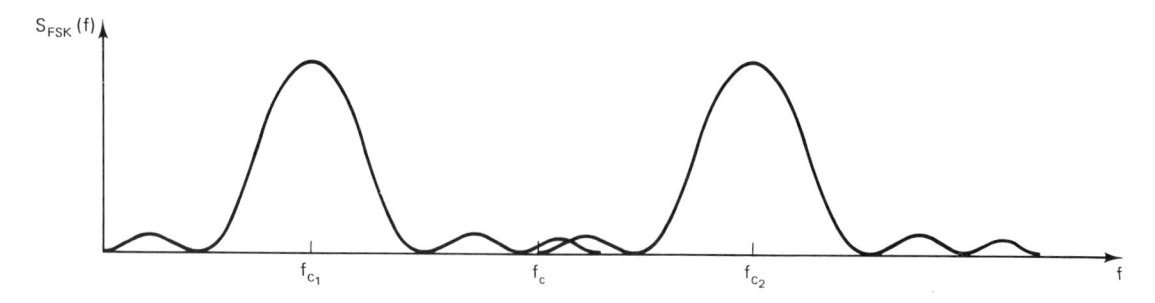

Figure 3.32 Power spectral density of a FSK modulated signal.

$$W = 2.5 + 2 \times 1 \text{ M Hz}$$
$$= 4.5 \text{ M Hz}.$$

In general, when multilevel modulation is used, equations 3.55 and 3.56 are given by

$$W = (1 + r)R / \log_2 M \tag{3.54a}$$

for ASK and PSK modulation, and

$$W = [2 \Delta F + (1+r)R] / \log_2 M \tag{3.55a}$$

for FSK modulation, where M is the number of symbols (amplitude, phase, or frequency) used in the modulation process.

Example

The IEEE 802.4 standard specified a three-level (i.e., M = 3) duobinary AM/PSK modulation scheme with R = 10 M bit/sec as one of the options. Calculate the required bandwidth assuming a pulse shaping filter with r = 0.89.

Solution Using Equation 3.54a, the required bandwidth is

$$W = (1 + 0.89) \times 10 \times 10^6 / \log_2 3 \text{ M Hz}$$
$$= 12 \text{ M Hz}.$$

The IEEE project 802 is currently considering other encoder and modulation schemes that will provide data rates higher than 10 M bps on a 12 M Hz channel.

3.9.2 Bit Error Rate (BER)

Bandwidth efficiency of modulation schemes provide one aspect of a receiver's performance. The other aspect is given by the detection *error probability*, also known as **bit error rate.** The detection **error probability** Pe is defined as the probability that a **0** is received when a **1** is transmitted, or that a **1** is received when a **0** is transmitted. Several factors contribute to the error probability, with perhaps the most important being the nature of the noise and the structure of the receiver. For the purposes of this section we make two assumptions regarding the nature of the noise and the structure of the receiver.

Regarding the nature of the noise, we assume that noise is additive, as shown in Figure 3.16. Furthermore, its amplitude follows a Gaussian probability distribution, and the noise has frequency components over all the frequency spectrum (white noise). Noise with these characteristics is referred to as **additive white Gaussian noise** (AWGN). The second assumption is that the receiver performs a signal processing operation that minimizes the probability of error. The minimization is achieved when the transfer function h(t) of the receiver is equal to the mirror image of the difference of the pulses used to represent a **1** and a **0** respectively. That is,

$$h(t) = s_1(T - t) - s_0(T - t) \tag{3.56}$$

where $s_1(t)$ and $s_0(t)$ are the encoded pulses corresponding to a **1** and a **0** respectively and T is the interval between bits.

Bit error rate for coherent demodulation. Receivers, upon receiving the transmitted signal, must be able to restore the transmitted symbols. Timing information is very important for receiver operation, because the received signal must be sampled at the appropriate times in order to decide what corresponding symbol was sent. When demodulators use a clock signal at the same frequency and in phase (synchronized) with the clock used for modulation, then the demodulation process is referred to as **coherent demodulation.** Noncoherent demodulators attempt to recover transmitted symbols using a clock at the same frequency as the clock used for modulation, but unsynchronized with the transmitted clock. If they can meet some performance requirements, noncoherent demodulators are preferred because they are simpler and therefore less expensive than their coherent counterparts. Coherent demodulators provide the best performance; thus, we present the results for coherent demodulation, since they can be used for comparison purposes.

Amplitude shift keying (ASK). The probability of error is

$$Pe = \frac{1}{2} \text{erfc}(\sqrt{z/2}) \tag{3.57}$$

where z is the signal to noise ratio SNR given by (see also Equation 3.31)

$$z = \frac{S_r \times BWE}{N\,R} \tag{3.58}$$

and S_r is the received power, $N/2$ is the noise power spectral density, R is the transmission rate in bit/sec, and BWE is the bandwidth efficiency.[18] The erfc(x) function is defined by

$$\text{erfc}(x) = \frac{2}{\sqrt{\pi}} \int_x^\infty e^{-t^2} dt \tag{3.59}$$

and is tabulated in most books on communication systems.

When z is much greater than 1 (i.e., $z \gg 1$), Pe can be approximated by

$$Pe \approx e^{-z/2}/2\sqrt{\pi z}, \qquad z \gg 1 \tag{3.57a}$$

Phase shift keying (PSK). The probability of error is

$$Pe = \frac{1}{2} \text{erfc}[\sqrt{(1-m^2)/z}] \tag{3.60}$$

$$\approx e^{-z}/2\sqrt{\pi z}, \; z \gg 1 \tag{3.60a}$$

The case for which $m = 0$ is referred to as Phase-Reversal Keying (PRK).

Frequency shift keying (FSK). The probability of error is

$$Pe = \frac{1}{2} \text{erfc} \sqrt{z/2} \tag{3.61}$$

which is the same expression as that of ASK.

[18] It is assumed that a filter with bandwidth $B = R/BWE$ is used to limit noise.

The probability of error versus the signal to noise ratio z for the three modulators considered in this section is shown in Figure 3.33. For the same Pe, PSK modulation is better than ASK or FSK, from the viewpoint of transmitted power.

Example

As noted in subsection 2.3.3, several factors contribute to noise in LANs. Assume that we have only a thermal noise contribution at room temperature, with power spectral density $N/2 = kT/2$, as given by Equation 2.101a. A MAP network station using a PSK demodulator receives a signal having an amplitude of $v = 0$ dBmW (i.e., 1 mv rms). Calculate the bit error rate of this particular receiver.

Solution The bit error rate is given by Equation 3.57, with the signal to noise ratio z given by

$$z = \frac{S_r \, BWE}{N \, R}$$

For the MAP network with PSK modulation, $R = 10$ Mbps, $BWE = 0.833$. The receiver power assuming a coaxial cable with $Z_0 = 75 \, \Omega$ is

$$S_r = v^2/Z_0 = (1/75) \times 10^{-6} \, W$$

The noise power spectral density for thermal noise is

$$N = kT = 1.38 \times 10^{-23} \times 293 = 404.34 \times 10^{-23} \, W/Hz$$

Thus,

$$z = 4.49 \times 10^5$$

Since $z \gg 1$, we can use the approximation of Equation 3.57a, yielding

$$pe \approx 10^{-97502.48}$$

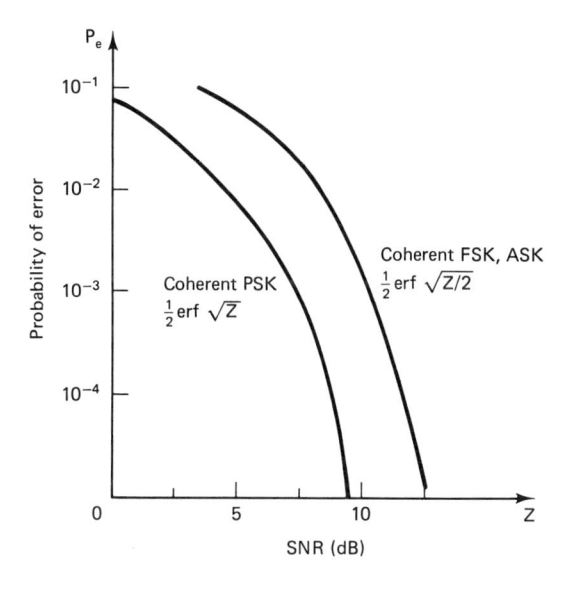

Figure 3.33 Probability of error vs. signal to noise ratio for ASK, FSK, and PSK coherent demodulators.

Sec. 3.9 Performance of Digital Modulation Systems

3.10 IEEE 802.4 PHYSICAL LAYER

3.10.1 Services

One of the main characteristics of a layer is the set of services it provides to the layer above by making use of the services from the layer below. The physical layer, being the lowest layer in the OSI reference model, is a special case, in that there is no layer below it. However, one can think of the physical medium as being layer **0**, even though such a layer is not defined in the OSI reference model.

The set of services provided by layer N, along with the rules and formats for using the services, constitute the interface between layers N and N+1. An important issue that arises in characterizing an interface is the specification of services.

As discussed in Section 2.9, services are specified as a set of procedure- or routine-like constructs referred to as **primitives,** which are called by the user of the service. The user of a physical layer service is located at the data link layer. In general, a service user is relative to the particular layer which provides the services. Primitives are named in the following general fashion, which is compatible with an ADA statement:

$$\text{primitive\_name.type(parameters)};$$

where *primitive_name* is the general category (or family) to which the primitive belongs, *type* specifies a particular primitive within the general category (i.e., request, indication, response, and confirmation), and *parameters* specify the data with which the primitive is to work.

Example

The IEEE 802.3 specification defines the following primitive between its data link and physical layers PLS_DATA.request(OUTPUT_UNIT). Thus, for this particular primitive, the primitive_name is PLS_DATA, its *type* is *request*, and its only parameter is OUTPUT_NAME. This primitive is called by a data link layer user requesting the transmission of a single data bit, represented by OUTPUT_UNIT, on the physical medium.

3.10.2 Physical Layer Description

The IEEE 802.4 standard provides three options for encoding and modulation based on AM/PSK, phase coherent FSK, and phase continuous FSK modulation schemes. Only the AM/PSK option is described in detail here. The reader is referred to the IEEE 802.4 standard for details on the FSK schemes.

Figure 3.34 depicts the block diagram for the IEEE 802.4 physical layer. The following is exchanged at the interface with the data link layer: clock (Phy_clock and Tx_clock) and symbols (Tx_MAC_symbol and Rx_MAC_symbol). The Tx_MAC_symbol is a set whose members are: *zero, one, non_data, pad_idle,* and *silence*. The Rx_MAC_symbol is another set whose members are: *zero, one, non_data, pad_idle, silence,* and *bad_signal*. Notice that the only difference in the two sets of symbols is that the element *bad_signal* is not present in the Tx_MAC_symbol set.

We can relate easily with elements *zero* and *one*, since they correspond to data bits **0** and **1**, respectively. Non_data symbols are used to indicate the beginning and ending of frames (i.e., delimiters). Framing is discussed in more detail in Chapter 4. *Pad_idle* is used to construct a special

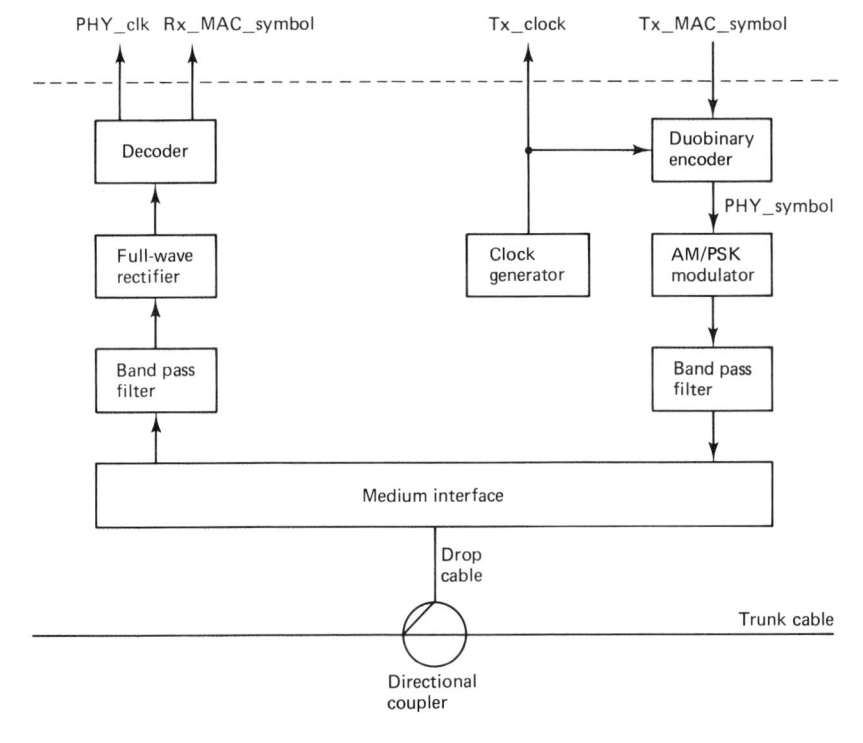

Figure 3.34 Physical layer model for the MAP network (IEEE 802.4, AM/PSK modulation).

sequence sent before the data (i.e., preamble) which is useful for bit synchronization. Data (either *zero* or *one*) should always be preceded by delimiters, which indicate where the data begins. Thus, data should not be preceded by *pad_idle* symbols. What if stations just want to synchronize their hardware elements (e.g., modems) without sending any data? To obey the preceding rules, a new symbol is necessary, called *silence*, which indicates that what follows preamble (*pad_idle* symbols) is neither data nor a delimiter.

At the receiver side, when the decoder decodes a symbol that the transmitter did not send, then it is considered a *bad_signal*. A *bad_signal* is also useful for indicating hardware malfunctions. When a *bad_signal* is received by a receiver, the receiver should resynchronize the decoding process as rapidly as possible.

As noted earlier, symbols received at the data link-physical layer interface are encoded using a *duobinary encoder*, with a pulse shape satisfying the second Nyquist criterion given by Equation 3.21. Data symbols (i.e., *zero* and *one*) receive a different treatment as compared to all other symbols, in that they are applied to a scrambler similar to the one described in Section 3.5, with $M=1$ and $N=6$ resulting in a scrambled *zero* or *one* MAC_symbol. The duobinary encoder allows the representation of incoming MAC_symbols as another set of PHY_symbols, whose elements are denoted as {0}, {2}, and {4}; thus, it is a ternary encoder. The main advantage of the duobinary encoder is that in cooperation with the specific modulator used for broadband modulation (AM/PSK), it allows better bandwidth efficiency as compared with other combinations of encoder-modulator. The AM/PSK modulator is a combined amplitude modulation/phase shift keying modulation in which the AM component uses three different amplitude levels of 0, max/2, and max, which correspond to the encoder outputs of {0}, {2} and {4} respectively, where max is the maximum amplitude for the pulse. The PSK component of the modulation does not carry any additional data. It is used to reduce the signal bandwidth (i.e., to improve bandwidth efficiency BWE).

The medium interface configuration is not specified in the standard. However, it should provide ac coupling between the transmitter (or receiver) and the medium. The station is interfaced with the communication medium by means of a flexible coaxial cable with a small diameter known as a *drop cable*. The communication medium is a larger diameter, semirigid coaxial cable with characteristic impedance $Z_o = 75$; thus, all loads should be terminated in 75 ohms to avoid reflections on the cable. The cable can be used to carry both ac power and radio frequency (rf) signals, because the frequency components of these two signals do not overlap. Bidirectional and unidirectional couplers constitute the medium attachment.

At the receiver end, the bandpass filter rejects signals from channels other than the one used by the network. Since the AM/PSK modulation scheme does not carry any information in the PSK component, it is not necessary to recover phase information. Thus, only AM demodulation is needed. The AM demodulator specified is of the full-wave rectifier type. The decoder performs functions which are the inverse of that of the duobinary encoder (with the exception of the *bad_signal* symbol).

Coaxial cables have several characteristics which make them well-suited for factory environments. One advantage is that coaxial cables use a well-developed technology, mostly because of their widespread use in CATV systems and for certain communication networks. The existence of many installations of transmission systems within General Motors, which are based on coaxial cable technology, was one of the reasons for its selection in the MAP specification. Another advantage of coaxial cables regards the possibility of having multiple networks simultaneously supported on the same medium, using the principle of frequency division multiplexing. Thus, one can have network *A* using channel *a*, network *B* using channel *b*, and so on, with all networks coexisting on the same cable. The networks do not interfere with each other, provided their channels do not overlap in frequency. Still another advantage of using coaxial cables is that, through modulation, it is possible to use as many channels as the cable bandwidth permits to transmit data, voice, video, and any other type of signal that requires finite channel bandwidth. Finally, the coaxial cable as a medium has been adopted or is under study for other important network standards such as the IEEE standards 802.3 (CSMA/CD) and 802.6 (Metropolitan Area Network).

Physical layer services. The IEEE 802.4 physical layer provides the following four primitives:

```
* PHY_MODE.request(mode);
* PHY_DATA.request(Tx_MAC_symbol);
* PHY_DATA.indication(Rx_MAC_symbol);
* PHY_NOTIFY.request;
```

Any station in the network can function as a repeater station. Some means are required to indicate whether a station is originating the messages or is simply relaying messages from other segments. Such means are provided by the PHY_MODE.request(mode) primitive, with mode = {originating, repeating}.

The PHY_DATA.request primitive is passed from the data link layer to the physical layer to request the transmission of a symbol on the communication medium. The physical layer, upon receipt of a PHY_DATA.request, will encode and transmit the symbol using the appropriate signaling technique (i.e., FSK or AM/PSK modulation). At the destination station, the recently arrived symbol is received and decoded by the corresponding physical layer and presented to its corresponding data link layer by means of the PHY_DATA.indication(Rx_MAC_symbol) primitive.

When the data link layer of a station is receiving data from another station and detects the end of frame, it is convenient to notify the corresponding physical layer. The notification is done using the primitive PHY_NOTIFY.request. The notify primitive is useful because it allows the physical layer to be prepared for detecting *silence*, *preamble*, or entering a high-speed acquisition mode for synchronization purposes.

3.11 IEEE 802.3 PHYSICAL LAYER

The IEEE 802.3 physical layer configuration, which is depicted in Figure 3.35, has the following major elements:

physical signaling (PLS) sublayer,
attachment unit interface (AUI),
physical medium attachment (PMA), and
medium dependent interface (MDI).

Together, the *physical medium attachment* and the *medium dependent interface* are referred to as the *medium attachment unit* (MAU). The physical signaling sublayer provides logical and functional coupling between the medium attachment unit and the data link layer. Although the PLS sublayer is located in the physical layer, like the MAC and LLC sublayers, the PLS sublayer is medium

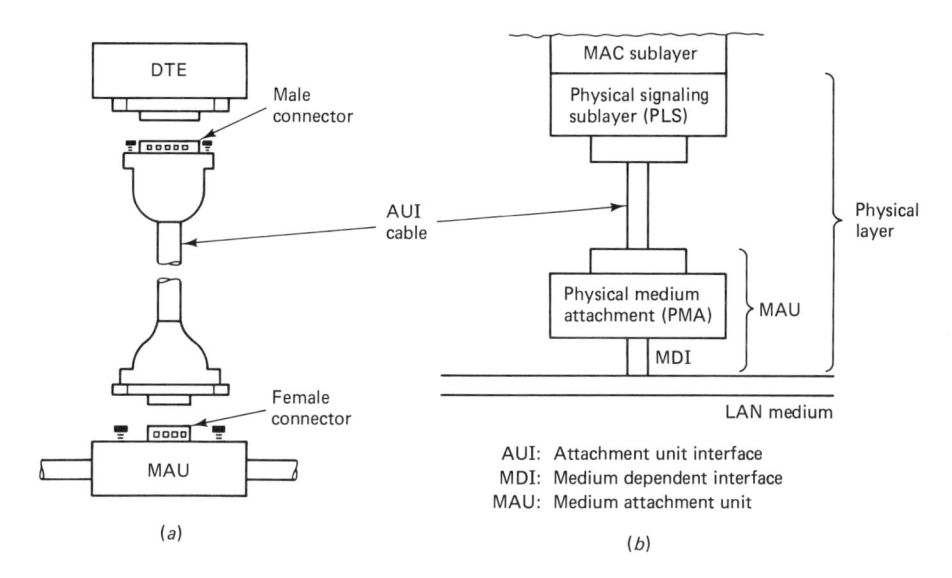

Figure 3.35 Hardware and architecture of the IEEE 802.3 physical layer.

independent; thus, the same PLS could work with a coaxial cable or optical fiber at any data rate. In addition, PLS supports baseband or broadband communications.

Whereas the PLS sublayer is located at the station side, (also referred to as the DTE side) the MAU is located on the cable side, as shown in Figure 3.35(a). Because the MAU may be difficult to access,[19] the majority of the physical layer functions are performed at the PLS sublayer, to provide flexibility in the location of network stations. The maximum separation between the station and the physical medium attachment is 50 m. Thus, the PLS sublayer is capable of driving a signal at least 50 m.

The major functions of the PLS sublayer are:

output,

input,

error sense,

carrier sense,

data encoding, and

electrical and mechanical interface with the attachment unit interface (AUI).

The *output* and *input* functions involve the PLS sublayer sending data to the MAU or receiving data from the MAU, respectively. Informing the MAC sublayer when certain conditions occur constitutes the *error sense* function. One of the special conditions occurs when there is a *collision* on the shared channel. Although the PLS does not actually detect collisions, it provides the means for passing information about collisions to the MAC sublayer. Collision detection is performed by the medium attachment unit. The *carrier sense* function involves the PLS determining whether any other station is using the channel.

Seven special *messages* are exchanged at the PLS-PMA interface. The messages *output*, *output-idle*, and *normal* carry information from the PLS to the PMA, whereas the messages *input*, *input-idle*, *signal-quality-error*, and *mau-available* carry information from the PMA to the PLS. A *collision* situation is reported as a special case of a *signal-quality-error* message.

The PLS sublayer performs a *data encoding* function using Manchester encoding, where a **1** is encoded as $-p(t)$ and a **0** is encoded as $p(t)$, where $p(t)$ is defined in Figure 3.6. The PLS-PMA interface distinguishes between control and data. Since either control or data can be input or output to the PLS sublayer, four signals result: *data in* (DI), *data out* (DO), *control in* (CI), and *control out* (CO). The four signals are carried by four different circuits by the attachment unit interface. Frames transmitted on the AUI have the following frame structure:

silence	data	end of transmission delimiter	silence

where the *silence* delimiter provides an observation window during which no transitions occur on the AUI. The *data* portion is the frame passed from the MAC sublayer. The *end of transmission* delimiter indicates the end of a transmission and serves to turn off the transmitter.

---

[19] For example, it may be located on roofs of buildings.

Medium Attachment Unit (MAU)

The MAU servers as an interface between the physical signaling sublayer and the medium dependent interface, as modeled in Figure 3.36. The IEEE 802.3 current specification (ISO/8802/3) specifies a data rate of 10 Mbps and the capability of driving a signal on the LAN medium up to 500 m without repeaters. A LAN medium involving no repeaters is called a LAN **segment.** The following notation has been developed in the IEEE 802.3 specification for identifying a particular implementation:

(Data rate)(Medium type)(Maximum segment length)

where the *data rate* is in M bps, the *medium type* is either *base* (i.e., baseband) or *broad* (i.e., broadband), and each unit of the segment length represents 100 m. For example, an implementation running at 10 M bps and maximum segment length of 500 m is denoted by *10 BASE 5*.

Since the MAU is an interface, it must perform functions involving transmission and reception of encoded symbols. Another major function performed by the MAU involves detecting collisions on the medium. A collision is detected when the signal on the coaxial cable equals or exceeds that produced by two or more MAU outputs transmitting at the same time under the condition that the MAU detecting the collision is transmitting.

Because the maximum frame size is 1518 bytes, it takes about 1.22 m sec to transmit the frame assuming a 10 Mbps data rate. If the MAU receives symbols to be transmitted corresponding to frames much longer than 1518 bytes, the MAU interrupts the ongoing transmission by means of the **jabber function.** The **jabber function** allows the MAU to transmit normal size frames for a nominal window between 20 and 150 msec before interrupting the transmission. As an option, the MAU also provides a **monitor function** for isolating the MAU transmitter from the rest of the network. The monitor function is intended to prevent a malfunctioning active component from bringing down the network.

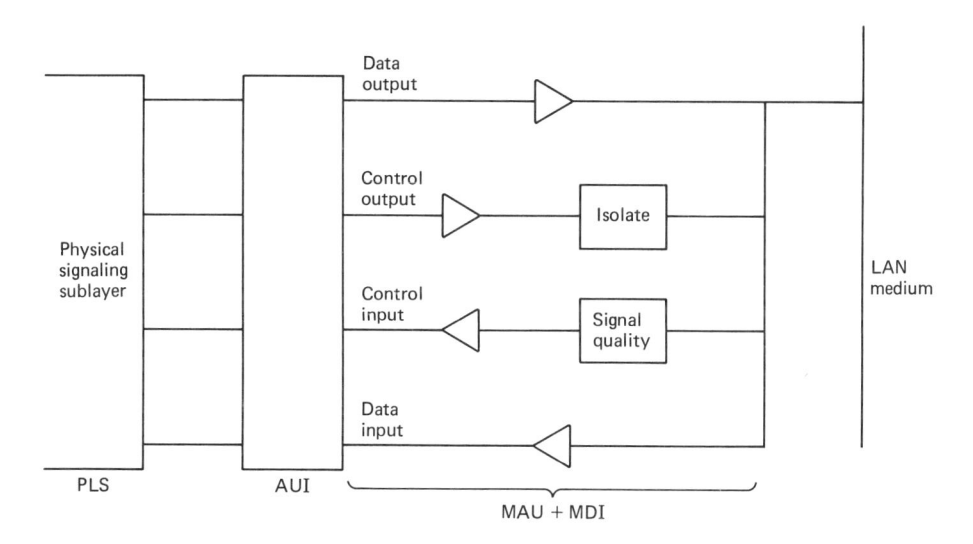

Figure 3.36 Conceptual model of the medium attachment unit (MAU).

Physical Layer Services

The services that the IEEE 802.3 physical layer provides to the data link layer are given by the following primitives:

> PLS_DATA.request
> PLS_DATA.confirmation
> PLS_DATA.indication
> PLS_CARRIER.indication and
> PLS_SIGNAL.indication

Whereas the first three primitives support data transfer between peer physical layer users, the last two primitives provide information to the data link layer for performing the medium access control function.

3.12 MAP PHYSICAL LAYER

The physical layer of the MAP 3.0 architecture consists of a backbone network with gateways, routers, and bridges connecting to other MAP and possibly some nonMAP subnetworks. Although an important issue, the network topology is left to the individual plant requirements. The two best known topologies applicable to MAP networks are the star and the tree (Campbell and Pimentel, 1986). The physical medium recommended as the network backbone in MAP 3.0 is a coaxial cable capable of supporting many channels (i.e., broadband). The modulation technique is AM-PSK, with duobinary encoding at a data rate of 10 Mbps. Channels on the broadband cable are chosen according to the midsplit channel allocation scheme, although a high-split scheme is also possible. To improve reliability, redundant media is recommended.

For applications not requiring broadband communications, a single channel network based on a phase coherent, Frequency Shift Keying (FSK) modulation scheme at a data rate of 5 Mbps is recommended. The corresponding network is referred to as a **carrierband** network. Installations using carrierband networks require that disturbance noise be carefully controlled. Specifically, it is recommended that the highest root mean square (RMS) noise level be -10 dBmV. Since carrierband subnetworks and broadband backbones use different modulation, encoding, and data rates, their interconnection requires appropriate routers, or bridges, to perform the required speed, modulation, and encoding conversions.

Broadband technology offer the following advantages:

1. Broadband allows multiple networks to coexist simultaneously on the same medium, with each network occupying a different channel. Frequency division multiplexing allows networks to use any desired channel. The channels can be dedicated or switched.

2. In addition to supporting data transmission, broadband also supports voice and video transmission, using the same or separate channels. Some applications benefiting from this option include security surveillance, closed circuit television (CCTV), teleconferencing, and education.

3. Broadband can also be used to support other network types (e.g., CSMA/CD).

Carrierband technology has the following advantages:

1. Since a single channel is used, the network interfaces are simpler and more inexpensive when compared to broadband interfaces. For example, channel cross talk noise is not a problem, because there is no interference with other channels. In addition, modulation schemes can be simpler, since there is no attempt to have high bandwidth efficiency.

2. Unlike broadband, carrierband technology is passive in nature, because there is no need for a *head end* and amplifiers. Thus, a higher degree of reliability is anticipated when compared with broadband technology.

3. Because there are no *head ends* nor amplifiers, signals travel directly from source station to destination station, thus incurring lower propagation delays than when compared with the broadband case. The savings in delays are attributed to head end and amplifier delays. Although the savings is in the order of 10s of μsec, it can make a difference for some time-critical applications.

4. Because of its passive nature, carrierband is limited to shorter distances and fewer stations than broadband. The limitations are 32 stations per segment, and 1 Km between most distant communicating stations.

3.12.1 TOP Physical Layer

The physical layer for the TOP 3.0 architecture specifies the version 10 BASE 5 of the IEEE 802.3 specification, supporting up to 1025 stations. Alternatively, the TOP 3.0 specification includes the following transmission systems: IEEE 802.4, IEEE 802.5, TOP packet switching, and 10 BROAD 36 (attachment unit interface (AUI) compatible). The 10 BASE 5 cable was selected for the following reasons (TOP, 1985):

1. There is widespread use of Ethernet local area networks with similar characteristics as that of 10 BASE 5.

2. The 10 BASE 5 cable permits a graceful migration from Ethernet version 2.0 to IEEE 802.3 CSMA/CD, which could coexist on the same cable.

3. The 10 BASE 5 is based on proven technology and provides very reliable and high-speed data transfer.

4. The 10 BASE 5 cable is capable of supporting TOP applications (i.e., design, office, etc).

One requirement of the TOP physical layer is that it should be independent (to a certain degree) of a variety of transmission media such as microwave, satellite, coaxial cable (baseband or broadband), twisted pair wires, and optical fibers. ISO is considering moving the IEEE defined media access control (MAC) sublayer to the physical layer. Accordingly, the TOP architecture includes MAC options as part of its physical layer. However, since in this book we discuss MAC schemes as part of the data link layer, we discuss the MAC sublayer for TOP in Chapter 4.

SUMMARY

In this chapter, we have discussed the functions, organization, and design techniques of the physical layer. The physical layers of the MAP and TOP network architecture were used to illustrate the main concepts.

The physical layer performs functions that overcome many of the limitations imposed by the transmission medium in an effective manner, from engineering and economics viewpoints. Functions performed by the physical layer include: encoding, decoding, modulation, providing a medium interface with the transmitter and receiver, rejecting noise, providing channels having a desired bandwidth and low error rate, generating control signals for the data link layer proper operation, and defining a physical connection with the medium.

If signals are modulated before transmission, the communication system is broadband; otherwise it is baseband. Two results, one due to Nyquist, and the other due to Shannon, give upper bounds for the data rate achievable in a noise-free, and noisy environment, respectively. Techniques for representing bits as electrical signals for transmission on a physical medium are known as **signaling techniques** or **data encoding** techniques. Data encoders also provide compensation for the following impairments: probability of error, finite bandwidth, and the presence of noise. The following criteria are useful when selecting an appropriate encoding scheme: adequate timing content, noise efficiency, error detection and correction capability, favorable power spectral density, and data transparency. The most common data encoding techniques are: on-off, polar, bipolar, duobinary, and Manchester (split-phase).

When rectangular pulses are sent over a communication channel, they experience a gradual decay in magnitude, which causes problems with neighboring pulses. The problems are known as **intersymbol interference** (ISI). Two well-known techniques for solving the intersymbol interference problem are based on the first and second Nyquist criterion for intersymbol interference. Having a long sequence of the same symbols (i.e., 1s or 0s) is undesirable. **Scrambling** allows the removal of long strings of 1s or 0s so as to make the data more random.

Broadband communications have the following advantages: radiation efficiency, noise and interference reduction, frequency assignment capability, multiplex capability, and optimum use of communication devices and equipment. Broadband communications often require specific devices for optimum operation, such as amplifiers, attenuators, couplers, splitters, taps, and head ends. The modulation techniques most used with broadband communications are: amplitude shift keying (ASK), frequency shift keying (FSK), and phase shift keying (PSK). The performance of a digital communication system can be characterized by two measures: bandwidth efficiency and bit error probability (BEP).

The IEEE 802.4 standard provides three options for encoding and modulation based on AM/PSK, phase coherent FSK, and phase continuous FSK modulation schemes. For the AM/PSK option, the standard specifies a duobinary encoder with pulse shaping satisfying the second Nyquist criterion. The data rate for this configuration is 10 Mbps occupying 12 M Hz of channel bandwidth. The medium interface should provide ac coupling between the transmitter or receiver with the medium. The station attaches to the communication medium by means of a *drop cable*. The communication medium is a larger diameter, semirigid coaxial cable with characteristic impedance $Z_o = 75$ ohm.

The physical layer of the MAP architecture consists of a backbone network with gateways, routers, and bridges connecting to other MAP and possibly some nonMAP subnetworks. The physical medium recommended as the network backbone in MAP 3.0 is a coaxial cable capable of supporting many channels (i.e., broadband), with an AM-PSK modulation scheme. For applications not requiring broadband communications, a single channel network based on a phase coherent, Frequency Shift Keying (FSK) modulation scheme at a data rate of 5 Mbps is recommended. The physical layer for the TOP architecture recommends the version 10 BASE 5 of the IEEE 802.3 specification, supporting up to 1025 stations.

Bibliographic Notes

Most physical layer issues are discussed in traditional books on digital communications. A partial list include Lathi (1983), Feher (1981, and 1983), Proakis (1983), Das et al (1986), and Ziemer and Tranter (1985). Certain books on data communications, such as Stallings (1985), Halsall (1988), and McNamara (1982) also include some physical layer material. Although the material presented in this chapter could be used with any physical media, the examples used only considered coaxial cables. A discussion of a physical layer using optical fibers for a MAP type networks is provided by Bergman (1987). Optical fibers for IEEE 802.3 type networks are discussed by Thompson (1987). Physical layer schemes with wireless transmission are discussed by Lessard and Gerla (1988). The IEEE Standards 802.4 and 802.3 have been adopted by ISO and are also known as ISO 8802/4 and ISO 8802/3 respectively.

PROBLEMS

1. List the main functions of the physical layer of the OSI reference model. Provide a brief explanation of each function.
2. Telephone circuits having a bandwidth of 3 K Hz are often used as channels for digital communications. Assume that reliable transmission can be achieved with a SNR of 20 dB. What is the maximum achievable data rate if binary signals are sent over this channel?
3. Using Eq. (3.2) find the threshold point for S/N (i.e., SNR) up to which the exchange of bandwidth for S/N is advantageous. (Hint: plot (B/C vs. S/N).
4. Using Eq. (3.4) find the limit (E_b/N) when B → ∞. This constitutes the fundamental limit of operation for modulator/encoder systems.
5. If the following bit pattern 11001010110 is the input to the following encoders a) Manchester, b) NRZ, and c) RZ. Draw the encoder output waveforms.
6. Suppose that you are making some design decisions regarding a special local area network for interconnecting *programmable devices* such as robots, numerically controlled machines, and their associated sensors and actuators. This special network is referred to as a *fieldbus network*. The major requirements that affects your decision are:
   (a) Low cost.
   (b) No bandwidth constraints (i.e., encoder can use the entire medium bandwidth).
   (c) Data encoder should have good timing capability.
   (d) Limited geographical coverage (e.g., less than 30 m). Recommend an encoding technique for this application. Provide two advantages and two disadvantages of your proposal.
7. Manchester type encoders are not unique. Develop your own version of a Manchester encoder different from that given in subsection 3.3.5.
   (a) Sketch the pulse shape p(t) and calculate P(ω) and $S_y(\omega)$.
   (b) For the bit pattern 11001010110, draw the corresponding encoder output.
   (c) List few advantages and disadvantages of your encoder.
8. Using Equation (2.80a), verify that $S_r = S_i/L_1$ and Equation (3.30a).
9. The IEEE 802.4 specification with FSK modulation specifies a maximum noise floor of −10 dBmV (rms). Assume a coherent demodulator, a coaxial cable with Z_o = 50 Ohm, and a received signal E_r = −2 dBmV. Find the bit error rate for the demodulator.
10. Write a computer program to calculate the power spectral density of a phase-continuous FSK modulated signal using Equation (3.49). Assume parameter values associated with the IEEE 802.4 specification and verify Equation (3.55).

11. What is the reason for having the *silence* symbol in the token bus protocol?
12. Given the broadband, single cable system of Figure P3.1, what is the maximum cable length for correct operation if the stations have receivers with a signal sensitivity of −2 dBmV and transmitters which deliver a signal level of 46 dBmV. Assume that all directional couplers are identical with 0.4 dB of insertion loss and 30 dB of tap loss. The directional couplers are evenly spaced every 100 foot on a coaxial cable with an attenuation of 3 dB/100 foot. Further assume that the stations are connected in close proximity to the directional coupler such that there is no appreciable signal loss in the drop cable.

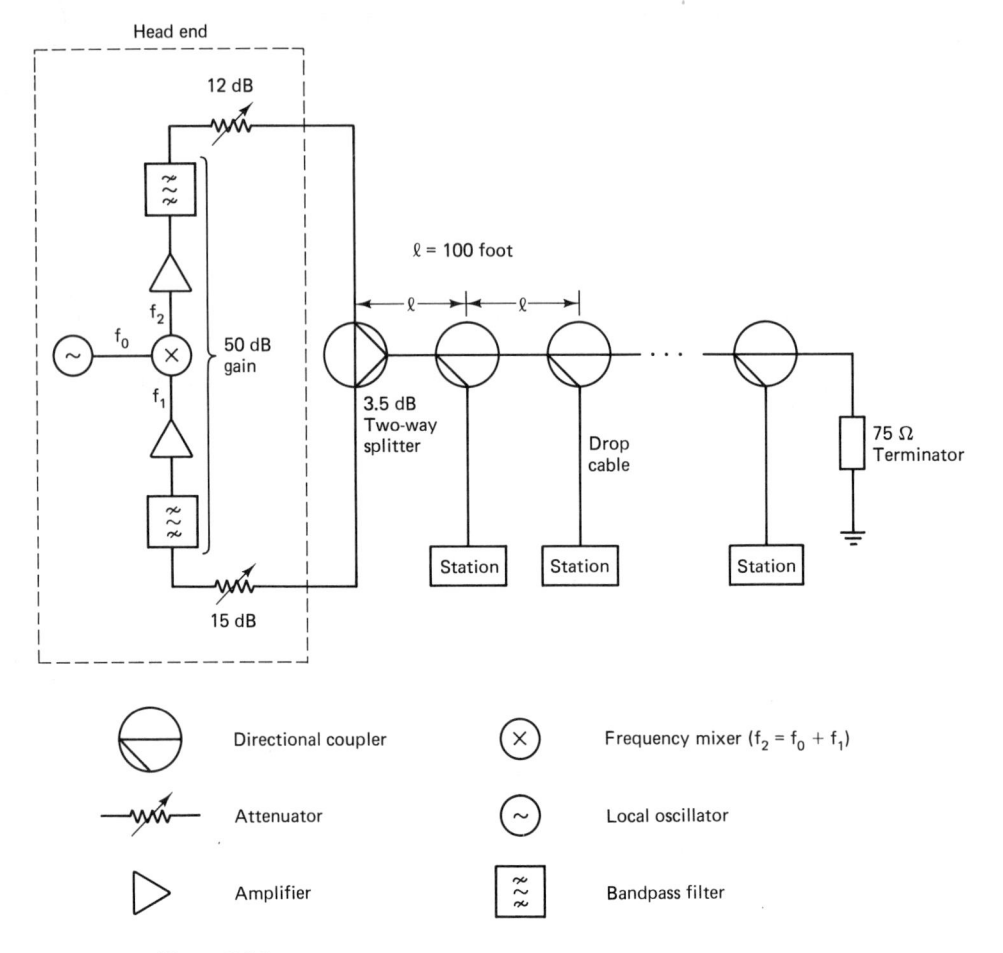

Figure P 3.1

13. Write a program for CAD (computer aided design) purposes that takes into account the location of network stations in a given installation and performs a signal analysis similar to that done in problem 12.

4

The Data Link Layer

Our objectives in this chapter are to discuss the functions of the data link layer, to provide a classification of data link protocols, and to explain schemes which are used to provide data link layer functions. We discuss channel access control, flow control, and error control in some detail, while focussing on schemes adopted by ISO as standard protocols, such as the token bus, CSMA/CD, and token ring schemes.

In the previous chapter, we saw how the physical layer takes a string of bits and performs the signal processing necessary so that the bits can be sent over a transmission channel. Ideally, one would hope that if the transmitter sends *10110*, the receiver will receive *10110*. Unfortunately, Mother Nature does not work in this way. The transmission medium is subject to several kinds of impairments that will cause some errors to occur from time to time. To make matters worse, the transmission medium is not the only culprit in causing errors. The complex signal processing operations done at the transmitter and receiver ends also contribute to the source of errors. For example, any time an amplifier is used, the amplifier is not happy by simply amplifying the signal. The amplifier also introduces noise to the amplified signal.

Another problem that arises at a level immediately above the physical layer is that a program handling bits to the physical layer at station A is clobbering a slower receiver that is receiving the bits from the physical layer at another station B. Still another problem is how to engage a sender and a receiver into a meaningful communication dialogue (i.e., a link). Finally, another problem that arises is that, without any form of synchronization or coordination, two or more stations may send bits through a shared channel to certain destination stations at the same time. Since there is only one shared channel, the bits coming from the different stations will collide with one another, thus making them unintelligible. Clearly, the collision process must be avoided or dealt with in some way if communication is to be successful.

4.1 DATA LINK LAYER FUNCTIONS

The data link layer deals with the major four problems just introduced, namely: error control, flow control, link management, and medium access control.[1] **Error control** is intended to improve the error performance characteristics provided by the physical layer. Typically, the physical layer guarantees that one bit could be lost every 1,000,000 bits transmitted. For most applications this is not good enough. The main function of error control is to improve this error performance value to error rates in the order of 1 bit lost every 10^{11} bits.

Flow control is intended to allow a fast sender to send data to a slow receiver. Some means must be used to slow down a fast sender while a slow receiver is handling previously received frames. **Link management** deals with the rules that the sender and receiver must follow in order to exchange information. For example, a sender and receiver must identify to each other and be willing and ready to communicate before exchanging any data.

Medium access control is only present in broadcast networks. Since other types of networks (i.e., point-to-point lines) have dedicated communication lines, no synchronization or coordination is needed to use the dedicated lines. For broadcast type networks, however, the medium access control problem is a very important one. The key function of *medium access control* is to assign the shared channel to the station that needs it in a way that avoids two or more stations sending data at the same time, or in a way that, even if two or more stations send data at the same time, the data collision that results is resolved.

4.2 SYNCHRONIZATION AT THE DATA LINK LAYER

Before going into the details as to how the data link layer performs the functions just noted, let us look at a model for the data link layer. Just as the overall communication system is modeled as a layered structure by means of the OSI reference model, the data link layer can also be modeled as a layered structure, as depicted in Figure 4.1(a). The model shows that the data link layer functions can be structured into a hierarchy of four layers of functions, referred to as the **hierarchical data link model** (Lam, 1983). Each level in the hierarchy depends on synchronism at the level below achieved over finer time intervals, as shown in Figure 4.1(b). Like the layers of the OSI reference model, each level in Figure 4.1 is offered a virtual communication channel by the level below, and in turn provides the level above with a virtual communication channel having improved characteristics. Together, the four levels corresponding to the data link layer in Figure 4.1 bridge the gap between what is provided by the transmission channel and the services provided by the data link layer. As noted in Chapter 3, bit synchronization is provided by the physical layer. For example, the IEEE 802.3 baseband specification for the physical layer specifies Manchester encoding for achieving bit synchronization.

---

[1] Although ISO is considering moving the medium access control function to the physical layer, we still consider it as part of the data link layer.

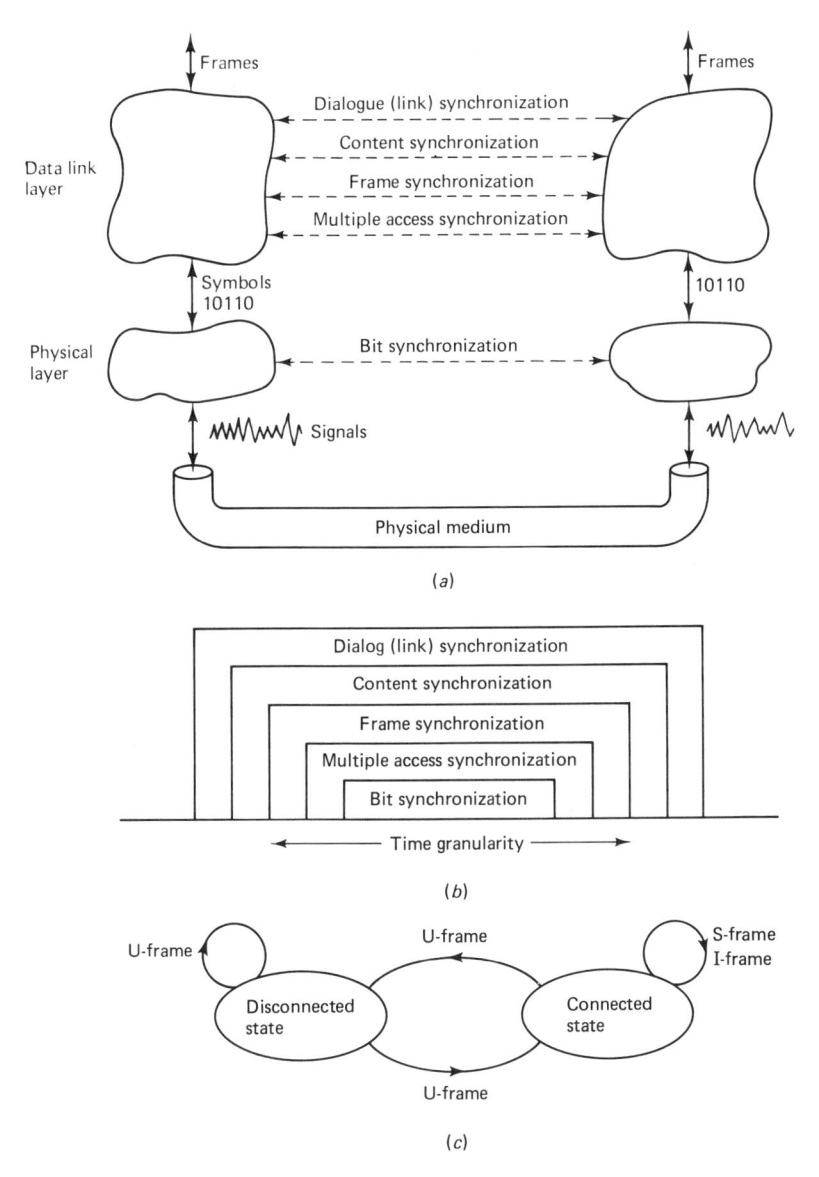

Figure 4.1 (a) Hierarchical data link model. (b) Time scale for synchronization functions. (c) Dialog synchronization and frame exchange.

Multiple access synchronization deals with the problem of sharing a transmission channel among different concurrent sender-receiver pairs (i.e., channel access schemes). There are two important aspects of multiple access synchronization. The first one relates the control signals and protocols necessary to synchronize senders to avoid (or resolve) access conflicts. The second aspect deals with the adoption of an addressing scheme for identifying senders and receivers. Another requirement that is not met by adopting an addressing scheme is the possibility of multiple destination of transmitted frames. The advantage of having a multiple access synchronization level is that the higher level protocol (i.e., the network layer) can view the data link and everything below it as a dedicated, almost error-free (it turns out that it is very difficult to remove all errors) virtual channel. The token bus protocol, token ring protocol, and the carrier sense multiple access with collision detection (CSMA/CD) are well-known schemes for achieving multiple access synchronization. Multiple access synchronization is treated extensively in Section 4.6.

The **frame synchronization** level establishes the conventions for delimiting the beginning and the end of frames. A **frame** is defined as a collection of bits which is the basic unit of transfer of data and/or control information from a transmitter data link layer to a receiver data link layer. Another function performed at this level is error detection. Usually, errors are detected by using special codes which are appended to the data. The codes are special cases of a code family known as **cyclic redundancy check** (CRC) codes, which are discussed in Section 4.11.

Two techniques are typically used for delimiting the beginning and end of frames. The first technique involves the use of a delimiter at the beginning of the frame and another at the end of the frame. In this way, a receiver is informed explicitly where the frame begins and where the frame ends. The family of IEEE 802 standards uses this technique for delimiting frames. The second technique involves the use of just one delimiter at the beginning of the frame and a length count indicating the size of the frame. In this case, a receiver is informed only where the frame begins, and it can determine where the frame ends based on the frame size. The DDCMP protocol uses this technique for delimiting frames.

Content synchronization is concerned with the information content of a frame transmitted from a sender to a receiver. The various aspects of content synchronization include differentiating between data and control information within the frame, encoding and decoding control messages, handling errors to ensure that a single error-free copy of each frame sent arrives at the receiver, and controlling the packet sequence so that packets are reassembled into the same sequence that they were sent. Some aspects of content synchronization are typically achieved by breaking the entire frame into sections (also known as fields) such as address, control, data, error check, etc. To further aid in the distinction between data and control information, frames are typically classified as belonging to three types: **information, supervisory,** and **unnumbered,** also known as *I-frames*, *S-frames*, and *U-frames*, respectively. Other aspects of content synchronization are achieved by exchanging *S-frames* and *I-frames*.

Dialog synchronization is concerned with the initiation and subsequent termination of a link (also referred to as a dialog) between the sender and receiver. For example, the sender can use dialog synchronization to inquire if the receiver is ready to *talk*. Likewise, the receiver uses dialog synchronization to respond affirmatively or negatively to the inquiry. The various aspects of dialog synchronization include coordination between the sender (or receiver) so that they send (or receive) whenever they are expected. Another aspect relates the detection and possible recovery of abnormal conditions, such as incomplete protocol specification and deadlocks.

As depicted in Figure 4.1(c), dialog synchronization is typically achieved by exchanging *U-frames*. Basically, dialog synchronization provides an orderly transition from the *disconnected state* to the *connected state*, and vice versa. While in the connected state the data link can achieve content synchronization, frame synchronization, and multiple access synchronization by exchanging *S-frames* and *I-frames*. Although *dialog synchronization* is achieved using a time granularity greater than the other forms of synchronization, dialog synchronization must occur before any other synchronization can take place.

4.2.1 Protocol Classification

Data link protocols can be classified according to the way the physical layer actually achieves bit synchronization. In an **asynchronous transmission system,** data is transmitted one character (five to eight bits) at a time. When a sender and receiver have nothing to send to each other (i.e., idle periods) no synchronization takes place. Bit synchronism is maintained only when data transmission is taking place. Thus, bit synchronization is performed one character at a time. In a **synchronous transmission system,** bit synchronism is maintained at all times. Data link protocols normally used with a synchronous transmission system are referred to as **synchronous protocols.** Likewise, data link protocols used with an asynchronous transmission system are referred to as **asynchronous protocols.** Because of their efficiency, *synchronous protocols* are prevalent in local area networks.

In the next section we discuss synchronous and asynchronous protocols in some detail. Since major functions performed by the data link layer include error control and flow control, the protocols are discussed in the context of error and flow control. Error control requires two mechanisms for dealing with errors, one for detecting them and another for dealing with them. Typically, error detection is performed using *cyclic redundancy check* (*CRC*) codes, which are discussed in Section 4.11. Errors are typically dealt with by message retransmission rather than using more sophisticated codes not only for detecting errors but also for correcting errors that might occur. Although flow control schemes can be performed by using only unnumbered frames, for efficiency purposes a mechanism for numbering frames is preferred. The frame numbering scheme used in the IEEE 802.4 protocols is discussed in Section 4.12.

4.3 ASYNCHRONOUS PROTOCOLS

Asynchronous protocols are also referred to as **start-stop** protocols. They are the simplest ones and historically the first ones to be developed. The main advantage of asynchronous protocols is their simplicity; however, their main disadvantage is their low efficiency. Asynchronous protocols are not used in applications requiring high throughput. Another term used for asynchronous protocols is that of **character-oriented protocols.**

4.3.1 Error Control

In general, two error control techniques are common for enabling a source station to determine whether a receiving station has correctly received a transmitted symbol: echo checking and automatic repeat request (ARQ). The latter is used with synchronous protocols and is discussed in Section 4.4.2.

4.3.2 Echo Checking

Echo checking is primarily used for terminal-to-computer communications. When a terminal is operating in the local mode, every time a user strikes a key the character is immediately displayed on the terminal. However, when the terminal is operating in the remote mode, the operation is different. When a user strikes a key, the character is not immediately displayed on the terminal. Rather, the character is sent to the computer, which, upon receipt of the character, sends the same character back to the terminal which then displays the character. When an error occurs, the character is not displayed at the user's terminal. Thus, the user knows when an error has occurred and is expected to retype and thus resend the character.

4.3.3 Flow Control (X-on/X-off)

For the simple case of terminal-to-computer communication, flow control is necessary when the computer load is high because of many programs being run or because there are many terminals connected to the computer. In either case, or both, when a character is typed at one of the terminals, it could be a while before one sees anything back at the terminal. One possibility is for the user to keep typing characters at the terminal. However, this would only make matters worse, because the computer will simply discard all characters that came after the one in error. What is needed is a mechanism whereby a terminal does not send any further characters until the overload condition at the computer is cleared. This is achieved by the computer, when it is overloaded, by returning a special control character, **X-off,** to the terminal, instructing it to stop transmitting. On receipt of the X-off character, the terminal ignores any further characters entered at the keyboard and hence does not contribute to an additional load to the computer. When the overload condition ends, the computer returns a companion character, **X-on,** to the terminal, indicating that the terminal may proceed sending characters. Although not generally used in local area networks, the *echo checking* and *X-on/X-off* techniques illustrate how some simple error and flow control mechanisms work.

4.4 SYNCHRONOUS PROTOCOLS

As noted, synchronous protocols differ in two major respects when compared with their asynchronous counterparts. First, synchronous protocols perform synchronization on a frame basis rather than on a character basis; and second, synchronous protocols maintain synchronization at all times rather than just when data is transmitted. Because of these differences, synchronous protocols have more degrees of freedom and are thus able to be more efficient. For instance, synchronous protocols need not associate data to be transmitted with certain character codes (e.g., ASCII, EBCDIC, etc). Thus, synchronous protocols are efficient, for example, when transmitting binary data collected from sensors in a factory environment. Synchronous protocols are also known as **bit-oriented protocols.**

4.4.1 Error Control

We begin our analysis of synchronous protocols by concentrating on the error control function, which involves a protocol mechanism for dealing with errors. One of the most effective ways for dealing with errors in local area networks involves the use of *acknowledgments*, and the corresponding mechanisms are called *automatic repeat request* (*ARQ*). In addition to using acknowledgments, the sender and receiver also rely on *retransmission timers*, or simply *timers*. The basic idea involves the sender sending a frame and starting a timer. If an acknowledgment is not received before the timer expires, the frame is retransmitted. The receiver on the other hand checks whether there is an error in the frame just received, and sends an acknowledgment if the frame is error free. In the remaining portion of this section we discuss several variations of the ARQ mechanism, such as *Idle RQ*, *Continuous RQ*, *Selective retransmission*, and *Go back N*. Error detection is addressed in Section 4.11.

t_{pr}: propagation delay
t_{fr}: frame transmission delay
t_{rd}: receiver frame processing delay
t_{ack}: acknowledgment transmission delay
t_{sd}: sender acknowledgment processing delay

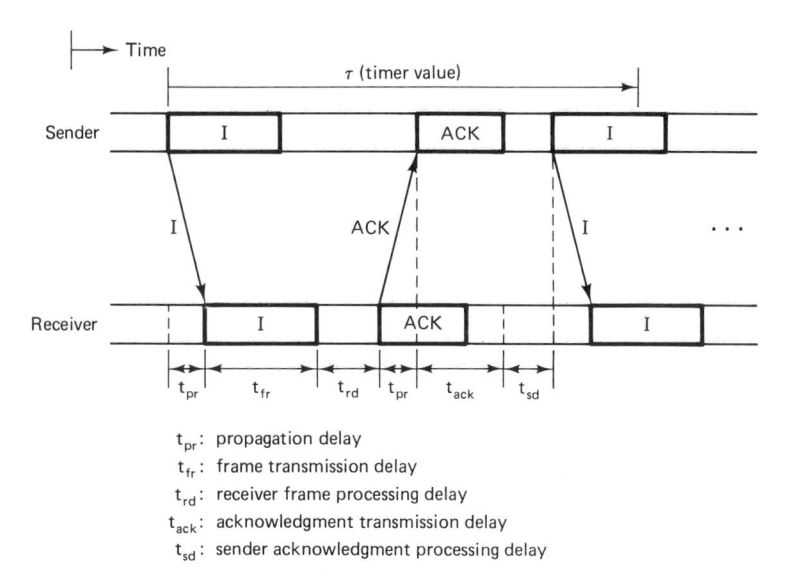

Figure 4.2 Error-free idle RQ sequences. (Adapted from Figure 4.1 with permission from *Data Communications, Computer Networks and OSI* by F. Halsall, © Addison-Wesley Publishers Ltd 1988.)

Automatic Repeat Request (ARQ). Echo checking is not appropriate for computer communications, since it is very inefficient. The reason for the inefficiency is twofold. First, most computers networks do not communicate on a character basis; rather the communication is on a frame basis; and second, it is clearly inefficient to send back entire frames just to see if they have been received correctly. Other schemes involving only a small control message are more efficient. Thus, a better technique for performing error control functions involves the use of special control messages for acknowledging correct receipt of each transmitted frame. The use of acknowledgments for error control purposes is referred to as **automatic repeat request** (ARQ). An acknowledging message is typically encoded as an *S-frame* and referred to as an *ACK-frame*. There are several versions of ARQ mechanisms used, with the two most important being *Idle RQ* (send and wait) and *continuous RQ*.

Idle RQ. Idle RQ is the simplest of the ARQ mechanisms. It requires the least amount of buffer storage but it is also the least efficient. The following simplifying assumptions are made: simplex operation (i.e., unidirectional flow of information)—the sender can have only one *I-frame* outstanding. As depicted in Figure 4.2, the operation of the Idle RQ mechanism is as follows. When the sender has a frame to send, it sends it immediately[2] and starts a timer. The *I-frame* takes T_{fr} sec (frame transmission delay) to reach the receiver. If the frame arrives to the receiver in an error-free manner, the receiver returns an ACK-frame to the sender. The receiver takes T_{rd} sec (receiver frame processing delay) to decode the I-frame and generate an acknowledgment. If the ACK-frame reaches the sender with no errors, the sender can continue to send subsequent I-frames. The time taken by the sender to process an ACK frame is T_{sd} (sender acknowledgment processing delay). If the receiver receives an I-frame or the sender receives an ACK-frame containing transmission errors,

---

[2] Actually, the frame is sent to the MAC sublayer.

the frame is discarded. After transmitting an I-frame, if the sender does not receive an ACK-frame before the timer expires, the sender retransmits the I-frame.

From Figure 4.2 it can be seen that the Idle RQ method is inefficient. Ideally (i.e., no errors in the transmission) a station must wait a total time of

$$T_{tot} = 2T_{pr} + T_{fr} + T_{rd} + T_{ack} + T_{sd} \tag{4.1}$$

before transmitting the next I-frame. Thus, the maximum throughput is

$$(Th)_{max} = X/T_{tot} \text{ (bit/sec)} \tag{4.2}$$

where X is the average frame length (in bits/frame). It is assumed that $T_{ack} = X_a/R$, where X_a is the average acknowledgment length (in bits/frame) and R is the data rate. When either the I-frame or ACK-frame contains errors

$$T_{tot} = \tau + 2T_{pr} + T_{fr} + T_{rd} + T_{ack} + T_{sd} \tag{4.2a}$$

where τ is the time-out interval and $\tau > (2T_{pr} + T_{fr} + T_{rd} + T_{ack} + T_{sd})$.

In general, after n retransmissions

$$T_{tot} = n\tau + 2T_{pr} + T_{fr} + T_{rd} + T_{ack} + T_{sd} \tag{4.2b}$$

Example

Calculate the maximum throughput on an already established link for a certain coaxial cable based LAN. The maximum distance between stations is 1Km, X = 1024 bytes, R = 10 Mbps, X_a = 26 bytes. Assume that $T_{rd} = T_{sd}$ = 10 μsec.

Solution

$$T_{pr} = 1000 \text{ m}/(0.85 \times 3 \times 10^8 \text{ m/sec}) = 3.92 \text{ μsec}$$

$$T_{fr} = 1024 \times 8 \text{ bits}/10 \times 10^6 \text{ bit/sec} = 819.2 \text{ μsec}$$

$$T_{ack} = 26 \times 8 \text{ bits}/10 \times 10^6 \text{ bit/sec} = 20.8 \text{ μsec}$$

Substituting in Equation 4.2, we obtain

$$(Th)_{max} = \frac{8 \times 1024 \text{ bits}}{(2 \times 3.92 + 819.2 + 20.8 + 20) \text{ μsec}}$$

$$= 9.47 \text{ Mbps}$$

Note that the preceding calculations do not take into account the delays involved in acquiring a shared channel. Thus, actual throughput values are lower than the value calculated in this example.

Continuous RQ. Since a sender waits until an acknowledgment is received before sending the next frame, the line utilization under the idle RQ method is very low. What is needed is a way for a sender to be able to number each frame sent and for a receiver to number each acknowledgment returned. In this way, the sender could just keep sending numbered frames without the need to wait for an acknowledgment right away. Conceivably, the sender could send 1000 frames without seeing an acknowledgment. Clearly, enough memory is required to keep track of unacknowledged frames by the sender, and missing frames by the receiver. Schemes whereby the sender keeps sending frames without receiving acknowledgments right away are called **continuous RQ**

protocols. In order for these schemes to work, however, the acknowledgments must eventually be received by the sender.

A continuous RQ protocol operates as follows. The sender keeps sending *I-frames* continuously without waiting for acknowledgments, as shown in Figure 4.3. Because of potential errors in the transmission, the sender retains a copy of each I-frame transmitted in a retransmission list, just in case. If an I-frame is correctly received, the receiver returns a corresponding ACK-frame. The receiver maintains an ordered list (the receive list) containing the identifiers from the last correctly received *I-frames*. The receive list is useful, for example, in situations where because of transmission errors, frames arrive out of order. The receiver can then reorder the received frames in the original order. As in the idle RQ case, associated with each frame sent by the sender is a timer which expires when no acknowledgment is returned within a time-out interval.

Depending upon the way transmission errors are handled, there are two classes of continuous RQ protocols. When the sender detects that a frame has been lost and retransmits just the unacknowledged frame, the method is referred to as **selective retransmission.** The other possibility is for the receiver to detect the receipt of an out-of-sequence *I-frame* and request the sender to retransmit

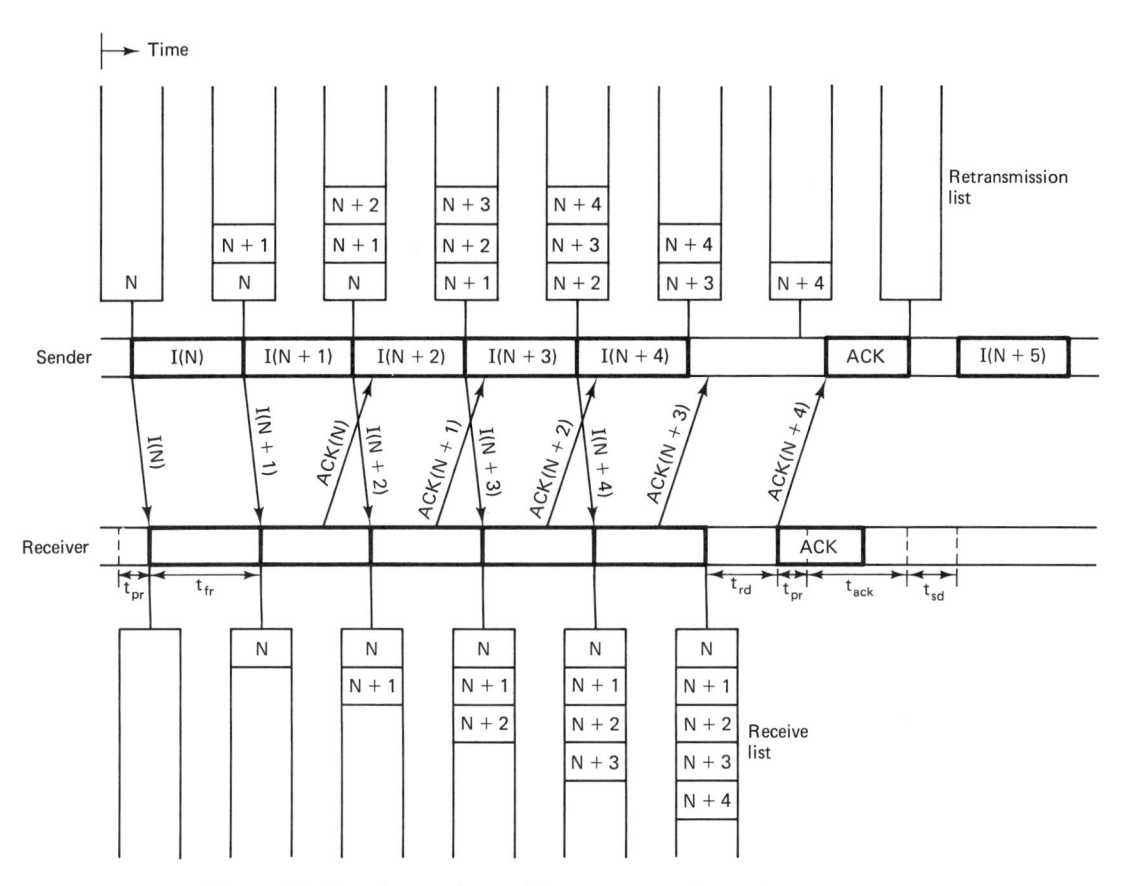

Figure 4.3 Error-free continuous RQ sequences. (Adapted from Figure 4.7 with permission from *Data Communications, Computer Networks and OSI* by F. Halsall, © Addison-Wesley Publishers Ltd 1988.)

Sec. 4.4 Synchronous Protocols 147

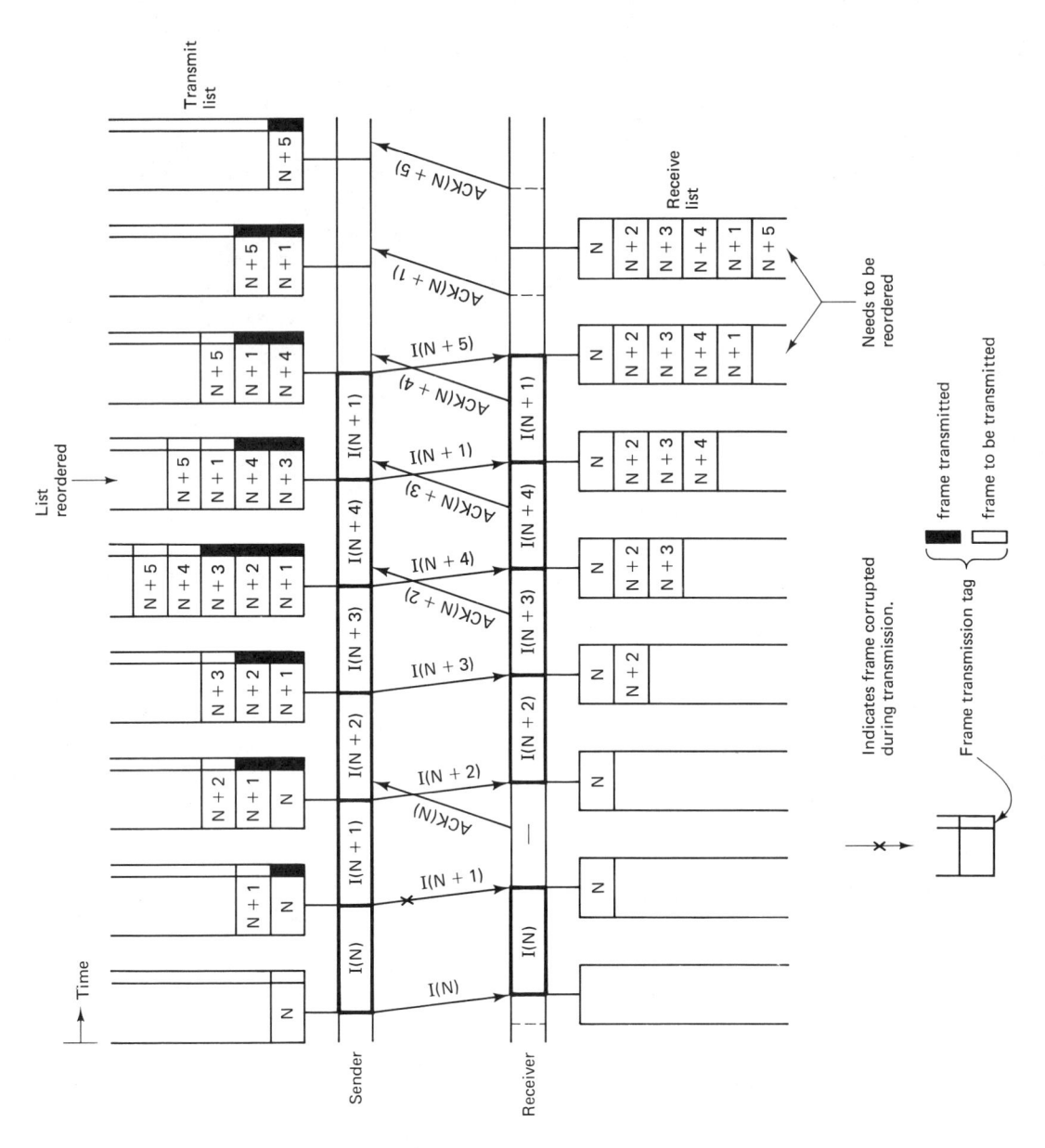

Figure 4.4 Selective retransmission, corrupted I-frame case. (Adapted from Figure 4.10 with permission from *Data Communications, Computer Networks and OSI* by F. Halsall, © Addison-Wesley Publishers Ltd 1988.)

all outstanding unacknowledged *I-frames* from the last correctly received, and therefore acknowledged frame. The latter technique is known as **Go-Back-N.** We discuss both classes of RQ protocols next.

Selective retransmission. Transmission errors are handled by *selective retransmission*, as follows. Let us assume that an error creeps in *I-frame N + 1*, as depicted in Figure 4.4. Since the receiver does not see frame N + 1, it returns acknowledgments for frames N − 1, N, N + 2, and so on. The sender detects that acknowledgments for frames N and N + 2 are out of sequence and safely assumes that the acknowledgment for frame N + 1 has been lost. Since the last acknowledgment received corresponds to frame N + 2, the sender proceeds to remove frame N + 2 from the retransmission list and retransmits frame N + 1 before transmitting frame N + 5.

The other error possibility is for an acknowledgment frame to be corrupted. The operation of the selective retransmission method is essentially the same as in the previous case, with one difference. After receiving two copies of the same frame, the receiver proceeds to get rid of one of them and sends an acknowledgment to the sender for that frame so that it is removed from the retransmission list.

Go-Back-N. In addition to the ACK-frame, the Go-Back-N protocol uses another kind of acknowledgment, known as NACK (negative acknowledgment). A receiver returns a NACK for a frame indicating that the frame was the last one received correctly. The sender uses this information to *go back* and resend frames following the last one received by the receiver. More specifically, assume that frame N + 1 is corrupted, and the receiver receives frames N − 1, N, N + 2, N + 3, and N + 4, and realizes that frame N + 2 is out of sequence (i.e., frame N + 1 is missing). The receiver then proceeds to return a NACK for frame N, indicating that the last frame correctly received was frame N. The receiver discards frames N + 2, and all subsequent ones (N + 3 and N + 4 in this case) until the next in sequence frame is received (i.e., N + 1). Upon reception of frame N + 1 by the receiver, the operation continues as in the normal continuous RQ protocol.

When ACK frames are corrupted, the operation of the Go-Back-N algorithm is sufficiently different from the previous case, so that it warrants additional explanation. Let us assume that the receiver receives each transmitted frame correctly but ACK frames N and N + 1 are both corrupted. After receiving ACK frame N + 2, the sender detects that there are two outstanding frames in the retransmission list (i.e., N and N + 1). Because the sender received an ACK frame, rather than a NACK frame (corresponding to N + 2), it safely implies that frames N and N + 1 correctly arrived at the receiver and that it was the ACK frames N and N + 1 that were corrupted. Hence, the sender accepts ACK(N + 2) as an acknowledgment for the two outstanding frames also (i.e., N and N + 1), and life goes on as usual.

4.4.2 Sequence Numbers

So far, frame identification by a sender or receiver was done by using arbitrary identifiers N, N + 1, N + 2, etc. (i.e., *I-frame* N + 1, ACK frame N + 3). In order to use a generic nomenclature for different kinds of frames, it is convenient to introduce the concept of sequence numbers for the sender and receiver. Basically, a **sequence number** is a number used to identify the frames in order to tell them apart. The **send sequence number** N(S) is associated with the sender, whereas the **receive sequence number** N(R) is associated with the receiver. In addition, to perform the error and flow control functions, it is necessary for the sender and receiver to keep track of the identifiers of the previously correctly received frames on the link. Thus, the sender maintains a **send state variable,** V(S), indicating the sequence number to be assigned to the next *I-frame* to be transmitted. Likewise, the receiver maintains a **receive state variable** V(R), indicating the next in-sequence *I-frame* to be received. Prior to the transmission of any frames on the link, the state variables V(S) and V(R) are initialized to zero. For each *I-frame* transmitted, the sender assigns N(S) = V(S). If the *I-frame* received by the receiver has N(S) = V(R), it is accepted and V(R) is incremented by 1. When the receiver returns an ACK or NACK frame, it sets N(R) = V(R). When the sender receives an ACK or NACK, the N(R) contained within it acknowledges those frames in the retransmission list up to, and including, N(R) − 1. The value of V(S) is incremented by one with each successive *I-frame* transmission.

4.4.3 Flow Control

In the foregoing subsections we have been dealing with error control, which is just one of the major functions of the data link layer. Another major function is that of flow control. Flow control is necessary in those situations in which the sender and receiver process frames at different speeds. It is possible for a fast sender to swamp a slow receiver. Techniques for slowing down a fast sender to a pace comfortable for the receiver are referred to as **flow control.**

Window mechanisms. For computer-to-computer communications using a frame-oriented link, the flow of *I-frames* across the link must be automatically controlled. For the Idle RQ protocol, flow control is achieved automatically, because a sender can transmit one *I-frame* only after receiving an error free ACK-frame for a previously transmitted frame. For the continuous RQ protocol, a sender may send many *I-frames* continuously before receiving any acknowledgments, and hence it is possible for a receiver to be swamped with frames. Flow control is achieved by limiting the number of *I-frames* a sender may send before receiving an acknowledgment for the corresponding *I-frame*. The sender monitors the number of outstanding (unacknowledged) *I-frames*, and when it reaches a limit, the sender simply stops transmitting further frames until acknowledgments start to flow again.

Recall that the outstanding frames are those frames currently held in the retransmission list. Thus, incorporating a flow control mechanism reduces to setting a limit on the number of *I-frames* in the retransmission list. Such limit is referred to as the **send window** for the link. For the Idle RQ scheme, the *send window* is 1. The following parameters influence the selection of an appropriate *send window*: maximum frame size, size of buffer available, and transmission data rate.

4.5 LINK CONNECTION MANAGEMENT

Error and flow control are mechanisms that operate on an already established link connection. Up to now, it has been assumed that a sender and receiver had somehow established a data link connection. In order for frames to be exchanged, a sender and a receiver must agree to start exchanging frames, to inquire about the identity of each other (in case they do not want to exchange anything), and to stop exchanging frames. The preceding mechanisms are collectively referred to as **link connection management.**

As noted earlier, in order to provide an efficient mechanism for link connection management, it is convenient to define three types of frames: information frames (*I-frames*), supervisory frames

(*S-frames*), and unnumbered frames (*U-frames*). The reason *I-frames* and *S-frames* are called numbered frames is that they are assigned sequence numbers. *U-frames* do not have sequence numbers associated with them, hence the name unnumbered.

When a sender needs to send frames to a receiver, the sender must first get the attention of the receiver and ask its willingness to accept frames. The receiver may either accept or reject the offer. If the receiver responds positively to the sender's request, then a **link connection** is established. A link connection is established using *U-frames*, since it is not necessary to number such frames. Once a link connection is established, additional coordination is required for successful frame transmission. For example, a receiver which is swamped with frames may want to request the sender to stop sending frames temporarily until further notice. This is achieved using *S-frames*. Finally, actual data frames are sent using *I-frames*.

It is also possible for a sender and a receiver to communicate without establishing a data link connection. In this situation, data frames may be exchanged using only U-frames.

Example

One of the MAP architectures specifies the IEEE 802.2 data link layer protocol, class I operation. Under this scheme, communication takes place without establishing a data link connection. Data frames are exchanged using only the following three *U-frames*:

UI	Unnumbered Information
XID	Exchange Identification
TEST	Test

Although the UI carries a limited amount of information, it is not an *I-frame*.

4.6 MEDIUM ACCESS CONTROL

A LAN consists of a collection of devices which communicate using some channel in a physical medium. If the communication is point-to-point, then there is no problem accessing the channel, since every pair of devices has a dedicated physical medium. However, when the communication is broadcast, the stations must communicate using the shared channel. At most, one device can make use of the channel at any one time. If more than one device attempts to access the channel at the same time, their signals will be garbled. The situation is known as **contention.** In general, contention occurs when information from various sources reaches the channel at the same time, thus making the messages unintelligible. Clearly, contention must be avoided or managed. Thus, a mechanism is needed to allow devices an orderly access to the channel so that the contention problem is resolved. These mechanisms are referred to as **medium access control** (MAC) mechanisms.

There are four important questions regarding MAC mechanisms:

1. How many significant MAC mechanisms are available?
2. How can these mechanisms be classified?
3. How can these mechanisms be quantitatively described or modeled?
4. What mechanisms are most suitable for a given application?

In this section we answer questions 1 and 2. Question 3 is addressed in Chapter 13, and question 4 is addressed in Chapter 14.

The answer to the first question is *too many*. A great deal of algorithms have been used recently, and many more have been proposed. Many of the MAC algorithms have achieved standard status. Even among the standard MAC algorithms, the situation can be best described by the saying, *the nice thing about standard protocols is that there are so many to choose from*.

Regarding the second question, several classifications are available in the literature which are similar to one another. We present two classification schemes for MAC mechanisms which use different classification criteria. The first classification is based on the *communication phases* and their *attributes*, whereas the second classification is based on *channel assignment strategies*. Both classifications are presented in Section 4.7. Before discussing the classification schemes, the remainder of this section provides some background on communication phases, their attributes, and channel assignment strategies

Communication Phases

Communication between a source station and a destination station involves the following three distinct phases:

 a. channel access phase,
 b. message transmission phase, and
 c. channel release phase.

When a source station has a message to send to a destination station, first the *channel access phase* is performed. After this phase, the source station has acquired the channel and the *message transmission phase* can begin. Finally, when the station is finished transmitting messages, it proceeds to perform the *channel release phase*. This process is repeated for every station, thus defining a message transfer cycle consisting of the preceding three phases.

Multiplexing Scheme

Depending upon the characteristics of the transmission system, there are two environments in which the channel access phase is performed. The first environment involves the transmission system providing only one channel. In this case, the channel access phase means accessing a single shared channel, and its solution is based on *time division multiplexing* (TDM). As discussed in Section 3.7, TDM schemes give every station a quantum of time of q secs per cycle to transmit. Every station has q secs to transmit part or an entire message. If a message needs more than q secs to be transmitted, the station will use several cycles until the entire message is transmitted. The quantum time q can be fixed (synchronous TDM) or variable (asynchronous TDM). Synchronous schemes find applications in voice networks, such as PBXs (private branch exchange). Schemes suitable for manufacturing applications are typically of the asynchronous type.

The second environment involves the transmission system providing several channels. In this case, the channel access phase means either accessing only one channel, or accessing any channel out of the many available. If only one channel is accessed out of the many available, then the situation is similar to the case described previously where there is only one channel available. If, however, any channel can be accessed, the solution involves using *frequency division multiplexing* (FDM). A transmission system with many channels can support multiple independent networks simultaneously. It is also possible that some stations connected to one channel communicate with stations connected to a different channel by using special devices called *bridges*.

Communication Phase Attributes

It is convenient to use certain attributes to characterize the communication phases. Attributes can be of two types: *location of control* attributes and *type of access* attributes.

Depending upon their *location of control*, the attributes are *centralized* (C) or *decentralized* (D), as defined next.

> Centralized (C): The operations within the phase are performed *with* the aid of a central function (i.e., centralized control).
>
> Decentralized (D): The operations within the phase are performed *without* the aid of a central function (i.e., decentralized control).

Depending upon the type of *channel access*, the attributes are *polling* (P) or *event driven* (E), as defined next.

> Polling (P): Access is performed by a *polling* mechanism.
>
> Event driven (E): Access is performed by an *event driven* mechanism.

The *channel access* phase can be centralized, decentralized, polled, or event driven. The *message transmission* phase can be performed centrally or decentrally. Central message transmission involves a source station indirectly transmitting messages via a central station to a destination station. In decentral message transmission, a source station directly transmits its message to a destination station without the need of a central station.

Likewise, the *channel release* phase, which can be performed in a central or decentral fashion, is equivalent to the termination of a transfer cycle. Channel release is performed centrally when stations use *passive couplers* to interface with the medium, and decentrally when stations use *active couplers* in their medium interfaces.

Centralized channel access mechanisms involves a central entity that is in complete control and decides when the individual stations can access the channel. The responsibility for deciding what station should get control of the channel is centralized in a **master** station. In this case, there is no contention, because the master assigns a permission to transmit to every station in a manner which is nonoverlapping. The advantages of this approach are that the master station can exert greater control over priorities, the required hardware at each station is simple, and it avoids problems of coordination between the slave station to find out whose turn it is to transmit. The disadvantages are that the central station constitutes a single point of failure, and it may act as a bottleneck.

In decentralized channel access mechanisms, all stations cooperate in accessing the shared channel. The responsibility for granting control to access the channel is shared among all stations that are members of the network. The access control mechanism can be done in a controlled (e.g., using a token) or random manner.

One can think of the controlled decentralized mechanism as a decentralized polling mechanism where the polling function is completely distributed. There are several schemes in this category, but our discussion is limited to the *token passing* schemes. A *token passing* access control is based on a control frame known as the **token,** which regulates the right to transmit. The token is passed from station to station in a cyclic manner. A station may transmit only if it has the token. There are two versions of token passing scheme: token bus and token ring.

Random Access Techniques

In random access techniques a station's turn to transmit is not predictable nor scheduled (i.e., a station transmission occurs randomly). In addition, no control is exercised to determine whose turn it is to transmit; thus, all stations contend for time in the network.

Using this approach, contention is almost guaranteed. The techniques in this family expect contention to occur, and work around it. An important term used to describe the details of these techniques is **collision**. A collision is an interference condition caused when two stations transmit over the same channel at about the same time. The interference makes the data frames unintelligible. The major random access techniques include ALOHA, Carrier Sense Multiple Access (CSMA), and Carrier Sense Multiple Access with Collision Detection (CSMA/CD), which are discussed in detail in Section 4.9.

Polling

Polling mechanisms for channel access are important for manufacturing networks because of their *deterministic* behavior and their simplicity of implementation.[3] By polling, we mean that all stations are polled either centrally or decentrally, regardless of whether the stations have any messages to communicate. In contrast, an event driven *channel access* allocates channel bandwidth dynamically in response to events generated by stations. The events usually indicate that there is a message ready to be transmitted. Figure 4.5 gives a general representation of a polling network used for interconnecting a variety of devices.

Centralized Polling Networks

A central station plays a crucial role in centralized polling networks by polling the remaining stations on the network in some predetermined order to provide access to the channel. If the polled station has any messages to transmit, it uses the channel to transmit its messages to the central station. While not being polled, stations accumulate messages but do not transmit until polled. Stations communicate with one another indirectly through the central station, which receives all incoming frames and retransmits them to the destination stations.

The lines coupling the polled stations to the central computer are typically high-speed and can be either half duplex or full duplex. If the lines are full duplex, the central computer can communicate outgoing messages to their destination stations over one-half of the full duplex connection, and simultaneously receive incoming messages from the current polled station over the other half. If the lines are half duplex, they must be shared between incoming and outgoing traffic, and a small amount of time is required each time the line is turned around at the central station.

Depending upon how the polling cycle is actually done, polling networks can operate in either of two modes: roll-call and hub polling. If the central station polls each other station directly in each cycle, the polling mechanism is called **roll-call polling.** The other possibility is for the central

---

[3] Simplicity mostly applies to centralized schemes, since decentralized polling schemes can be very complex.

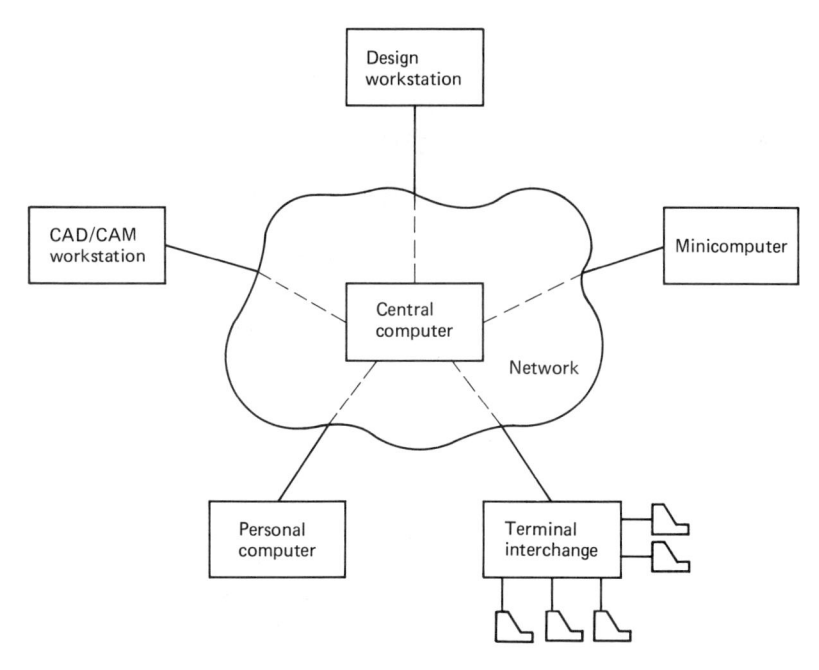

Figure 4.5 A general configuration for a polling network.

station to initiate the polling cycle by polling one station, which in turn polls the next one, until the polling cycle is completed. The latter polling mechanism is called **hub polling.** For roll-call polling, the central station initiates the polling sequence by sending a polling message to the first station in the polling sequence. After this station has transmittted its messages, it notifies the central station, using a special suffix at the end of its last frame. After receiving the special suffix, the central computer sends a poll to the next station in the polling sequence, and the process is continued.

For hub polling, the central station sends out the polling message to the initial station, just as in the call polling case. When the polled station has completed its transmission, it not only sends a special suffix, but also the address of the station to be polled next.

After a station completes its transmission, the next station in the polling sequence (which is continually monitoring incoming traffic to the central computer) reads the go-ahead message, recognizes its own address, and begins transmitting immediately. Listening to other stations as well as to the central station in hub polling can speed up the polling operation. Transmission of the go-ahead to the central computer and of the poll from the central computer to the next station in the polling sequence is, in effect, replaced in hub polling by transmitting a go-ahead directly from one station to another.

Polling networks can be configured in ring, bus, star, or tree topologies. Roll-call polling is straightforward for any of these topologies. Implementation of the monitor function for hub polling may not be obvious in all cases. For ring topologies, however, polling can be implemented in an obvious manner if the polling sequence progresses between adjacent stations. For the bus topology, some sort of monitoring mechanism is required to enable each station to monitor incoming traffic on the shared medium.

In this section, we have mostly discussed centralized polling schemes in a general fashion to illustrate the concept of polling. The best known examples of decentralized polling are the token bus and token ring protocols, which are discussed in detail in Sections 4.8 and 4.10. Before discussing the major channel access schemes, we present two access classifications.

4.7 CLASSIFICATION OF ACCESS SCHEMES

4.7.1 Communication Phase-based Classification

Our first access scheme classification takes into account the communication phases and their attributes, and is due to Heger (1983). Since the channel access phase can be performed in 4 ways, the message transmission phase in 2 ways, and the channel release phase in 2 ways, we have a total of 16 different ways in which channel access mechanisms can be performed. The 16 ways are shown in Table 4.1. Although it is possible to have medium access control schemes belonging to any of the 16 mechanisms, some of them are not technically sound, and thus they are not used in practice. In what follows we discuss characteristics of selected medium access schemes.

CPCC medium access control scheme. A typical network configuration using this scheme is depicted in Figure 4.6. The central station C(0) polls a station and, when it has a message to send, the central station allows it to use the channel. Since the message transmission phase is indirect, the source station sends its data message to the central station, which in turn sends the data message to the destination station (i.e., indirect transmission). Examples of this MAC scheme include the first definition of the PDV bus, US Department of Defense (MIL-STD-15538), and Intel's Bitbus.

DPDC medium access control scheme. In this scheme, the channel assignment is controlled in a decentralized (i.e., distributed) fashion. Messages go directly from the source to the destination without going to a central station, and stations are passively coupled to the medium. Examples of systems using this MAC scheme include the IEEE token bus protocol, the Cambridge Ring with its empty slot procedure, and other schemes which are variations of the token protocol.

TABLE 4.1 CLASSIFICATION OF CHANNEL ACCESS SCHEMES

Channel assignment	Data message transmission	Central (indirect)		Decentral (direct)	
C	POLLING	CPCC	CPCD	CPDC	CPDD
	EVENT DRIVEN	CECC	CECD	CEDC	CEDD
D	POLLING	DPCC	DPCD	DPDC	DPDD
	EVENT DRIVEN	DECC	DECD	DEDC	DEDD
		CENTRAL (PASSIVELY COUPLED)	DECENTRAL (ACTIVELY COUPLED)	CENTRAL (PASSIVELY COUPLED)	DECENTRAL (ACTIVELY COUPLED)
		CHANNEL RELEASE			

C: CENTRAL
D: DECENTRAL

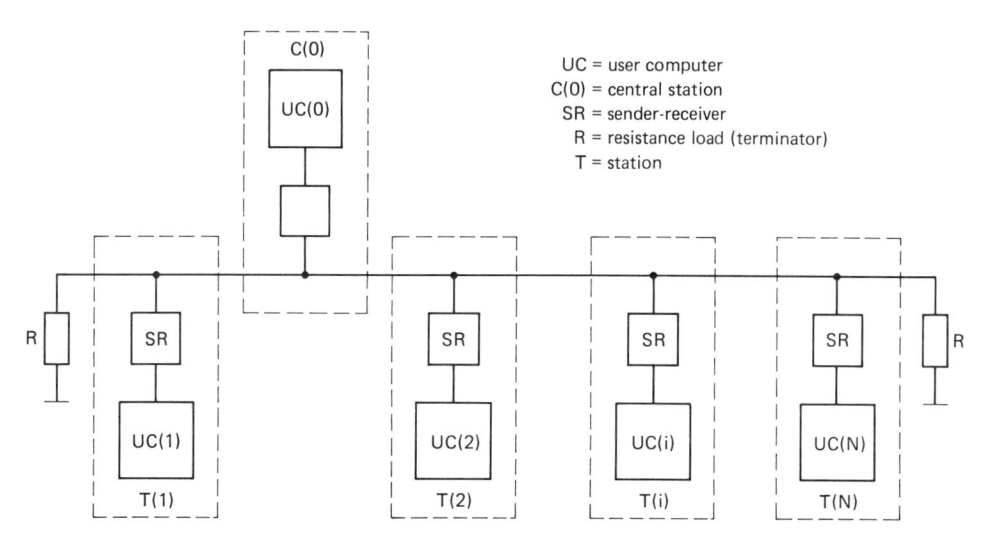

Figure 4.6 Topological structure, configuration, and coupling scheme for a data highway with passively coupled stations and a central control station.

DEDC medium access control schemes. A disadvantage of a DPDC scheme is that channel bandwidth is wasted by the polling mechanism if the polled station has no messages to send. An event driven channel assignment scheme such as the DEDC improves channel bandwidth utilization by assigning the channel on an event basis (i.e., when needed). There are many schemes that fall in this category. We present three schemes.

1. We begin by considering a token passing system with an indifferent token, where the token carries no source or destination address. The frame format has a bit position which can be set disjunctively by the stations with messages to send. The station with the right to send detects such an event and sends out the indifferent token, in which a specific bit position is reserved for each station. Every station with messages to send sets its bit position in this token, and thus notifies all other stations of its willingness to send. This token is received by all stations which have set a bit in the token. It is assumed that at this point the station's priorities are already known and fixed (e.g., in order of station addresses 1, 2, . . . , N) and the station with messages to send having the highest priority sends messages until interrupted by another station with messages to send. After completing the transmission of its current message, the transmitting station sends out the indifferent token, and the decentralized priority decision is carried out again. This scheme leads to a preferential treatment for stations with high priority especially under high loads.

2. The disadvantage of the fixed station priorities in the first scheme is avoided in this scheme, which is depicted in Figure 4.7. Scheme 2 is based on an event registration and token passing with destination-addressed token. Like scheme 1, each station with messages to transmit set its bit in a special registration message, which is received by all the other stations. The station with highest priority (e.g., lowest station address) may send first, but after completing its transmission it signals the next station, which is to begin transmission by means of a destination-addressed token. The next station to begin transmission is the next station to have registered its request to send based on its priority. When all registered stations (i.e., stations with messages to send) have used the channel, the last station in this cycle sends a new registration message. It is essential that every station

Sec. 4.7 Classification of Access Schemes

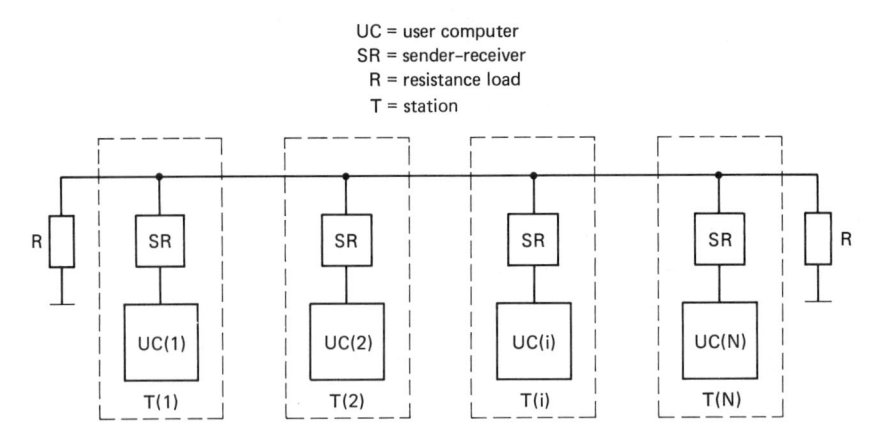

Figure 4.7 Topological structure, configuration, and coupling scheme for a data highway with passively coupled stations and decentralized control for message transfer.

receives only limited transmission time (i.e., may send only one message). This is a round robin scheduling algorithm, as described in Kleinrock (1976).

3. Our third scheme corresponds to the so called *random access techniques*. The main scheme in the random access family is that of CSMA/CD and its predecessors (e.g., Ethernet). Briefly, Ethernet-like protocols work in the following way: Every station with messages to send tests to see if the channel is free. If the channel is free, the station starts sending immediately, otherwise the station waits until the end of the ongoing transfer and attempts to send again. There are no control messages exchanged among the stations for the purpose of channel assignment. If stations wait the same time interval before message transfer attempts, their signals collide in the channel. It is assumed that stations can detect the collision by listening on the channel. When a collision is detected, the corresponding station stops transmitting and waits a random amount of time before attempting to transmit again.

DEDD medium access control schemes. As an example of the DEDD access techniques, we describe the RDC-Ring, a DEDD medium access scheme developed at the Fraunhofer Institute in West Germany, Heger (1985). Stations are actively coupled to the medium, as depicted in Figure 4.8, with the message transmission phase carried out without assistance from a central station. We consider only the normal mode of operation, in which the transfer direction is fixed. When a station receives a message not addressed to it, the station immediately forwards the message to its neighbor. A station with frames to send listens at its receiving side R and starts sending a data message via its sender S, as long as the station has no messages to be forwarded and its buffer is empty. If a message to be forwarded arrives during a message transmission, it is stored in the buffer B. Storing incoming messages to be retransmitted while the station is transmitting is referred to as the **buffer insertion principle**. When the station has finished sending its own data message, it then sends all messages or parts of messages waiting in the buffer B with priorities over messages of its own. Since the channel release phase is decentralized, each station is responsible for taking messages destined to it from the ring. Failure to remove messages from the ring results in the message circulating indefinitely. Thus, the feeding of messages into the ring is event driven, and several messages can be on the ring at the same time.

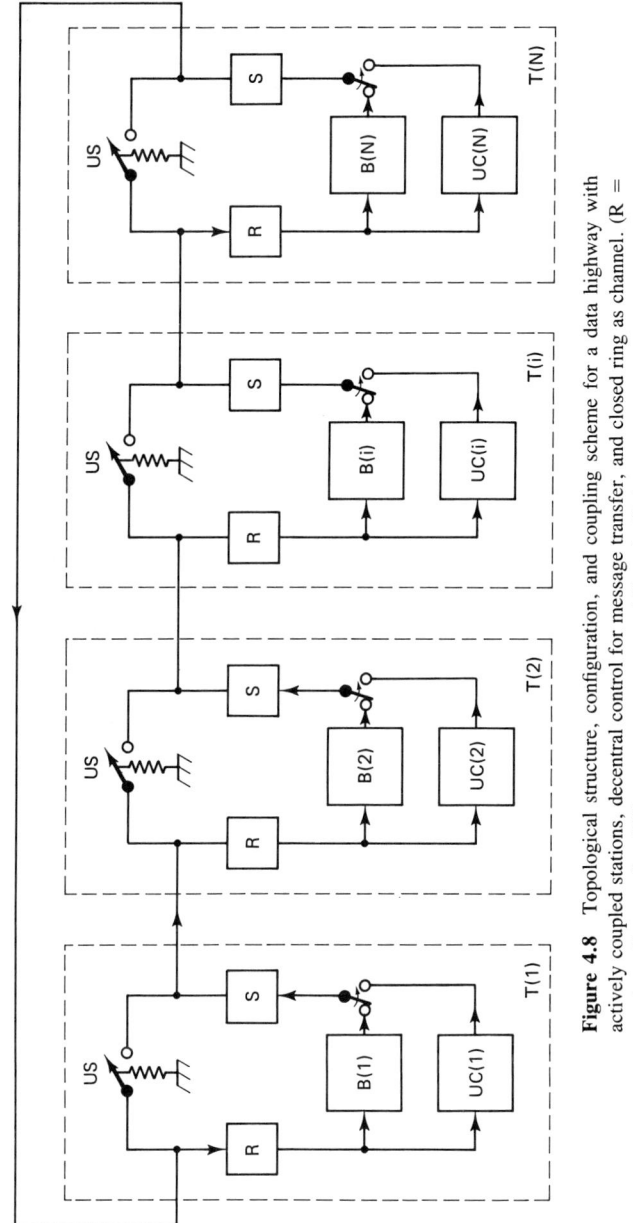

Figure 4.8 Topological structure, configuration, and coupling scheme for a data highway with actively coupled stations, decentral control for message transfer, and closed ring as channel. (R = receiver, S = sender, UC = user computer, and B = buffer)

Sec. 4.7   Classification of Access Schemes   159

4.7.2 Channel Assignment-based Classification

Our second channel access classification is based on how the channel is assigned to the different stations. Hammond and O'Reilly (1986) provide the following channel access classification according to the channel assignment: *fixed assignment*, *random assignment*, *demand assignment*, and *adaptive assignment*.

Fixed assignment strategies make a fix allocation of channel resources to each station on a predetermined basis. Two common schemes in this category are frequency division multiple access (FDMA) and time division multiple access (TDMA). Whereas FDMA assigns each station a fixed channel in a common transmission medium, TDMA assigns each station a *time-slot* in a repetitive manner so that all stations are served periodically in some fixed order. FDMA is an application of frequency division multiplexing (FDM), and TDMA is an application of time division multiplexing (TDM).

In *fixed assignment* strategies, each station is allocated its assigned time slot or its assigned frequency band regardless of whether stations have messages to transmit. For typical bursty computer data, these schemes can be inefficient in the use of bandwidth, because the resources are wasted when stations have nothing to send.

At the other extreme from fixed assignments are the **random assignment** methods. For the simplest of these methods, referred to as pure ALOHA, each station transmits whenever it is ready. If the channel is free, the transmission is successful; otherwise, a collision occurs, and the colliding packets are retransmitted later. Such an access mechanism is well suited to bursty traffic, since a station does not use the channel when it has no data to transmit. The disadvantage of pure ALOHA is that network performance deteriorates due to excessive collisions at medium and high loads.

Demand assignment and adaptive assignment strategies *require a network control mechanism* that operates *in real time* and attempts to allocate channel capacity to the multiple stations in an optimum or near-optimum fashion. **Demand assignment** methods are further classified as *central control* or *distributed control*. In either case, the control algorithm does not change with traffic conditions, and is designed to allocate channel usage to stations with packets to transmit. Idle stations are ignored to make efficient use of the channel. Polling algorithms are examples of *central control*, whereas ring networks generally make use of *distributed control*.

Adaptive assignment methods attempt to refine further either random or demand assignment protocols. These strategies not only attempt to make efficient use of the channel by avoiding idle stations, but also attempt to adapt to network conditions. Such adaptations can make a more efficient assignment of channel usage among those stations that require service. Adaptive assignment protocols are often limited-contention protocols, since collisions are usually permitted at low loads to minimize access times. At high loads, however, these procedures usually adjust to some form of polling or TDM.

Although the emphasis in this book is on packet switched networks, there are fixed assignment access mechanisms belonging to circuit switched networks. Perhaps the best example is that utilized by the Computerized Branch Example (CBX) or its frontrunner, the digital Private Branch Example (PBX). The channel assignment of a CBX is called **synchronous time division multiplexing** (TDM), because time slots of fixed duration are assigned to all users. The reader is referred to the books by Stallings (1987) and Schwartz (1987) for additional details.

The main objective of this text is to present the fundamentals of networks suitable for supporting applications in Computer Integrated Manufacuring (CIM). To accomplish this objective, we focus on a subset of available access techniques, choosing those that have the functionality required by the applications. It is generally agreed that the standards being developed by the IEEE 802 Committee, ISO, and the CCITT will play a crucial role in the development of networks for manufacturing. More specifically, we concentrate on polling methods, including the token bus and token ring, and random access methods. The token bus and token ring access schemes have evolved into protocol standards known as the IEEE 802.4 and IEEE 802.5, respectively. Likewise, CSMA/CD, which is one of the most useful random access methods, has also evolved into a standard known as IEEE 802.3.

4.8 TOKEN BUS

As depicted in Figure 4.9 a physical bus interconnects stations using the token bus scheme. Since the token bus algorithm is a *decentralized* polling channel access mechanism, all stations connected to the bus cooperate in using the shared channel. The basic idea behind the channel access mechanism involves the concept of the *right to use the channel*. Basically, only the station having the right to use the channel is allowed to send messages. The right to use the channel is referred to as the **token**, and sometimes is also known as **baton**. The station receiving the token is granted control of the channel for a specified time. Thus, a station can send messages (i.e., use the shared channel) only if it has the token. While holding the token, the station can send messages to any other station connected to the physical bus. After a station is finished sending messages, it passes the token to another station, which proceeds likewise.

The token is passed from station to station in a cyclic fashion, thus defining a *logical ring* which is shown in Figure 4.9. Therefore, the logical ring determines the sequence for passing the token from station to station. As far as the logical ring is concerned, each station only knows the identity (i.e., the address) of the station preceding it and the one following it. Naturally, a station must know the identity of all remaining stations for the purpose of communicating with them, but it has no idea about their location in the logical ring. Although any station is capable of sending and receiving messages, stations not included in the logical ring cannot send messages, since they are never given the token. These stations are called *listen only* stations, because they can receive messages but can't send them.

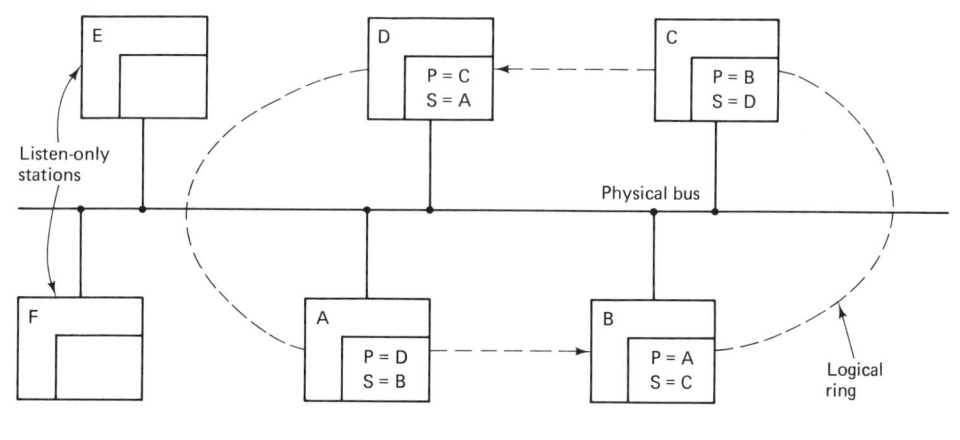

Figure 4.9 Principle of the token bus protocol.

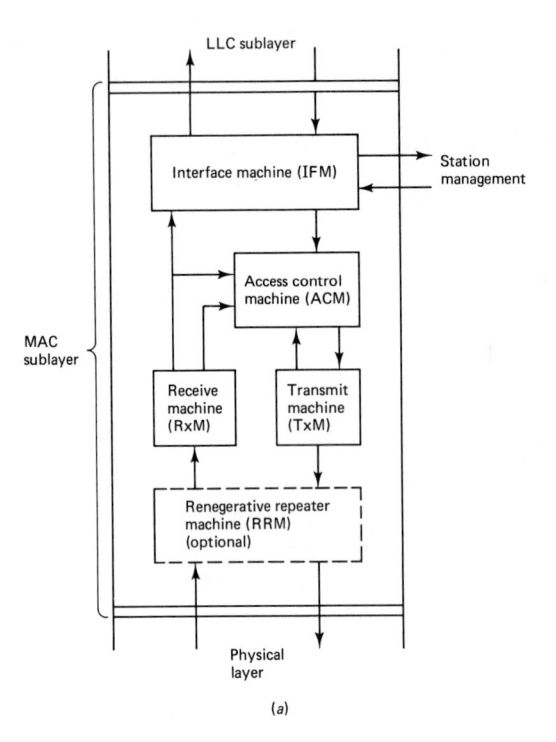

Figure 4.10 (a) Functional configuration of the MAC sublayer.

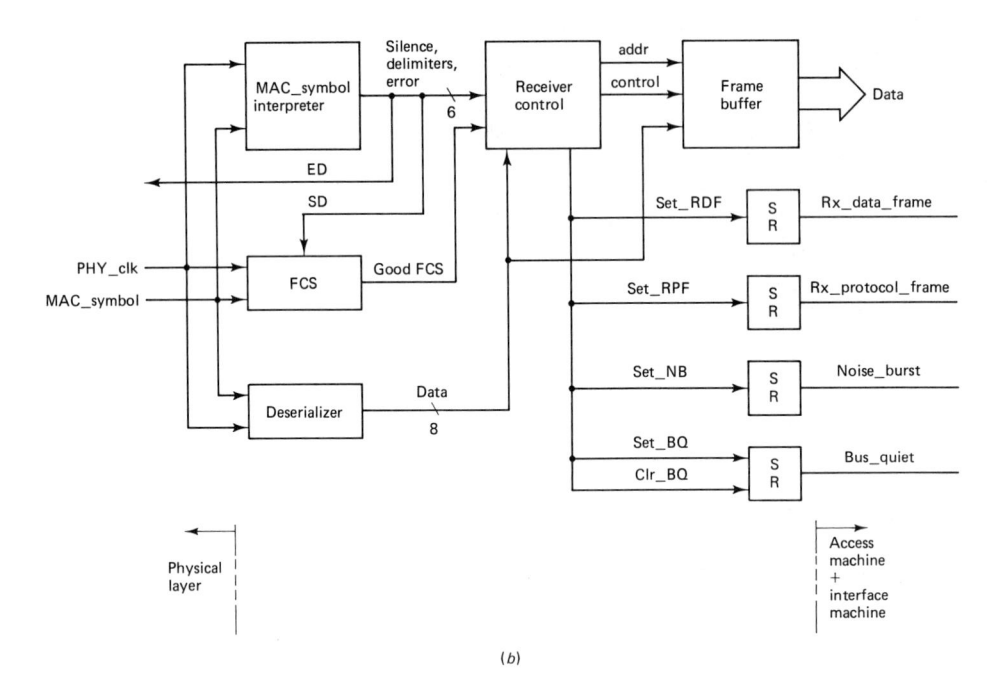

Figure 4.10 (b) Receive machine configuration.

Before discussing additional details of the token bus protocol, let us discuss the general structure of the data link layer of the IEEE 802 set of standards. The data link layer is divided into two sublayers, called the logical link control (LLC) and medium access control (MAC) sublayers. The major elements of the MAC sublayer are the *interface machine* (IFM), *access control machine* (ACM), *Receive Machine* (RxM), and *Transmit Machine* (TxM), as depicted in Figure 4.10(a).

The *interface machine* acts as an interface and buffer between (a) the LLC and MAC sublayers and (b) station management and the MAC sublayer. It interprets all incoming service primitives from the LLC sublayer and generates appropriate outgoing primitives. It handles the queueing of service requests and performs the *address recognition function*.

In order to perform the distributed token bus protocol, the *access control machine* cooperates with the ACM of all other stations in the logical ring. As an option, the MAC handles messages with priorities. The ACM is also responsible for initialization and maintenance of the logical ring, including admission of new stations, failure detection, and recovery, and handling other failures in the token bus network.

The *receive machine* accepts symbols from the physical layer, assembles them into frames, performs frame validation, and passes the frames to the ACM and IFM. The RxM accomplishes this by recognizing the delimiters for the start of a frame (i.e., the start delimiter, SD) and the end of a frame (i.e., the end delimiter, ED), checking the frame check sequence (FCS), and validating the frame structure. The RxM also identifies and indicates the reception of noise bursts, and bus quiet conditions. Details of the receive machine are shown in Figure 4.10(b).

Likewise, the transmit machine accepts a data frame from the ACM and transmits it as a sequence of symbols, in the proper format to the physical layer. The TxM builds a MAC protocol data unit by prefacing each frame with the required preamble and SD, and appending the FCS and ED.

In the rest of this section we concentrate on further details of the token bus protocol. As noted, the token bus protocol is performed by the access control machine. Accordingly, we discuss next the major characteristics of the MAC sublayer of the IEEE 802.4 specification. In Section 4.14, we discuss the service aspects of the IEEE 802.4 specification.

Access Control Machine (ACM)

As discussed, the basic idea of the token passing algorithm is very simple. However, to make it practical and robust, there are important requirements that the algorithm must meet. Some requirements are:

> fairness,
> bounded access delays,
> priority mechanisms,
> dynamic ring maintenance, and
> fault tolerance aspects.

We next consider each requirement in more detail and discuss how the token passing algorithm handles each requirement.

Fairness. A station should not monopolize the use of the shared channel. Without this requirement, a station having large amounts of data could transmit for hours without giving up the token. This is very good for the transmitting station, but very bad for the other stations in the logical ring which are waiting for their turn to transmit.

The token bus protocol resolves the fairness requirement by limiting the time a station can send messages (i.e., hold the token). Associated with each station, there is a special timer called the **token hold timer** for limiting how long the station can keep the token and thus transmit frames. Depending upon the value loaded in the *token hold timer*, two situations can happen after a station has started sending frames. The first situation involves the station completing the message transfer before the timer expires. In this case, the station simply passes the token to the next station in logical sequence. The second situation involves the station's timer expiring before the station completes the message transfer. In this case the station must pass the token and continue sending the remaining portion of the message the next time it receives the token. In this way, the protocol ensures that one station does not monopolize the use of the token.

Bounded access delays. Once a message is ready for transmission by the MAC sublayer, transmission should start within a calculable delay. The delay only involves accessing the medium and does not involve queueing delays.

Because the time taken by each station for transmission, per token rotation, is limited, the medium access delay is bounded. Assuming that no priority scheme is used, the maximum medium access delay is given by

$$W = N(THT + \omega) \qquad (4.3)$$

where N is the number of stations in the logical ring, THT is the token hold timer, and ω is the maximum time it takes the token to go from one station to the next. More accurate calculations are derived in Chapter 13.

Priority mechanisms. Some applications using the token bus scheme can have messages involving several degrees of priorities. For example, alarm messages should be sent before any other kind of message.

The IEEE 802.4 standard provides an optional priority mechanism. The priority of each frame is indicated when the LLC sublayer submits a data frame to be transmitted to the MAC sublayer. The MAC sublayer offers four levels of priority classes, called **access classes.** The access classes are named 0, 2, 4, and 6, with 6 corresponding to the highest priority and 0 to the lowest. We use the term *class H* to denote the highest priority class, and *class l* to denote any of the lower three priority classes. There is a separate queue for frames in each class to wait pending transmission. Any station not having the priority option transmits every data frame with the highest priority value. The objective of the priority scheme is to use the channel bandwidth to transmit the low priority frames when there is sufficient bandwidth available. Each access class acts as a virtual substation, in that the token is passed internally from the highest access class downward, through all access classes before being passed to the successor station.

The priority scheme works as follows: any station receiving the token initiates transmission of frames of the highest priority class in a time interval not exceeding some maximum value called the *high-priority token-hold time* (HPTHT). This high-priority token-hold time prevents any single station from monopolizing the network. After sending the high-priority frames, the station starts servicing the queue of the next access class. Each of the three lower access classes at a station is assigned a timer, called *target token-rotation time* TTRT (*l*). For these three access classes, the station measures the time it takes for the token to circulate around the logical ring. If the token returns to the queue in less than the target token-rotation time, the station is allowed to send frames of that particular access class until the corresponding target token-rotation timer has expired. If the target token-rotation timer has expired by the time the token returns, the station is not allowed to send further frames of that access class. The fraction of bandwidth that will be allocated to various classes is controlled by the target token-rotation time of each access class. The responsibility of setting these values lies with the station management.

Dynamic ring maintenance. Stations should be added or deleted from the logical ring on a dynamic basis without the need to shut down the network and initialize the network on an offline basis.

New stations are allowed to enter the logical ring in the following way: Periodically, each station invites stations having addresses between the *token holder station* and the *successor station* to enter the logical ring. The invitation is done by sending special messages, called **solicit successor frames,** indicating the range of addresses. Stations whose addresses fall within this range and wish to enter the logical ring respond to the special frame. If no station responds to the *solicit successor frame*, then no station having addresses in the specified range wants to enter the logical ring. When one station responds to the *solicit successor frame*, the inviting station modifies its pointers so that the responding station is inserted into the ring. There is the possibility that more than one station may respond to the *solicit successor frame* simultaneously. In this case, the inviting station uses a special algorithm to identify a single responder, which then is inserted into the logical ring.

Fault tolerant aspects. As much as possible, problems with one station should not affect the network. For example, a station with a bad receiver expecting the token should not prevent other stations from transmitting. Other aspects involve lost tokens, duplicated tokens, noisy transmitters, and so on. We consider each of these aspects in turn.

Station with Bad Receiver. As part of the protocol, once a station is finished sending frames, it sends the token to the next station in logical sequence and listens for activity on the channel just to be sure that the intended station received the token. The station that just sent the token listens for activity for four *slot times*.[4] After this period, if some activity is heard, the token-sending station assumes that everything is fine, and life goes on normally. However, if nothing is heard, the station sends the token one more time and listens for an additional period of four slot times, performing the same monitoring as in the first attempt. If the successor station does not respond to the second attempt, the sender assumes that the successor has a bad receiver (i.e., it is deaf) or has failed. The token-sending station then attempts to identify the station that follows the one that just failed. This is accomplished by sending a special frame, called *who follows frame*. If a station responds to the *who follows frame*, the token-sending station proceeds to modify its pointers so that the failed station is bypassed and the station responding to the *who follows frame* becomes the new successor. If no station responds to the *who follows frame*, the token holding station repeats the attempt one more time just in case, proceeding as in the first one.

If no station responds to the second *who follows frame*, the situation is turning sour for the token-holding station. By then, the token-holding station knows that its successor has probably failed, and that there is no other station following the successor station in the logical ring. The

---

[4] A slot time is defined as the maximum time any station need wait for an immediate-response from another station. It is roughly equal to twice the propagation delay plus twice the station delay plus some safety margin.

token-holding station begins to wonder as to what is going on. As a last attempt to find out what is really happening, the token-holding station tries to determine if there is any other station in the logical ring, by sending a special frame called a *solicit successor frame*.[5] If a station responds to this final attempt, the token-holding station sends the token to the responding station and the problem is resolved. The worst case is when no station responds to the last attempt. By now, the token-holding station is really confused. It does not know if all other stations have failed or left the ring, whether the medium is broken, or whether its own receiver has failed, since it cannot hear the activity from the other stations. Under these circumstances, the token-holding station gives up by becoming silent and listening for any activity on the channel.

Lost Tokens. Every station maintains a special timer, called the *bus idle timer*, for deciding when there is no activity of any kind on the network. While listening, when the *bus idle timer* for a station runs out, the station assumes that the token is lost, since the bus is idle for a period of time much longer than what is expected. When stations determine that the token has been lost, they cooperate in the execution of a special distributed algorithm for finding a single station which becomes the new token holder station.

Duplicated Token. When a token holding station hears activity on the network indicating that another station also has a token, it simply *drops* its own token by becoming silent and listening for other station's transmissions. By *dropping* the token we mean that the station stops transmitting (i.e., using its token) and it does not attempt to send the token to the next station in the logical ring. The worst that could happen is that the two stations drop their token at the same time, and thus there is no token. This situation is resolved using the *lost token* procedure discussed previously.

Noisy Transmitters. The token bus protocol explicitly takes into account the noisy nature of the transmission system, including noisy transmitters. A special boolean signal, called *noise burst*, is used to indicate reception of invalid frames caused by noise. When the *noise burst* signal is *set* during a frame reception, the frame is simply discarded.

A Simplified Token Bus Protocol. As specified in the IEEE 802.4 standard, the token bus protocol is quite complex. In order to illustrate some details of the protocol, we make use of a simplified version of the protocol as presented by Muralidhar and Pimentel (1987). As described previously, the token bus protocol is a complex protocol that has special features, such as concurrency, degradable performance, timeliness, and fault tolerance characteristics. The token bus protocol allows concurrency by permitting different stations on the network to proceed in parallel in performing their communication functions. The degradable aspect of the protocol allows, for example, stations with bad receivers to be bypassed by the token passing mechanism. The token bus protocol meets timeliness requirements by providing an upper bound to token rotation times. Finally, the protocol can tolerate such faults as token losses and noise bursts.

In order to arrive at our simplified version of the token bus protocol, we make the following simplifying assumptions:

STATE ASSUMPTIONS

1. The station under consideration is already in the logical ring. Thus, there are no new stations desiring entry into the logical ring.

[5] The parameters in this frame (solicit_successor) are different from those used for allowing new stations to enter the logical ring.

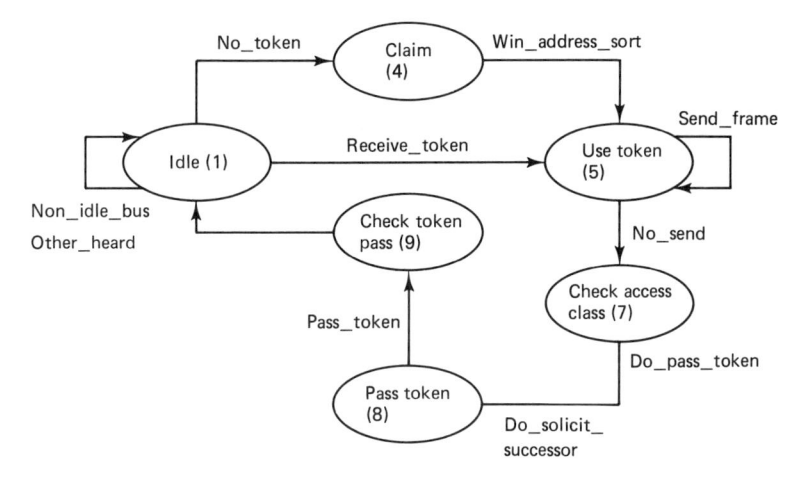

Figure 4.11 State transition diagram for a simplified token bus protocol. Numbers correspond to state numbers of the IEEE 802.4 protocol.

2. The station is up and operational. Thus, the protocol does not handle situations in which stations need to be powered and brought into an operational state from an *off-line* state.
3. All frames sent expect no acknowledgment. This is in accordance with one of the MAP network architectures (i.e., IEEE 802.4 with class I option).

OTHER ASSUMPTIONS

1. Only the highest priority class (class 6) is considered.
2. The station always knows its successor and its predecessor in the logical ring. In addition, it is also assumed that the token is passed only once, and that the next station in the logical ring gets the token the first time.

As a result of the previous assumptions, we need only 6 protocol states rather than 10 used by the IEEE specification. The simplified state transition diagram is shown in Figure 4.11, and the corresponding state transition table is given in Table 4.2. The numbers associated with each state (i.e., 1 with state IDLE) correspond to the numbers used by the IEEE specification.

A brief explanation of each state follows. A station is in the *idle* state when it is listening and not transmitting. The *claim token* state is entered from the idle state after the *bus_idle_timer* expires. In this state, the station attempts to initialize or reinitialize the logical ring by sending *claim_token frames*. When a station receives a token or wins a claim token procedure, it enters the *use token* state. This is the state in which a station can send data frames. The *check access class* state only serves to control entry to the pass token state.[6] The *pass token* state is the state in which a station attempts to pass the token to its successor. Stations wait in the *check token pass* state while making sure that the successor station received the token.

---
[6] In the IEEE 802.4 standard, the *check access class* state also controls the transmission of frames for different access classes.

TABLE 4.2 SIMPLIFIED ACM STATE TRANSITION TABLE SUMMARY

Present state	Transition name	Next state
1 IDLE	receive_token	5 USE_TOKEN
	non_idle_bus	1 IDLE
	no_token	4 CLAIM_TOKEN
	other_heard	1 IDLE
4 CLAIM_TOKEN	win_address_sort	5 USE_TOKEN
5 USE_TOKEN	send_frame	5 USE_TOKEN
	no_send	7 CHECK_ACCESS_CLASS
7 CHECK_ACCESS_CLASS	do_pass_token	8 PASS_TOKEN
	do_solicit_successor	8 PASS_TOKEN
8 PASS_TOKEN	pass_token	9 CHECK_TOKEN_PASS
9 CHECK_TOKEN_PASS	pass_ok	1 IDLE

The simplifed token bus protocol uses the following variables:

1. Rx_protocol_frame. A boolean variable indicating that a valid frame has been received, and that the frame type is one of the MAC protocol frame types.

2. Rx_data_frame. A boolean variable indicating that a valid frame has been received, and that the frame contains data rather than control information (e.g., a token).

3. Rx_frame. A record containing the most recently received valid frame. The record structure is shown in the ADA program at the end of this section.

4. Bus_quiet. A boolean variable set to TRUE whenever the physical layer detects no activity on the channel.

5. Noise_burst. A boolean variable indicating that something has been heard on the channel which is neither a Rx_protocol_frame nor a Rx_data_frame.

6. Pass_state. A two-state variable used for passing the token to the next station or offering entry to new stations with values *pass_token* and *solicit_successor*, respectively. Although our model assumes that no stations enter the logical ring, the simplified protocol nevertheless invites stations to join the logical ring (unsuccessfully).

7. Send_pending. A boolean variable set if there is a pending frame to be transmitted.

8. Inter_solicit_count. A counter indicating how often (in terms of the number of token rotations) a token holding station invites new stations to join the logical ring.

9. Bus_idle_timer. Controls how long a station listens in the IDLE state for any data on the channel before entering the CLAIM_TOKEN state and reinitializing the network.

10. Claim_timer. Controls how long a station listens before claiming the token and entering the USE_TOKEN state.

11. Token_pass_timer. Controls how long a station listens after passing the token to its successor.

12. Token_rotation_timer. Controls situations when a station invites other stations to join the ring. Since our model assumes just one class (i.e., the highest priority), this timer corresponds to the *ring_maintenance* class in the IEEE 802.4 specification.

13. Token_hold_timer. A station may send data frames as long as the *token_hold_timer* has not expired.

The first three timers are expressed in units of *slot_time*, whereas the last two are expressed in units of *octet_time*.[7]

We next present the section of an ADA program containing the specification and body sections of our simplified token bus protocol. Associated with a timer there is a procedure named *xx_timer.start(value)* and a boolean variable named *xx_timer.expired*, where *xx* is the timer name (e.g., *token_hold*) and *value* is an integer that sets the timer delay. The boolean variable has a value of FALSE while the timer is running, and TRUE when the timer has expired.

In addition, we assume the existence of two procedures for fetching a frame from the queue and for sending the frame to the physical layer for transmission, called respectively *get_pending_frame*, and *send*, declared in the ADA program below.

```
type bit_string is array (positive range <>) of boolean;
type t_address is integer range 0.. (2**48–1);
type t_frame_ctrl is bit_string(1..8);
type t_fcs is integer range 0.. (2**32–1);
type t_data_unit is
    record
            length: integer range 0..max_du_length;
            data: array (0..max_du_length) of data_octet;
    end record;
type t_pass_state is (solicit_successor, pass_token);
type t_Rx_frame is
    record
            FC : t_frame_ctrl;      — Frame control field
            DA : t_address;         — destination address field
            SA : t_address;         — source address field
            data_unit : t_data_unit; — data field
            FCS : t_fcs;            — frame chech sequence field
    end record;
procedure get_pending_frame (FC:      out t_frame_ctrl;
                             DA:      out t_address;
                             SA:      out t_address;
                             data_unit: out t_data_unit);

procedure send (FC: in t_frame_ctrl;
                DA: in t_address;
                SA: in t_address;
                data_unit: in t_data_unit);

Rx_frame : t_Rx_frame;
claim_timer.expired : boolean;
```

[7] An octet is defined as eight bits.

```
token_hold_timer.expired : boolean;
token_pass_timer.expired : boolean;
token_rotation_timer.expired : boolean;
bus_idle_timer.expired : boolean;
inter_solicit_count : integer range 0..max_inter_solicit_count;
noise_burst : boolean;
bus_quiet : boolean;
Rx_protocol_frame : boolean;
Rx_data_frame : boolean;
send_pending : boolean;
pass_state : t_pass_state;

((IDLE))      — receive_token transition
if Rx_protocol_frame and (Rx_frame.FC = token) then
    Rx_protocol_frame := FALSE;
    token_hold_timer.start(5000);    — start token hold timer
      goto USE_TOKEN;      — Go to USE_TOKEN state
endif;

((IDLE))       — non_idle_bus transition
if noise_burst then
    noise_burst := FALSE;
    bus_idle_timer.start (40);   — start bus idle timer
      goto IDLE  ;       — Go to IDLE state
endif;

((IDLE))       — no_token transition
if send_pending and bus_idle_timer.expired
    and not (Rx_protocol_frame or Rx_data_frame or noise_burst)
    and bus_quiet then
    claim_timer.start (2);   — start claim timer
    goto CLAIM_TOKEN;       — Go to CLAIM_TOKEN state
endif;

((IDLE))       – other_heard transition
if Rx_data_frame or Rx_protocol_frame
    and not (Rx_frame.FC = token) then
    Rx_protocol_frame := FALSE;
    Rx_data_frame := FALSE;
    bus_idle_timer.start (40);    — start bus idle timer
      goto IDLE  ;       — Go to IDLE state
endif;

((CLAIM_TOKEN))         — win_address_sort transition
if claim_timer.expired and bus_quiet then
    token_hold_timer.start (5000);
    token_rotation_timer.start (500000);
    inter_solicit_count := 0;
      goto USE_TOKEN   ;       — Go to USE_TOKEN state
endif;
```

```
((USE_TOKEN))           — send_frame transition
if send_pending  and not token_hold_timer.expired then
    get_pending_frame (..)    — fetch frame from queue
    send (..)                 — send frame to physical layer
    goto USE_TOKEN ;          — Go to USE_TOKEN state
endif;

((USE TOKEN))           — no_send transition
if not send_pending or token_hold_timer.expired then
    goto CHECK_ACCESS_CLASS ;  — Go to CHECK_ACCESS_CLASS state
endif;

((CHECK_ACCESS_CLASS))         — do_pass_token transition
if token_rotation_timer.expired or (inter_solicit_count > 0) then
    pass_state := pass_token;
    token_rotation_timer.start (500000);
    inter_solicit_count = max(inter_solicit_count − 1, 0);
    goto PASS_TOKEN ;         — Go to PASS_TOKEN  state
endif;

((CHECK_ACCESS_CLASS))          — do_solicit_successor transition
if not token_rotation_timer.expired and (inter_solicit_count = 0)
then
    pass_state := solicit_successor;
    token_rotation_timer.start (500000);
    goto PASS_TOKEN ;         — Go to PASS_TOKEN  state
endif;

((PASS_TOKEN))          — pass_token transition
if pass_state = pass_token then
    noise_burst := FALSE;
    token_pass_timer.start(4);
    Rx_protocol_frame := FALSE;
    goto CHECK_TOKEN_PASS  ;  — Go to CHECK_TOKEN_PASS state
endif;
((CHECK_TOKEN_PASS))           — pass_ok transition
if Rx_data_frame or Rx_protocol_frame then
    goto IDLE   ;             — Go to IDLE    state
endif;
```

4.9 RANDOM ACCESS SCHEMES

In this section, we concentrate primarily on the major random schemes that have been developed for accessing a shared channel. The schemes to be discussed are: ALOHA, Slotted ALOHA, Carrier Sense Multiple Access (CSMA), and Carrier Sense Multiple Access with Collision Detection (CSMA/CD).

4.9.1 The ALOHA Random Access Scheme

The ALOHA scheme is one of the simplest of the random access schemes, incorporating a limited form of distributed control that effectively allows every station to operate independently of the others. When compared to other random access schemes, such as CSMA and CSMA/CD, the ALOHA scheme is the least civilized. Whenever a station has a message to send, it just sends it regardless of whether other stations are doing so. Thus, the station does not even bother to check if other stations are using the shared channel before starting to transmit. This is similar to a person talking regardless of whether other persons are talking, assuming that all persons can hear one another.

Although ALOHA is generally not used with local networks, we discuss it because it serves as the basis for other important random schemes. We assume that each station is coupled to a simple passive channel, such as one provided by a coaxial cable, as shown in Figure 4.9.

The ALOHA scheme is quite simple and can be summarized by the following rules:

1. When a station has any frames to transmit, it does so immediately, starts a timer, and waits for an acknowledgment.
2. If the acknowledgment for the frame just sent is not received before the timer expires, the station waits a random amount of time and retransmits the frame.

When stations have no frames to send, of course nothing happens. However, when stations have frames to send, two situations arise. The first situation occurs when only one station transmits in a given time interval. In this case, the frames are received without error at the receiving station, which then responds with an acknowledgment, often over a separate channel. Thus, this situation results in a successful transmission.

The second situation involves two or more stations transmitting so that their frames overlap in time, causing interference and errors in the overlapping frames. Since the frames are in error, no acknowledgments are sent by the receiving stations. After an appropriate time-out, which is at least the maximum two-way propagation time on the cable, the original transmitting stations conclude that a collision has occurred and schedule retransmissions of the frames at later times. To avoid repeat collisions of the collided frames, the retransmission times are usually chosen at random by the stations involved.

As noted earlier, ALOHA is seldom used for local networks. However, a number of practical access schemes in current use for local networks have been derived from the ALOHA method. For example, to improve operating characteristics, other schemes to be discussed later use some form of synchronization and/or the ability to realize if other stations are transmitting. To distinguish the basic ALOHA procedure from these other networks, it is often referred to as *pure ALOHA*.

4.9.2 Slotted ALOHA

In the pure ALOHA scheme, once a frame is transmitted, a collision will occur if at least one additional frame arrives for transmission at any station within 2 X/R secs after a transmission has started where X is the frame size and R the data rate. The maximum utilization of the ALOHA scheme is about 18 percent. The slotted ALOHA scheme attempts to reduce the collision interval 2 X/R by segmenting time into slots of a fixed length, m = X/R. Frame transmission is synchronized so that each transmission starts at the beginning of each slot. In this way, the collision interval

2 X/R is reduced by half to X/R. Consequently, the efficiency of the slotted ALOHA is about 36 percent, which is twice that of the pure ALOHA.

To accomplish synchronization, a frame arriving to be transmitted at any given station must be delayed until the beginning of the next slot. Recall that for pure ALOHA, a frame transmission can begin at any time. Clearly, slotted ALOHA requires additional overhead to provide the synchronization required between different stations in the network. Like the pure ALOHA scheme, slotted ALOHA is not generally used with LANs; we nevertheless explain the slotted ALOHA scheme in the context of a LAN with a shared bus, as shown in Figure 4.9.

As already noted, the rules for the slotted ALOHA are similar to that of the pure ALOHA. More specifically, the rules are:

1. When a station has any frames to transmit, it waits until the beginning of the next slot and transmits immediately. After transmission, the station starts a timer and waits for an acknowledgment.
2. If an acknowledgment for the frame just sent is not received before the timer expires, the station waits a random amount of time and retransmits the frame according to rule 1.

Notice that the second rule is the same in the pure and slotted ALOHA schemes. A station having frames to transmit can be in one of two states: transmitting or backed-off. In the transmitting state, a frame is delivered in a time m = X/R. The backed-off state results after a collision. Rescheduling collided frames after a random delay avoids further collisions.

One method for rescheduling collided frames is to select an integer, k, from 0, 1, 2, . . . , K − 1, under the condition that the selection of each integer is equally likely with a probability 1/K (i.e., a discrete uniform distribution). The backoff time for a chosen integer, k, is then set at k *frame times* or km seconds.

As in the pure ALOHA case, after a frame is transmitted, two situations can arise: The first situation occurs when the frame is successfully received (i.e., a collision does not occur) by the receiver, which then sends a positive acknowledgment.[8] The second situation involves a collision and causes the transmitter's timer to run out, since no acknowledgment is received. The sending station then selects a backoff time for retransmitting the frame and remains backed off, or in a waiting state, until the frame is retransmitted. A frame scheduled for retransmission is handled just like a new frame. A diagram for the slotted ALOHA access process is given in Figure 4.12. Because of their operation, ALOHA techniques are nicknamed *send and pray* schemes.

4.9.3 Carrier Sense Multiple Access (CSMA)

ALOHA schemes are inefficient, because under these schemes stations do not bother to determine if other stations are transmitting before they start doing so. Transmitting when the channel is used by other stations is wasteful and surely leads to collisions. An obvious improvement is for a station to refrain from transmitting if the station can determine when other stations are doing so. ALOHA-like schemes that sense whether the channel is busy before transmitting are called **carrier sense multiple access** (CSMA) schemes. The reason for the name *carrier sense* is that sensing whether the channel is busy is similar to sensing the presence of a carrier[9] signal on the channel.

---

[8] Assumed to be transmitted over an error-free channel.

[9] When information is modulated onto the carrier.

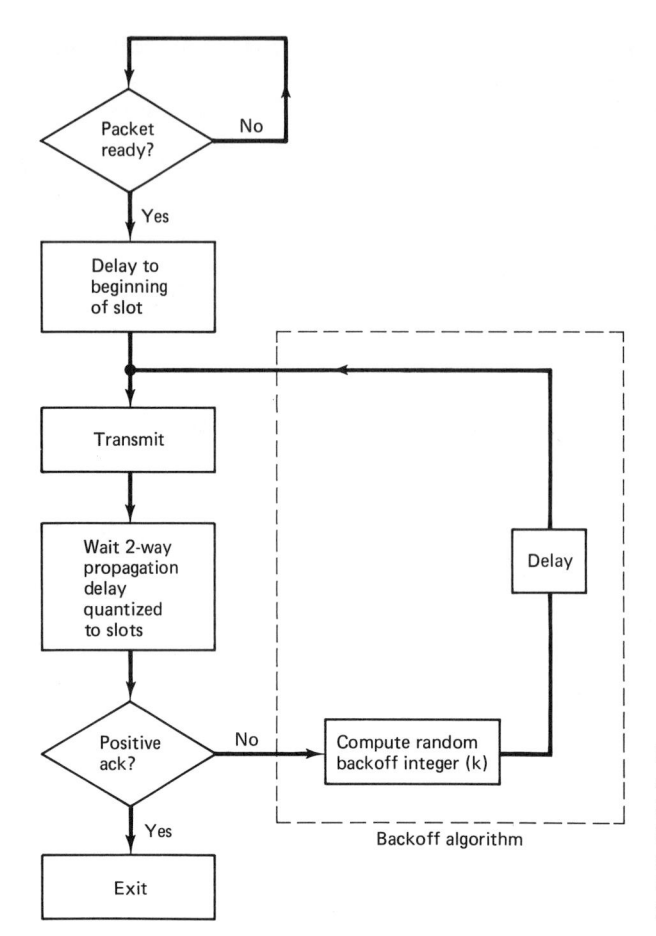

Figure 4.12 Flow diagram for the slotted ALOHA access scheme. Adapted from Figure 9.5 with permission from Hammond/O'Reilly, *Performance Analysis for Local Computer Networks*, © 1986, Addison-Wesley Publishing Co., Inc., Reading, Massachusetts. Reprinted with permission.)

Thus, CSMA schemes are more civilized than ALOHA schemes, in that CSMA schemes listen for activity on the channel before transmitting. For this reason, CSMA schemes are also known as **listen before transmitting** (LBT) schemes.

Although there are several CSMA schemes, their general behavior can be characterized by the following rules:

1. When a station has any frames to transmit it *listens* (i.e., senses the channel) to determine if other stations are doing so.
2. a) If no other station is transmitting (i.e., the channel is idle), the station transmits immediately, starts a timer, and waits for an acknowledgment.
   b) If other stations are transmitting (i.e., the channel is busy), the station waits a random amount of time and goes to step 1.
3. If an acknowledgment for the frame just sent is not received before the timer expires, the station waits a random amount of time and retransmits the frame.

As previously noted, CSMA protocols are refinements of the pure and slotted ALOHA protocols. By listening before transmitting, there are less collisions as compared with the ALOHA schemes. However, these advantages do not come without a disadvantage. In order for CSMA schemes to work, the frame length X in bits must be greater than a minimum value, which is calculated as follows. Assume that a network contains many stations, with stations A and B located furthest away from one another. After station A sends a frame, it takes T_{prop} sec to reach station B, where T_{prop} is the end-to-end propagation delay. The worst situation occurs when B senses the channel just before the frame arrives, and thus B starts transmitting, causing a collision almost immediately. The collision takes another T_{prop} sec to reach station A. Thus, it takes up to 2 T_{prop} sec for the collision to reach any station on the network. The frame transmission interval m = X/R has to be greater than 2 T_{prop}, otherwise the collision in question could be interpreted as a collision with other stations and not with the station which just sent the frame. The constraint on the frame length is then X/R > 2 T_{prop}, or

$$X \geq 2.R.T_{prop} \quad (4.4)$$

The term $2T_{prop}$ is also referred to as **channel slot time** (CST). Thus,

$$X \geq R.CST \quad (4.5)$$

CSMA schemes have most of the characteristics of slotted ALOHA, with additional improvements made on the basis of the carrier-sense information. Depending upon how the carrier-sense information is used, we distinguish two general classes of CSMA protocols: *nonpersistent* and *p-persistent*. Operation for each of these classes can be *slotted* or *nonslotted*.

Slotted CSMA schemes quantize time into *slots* of at least 2 T_{prop} seconds. Like the slotted ALOHA, all stations in a slotted CSMA network must synchronize by starting transmission only at the beginning of a slot.

Persistent and nonpersistent CSMA protocols. As with other contention type schemes, networks based on CSMA protocols are based on a bus topology, as depicted in Figure 4.9. The bus interface unit (BIU) contains hardware to perform the carrier sense function (i.e., listening before talking).

Since the operation of ALOHA type and CSMA type schemes are somewhat similar, the several CSMA protocols can be described with the flow chart of Figure 4.13, which is an extension of that given in Figure 4.12 for slotted ALOHA, including a **carrier-sense strategy** box. The dashed delay box is included for slotted operation, along with a quantization of all variables to slots. In particular, Figure 4.13 becomes Figure 4.12 for slotted ALOHA if the carrier-sense box is replaced by the direct connection shown in the figure, and if slotting to frame transmission times is used.

Whereas the major difference between CSMA and ALOHA schemes is that the former is able to make decisions based on carrier sensing, the several CSMA schemes differ from one another in how the decisions are made. In all cases, as Figure 4.13 shows, after detecting a collision, the station reschedules the transmission of the frame to a later time by using some specified backoff algorithm. After the backoff, the station again senses the channel and repeats the algorithm. A **ready station** is one that has a frame ready for transmission regardless of whether the frame is new (just generated) or a retransmission.

We discuss *nonpersistent CSMA* first using the appropriate carrier-sense box in Figure 4.13. Since a frame is always rescheduled upon finding the channel busy, interference between frame

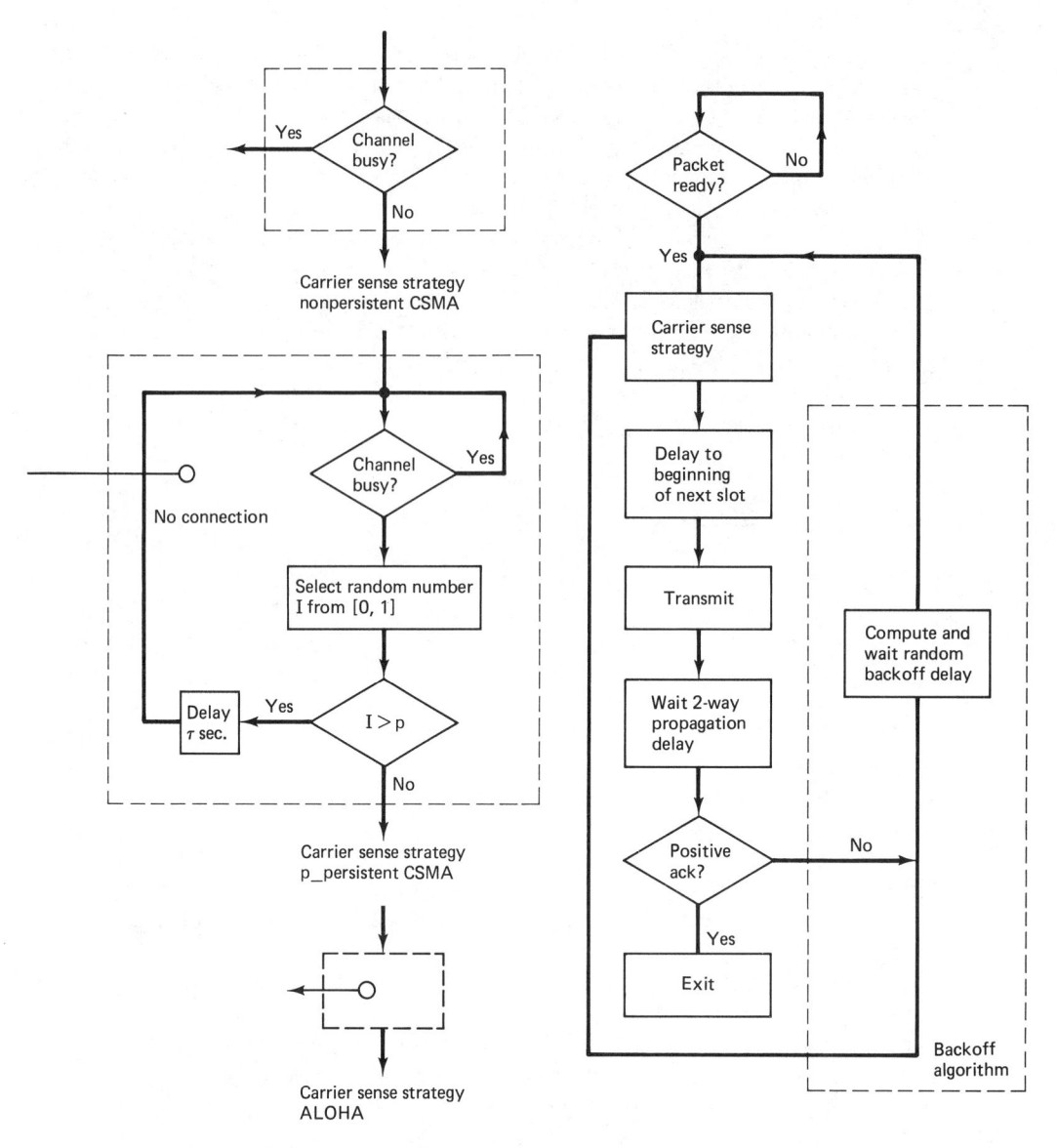

Figure 4.13 Flow diagrams for CSMA random access schemes. Adapted from Figure 9.14 with permission from Hammond/O'Reilly, *Performance Analysis for Local Computer Networks*, © 1986, Addison-Wesley Publishing Co., Inc., Reading, Massachusetts. Reprinted with permission.)

transmissions is minimized. When a station has a frame to transmit, the channel is sensed, and the following algorithm is carried out:

1. If the channel is idle, the frame is transmitted.
2. If the channel is busy, the station uses the backoff algorithm to reschedule the frame to a later time. After the backoff, the channel is sensed again, and the algorithm is repeated.

176   The Data Link Layer   Chap. 4

P-persistent CSMA. First, let us consider a special case of the p-persistent CSMA protocol with p = 1, as depicted in the appropriate carrier-sense strategy in Figure 4.13. Under the 1-persistent scheme, a station always uses the channel when it is sensed idle. After the station senses the channel, the following rules are applied;

1. If the channel is idle, the frame is transmitted (in the flow chart of Figure 4.13, the random number selected is always between 0 and 1, and the test always results in **YES**).
2. If the channel is busy, the station continues sensing the channel (i.e., persists) until the channel goes idle, and then it transmits the frame (again with probability 1).

We now consider the general case of p-persistent CSMA. An advantage of making p less than 1 is to reduce the number of collisions in the following way: When two (or more) stations become ready during a busy interval, with 1-persistent CSMA, they all wait until the end of the transmission in progress; when it ends, all transmit, thus causing a collision. By reducing p to a value less than 1, the probability of such a collision occurring is reduced.

For general p-persistent operation, a ready station operates as follows after the channel is sensed:

1. If the channel is idle, then with probability p the station transmits the frame, or with probability (1 − p) the station waits t seconds, where t is the end-to-end propagation delay on the bus, and the algorithm is repeated.
2. If the channel is busy, then the station persists in sensing the channel until it becomes idle, and then it operates as in step 1.

As noted, slotted versions of all the preceding schemes can be obtained by quantizing time into slots of length 2 X/R seconds by synchronizing stations so that transmission can begin only at the start of a slot.

4.9.4 Carrier Sense Multiple Access with Collision Detection (CSMA/CD)

Although CSMA schemes are much more efficient than ALOHA schemes, they are still not good enough. Consider the following scenario involving many stations: After sensing an idle channel, station A sends its frame, which takes some time $t \leq T_{prop}$ to reach station B. Further assume that station B senses the channel just before the arrival of the frame sent by A. According to the CSMA scheme, station B proceeds to send its frame, which will collide with the one coming from A almost immediately. Of course, the associated timers at both stations will expire, causing both frames to be retransmitted. What is needed is a way for a station that just sent a frame to continue sensing the channel, *just in case* there is a collision similar to the one just described. If a collision is detected, it is counterproductive to finish sending the remainder of the frame. CSMA schemes that continue sensing the channel after transmission are known as **Carrier Sense Multiple Access with Collision Detection** (CSMA/CD). Thus, CSMA/CD schemes not only *listen before transmitting* (LBT) like CSMA, but also *listen while transmitting* (LWT) to further decrease the probability of collision.

Networks based on CSMA/CD schemes are also based on a bus topology, as shown in Figure 4.9. To implement the additional feature of collision detection, the transceiver must include hardware not only for monitoring the channel before transmitting, but also for monitoring while transmitting. In a baseband system, for example, the collision detection circuitry observes the signal waveform directly from the medium. Thus, when signals from two or more stations are present simultaneously, the composite waveform is distorted from that for a single station in such a manner that collisions can usually be identified by larger than normal voltage amplitudes on the cable.

Since CSMA/CD schemes are basically CSMA schemes with the *listen while talking* feature, CSMA/CD schemes can also have the same variations as CSMA: *slotted* and *unslotted*, and *nonpersistent* and *p-persistent*. For all these variations, the additional feature of collision detection gives improved performance.

The following rules describe the general features of CSMA/CD schemes (as will be shown in Chapter 13, the performance of CSMA/CD schemes in terms of throughput is superior to those of other types of random access schemes):

1. When a station has any frames to transmit, it *listens* (i.e., senses the channel to determine if other stations are doing so.

2. If other stations are transmitting (i.e., the channel is busy), the station waits a random amount of time and goes to step 1.

3. a) If no other station is transmitting (i.e., the channel is idle), the station transmitts immediately, starts a timer, and waits for an acknowledgment.

b) After the station has started transmitting, it continues listening to the channel (listen while talking). If a collision is detected, the transmission is aborted and the station transmits a brief *jamming signal*. The jamming signal ensures that all other stations are aware of the collision. The stations of all colliding frames then abort their transmission, wait a random amount of time, and go to step 1.

4. If an acknowledgment for the frame just sent is not received before the timer expires, the station waits a random amount of time and retransmits the frame.

We describe next the basic CSMA/CD operation in terms of Figure 4.14, including refinements such as collision consensus reinforcement and dynamic backoff schemes. Figure 4.14(a) shows the algorithm for CSMA, discussed in subsection 4.9.3. The *listen while transmitting* feature of the CSMA/CD scheme is illustrated in Figure 4.14(b).

As Figure 4.14 shows, the logic of the algorithm is the same as that of CSMA through the transmit operation. After the frame is transmitted, CSMA/CD employs hardware to listen while the transmitted frame is in transit over the medium. If no collisions are detected, the frame is successfully transmitted, and the algorithm is exited. On the other hand, if a collision is detected, transmission is immediately aborted, a *jamming signal* is transmitted, and the collided frame is backed off in the same manner as for CSMA. Whereas CSMA requires an acknowledgment indicating that the frame transmission was successful, CSMA/CD does not require such feedback, because by monitoring the channel after transmission (i.e., listening while talking) a station can ensure that the transmission was successful.

Under the CSMA/CD scheme, stations with messages to transmit use the following rules after sensing the channel:

1. If the channel is sensed idle:

a) For nonpersistent and 1-persistent CSMA/CD, the frame is transmitted immediately.

b) For p-persistent CSMA/CD, the frame is transmitted with probability p, and is delayed by the end-to-end propagation delay, t seconds, with probability $(1 - p)$.

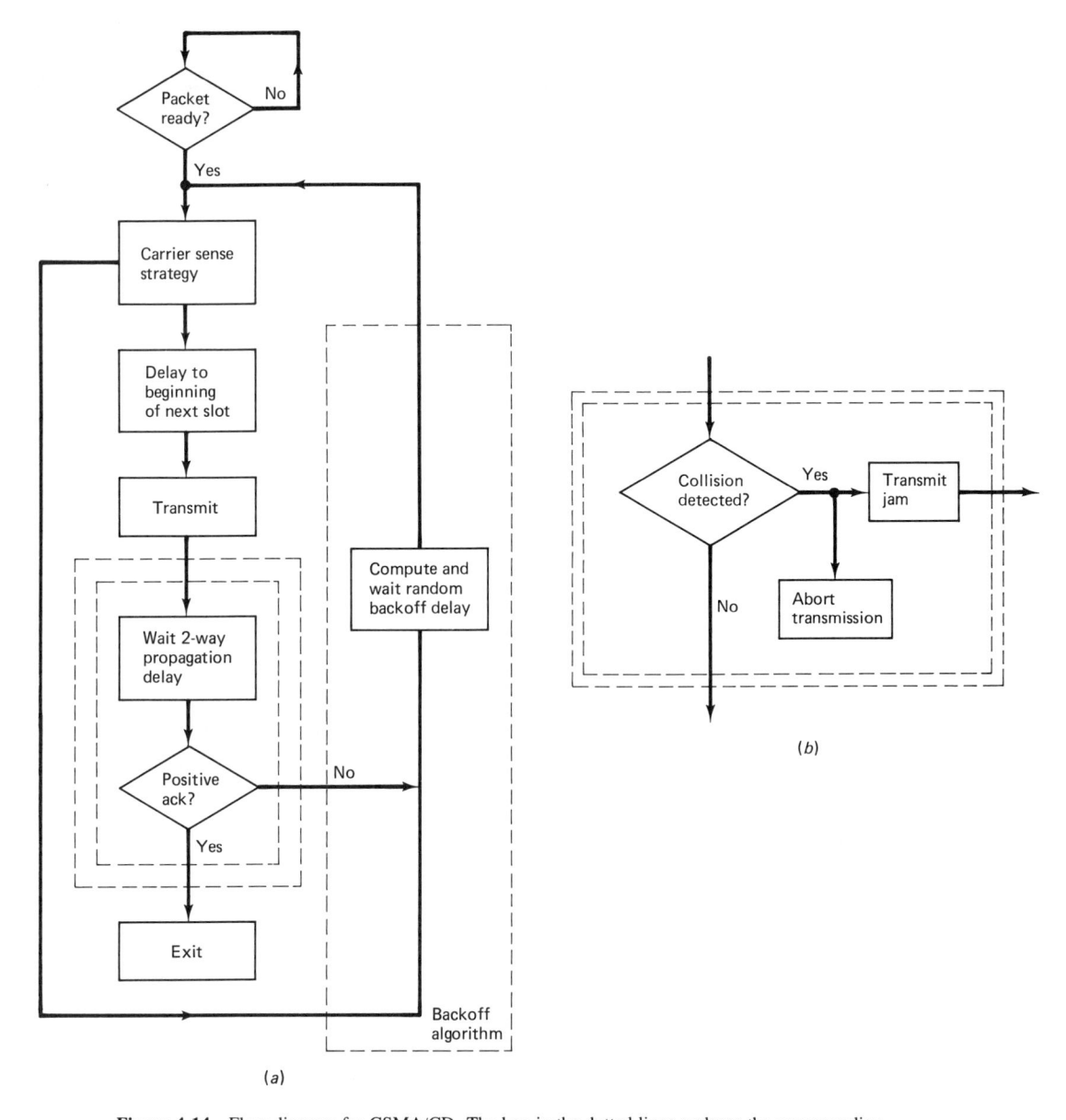

Figure 4.14 Flow diagram for CSMA/CD. The box in the dotted lines replaces the corresponding box for CSMA. The carrier sense options are the same for CSMA as in Figure 4.13(a) CSMA operation. (Adapted from Figure 9.24 with permission from Hammond/O'Reilly, *Performance Analysis for Local Computer Networks*, © 1986, Addison-Wesley Publishing Co., Inc., Reading, Massachusetts. Reprinted with permission.)

Sec. 4.9 Random Access Schemes

2. If the channel is busy, then:

a) For nonpersistent CSMA/CD, the channel is backed off and the algorithm is repeated;
b) For 1-persistent CSMA/CD, the station defers until the channel is sensed idle and then transmits a frame;
c) For p-persistent CSMA/CD, the station defers until the channel is idle and then, with probability p, transmits a frame, and with probability (1 − p) delays transmission by t seconds. In the latter case, after the t seconds delay, the procedure is repeated.

3. If a collision is sensed, the station aborts the frame being transmitted and transmits a jamming signal. The stations of all colliding frames then abort their transmission and back off.

4. At the time a backed off frame is to be retransmitted, the algorithm is repeated.

Although the jamming signal is not an essential feature of CSMA/CD, it is used by common implementations such as Ethernet.

Some commercial CSMA/CD networks favor the 1-persistent CSMA/CD protocol, using a backoff algorithm such as that used by Ethernet. The Ethernet backoff algorithm is called a *truncated binary exponential backoff algorithm*, with one version allowing an initial attempt plus 15 retransmissions, each delayed by an integer r times the base backoff time. The integer r is selected randomly from a discrete uniform distribution on the range $\{0, \ldots, 2^{k-1}\}$, where k is the minimum of the number of current attempted transmissions and the integer 10. After 16 attempts, the frame is discarded. The base backoff time is tyically 2P, where P is the end-to-end propagation delay.

Since the distribution from which the backoff time is selected changes with the number of collisions, the backoff algorithm described previously is an example of a dynamic backoff strategy. The term *linear incremental backoff* is sometimes used to identify any dynamic backoff strategy for which the mean backoff time is linearly proportional to the number of collisions experienced by a particular frame.

4.9.5 Deterministic CSMA/CD

One characteristic of random access schemes is that maximum values of performance variables of interest (i.e., response time) cannot be predicted in advance. As discussed in detail in Chapter 13, random access schemes exhibit good performance at low loads; however, at high loads their performance deteriorates. Recently, there have been several proposals for modifying the CSMA/CD scheme so that at low loads it retains its random behavior and at high loads it behaves in a deterministic fashion. One advantage of the deterministic behavior at high loads is that maximum values of performance values can still be predicted. In this subsection we discuss one of the proposals for a deterministic CSMA/CD, referred to as CSMA-DCR (Boudenant et al, 1987).

CSMA-DCR is one example of an *adaptive assignment* scheme, as discussed in subsection 4.7.2. The acronym DCR stands for Deterministic Collision Resolution. The CSMA-DCR is currently being evaluated experimentally as part of a network called LYNX at INRIA in France.

Briefly, we describe the CSMA-DCR protocol as follows: The CSMA-DCR protocol is a special case of the IEEE 802.3 standard, with which it is fully compatible at the physical layer and at the LLC sublayer. It can be implemented either by replacing the *Binary Exponential Backoff* (BEB) algorithm on an existing VLSI circuit or via an additional hardwired controller that disables the BEB algorithm. Basically, the DCR is not only compatible with the 802.3 standard, but also adds value to it. Although available 802.3 protocols and DCR protocols can coexist within the same network, the deterministic properties of the DCR protocol cannot be guaranteed.

In the absence of collisions, the channel is randomly accessed, just like CSMA/CD. The determinisic scheme acts only when a collision occurs, opening a time interval called an **epoch.** There is no privileged station. When a collision occurs, there are two modes of operation: *general* and *periodic*. In the *general* mode, all messages involved in the initial collision are transmitted during an *epoch*, while other messages may be deferred until the end of the epoch. This guarantees a bounded delay to transmit any message. The periodic mode is equivalent to a TDMA[10] protocol.

The collision resolution scheme is based on a tree, as shown in Figure 4.15. Every station is assigned a unique and private name which is used to make a local decision when a collision occurs. After every collision, the entire branch of the tree containing loosers stops transmitting until winners transmit their messages successfully. A branch is completely analyzed when a message is transmitted successfully on the channel or when an *idle slot time* (*ist*) is observed. The slot time is the unit for collision handling as defined in the IEEE 802.3 protocol.

Figure 4.15 depicts the resolution of a collision with seven messages. After the initial collision, the stations belonging to the lower part of the tree lose by a self-elimination process. Stations in the upper part of the tree continue to resolve the collisions. Since there is more than one message, a new collision occurs and the lower branch of the remaining subtree loses. Three messages remain in the winner branch where a new collision occurs. Since stations 3 and 4 lose, the message from station 1 is successfully transmitted. The most recently eliminated subtrees try to transmit again causing stations 3 and 4 to collide, after which messages from 3 and 4 are sequentially transmitted. The most recently eliminated subtree now contains stations 5 to 8, with stations 5 and 6 having no message to transmit. This leads to a new collision, and stations 7 and 8 lose. A channel idle slot time can be observed, informing all other stations that this subtree has been fully analyzed. The resolution scheme continues until the complete tree is analyzed. As already noted, the protocol accepts two different modes: a general and a periodic mode, which are described next.

General mode. Under the general mode, two compatible options within the same network are available: blocked-entry and free-entry. Whereas the blocked-entry option does not accept new messages after the beginning of an epoch, free-entry does accept messages after the epoch has begun. The latter option reduces the maximum delay to transmit a message. Moreover, the general mode can accept a predefined number of static priorities with high priority messages transmitted first during an epoch.

Protocol performance in the worst case situation is as follows: Let N be the number of stations and T_m the longest message transmission duration. Let T_s be the slot time duration, which is a function of the bus length. The maximum duration of an epoch is $(N-1)T_s + NT_m$.

According to the IEEE 802.3 standard, the worst case values are $T_s = 50$ μs, m = 1518 bytes and $T_m = m/R$, where R = 10 Mbps (IEEE 802.3). For 64 stations, the worst case epoch duration would be equal to 80.9 ms, corresponding to 64 successfully transmitted messages.

For the LYNX prototype, the maximum message length m is 1024 bytes, R = 2 Mbps, and with the HDLC[11] bit-stuffing used the maximum message duration T_m is 5.3 ms. The slot time, T_s, is fixed at 120 μ sec. The worst case epoch duration for 64 stations is 346.88 ms, where measurements are made in the blocked-entry mode.

[10] Time Division Multiple Access.
[11] High Level Data Link Control, a forerunner of the IEEE data link layer protocols.

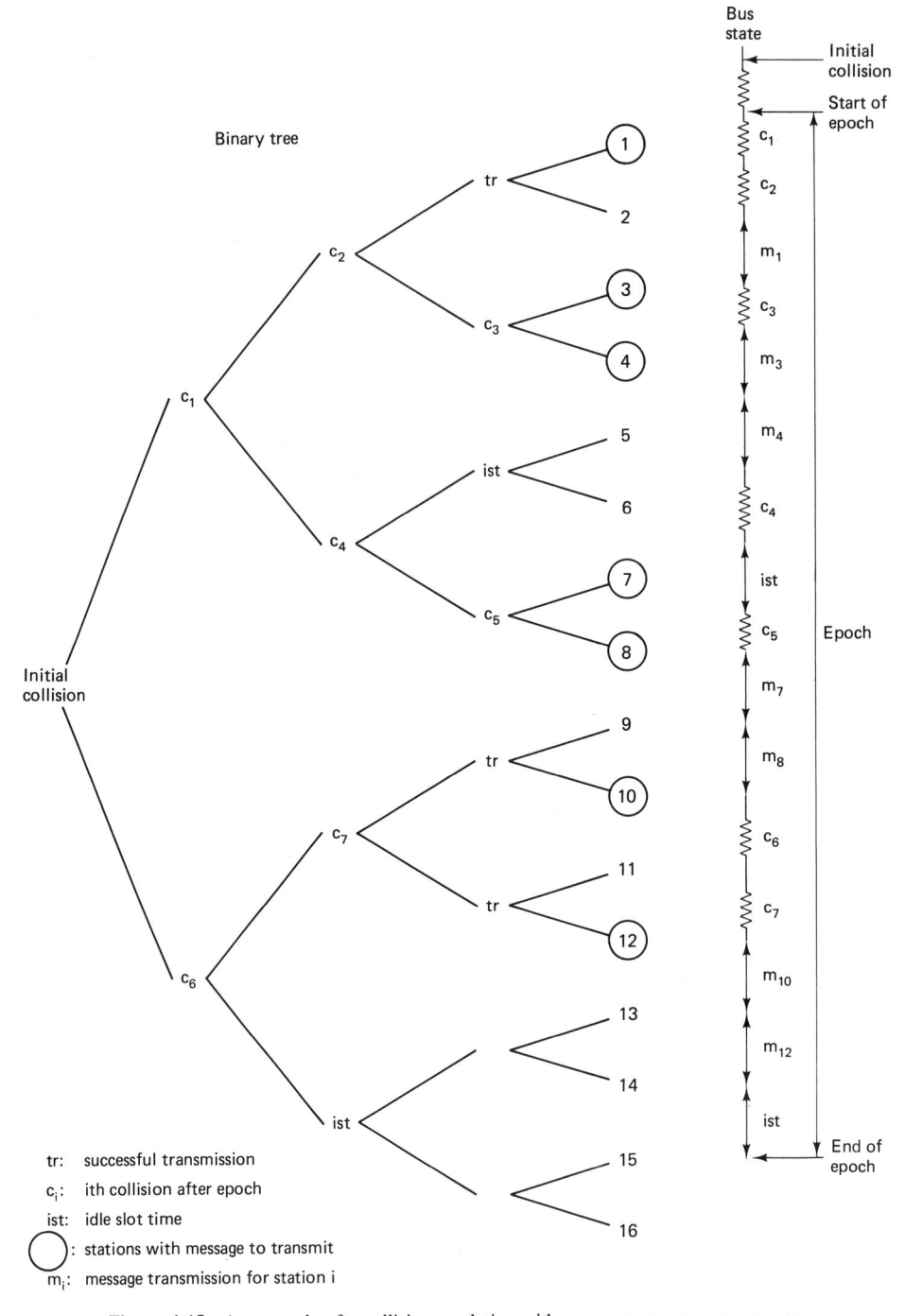

Figure 4.15 An example of a collision resolution with messages m_1, m_3, m_4, m_7, m_8, m_{10}, and m_{12} in the epoch.

182   The Data Link Layer   Chap. 4

On the average, the response time for any message will be shorter than the worst case value. For a 100 percent channel utilization, *epoch* duration is a linear function of the message length. If, for a specific application, the message length never exceeds the worst message allowed on a CSMA/CD LAN, then the maximum epoch duration is reduced to $(2N - 1) T_s$.

Periodic mode. At high loads, the periodic mode is better adapted because only the time due to the initial collision is lost. The periodic mode is equivalent to a TDMA protocol synchronized by the initial collision. The maximum epoch duration is then reduced to $N T_m + T_s$ with a minimum value $= (N + 1) T_s$.

Throughput considerations. At high loads, where the periodic mode is optimal, the general mode is less efficient. The worst case occurs when messages are short (i.e., $T_m = T_s$). Then the throughput in the general mode is restricted to R/2 where R is the data rate. In the general case, $(T_m \geq T_s)$, the throughput is $R.T_m/(T_s + T_m)$; thus, from the throughput point of view, it is better to send long messages.

4.10 TOKEN RING PROTOCOL

Using our classification of Section 4.7, the token ring protocol belongs to the category of decentral polling, actively coupled. The general structure of a ring network was shown in Figure 1.4, with the *ring interface processor* (RIP) depicted in Figure 1.5. A specific example of a ring network is shown in Figure 4.8. One of the main examples of a ring network is the one developed by IBM and referred to as the *token ring network*. In this section, we discuss ring networks in general and concentrate on the *token ring protocol*. Another well-known ring network is the Cambridge ring.

The token ring protocol is somewhat similar to the token bus protocol, with the exception that the token ring protocol is based on a physical ring rather than on a physical bus. Although, strictly speaking, ring networks are point-to-point, because of the special configuration of the ring interface processors (RIP), they have many of the properties of broadcast networks. More specifically, the delay Q/R associated with the RIP is comparable to the propagation delay L/v on the medium, where Q is the number of bits in the shift register (see Figure 1.4), R is the data rate, L is the station to station medium length, and v is the propagation velocity. Thus, shared channel access schemes are also applicable to ring networks.

Another RIP configuration is depicted in Figure 4.16(a), which includes a line driver and a receiver for coupling to the ring, and appropriate transmitter and receiver for communicating with the station. Operation of the ring interface processor is controlled by a controller, as shown in the figure. Bits from the ring enter the RIP in one direction in a serial fashion, are read by the interface, and then, after a delay of several bits, are retransmitted over the ring unchanged or after some modification. Depending on whether stations have messages to transmit, the controller configures the RIP in a *listen* (also called bypass) or *transmit* (also called active) mode, as shown in Figure 4.16(b). Stations are normally in the listen mode, in which the station can detect its address on the traffic circulating on the ring and read the contents of packets addressed to it.

Like the token bus protocol, a *token* regulates access to the channel, with the token being passed from station to station in the order of their physical connection. Since the order of token passing defines a logical ring, the physical ring and the logical ring are identical. When the ring is initialized, an *idle token* circulates around the ring from station to station. A station wishing to

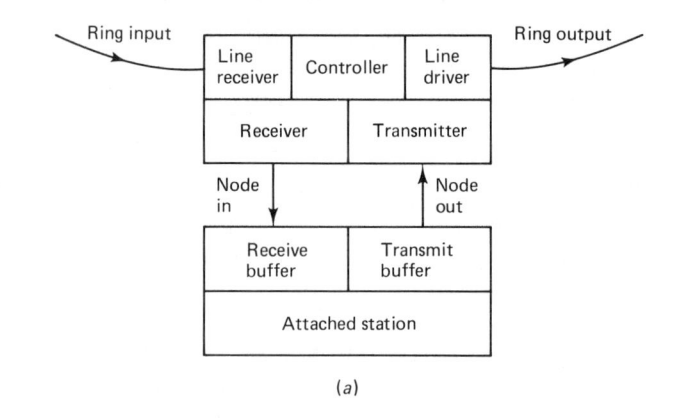

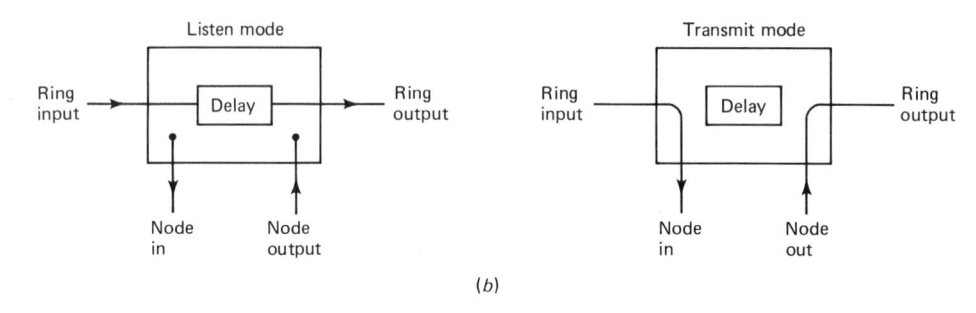

Figure 4.16 (a) A ring interface processor; (b) Listen and transmit modes.

transmit must wait until it detects a free token passing by. The station changes the token from *free token* to *busy token*, and then transmits a frame immediately following the busy token, as depicted in Figure 4.17. Meanwhile, a station down the ring examines the frames passing by; if the frame has a free token, then this station can send messages. However, if the frame has a busy token, the station examines if the frames are addressed to it. The station copies the frames addressed to it, and lets other frames go through.

Since the channel release phase is decentralized, stations cooperate in releasing the channel as follows: A frame on the ring will make a round trip and be purged by the transmitting station. A released channel is indicated by a new free token, which is inserted into the ring by the transmitting station. After a new token release, the next station downstream with data to send will be able to seize the token and transmit.

4.10.1 IEEE 802.5 Token Ring Protocol

In this subsection, we provide additional details about one ring protocol which has achieved standard status, the IEEE 802.5 token ring protocol.

As noted, the access to the channel is regulated by a token which is a unique data pattern. For example, the token could consist of a sequence of eight 1s, and because of transparency requirements it is necessary that the same pattern does not occur in a run of data. One solution often used involves monitoring the data and breaking up the data pattern that duplicates the token

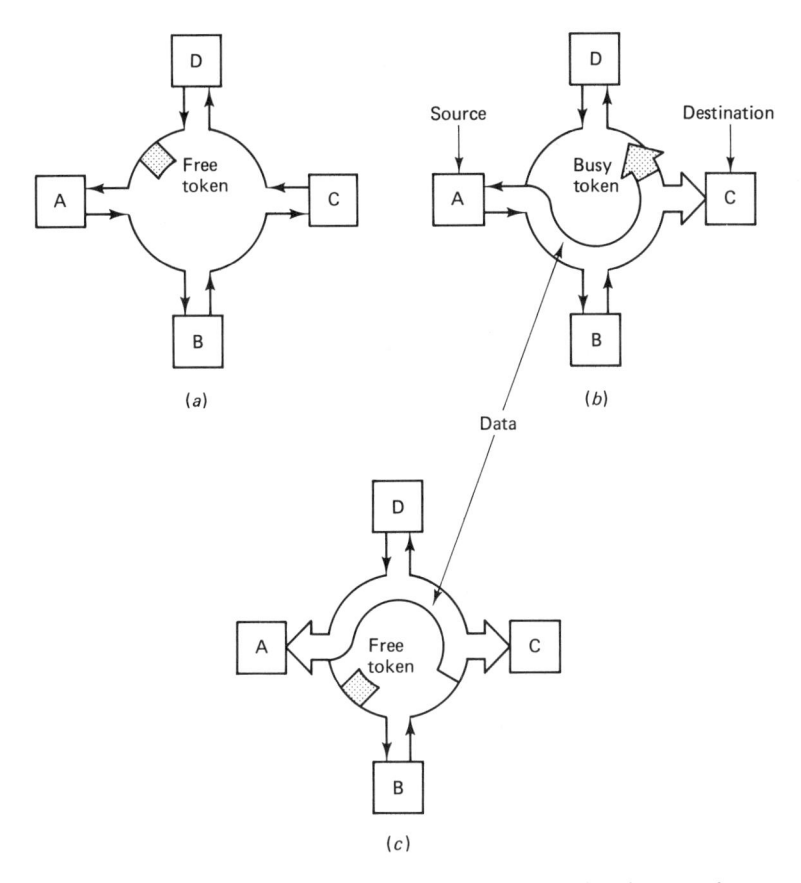

Figure 4.17 Free token and busy token circulation on a token ring network.

by adding or stuffing extra bits; hence the name *bit stuffing*. The disadvantage of the *bit stuffing* technique is the extra bits added to disguise data that may otherwise be detected as a token, thus contributing to overhead. A better technique involves the use of special symbols to mark the beginning and ending of control fields. The token ring protocol uses the latter technique.

Recall from our discussion in Section 3.3 that Manchester encoding always has a transition at the middle of a bit cell, which could be used for error detection. A missing transition simply indicates that there has been an error in the transmission. Since error detection is normally done using cyclic redundancy codes, the token ring protocol uses the error detection property of Manchester encoding for marking the beginning and ending of control fields. The encoding technique is actually a modified version of Manchester encoding, called *differential Manchester encoding*, with the rules depicted in Figure 4.18. The symbols **J** and **K**, which are code violations, are used for constructing a *start delimiter* and *end delimiter*, as shown in Figure 4.19(a), which shows the token frame, with the data frame depicted in Figure 4.19(b).

Token frame. Regarding the *token frame*, the Access Control (AC) byte consists of three *priority bits*, a *token bit*, a *monitor bit*, and three *reservation bits* denoted as P P P T M R R R. The *priority bits* (PPP) indicate the priority of the token, the *token bit* (T) is **1** for a *busy token* and **0** for a *free token*, M is a *monitor bit*, and RRR are *reservation bits*.

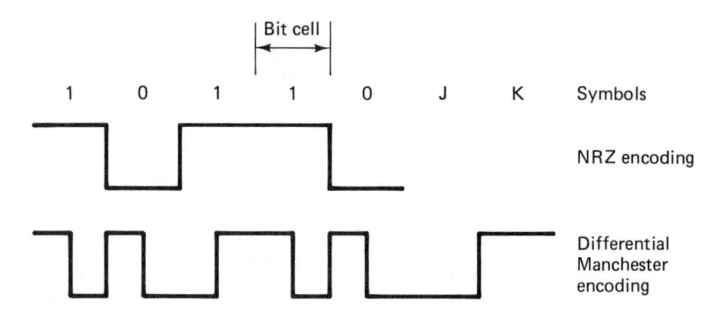

Figure 4.18 Special differential Manchester encoding used in the token ring protocol. Data "0" defined by transition at the beginning of bit/cell. Data "1" defined by no transition at beginning of bit cell. Non-data "J" has no transition at center of bit cell and same polarity from previous bit. Non-data "K" has no transition at unit of bit cell and opposite polarity from previous bit.

The *priority bits* determine the priority of a token, which is used for determining which station (or stations) may transmit per token circulation. To recover from potential error situations, there is a special station called the *active monitor* with exclusive control over the *monitor bit*. The *active monitor* can recover from the following error conditions: lost token, persistently circulating data frame, failure in the priority mechanism, multiple active monitors. The *monitor bit* is always initially transmitted as **0,** with all stations repeating this bit unchanged. The *reservation bits* are used by repeating stations to request that the next token be issued at a requested priority. A station may only modify these bits if it holds a message of higher priority than the value of the reservation bits currently being repeated.

Because of its implication on performance, let us consider the propagation delay in going through the *ring interface processor*. The worst situation, of course, occurs when a station has frames to transmit and monitors the channel for a free token. Electronics in the receiver portion of the RIP can detect the start delimiter field and read the token bit. Assuming that the token is free, the RIP can then change the token bit to a **1** to indicate a busy token before transmission. Since

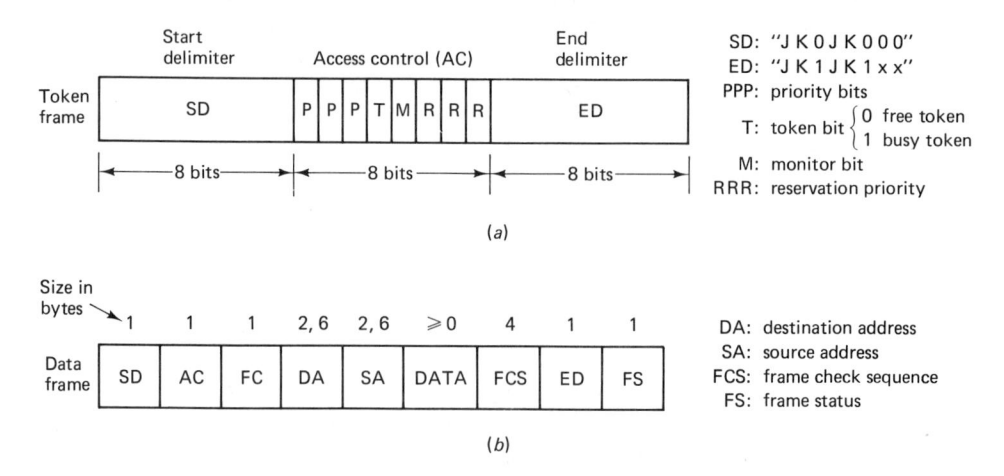

Figure 4.19 Frame formats for the token ring protocol (IEEE 802.5).

186 The Data Link Layer Chap. 4

only one bit is changed, the RIP introduces a delay of just one bit. The one bit delay of the RIP in a token ring network means reduced overhead and hence improved performance.

Frame format. As noted, when the token bit T = **1,** the token is busy and the data frame is as shown in Figure 4.19(b), where the SC, AC, and ED are the same fields in the token bus protocol format. The FC field contains two bits for indicating whether the data corresponds to an LLC data frame, and six bits for controlling the operation of the MAC protocol. The DA and SA fields are the destination and source addresses, respectively. Information coming from the LLC sublayer is contained in the DATA field. The frame check sequence (FCS) field is a cyclic redundancy code, as discussed in Section 4.11. Finally, the frame status (FS) field is used for indicating when a station recognizes the DA as its own, and when a receiving station successfully copied the message into its receive buffer (i.e., no error was detected).

4.11 ERROR DETECTION AND CORRECTION CODES

After reading Chapter 3, it should be clear that communication channels are subject to noise, which may corrupt some of the data being transmitted. In digital communications, the effect of noise is such that if the sequence 10110101 is sent by the sender, the receiver can receive 10110100, 10110110, or any other sequence which can be caused by errors in detecting the bits because of channel noise. Our primary objective in this section is to discuss techniques for error detection and correction applicable for local area networks.

An important question that arises in the following: In the presence of channel noise, how can a sender make sure that a receiver will receive precisely what was sent? There are several possible techniques that could be used for dealing with this question.

One technique which could be used by the sender consists of sending the sequence an odd number of times (e.g., 3) and having the receiver perform a decision based on the majority rule. For example, if three copies of a sequence are sent over the channel and the receiver gets 10101100, 10101100, and 10101111, the receiver will conclude that the sequence sent was 10101100 because it occurred twice.

A second technique that the sender could use is to send the sequence and wait for the receiver to send back the same sequence to the sender, which can then compare the two sequences. If the received sequence matches the sequence sent by the sender, then it can be concluded that the transmission was without errors. This technique is used for correcting errors in terminal-to-computer communications, where it is also known as *echo checking*, and was briefly discussed in subsection 4.3.2. A user sitting on a terminal types characters which go to the computer directly instead of being displayed on the terminal right away. The computer echoes what it receives back to the terminal, where it is finally displayed. The user now compares the character echoed by the computer with the one intended. If an error has occurred, the user can correct it by just retyping the character.

Still another technique for making sure that a receiver receives exactly what was sent by the sender is to include enough *redundancy* in the source data so that the receiver can check whether errors have occurred during transmission. Depending upon whether error correction is done by just the receiver or if error correction requires the cooperation of both sender or receiver, one can distinguish two situations. The first situation occurs when the receiver detects (but does not correct) errors in the transmission and requests that the sender retransmit the symbol sequence. Upon receiving an indication that an error has occurred in the transmission, the sender then retransmits the symbol sequence. This technique is known as *automatic repeat request* (ARQ) and is widely used in computer communications (Stallings, 1987). The second situation involves the receiver detecting and correcting a certain number of errors without the cooperation of the sender. The complexity of the codes for detecting and correcting errors is greater than the complexity of the codes for just detecting errors.

Several advantages and disadvantages exist with each of the preceding techniques. The disadvantage of the first technique is that it requires the message to be sent several times, which is considerable overhead. The receiver needs to store each version of the sequence and compare them to decide what was sent. The second technique involves a handshake between the sender and receiver. The sender will wait until the sequence is echoed back before sending the next sequence. Thus, the disadvantages of the second technique is due to the handshaking overhead and any retransmissions that may take place. Because the third method is the most advantageous for computer communication networks, it will be considered in more detail next.

BLOCK CODES

As noted, the key to overcoming errors caused by channel noise is the use of *redundancy*. One of the most effective ways of introducing redundancy in the source is to deal with the source symbols as blocks of fixed size called *source words*. In **block codes,** a block of k data bits is encoded by a codeword of n bits where $n > k$. For each sequence of k data bits, there is a distinct code word of n bits. There is another class of codes, referred to as **convolutional codes,** in which the coded sequence of n bits depends not only on the k data bits but also on the previous $(N - 1)$ data bits where $N > 1$. Because of its widespread use in computer networks, we will only consider block codes.

The block encoder is only a component of the *channel encoder* block of a general communication system, as depicted in Figure 4.20. Other components of the channel encoder not considered here are modulators, filters, scramblers, and so on, which were discussed in Chapter 3. Thus, a block encoder receives a *data word* **d** of k-bits as its input and produces a *code word* **c** of n-bits as its output where $n > k$. In fact, the number of redundant bits is $m = n - k$. The code

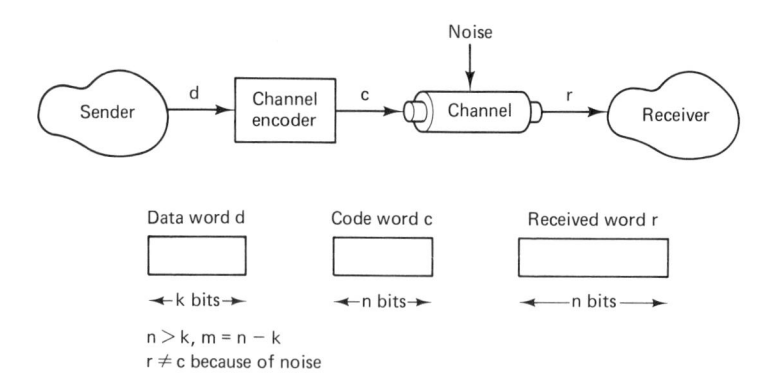

Figure 4.20 Block encoder as a component of channel encoder.

TABLE 4.3 DATA WORDS AND CODE WORDS CORRESPONDING TO A PARITY CHECK BLOCK CODE

d (k = 3) data word	c (n = 4) code word
0 0 0	0 0 0 0
0 0 1	0 0 1 1
0 1 0	0 1 0 1
0 1 1	0 1 1 0
1 0 0	1 0 0 1
1 0 1	1 0 1 0
1 1 0	1 1 0 0
1 1 1	1 1 1 1

word is sent over the channel and it appears at the receiver side as a *received word* **r** having also n-bits in length. Because of channel noise, in general **r** ≠ **c**.

Example

The even parity check bit often used in data and computer communications is a good example of a block code. Data words usually consist of seven-bit ASCII characters. In this example, however, let us consider three-bit data words (i.e., k = 3). A parity bit encoder encodes three-bit data words into four-bit code words in the following manner. The first three bits of the code word are identical to the data word. A fourth bit in the code word (also called the parity bit) is included, in such a way so that the total number of **1**s in the code word is an even number. Table 4.3 shows all the possibilities of data words, along with the corresponding code words.

Conditions for Error Detection and Error Correction

For the previous example, let us assume that the receiver receives r = 0001. Further assume that the receiver does not know how the encoding is done. Under this situation, is the receiver able to detect and possibly correct any errors? The answer to this question is in terms of the **Hamming distance,** which is defined as the number of bits by which two code words differ. For example, 0000 and 0011 differ in two bits; thus, their Hamming distance is two. While trying to answer the preceding question, it is equally likely that the code word sent was 0000, 0011, 0101, or 1001. Thus, the receiver cannot correct the error because of the uncertainty involved with the four choices. However, we see that in this case, it is always possible to detect one error, since the Hamming distance between any two code words is at least two, In general, the condition for detecting up to *t* errors is that the minimum Hamming distance d_{min} between any two code words satisfies

$$d_{min} = t + 1 \tag{4.6}$$

Likewise, in order to detect and correct up to *t* errors, the minimum Hamming distance between any two code words satisfies

$$d_{min} = 2t + 1 \tag{4.7}$$

Example

Consider the even parity check example again. From Table 4.3, it can be seen that the minimum distance between any two code words is $d_{min} = 2$, satisfying $d_{min} = t + 1$ for $t = 1$; thus, the code can only detect up to one error but not correct it. In order for a code to correct one error, the minimum distance d_{min} must be three.

Example

A particular channel has the nasty habit of making exactly two errors per code word transmitted. Assume that $k = 3$ and $n = 4$. If $c = 0000$ is transmitted, list all the possible received words.

Solution Since the received word also has four bits, there are $\binom{4}{2} = 4!/(2!)(2!) = 4 \times 3 \times 2/2 \times 2 = 6$ possible received words which are 0011, 0110, 1100, 1001, 1010, and 0101.

We next find a necessary condition for the parameters n, k, and $m = n - k$ associated with an encoder, such as the one depicted in Figure 4.20, to detect and correct up to t errors. From the previous example, the number of possible received words is

$$N_r = \sum_{j=0}^{t} \binom{n}{j} \tag{4.7a}$$

which is simply the sum of all possible received words having 0, 1, up to t errors. Since there are $m = (n - k)$ additional bits to encode each data word, the condition is

$$2^m \geq \sum_{j=0}^{t} \binom{n}{j} \tag{4.8}$$

which is known as the Hamming bound. Codes producing n-bit *code words* from k-bit *data words* are called (n,k) codes.

Example 4.8

Consider the even parity check example once more. Use Equation 4.8 to determine if the code can correct one error.

Solution Direct application of Equation 4.8 for $m = 1$, $n = 4$, and $t = 1$ yields, $2^m = 2$, $\sum_{j=0}^{t} \binom{4}{j} = 1 + 4 = 5$; thus, since Equation 4.8 is not satisfied, the code cannot correct one error.

Because of efficiency in their implementation and other useful properties, error control codes used in local area networks are primarily systematic codes, which are discussed next.

Systematic Codes

A **systematic code** is a *block code*, where the first k bits of the code word are the same as the k bits in the data word. If we denote the data word as $\mathbf{d} = (d_1, d_2, \ldots, d_k)^T$, where T denotes the matrix transpose operation, and the code word as $\mathbf{c} = (c_1, c_2, \ldots, c_n)^T$, where d_i and c_i are bits, then a systematic code satisfies the following

$$c_1 = d_1$$
$$c_2 = d_2$$
$$\vdots$$
$$c_k = d_k$$
$$c_{k+1} = h_{11}d_1 + h_{12}d_2 + \ldots + h_{1k}d_k$$
$$c_{k+2} = h_{21}d_1 + h_{22}d_2 + \ldots + h_{2k}d_k$$
$$\vdots$$
$$c_n = h_{m1}d_1 + h_{m2}d_2 + \ldots + h_{mk}d_k$$

(4.9)

or, in matrix form

$$\mathbf{c} = \mathbf{G}\mathbf{d} \qquad (4.10)$$

where **c** and **d** are $n \times 1$ and $k \times 1$ column vectors and G is an $n \times k$ *generator matrix* given by

$$G = \begin{bmatrix} 1 & 0 & 0 & \ldots & 0 \\ 0 & 1 & 0 & \ldots & 0 \\ \vdots & & & & \\ 0 & 0 & 0 & \ldots & 1 \\ h_{11} & h_{12} & h_{13} & & h_{1k} \\ h_{21} & h_{22} & h_{23} & & h_{2k} \\ \vdots & & & & \\ h_{m1} & h_{m2} & h_{m3} & & h_{mk} \end{bmatrix} \qquad (4.11)$$

In Equation (4.9) all addition operations are performed modulo 2.

Example

For a (6,3) code, the generator matrix G is

$$G = \begin{bmatrix} 1 & 0 & 0 \\ 0 & 1 & 0 \\ 0 & 0 & 1 \\ 1 & 0 & 1 \\ 0 & 1 & 1 \\ 1 & 1 & 0 \end{bmatrix}$$

Find all code words corresponding to all eight possible data words. Up to how many bits can this code correct?

Solution Using $\mathbf{c} = \mathbf{G}\mathbf{d}$, Table 4.4 shows all data words with the corresponding code words. Since the minimum Hamming distance is $d_{min} = 3 = 2t + 1$ for $t = 1$, this code can detect and correct up to one error.

Block Codes

TABLE 4.4

Data word	Code word
1 1 1	1 1 1 0 0 0
1 1 0	1 1 0 1 1 0
1 0 1	1 0 1 0 1 1
1 0 0	1 0 0 1 0 1
0 1 1	0 1 1 1 0 1
0 1 0	0 1 0 0 1 1
0 0 1	0 0 1 1 1 0
0 0 0	0 0 0 0 0 0

Designing a block encoder involves finding the components of the generator matrix G. In general, there is no systematic way for designing block encoders, except for the case of single-error-correcting codes, which are known as Hamming Codes (Lathi, 1983). Procedures for designing block encoders can be simplified for a particular class of linear *block codes* known as *cyclic codes*, which are considered next.

Cyclic Codes

One simple way of obtaining the n-bit codeword **c** from a k − bit data word **d** is to obtain c_i as the coefficients of the polynomial $c(x) = \Sigma c_i x^{n-i}$ produced by multiplying $d(x) = \Sigma d_i x^{k-i}$ by a fixed **generator polynomial** g(x) of degree (n − k); thus

$$c(x) = d(x)g(x) \qquad (4.12)$$

Codes obtained in this way are called **cyclic codes.**

Properties of Cyclic Codes

    a. The generator polynomial g(x) of an (n,k) cyclic code is a factor of

$$(x^n + 1) ; \text{i.e.,} \qquad (4.13)$$
$$x^n + 1 = g(x) h(x)$$

for some polynomial h(x).

    b. Any polynomial of the form d(x)g(x) is a *code polynomial*, where g(x) is a generator polynomial of degree (n − k) and d(x) is any polynomial of degree (k − 1) or less.

    c. Code words obtained from the code polynomial c(x) as generated by g(x) (i.e., c(x) = d(x)g(x)) are cyclic.

Property c) can be verified in the following way:

$$c(x) = d(x)g(x)$$

Since the code polynomial is given by

$$c(x) = c_1 x^{n-1} + c_2 x^{n-2} + \ldots + c_n \qquad (4.14)$$

and

$$xc(x) = c_1 x^n + c_2 x^{n-1} + \ldots + xc_n$$
$$= c_1(x^n + 1) + (c_2 x^{n-1} + \ldots + c_n + c_1)$$
$$= c_1(x^n + 1) + c^{(1)}(x) = xd(x)g(x)$$

From property a), $(x^n + 1)$ is a multiple of $g(x)$; thus $c^{(1)}(x)$ must also be a multiple of $g(x)$. That is, $c^{(1)}(x) = d_1(x)g(x)$, which implies that $c^{(1)}(x)$ is also a code polynominal corresponding to some data word d_1. The procedure can be continued in this way, and it can be seen that $c^{(2)}(x), c^{(3)}(x), \ldots$ are all generated by $c^{(i)}(x) = d_i(x)g(x)$ for source data word d_i. Therefore, codes generated by $g(x)$ are cyclic.

Systematic Cyclic Codes

Codes obtained from $c(x) = d(x)g(x)$ are not systematic. However, the following procedure generates systematic cyclic codes:

A systematic cyclic code $c(x)$ can be obtained as

$$c(x) = x^{n-k} d(x) + p(x) \qquad (4.15)$$

where $p(x)$ is the remainder from dividing $x^{n-k} d(x)$ by $g(x)$; that is,

$$p(x) = \text{Rem}[x^{n-k} d(x) / g(x)] \qquad (4.16)$$

This can be verified by observing that

$$x^{n-k} d(x) = q(x)g(x) + p(x) \qquad (4.16a)$$

where the quotient of the division $q(x)$ is of degree $(k-1)$ or less. Since additions and subtractions in modulo 2 operations are the same operations, Equation 4.16a can be written as

$$q(x)g(x) = x^{n-k} d(x) + p(x) \qquad (4.16b)$$

From property b), listed previously, $q(x)g(x)$ is a code word. An advantage of obtaining systematic code words using the procedure just described is that its implementation is straightforward, as explained next.

Example

Determine the systematic cyclic code generated by the generator word **g** = 11001 corresponding to the data word **d** = 110011.

Solution For this problem, $n = 10$, $k = 6$, and $m = n - k = 4$. The data and generator polynomials are

$$d(x) = x^5 + x^4 + x + 1$$
$$g(x) = x^4 + x^3 + 1$$

$p(x)$ is calculated using Equation 4.16 as $p(x) = \text{Rem } [x^4 d(x)/g(x)]$, which can be evaluated using long division as follows

$$
\begin{array}{r}
x^5 + 1 \\
x^4 + x^3 + 1 \overline{)\; x^9 + x^8 + x^5 + x^4} \\
x^9 + x^8 + x^5 \\
\hline
x^4 + x^3 + 1 \\
x^3 + 1
\end{array}
$$

Thus, $p(x) = x^3 + 1$.

Block Codes 193

Using Equation 4.15, the systematic cyclic polynomial is

$$c(x) = x^4 d(x) + p(x)$$
$$= x^9 + x^8 + x^5 + x^4 + x^3 + 1$$

and the corresponding codeword is **c** = 1100111001.

Actually, there is a simpler way to obtain **c** directly from **d** and **g** without involving polynomials. The procedure simply involves treating **c, d,** and **p** as binary numbers and performing a binary division to obtain **p** and **c** in the following way.

```
                    1 0 0 0 0 1
        1 1 0 0 1 ⌋ 1 1 0 0 1 1 0 0 0 0
                    1 1 0 0 1
                    ─────────
                          1 0 0 0 0
                          1 1 0 0 1
                          ─────────
                            1 0 0 1
```

Thus, **p** = 1001 and **c** = 1100110000 + 1001 = 1100111001. In the previous division, recall that all operations are done modulo 2, and that addition is the same as subtraction when working with binary digits. A circuit implementing the previous operations is straightforward since modulo 2 is equivalent to an exclusive-or operation.

Error Detection and Correction Using Systematic Cyclic Codes

The systematic cyclic codes just discussed constitute the basis for error detection and correction applicable for local area networks. We summarize next a procedure for error detection and correction based on systematic cyclic codes. Other terms used for the code words obtained using this procedure are **cyclic redundancy check** (CRC) and **frame check sequence** (FCS).

We assume that the sender is given a *data word* **d** having k bits, which is to be converted into a *code word* **c** of n bits by means of a (n,k) cyclic code with *generator polynomial* g(x) of order m = (n − k). Bit components of the data word and code word are used to construct a data polynomial d(x) and code polynomial c(x), respectively.

The procedure is as follows:

1. The sender calculates p(x) using Equation 4.16. Note that multiplying d(x) by x^m is equivalent to appending m zeroes to **d**.

2. The sender transmits a code word **c** obtained from the code polynomial c(x) given by Equation 4.15.

3. The receiver, upon receiving **r**, calculates the remainder of the division r(x)/g(x). If the remainder is zero, the message has no errors, with a high degree of probability.

4. If the remainder is different from zero, the received code word is in error. In this case, the sender and receiver use appropriate error control schemes (e.g., go-back-N or selective retransmission) so that the message in error is retransmitted by the sender. Thus, error correction is performed by retransmitting the message.

Some of the most used generator polynomials are:

CRC-12: $\quad g(x) = x^{12} + x^{11} + x^3 + x^2 + x + 1$

CRC-16: $\quad g(x) = x^{16} + x^{15} + x^2 + 1$

CRC-CCITT: $g(x) = x^{16} + x^{12} + x^5 + 1$

IEEE, 802.4: $g(x) = x^{32} + x^{26} + x^{23} + x^{22} + x^{16} + x^{12} + x^{11} + x^{10} + x^8$
$\qquad + x^7 + x^5 + x^4 + x^2 + x + 1$

Example

In the previous example, assume that the receiver receives a word r = 1100111001. Has an error occurred in the transmission? What is the degree of certainty with the receiver's conclusion?

Solution According to the procedure just outlined, the receiver performs the division r/g in the following way:

```
              1 0 0 0 0 1
     1 1 0 0 1 ⟌ 1 1 0 0 1 1 1 0 0 1
              1 1 0 0 1
              ─────────
                    1 1 0 0 1
                    1 1 0 0 1
                    ─────────
                    0 0 0 0 0
```

Since the remainder is zero, the receiver concludes that no error has occurred in the transmission. Actually, the receiver cannot be absolutely certain that no error has occurred. The properties of cyclic codes given next attempt to characterize the degree of certainty of a receiver's decision.

Properties of Systematic Cyclic Codes

As noted, systematic cyclic codes are advantageous for local area networks because of the following properties:

1. A cyclic code generated by any polynomial $g(x)$ with more than one term detects all single errors.

2. Every polynomial divisible by $(x + 1)$ has an even number of terms.

3. A code generated by the polynomial $g(x)$ detects all single errors and double errors if the length n of the code is less than $(2^m - 1)$.[12]

4. A code generated by $g(x) = (1 + x)g1(x)$ detects all single, double, and triple errors if the length n of the code is less than $(2^m - 1)$.

5. Any cyclic code generated by a polynomial of degree m detects any burst error of length m or less.

[12] Actually, this result is only true for a special class of codes called *primitive polynomials*. Generator polynomials used in practice are of the form $(1+x)g1(x)$, where g1(x) is a primitive polynomial.

6. The fraction of burst errors of length b > m that are undetected is

$$\text{a) } 2^{-m} \qquad \text{if } b > m + 1 \qquad (4.17)$$

$$\text{b) } 2^{-(m-1)} \qquad \text{if } b = m + 1 \qquad (4.17a)$$

7. The cyclic code generated by g(x) does not detect errors involving a factor of g(x).

Example

Apply the cyclic code properties just stated and derive characteristics of the CRC code used by the IEEE 802.4 standard.

Solution The IEEE code is generated by a generator polynomial g(x) having 15 terms, as given previously. The IEEE CRC has the following properties:

  a. Since g(x) has more than one term, the code can detect all single bit errors.
  b. Since g(x) has an odd number of terms, it is not divisible by (1 + x).
  c. The code can detect all single and double errors as long as the length of the data word $n < (2^{32} - 1) = 4294967295$ bits.
  d. The code can detect any burst errors of length 32 or less.
  e. The code can detect 99.99999977 percent of all burst errors of length greater than 32.
  f. The code cannot detect errors involving a factor of g(x), but these are extremely rare.

4.12 IEEE 802.2 LOGICAL LINK CONTROL (LLC)

The IEEE 802.2 logical link control (LLC) protocol is a set of mechanisms for transferring information and control between any pair of data link layer users in a LAN. The LLC protocol is independent of the medium access control method and also independent of the physical medium used. In particular, the IEEE 802.2 protocol can work with three different medium access control methods also standardized by the IEEE: token bus, token ring, and CSMA/CD (e.g., Ethernet). More specifically, as discussed in Chapter 3, the token bus protocol offers three options for modulation and encoding techniques. The overall choices available in IEEE 802 protocols for layers 1 and 2 are depicted in Figure 4.21. Each medium access control method in turn specifies compatible physical media. For example, token bus and Ethernet can specify coaxial cable, whereas token ring can specify twisted pair wires or optical fibers.

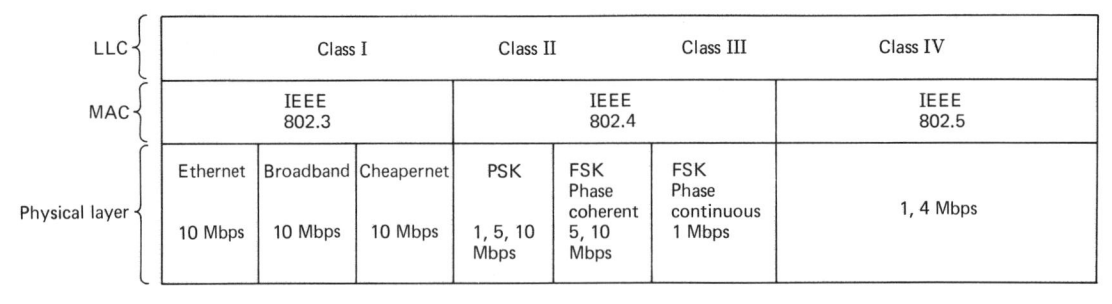

LLC	Class I	Class II	Class III	Class IV
MAC	IEEE 802.3		IEEE 802.4		IEEE 802.5
Physical layer	Ethernet 10 Mbps	Broadband 10 Mbps	Cheapernet 10 Mbps	PSK 1, 5, 10 Mbps	FSK Phase coherent 5, 10 Mbps	FSK Phase continuous 1 Mbps	1, 4 Mbps

Figure 4.21 Several choices for LLC and MAC sublayers and the physical layer. Only ISO protocols are considered.

TABLE 4.5 TYPES OF LLC OPERATION SUPPORTED AND CORRESPONDING CLASSES

		Class of LLC			
		I	II	III	IV
Types of	1	x	x	x	x
Operation	2		x		x
Supported	3			x	x

Table 4.5 lists three types of service organized in four different classes provided by the LLC sublayer. The LLC classes are defined in terms of three different types of operation: type 1 or **unacknowledged connectionless,** type 2 or **connection-oriented,** and type 3 or **acknowledged connectionless.** With type 1 operation, data units are exchanged between LLC users without the need for the establishment of a data link connection. In the LLC sublayer, the data units (i.e., PDUs) are not acknowledged, and there is no provision for error control nor for flow control. With type 2 operation, a data link connection is established between two LLC users prior to any exchange of information. In addition, data units are acknowledged and error control and flow control is also provided.

Type 3 can be thought of a mix of type 1 and type 2, in that data units are acknowledged without the need of a connection. Type 3 is intended for applications that require acknowledgment of data units transfer while avoiding the complexity associated with type 2 connection oriented services. Type 3 provides an acknowledged connectionless data unit exchange service, allowing a station not only to send data but also request the return of data at the same time. Because of this latter mechanism, type 3 service is also known as an **immediate response** mechanism. Although the exchange service is connectionless, sequenced delivery is guaranteed for data sent by the initiating station.

We present the description of the LLC sublayer in the following order: First, the user services provided by the LLC sublayer are described, then the operation of the protocol itself, and finally the services used by the LLC sublayer.

4.12.1 Services Provided by the LLC Sublayer

As noted, the LLC sublayer provides three types of services to a user (e.g., the network layer):

unacknowledged connectionless-oriented service,
connection-oriented service, and
acknowledged connectionless service.

The **unacknowledged connectionless**-oriented service is used in situations where the upper layers provide a connection-oriented type of service if one is desired. A connectionless service allows for data to be exchanged without the need of establishing a data link connection. A **connection-oriented service** establishes a special dialogue between a sender and receiver, called a **data link connection.** As noted in Chapter 2, there are three distinct phases that take place when communication takes place using a connection-oriented service: connection establishment, data transfer, and connection deestablishment (i.e., release or termination). The **acknowledged connectionless** service

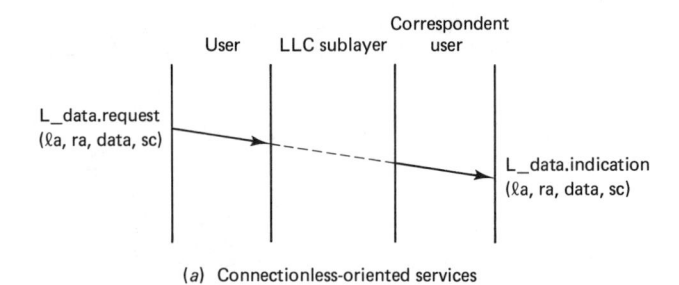

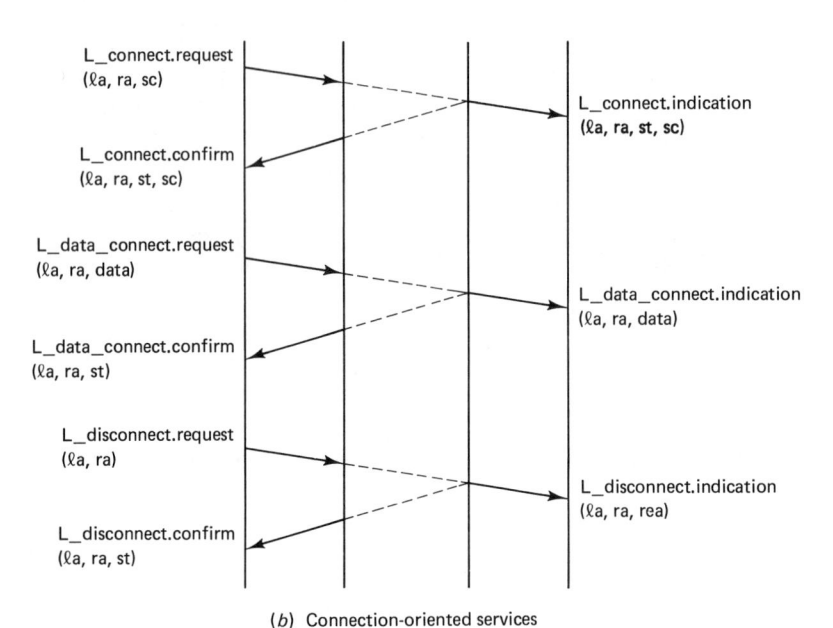

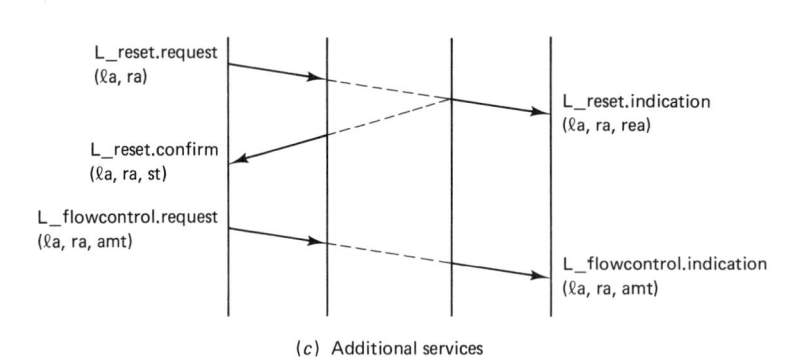

Figure 4.22 LLC Type 1 and Type 2 services.

is useful for applications requiring fast response, such as the ones encountered in some process control and manufacturing applications. Acknowledged connectionless services allow one station to poll another for data and perform data exchange in a *send one frame, receive one acknowledgment* fashion. Go-back-N type protocols are not allowed; thus, there is no multiple frame transfer with a single response capability.

LLC services. One of the major reasons for the existence of a layer in the OSI reference model is for providing services to the layer above it. The services provided by the LLC sublayer to the layer above it (i.e., the network layer) are divided into three types, depending upon whether the service is unacknowledged connectionless, connection-oriented, or acknowledged connectionless.

   1. Unacknowledged connectionless services.

Two primitives are defined in this category of service: L_DATA.request and L_DATA.indication, with Figure 4.22(a) depicting their format and indicating how they can be used. Regarding Figure 4.22, *la* indicates the local address, *ra* the remote address, *data* the actual data being transferred, *sc* the service class, *st* the status for the primitive's response and indication, *rea* the reason for requesting specific primitives (e.g., disconnect), and *amt* the amount of data the LLC sublayer is permitted to pass. The address identifiers refer to link layer service access points (LSAPs), and the *service class* parameter specifies the priority for the data unit transfer. PROWAY[13] refers to LLC type 1 as a *send data with no acknowledgment* (SDN) service.

   2. Connection-oriented services.

Five families of primitives are incorporated in this category of service: L_CONNECT, providing data link setup (i.e., connection establishment), L_DATA_CONNECT, providing data transfer, L_DISCONNECT, providing data link disconnection (i.e., connection termination), L_RESET, providing connection reset, and L_FLOWCONTROL, providing connection flow control. The primitives within each of the families are depicted in Figures 4.20(b) and 4.20(c). The *service class* parameter specifies the priority desired for the connection, and the *status* parameter (st) indicates the result to the request on the connection in question.

   3. Acknowledged connectionless services.

The primitives in this category of service fall into three families: L_DATA_ACK, providing acknowledged data unit transfer between two LLC users, L_REPLY, requesting that data units be returned from a remote station or that data units be exchanged between stations, and L_REPLY_UPDATE, for passing data units to the LLC sublayer and requesting that they be stored temporarily until requested by another station. Figure 4.23 shows the formats and parameters associated with the preceding primitives. PROWAY refers to LLC type 3 as *send data with acknowledgment* (SDA) when the data are in a command PDU, or *request data with reply* (RDR) when the data are in a response PDU.

4.12.2 LLC Protocol Operation

Figure 4.24 depicts the protocol data unit (PDU) for the LLC sublayer. DSAP specifies the address of the destination service access point (SAP), whereas SSAP specifies the address of the source

---

[13] Process Control data highway, a standard of the Instrument Society of America (ISA s72.01) describing a token passing bus system similar to IEEE 802.4 for process control applications.

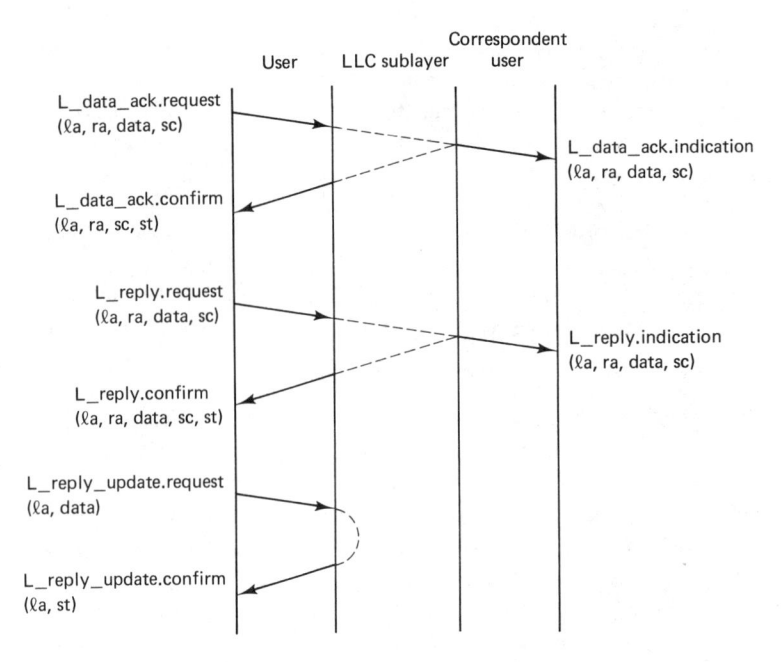

Figure 4.23 Acknowledged connectionless services (Type 3).

service access point. The *control* field of the frame provides the variables required to implement error control, flow control, and link management functions associated with the protocol. The medium access control function is implemented at the MAC sublayer. The size of the control field is two bytes if sequence numbers are used, or one byte if sequence numbers are not used. The *information* field contains the data to be sent to the receiver.

The address fields each contain a single address (i.e., a number). It is possible to identify one or more destination addresses for which the data is intended, by means of the least significant bit (I/G bit) of the DSAP. If the I/G bit is 0, the data is for an individual SAP address; if the I/G bit is 1, the data is for a group of SAP addresses. Frames could be generated by a LLC entity autonomously (i.e., a command or inquiry) or in response to a command or inquiry from other LLC

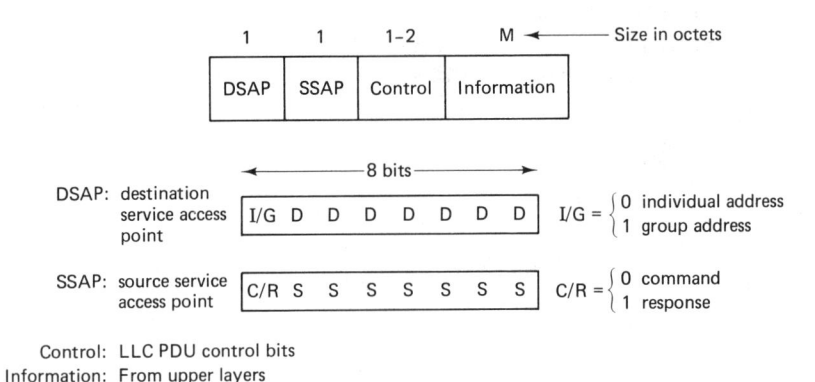

Figure 4.24 LLC protocol data unit (PDU) structure.

200   The Data Link Layer   Chap. 4

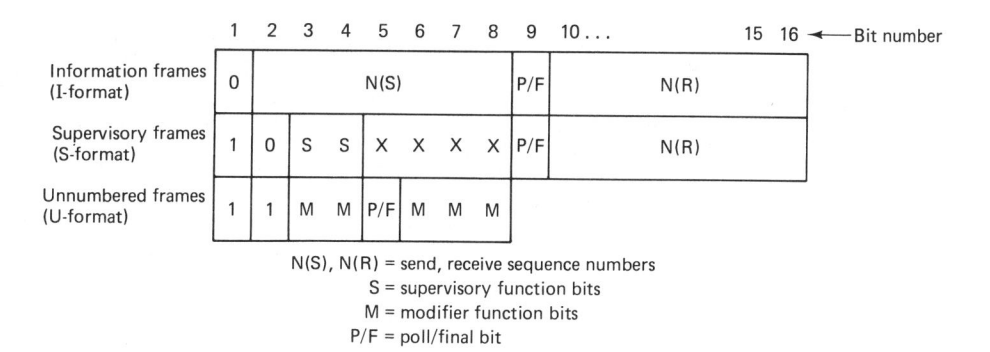

```
                    1   2   3   4   5   6   7   8   9   10...          15  16  ← Bit number
Information frames  | 0 |       N(S)          | P/F |       N(R)           |
(I-format)

Supervisory frames  | 1 | 0 | S | S | X | X | X | X | P/F |    N(R)       |
(S-format)

Unnumbered frames   | 1 | 1 | M | M | P/F | M | M | M |
(U-format)
```

N(S), N(R) = send, receive sequence numbers
S = supervisory function bits
M = modifier function bits
P/F = poll/final bit

Figure 4.25 Format of LLC control field.

entities in other stations. When the least significant bit (C/R bit) of the source SSAP address is 0, the frame is a command; if the C/R bit is 1, the frame is a response. Actually, the I/G and C/R bits are control bits, which should be in the control field but had to be located somewhere else, because the designers ran out of control bits.

Figure 4.25 depicts the format for the control field of the LLC-PDU. The bit groups N(S) and N(R) are used to encode the send and receive sequence numbers, which were discussed in subsection 4.4.2. The bit groups S and M are used to encode different *supervisory* and *unnumbered* frames respectively (e.g., receive ready, disconnect, etc). The P/F bit is referred to as the Poll (P) bit for commands or the Final (F) bit for responses. When the P bit is a **1**, the sender is soliciting a response from the remote receiver. A receiver can acknowledge the receipt of a command by setting the F bit to **1**. The bit group X is reserved and set to zero.

With 2 S-bits, one can define up to 4 supervisory frames (i.e., *S-frames*). However, only three are used: *receive ready* (RR), *receive not ready* (RNR), and *reject* (REJ). Only 10 of the possible 32 *U-frames* are used: unnumbered information (UI), exchange identification (XID), test (TEST), set asynchronous balanced mode extended (SABME), disconnect (DISC), unnumbered acknowledgment (UA), disconnect mode (DM), frame reject (FRMR), acknowledged connectionless sequence 0 (AC0), and acknowledged connectionless sequence 1 (AC1).

4.12.3 Classes of LLC

As noted, the LLC protocol supports three types of operation: type 1, supporting connectionless service, type 2, supporting a connection-oriented service, and type 3, supporting acknowledged connectionless service. Type 1 operation is very simple. Frames are not acknowledged, flow control is not exercised, and no error recovery is used. The implicit assumption with type 1 is that error control, flow control, and error recovery functions are performed by higher layer protocols. The only frame type supported by type 1 is U-frames. Thus, the only frames supported by type 1 operation are UI, XID, and TEST. Type 2 operation requires the establishment of a connection between the sender and receiver prior to information exchange.

As illustrated in Table 4.5, for implementation purposes four classes of protocols are defined. Class I supports type 1 operation only. Class II supports both type 1 and type 2. Thus, class I supports a connectionless service only, whereas class II supports either a connectionless or a connection-oriented service. Class III supports both type 1 and type 3, whereas type IV supports all types of operation. The frame types associated with class III and class IV are listed in Table 4.6.

TABLE 4.6 FRAME TYPES ASSOCIATED WITH CLASSES III AND IV.

		Commands	Responses
Class III	Type 1:	UI	
		XID	XID
		TEST	TEST
	Type 3:	AC0	AC0
		AC1	AC1
Class IV	Type 1:	UI	
		XID	XID
		TEST	TEST
	Type 2:	I	I
		RR	RR
		RNR	RNR
		REJ	REJ
		SABME	UA
		DISC	DM
			FRMR
	Type 3:	AC0	AC0
		AC1	AC1

MAC services. The MAC services specify how the LLC sublayer makes use of the services provided by the MAC sublayer. Figure 4.26 depicts the time sequence diagram for the three primitives supported by the MAC sublayer: MA_DATA.request, MA_DATA.indication, and MA_DATA.confirmation. The (station) source and destination addresses are indicated in the *sa* and *da* parameters, respectively. The data unit is specified by the *du* parameter. The parameters *sc* and *st* are used to specify the *service class* and *status* of requested, or already provided services.

4.13 IEEE 802.4 MEDIUM ACCESS CONTROL (MAC) SUBLAYER

In this section, we discuss the organization of the IEEE 802.4 MAC sublayer, the MAC frame format, and the MAC sublayer relationship with the LLC sublayer and the token bus protocol.

The functional organization of the MAC sublayer was depicted in Figure 4.10(a). Services

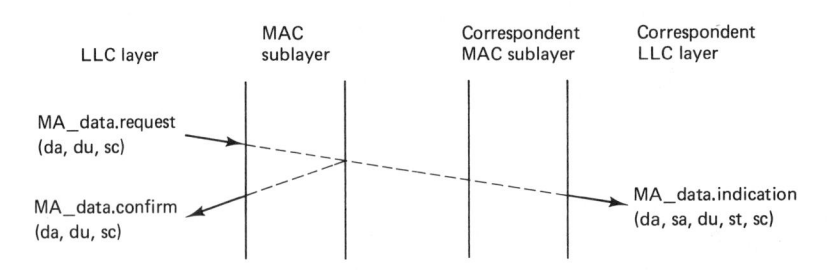

Figure 4.26 MAC sublayer user service primitives.

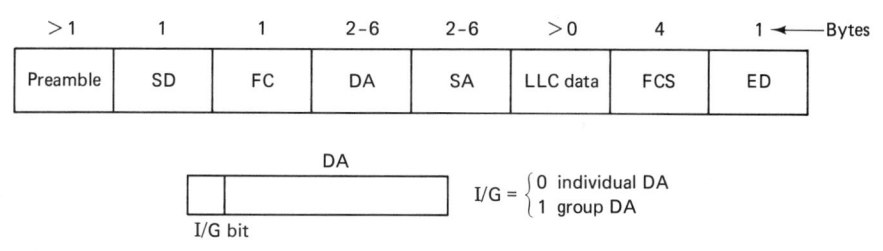

```
   >1        1        1       2-6      2-6      >0         4        1  ←——Bytes
┌──────────┬──────┬──────┬──────┬──────┬──────────┬──────┬──────┐
│ Preamble │  SD  │  FC  │  DA  │  SA  │ LLC data │ FCS  │  ED  │
└──────────┴──────┴──────┴──────┴──────┴──────────┴──────┴──────┘
```

```
                    DA
            ┌─────────────┐              ⎧ 0 individual DA
            │             │       I/G = ⎨
            └─────────────┘              ⎩ 1 group DA
              I/G bit
```

SD: starting delimiter
FC: frame control
DA: (station) destination address
SA: (station) source address
LLC: LLC frame
FCS: frame check sequence (CRC)
ED: end delimiter

Figure 4.27 MAC frame format for the IEEE 802.4 standard.

provided by the MAC sublayer are made up of just one primitive family, MA_DATA, whose primitive components are given in Figure 4.26. The MAC sublayer performs the following functions:

multiple access synchronization,

frame synchronization, and

content synchronization.

Multiple access synchronization is performed using the token bus protocol, as discussed in Section 4.8. Frame synchronization is performed by using delimiters for marking the beginning and end of frames, as depicted in the MAC frame format of Figure 4.27. Actually, the MAC frame format also helps the physical layer in performing bit synchronization by including a *preamble* field used for synchronizing the transmitter and receiver. Content synchronization is achieved by dividing the MAC frame into control and information fields, handling errors, and encoding control messages to perform the various token bus protocol functions.

Bits in the *frame control* (FC) field are crucial to the operation of the token bus protocol. More specifically, when FC = 10 (Hex) the frame in question represents a *token frame*. Other FC values of interest are 00 (Hex) and 80 (Hex) for the *claim-token* and *solicit-successor* frames, respectively. Recall that the token is passed from station to station in the logical ring, with station addresses identified in the DA (destination address) and SA (source address) fields, respectively. Information from[14] the LLC sublayer is identified in the *data* field. The FCS field contains the word **p,** as obtained from the remainder polynomial given by Equation 4.16 using a 32-bit generator polynomial given in Section 4.11. The word **p** is the remainder, obtained by dividing the FC, SA, DA, and DATA fields of the MAC frame format by the generator polynomial.

4.14 IEEE 802.3 MEDIUM ACCESS CONTROL (MAC) SUBLAYER

In this section, we discuss the organization of the IEEE 802.3 MAC sublayer, the MAC frame format, and the MAC sublayer relationship with the LLC sublayer and the CSMA/CD protocol.

---

[14] We are assuming that data flows from the upper layers to the lower layers in our explanations.

```
     7      1    2-6   2-6   2    >0    ≥0    4  ← Bytes
  ┌────────┬────┬────┬────┬──────┬────────┬─────┬─────┐
  │Preamble│SFD │ DA │ SA │Length│LLC data│ PAD │ FCS │
  └────────┴────┴────┴────┴──────┴────────┴─────┴─────┘
```

```
    48 bit address format              16 bit address format
  ┌───┬───┬──────────────┐            ┌───┬──────────────┐
  │I/G│U/L│ 46 bit address│            │I/G│ 15 bit address│
  └───┴───┴──────────────┘            └───┴──────────────┘
```

I/G = { 0 individual address
        1 group address

U/L = { 0 globally administered address
        1 locally administered address

SFD: start frame delimiter

Figure 4.28 MAC frame format for the IEEE 802.3 standard.

The services of the MAC sublayer are the same as that of the corresponding MAC sublayer of the 802.4 standard, consisting of just one primitive family MA_DATA, whose primitive components are given in Figure 4.26. As with the 802.4 standard, the MAC sublayer for the 802.3 standard performs the following functions:

multiple access synchronization,

frame synchronization, and

content synchronization.

Multiple access synchronization is performed using the CSMA/CD protocol, as discussed in Section 4.9. Frame synchronization is performed by using one delimiter for marking the beginning of the frame (i.e., *start frame delimiter*) and a length count indicating the size of the frame, as depicted in the MAC frame format of Figure 4.28. The *length* field contains the number of LLC data bytes in the *data* field. If the value of the *length field* is less than the minimum required for proper operation of the protocol as given by Equation 4.5, additional bits are appended to the data in the *pad* field so that Equation 4.5 is satisfied. Actually, the MAC frame format also helps the physical layer in performing bit synchronization, but including a *preamble* field used for synchronizing the transmitter and receiver.

Content synchronization is achieved by dividing the MAC frame into control and information fields, handling errors, and encoding control messages to perform the CSMA/CD protocol. Recall that in the CSMA/CD protocol, after the channel has been acquired, information is sent to stations using address identification given by the DA (destination address) and SA (source address) fields, respectively. Information from the LLC sublayer is identified in the *data* field. The FCS field is obtained in the same manner as that of the 802.4 standard.

4.15 MAP DATA LINK LAYER

Since the MAP 3.0 architecture is based on the IEEE 802 protocols, its data link layer is divided into two sublayers: logical link control (LLC) and medium access control (MAC). The LLC sublayer corresponds to the IEEE 802.2 standard under the class I or class III operation, whereas the MAC sublayer corresponds to the IEEE 802.4 standard.

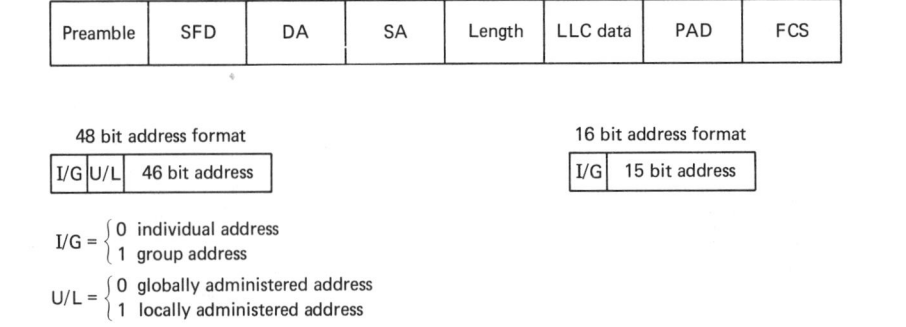

Recall that the main function of the MAC sublayer is to manage the access to a shared channel, and that the main functions of the LLC sublayer are to perform error control, addressing, and flow control in order to ensure reliable data transmission between nodes. For the MAP 3.0 network architecture, the MAC sublayer is the token bus protocol specified in the ISO 8802/4 standard, whereas the LLC sublayer is a subset of the ISO 8802/2 protocol known as class I (connectionless-oriented) services. Alternatively, for applications requiring improved performance class III (acknowledged, connectionless-oriented) is recommended.

4.15.1 Logical Link Control (LLC) Sublayer

Class I operation of the IEEE 802.2 protocol operation specifies a connectionless type of service. Initially, the MAP network was designed with a connectionless type of service for layers 1,2, and 3, and with a connection oriented type of service for layers 4,5,6, and 7. As noted earlier, the IEEE 802.2 with class I operation is a very simple protocol. One of the reasons for its simplicity is that it could be readily incorporated into VLSI designs. The disadvantages of a simple data link layer protocol are: delivery of data cannot be guaranteed, data could arrive at the destination in a sequence different to the one in which it was sent (because of transmission errors and subsequent retransmissions), no flow control is exercised, and only a limited number of error recovery procedures is available. For the MAP network, however, the physical layer alone provides low error rates; thus, a complex data link layer is not required. Accordingly, MAP uses the simplest data link layer protocols offered by the 802 standards IEEE project 802, namely IEEE 802.2 class I and class III.

As noted earlier, the LLC sublayer of the MAP network architecture is the ISO 8802/2 standard protocol, using class I services to provide connectionless communications, or when required by certain applications, class III. Since the ISO 8802/2 class 1 protocol does not provide message sequencing, acknowledgments, flow control, or error recovery, other layers in the MAP network architecture must provide these important functions. However, the IEEE 802.2 standard does provide other options, known as class II and class IV operations, based on a connection-oriented service known as **data link connection,** but classes II and IV are not part of MAP.

The IEEE 802.2 class I operation basically performs data exchange without establishing a

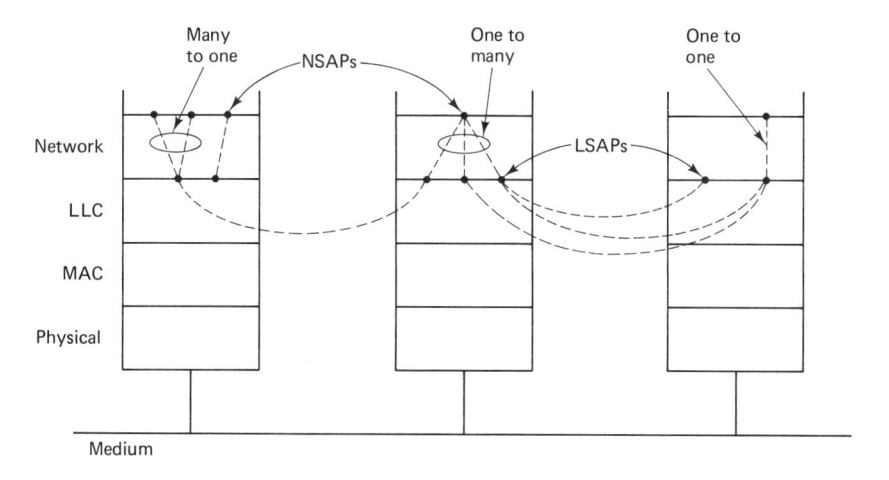

Figure 4.29 Possible configurations for data exchange at the logical link sublayer.

data link connection. This mode of communication is referred to as **logical data link.** As depicted in Figure 4.29, data could be exchanged in a variety of configurations, as described by the following:

1. One or several entities at one source station exchange data with one or several peer entities at one destination station.
2. One or several entities at one source station exchange data with one or several peer entities at different destination stations.
3. Mapping of entities to service access points can be one to one, many to one, or one to many.

The IEEE 802.2 class III operation provides unacknowledged connectionless and/or acknowledged connectionless services. In the acknowledged connectionless type (i.e., *immediate response* mechanism) data units are exchanged without the need for the establishment of a data link connection. The LLC protocol is responsible for providing acknowledgments for individual protocol data units (PDUs) regardless of whether they carry user information.

The following reasons for the selection of the ISO 8802/2 LLC protocol are cited by MAP designers (MAP, 1986):

It supports data transfers at very high rates.
It can be used on multiple media (twisted pair, coaxial cable, optical fibers, etc.).
It provides connectionless services.
It provides an acknowledged single frame service.
If widely accepted, VLSI chips will emerge and substantially reduce the cost of network interfaces.

4.15.2 Medium Access Control (MAC) Sublayer

As noted, the MAC sublayer of the MAP architecture specifies the token bus protocol. At the time the token bus protocol was selected as the medium access method for the MAP architecture, MAP designers offered the following reasons for the selection:

Token bus was the only protocol presently supported on broadband by the IEEE 802 project.
Many protocols used by programmable device vendors were already somewhat token bus-based.
The token bus protocol supported a message priority scheme.
In the token bus protocol, high priority messages are delivered within a specified time limit. The time limit can be easily determined knowing details of a network configuration (e.g., number of stations, etc.).

In the MAP architecture, the MAC frame address field length is 48 bits to allow for a sufficient number of stations on the network. Although a particular MAP network segment is not expected to have as many stations as allowed by the 48-bit field, it is expected that the 48 bits are sufficient to identify stations not only in a particular segment but also between segments, local area networks, and wide area networks (i.e., a global address). For this purpose, the 48-bit address field can be segmented into network address and station address, as shown in Figure 4.30.

Network address	Station address
←—— 48 bits ——→	

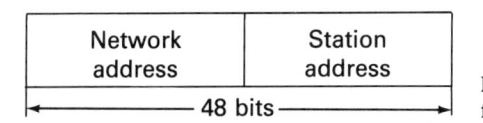

Figure 4.30 Address field within the MAC format of a MAP network architecture.

4.15.3 TOP Data Link Layer

Like MAP 3.0, the TOP 3.0 architecture for the data link layer is composed of the MAC and LLC sublayers. The primary MAC sublayer corresponds to the CSMA/CD protocol, as specified in the ISO 8802/3 standard. Alternate MAC options include IEEE 802.4 and IEEE 802.5. The LLC sublayer of the TOP network architecture for local area networks is the same one as one of the options of the MAP data LLC sublayer (ISO 8802/2 class 1) with a *link service access point* (LSAP) value of FE (Hexadecimal). For wide area networks (i.e., metropolitan and long haul networks) the TOP data link layer is the CCITT X.25 (LAPB) protocol with CCITT X.121 addressing.

SUMMARY

In this chapter, we have discussed the functions and classification of data link layer protocols, and medium access control schemes. We next discussed the token bus, CSMA/CD, and token ring protocols in some detail. The data link layer of the MAP and TOP networks were used to illustrate the concepts.

The data link layer deals with the following four major functions: error control, flow control, link management, and medium access control.

Data link layer functions can be structured into a hierarchy of four layers of functions, referred to as the **hierarchical data link model.** The layers are: multiple access synchronization, frame synchronization, content synchronization, and dialog synchronization. Data link protocols can be classified as asynchronous protocols and synchronous protocols. One of the most effective ways for dealing with errors in local area networks involves the use of *acknowledgments*, and the corresponding mechanisms are called *automatic repeat request* (*ARQ*). Variations of the ARQ mechanism include *Idle RQ*, *Continuous RQ*, *Selective retransmission*, and *Go back N*.

Link connection management allows a sender and a receiver to start exchanging frames, to inquire about the identity of one another, and to stop exchanging frames.

When the communication is broadcast, stations must communicate using a shared channel. At most, one device can make use of the channel at any one time. If more than one device attempt to access the channel at the same time, the signals will be garbled.

Channel access mechanisms can be based on time division multiplexing (TDM) or frequency division multiplexing (FDM). Depending upon their location of control, channel access attributes are *centralized* (C) or *decentralized* (D). Depending upon the type of channel access, the attributes are *polling* (P) or *event driven* (E). Centralized channel access mechanisms involve a central entity that is in complete control, and decides when the individual stations can access the channel. In decentralized channel access mechanisms, all stations cooperate in accessing the shared channel.

The token bus scheme is a decentralized polling channel access mechanism, with the network stations interconnected by a physical bus. The station receiving the token is granted control of the channel for a specified time. After a station is finished using the channel (i.e., sending messages), it passes the token to another station, which proceeds likewise. The token is passed from station to station in a cyclic fashion, thus defining a *logical ring*.

The major random schemes that have been developed for accessing a shared channel are: Aloha, Slotted Aloha, Carrier Sense Multiple Access (CSMA), and Carrier Sense Multiple Access with Collision Detection (CSMA/CD). Although there are several CSMA schemes, their general behavior can be characterized as follows: When a station has any frames to transmit, it *listens* to determine if other stations are doing so. If no other station is transmitting, the station transmits immediately; otherwise, the station waits a random amount of time and starts all over. CSMA schemes that continue sensing the channel after transmission are known as **Carrier Sense Multiple Access with Collision Detection** (CSMA/CD).

Transmission channels are subject to noise, which may corrupt some of the data being transmitted. A solution involves the use of enough *redundancy* in the source data so that the receiver can check whether errors have occurred during transmission. Error control in local area networks are primarily based on systematic cyclic codes.

The IEEE 802.2 logical link control (LLC) protocol is a set of mechanisms for defining the transfer of information and control between any pair of data link layer users in a LAN. The LLC protocol is independent of the medium access control method, and also independent of the physical medium used. The LLC sublayer provides three types of service organized in four different classes. The three types of operation are: type 1, or **unacknowledged connectionless,** type 2, or **connection-oriented,** and type 3, or **acknowledged connectionless.**

Since the MAP network architecture is based on the IEEE 802 protocols, its data link layer is divided into the sublayers: logical link control (LLC) and medium access control (MAC). The LLC sublayer corresponds to the IEEE 802.2 standard under the class I or class III operation, whereas the MAC sublayer corresponds to part of the IEEE 802.4 standard. MAP uses the IEEE 802.2 class I and class III. The MAC sublayer of the MAP architecture specifies the token bus protocol. Like MAP, the TOP architecture for the data link layer is composed of the MAC and LLC sublayers. The MAC sublayer corresponds to the CSMA/CD protocol. The LLC sublayer for TOP is the same one as one of the options of the MAP data LLC sublayer (ISO 8802/2 class 1).

Bibliographic Notes

Prior to the development of the ISO reference model, most communication protocols had functions now assigned to the data link layer. Thus, a great deal of material exists on the data link layer, since it is one of the first layers which was developed. In particular, the following books contain a good treatment of the data link layer: Schwartz (1988), Hammond and O'Reilly (1986), Stallings (1987), Tanenbaum (1988), McNamara (1982), Chou (1983), Meijer and Peeters (1982), and Ahuja (1982). The hierarchical data link layer model is due to Lam (in Chou, 1983), and the classification based on communication phases is due to Heger (1985). The token bus protocol standard is detailed in IEEE 802.4. The time division multiple access protocol is described by Capetanakis (1979). The Aloha protocol was developed by Abramson (1973), and the CSMA/CD scheme was developed by Metcalfe (1976). The books by Hammond and O'Reilly (1986), and Franta and Chlamtac (1981) also provide a good discussion of random access protocols. The Cambridge ring network is discussed by Hooper (1980) and Temple (1984), whereas the token ring protocol is described by Dixon et al. (1983). Error correction and detection codes are described in digital communication books such as Lathi (1983), and Das (1986), or in some data network books such as Bertrekas and Gallager (1987). The CSMA/CD and token ring standards are detailed in IEEE 802.3, and IEEE 802.5, respectively. The IEEE 802.2, 802.3, 802.4, and 802.5 are also ISO standards with identifiers ISO 8802/2, 8802/3, 8802/4, and 8802/5 respectively.

PROBLEMS

1. (a) Explain the major differences between the following frame types: Information (I-frame), Supervisory (S-frame), and Unnumbered (U-frame).
   (b) For the IEEE 802 standards, name two specific frames belonging to each of the preceding types.
2. (a) How is *frame synchronization* typically achieved at the data link layer?
   (b) Explain the difference between the techniques for achieving frame synchronization used by the IEEE 802.4 and IEEE 802.3 standards.
3. How is *content synchronization* typically achieved at the data link layer?
4. Produce a time sequence diagram similar to that of Figure 4.3 for the following cases:
   (a) Go Back N, error free case.
   (b) Go Back N, Ack frame corrupted.
   (c) Selective retransmission, Ack frame corrupted.
5. Discuss the advantages and disadvantages of the DPDD, CPDD, DECC, and DPCC channel access schemes.
6. Calculate the maximum throughput on a data link using an HDLC link format as shown in Figure P4.1. Unlike the HDLC protocol, assume that an *Idle RQ* mechanism is used for flow and error control purposes. Additional assumptions: $T_{rd} = T_{sd} = 1$ msec, maximum medium (wire) length = 5 Km, data frame length (not including overhead) = 500 bytes, data rate = 1 M bit/sec.

1	1	1	≥ 0	2	1	Bytes
FLAG	ADDRESS	CONTROL	DATA	FCS	FLAG	

Figure P4.1

7. The implementation of window mechanisms for flow control requires the management of circular buffers in the following way. As shown in Figure P4.2, two pointers H and T are maintained for the Header and Trailer portion of the buffers containing data. The buffer empty condition is detected when H = T, and the full condition is detected when H = T − 1. To put data in the buffer, the header H is incremented by 1 and the message is written into the buffer pointed to by H. Likewise, to get data from the buffer, the buffer trailer T is incremented by 1 and

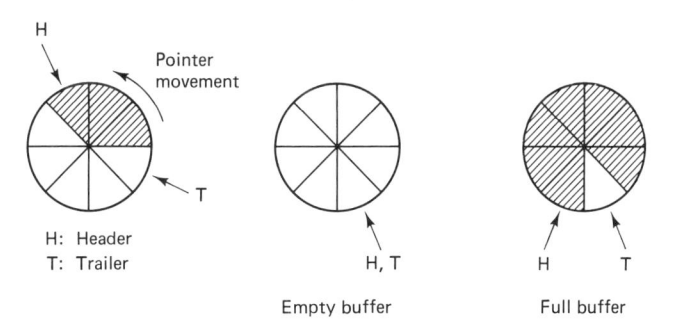

Figure P4.2

Chap. 4　Problems

the data is read from the buffer pointed to by T. All arithmetic operations are done modulo N, where N is the number of buffers available.
  (a) If n bits are used to number frames, what is the maximum size of usable buffers (i.e., the maximum window size)?
  (b) Write an ADA program for managing data in the circular buffer. Include two procedures *put_data*, and *get_data* for writing and reading data into and from the buffer respectively.
8. Some network architectures do not include some of the OSI layers for performance or other reasons.
  (a) Discuss the implications of not including the data link layer.
  (b) Regarding the decision of whether the data link layer should be included in a certain network architecture, give two reasons for including it and two reasons for not including it.
9. (a) Explain the concept of dialog synchronization.
  (b) How does the IEEE 802 standards achieve dialog synchronization?
10. (a) Explain the operation of the token bus protocol.
  (b) List and explain the potential problems that the protocol must consider in a well designed network (i.e., a practical and robust network).
11. (a) Determine the *Hamming bound* for a ternary code.
  (b) A ternary (11,6) code exists that can correct up to two errors. Verify that this code satisfy the Hamming bound exactly.
12. Analyze the (6,3) code with generator matrix G by answering the following:
  (a) Find the minimum Hamming distance between code words.
  (b) Up to how many bit errors can this code correct?
  The generator matrix is:

$$G = \begin{bmatrix} 1 & 0 & 0 \\ 0 & 1 & 0 \\ 0 & 0 & 1 \\ 0 & 1 & 1 \\ 1 & 0 & 1 \\ 1 & 1 & 0 \end{bmatrix}$$

13. A receiver receives the word $\mathbf{r} = 101011000110$ using a generator polynomial $g(x) = x^6 + x^4 + x + 1$. Is the received word correct?
14. Consider a token bus protocol like the one used in the MAP network architecture with a frame overhead of 26 bytes (trailer + header). Assume that there is no priority classes and that THT is the maximum time a station can hold the token. Calculate the maximum number of information bits that the station can send every time it gets the token. Let THT = 500 msec.
15. An appropriate formula for the *channel efficiency* of a data link layer protocol (not including channel access mechanisms) such as the *stop and wait* protocol is given by

$$\text{Chann. Eff.} = \frac{L}{H + L + \text{Ack} + 2RT}$$

where L is the data length, H is the overhead length, Ack is the acknowledgment frame length (S-format), R is the data rate, and T is the station service time including round trip propagation delays. All lengths are in bits. Calculate the channel efficiency for a *stop and wait* protocol with frame format such as the one used by the IEEE 802.3 standard. Assume L = 1024 bytes, pad length = 0, R = 10 M bps and T = 15 μ sec.

5

The Network Layer

Our primary purpose in this chapter is to discuss the functions of the network layer, concentrating on routing and congestion control schemes and their relationships. In Section 5.2, we provide two classifications of routing algorithms. Since the network layer plays a crucial role when interconnecting several networks together, network interconnection is discussed in Section 5.7. The chapter concludes with a discussion of the ISO network layer standard and characteristics of the network layer of the MAP and TOP architectures.

5.1 NETWORK LAYER FUNCTIONS

The network layer of the OSI reference model is concerned with functions such as routing, addressing, and congestion resolution of data packets as they find their way from a source station to a destination station. The network layer performs the aforementioned functions on behalf of higher layers (i.e., transport, session, etc). The functions performed by the network layer are made available to higher layers as a set of network services.

Three major contexts exist in which the network layer performs its functions. The first context involves a single network with a shared medium (i.e., a broadcast network). The second context involves a single point-to-point network, which contains at least two paths between any two source and destination stations, like the one shown in Figure 5.1, depicting a packet switched network similar to the ARPANET network. The third context for performing network layer functions involves

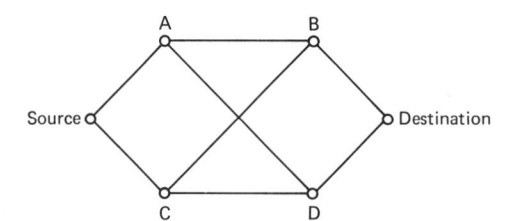

Figure 5.1 A packet switched network. Nodes A, B, C, and D are switching nodes.

several networks, with the source station located in one network and the destination station located in a different network, as shown in Figure 5.2. Interconnecting several networks is referred to as **internetworking.**

Routing, addressing, and congestion resolution functions are performed in the three contexts just mentioned. In broadcast networks, routing and addressing involve segmentation, reassembly, source routing, managing address headers, etc. In point to point networks, an intermediate node, such as A in Figure 5.1, must make a decision to route packets to the destination, either through nodes B or D. Finally, regarding internetworks, routing and addressing problems occur when there are at least two paths between the source and destination stations. For example, messages going from source to destination in Figure 5.2 have two possible paths: a path through networks A and C and another path through networks A, B, and C.

Routing aims at forwarding protocol data units (PDU) closer to their final destination. The PDU final destination may be a few hops away in a point-to-point network similar to the one shown in Figure 5.1, or it may be a few networks away in an internetwork configuration such as the one shown in Figure 5.2. While forwarding PDUs, a station needs to switch the PDU to one of several possible subsequent nodes that will eventually get the PDU closer to its final destination. Switching PDUs requires a way of naming stations (i.e., addressing) in a way suitable for a station to perform its routing function.

Congestion control deals with the problem of more packets arriving at nodes responsible for routing than there are buffers to store them all. Congestion problems may arise on an end-to-end (i.e., involving source and destination stations) basis or on an intermediate (i.e., involving intermediate nodes) basis. The network layer is concerned with congestion at the intermediate nodes.

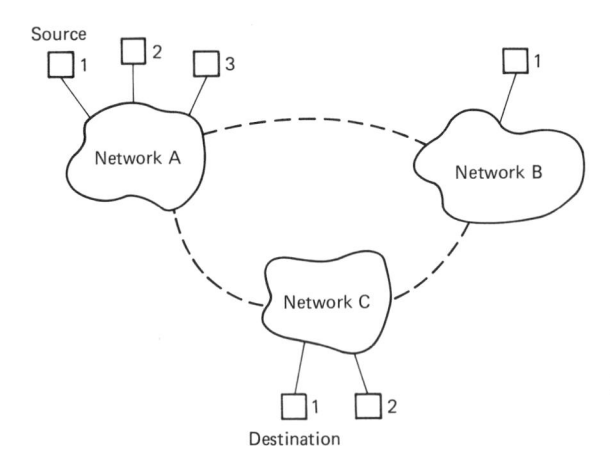

Figure 5.2 Communication between a source and destination stations located in different networks.

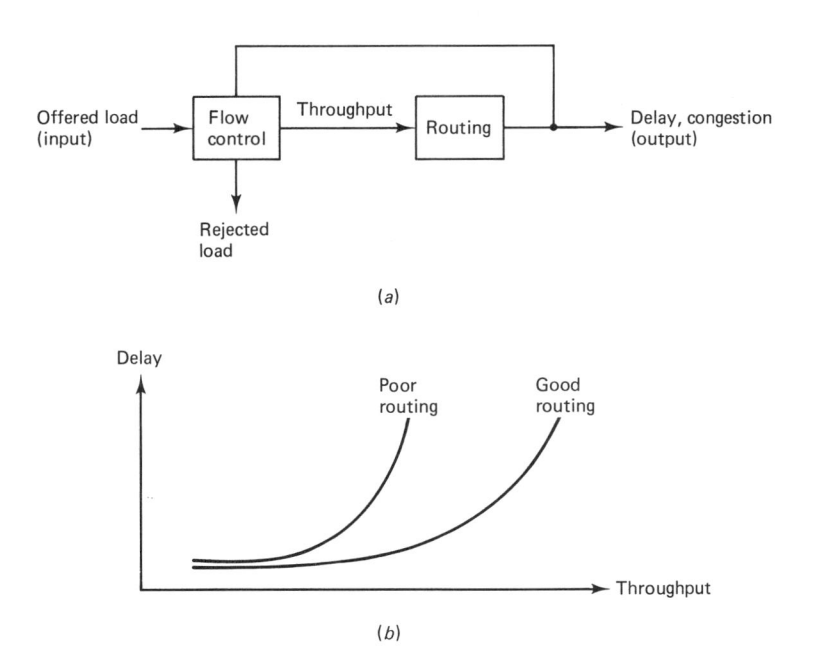

Figure 5.3 (a) Relationship between subnetwork flow control, routing, congestion, and delay; (b) Effect of poor or good routing on delay.

Resolving congestion on an end-to-end basis is a function of the transport layer by means of flow control techniques.

Intermediate nodes performing congestion control functions may involve the use of flow control techniques. The relationship between flow control, routing, and congestion is depicted in Figure 5.3(a), which is configured as a feedback system. The subnetwork[1] accepts an offered load as input and applies flow control for determining if some of the load is to be accepted or rejected. The accepted load is known as the *throughput*. Depending upon the routing algorithm, the subnetwork exhibits a certain level of performance, which can be used to decide if packets should be rejected. Examples of performance include packet delay or subnetwork level of congestion. Figure 5.3(b) depicts the effect on delay of poor or good routing schemes.

Switching and Cascading

Before discussing each of the previous functions in more detail, let us discuss two design principles useful in analyzing and designing services and protocols of different layers of the OSI reference model, particularly the network layer. The first principle is one of switching (Gien and Zimmerman, 1979). When one resource, or more generally any logical entity, is shared among several entities (through multiplexing), the resource must be able to identify which activity is concerned with subsequent actions and be able to forward a request to those entities (see Figure 5.4). **Switching** implies interpretation of addresses and routing of requests. Examples include switching a packet to

---

[1] When discussing issues concerning the network layer, computer networks are sometimes referred to as *subnetworks* to avoid confusion with the word *network*, representing a layer.

Sec. 5.1   Network Layer Functions

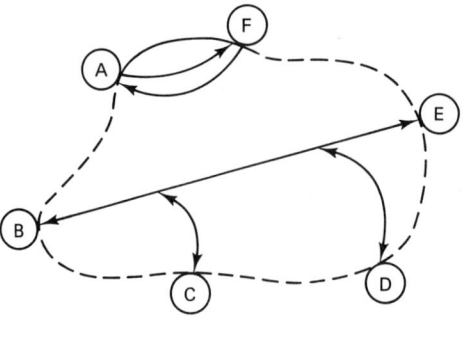

Figure 5.4 A resource B shared among several activities (C, D, and E) through multiplexing.

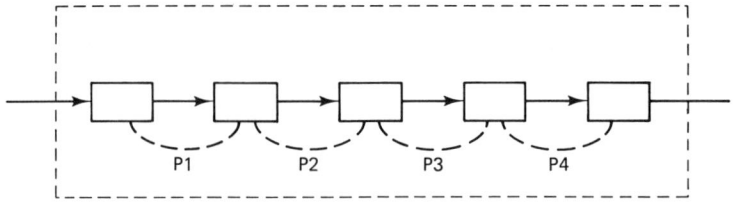

Figure 5.5 Cascading principle. Requests are forwarded or activities are propagated along the cascade.

the proper output line of a packet switching node, or forwarding a message to the proper process in a server host.

The second principle involves cascading. A linear string of entities (see Figure 5.5) built for forwarding requests or propagating activities along the cascade is referred to as **cascading.** For example, intermediate nodes not capable of performing certain functions cascade the requests to other nodes.

5.2 NAMING, ADDRESSING, AND ROUTING

Names, addresses, and routes are all different concepts that help clarify important communication issues in computer networks. Since a computer network involves the use of resources (e.g., buffers, nodes, stations, etc.), names, addresses, and routes can be defined in terms of resources. Whereas the **name** of a resource indicates *what* we seek, an **address** indicates *where* it is, and a **route** tells us *how to get there* (Shoch, 1978). Sometimes, a name is also referred to as a **logical name,** and an address is known as a **physical address,** to emphasize that the name is something agreed upon for representing physical resources.

A name is a symbol[2] identifying some resource or set of resources. For example, a string representing a name can identify service access points (SAP), connections, processes, places, people, machines, functions, or anything else a user chooses. The usefulness of names is enhanced through a mechanism that maps names into addresses. In the MAP architecture, such a mechanism is provided by the *MAP Directory Services*. The main advantage of separating names from addresses is that a

---

[2] Usually a human readable string.

name need not be bound to the corresponding address until the mapping takes place. Thus, physical addresses can change at will without the need to change the programs that deal with the corresponding resources. The only thing that needs to be changed is the name-to-address mapping. Another advantage of keeping names and addresses separate is that it is easier to remember names than to remember addresses. For example, it is easier to remember *cell controller #12* rather than 7BA2G26.

An address is typically a data structure for uniquely identifying the addressable object (i.e., a resource). An address must be meaningful throughout the domain, and must be drawn from some uniform address space. The address space may be *flat* or *hierarchical*. A **flat** address spans the entire domain (e.g., Social Security numbers) whereas a **hierarchical** address has several components, with each component belonging to a different level in the hierarchy. A telephone number is an example of a hierarchical address with the following hierarchical levels: area code, exchange, and number. For example, the number (313) 555-4453 has 313 as the area code, 555 as the exchange, and 4453 as the number.

Just as there is a mapping between a name and its corresponding address, there is also a mapping between an address and the corresponding route indicating how to get to that address. However, unlike the name-address mapping, the address-route mapping is not unique, because there may be many possible ways to get to the address. Consequently, there must be a mechanism to perform the address-route mapping. Typically, the mechanism exists as a **routing algorithm** or a **routing table.**

Although an address need not be bound to a route until the corresponding mapping takes place, we can think of an address as an identifier useful for forwarding information (i.e., finding a path) to a given destination. As shown in Figure 5.6, an address has two aspects: external (user) and internal. The user aspect is used by user entities for naming their correspondents. The internal aspect is processed within the network (i.e., the subnetwork) to forward a request to its destination.

In addition to an address, forwarding information to a destination station requires specific instructions indicating how to get the information from its current location to the desired address. The specific instructions exist as a **route** or **path,** and generating the instructions is referred to as **routing.** The routing action may only require one step to reach a destination (i.e., a direct route), or it may require a series of steps in forwarding the information on its way to the destination. The routing decision may be very straightforward in simple topologies, or more involved in complex topologies.

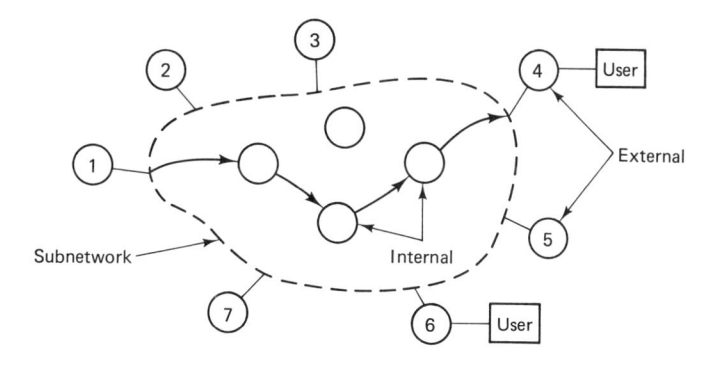

Figure 5.6 External (user) and internal aspects of addressing.

5.2.1 Classification of Routing Algorithms

In this subsection, we provide two classifications of routing algorithms. Before presenting the classifications, however, we provide a preliminary discussion of routing issues as background material for understanding the classifications.

Packet switched networks (e.g., ARPANET) can be viewed as a collection of shared resources such as processors, buffers, and communication links. The links, buffers, and CPUs all have limits on their respective speeds and capacities. As the influx of messages into the network increases, these limits may well be approached. When these limits are exceeded, the network experiences a great deal of difficulty in processing messages. Queue lengths and service times tend to grow exponentially, and the probability of deadlock increases (Glazer and Tropper, 1987). The effect of busy resources spreads to adjacent nodes while they wait for acknowledgments. As noted earlier, such network degradation is known as *congestion*.

With this view in mind, packets traveling from a source station to their destination compete for these resources. Efficient utilization and sharing of the communication resources require various types of control, with perhaps the most important being packet routing. As mentioned previously, selecting paths or links along which packets are to be forwarded through the network is referred to as *routing*. One way of implementing a routing algorithm involves setting a routing table on each station for selecting an outgoing link that will hopefully forward packets closer to their final destination. The selection of an appropriate outgoing link is done using the destination address contained in the incoming packets. Another way of implementing routing algorithms does not involve routing tables at all. Packets have additional fields indicating the sequence of nodes that make up their route. Routing nodes simply read this information and route packets accordingly.

Most packet routing schemes involve an optimization problem of some sort. The objective is to minimize or maximize a set of performance variables while satisfying certain constraints. Depending upon the type of performance variables and the corresponding constraints, one has different types of routing algorithms. A list of routing performance variables includes end-to-end network delay, throughput (i.e., the sum of actual flows in all network links), congestion, and so on. Examples of constraints include the capacity of links, buffer sizes, costs, simultaneous link access, network reliability, and others.

First classification. The first classification is based on two attributes useful for describing *routing algorithms*. The attributes characterize the *place* where each intermediate routing decision is specified, and the *time scale* used for specifying and modifying the information upon which routing decisions are based.

Regarding the *place attribute*, the following routing types exist:

1. *Source routing*. The source specifies all of the intermediate routing decisions, and includes this information along with the data being sent. The disadvantage is that in order to have a good route, the source must have fairly comprehensive information about the environment. The advantage is that the switching nodes need not maintain routing tables.

2. *Incremental routing*. The source may only specify the destination address, with the intermediate nodes choosing the next portion of the route. The incremental routing type is also called *intermediate routing* or *hop-by-hop routing*. The advantage is that the source needs only enough information to reach the next switching node. The disadvantage is that the switching nodes must have appropriate routing tables or algorithms.

3. *Hybrid routing.* The source specifies certain major intermediate points, but allows nodes to choose routes between those points. Thus, hybrid routing is a combination of source routing and intermediate routing.

Regarding the *time scale* attribute, the following routing types exist:

1. *Fixed routing.* Routing tables may be set once, left unchanged for relatively long periods of time, and only changed to reflect major system modifications. Fixed routing is also called *deterministic routing*.

2. *Dynamic routing.* Routing tables may be updated relatively frequently, reflecting short-term changes in the environment. Dynamic routing is also referred to as *adaptive routing*.

For dynamic routing algorithms, there is a third attribute which is useful for characterizing them. The attribute involves a **control** mechanism for locating information regarding changes in the environment and forwarding this information to nodes involved in the routing process. From the viewpoint of their control mechanism, dynamic routing algorithms can be further classified as:

1. *Isolated routing.* Individual switching nodes update their information in an *isolated* manner, perhaps by periodically trying various routes and observing performance measures such as delay.

2. *Centralized routing.* Changes in the environment are collected by one *centralized* point, which then forwards this information to the appropriate nodes responsible for making routing decisions.

3. *Distributed routing.* Control of the dynamic update process is *distributed* among all of the nodes which individually obtain information about changes in the environment.

Second classification. Providing a good classification of routing schemes is difficult, because most schemes do not fit neatly into the categories given earlier. There are numerous routing algorithms that have been proposed, and many of them are operating in installations around the world. In analyzing the different routing algorithms, one can distinguish the following class pairs which constitute the second classification: *central* vs. *distributed*, *static* (fixed) vs. *dynamic* (adaptive), and *deterministic* vs. *random*.

Central routing schemes involve one station (usually centrally located) responsible for constructing the routing tables for all other stations and sending the updated tables periodically. In local routing, all nodes are responsible for constructing their routing tables.

Fixed routing algorithms result in routing tables that do not change with time, whereas routing tables for *dynamic algorithms* change with time. There are many factors that can cause dynamic algorithms to change the routing tables. One factor involves topological changes in the network. If one station goes down, then that station cannot be in the route to be followed by packets. Another factor involves queue lengths. If one station has all of its buffers full, then the routing algorithm attempts to find another route through a station whose buffers are not so full. Depending upon how routing tables are updated by dynamic algorithms, the resulting algorithm is deterministic or random.

If factors causing a change in routing tables are known and the change is always predictable, the routing scheme is *deterministic*. If the change cannot be predicted, then the routing scheme is *random*. An example of a deterministic scheme is an adaptive algorithm that depends on the topology of the network. Specifically, let us assume that the algorithm is of the shortest path type, where the metric is the number of hops. Clearly, given that the station goes down, one can always predict the resulting new path.[3] An example of a random scheme is an adaptive algorithm that routes packets according to the queue lengths at some nodes. Clearly, one cannot predict instantaneous values for queue lengths, because they depend on random (i.e., unknown) variables such as how fast stations are generating messages to be transported by the network,

Before we discuss routing algorithms in more detail, we describe an algorithm for finding the shortest path between two nodes, which is extensively used in computer networks. For example, ARAPANET uses a dynamic routing algorithm known as *shortest path first* (SPF).

Shortest path algorithms. Although routing functions differ when applied to LANs, WANs, and a combination of LANs and WANs, most of the routing algorithms in these networks are variants, in one form or another, of shortest path algorithms (SPA), which forward packets from source to destination over a path of least cost. The following criteria can be used for estimating cost: link capacity, link traffic, number of hops, buffer levels at switching nodes, link error rate, link cost, link delay, etc.

The two most commonly used algorithms for routing in communication networks are due to Dijkstra (algorithm I) and Ford and Fulkerson (algorithm II) (Schwartz and Stern, 1982). For illustration purposes, consider the network in Figure 5.7, in which the numbers associated with the links are the link costs. Each link is bidirectional, with the same cost in each direction. However, both algorithms handle the case of links with different costs in each direction.

Let us use algorithm I to find the shortest paths from a single source node to all other nodes. The algorithm is a step-by-step procedure where, by the kth step, the shortest paths to the k nodes closest to the source have been calculated and included in a set N. At the next step (i.e., k+1), the node whose distance to the source is the shortest of the remaining nodes outside of N is added to N. The algorithm is briefly described as follows.

1. Initially, set N={1}, and for each node n not in N, set D(n) = d(1,n) where d(1,n) is the length of the link from node 1 to node n. In general, if no link exists between i and j, d(i,j) is assumed to be ∞.

2. At each subsequent step, find a node m not in N for which D(m) is a minimum and add m to N. Then update the distances D(n) for the remaining nodes not in N by evaluating

$$D(n) \leftarrow Min[D(n), D(m) + d(m,n)] \qquad (5.1)$$

Example

To illustrate the application of algorithm I, consider the network of Figure 5.7, where we wish to find the routing table for node 1.

Solution The routing table for node 1 can be determined by finding all the shortest paths to node 1. Application of algorithm I allows the construction of Table 5.1 where intermediate results are tabulated at each step, new nodes with shortest distance to node 1 are encircled. The routing table for node 1 can be constructed in the following manner: Construct a spanning tree rooted at node 1 and starting with the topmost node of the last column of Table 5.1, continuing with the next topmost node until all nodes are added. The resulting tree is depicted in Figure 5.7(b). The routing table can be constructed by inspection of Figure 5.7(b).

---

[3] With the assumption that all other nodes and links are operational.

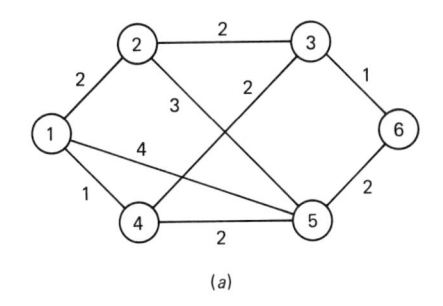

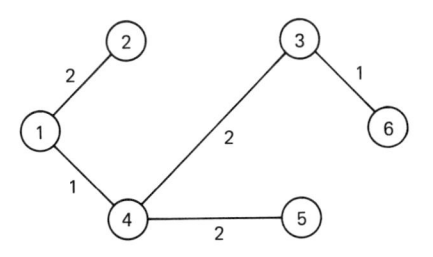

Figure 5.7 (a) A point-to-point network; (b) Example of shortest path routing.

5.3 FIXED ROUTING SCHEMES

Fixed (static) routing schemes establish one path from source station to destination station, and each successive packet follows this route. The path is typically established when the network is first installed by a network operator or after the network is operational by means of network management. Paths can either remain fixed or change infrequently. Static routing algorithms are generally im-

TABLE 5.1 INTERMEDIATE RESULTS FOR FINDING ROUTING TABLE FOR NETWORK OF FIGURE 5.7 USING ALGORITHM I.

Step	N	D(2)	D(3)	D(4)	D(5)	D(6)	Tree node
Initial	{1}	2	∞	①	4	∞	4
1	{1,4}	②	3	1	3	∞	2
2	{1,4,2}	2	③	1	3	∞	3
3	{1,4,2,3}	2	3	1	③	4	5
4	{1,4,2,3,5}	2	3	1	3	④	6
5	{1,4,2,3,5,6}	2	3	1	3	4	

Encircled numbers indicate nodes with minimum distance.

plemented by using a fixed look-up table based on the destination address of the incoming packet. The following are well-known fixed routing schemes.

1. *Flooding.* Under this scheme, a packet arriving at a station is sent to all links attached to that station except the one on which it arrived. The advantage of this approach is that the algorithm is very robust; namely, when certain stations go down, there is still a good chance that packets will reach their destination.

A good application for this scheme is a network comprised of an array of seismological stations in regions prone to earthquakes (e.g., California). When an earthquake takes place, there is a good chance that some stations would be destroyed. A flooding scheme will increase the probability that the data from most stations would not be lost. The major disadvantage of flooding is that it increases congestion[4] in the network. Thus, one application of flooding algorithms involves systems that are prone to earthquakes, fires, wars, and the like.

2. *Directory routing.* The simplest directory routing scheme is of a fixed type and is one of the most widely used. The routing table contains a row for each destination. A row is noted with the best, second best, . . . routing for a particular destination, as shown in Figure 5.8. Under

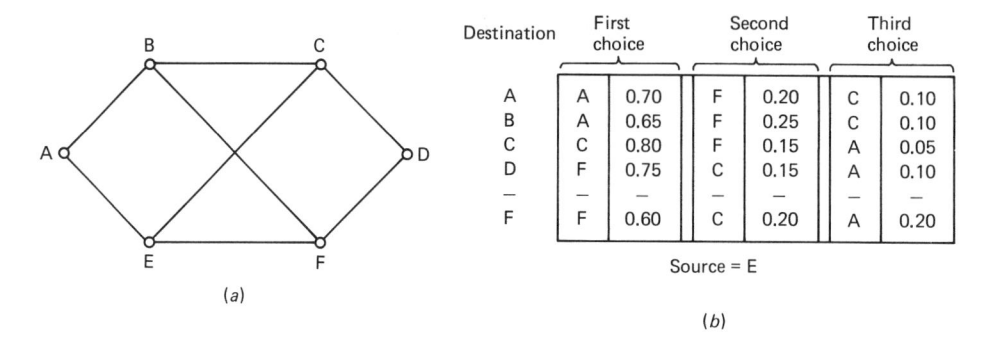

Destination	First choice		Second choice		Third choice	
A	A	0.70	F	0.20	C	0.10
B	A	0.65	F	0.25	C	0.10
C	C	0.80	F	0.15	A	0.05
D	F	0.75	C	0.15	A	0.10
—	—	—	—	—	—	—
F	F	0.60	C	0.20	A	0.20

Source = E

Figure 5.8 (a) A substructure network example; (b) Routing table for mode E.

normal circumstances, the best routing (i.e., first column) is chosen as the next station in the path. If for some reason the station in the first routing is not available (e.g., it goes down), the second best routing is chosen. This procedure is repeated until one runs out of routings, in which case new routing tables must be loaded.

As an example, consider the subnetwork of Figure 5.8(a) when the source is node E. The corresponding routing table is shown in Figure 5.8(b). When node E receives a node forwarded to A, three choices are available. The choices indicate the next node in the path to the destination station. The first choice is through A, followed by F and C, respectively. To decide, E generates a random number between 0 and 1. If the number is below 0.7, node A is used; if the number is between 0.7 and 0.9, F is used; otherwise, C is used. Thus, the three weights are the respective probabilities that A, F, or C will be used.

The main advantage of static routing is its simplicity. If the actual mean traffic is nearly the same as the estimated traffic used to develop the tables, the system will operate efficiently. However,

---
[4] Network congestion is addressed in Section 5.5.

if the topology and/or the traffic change even slightly from the ones assumed, the tables must be updated to avoid congestion and flow control problems. If the traffic is subject to dramatic changes, static schemes may not be appropriate at all.

Adaptive versions of directory routing also exist. Let us suppose that the adaptive scheme is based on the network's traffic matrix. From analyzing a traffic matrix, one can determine routes that are likely to be congested. Thus, good routes can be obtained by using links that are the least congested. The routing table for this case is similar to the previous case, except that each route has an extra column assocciated with it, indicating the probability of using the route. Links that are more likely to be congested are assigned a lower probability.

5.4 DYNAMIC ROUTING SCHEMES

Dynamic routing algorithms lessen the probability of congestion by taking into account the conditions that cause congestion. One such condition is the change of traffic flow. Under this condition, routing tables might be updated periodically to adjust for changing traffic. The following types of dynamic routing can be distinguished.

1. *Centralized Routing*. Centralized routing is a variation of directory routing. As in the case of static routing, a table is maintained by each station listing the routes where packets are directed. The difference is that centralized routing utilizes a routing control center (RCC) which periodically updates the tables of all stations. The RCC is able to collect and analyze status data from each station and determine new routes based on this information.

The obvious advantage of this scheme is the adaptability to changing traffic conditions. The control center has access to the status of the network and is able to make decisions to optimize the routing paths. A fairly obvious disadvantage is the processing time used to perform the routing calculations. These calculations must be performed quite often (e.g., on the order of second or minutes) if the tables are to accurately reflect the traffic flow conditions of the network. Another disadvantage is the network's dependence on the RCC; if it goes down, the routing scheme defaults to a fixed one with perhaps inefficient routing tables. Undoubtedly, stations closer to the RCC will receive new and updated tables first and route incoming packets according to the new paths. Stations which are further away will continue to use outdated tables, possibly contributing to congestion. Still another disadvantage of centralized routing is the increased data flow (i.e., updated routing tables) from the RCC to all stations, which further contributes to congestion.

2. *Isolated Routing*. Instead of having the RCC collecting network-wide information and making routing decisions based on this information, a variation is to allow each station to make its own routing decisions based on information it has collected.

A version of isolated routing is the *hot potato* scheme. Under this scheme, a station puts an incoming packet on the shortest outgoing queue, regardless of its destination. The packet must be directed in the approximate direction of the destination station or a packet may not ever reach the destination. We assume that each outgoing line is associated with just one queue. For example, in Figure 5.9 the packet to be forwarded is sent to node E because it has the shortest outgoing queue.

Another version of isolated routing is the *backward learning* scheme. Each packet is tagged with the source station identification and the number of hops the packet has traveled. Using this information, the station can tabulate the approximate distances to particular destinations and route packets accordingly. Under this approach, a station only gets good news (i.e., best routes to all

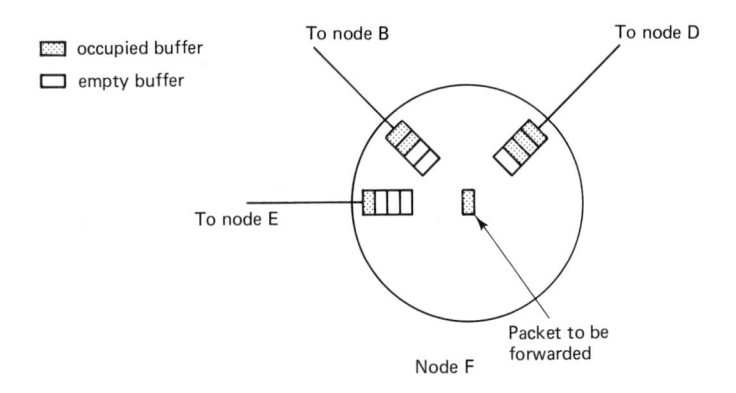

Figure 5.9 Queueing within a node.

destinations). If a link or another station goes down, there is no way for the tabulating station to be aware of these facts. A solution to this problem is to have all stations forget about everything they know and start all over in learning best routes to destinations. The advantage is the absence of data being exchanged with a central node or even exchanging data between stations, which contributes to congestion.

A few combinations of the schemes previously discussed are interesting. A combination of directory and hot potato routing schemes allows the station to prioritize which scheme is optimal based on relative weights (obtained based on average traffic and queue lengths). The advantage here is the choice of options from which to pick the route. The disadvantage is the additional processing required.

Another combination of the centralized and isolated routing is called *delta routing* (Tanenbaum, 1988). In this scheme, a common variable is compared for each link, such as queue length, packet delay, traffic, and so on. This information is delivered to the control center (i.e., the RCC) where routing tables are calculated. Again, the advantage is in the additional information on which to base the routing decisions. The cost is the additional data traffic to transfer the information and the processing time to calculate the new tables.

More specifically, delta routing works as follows: Based on the information received by the various nodes, the RCC calculates the best k paths from node i to node j, for all i and all j, where only paths that differ in their initial line are considered. Let $C_{ij}(1)$ be the total cost of the best i-j path, $C_{ij}(2)$ be the total cost of the next best path, etc. If $C_{ij}(n) - C_{ij}(l) < d$, where d is a small number, path n is declared equivalent to path l, since their costs are about the same. Upon finishing the routing computations, the RCC sends a list of all the equivalent paths for each of its possible destinations to each node.

Actually, a node is allowed to choose any of the equivalent paths randomly or based on the current measured values of line costs. By adjusting k and d, network operators can transfer authority between the RCC and the nodes. When d is small, all other paths are inferior relative to the best path, and the RCC makes all the decisions. When d is large, the RCC cannot distinguish between paths, and the routing decisions are made by the nodes based on information collected locally only. The French public packet switching network, Transpac, uses delta routing.

3. *Distributed Routing.* Instead of sending status information to a central node, each station exchanges explicit status information with its neighbors. For each destination, the station has an entry of the optimal outgoing link and estimated distance to the destination. Each station compares an actual measured distance to another station, and that station's estimate and proceeds to update its own table to ensure that the information is current and as correct as possible. Under this scheme, every station performs the function of the central station in the centralized algorithm. This requires many calculations, as each station calculates the new table independently. The data flow is far less concentrated over a few lines than the traffic required to update a central node. Furthermore, the network is not dependent on just one node for the calculation of the tables.

As an example, consider the subnetwork of Figure 5.8 again. Assume that the delay is used as a metric and that the node knows the delay to each of its neighbors. Figure 5.10 shows the delay tables at nodes A, F, and C where A claims to have a delay to B of 3 msec, to C of 5 msec, etc. Once every T msec each node sends to each neighbor a list of its established delays to each destination. Likewise, the node also receives a similar list from each neighbor. Assume that a node receives from node X the estimate T_i indicating how long it takes a packet to go from X to i. Further assume that the delay to reach node X from the current node is m. Thus, the current node knows that it can reach node i via X in $(m + T_i)$ secs. The current node can construct a new routing table by performing similar calculations and keeping the best values.

The construction of new routing tables is illustrated in Figure 5.10, with the new routing table from node E in the last column. Consider a new delay from E to D. The current node (i.e., node E) knows that it can reach node F in 4 msec, and node F can reach node D in 4 msec, thus a total delay of 8 msec. Similarly, delays from E to D via C and A are $(6+4) = 10$ and $(5+9) = 14$, respectively. The best delay is 8 msec via node F, and an entry is made in the table for the best delay and the outgoing link. The calculation is repeated for all other nodes.

One of the main disadvantages of dynamic routing algorithms is the possibility of loops. For example, in the subnetwork of Figure 5.8, a packet going from E to D may be routed initially to node F, as illustrated in Figure 5.10. Because of the dynamic nature of the algorithm, the packet may be routed to B (e.g., due to a change in the tables involving less delay) and then to A and finally back to E again. The packet will loop in the circuit EFBAE until a change in the routing tables causes the packet to leave the loop. This situation is known as **looping.**

5.5 NETWORK CONGESTION

A network can be viewed as a collection of resources such as buffers, processors, and links, which can be shared on a dynamic basis. However, advantages offered by dynamic sharing do not come

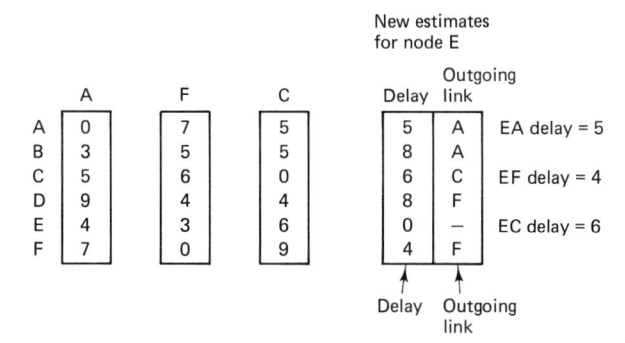

	A		F		C	New estimates for node E Delay	Outgoing link	
A	0		7		5	5	A	EA delay = 5
B	3		5		5	8	A	
C	5		6		0	6	C	EF delay = 4
D	9		4		4	8	F	
E	4		3		6	0	—	EC delay = 6
F	7		0		9	4	F	

Figure 5.10 Delay tables at nodes A, F, and C of Figure 5.8 (a) and new routing table for mode E.

without a certain danger. Unless careful control is exercised on the user demands, users may seriously abuse the network. In fact, if the demands are allowed to exceed the system capacity, a highly unpleasant situation occurs which rapidly neutralizes the delay and efficiency advantages of packet switched networks. The situation is referred to as **congestion.** Although it is very difficult to pinpoint exactly when congestion begins, one way to determine if a network is congested is to evaluate the resource (e.g., buffer) utilization. If the utilization is near or above 100 percent, then the network is probably congested. Another way to determine congestion is to evaluate message delays. If the delay is larger than the maximum value expected, then the network might be congested.

Congestion is similar to traffic jams in large cities. At *rush hour*, car traffic increases, causing streets and highways to experience car buildup, which proliferates to adjacent streets and highways. As everyone knows, traffic congestion can cause delays ranging from a few minutes to a few hours.

When message congestion builds up in a network, the throughput rate decreases, as shown in Figure 5.11. When congestion builds up even further, it may ultimately lead to deadlock, in which no message flow takes place. When no corrective action is taken, the performance of the network degrades as traffic increases. Congestion control techniques attempt to provide an acceptable level of performance even when traffic increases.

Congestion control schemes. As depicted in Figure 5.3(a), two major schemes for dealing with congestion are through the use of *flow control* and *routing* algorithms. Thus, the performance of flow control or routing algorithms can be judged by the level of congestion that they produce in the subnetwork. Subsections 5.5.1 and 5.5.2 describe how flow control and routing algorithms can be used to control congestion. Flow control, as used in the network layer, differs from that used in the data link or transport layers. This difference is explained in Section 5.5.1.

5.5.1 Flow Control Techniques

Network congestion can be managed using some flow control techniques. It is important to realize that the flow control schemes discussed in this section are different from the ones studied in the data link and transport layers. They are similar in that both schemes attempt to limit the flow of incoming messages. They differ in that the data link flow control attempts to keep a fast sender from swamping a slow receiver with data, regardless of whether the network is congested. In contrast, a flow control scheme to resolve congestion attempts to keep a sender from congesting

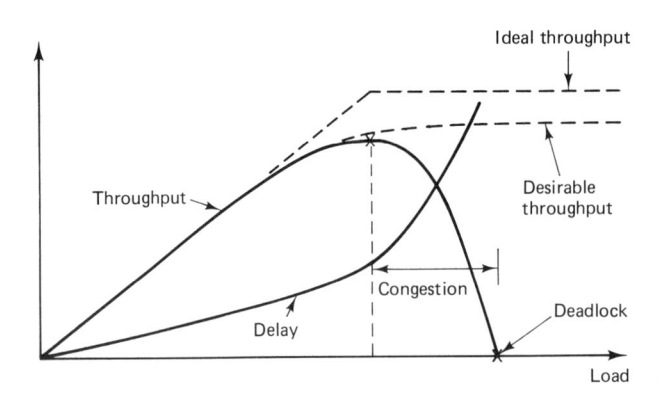

Figure 5.11 Throughput and delay curves as a function of network load.

the network, even in cases in which the receiver is faster than the sender. Flow control techniques can be *centralized* or *decentralized*. In the following, we discuss each in turn.

Centralized flow control. Centralized flow control schemes operate in the following order:

1. A network control center (NCC) gathers information on current traffic patterns.
2. The NCC applies some congestion algorithm for evaluating message flow assignments for each node.
3. The NCC communicates the new message flow assignment to nodes for which the flow assignments have changed.

Algorithms for providing centralized flow control involve the following:

1. recording or estimating the throughput for each node;
2. checking each node or link to determine if its message rate exceeds the acceptable rate (if such a node or link exists, continue; otherwise terminate the algorithm);
3. for each node or link on which the message traffic exceeds a predefined limit, calculating a new set of message flows so that the excess traffic on overloaded links and nodes is directed through the less heavily loaded nodes and links; and
4. transmitting new message flow assignments to each node.

It is possible in the preceding step 3) that a calculation of new flow assignments is not feasible without violating some constraints (e.g., link capacities). In such cases, satisfactory network performance can be achieved by increasing link capacities, adding new physical links, or restricting access to the network by some other procedure.

Since message delay is an indicator of network congestion, a method for dealing with congestion is to minimize the average message delay through the network. One approach for determining an acceptable message delay is to limit the message flow to a level that will not introduce excessive delays. The following analysis of this approach is based on the assumption that each network link can be modeled as a M/M/1 queue.[5] The link packet delay T is given by $1/(\mu - \lambda)$ where μ is the service rate of the node and λ is the rate of arriving packets. By limiting λ to about 70 percent of the service rate capacity (i.e., $\lambda = 0.7 \mu$), the delay T is less than $(3.33/\mu)$ sec.

As an example of the evaluation of message flow assignments, we describe the *flow deviation method*.

Flow deviation method. Given a network topology consisting of N nodes and M links and a traffic matrix γ_{ij} (packets/sec), the flow deviation method assigns flows within a network so as to avoid congestion by minimizing the average packet delay through the network. The traffic matrix γ_{ij} represents the number of packets sent from the node i to node j per unit of time. The delay T_i on link i is given by (Tanenbaum, 1981)

$$T_i = \frac{1}{(\mu C_i - \lambda_i)} \quad (5.2)$$

---

[5] The M/M/1 queue is analyzed in Chapter 13.

The average packet delay T over all links can be estimated as

$$T = \sum_{i=1}^{M} \frac{\lambda_i/\gamma}{(\mu C_i - \lambda_i)} \tag{5.3}$$

where M is the number of simplex links, λ_i is the rate for the arriving packets per link (packets/sec), the product μC_i is the service rate of the nodes in packets/sec, C_i is the link capacities (bit/sec), and γ is the sum of traffic on all links. That is,

$$\gamma = \sum_{i=1}^{N} \sum_{j=1}^{N} \gamma_{ij} \tag{5.3a}$$

Clearly, when $\lambda_i = 0$, the delay T is zero and we must find minimum values for $T \neq 0$ using other techniques. As in many optimization problems, a solution can be found by obtaining the partial derivative of T with respect to (λ_i/μ) and setting it to zero, in the following way:

$$l_i = \frac{\partial T}{\partial(\lambda_i/\mu)} = \frac{C_i}{\gamma(C_i - \lambda_i/\mu)^2} \quad i = 1, 2, \ldots, M \tag{5.4}$$

Setting $l_i = 0$ for all values of i leads to the trivial solution $\gamma = \infty$. This solution is expected, since generating packets infinitely fast results in a zero packet delay. However, packet flows γ_{jk} cannot be increased above link capacities (i.e., $\gamma_{jk} < C_i$), and one is dealing with a constrained minimization problem. Fratta, Gerla, and Kleinrock (1973) have developed the following algorithm that solves the constrained minimization problem:

1. Assume a feasible initial routing flow f(k); thus

$$f(k) = (\lambda_1(k)/\mu, \lambda_2(k)/\mu, \ldots, \lambda_M(k)/\mu) = G$$

where k is the iteration number.

2. Calculate the length

$$l_i = \frac{C_i}{\gamma(C_i - \lambda_i(k)/\mu)^2} \quad , \quad i = 1, 2, \ldots, M \tag{5.5}$$

Since l_i cannot be set to zero without violating capacity constraints, the next best thing to do is to work with the smallest values of l_i giving the shortest routes, as outlined in step 3.

3. For each node pair (j, k), obtain the shortest routes based on l_i. Shortest routes can be obtained using suitable shortest route algorithms.

4. For each flow γ_{jk}, proceed as follows:

a) Create a vector V that represents the new flow obtained from G by directing all the traffic γ_{jk} for node pair (j,k) through the shortest j-k route.

b) If V is feasible, and if the value T corresponding to V is less than the value T corresponding to G, then let G = V. Repeat step 4 until all γ_{jk} flows have been examined.

5. If G = f(k), the algorithm terminates, since no improvement is possible. Otherwise, let f(k+1) = G, and return to step 3 and proceed with the (k+1)th iteration.

Example

Consider the network of Figure 5.12(a) with associated arrival rates λ_i shown in parenthesis. Find a flow assignment to minimize message delay using the flow deviation method. Assume that $1/\mu = 800$ bit/packet.

	Destination					
Source	A	B	C	D		
A		6 AB	6 AC	10 AD	4 ACD	2 ABD
B	6 BA		3 BDC	5 BD	—	—
C	6 CA	3 CDB		3 CD	—	—
D	2 DBA	4 DCA	10 DA	5 DB	3 DC	

(b)

i	Line	λ_i	C_i	T_i (msec)	ℓ_i ($\times 10^{-6}$)
1	AB	8	10	222	9.76
2	AC	10	10	400	31.64
3	AD	10	20	67	1.75
4	BD	8	10	222	9.76
5	CD	3	15	63	1.19

T = 107.83 msec

(d)

	A	B	C	D
A		6 AB	6 ADC	16 AD
B	6 BA		3 BDC	5 BD
C	6 CDA	3 CDB		3 CD
D	16 DA	5 DB	3 DC	

T = 130.96 msec

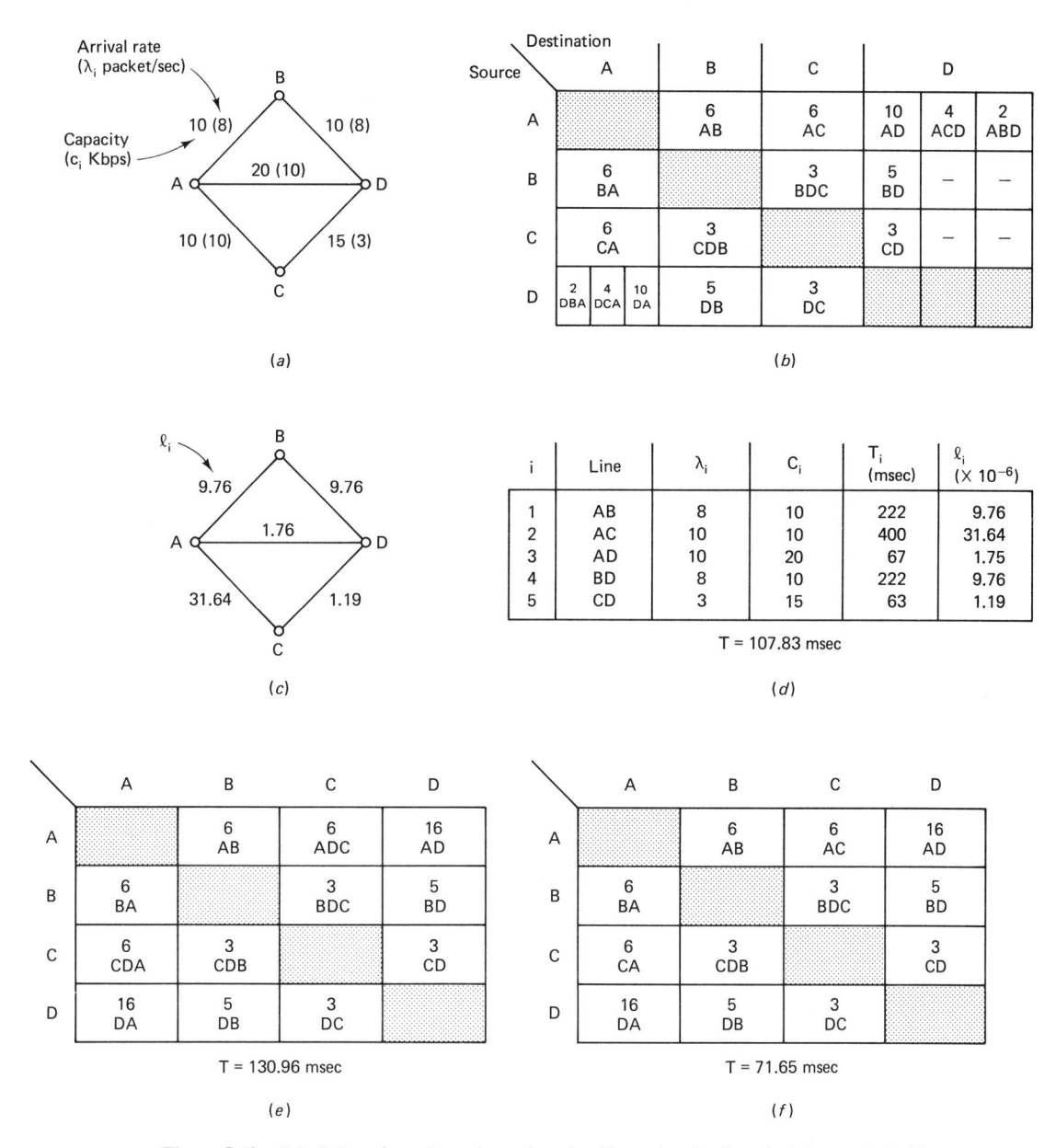

(e)

	A	B	C	D
A		6 AB	6 AC	16 AD
B	6 BA		3 BDC	5 BD
C	6 CA	3 CDB		3 CD
D	16 DA	5 DB	3 DC	

T = 71.65 msec

(f)

Figure 5.12 Calculations for a dynamic routing algorithm using the flow deviation method: (a) Initial network; (b) Initial flow assignment; (c, d) Shortest path calculation; (e) Feasible solution with unacceptable delay; (f) Feasible solution with acceptable delay.

Solution The following steps correspond to those of the flow deviation method. In order to show the details of the algorithm, we consider only one iteration.

Step 1. The feasible initial routing flow is shown in table form in Figure 5.12(b). For example, the total flow of 16 packets/sec from A to D is partitioned into 3 paths: AD, ACD, and ABD, with flows 10, 4, and 2 packet/sec respectively. Using Equation 5.2, the average delay is 107.83 msec with the intermediate calculations shown in Figure 5.12(d).

Step 2. Using Equation 5.5, we calculate the length l_i which is given in the last column of Figure 5.12(d).

Step 3. Shortest routes can be obtained graphically from Figure 5.12(c). For more complicated examples, computer-based solutions are required.

Step 4a. A new flow is obtained by redirecting all of the traffic through AD, since it is the shortest path for the AD and AC traffic. The resulting flow is shown in Figure 5.12(e), with an average delay T = 130.96 msec. Since this average delay is greater than the initial value of 107.83 msec, we discard this flow assignment. Another flow assignment is shown in Figure 5.12(f), yielding an average delay of 71.65 msec.

Step 4b. Since the average delay obtained in the last step (i.e., 71.65 msec) is less than the initial value of 107.83 msec, we make the flow of Figure 5.12(f) and the average delay of 71.65 msec as the initial values of the next iteration.

Step 5. This step is reached when no improvements are possible. It is left as an exercise to the reader to perform the calculations for subsequent iterations.

Distributed flow control. As in any decentralized approach, the entire network is responsible for managing flows in order to avoid congestion. There are many techniques that have been proposed and implemented to solve the congestion problem. The main approaches are the following:

1. End-to-end flow control. Keeping a sender from transmitting when the receiver's buffers are full helps in solving the congestion problem. However, this end-to-end flow control function actually belongs to the transport layer, and will be treated in Chapter 6.

2. Isarithmic flow control. Since the main reason for network congestion is the excessive number of packets circulating in the network, it makes sense to prevent congestion by limiting the total number of packets circulating in the network at any one time. The Isarithmic scheme is based on the concept of a *permit* (i.e., a ticket allowing a packet to travel from source to destination). Under this scheme, network congestion is controlled by limiting the total number of data packets in the network.

A version of the isarithmic flow control described by Ahuja (1982) keeps the total number of data packets plus *permits* (also called empty packets) in the network constant. As soon as data packets leave the network, *permits* are created. Data packets enter the network only by destroying *permits*. *Permits* are moved randomly within the network to increase the probability that incoming data packets encounter *permits* at the nodes where data packets enter the network.

The performance of the isarithmic scheme depends on the total number of packets allowed in the network, number of nodes, number of buffers in each node, and so on. Simulation experiments show that the total network throughput increases as the number of messages per node P increases (Davies, 1972), where P is the ratio of the total number of packets allowed in the network over the number of nodes. As P increases, throughput reaches a maximum value, and then decreases as congestion occurs.

5.5.2 Routing Techniques

As noted earlier, some adaptive routing algorithms also solve the congestion problem. For example, a routing algorithm that finds routes based on buffer utilization of intermediate nodes clearly aids in reducing congestion. The following is an example of a dynamic algorithm that reduces congestion.

A congestion-based dynamic routing algorithm. In this subsection we discuss a routing algorithm for controlling network congestion, proposed by Glazer and Tropper (1987). The algorithm is similar to the current routing algorithm used in the ARPANET. Glazer and Tropper's algorithm replaces delay as a metric by a combination of link and buffer utilization.

As depicted in Figure 5.3(a), routing is closely related to congestion control. Congestion control attempts to prevent the overutilization of network resources, and thus to maintain high throughput. Routing affects congestion in that it decides which resources are used to transport messages.

As noted a number of times, a network can be viewed as a collection of *shared links, buffers*, and *processors*. The key to the dynamic routing algorithm is that it is based on the concept of *resource utilization*. Of the three resources identified, congestion is mostly due to *link* and *buffer* utilizations. Simulation suggests that an appropriate general expression for resource utilization is

$$G_u(i) = \begin{cases} B_u(i), & \text{if } B_u(i) \geq 90\% \\ L_u(i), & \text{otherwise} \end{cases} \quad (5.6)$$

where $B_u(i)$ is the buffer utilization and $L_u(i)$ is the link utilization.

Buffer utilization is defined as the percentage of the maximum possible buffer allocation to each link. This definition not only reflects the ability of a node to accept a new packet for transmission along a specific link, but also takes into account the existence of different types of buffers (e.g., private, pool, and flow control type buffers). *Link utilization* is defined as the fraction of time in which all logical channels associated with a link are in use. According to this definition, a link can have up to seven out of eight of its logical channels in use at all times and still have 0 percent utilization, since access to the server is never completely restricted. As defined, the link utilization reflects the percentage of time in which incoming packets cannot be served and therefore will be queued.

The algorithm calculates paths as a set of links whose utilizations have the smallest sum. Thus,

$$\text{path} = \{\text{link}(i)\} \quad (5.7)$$

where the links are the ones minimizing the following cost function C,

$$C = \sum_{i=\text{source}}^{\text{dest}} (G_u(i) + 1) \quad (5.8)$$

The constant 1 is added so that there is a distinction between paths with equal utilization but different hop lengths. Figure 5.13 shows simulation results of the algorithm compared with the current ARPANET algorithm. The network used in the simulation corresponds to an 8-node network,

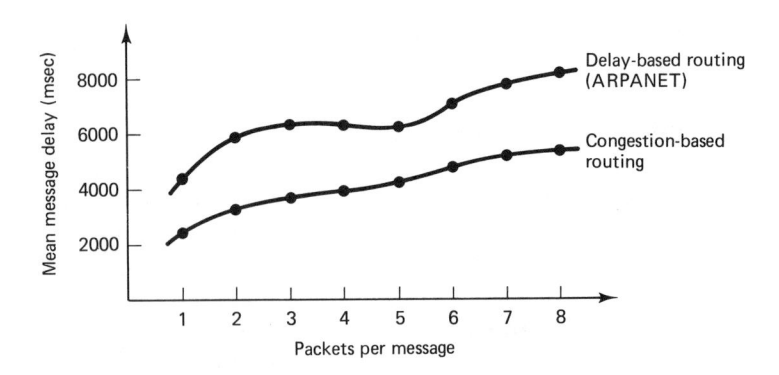

Figure 5.13 Results for the congestion-based dynamic routing algorithm.

with each node having 64 buffers available. Transmission lines are full duplex, with some running at 50 Kbps and others at 100 Kbps. Maximum packet lengths are 1008 bits and messages arrived at the hosts according to a Poisson process.[6] Results clearly show considerable improvement as compared with delay-based metrics. Higher throughput and lower delays are observed at all traffic levels, with the most dramatic improvements occurring at high levels of congestion.

5.6 DEADLOCKS

Under certain conditions, a network (or part thereof) cannot provide any communication service at all, because a certain node needs resources being used by another node. Both nodes are not willing to give up the resources they have, and both need resources available at the other node. This situation is referred to as **deadlock**. Figure 5.14 depicts a deadlock situation involving four nodes with two buffers in each node. Node 4 intends to deliver a packet to node 2 and another packet to node 1. However, neither node 1 nor 2 can accept the packet, because their buffers are full. To make matters worse, nodes 1 and 2 cannot deliver packets, because the destination nodes have their buffers full. Deadlocks can result from a protocol condition or from a resource[7] condition. Accordingly, deadlocks are classified as a *protocol deadlock* or *buffer deadlock*.

Protocol Deadlock

Protocol deadlock results when two or more peer processes are waiting on each other for some type of control message (e.g., acknowledgments) in a manner that no further communication can take place. A protocol deadlock situation caused by out-of-sequence transmission and delivery is shown in Figure 5.15. Because of different available routes, control messages used to *establish* and terminate connections can arrive in opposite sequence as compared to their transmission sequence. As a result, station A assumes that it does not have a connection, whereas station B assumes it has. Other protocol deadlocks occur when stations are exchanging control information under link failures and subsequent link repairs. Two simple techniques for dealing with protocol deadlocks involve the use

---

[6] See Stark and Woods (1986), for an introductory review of probabilities.

[7] Most likely, a buffer.

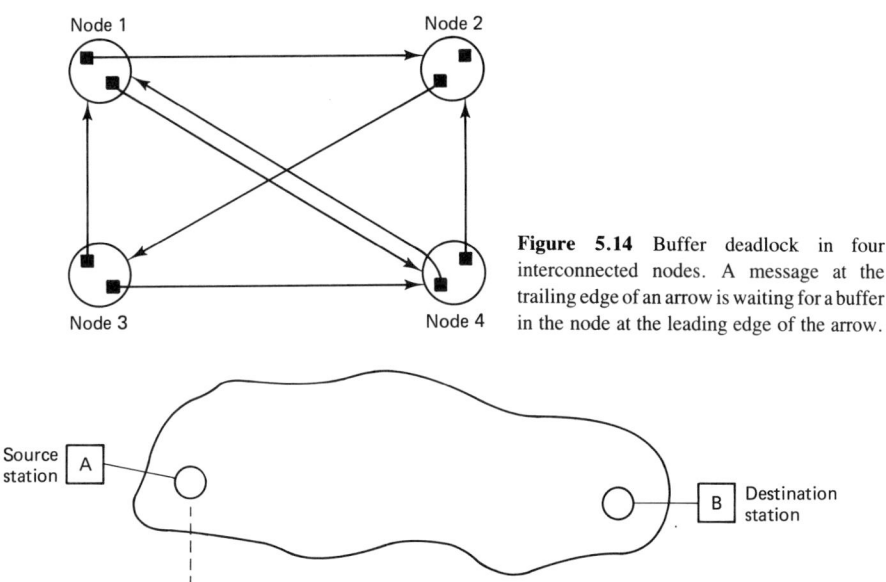

Figure 5.14 Buffer deadlock in four interconnected nodes. A message at the trailing edge of an arrow is waiting for a buffer in the node at the leading edge of the arrow.

Figure 5.15 Protocol deadlock. Because of variable message delays, stations A and B have inconsistent information.

of timers and special protocol rules, such as the *two-way handshake* and the *three-way handshake*. Timers were discussed in the context of the data link layer, and they are also discussed in Chapter 6 in the context of the transport layer. Handshake protocols are discussed in Chapter 6.

Buffer Deadlock

A buffer deadlock occurs when two or more nodes do not have free buffers, and each node is waiting for some other node to provide a buffer. Nodes are unwilling to give up the buffer they have, thus causing a lockup. When the nodes involved in the deadlock form a loop, the corresponding lockup is referred to as a **store-and-forward lockup. Direct store-and-forward** occurs when only two nodes are present. **Indirect store-and-forward** takes place when there are more than two nodes involved in the deadlock.

Example

Consider the network shown in Figure 5.16. Let us assume that nodes A, B, and C have no buffers available to store new messages. Furthermore, assume that each message in node A requires assignment of a buffer in node B before the message can be transmitted. If messages in node B are also waiting for a buffer in node C, and those in C are waiting for a buffer

Figure 5.16 A network with two buffer deadlocks. Nodes A, B, and C constitute a store-and-forward wait deadlock and nodes F,G,H,M,J, and K constitute a mutual wait deadlock.

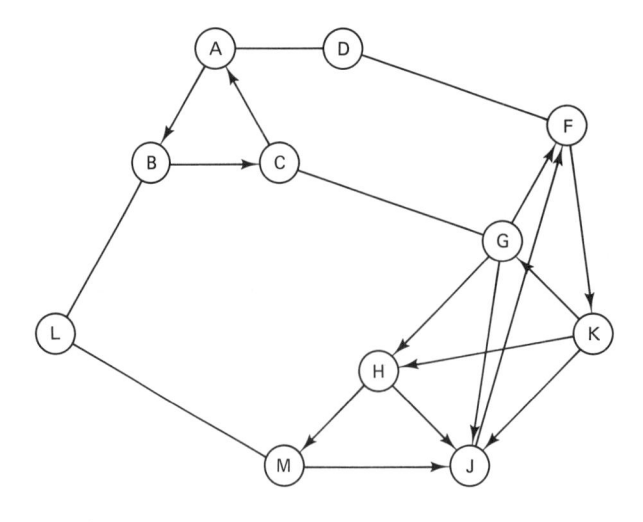

X ⟶ Y : Arrow indicates that Node X is waiting for a buffer in Node Y

X —— Y : Solid line indicates a link between Nodes X and Y

in A, then nodes A, B, and C are in a store-and-forward buffer deadlock. Now consider another buffer deadlock in the same network. Again assume that there is no free buffer in any node in the set of nodes X = (F, G, H, J, K, M). If messages in each of these nodes are waiting for buffers in one or more nodes in X, then the set of nodes X is in a buffer deadlock. This deadlock results from the mutual wait among nodes in the set X.

Two important observations can be made regarding deadlock occurrence. First, the set of nodes in a deadlock must be connected. For example, in Figure 5.16, the set X = (F, G, H, J, K, M) is connected, since each node in X is linked to every other node in X through nodes in X. Second, the preceding deadlocks can occur only if each message in the network follows a fixed route. On the other hand, if the message routes are adaptive, it is possible that the preceding two deadlocks may be resolved. For example, consider messages in node M destined for node A. Assuming that there is no free buffer in nodes H or J, the message can be directed through node L. Thus, for adaptive routing, local congestion can be prevented, at least for short periods of time. With adaptive routing, a buffer deadlock usually occurs only when most of the network nodes have no free buffers. For the remainder of this section, we restrict our treatment to networks *with fixed routing*.

Given a network design (in terms of nodes, links, and buffers) several schemes exist to determine if a deadlock can occur. In the **state enumeration scheme,** each network state is checked for deadlock. This scheme is useful only if the number of nodes is not excessive. In the **network flow scheme,** buffers are incorporated into packet flows so that results from graph theory can be utilized. Alternatively, one can design the network so that deadlocks can be avoided to start with. The following deadlock-free buffer allocation algorithm (Raubold and Haenle, 1976) divides buffers in each node into an ordered set of buffer classes.

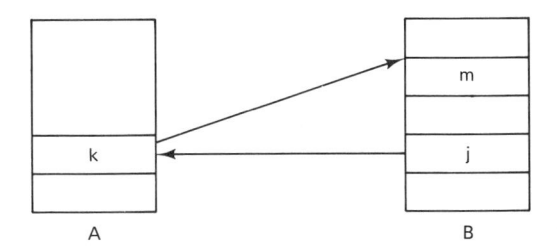

Figure 5.17 Deadlock prevention using a buffer allocation scheme.

Deadlock-free buffer allocation. Each buffer class can have at least one buffer and the remaining buffers are kept in a pool for dynamic allocation to buffer classes. As packets traverse the network, their buffer class index increases. A packet with a buffer class index i has buffers available from buffer classes with an index less than or equal to i. The following example adapted from Ahuja (1982) illustrates the deadlock prevention technique.

Example

Consider two adjacent nodes in a network, as shown in Figure 5.17, so that certain messages in each node are waiting on the other node for a buffer. We assume that messages in class j of node B are waiting for a buffer in class k of node A. Therefore, if we show that messages in class k are waiting for a buffer in a class other (in fact higher) than j, then circularity in the wait is prevented. Since the buffer class increases as a message traverses the network, k = j + 1. Now, messages in class k are waiting for buffers in a class, say m. Then m = k + 1, which implies m > j. Therefore, the circular wait is avoided. This is true since, as noted earlier, circular wait results when messages in two classes are waiting on each other, either directly or indirectly, through other message classes.

5.7 NETWORK INTERCONNECTION

Just as stations can be interconnected to form networks, one can interconnect networks to form a system of networks. The interconnected networks are often referred to as **catanets.** The need for network interconnection is not different from the need for station interconnection. Individual computers or stations can be likened to human minds, and networks can be likened to human societies. The need for societies (e.g., countries) to interact with one another is similar to the need of networks to interact with one another.

Some problems arising in the interconnection of networks are similar to the problems encountered in the interconnection of stations. Thus, one must deal with routing, addressing, fault isolation, flow control, congestion control, and the services offered, all in the context of internetworking. Figure 5.18 depicts a view of network interconnection. The interface block is similar to the network interface unit (NIU) of conventional networks. The major difference is that NIUs provide an interface between stations and the network's transmission system, whereas the interface block in Figure 5.18 provides an interface between a network and the catanet's transmission system. Unlike Figure 5.18, local networks can be interconnected directly with one another. That is, the *interface boxes* of Figure 5.18 could provide an interface between two local networks.

Since a catanet involves several networks with perhaps widely different characteristics, the interconnection schemes must provide enough flexibility to accommodate different networks. Table 5.2 shows some characteristics featured by local and long haul networks which must be taken into

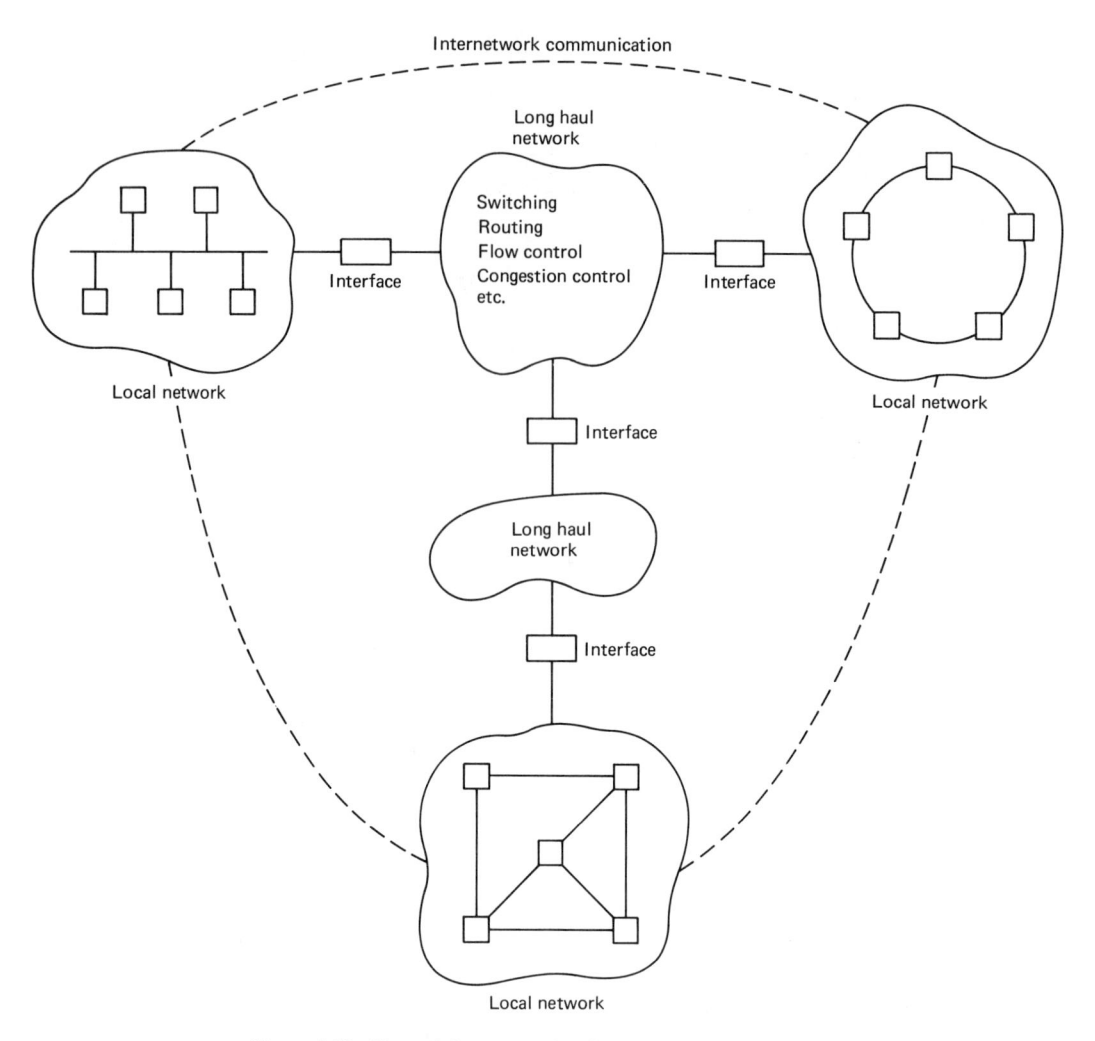

Figure 5.18 Network interconnection featuring local and long haul networks.

consideration when interconnecting these two networks. There are many ways for interconnecting networks to form catanets. Figure 5.18 depicts a local network and long haul network interconnection. Two other possibilities involve interconnecting just local networks or just long haul networks.

Analysis of the main characteristics of network interconnection leads to the following major interconnection issues:

How should networks be physically attached to one another?
How should one station in one network access the medium in another network for communication purposes?
To what extent should the protocols used in one network be used in another network?
Since data rates affect acknowledgment handling and flow control, how is the problem of

TABLE 5.2 COMPARISON OF TYPICAL LOCAL AND LONG HAUL NETWORK CHARACTERISTICS

Characteristic	Local network	Long haul network
Data rate	10 million bit/sec	50,000 bit/sec
Propagation delay	Small due to short distance	Large due to long distance (e.g., satellite)
Flow/congestion control; Message sequence	Minimum due to high data rate and simple topology	Major due to low data rate and complex topology
Error rate	Relatively low due to efficient signal processing (e.g., modulation)	Relatively high. Operated in noisy environment of telephone network
Addressing	Simple if not interconnected to other networks	Complex because of many nodes and links
Network Management	Extensive because of complexity of protocols	Extensive due to large number of nodes and links and complex topology

connecting networks with widely differing data rates resolved?

Some networks provide different services than others (i.e., datagrams and virtual circuits). How are the different services reconciled?

How is the difference in delay time, as it affects the user's response time, to be reconciled?

How should network addressing capability be provided?

Interconnection Approaches

The OSI reference model can provide the basis for network interconnection. More specifically, networks can be connected by interfaces having some of the OSI layers common to both networks, as depicted in Figure 5.19. The common layers are the layers above the kth layer of the OSI reference model.

Interfaces are classified into repeaters, bridges, routers, or gateways, depending upon the number of layers that are common to networks on both sides of the interface. A **repeater** is a device that interconnects networks at the physical layer. When the interconnection is done at the data link layer, the corresponding interface is referred to as a **bridge.** Other interfaces include **routers** and **gateways,** which interconnect networks at the network and application layers, respectively.

Since *bridges* do not work above a network layer, stations in networks connected by bridges share the same address space (i.e., bridges are transparent) with stations in other networks, as shown in Figure 5.20. In most cases, the physical and data link layers are different. Examples of networks interconnected by bridges include two MAP networks that have identical layers 2 through 7 but run on two different media (e.g., coaxial cable and optical fibers). Message transfer between a source station located in the coaxial cable and a destination station located in the optical fiber cable takes place in the following way: The source station puts the message on the medium with the destination address attached to it. The bridge contains a table with a list of addresses for stations in the optical fiber network. Since the destination address for the message traveling on the medium is contained in the bridge's table, the message is captured by the bridge and forwarded into the other network.

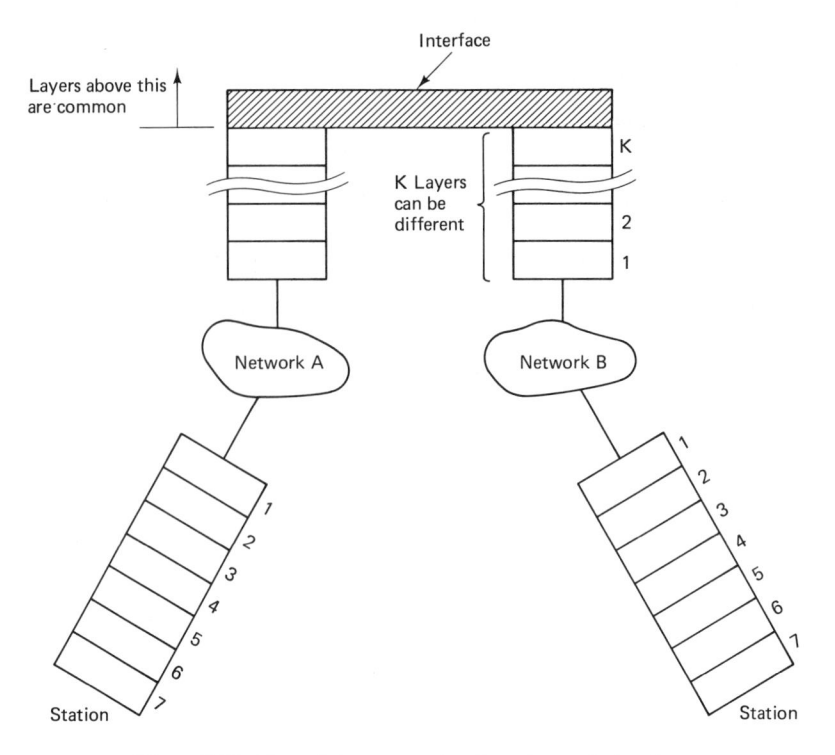

Figure 5.19 Network interconnection through generic interfaces.

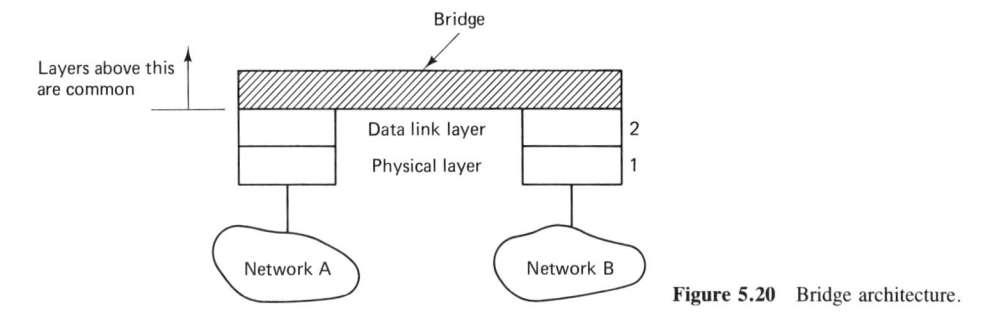

Figure 5.20 Bridge architecture.

The destination station located in the optical fiber medium is now able to receive the message, since the address contained in the message matches its own. The bridge thus performs a store-and-forward function.[8]

One of the main advantages of using bridges is the decoupling of networks, which translates into improved performance. A group of stations that have high communication requirements within the group can be put in one network. Likewise, another group of stations that have high communication requirements can be put in another network. Performance is improved, because stations not actively

---

[8] Although the bridge described here is the most likely implementation, it is, strictly speaking, a filtering bridge. A pure OSI bridge would pass all messages in both directions.

communicating with other stations in one group are excluded from that group, thus minimizing the overhead involved (e.g., relaying or token passing). The disadvantage of using a bridge is the increased overhead involved in going through it. The overhead translates into lower throughput, increased response time, and increased congestion. However, the disadvantages can be minimized through proper network design. Traffic requirements should dictate the number of networks in the catanet and what stations should be in what networks.

Unlike bridges, which are able to interconnect just two networks, *routers* allow the interconnection of any number of networks (see Figure 5.21). Obviously, a routing functionality must be present in the router to achieve this function. Since the interconnected networks can use different addressing schemes and internal routing schemes of their own, layers 1, 2, and 3 can be different. An advantage of using routers instead of bridges is the flexibility in interconnecting a number of heterogeneous networks in a more flexible topology. The disadvantage again is the decreased performance caused by the additional overhead. Transport layer relays also exist.

When interconnected networks have different transport or higher level layers, *gateways* are required. Gateways have the functionality of bridges and routers. Moreover, gateways must provide protocol conversion for the layers that differ in both networks. As depicted in Figure 5.22, in general, gateways provide network interconnection by using the services provided by the application layer. The advantage of using gateways is that it allows networks which are entirely different to be interconnected. The disadvantage, again, is the decrease in performance as a result of protocol conversion functions.

Stations in different networks connected by either *routers* or *gateways* do not share the same network address space. Thus, a station in network A can have the same address as another station in network B. Consequently, routers and gateways are not transparent devices, because one must specify that a message is for station 1 in network B rather than station 1 in network A. In this case, internetworking requires an addressing scheme that includes both a network and stations within that network. The following hierarchical addressing scheme is common.

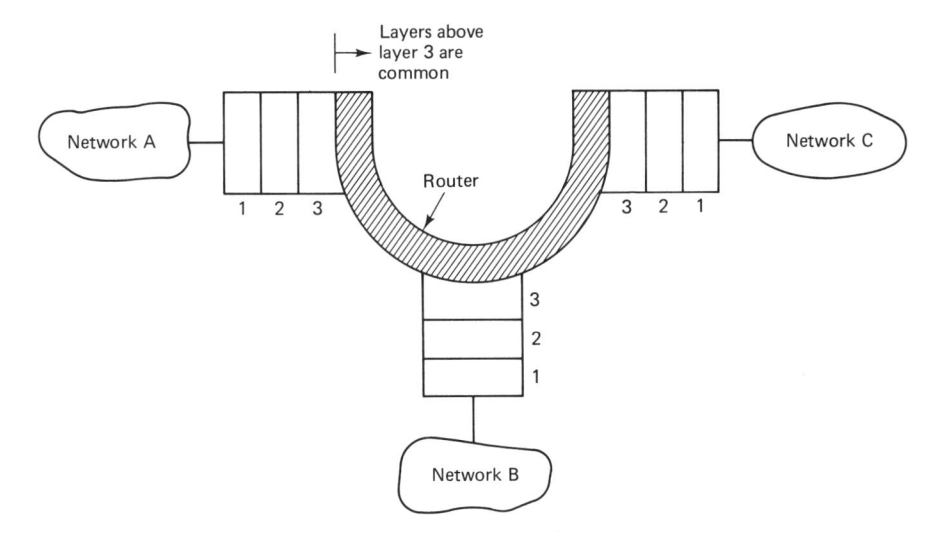

Figure 5.21 Router architecture.

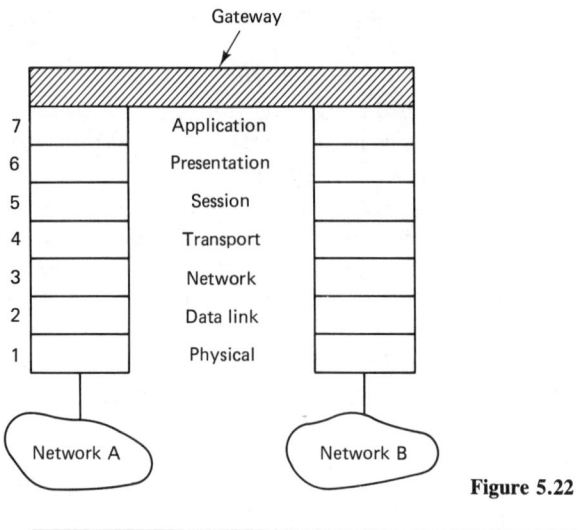

Figure 5.22 Gateway architecture.

| NETWORK ADDRESS | LOCAL ADDRESS |

The preceding addressing scheme introduces an *individual network address* space and a *global network address* space, as the one shown in Figure 5.23. An individual network address space encompasses all stations connected to that network and all gateways (or routers) that interconnect to other networks. The global network address uniquely identifies any station in the context of all networks.

LAN-to-LAN Interconnection

Interconnecting LANs provide the following benefits:

> geographical extension of LAN coverage,
> better fault diagnosis and fault isolation,
> improved network security and access control,
> heterogeneous LAN interconnection, and
> improved performance (e.g., higher throughput).

However, achieving these benefits is not easy because of the following difficulties:

1. The various links interconnected may have a dramatic data rate mismatch, such as when interconnecting a 10 Mbps CSMA/CD, a 100 Mbps fiber distribution data interface (FDDI), and a 4 Mbps token ring.
2. Even if the LANs are of the same type and have the same rates, the loads may be unbalanced, thus causing congestion at the boundaries.
3. State-of-the-art bridge implementation can forward only a few thousand packets/sec. Because of protocol overhead, the situation with routers is even worse. Thus, there is also a dramatic throughput mismatch between bridges (or routers) and high-speed LANs. Unlike wide area

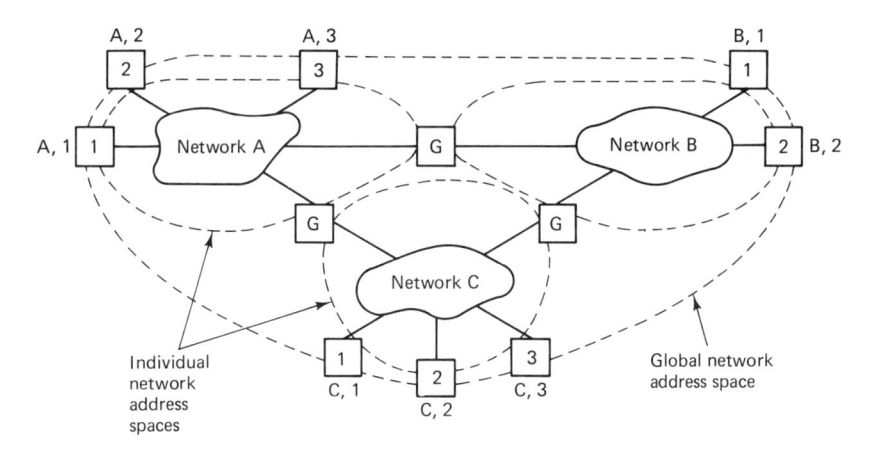

Figure 5.23 Individual and global network address spaces in catanets.

network (WAN) interconnection, the bridge and routers used in LAN interconnection are not only the communications bottleneck, but also contribute to congestion.

A new type of network interconnection device, called **brouters,** has been proposed which incorporates many of the congestion control features of a router and yet retains the transparency of the bridge (Gerla and Kleinrock, 1988).

5.8 THE ISO NETWORK LAYER STANDARD PROTOCOL

In this section we provide an overview of the network layer standard protocol developed by the International Organization for Standardization (ISO). The protocol portion of the standard is detailed in (ISO 8473) and the service portion in (ISO 8348). The ISO standards cover two key aspects of the OSI network layer, involving the *service* provided by the network layer to the transport layer or to any other higher layer, and the *specification* of the way in which the network layer is used in the context of internetworking (i.e., its architecture) (Ware, 1983). The ISO network layer service and architecture are discussed in subsections 5.8.1 and 5.8.2, respectively.

5.8.1 The OSI Network Service

Two kinds of service are provided by the OSI Network Service definitions: connection-oriented network service and connectionless.

Connection-oriented network service. The connection-oriented network service provides communications capability to service users by means of *network connections*. After a network connection is established, the characteristics (i.e., quality of service) of the network services are always perceived by the service users at the two ends of the connection to be identical. Since a connection-oriented service has three distinct phases, (i.e., connection establishment, data transfer, and connection release). The network services are grouped accordingly and listed on Table 5.3 along with their corresponding parameters. Of the six services, N_CONNECT and N_RESET are

TABLE 5.3 SUMMARY OF NETWORK SERVICE PRIMITIVES AND PARAMETERS

Phase	Primitive	Parameters
Connection establishment	N_CONNECT.req	(Called Address, Calling Address, Receipt Confirmation Selection, Expedited Data Selection, Quality of Service Parameter Set, NS* User-Data)
	N_CONNECT.ind	(Called Address, Calling Address, Receipt Confirmation Selection, Expedited Data Selection, Quality of Service Parameter Set, NS User-Data)
	N_CONNECT.resp	(Responding Address, Receipt Confirmation Selection, Expedited Data Selection, Quality of Service Parameter Set, NS User-Data)
	N_CONNECT.conf	(Responding Address, Receipt Confirmation Selection, Expedited Data Selection, Quality of Service Parameter Set, NS User-Data)
Data Transfer	N_DATA.req	(NS User-Data, Confirmation request)
	N_DATA.ind	(NS User-Data, Confirmation request)
	N_DATA_ACKNOWLEDGE.req	—
	N_DATA_ACKNOWLEDGE.ind	—
	N_EXPEDITED_DATA.req	(NS User-Data)
	N_EXPEDITED_DATA.ind	(NS User-Data)
	N_RESET.req	(Originator, Reason)
	N_RESET.ind	(Originator, Reason)
	N_RESET.resp	—
	N_RESET.conf	—
Connection Release	N_DISCONNECT.req	(Originator, Reason, NS User-Data, Responding Address)
	N_DISCONNECT.ind	(Originator, Reason, NS User-Data, Responding Address)

* NS: Network layer service.

confirmed services, whereas N_DATA, N_DATA_ACKNOWLEDGE, N_EXPEDITED_DATA, and N_DISCONNECT are *unconfirmed* services. The meaning of the service parameters should be clear after the following description of the services.

The connection establishment phase of the network service consists of just the N_CONNECT service, which provides the means for network users to establish a network connection. As part of the connection establishment, each user can transfer up to 128 bytes of data. In addition, service users can negotiate the quality of service of the network connection, and the availability of the N_DATA_ACKNOWLEDGE and N_EXPEDITED_DATA optional services to be used during the data transfer phase.

Four services make up the data transfer phase: N_DATA, N_DATA_ACKNOWLEDGE, N_EXPEDITED_DATA, and N_RESET. The N_DATA service is used for transferring user data over the network connection. User data transferred by the N_DATA service is also referred to as *Network Service Data Unit* (NSDU). The network service provides flow control and preserves both the sequence and the boundaries of the NSDUs transferred. The network service imposes no constraints on the size or content of the data to be transferred.

The N_DATA_ACKNOWLEDGE service, also referred to as *receipt confirmation*, provides a means for a service user to acknowledge the receipt of data sent by means of the N_DATA service. For each NSDU sent, the sending user can indicate whether a confirmation of its receipt is desired. If the confirmation is requested, the N_DATA_ACKNOWLEDGE service is issued by the receiving user to respond positively to the sender when the NSDU is successfully received. Since the N_DATA_ACKNOWLEDGE service is optional, its use is negotiated while establishing a network connection. It is possible that either of the network service users or the service provider can refuse the use of N_DATA_ACKNOWLEDGE.

In manufacturing applications, some data (e.g., orders to machines) need to be sent before other normal data, because they may affect production throughput. The N_EXPEDITED_DATA service provides a means of information transfer which is distinguished from normal data transfer using the N_DATA service. Expedited NSDUs[9] can bypass normal NSDUs being transferred in the same direction and can still be delivered when normal NSDUs are not being accepted by the receiver. However, the degree to which expedited NSDUs will bypass normal NSDUs is not predictable nor guaranteed. Expedited NSDUs are subject to a different quality of service and separate flow control from that applying to normal NSDUs. The N_EXPEDITED_DATA allows a user to send information even when the peer user is refusing to accept normal NSDUs. It is useful for transmitting exception conditions or providing an *expedited* service to higher layers.

When things go wrong in a message transmission, sometimes it is best to start all over. For example, a process generating data to be transmitted may simply stop operating in the middle of the transmission, or a modem failure may occur during message transmission. When situations such as these happen, the network layer allows users to start all over (i.e., resynchronize) by means of the N_RESET service. N_RESET can be invoked by either of the service users or by the service provider.

When initiated by a service provider, N_RESET is used to report unrecoverable loss of data without releasing the network connection. As a result of an N_RESET, service users may determine that a recovery procedure must be performed. When initiated by a service user, N_RESET is used to halt message transmission and to initiate a resynchronization operation. In response to a N_RESET service, the service provider discards all data on the network connection which have not been delivered to the service user. In addition, the network service provider also notifies any service user which did not initiate the N_RESET service that a resynchronization is taking place.

Like the connection establishment phase, the connection release phase consists of just one service, called N_DISCONNECT. The N_DISCONNECT service is used for terminating a network connection. It can be invoked by either of the service users of the connection or by the service provider. The delivery of data which is being transferred over a connection when an N_DISCONNECT is invoked cannot be guaranteed.

When requesting services from the network layer, a service user can request that the service be provided with a certain level of performance or other characteristics, referred to as **quality of service** (QOS). Performance aspects of LANs are discussed in detail in Chapter 13. Thus, we

---

[9] Limited in size to a maximum of 32 bytes.

provide here only a list of QOS parameters and we leave further performance discussions for Chapter 13. The following QOS parameters have been identified for the connection-oriented network services:

Connection establishment delay,
Connection establishment failure probability,
Throughput,
Transit delay,
Residual error rate,
Connection resilience,
Transfer failure probability,
Connection release delay,
Connection release failure probability,
Connection protection,
Priority, and
Maximum acceptable cost.

Connectionless network services. The connectionless network service transfers data units which are independent of one another without the establishment and maintenance of a network connection. Unlike the connection-oriented network service, the connectionless service is very simple, consisting of just one service, called N_UNITDATA. The N_UNITDATA service is used to transmit a single, discrete NSDU from one service user to another without establishing and utilizing a network connection. From the viewpoint of the service provider, a data unit transferred with an N_UNITDATA service bears no relationship with any other data unit. Thus, data units are not necessarily received in the same order that they were transmitted. In addition, flow control is not provided by the service provider. Clearly, QOS parameters for connectionless network services refers to transmission characteristics of single data units, such as transit delay, residual error probability, cost, and protection from authorized access.

5.8.2 ISO Network Layer Architecture

Unlike the transport, session, presentation, and application layers, which communicate strictly in pairs (i.e., a source and a destination station), the network is functionally more complex, because it contains additional components which are outside of end systems. The additional components include *relay systems* and *relay functions* in subnetworks, as depicted in Figure 5.24.

Ideally, all subnetworks should be identical from the viewpoint of services and characteristics. In reality, subnetworks are different and do not provide the equivalence of an OSI network service. Rather, these subnetworks vary considerably in the functions performed, services provided, and method of access. For example, some subnetworks may provide a connection-oriented service, whereas others may provide a connectionless. Thus, when interconnecting subnetworks via an OSI network layer, additional functions need to be performed by the network layer at adjacent ends and intermediate systems. As a result, the functionality and internal organization of a network layer is highly variable and very much dependent upon the characteristics of subnetworks to be interconnected.

The purpose of specifying a network layer **internal architecture** is to take into account the wide variance in network layer functionality and to understand its effect on critical aspects of the

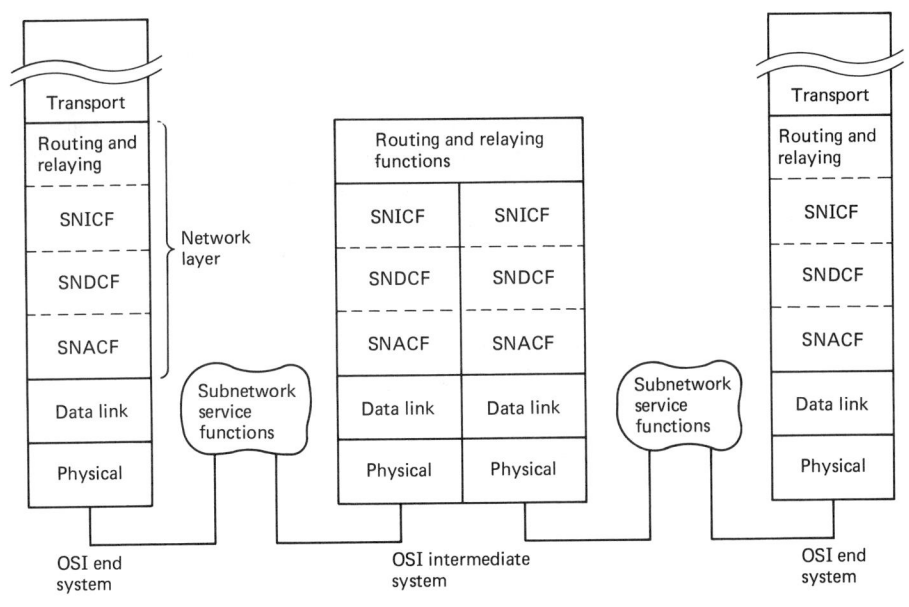

Figure 5.24 Subnetwork interconnection of OSI end systems and intermediate systems showing the network layer internal architecture.

SNICF: subnetwork independent convergence facility
SNDCF: subnetwork dependent convergence facility
SNACF: subnetwork access facility

network layer, such as routing, addressing, protocol, and interworking strategies. In the network layer internal architecture, functions are classified as those performed completely independent of the subnetworks and those which are performed in a subnetwork specific manner. As depicted in Figure 5.24, the ISO network layer consists of the following sublayers:

Subnetwork Access Facility (SNACF),
Subnetwork Dependent Convergence Facility (SNDCF),
Subnetwork Independent Convergence Facility (SNICF), and
Routing and Relaying.

Whereas the first two sublayers are subnetwork dependent, the latter two are subnetwork independent. SNICF functions are performed entirely by cooperative action of peer network entities in end or intermediate systems, regardless of whether subnetworks are being used. It is expected that any subnetwork specific functions be done below the SNICF. A protocol implementing the SNICF is referred to as a *SNICF protocol* (SNICFP).

Routing and relaying are also subnetwork independent. Routing involves the interpretation of address and QOS parameters along with some criteria in selecting a route. Relaying functions are internal to the intermediate system involving the switching of information flow when it goes from one subnetwork to another.

The subnetworks perform a number of functions, referred to as the **subnetwork service.** The *Subnetwork Access Facility* is the portion of the network layer that makes use of the subnetwork

Sec. 5.8 The ISO Network Layer Standard Protocol

service. Thus, the SNAF acts as an interface to the subnetwork. Because subnetworks vary considerably in functionality and services offered, the approach taken by ISO is to include a sublayer that translates the specific service provided by subnetwork into a uniform set of services expected by the SNICF sublayer. The translation is performed by the Subnetwork Dependent Convergence Function (SNDCF) sublayer. In performing the translation function, the SNDCF may provide additional capabilities, or it may abrogate the functionality provided by the subnetwork. A protocol implementing the functions of the SNDCF is called a *Subnetwork Dependent Convergence Function Protocol* (SNDCFP).

Because of the diversity of available subnetwork services, the network layer architecture just outlined is flexible enough to support different internetworking strategies, depending upon the circumstances. For example, when highly functional subnetworks are interconnected, it is advantageous to fully utilize the subnetwork-specific functions and define minimal or no SNIDF. At the other extreme, in a configuration composed of subnetworks with a low degree of functionality, the preferred internetworking strategy is one where most of the functions are performed by a SNICF. In this case, only the functionality which is common to all subnetworks is utilized from each subnetwork.

5.9 MAP NETWORK LAYER

As noted a number of times in this chapter, the main function of the network layer is to provide message routing between end nodes, either in the same subnetwork or any other subnetwork, regardless of their location. Additional functions include addressing, congestion control, and message segmentation. The MAP network layer performs the routing function by converting global address information into routing information, maintaining message routing tables and/or algorithms, and switching each incoming message to its proper outgoing path. Associated with the preceding operations are special procedures and/or databases for translating global addresses into the required routing information. The databases are part of the *MAP directory services*.

End-to-end routing is performed in the MAP 3.0 network by means of a global routing function, as specified in the ISO 8473 *Connectionless Mode Network Service* (*CLNS*), also referred to as the **CLNS protocol.** The CLNS protocol is an internetworking protocol for allowing packets to traverse multiple LANs, regardless of the routing algorithm used in each LAN. Specifically, the protocol provides exchange of data and control information (CI) via connectionless transmission, IPDU (Internet Protocol Data Unit) information encoding, procedures for interpreting the information, and a formal specification to be met to be in compliance with the standard.

The major functions of the CLNS protocol as used in the MAP 3.0 architecture are *PDU segmentation/reassembly*, *routing*, and *congestion control*. Segmentation is performed when the PDU size is greater than a predefined maximum size. At the receiver, the initial PDU is reconstructed from the derived PDUs. Routing is performed using a hierarchical routing algorithm with tables and routing control centers (RCCs). The routing algorithm has provisions for complete source routing and partial source routing. Congestion control is performed by simply throwing packets away (i.e., packet discarding). The protocol machine discards packets when it encounters a violation of the protocol, a PDU with incorrect checksum, not enough buffers, or a PDU header which cannot be analyzed. The PDU format at the network layer is shown in Figure 5.25.

Depending on whether the communication nodes belong to a single subnetwork (i.e., segment)

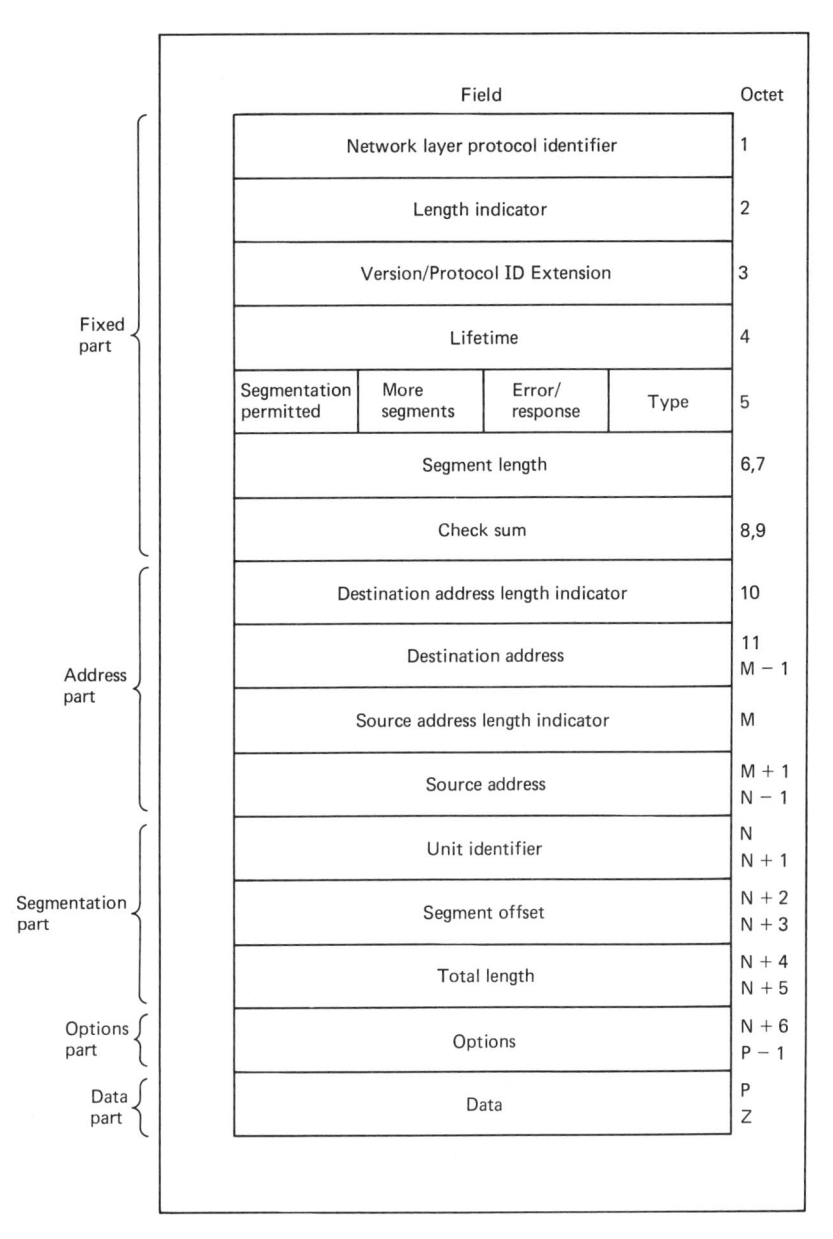

Field	Octet
Network layer protocol identifier	1
Length indicator	2
Version/Protocol ID Extension	3
Lifetime	4
Segmentation permitted | More segments | Error/response | Type	5
Segment length	6,7
Check sum	8,9
Destination address length indicator	10
Destination address	11 / M − 1
Source address length indicator	M
Source address	M + 1 / N − 1
Unit identifier	N / N + 1
Segment offset	N + 2 / N + 3
Total length	N + 4 / N + 5
Options	N + 6 / P − 1
Data	P / Z

Fixed part: rows 1–9
Address part: rows 10 through source address
Segmentation part: unit identifier, segment offset, total length
Options part: Options
Data part: Data

Figure 5.25 ISO network layer protocol data unit.

two subsets of the CLNS protocol are defined: *inactive network layer protocol*, and *full conformance protocol*. The inactive network layer protocol is used when the following three conditions are met:

1. the source and destination stations are on the same subnetwork,
2. the size of transport protocol data unit (TPDU) is less than the size of maximum link protocol data units (LPDU) at both ends of the communication, and

3. the destination network service access point (NSAP) is accessible via an inactive network layer header.

When any of the preceding conditions are not true, the full conformance network protocol is used. MAP supports the following *type 1* functions of the CLNS protocol:

- PDU composition and decomposition,
- Header format analysis,
- PDU lifetime control,
- PDU routing and forwarding,
- PDU segmenting, reassembly, and discard,
- Error reporting, and
- PDU header error detection.

The implementation of the CLNS protocol *type 2* functions is not required. *Type 2* functions include security and complete source routing. If a network implementation does not support a *type 2* function which is requested by an incoming packet, the packet is discarded and an error report PDU is sent back to the source station.

Although CLNS protocol *type 3* functions are also optional, unlike *type 2* functions, when *type 3* functions are requested by an incoming packet, the packet is not discarded. Rather, the function parameters are recognized as valid but ignored. Thus, if *type 3* functions are not implemented, a *type 3* request should be processed as if the request were a *type 1* and the *type 3* parameters ignored. *Type 3* functions include padding, partial source routing, priority, record route, and quality of service maintenance.

5.9.1 TOP Network Layer

The TOP 3.0 network layer is identical to that of the MAP 3.0 network layer.

SUMMARY

In this chapter we have discussed the functions of the network layer and schemes for performing these functions. We began by defining key concepts such as internetworking, routing, congestion, naming, and addressing. Next, we provided two classifications of routing algorithms, followed by further discussion of routing schemes, congestion control, deadlock, and internetworking. The chapter concluded with a discussion of the ISO network layer standard, and the MAP and TOP network layers.

The network layer of the OSI reference model is concerned with routing, addressing, and congestion resolution. The network layer also deals with the interconnection of several networks (i.e., internetworking). A repeater is a device that interconnects networks at the physical layer. When the interconnection is done at the data link layer, the corresponding interface is referred to as a **bridge**. Other interfaces include **routers** and **gateways**, which interconnect networks at the network and application layers, respectively. A **brouter** is a combination of bridge and router.

Routing aims at forwarding protocol data units (PDU) closer to their final destination. **Con-**

gestion control deals with the problem of more packets arriving at nodes responsible for routing than there are resources to deal with them. Whereas the **name** of a resource indicates *what* we seek, an **address** indicates *where* it is, and a **route** tells *how to get there*. A mechanism for performing the address-route mapping is referred to as a **routing algorithm** or a **routing table.**

From the viewpoint of the place where intermediate routing decisions are made, the following routing types exist: source routing, incremental routing, and hybrid routing. From the viewpoint of the time scale used for specifying or modifying routes, the following routing types exist: fixed routing, and dynamic routing. From the viewpoint of their control mechanism, dynamic routing algorithms can be further classified as isolated routing, centralized routing, and distributed routing.

A network can be viewed as a collection of resources, such as buffers, processors, and links, which can be shared on a dynamic basis. Unless careful control is exercised on the user demands, users may seriously abuse the network. If the demands are allowed to exceed the system capacity, *congestion* may occur. When message congestion builds up in a network, the throughput rate decreases. When congestion builds up even further, it may ultimately lead to *deadlock* in which no message flow takes place. When no corrective action is taken, the performance of the network degrades as traffic increases. Congestion control techniques attempt to provide an acceptable level of performance even when traffic increases. Two major schemes for dealing with congestion are through the use of *flow control* and *routing* algorithms. Congestion control attempts to prevent the overutilization of network resources, and thus to maintain high throughput. Routing affects congestion in that it decides which resources are used to transport messages.

The ISO standards cover two key aspects of the OSI network layer, involving *service* and *architecture*. The OSI Network Service provides two different kinds of service: connection-oriented network service and connectionless. The connection-oriented network service provides communications capability to service users by means of *network connections* via six services: N_CONNECT, N_RESET, N_DATA, N_DATA_ACKNOWLEDGE, N_EXPEDITED_DATA, and N_DISCONNECT. The connectionless service is very simple, consisting of just one service, called N_UNITDATA.

The MAP architecture is based on the ISO connectionless protocol known as *Connectionless Mode Network Service* (*CLNS*). The major functions of the CLNS protocol as used in the MAP architecture are PDU segmentation/reassembly, routing, and congestion control. Depending on whether the communication nodes belong to a single subnetwork (i.e., segment) two subsets of the CLNS protocol are defined: inactive network layer protocol and full conformance protocol. The TOP network layer is identical to that of the MAP network layer.

Bibliographic Notes

A fair amount of information exists on describing the problems associated with performing network layer functions, especially internetworking. However, many problems are still unresolved, particularly for LAN to LAN interconnection, because of more stringent constraints. The books by Bertrekas and Gallager (1987), Chou (1983), McNamara (1982), Schwartz (1977), Schwartz (1987), Stallings (1987), and Tanenbaum (1988) contain various degrees of discussion on network layer issues. Sunshine (1977) provides a good introduction to the subject, Hawe et al. (1984) discuss network interconnection with bridges, Bux and Grillo (1985) investigate flow control issues when interconnecting several ring networks, and Pitt et al. (1985) suggest the use of source routing for LAN interconnection. The articles by Callon (1983) and Hinden and others (1983) provide a good discussion of internetwork issues. Because of its current importance, the January, 1988 issue of *IEEE Network* is devoted to bridges and routers. In this issue, Backes (1988) addresses bridges which are appropriate for IEEE 802 LANs, Seifert (1988) provides a contemporary review of bridges and routers, and Perlman et al. (1988) discuss the issue of choosing the appropriate ISO Layer for LAN interconnection. The service definition and the protocol specification for the ISO network layer standard are ISO 8348 and ISO 8473, respectively.

PROBLEMS

1. Discuss the advantages and disadvantages of using:
   (a) logical names versus physical addresses.
   (b) flat versus hierarchical addresses.
2. List problems that one may encounter when interconnecting two local area networks rather than a local area network with a wide area network.
3. For the network shown in Figure P5.1 and the associated traffic matrix, find the average network delay.

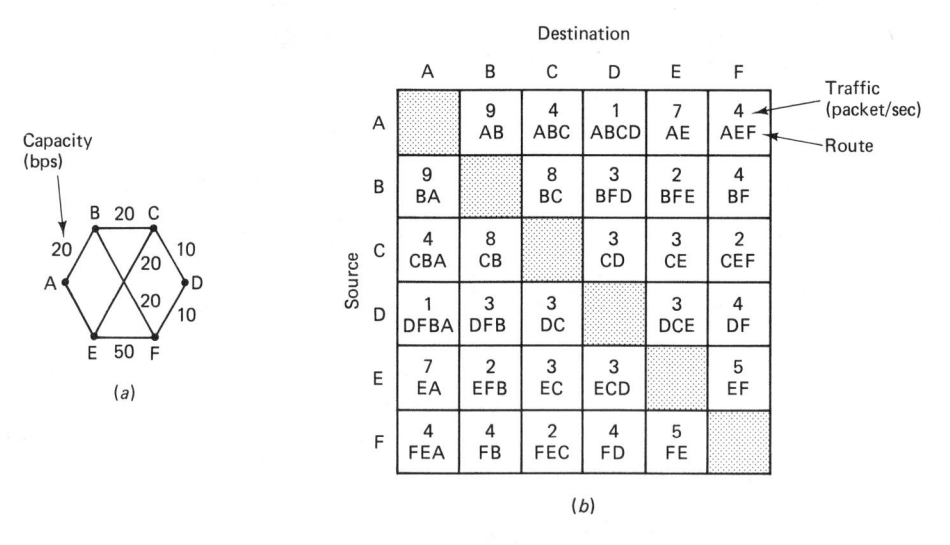

Figure P5.1

4. A network address must be unique, but a logical representation (i.e., name) is also important. Suggest a way to perform a name to address translation in a LAN environment.
5. Write a program to find the shortest path in an arbitrary network using Dijkstra's algorithm. The program should accept the network topology with associated link costs and the node for which the shortest path to all remaining nodes is desired. The program should also provide the routing table for the node.
6. The network shown in Figure P5.2, uses an incremental routing scheme which works as follows. Each station uses a table to determine the next hop that the next packet has to travel on its way to a destination. Upon receipt of a packet, a routing node finds the packet destination, and uses the appropriate link in its table to route the packet.
   (a) Identify the route that a packet must follow to go from A to E.
   (b) What happens when trying to send a packet from A to F? What can be done to improve the network routing?

Link number

A —1— B —4— C

2, 3, 5, 6

D —7— E —8— F

(a)

Routing matrix

| | From use link |||||||
To	A	B	C	D	E	F
A	—	1	4	2	5	6
B	1	—	4	3	5	6
C	1	4	—	7	5	6
D	2	3	5	—	7	6
E	1	4	5	7	—	8
F	1	3	6	2	8	—

(b)

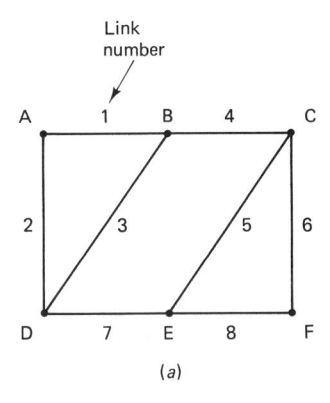

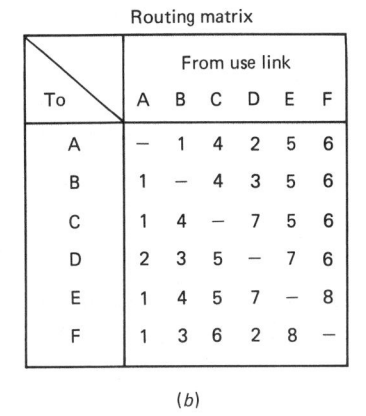

Figure P5.2

(c) Describe the level of congestion and bottleneck present in this network. How can a routing node improve performance?
(d) Why is this form of incremental routing also called *minimal-addressing* and *minimal-routing*?
(e) What header information is required to route messages? How can header information flag problems such as the one encountered in part (b)?

7. The Fizzletech Corp. has just designed a computer network with centrally controlled routing. If a routing node goes down, describe how the system can approach recovery if the failed routing node is
   (a) not a single point of failure.
   (b) a single point of failure.
8. Find the delay table for node B using distributed routing for the network of Figure 5.10 with the following delays BA = 4, BF = 3, and BC = 5. Assume that the delay tables for nodes A, F, and C are unchanged.
9. For the network of Figure P5.1, calculate the minimum delay using the flow deviation method.
10. Finish the example involving Figure 5.12.
11. The example corresponding to Figure 5.12 shows just one iteration step of the flow deviation method. Write an interactive computer aided design CAD program to aid with the application of the flow deviation method. The program should provide the following at each iteration:
    (a) link length l_i.
    (b) shortest route for each node pair.
    (c) average message delay.
12. Consider 2 subnetworks, one with stations having a seven layer architecture and the other one having a three layer architecture consisting of the physical, data link, and application layers. Discuss the use of repeaters, bridges, routers, brouters, and gateways for interconnecting these two networks. Which of these devices provides the most appropriate interface?
13. For the MAP architecture, discuss the advantages of using an inactive network layer protocol instead of a full conformance network layer in the following situations:
    (a) a time-critical application.
    (b) a non time-critical application.

6

The Transport Layer

A fundamental difference exists between the lower three layers and the upper three of the OSI reference model. The physical, data link, and network layers of the OSI reference model are concerned with *basic data transmission functions*, either through one link or a cascaded system of links. On the other hand, the upper three layers, namely the session, presentation, and application layers basically provide *data communication functions* to network end users. The transport layer is responsible for bridging the gap between the layers that provide data transmission functions and the layers that provide communication functions, as depicted in Figure 6.1(a). The lower three layers are often referred to as the *lower layers*, with the upper three layers constituting the *upper layers*. Like all chapters in this book dealing with individual layers, the purpose of this chapter is to discuss the functions, services, and the protocols for the transport layer. The ISO transport layer standard protocol is discussed in Section 6.4, where we concentrate on the class IV protocol, and the features of the MAP and TOP transport layers are covered in Section 6.5.

6.1 TRANSPORT LAYER FUNCTIONS

The essential functions of the transport layer involve performing *end-to-end control* and *end-to-end optimization* of data transfer between end systems. Unlike the data link and network layers, the transport layer always operates end to end. In other words, the network and data link layers operate on a single link basis, which do not necessarily involve the stations at both ends of the communication.

```
                End system         Intermediate         End system
                                   system (node)

       OSI Layer
        ┌─────────────────────────────────────────────────┐
        │    7                              │           │ │ Layers performing
        │    6                                            │ communication
        │    5                                            │ functions
        └────────────────                    ─────────────┘
             4   Transport                     Transport
        ┌────────────────                    ─────────────┐
        │    3                                            │
        │    2                                            │ Layers performing
        │                                                 │ data transmission
        │    1                                            │ functions
        └─────────────────────────────────────────────────┘
                                                            Physical medium
                  Network A              Network B
                              (a)
```

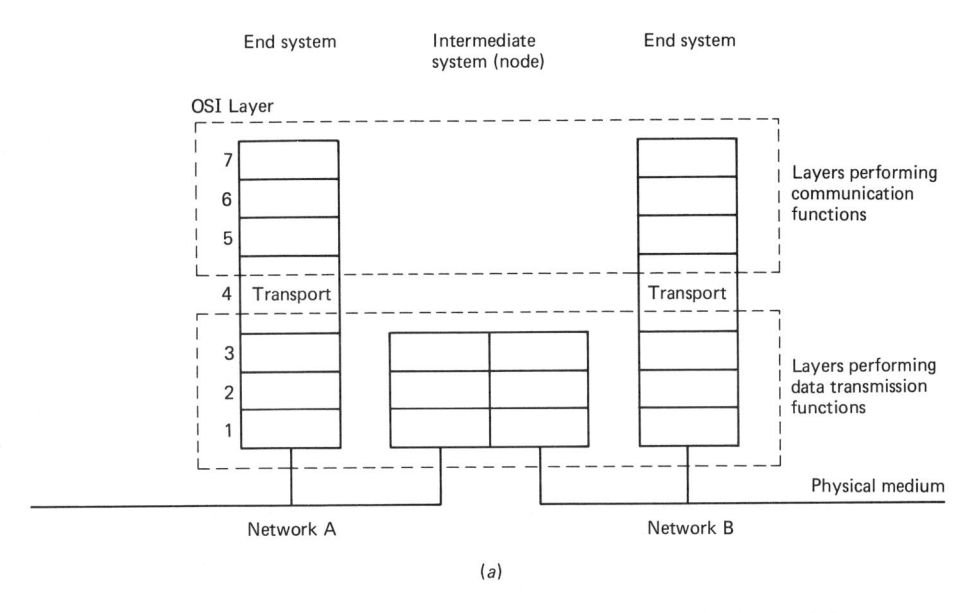

Figure 6.1 (a) Separation of layers performing communication functions and data transmission functions.

A link may or may not connect end systems, as depicted in Figure 6.1(b). If the link connects both end systems it is end to end, otherwise it is not. The physical layer can be thought of as operating on a half-link basis, that is, as an interface between the data link layer and the medium on one side and the same type of interface on the other side.

All functions related to the transport or transfer of information between systems are performed within the transport layer or in the layers below. Thus, the view that the transport layer presents to the session layer (or any layer above the session layer) is one of a *virtual point-to-point link*, regardless of the methods used for actual information transfer and regardless of the network's physical topology or medium. The session layer does not realize if the link provided by the data transmission layers goes halfway around the world through wide area networks, bridges, radio links, satellite relays, and so on, or if it simply goes a few feet away in a LAN bus topology.

More specifically, the transport layer and the layers below it hide from the upper layers the following details of the communication system:

Message segmentation,

Message routing and congestion,

Flow control and error control,[1]

Channel access scheme,

Modulation, encoding,

Network topology, and

Network Interface Unit (NIU) hardware.

---

[1] The transport layer also provides flow and error control, but on an end-to-end basis.

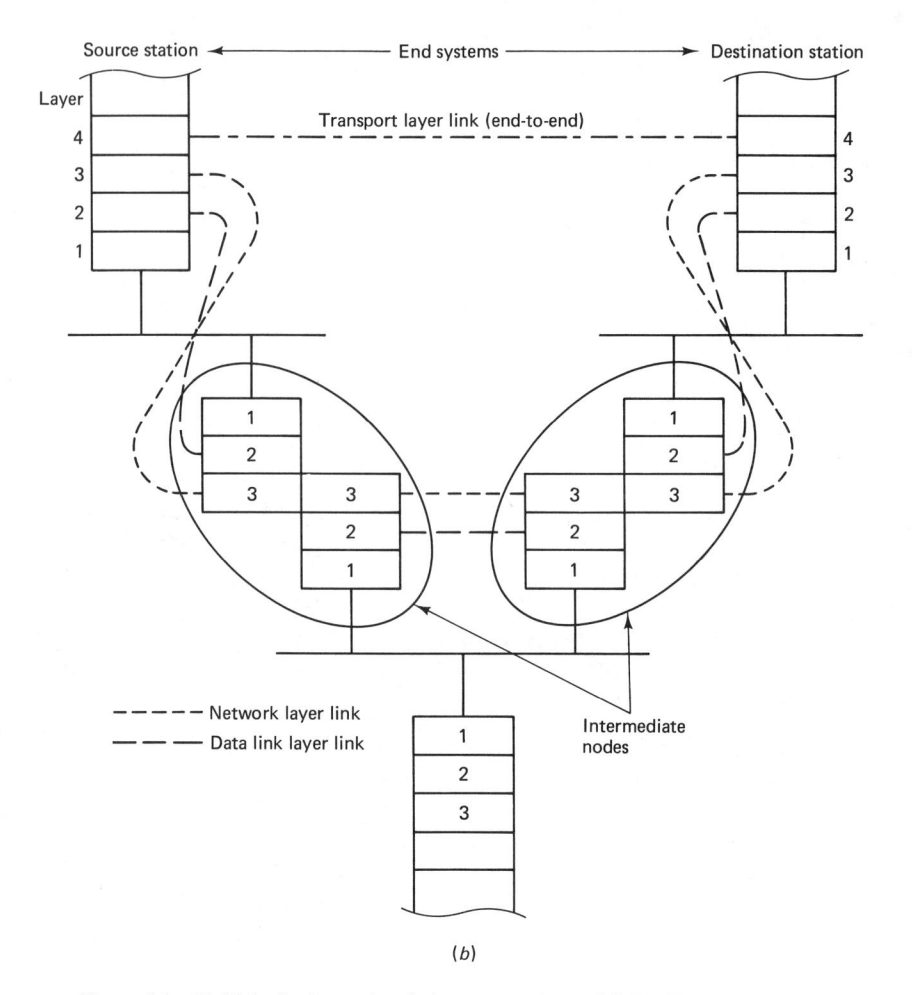

Figure 6.1 (b) Links for layers 4 and above are end-to-end links. Network and data link layer links are not end-to-end.

Because the preceding functions are performed in a transparent fashion on behalf of the upper layers, transport layer users can concentrate on the distributed processing aspects of their applications. Chapter 7 provides sufficient background for understanding the upper layers, which are covered in Chapters 8 through 10.

6.1.1 Transport Layer Services

Like the network layer, services provided by the transport layer can be connection-oriented (i.e., virtual circuits) or connectionless (i.e., datagrams). From the transport protocol design point of view, the difficulty in providing transport layer services depends on the services already provided by the network layer. Accordingly, it is easier to provide a connection-oriented transport service using a connection-oriented network service than using a connectionless-oriented network service. This is because many of the functions to be offered by the transport layer are already provided by the network layer if both layers provide connection-oriented services. For example, if the network layer provides packet delivery in the same order that packets entered the network, then the transport layer should have no difficulty in providing sequenced message delivery.

The rationale for providing datagram services rather than virtual circuit services is basically the same for all layers of the OSI reference model (with the exception of the physical layer, where the choice does not exist). Since datagram services involve less overhead than virtual circuit services, datagram services provide better performance from the viewpoint of message delays and throughput. Datagram services find applications in data acquisition systems, special control messages, single request response, and real time applications. For applications requiring reliable data transfer with sequenced message delivery, the virtual circuit approach is appropriate.

Recall that in a connection-oriented service, three distinct phases are required for successful communication: connection establishment, data transfer, and connection termination. In principle, the connection phases of the transport layer are similar to those of lower protocols (i.e., network and data link layers). From the viewpoint of design, implementation, and operation, however, the corresponding functions for the transport layer are much more complicated than their counterparts in the lower layers.

For example, a data link layer flow control scheme need not be concerned when the physical medium breaks or fails.[2] On the other hand, a transport layer flow control scheme needs to recover from link failures at the network layer level. This is because when one link fails, it is not usually a catastrophic failure as it is for the data link layer. The transport layer can request that another connection be established transparently between the participating stations, possibly involving other links not used by the initial connection. Thus, if the communicating stations are in the midst of a message exchange involving flow control, the link failure should be transparent to the flow control mechanism being performed by the transport layer.

Because of the preceding reasons, it is not just enough to open a connection, transfer data, and close the connection. Since many nodes may exist between the two end systems, with the possibility of a variety of contingencies, it is necessary to monitor the connections through **connection management** mechanisms. For example, the ISO transport protocol maintains a parameter MRC, called the *maximum retransmisssion count*, for managing retransmissions. When a message sent by the transport layer is lost, the message is retransmitted up to MRC times. If the last retransmitted message is still lost, the transport layer simply gives up and informs the upper layers accordingly.

Before describing typical transport layer services, let us look at a transport service model to clarify nomenclature. The model is shown in Figure 6.2 and depicts the interrelationship of the following service primitives: request, indication, response, and confirmation. Each primitive involves a relationship between the *service user* and the *service provider* (i.e., the transport layer). The service user could be part of a protocol entity at the session layer, presentation layer, application layer, or an end user entity that is directly accessing the services provided by the transport layer.

The **request** primitive originates at the user side and is directed toward the protocol entity side. As the name implies the request primitive asks the protocol entity to perform a service. Because of the layered nature of the overall network architecture, the transport protocol entity performs some housekeeping functions and passes the request to the network layer. As shown in Figure 6.2(a), the request makes its way through the network layer and the other lower layers and is finally delivered by the peer protocol entity as an **indication** to the correspondent user. The peer protocol entity

---

[2] When this happens, the network simply stops operating unless redundancy is available. Even in case of failure, higher layer software can detect this problem.

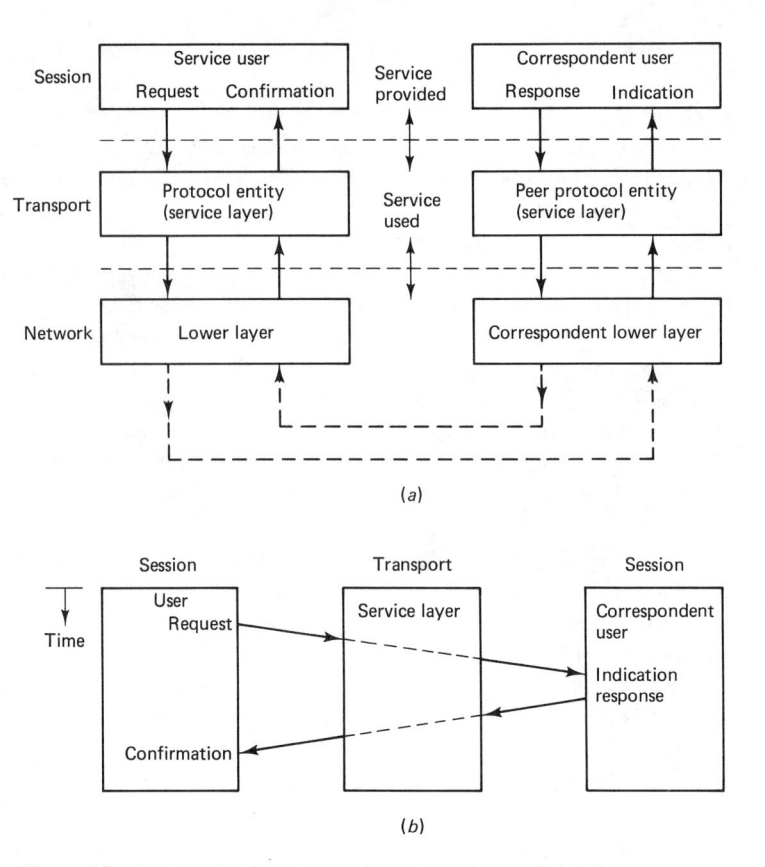

Figure 6.2 Service primitive relationships: (a) Architectural; (b) Time sequence.

obtains a **response** primitive from the correspondent user, which follows a similar path as the request primitive and is finally delivered by the transport protocol entity as a **confirmation** primitive to the user.

6.2 A TRANSPORT LAYER MODEL

In order to describe the services of a typical transport layer, we make use of a model similar to the OSI transport protocol but greatly simplified. The OSI transport model is discussed in detail in Section 6.4. Our transport service model divides services into two main categories: **connection management** and **data transfer** service. As the name implies, connection management services are useful for creating and maintaining a data path to a corresponding user. Data transfer services support the exchange of data between a pair of users.

Figures 6.3(a) and 6.3(b) depict the transport services for our model for the connection-oriented and connectionless-oriented cases, respectively. The T_CONNECT and T_DISCONNECT family of primitives make up the connection management services, whereas the T_DATA and T_UNIT_DATA make up the data transfer services. Notice that when using connectionless-

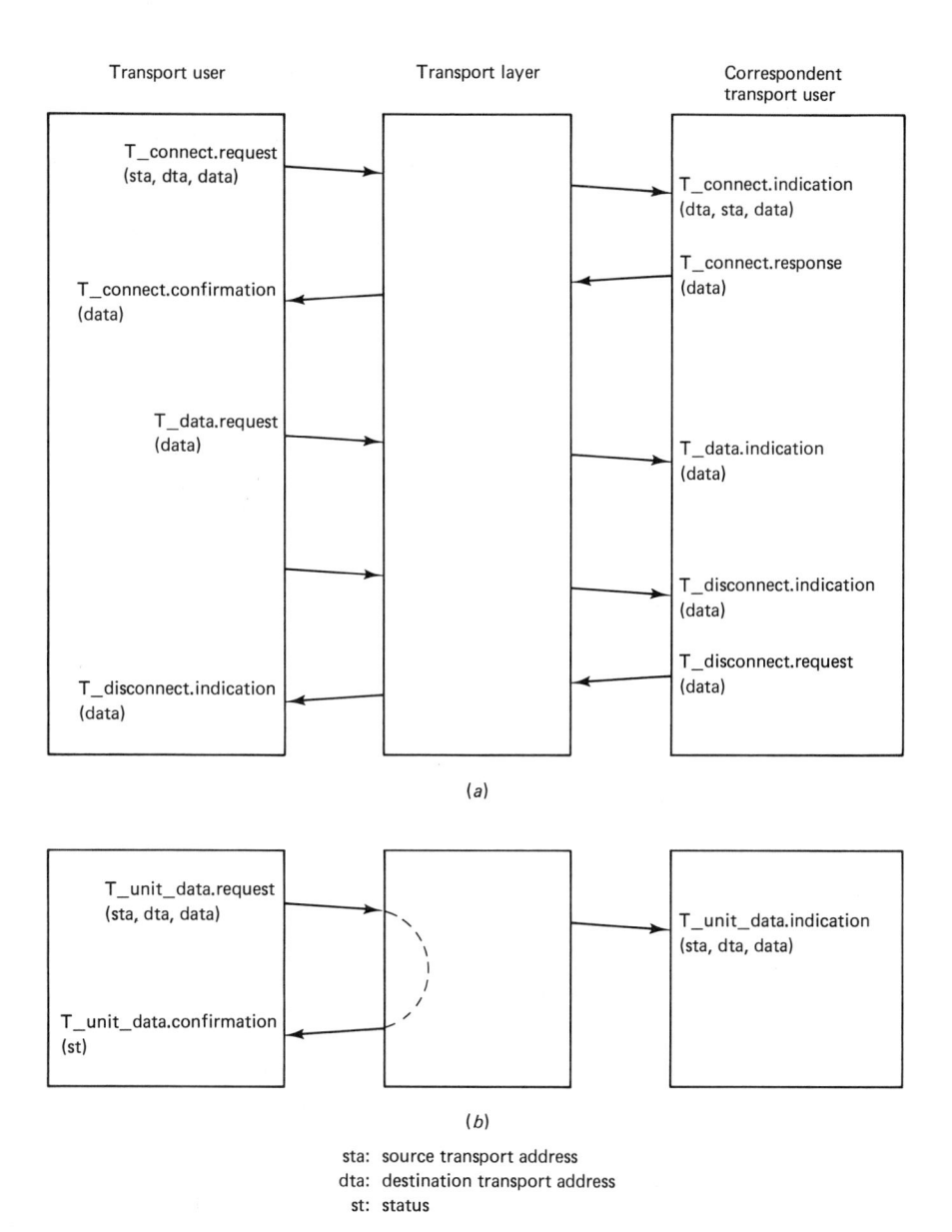

Figure 6.3 Service primitives for the transport model: (a) Connection-oriented services; (b) Connectionless-oriented services. (Adapted from Figure 6.16 with permission from *Data Communications, Computer Networks and OSI* by F. Halsall, © Addison-Wesley Publishers Ltd. 1988.)

oriented services (i.e., T_UNIT_DATA) it is not necessary to set up a connection. Primitive parameters are inside parentheses.

Regarding the T_CONNECT family of primitives, the *request* primitive is first issued by the local transport user requesting its transport layer to attempt the establishment of a connection with a specified remote transport user. Upon receipt of the request primitive, the remote (peer) transport protocol entity uses the *indication* primitive to inform its user of the connection request. The correspondent user then uses the *response* primitive for indicating its response to the connection request. The response primitive goes through the lower layers, the transmission channel, and appears at the local transport entity. Finally, the local transport entity uses the *confirmation* primitive for informing the initiating transport user of the correspondent user's willingness to accept (or reject) the connection request.

Other primitive families function similarly. However, a major difference is that primitive families that do not have the confirmation primitive (e.g., T_DISCONNECT) perform the indicated function on a half-connection basis. In other words, in order to clear a connection completely, both users are required to issue a T_DISCONNECT.request primitive.

The parameters *sta*, *dta*, and *data* of the service primitives depicted in Figure 6.3 represent the source transport address, destination transport address, and the message to be sent by the primitive, respectively. The *st* is a status parameter used to indicate whether the unacknowledged data transfer was sent by the local transport layer. Acknowledgments at the transport layer are sent using special messages, as detailed in subsection 6.3.3.

6.2.1 Use of Network Services

Like all layers in the OSI reference model, the transport layer provides its services by making use of the services of the layer below (i.e., the network layer). The network layer services were discussed in Chapter 5. The intent of this section is to indicate how certain network layer services are used by the transport layer. As illustrated in Figure 6.4, the transport layer makes use of the following network layer[3] service primitives:

```
N_CONNECT
N_DATA
N_DISCONNECT
```

Regarding Figure 6.4, upon receipt of the T_CONNECT.request from the session layer, the transport layer makes use of several services provided by the network layer until a T_CONNECT.confirmation is received by the originating transport user. Note that the processing of a single request primitive by the transport layer involves several primitives to be processed by the network layer. For example, processing a T_CONNECT.req by the transport layer involves the processing of N_CONNECT.req, N_CONNECT.ind, N_CONNECT.resp, N_CONNECT.conf, N_DATA.req, and N_DATA.ind by the network layer. The N_DATA service is used for transferring data associated with the parameters of the transport primitive (i.e., T_CONNECT.req).

The transport protocol makes use of the following types of Transport Protocol Data Units (TPDUs):

```
Connection request (ConReq),
Connection confirm (ConCfm),
Data (Data),
Data acknowledgement (Ack), and
Disconnect request (DiscReq).
```

[3] We assume that we use the ISO connection-oriented services discussed in subsection 5.8.1.

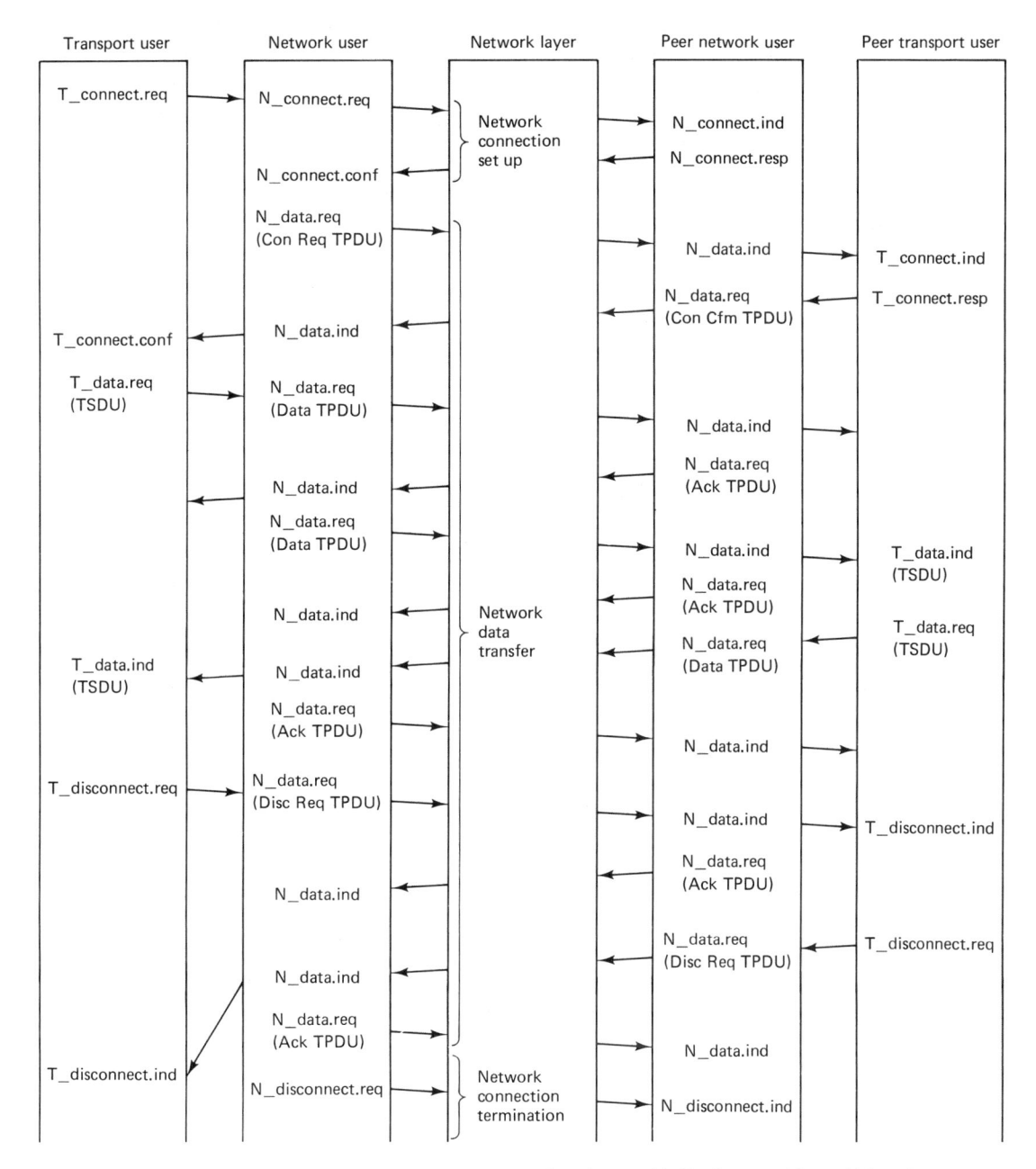

Figure 6.4 How the transport protocol makes use of services provided by the network layer. (Adapted from Figure 6.23 with permission from *Data Communications, Computer Networks and OSI* by F. Halsall, © Addison-Wesley Publishers Ltd. 1988.)

Sec. 6.2 A Transport Layer Model   257

Data exchanged by peer transport protocol machines regarding a T_CONNECT.req is contained in the *ConReq TPDU*. Likewise, *ConCfm TPDU* contains the data exchanged by peer transport protocol machines regarding a T_CONNECT.resp. *Data* and *Ack* TPDUs are used for delivering the information and acknowledgment messages associated with a T_DATA.req, respectively. And finally, a *DiscReq TPDU* is the data exchanged by peer transport protocol machines regarding a T_DISCONNECT.req.

6.3 TRANSPORT LAYER PROTOCOL ISSUES

Having examined the services offered by our transport model and how services offered by the network layer are used, it is time to look at the transport protocol mechanisms. The most important protocol mechanisms at the transport layer are: addressing, multiplexing, flow and error control, information units, and connection management.

6.3.1 Addressing

In sophisticated protocols such as the ISO transport protocol, it is necessary to identify protocol entities and service users in the context of the entire network or catanet under which the transport protocol operates. One could think of a transport address as being composed of two fields: *network address* and *transport suffix*. The *network address* component is used to locate the transport entity in the network or catanet. The *transport suffix* is used to identify the transport user within the local system. Thus, whereas the network address is unique and absolute in the network context or catanet, the transport suffix is relative to the session-transport layer interface, and furthermore not unique. The nonunique aspect of the *transport suffix* is treated in the *multiplexing* section.

A transport suffix assigned at system generation time and unchanged thereafter is referred to as a **static suffix,** whereas a **dynamic suffix** is allowed to change and result from cooperation and negotiation between a transport user and the transport entity.

A problem that arises at the transport layer regards the identification of required addresses in a different station. For example, a transport user at station A may want to send a message to another transport user at station B. One solution involves the transport user at station A *looking up* the transport address for the correspondent user at station B in a directory. The directory is analogous to a telephone book in telephone communications.

Another solution involves using a *server* instead of a *directory* for obtaining the transport address of the peer user. The latter solution is useful when the directory does not have the transport address of a peer user (e.g., a new user in the system) or when a directory is not available. The assumption is that the server is well-known throughout the network and in fact it has a **well-known address** or **well-known suffix** for the transport address case. The situation is similar to calling *information services* when a telephone book is not available. In this case, the telephone number of *information services* is the *well-known address*. The procedure for establishing a connection to an unknown transport address by means of a server is the following:

1. It is assumed that the server is attached to its well-known address.
2. A transport user in station A makes a connection to the well-known address, requesting the creation or identification of the desired peer transport user address.

3. (a) The well-known server either creates or identifies the address of the peer transport user.
   (b) The well-known server then requests that the user be attached to the transport address.
4. The well-known server tells the initiating user where to connect in order to communicate with the peer transport user.
5. After connecting to the transport address of the peer transport user, the initiating user can now proceed to exchange information.

The peer transport user could represent a desired server whose address is not known initially. The previous procedure is referred to as the **initial connection protocol,** and is depicted in Figure 6.5.

6.3.2 Multiplexing

In the previous section, we noted that a single transport user may be associated with several transport suffixes (i.e., a transport suffix is not unique). A transport protocol user may be part of the session protocol entity responsible for providing specific functions to the presentation layer. Protocol users perform their functions by associating themselves with service access points at the interfaces just above and just below the protocol entity, as shown in Figure 6.6. Associating several SAPs at adjacent interfaces in the OSI reference model with protocol service users is referred to as multiplexing. In terms of the transport layer, **downward multiplexing** associates one TSAP to several NSAPs, and **upward multiplexing** associates several TSAPs with one NSAP.

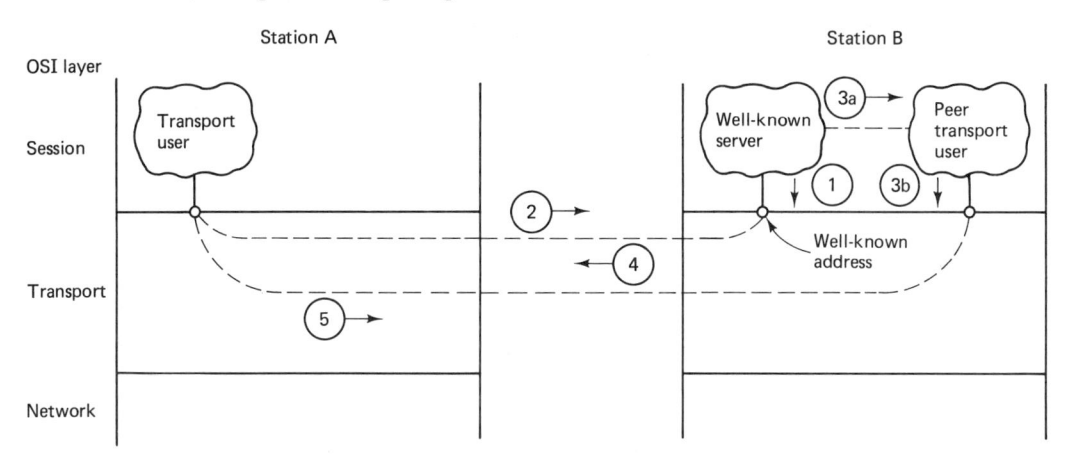

① Server attaches to its well-known address
② User connects to well-known address
③a Server creates or identifies address of peer transport user
③b Peer transport user attaches to transport address
④ Well-known server tells user where to connect and closes its own connection
⑤ Transport user connects to peer transport user

Figure 6.5 Initial connection protocol. How a transport user in station A connects to a corresponding peer transport user with unknown address at station B.

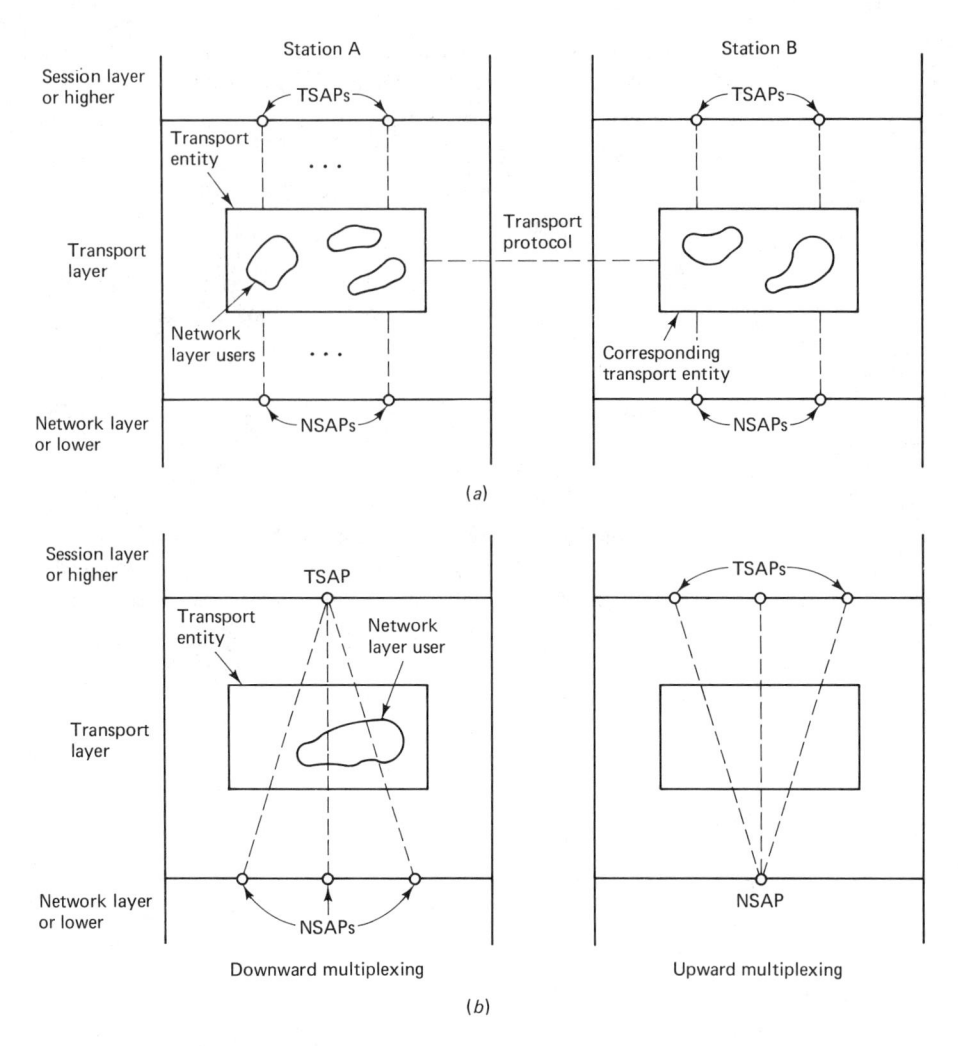

Figure 6.6 (a) Transport layer model; (b) Splitting a transport connection into several network connections (downward multiplexing) and multiplexing several transport connections onto one network connection (upward multiplexing).

6.3.3 Flow and Error Control

Flow and error control techniques used at the data link layer are not directly applicable at the transport layer. As discussed in detail in Chapter 4, error control is a mechanism for handling errors in the message transmissions. Flow control, on the other hand, attempts to limit the rate of messages sent by the sender to a pace that is comfortable for the receiver. At the data link layer, error and flow control are handled together by appropriate mechanisms, such as the window mechanism discussed in subsection 4.4.3. At the transport layer, it is convenient to handle error control separate from flow control, as explained in the remainder of this subsection.

One of the most effective techniques for implementing a flow and error control function at the data link layer is through the use of a *sliding window flow control* (SWFC) mechanism. Since the SWFC protocol works so well for the data link layer, could it be used for the transport layer as well? The answer to this question is yes, but not without difficulties.

The difficulties in applying SWFC mechanisms at the transport layer are varied, with perhaps the most important ones being long message delays experienced by messages going through the lower layers (and possibly through other networks) and large message sizes. Unlike the data link layer case, message delays could range from a few milliseconds to several minutes, and even hours. Larger message sizes at the transport layer increase the difficulty in providing required transmission buffers and performing buffer management.

At the data link layer, the use of acknowledgment frames serves a dual purpose: It acknowledges the receipt of a frame and indicates that a new buffer area was just made available at the receiver, so that the sender can send another frame. Because of larger message delays, this is no longer true for the transport layer. Consider the following scenario: A receiver at the transport layer receives message N and proceeds to send ACK N to the sender, indicating that it could send another message. Because of large message delays and large messages sizes, it is possible that messages that were sent earlier (i.e., $N-1$, $N-2$, . . .) arrive at the receiver after frame N and fill up all available buffers. In the meantime, the sender will send message $N+1$, which will be discarded by the receiver because of insufficient buffer space. Thus, the acknowledgment sent by the receiver does not necessarily mean that a buffer space is available to store the next message. In general, this problem is difficult to solve, since it requires the receiver to guess its free buffer size and respond accordingly.

A solution that is often used consists in decoupling acknowledgments (which deal with error control) from flow control information. Instead of the receiver sending just ACK information, additional information is returned with ACK messages which indicates how much buffer space is available at the receiver at the time the message was received. The additional information regarding buffer space is referred to as **credit** (CDT). Thus, the receiver, upon receipt of a valid message, returns (ACK N, CDT M), indicating the correct receipt of messages up to the Nth one and granting permission to send messages $N+1$ through $N+M$. In effect, (ACK N, CDT M) enables the sender to send M additional messages until instructed otherwise by means of another credit.

In order to illustrate how the sliding window flow control works with a *credit* scheme, let us consider the example of Figure 6.7. We assume that the sender is initially granted a credit of 7 (i.e., CDT = 7), and that the sender receives a number of messages to transmit which is greater than the credit allowed at any instant (i.e., the sender always has messages to send). The sender starts by sending messages 0, 1, 2, 3, and 4 right away. As depicted in Figure 6.7, upon receipt of message 2, the receiver sends back (ACK 2, CDT 5), thus acknowledging the receipt of the first 3 messages and granting permission to the sender to send messages 3 through 7. However, at the time the sender receives (ACK 2, CDT 5), messages 3 and 4 have already been sent. Since the sender was granted permission to send up to message 7, it will proceed to send messages 5, 6, and 7, after which its credit runs out and it therefore must stop sending further messages until the receiver acknowledges current messages received and updates the sender's credit.

Example

After sending message I(4), a sender receives (ACK 1,CDT 6) as an acknowledgment. How many more messages can the sender send before its credit is exhausted?

Solution Since the sender has received (ACK 1, CDT 6), it knows that the receiver has received messages I(0) and I(1) and that it has available memory for 6 more messages. Since the sender has already sent messages I(2), I(3), and I(4), it can proceed to send messages

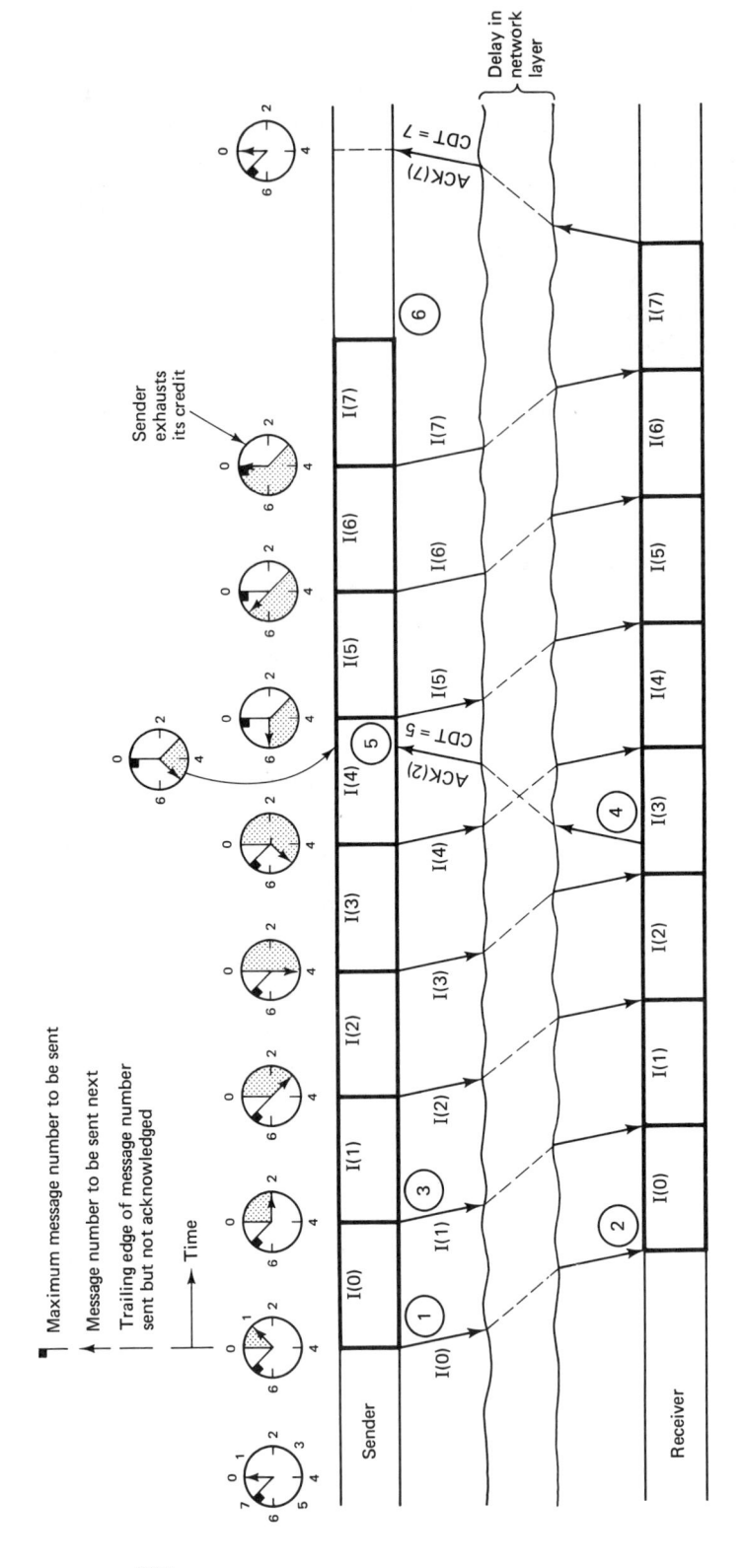

Figure 6.7 Sliding window flow control with a credit scheme.

I(5), I(6), and I(7), which will exhaust its credit and it must stop. Thus, after sending I(4), the sender can send 3 additional messages. The situation is depicted in Figure 6.8.

6.3.4 Information Units

As messages are passed from layer to layer, they change sizes. Generally, a header and a trailer is added to the session layer PDU (i.e., STDU) to form the transport layer PDU (i.e., TPDU). Before continuing with the various transport protocol issues being discussed in this section, let us state some assumptions about our transport model, since it is being used to illustrate some concepts.

We assume that our transport layer model performs no message segmentation. This assumption is easily met if the transport user sends messages of size less than the maximum size handled by the transport protocol machine. We assume further that the transport protocol machine handles only one virtual circuit. This assumption basically reduces the level of management to be performed by the protocol machine. An additional assumption involves the use of a sliding window flow control with credit allocation for buffer management. Another assumption is that our transport model does not handle urgent or expedited data. Still another assumption is that the possibility of *downward multiplexing* is not precluded. The final assumption is that service requests issued by transport users are always successful; thus, there is no need for status information to be provided by the protocol machine concerning the *reason* for a possible failure in the execution of the service request.

Figure 6.9 depicts the different types of transport layer protocol data units for our transport model. The field *LI* indicates the length (in otects) of the header field alone (i.e., excluding LI itself and the data, if any). The first nibble (i.e., first four bits) of the second byte is the *TYPE* field, indicating the type of message, which was listed in Section 6.2.1.

The remaining bits of the second byte is the *CDT* (credit) field used for flow control with a credit scheme, as discussed in the previous subsection. The field *PARAMETERS* is used to interchange certain parameters, such as service access points (TSAPs) etc. The $N(S)/N(R)$ field is used for exchanging the message sequence numbers N(S) and N(R) corresponding to the sliding window flow control (SWFC). N(S) is associated with the sender, whereas N(R) is associated with the receiver. Finally, the *DATA* field contains the actual message to be transferred between the two transport protocols.

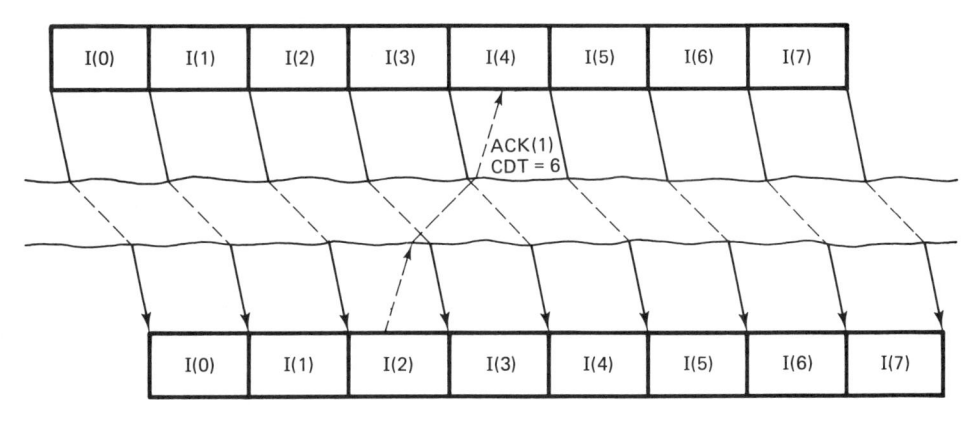

Figure 6.8 An example using the sliding window flow control (SWFC) mechanism.

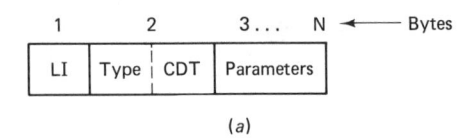

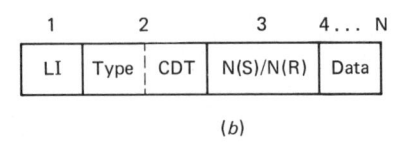

Figure 6.9 Transport layer protocol data units (TPDUs) for simplified transport model: (a) TPDU used for ConReq and ConCfm message types; (b) TPDU used for DiscReq, Data, and Ack message types.

6.3.5 Protocol Operation

Although our transport model provides connection-oriented and connectionless services, we only discuss the connection-oriented case. We discuss the protocol operation in terms of the three major phases of a connection-oriented service: connection establishment, data transfer, and connection termination. The reader is referred to Figure 6.4 for the remainder of this subsection.

A **connection establishment** phase begins with the receipt of a T_CONNECT.request from a transport user. The transport protocol entity then issues a message containing a *ConReq* PDU to its peer transport protocol entity at the remote station. Upon receiving the *ConReq* PDU message, the remote protocol peer entity notifies its correspondent user by means of a T_CONNECT.indication and waits for either a T_CONNECT.response or a T_DISCONNECT.request. The former is used when the remote correspondent user accepts the call, whereas the latter is used when the call is rejected.

Message types used for the connection establishment phase correspond to Figure 6.9(a), with *TYPE* = *ConReq* or *ConCfm*. The *PARAMETERS* field contained in this message type is used for locating a local identifier at the correspondent user. The *PARAMETERS* field can also be used for exchanging additional information regarding the connection being established, such as the quality of service required and the maximum length of subsequent *DATA* TPDUs.

Once a transport connection has been established, the protocol entities are now ready to exchange actual messages in the **data transfer phase.** A transport user initiates the transfer of data to its correspondent user across a previously established connection using the T_DATA.request primitive. The local transport protocol entity receives the information to be sent as a transport protocol service data unit (TSDU), which is then sent using *data* PDUs corresponding to the type shown in Figure 6.9(b) with *TYPE* = *data*. Unlike data frames at the data link layer, in which the *send sequence number* N(S) and *receive sequence number* N(R) can be piggybacked in the same frame, the data messages for the transport layer uses only send sequence number N(S). As shown in Table 6.1, the only message type using *receive sequence numbers* N(R) is the *ACK* message.

TABLE 6.1

Type	N(S) or N(R)	Message body
DiscReq	N(S)	Reason
Data	N(S)	User data
Ack	N(R)	— (null)

As is the case for the data link layer, ACK messages are used by the receiver for indicating the correct receipt of messages. When all TPDUs corresponding to a single TSDU have arrived correctly and are acknowledged by the receiver, the receiver generates a T_DATA.indication to its corresponding user, signaling the successful reception of a TSDU.

Actually, the degree of error recovery in the *data transfer phase* depends on the nature of the service to be provided by the transport protocol. The nature of the service may range from a very simple service, such as the one considered in our example, to a very sophisticated service providing message segmentation, error reporting, recovery from network layer errors and failures, multiplexing, and message sequencing. An example of a sophisticated transport protocol is that of the ISO class IV protocol, which is discussed in Section 6.4.

Finally, the **connection termination** phase begins with the transport entity receiving a T_DISCONNECT.req from the transport user. The transport entity sends a *DiscReq* TPDU to its peer at the receiver side and waits for an *Ack* TPDU. Although the *Ack* TPDU just received by the initiating protocol entity indicates that its corresponding peer received the previous *DiscReq* TPDU, it does not indicate that the responding transport user has agreed to the disconnection request. Thus, the transaction is completed by the responding transport user issuing another T_DISCONNECT.req.

6.3.6 Protocol Specification

One method commonly used for specifying protocol operation is by means of a *state transition diagram*. Other methods often used include *Petri Nets*, and *high level languages* such as Pascal or ADA. Figure 6.10 depicts the state transition diagram for our transport protocol model. The protocol changes states when the exit condition (EC) is true and it performs the indicated action (A). For example, the protocol leaves the state *idle* when an N_CONNECTION.ind is received. The protocol then generates N_CONNECT.resp and goes into the *called* state. Implementing a transport protocol involves writing a program that behaves like the transition diagram shown in Figure 6.10. Protocol implementation is discussed in detail in Chapter 12. As is the case with statements in a programming language, formats associated with protocol data units may be quite complex. Accordingly, special notations for defining formats, such as the *Backus-Naur-Form* (BNF) or *syntax graphs*, can be used. For protocols, however, a more recent notation, called *Abstract Syntax Notation One* (ASN.1),[4] is used because it can be computer automated and thus more effective. ASN.1 is summarized in Appendix E.

In this book, the protocol viewpoint taken is primarily that of a user; thus, we concentrate on services rather than on details of the protocol machine. Hence, we do not include much material on protocol specification.

6.4 ISO TRANSPORT LAYER

In this section, we describe the transport layer standard protocol developed by the International Organization for Standardization (ISO), focusing on one of the five classes defined for this protocol. The protocol that we have chosen to discuss in detail is the class 4 protocol, which is used in the MAP and TOP architectures. Recall that one of the main functions of the transport layer involves providing reliable end-to-end data communication functions to the upper layers of the ISO reference

---

[4] Some ISO standard protocols use the ASN.1 notation, which is itself another ISO standard.

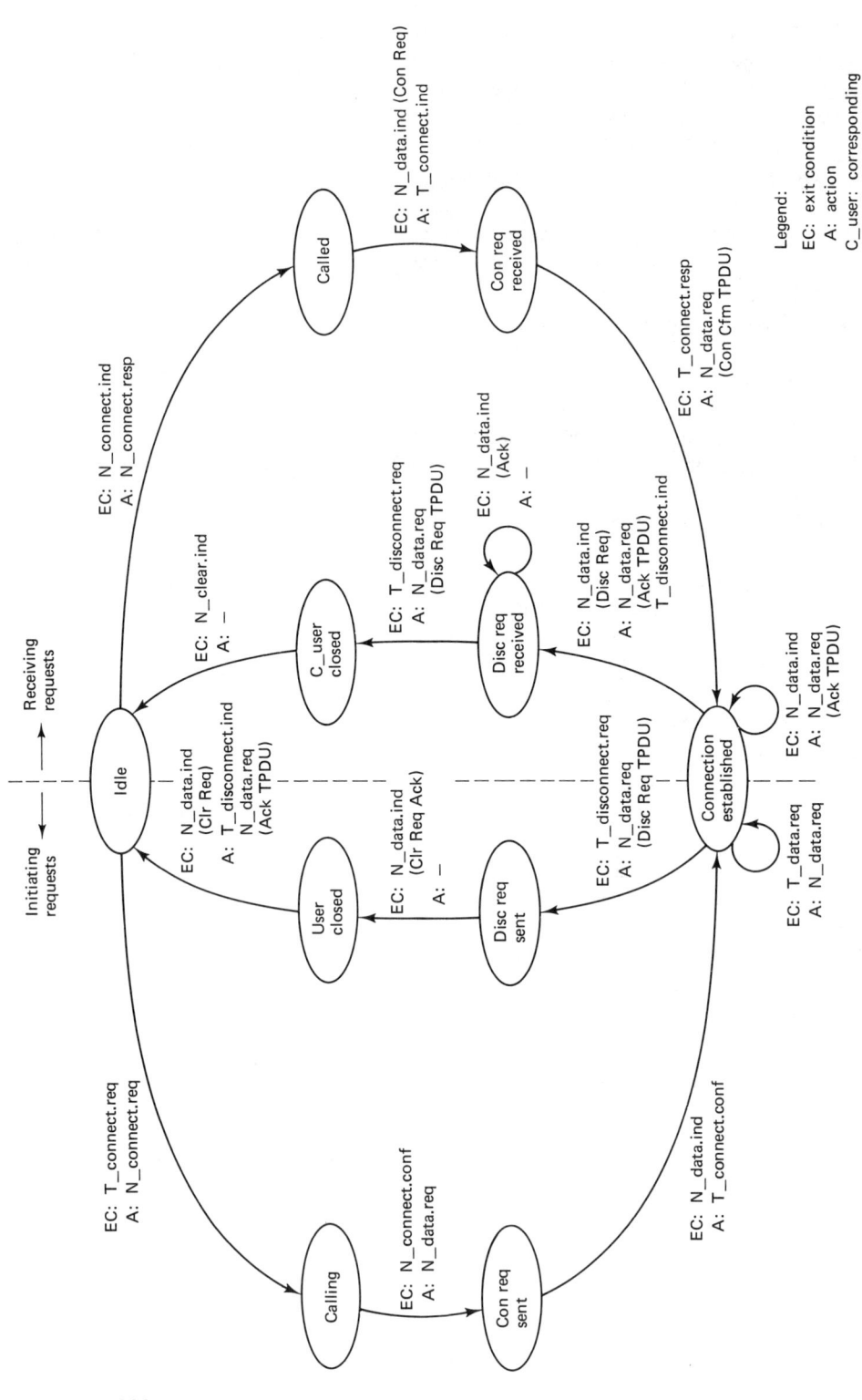

Figure 6.10 Transport protocol model state transition diagram. (Adapted from Figure 6.17 with permission from *Data Communications, Computer Networks and OSI* by F. Halsall, © Addison-Wesley Publishers Ltd. 1988.)

model. Since the underlying layers may be unreliable, error detection and error recovery mechanisms play important roles in the operation of the ISO transport protocol.

In Section 6.3 we considered a simplified transport model to illustrate the main concepts in a simple fashion. The simplification was possible because of several assumptions made regarding the environment in which the protocol operated. In this section, we remove all assumptions made in Section 6.3.

More specifically we assume that the transport layer can perform message segmentation when the message received from the transport user is greater than the maximum size allowed by the transport protocol machine. In addition, we assume that the transport protocol machine can handle several virtual circuits; thus, the need to manage them appropriately. Furthermore, we assume that the transport protocol machine uses some form of sliding window flow control with credit allocation for buffer management. We also assume that the transport protocol can now handle urgent or expedited data. An additional assumption involves the possibility of both upward and downward multiplexing. The final assumption is that the service requests issued by the transport users may not be successful, thus requiring status information from the protocol machine regarding the state of a service request or whether the request was completed successfully. The preceding assumptions basically mean that the transport protocol and its TPDUs are more complex than the ones considered in Section 6.3.

Because of the different types of data transfer that might be expected and the wide variety of subnetworks that might be available for providing network services, five classes have been defined for the ISO transport protocol. The classes are known as classes 0, 1, 2, 3, and 4.

The simplest class of service is *class 0*, which is compatible with an earlier CCITT recommendation for providing transport service for teletext terminals. Class 0 transport service assumes that the underlying network service provides an acceptable error rate, as well as an acceptable rate of network layer connection failures. Thus, this class of transport protocol is required only to set up a simple end-to-end transport connection and, in the data-transfer phase, to have the capability of segmenting data if necessary. It has no provision for recovering from errors and cannot multiplex several transport connections onto a single network connection. Error conditions signalled by the network layer are passed to higher layers in a pass-through manner.

Class 1 provides similar functionality to that of class 0, with an additional error recovery capability. Examples of errors that the class 1 transport protocol can recover from include a network disconnection or failure, the receipt of a data unit from an unrecognized transport connection, and others.

Unlike classes 0 and 1, *class 2* and higher provide the capability of multiplexing several transport connections onto the same network connection. Class 2 provides similar functionality as class 0, with the additional multiplexing capability. Classes 3 and 4 are supersets of class 2. Whereas *class 3* can just detect network layer failures, *class 4* not only detects network failures, but also recovers from them. Thus, class 4 is the most comprehensive of the protocols developed by ISO.

The following criteria can be used when choosing the class of service to be provided:

1. *User requirements.* Transport users specify their requirements when establishing a transport connection. In addition, end users may also specify their requirements in terms of reliable data transfer, and level of error recovery.

2. *Quality of service* offered by the underlying data link layer. In a network involving only one segment (where an ISO inactive network layer protocol can be used) the multiplexing, error, and flow control characteristics of the data link and transport layers are basically the same. Thus, the user may choose to provide error control (or flow control) at the data link layer or at the transport layer but not both.

3. *Quality of service* offered by the underlying network layer. More specifically, the standard classifies the functionality received from the network layer into three types:

Type A: Network layer connection with acceptable residual error rate and acceptable rate of signaled failures.

Type B: Network layer connection with acceptable residual error rate but unacceptable rate of signaled failures (e.g., provider-initiated N_DISCONNECT or N_RESET)

Type C: Network layer connections with residual error rate not acceptable to the transport service user.

In a network layer with type A services, packets are assumed not to be lost or misordered, and the services are assumed to be reliable. Consequently, there is no need for the transport layer to provide failure recovery, error control, and resequencing mechanisms. An example of type A services is a network with virtual circuit services at the network layer. Type A network services provide the functionality over which transport protocols class 0 and 2 are designed to operate.

Type B network services are inherently unreliable, thus requiring reliable transport protocols such as class 3 or 4. Finally, a type C network service is the most unreliable, thus requiring robust and reliable transport protocols for detecting and recovering from network failures, detecting and correcting out of sequence, duplicate, or misdirected messages, and so on. An example of a type C network service might be provided by a datagram-based network layer with underlying noisy communication lines, such as long distance communications using the telephone network. The class 4 transport protocol is designed to operate over a network layer with a type C service. In the remainder of this section, we focus our attention on the ISO class 4 transport protocol.

6.4.1 Class 4 Transport Services

As noted, the class 4 transport protocol does not trust the network layer for providing reliable transmission services. Thus, it incorporates means for detecting and handling a variety of error or fault conditions, choosing appropriate data unit sizes, allowing expedited data flow, and maintaining appropriate flow control. Furthermore, the transport layer attempts to optimize the services provided based on the characteristics of the underlying network layer. For example, the transport layer is involved in appropriately choosing network connections, and deciding whether multiplexing or splitting transport connections are possible or advantageous. Users can request the desired quality of service by specifying values for certain parameters.

Although the primary purpose of the transport protocol is to provide reliable, end-to-end message transfer, appropriate management services must also be provided. Therefore, the services offered by the transport protocol are grouped into two groups:

1. connection management, and
2. data transfer.

Whereas the *connection management* services establish and terminate the transport connection, the *data transfer* services actually perform data transfer on an already established transport connection.

A class 4 transport *connection release* does not guarantee data integrity. If the *service provider*[5] receives a request to release the transport connection in the middle of a data transfer, then some data is lost. The responsibility of providing connection release while maintaining data integrity lies in higher layers (i.e., session, presentation, and application). In the data transfer services, provision is made for the transfer of higher-priority or *espedited* data outside the normal data flow.

Recall from subsection 6.1.1 that the transport layer performs services on behalf of the session layer and other higher layers. Just like any other layer, the transport layer makes its services available to higher layers via *service primitives*. Table 6.2 lists the services offered by the transport layer to higher layers along with the service type. Recall that a confirmed service includes four primitive types: request, indication, response, and confirm; and an unconfirmed service includes two primitive types: request and indication. Table 6.3 lists the *primitives* associated with each transport service.

TABLE 6.2 TRANSPORT LAYER SERVICES WITH THEIR TYPE

Service Group	Service	Service Type
Connection Management	T_CONNECT	Confirmed
Services	T_DISCONNECT	Unconfirmed
Data Transfer	T_DATA	Unconfirmed
Services	T_EXPEDITED_DATA	Unconfirmed

TABLE 6.3 TRANSPORT LAYER SERVICE PRIMITIVES WITH PARAMETERS

Service Primitive	Parameters
T_CONNECT.req	(Called address, calling address, options, QOS, user data)
T_CONNECT.ind	(Called address, calling address, options, QOS, user data)
T_CONNECT.res	(QOS, responding address, options, user data)
T_CONNECT.con	(QOS, responding address, options, user data)
T_DISCONNECT.req	(User data)
T_DISCONNECT.ind	(Disconnect reason, user data)
T_DATA.req	(User data)
T_DATA.ind	(User data)
T_EXPEDITED_DATA.req	(User data)
T_EXPEDITED_DATA.ind	(User data)

The connection request service (i.e., T_CONNECT) is depicted in the time diagram of Figure 6.11, with the parameters carried in each of the four primitives listed in Table 6.3. The connection establishment process is initiated by the transport user by issuing the T_CONNECT.request primitive to the transport service provider. Since the class 4 transport protocol provides a connection-oriented

---

[5] We are using *protocol machine* and *service provider* interchangeably.

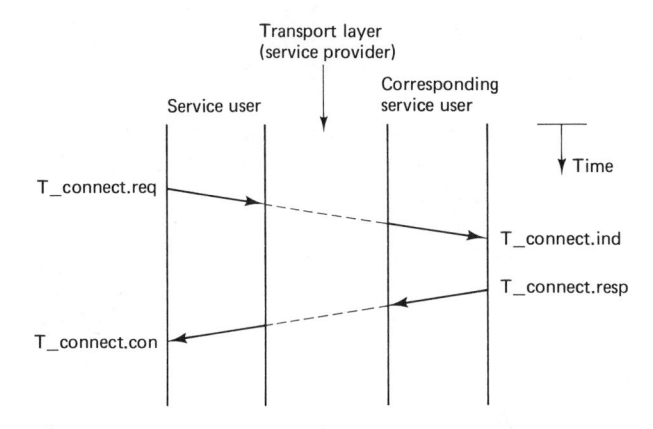

Figure 6.11 Time sequence diagram showing primitives corresponding to the T_CONNECT service for establishing a transport connection.

service, establishing a connection is necessary before any data transfer can take place. The connection request includes the source and destination addresses (called and calling addresses),[6] *quality of service* (QOS) parameters, and up to 32 bytes of user data. In addition, an indication as to whether expedited data service is requested is included as well. The quality of service parameters represents the user's requirements for throughput, transit delay, reliability (e.g., acceptable residual error rate), and priority of this connection, relative to other connections. The transport protocol will in turn forward these parameters to the peer *transport entity* at the destination station as part of the negotiation process. The transport protocol uses these parameters to determine appropriate network services, transport class to choose, credit allocation, whether a transport layer checksum is needed, and so on.

Once the connection request reaches the destination station, it appears as a connection indication (i.e., T_CONNECT.indication). The service user at the destination station responds to the connection request by means of the T_CONNECT.response primitive, which appears at the source station as a T_CONNECT.confirmation. It is possible that the quality of service be reduced by the service provider or by the called transport user. The reduction in quality of service may be caused by insufficient buffers available and characteristics of the underlying network services.

The connection establishment process produces three possible outcomes: the connection request is accepted with the required quality of service, the connection request is accepted with a reduced quality of service, or the connection request is not accepted. A service user at the destination station can reject a transport connection request by means of the T_DISCONNECT.request primitive, which appears at the initiating service user as a T_DISCONNECT.indication, as shown in Figure 6.12(a). Thus, in this context, the T_DISCONNECT.indication primitive is analogous to the familiar message *your call did not go through, all circuits are busy now, would you try again later* in telephone communications. A service provider can also terminate the connection and inform the service user accordingly by means of the T_DISCONNECT.ind primitive, as depicted in Figure 6.12(b). The T_DISCONNECT.request can also be used by the initiating service user to release the connection at any time during data transfer.[7]

Once a transport connection is established, data can be exchanged over the connection via

---

[6] These parameters can also be symbolic names, in which case a mapping between names and addresses must be provided.

[7] With possible loss of data.

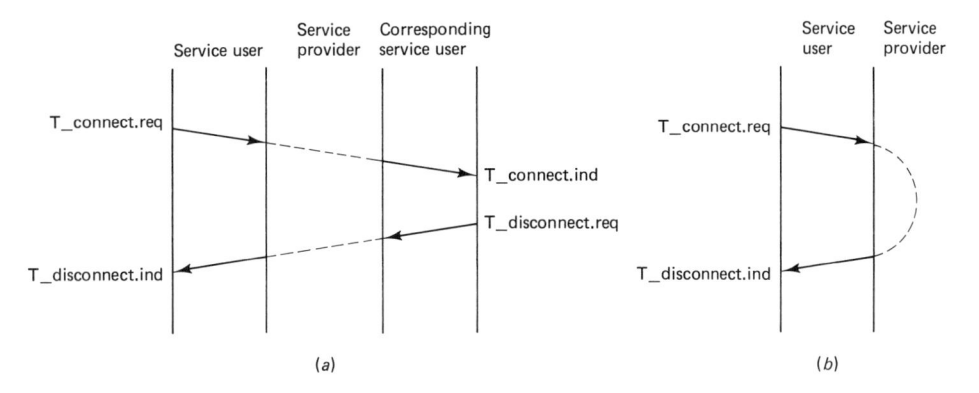

Figure 6.12 Rejection of a request for connection establishment: (a) Rejection by a service user; (b) Rejection by a service provider.

the T_DATA or T_EXPEDITED_DATA services, depending upon whether the data is normal or urgent. These services are *nonconfirmed*; thus the transport protocol is trusted by the users for reliable data transfer.

The data transfer phase begins with the initiating service user issuing a T_DATA.request, which is delivered to the responding service user as a T_DATA.indication. There is no length restriction on the data exchanged using T_DATA. Since the transport class 4 protocol provides flow control, data is delivered in sequence to the receiving transport user. The T_EXPEDITED_DATA service is similar to that of the T_DATA, with two differences: first, the length of the data exchanged is restricted to 16 bytes, and second, expedited data has priority relative to normal data.

Figure 6.13 depicts the state transition diagram associated with a transport user process responsible for interfacing with the transport layer. The user process not only issues *requests* for services or *responses* to service requests, but also receives *indications* for services and service *confirmations*. The diagram consists of 4 states: *idle, outgoing connection pending, incoming connection pending,* and *data transfer ready*. The states attempt to model the process of establishing and using a transport connection, with state 1 representing an initial condition where no transport connection exists and state 4 representing the existence of a connection. States 2 and 3 are transition states where the user process waits for a T_CONNECT.confirm[8] from a remote user process or the user process decides whether it can respond positively or negatively to a connection request.

6.4.2 Class 4 Transport Protocol

Having looked at the transport services, it is now time to see how these services are provided by the transport layer. Recall that the transport class 4 protocol makes no assumption that the underlying network layer is reliable. Therefore, the class 4 protocol is designed to work with a network layer that may fail or garble, lose, misorder, or duplicate data. Furthermore, the network layer cannot be trusted to notify the transport layer as to a possible problem with the lower layers.

Like most error control schemes used in Local Area Networks, the transport class 4 uses a

---

[8] This is the optimistic case. The other possibility is that the connection request is rejected by the service provider or the remote service user. In either case, the transport user process receives a T_DISCONNECT.indication.

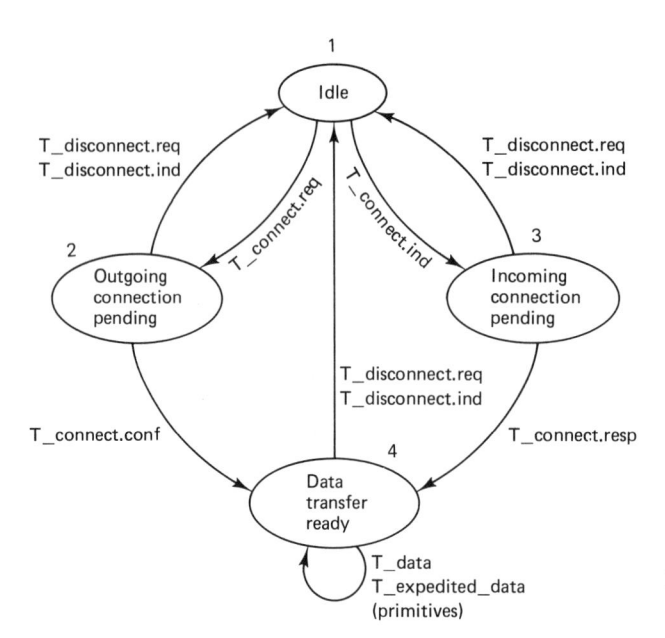

Figure 6.13 State transition diagram associated with a transport user process.

positive acknowledgment and retransmission scheme for dealing with errors. In addition, there is a timer associated with every transport data unit sent. Basically, the scheme works as follows: The transport protocol sends a *data unit* and starts a timer. If an acknowledgment for the data unit sent is not received before the corresponding timer expires, it is assumed that the data unit or the corresponding acknowledgment has been lost. The transport protocol then proceeds to retransmit the data unit.

Example

>This example shows a situation where the data sent by a transport user can be duplicated at the receiver. A transport user at a source station sends messages $M(1)$, $M(2)$, and $M(3)$ to a peer transport user at a destination station located in another subnetwork. The routing algorithm at the network layer routes messages $M(1)$ and $M(3)$ through subnetwork A. Message $M(2)$ does not go through any intermediate subnetwork, but rather reaches the destination subnetwork directly. Further, assume that message $M(1)$ takes much longer to reach the destination station relative to $M(2)$ and $M(3)$. After the timer associated with $M(1)$ expires, the transport protocol at the source station assumes that $M(1)$ has been lost and proceeds to send another copy of the same message. Since $M(1)$ has not been lost, the peer transport user eventually receives two copies of $M(1)$, and thus $M(1)$ is duplicated.

Transport services are provided at both ends of a transport connection by **transport protocol entities.** Although the exact relationship between a *service provider* and *protocol entities* are highly dependent on the particular implementation, for the purposes of this chapter we assume that a *service provider* is equivalent to a set of *protocol entities*. Conceptually, we can view a *protocol entity* as one or several processes implementing the functions of the transport layer. In performing their functions (e.g., exchanging messages), *protocol entities* communicate by exchanging transport protocol data units (TPDUs). Table 6.4 lists the ten TPDUs that are used in the transport class 4 protocol.

TABLE 6.4 TRANSPORT PROTOCOL DATA UNITS

TPDU	Type	Amount of Data Carried
CR	Connection request	Up to 32 bytes
CC	Connection confirm	Up to 32 bytes
DR	Disconnect request	Up to 64 bytes
DC	Disconnect confirm	None
ERR	TPDU error	None
DT	Data	Up to negotiated length
ED	Expedited data	Up to 16 bytes
AK	Acknowledgment	None
EA	Expedited data acknowledgment	None
UD	Unit data	Up to maximum value of network service data unit (NSDU)

TPDUs are related to services primitives in the following way: In general, receipt of primitives causes the protocol entities to be engaged in a dialog, using the protocol rules and exchanging TPDUs. More specifically, upon receipt of a T_CONNECT.request, the transport protocol at a source transport layer sends a CR TPDU to its peer protocol entity at the destination station. The CR TPDU is actually sent using the services provided by the network layer. Thus, a CR TPDU is a special message assembled by the transport entity requesting that a transport connection be established and indicating the characteristics of the connection by means of parameters.

In order to establish a connection at the transport layer, three TPDUs are exchanged, as shown[9] in Figure 6.14. The establishment of the transport connection begins with the requesting protocol entity issuing a CR TPDU to the responding protocol entity. After coordinating with its service user and assuming that all connection requirements can be met, the responding protocol entity responds with a CC TPDU, which upon its arrival to the initiating transport entity, causes it to respond with an AK TPDU. The explicit exchange of three different messages back and forth in a negotiation process is referred to as a **three-way handshake.** Reasons for establishing a transport connection as a three-way handshake protocol are illustrated in the next two examples.

Example

This example illustrates one situation where issuing an acknowledgment for a CC TPDU is advantageous. Let us assume that the sender crashes right after sending the CR TPDU. If an AK TPDU is not used, the responding protocol entity, upon receipt of the CR TPDU, proceeds to send a CC TPDU and assumes that a connection is now established. This situation leads to a conflicting view of the system, because the initiating protocol entity (whenever it comes up) assumes that a transport connection does not exist since it did not receive the CC TPDU, whereas the responding protocol entity assumes that a transport connection does exist. The AK TPDU avoids this probem in the following way: After replying with a CC TPDU, the responding protocol entity starts a timer and expects an acknowledgment (AK) before the timer expires. Obviously, since the initiating protocol entity is down, no acknowledgment is generated, causing the receiver to time-out and retransmit the CC TPDU. After a few such attempts, the receiver gives up and assumes that there is something wrong with the initiating protocol entity or the communication system. Thus, both transport protocol entities now have the same view of the system.

[9] The AK TPDU is not used in the ISO class 2 protocol.

Figure 6.14 A three-way handshake at the transport layer.

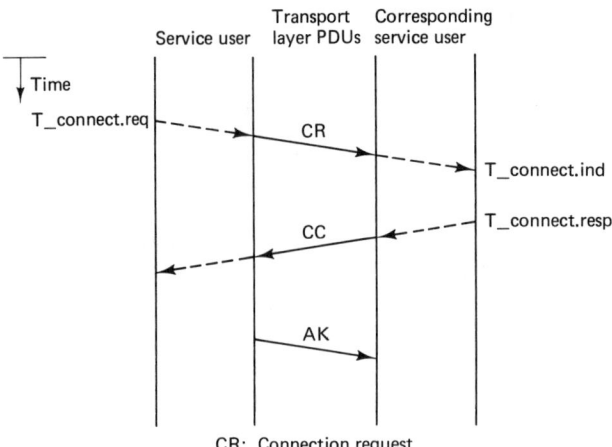

CR: Connection request
CC: Connection confirm
AK: Acknowledgement

Example

This example illustrates how the AK TPDU solve the problem of *reincarnated CR TPDUs*. Assume that the initiating protocol entity sends a CR TPDU which is delayed unnecessarily by the network layer. After the timer associated with the CR TPDU expires, the initiating protocol entity assumes (incorrectly) that the CR has been lost and proceeds to send another one, which arrives sooner than the first CR (perhaps due to a shorter route). Upon receipt of the CR TPDU which was sent later, the responding protocol proceeds to establish the connection and exchange some data with the initiating protocol entity. In addition, let us assume that the transport connection is released immediately after a short data exchange.

In the meantime, the CR TPDU which was sent first finally makes its way through the network layer and is delivered to the responding protocol entity as a *reincarnated CR TPDU*. Naturally, the responding protocol entity assumes (incorrectly) that the reincarnated CR TPDU is a new request for a connection and proceeds to establish one accordingly and sends a CC TPDU. The resulting situation is again a conflicting view of the system, because the initiating protocol entity believes there is no transport connection, whereas the responding protocol entity believes there is one.

The AK TPDU helps solve this problem in the following way: After the responding protocol entity sends a CC TPDU corresponding to the second CR, it expects an acknowledgment (AK TPDU) before establishing the connection. Since the initiating transport entity did not really request another connection to be established, it treats the incoming CC TPDU as an error and proceeds to send a disconnect request (DR TPDU), thus canceling the connection.

Recall that a transport connection is established by a negotiation process between two protocol entities: the initiating one and the responding one. The negotiation process involves the exchange of several parameters, such as class number, flow control option, maximum data unit (i.e., TPDU) size, use of checksum, and quality of service. Thus, the formats for the different transport protocol data units must be flexible in order to support the exchange of many connection parameters. Since the formats for all TPDUs are similar, we will explain one in detail. Readers interested in additional details should consult the ISO 8073 standard.

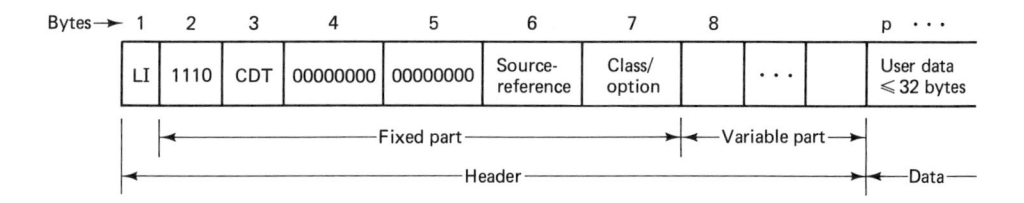

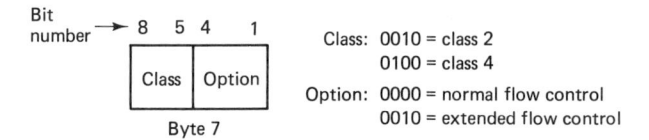

Figure 6.15 Format for the connection request (CR) TPDU of the ISO transport protocol class 4.

The connection request transport PDU. Figure 6.15 depicts the format for the connection request (CR) TPDU. The field LI indicates the length in bytes of the rest of the header, up to 256 bytes excluding any data carried. The remaining portion of the header is grouped in two parts, a fixed part and a variable part. The variable part contains addresses of the communicating transport users.

The fixed part of the CR TPDU begins with a code (i.e., 1110) indicating that this frame is a CR frame and a 4-bit *credit allocation* (CDT) parameter is used for flow control. The source reference in bytes 5 and 6 indicates the proposed transport connection identifier[10] that, if accepted, will be used in the data transfer phase. Byte 7 indicates the class of ISO transport protocol being requested (i.e., 0 through 4) and whether normal or extended flow control is desired. Whereas normal flow control requires 7-bit sequence numbers and 4-bit credit fields, extended flow control requires 31-bit sequence numbers and 16-bit credit fields.

Users can select the *class* and *options* for the connection by means of a negotiation process. A fundamental rule used in the negotiation process is that the responding protocol entity may reduce but never increase the service options requested by the initiating transport protocol. For example, the responding protocol entity may reduce the value of the sequence number window size requested by the initiating protocol entity. Likewise, a request for class 4 may be turned down, and a class 2 connection confirm (CC) may be returned instead. Thus, the values returned by the CC TPDU can be equal to or less than those sent by the CR TPDU.

Whereas the fixed part of the PDU remains fixed in size, the variable part includes optional parameters, each preceded by its own identifying code of specified or variable length. For example, the variable part contains the complete source and destination addresses of the transport users at either end of a transport connection. Other parameters carried in the variable part are listed in Table 6.5.

The transport service access point (TSAP) identifiers are the source and destination addresses of *socket-like points*, where the services of the transport layer are made available. Protocol entities map TSAPs into transport connection identifiers to be used during data transmission. Security parameters are not specified and are left for specific implementations.

---

[10] The identifier is similar to the virtual circuit number used in the network layer.

TABLE 6.5 SELECTED PARAMETERS IN THE VARIABLE PART OF A CR TPDU FOR THE CLASS 4 TRANSPORT PROTOCOL

Parameter	Parameter Length (Bytes)
Maximum TPDU size	1
Calling transport SAP* identifier	
(Calling transport address)	variable
Called transport SAP identifier	variable
Security parameters	variable
Checksum	2
Additional options (Checksum/expedited service)	1
Quality of Service Parameters	
Acknowledge time	2
Throughput	12
Residual error rate	3
Priority of connection	2
Transit delay	8

* SAP: Service Access Point

Although the data link protocol may perform error control functions, the two-byte checksum option at the transport layer provides additional error control capability. In some cases (e.g., the MAP architecture with class I LLC) the data link protocol does not provide error control. Thus, the two-byte checksum option must be used in this case if the transport protocol is to provide a reliable service. The *additional options* parameter indicates whether checksumming or expedited data is used. The *quality of service parameters* is precisely that discussed in the context of the T_CONNECT.request primitive.

6.5 MAP TRANSPORT LAYER

The MAP 3.0 architecture uses a subset of the ISO 8073 Class 4 transport specification. Since the MAP data link layer does not provide flow and error control functions it is up to the MAP transport layer to provide these functions. This is one of the main reasons why the MAP transport layer specifies *class 4*, the largest and most complex class of transport services as specified by ISO. As explained in the previous section, in addition to providing flow and error control functions, the ISO Class 4 transport provides the ability to multiplex user transmissions, recover from network layer errors and failures, and the ability to support datagrams.

Since the ISO standard classifies all transport services into two groups, connection management and data transfer, Table 6.6 shows the MAP service requirements from each group.

TABLE 6.6

CONNECTION MANAGEMENT	DATA TRANSFER
T_CONNECT	T_DATA
T_DISCONNECT	T_EXPEDITED_DATA

In addition, the MAP subset of the class 4 ISO transport protocol has the following characteristics:

1. Ability to negotiate a Class 2 service from a Class 4 request.

2. The following parameter list, which is normally used as acceptance criteria, is ignored if received: security, acknowledgment time, throughput, transit delay, priority, and residual error rate.

3. Both 7-bit and 31-bit sequence numbers must be supported and negotiated during connection establishment. All implementations shall request 31-bit sequence numbers in the CR TPDU.

4. Expedited data support is required.

5. Checksums are required in connection requests (CR TPDU) per ISO rules, but are optional on data transfer (DT PDU). Using checksums for data transfer is application-dependent and negotiated during connection establishment.

6. With the exception of a connection request service, a parameter which is not defined in any other transport service or not implemented at the receiver is treated as a protocol error. In the connection request case, the parameter is ignored.

7. A specific implementation is required to support the concurrent use of multiple transport connections via one or more TSAPs.

8. Whereas all transport machines must receive concatenated TPDUs, sending concatenated TPDUs is optional.

9. Although the transmission of flow control information (i.e., AK TPDUs) by the transmitter is optional, the receiver must recognize flow control information and act in accordance with the ISO specification.

6.5.1 TOP Transport Layer

The TOP 3.0 transport layer is identical to that of MAP 3.0.

SUMMARY

In this chapter we have addressed the functions, services, and protocols associated with the transport layer. First, a simplified transport protocol model was used to illustrate concepts associated with addressing, multiplexing, flow and error control, and information units. The ISO transport layer standard protocol was then analyzed, focusing on the class 4 protocol. Finally, features of the MAP and TOP architectures were presented.

The transport layer is responsible for bridging the gap between the layers that provide data transmission functions and the layers that provide communication functions. The essential functions of the transport layer involve performing *end-to-end control*, and *end-to-end optimization* of data transfer between end systems. The view that the transport layer presents to the session layer (or any layer above the session layer) is one of a *virtual point-to-point link,* regardless of the methods used for actual information transfer, and regardless of the network's physical topology.

Like the network layer, services provided by the transport layer can be connection-oriented or connectionless. The most important protocol mechanisms at the transport layer are: addressing, multiplexing, flow and error control, information units, and connection management. Flow and error control is typically achieved using a sliding window flow control (SWFC) mechanism similar to that used at the data link layer. A feature of the SWFC mechanism used at the transport layer consists of decoupling error control from flow control information by using a *credit* scheme.

One way of specifying protocol operation is by means of a *state transition diagram*. Other methods often used for specifying protocols include *Petri Nets*, and *high level languages* such as Pascal or ADA.

Because of the different types of data transfer that might be expected and the wide variety of subnetworks that might be available for providing network services, five classes have been defined for the ISO standard transport protocol. The classes are known as class 0, 1, 2, 3, and 4.

The simplest class of service is that of *class 0*, which assumes that the underlying network service provides an acceptable error rate, and an acceptable rate of connection failures. *Class 1* provides similar functionality to that of class 0, with an additional error recovery capability. Class 2 provides similar functionality as class 0, with an additional multiplexing capability. Classes 3 and 4 are supersets of class 2. Whereas *class 3* can only detect network layer failures, *class 4* not only detects network failures but also recovers from them.

Services offered by the transport protocol are grouped into two groups: *connection management* and *data transfer*. The *connection management* group include the T_CONNECT and T_DISCONNECT services whereas the *data transfer* group include the T_DATA and T_EXPEDITED_DATA services. The transport class 4 uses a positive acknowledgment and retransmission scheme for dealing with errors. In order to establish a connection at the transport layer, three TPDUs are exchanged, constituting a three-way handshake.

The MAP architecture uses a subset of the ISO 8073 Class 4 transport specification. Since the MAP data link layer with class I operation does not provide flow and error control functions, it is up to the MAP transport layer to provide these functions. The TOP transport layer is identical to that of the MAP transport layer.

Bibliographic Notes

Transport layer issues are discussed in the books by Tanenbaum (1988), Schwartz (1987), and Stallings (1987). The latter two books also contain some material on the ISO standard protocol. The articles by Cerf and Kahn (1974) and Cerf and Kirstein (1978) contain packet-network design issues which are relevant to the transport layer. Protocol specification is addressed in Diaz (1986). Naturally, the most accurate information on the ISO transport layer standard are ISO 8072 and ISO 8073 dealing with the service definition and protocol specification, respectively.

PROBLEMS

1. What is meant by the terms end-to-end control and end-to-end optimization?
2. What is the main use of the transport suffix?
3. Why is error control decoupled from flow control at the transport layer? Explain how each type of control is typically performed.

4. Draw a time diagram for the T_DATA and T_EXPEDITED_DATA primitives assuming a reliable data transfer (i.e., no contingencies).
5. Problem 7 of Chapter 4 involves writing a program for managing a circular buffer. Write a procedure for returning the number of available buffers in the circular list. This procedure could be used for returning credit information associated with the sliding window flow control used in transport protocols.
6. Figure 6.10 depicts a transport protocol specification using a state transition diagram. Change this specification into an ADA program specification similar to the token bus simplified model specification at the end of section 4.8.
7. Discuss the implications of using transport protocols with varying degrees of functionality such as the ISO transport protocol class 0, 1, 2, 3, and 4 with a sophisticated data link protocol such as the ISO logical link control class 2. Compare this solution with the options specified in the MAP architecture. In your discussion, consider the following scenarios:
   (a) A connection oriented network layer.
   (b) A connectionless inactive ISO network layer.
   (c) A connectionless full conformance ISO network layer.
8. Assume a station architecture with an ISO inactive network layer. This architecture is useful for time critical applications involving just one network segment. Discuss the implications of using transport protocols with varying degrees of functionality such as the ISO transport protocol class 0, 1, 2, 3 or 4 in combination with the following:
   (a) ISO LLC class 1,
   (b) ISO LLC class 2, and
   (c) ISO LLC class 3.
9. Whereas the ISO network layer standard provides a N_DATA_ACK service, the ISO transport layer standard does not provide an equivalent T_DATA_ACK service. Rather, the transport protocol uses acknowledgement PDUs for error control purposes. When an error occurs, TPDUs are retransmitted a maximum number of times N. If the error persists, the transport connection is closed. In time critical applications, discuss the advantages and disadvantages of error recovery using the standards for the network and transport layers. Assume that the value N is arbitrary.
10. Write two procedures for implementing the services T_DATA.req and T_DATA.ind and the associated transport protocol for the model of Section 6.2 where the following assumptions were made:
    —no message segmentation,
    —only one connection,
    —no credit scheme,
    —no urgent data is handled,
    —no multiplexing is provided, and
    —there are no errors during message transmission (ideal case).
    Assume the existence of two procedures N_DATA.req and N_DATA.ind for sending a message to or receiving a message from the network layer.
11. Extend the procedures of the previous problem to remove the assumptions made.
12. In a certain datagram internetwork, routers operate at the network layer, replacing the network layer overhead of the source by the destination subnetwork overhead. A transport layer message consisting of 1024 bytes of data and 16 bytes of overhead is sent into a network by attaching a 12 byte network layer overhead to it. The destination subnetwork has a maximum packet size of 520 bytes, including its own 10 byte network overhead. How many bits of information, including overhead, are ultimately delivered to the network layer at the destination?

PART 2

7

Background for the OSI Upper Layers

As noted in Chapter 6, the session, presentation, and application layers are known as the **upper layers** and deal mostly with *communication* aspects rather than with *transmission* aspects of computer networks. Thus, it is not surprising that the issues of the upper layers vary markedly when compared with the issues of the lower layers. The upper layers assume that the service provided by the lower layers is a reliable, virtual *point to point* link regardless of the actual method used for data transmission and regardless of the network physical topology. The upper layers basically deal with the communication aspects for the appropriate support of *distributed systems*. Accordingly, we begin Part II by providing sufficient background in operating systems and distributed systems to understand the upper layers of the OSI reference model.

Our discussion of operating systems is brief, and we concentrate on those aspects directly related to the book, *processes* and *scheduling techniques*. The purpose of this chapter is to provide an introduction to operating systems, emphasizing the concepts of processes and scheduling, and to provide an introduction to distributed systems.

7.1 INTRODUCTION TO OPERATING SYSTEMS

Imagine for a moment that someone is programming one of the earliest computers (late 1940s), which were very rudimentary. One had to enter a program by setting switches for the memory contents containing the instructions one address at a time. It took almost an eternity just to enter one program, not to mention the problems involved with running it. If any error occurred (e.g., the failure of one memory element) the computer did not give any indication whatsoever about the nature of the problem, thus making the debugging extremely difficult. Once one programmer finished running his or her program, the computer was idle for hours while the next programmer entered his or her program. Consequently, computer utilization was extremely low. It was a nuisance to work with these machines because they had *no operating system*.

An **operating system** is a software system that manages the resources of a computer for efficient and user friendly use. Examples of computer resources include memory, secondary storage (i.e., hard disk, tapes, and so on), central processing unit (CPU), printers, etc. The operating system is made up of a set of programs, each dealing with one aspect of the overall resource management. Typically, a portion of the operating system deals with human users, whereas other portions deal with file systems, main memory, etc. An important aspect of resource management involves the control of the overall computer resources. For example, an important portion of the operating system controls the use of the CPU[1] among the various programs submitted to the computer system for execution.

7.1.1 Generation of Operating Systems

Just as computer hardware has evolved through several generations, so have operating systems. However, it is more difficult to visualize the evolution of operating systems, because they deal with intangible changes involving functions and capabilities. Operating systems have evolved through the following generations (Deitel, 1984):

1. Zeroth generation (1940s):
The computers in this generation had no operating systems.

2. First generation (1950s):
The major function of operating systems in this generation was to improve the utilization of the CPU after one program finished execution and while the next one was being loaded. The CPU utilization was improved by organizing the programs into batches. Many programs were collected off-line and submitted to the computer at once. The operating system could then switch between programs quickly and in an efficient manner.

3. Second generation (1960s)
This generation incorporated two major developments: multiprogramming and multiprocessing. In addition, the following features also began to appear:

Device independence: This feature allows programs to reference input/output devices in a logical fashion, rather then specifying the actual physical device. For example, the FORTRAN statement *WRITE(5,10) A,B* writes the value of the variables A and B to *logical device* number 5, which might represent a printer or a console or any other physical device to be specified by the programmer.

Time-sharing systems.

Real-time systems.

---

[1] Although a computer system can have more than one CPU, we restrict our discussion to the single CPU case.

4. Third Generation (Mid-1960s to mid-1970s)

This generation started with the introduction of the Operating System for the IBM System/360 family of computers in 1964. The main characteristic of this generation of operating systems is that they were general purpose. They were also very complex. Some of them simultaneously supported batch processing, time sharing, real-time processing, and multiprocessing.

5. Fourth Generation (mid-1970s to present)

These operating systems represent the current state of the art. They are characterized by incorporating some of the following developments: computer networks, fault tolerance, very user friendly, databases, artificial intelligence, distributed data processing, and distributed operating systems.

Depending upon whether a program is part of the operating system, programs are classified into (operating) *system programs* and *application programs*. Thus, a **system program** is a subset of an operating system.

Example

The operating system for the popular IBM PC personal computer is called DOS. A portion of DOS dealing with input/output devices is called *Basic Input/Output System* (BIOS). Thus BIOS is a *system program*.

Programs other than *system programs* are called **application programs.** An *application program* executes under control of the operating system.

Example

A program in any programming language (i.e., Pascal) running under PC-DOS is an *application program*.

7.1.2 Processes or Tasks

In this subsection, we discuss the concept of a *task* or *process* and provide definitions of important terms associated with processes. In operating system terminology, the term *process* is used interchangeably with *tasks*. Because we are using established terminology in the field, we use both terms in this chapter. To avoid confusion with other terms, we use the term *process* in any other chapter of this book. A **task** is an *application program* used by the operating system as a unit of management and control. For example, an operating system may be able to list the tasks currently residing in the system, to start execution of a new task, or it may indicate which task is currently running. We provide a more detailed discussion of processes in Section 7.2.

When an operating system allows more than one partially completed task to be processed concurrently, the system is referred to as a **multiprogramming system.** Since we are assuming only one CPU, the term *concurrently* indicates that the CPU runs a task for a short interval, and before the task finishes execution, the CPU runs another task and the same rule applies. Unfinished tasks run again so that eventually they complete execution.

Example

An example of a multiprogramming system is one where the operating system allows each task to run for a predefined interval and the CPU is switched to another task, regardless of whether the task finished execution. Thus, task 1 can execute for T1 sec, task 2 for T2 sec. . . . Then the cycle repeats.

A special class of *multiprogramming systems*, in which the tasks handle requests from several users which are located remotely or locally from the computer system, is known as a **multiuser system**. A multiuser system is also called a **time-sharing** system, because the CPU is shared among the users on an interactive basis. Since CPU speeds are much faster than human speeds, human users interacting with a *time-sharing system* are not often aware that they are sharing the CPU with other users.

A computer system containing more than one CPU and thus being able to process more than one task simultaneously is known as a **multiprocessing system**. A multiprocessing system is in fact a multiprocessor network using the classification given in Chapter 1. Since we are interested primarily on LANs, *multiprocessing systems* are outside the scope of this book.

Because of their importance in implementing complex software systems such as ISO protocols and manufacturing systems, a subset of multiprogramming systems deserves special attention. A highly flexible multiprogramming system in which tasks can control each other is referred to as a **multitasking system**. A task controlling another task involves, for example, task A starting, suspending, delaying, or stopping the execution of task B. A **multitasking operating system** is one that supports multitasking systems. Thus, from our definition, a multitasking system supports a high degree of concurrency and flexibility.

Another system that deserves special consideration is a *real-time system*. A system that responds sufficiently quickly to affect its environment within a predefined time interval is referred to as a **real-time system**. Note that in the definition of a real-time system, we are not specifying that the system responds within a specific time limit, such as 100 msec. Thus, our definition of a real-time system is a generic one. Whether a system can be classified as a *real-time system* depends on specific applications. For example, a system having a response time of 50 msec may be qualified as being real-time for some applications, but not real-time for others.

Depending upon the relative values for system response times, *real-time systems* are further classified into **hard real-time systems** and **soft real-time systems**. Hard real-time systems have more stringent response time requirements than soft real-time systems. Typical response time values for hard real-time systems range from 0.1 to 10 msec, whereas typical values for soft real-time systems range from 10 msec to several sec. Hard real-time systems find applications in avionics, military, and process control systems, whereas automated manufacturing mostly involves soft real-time systems.

Multitasking operating systems which are able to meet real-time system requirements are known as **real-time multitasking operating systems**. Thus, from the previous discussion, it should be clear that *real-time multitasking operating systems* are important when designing application software for complex systems, such as automated manufacturing systems, or when implementing ISO higher layer protocols.

7.2 PROCESS CONCEPTS

As noted in the previous section, the concept of a *process* is crucial to understanding operating systems and communication networks. There has been some misunderstanding about the meaning of a process, mostly because there is no unique definition. Although the main concept is basically the same, some authors define it in a slightly different way. The idea behind a process is that an operating system needs a management entity or *unit of management* to work with in an efficient manner. There are several possibilities for this unit of management: a statement, 100 statements, a module, a program, etc.

A single statement is not effective, since it would involve too much overhead. Furthermore, by having the operating system (OS), deal with one statement at a time, the OS function is almost indistinguishable from that of a language. The difficulty with the second possibility is that the number 100 is completely arbitrary. What if the 100th statement falls right in the middle of a loop? This causes problems, because the OS would need to save information such as the loop iteration, etc. The idea of having the OS deal with modules is a good compromise. However, the effectiveness depends on the definition of a module (more on this later). Finally, the possibility of having the OS deal with programs is not a good one, because one does not know in advance the complexity and size of a program. Typically, a program can range in size from a few lines to thousands (perhaps millions) of lines. Thus, the OS would deal with entities with size variation of a few orders of magnitude.

Modules

How is a module defined? One possibility is to assign a certain number of statements to a module. Thus, a module could be defined as any set of instructions of size 500 or less. Of course, the number 500 is open for discussion, and there are proponents to increase it or decrease it.

A better definition for a module results from applying the principle of *divide and conquer*, which was successfully used by Alexander the Great many years ago for military purposes. The idea is to decompose (divide) a problem (usually large and complex) into several subproblems. By solving each subproblem separately, and effectively integrating the solution of the subproblems, the next thing you know is that the overall problem has been solved. The advantage of this approach is that solving each subproblem is much easier than solving the entire problem.

However, there are two major stumbling blocks that one has to overcome. First, decomposing a complex problem is not sraightforward. It requires intuition and some degree of experience to come up with an effective *problem decomposition*. The second stumbling block is to identify the relationships between the subproblems, so that taken together their solutions can be integrated to provide the solution of the original problem.

Functional programming is a good approach to follow for problem decomposition. This approach consists, basically, of identifying the functions associated with the solution to the overall program. Examples of some functions include: initialize many variables, create and initialize several files, input data to one or more files, write a report, and others. Undoubtedly, some functions are trivial (e.g., initialize 3 variables) while others are very complex (e.g., input data and sort 30 large files). The next stage in the functional programming approach involves identifying inputs and outputs for each function. For example, if the function is to write a report from data contained in one file, the input is given by the filename (with some data in it) and the output is given by the printout. The final stage in the approach consists of matching functions to modules. Depending upon the complexity of the functions, the matching can be *one-to-one* or *several*-(functions)-*to-one* (module).

We are now in a position to provide a definition of a process. We define a **process** as a module-like entity that the OS knows about (i.e., it is registered in the OS tables). The reason that processes (i.e., tasks) are important is because they help keep track of the separate management entities in a computing system. For example, one can list, delete, suspend, or start processes.

Although the process concepts have been introduced from the viewpoint of operating systems, they could also be introduced from the viewoint of application requirements. When an application is very complex, we can decompose the application into a set of **application process.**

One key characteristic of processes is that they proceed at their own pace, independent of one another, and make no assumptions whatsoever about the speed of other processes. Processes operating in this manner are referred to as *asynchronous concurrent processes.*

Disjoint and Overlapping Processes

Two processes, A and B, are **disjoint** if they do not share data; otherwise they are **overlapping.** Sharing data among asynchronous concurrent processes can cause problems, with perhaps the major problem being the *simultaneous access to the database*. This problem is illustrated in subsection 7.2.3. Even disjoint processes experience problems if they are required to *synchronize* their operation. A form of synchronization consists of allowing Task B (or a statement in it) to execute *only after* Task A (or a statement in it) has executed. Synchronization is further discussed in subsection 7.4.2.

7.2.1 Process States

Let us assume a multitasking OS which is running two tasks, TASK1 and TASK2, concurrently. If, at any instant we inquire what is happening to TASK1, here are some possibilities.

a. TASK1 has the CPU.
b. TASK1 is waiting for I/O to complete while TASK2 has the CPU.
c. TASK1 is waiting for a synchronization signal from TASK2.
d. TASK1 is waiting for a message from TASK2.

The preceding possibilities can be summarized using the concept of a *task state*. The minimum information required to characterize a task is referred to as the **task state.** Thus, there must be a criterion to evaluate the minimum information requirements. One criterion often used is the size and complexity of the tables that the OS maintains to keep track of task states. The following is a set of states generally used to characterize tasks:

1. *Undefined*—The process is unknown to the OS (i.e., it is not registered in the OS tables).
2. *Ready*—A process is said to be ready if it could use a CPU if one were available.
3. *Running*—A process is said to be running if it currently has the CPU.
4. *Blocked*—A process is said to be blocked if it is waiting for some event to happen (e.g., I/O completion) before it can proceed.

Process state transitions. When a task is first created, it changes its state from *undefined* to *ready*. While in the *ready* state, a task is at the mercy of a portion of the OS called the *scheduler* (or dispatcher). The scheduler basically chooses one task to be run from all tasks entered into the scheduler's *ready list*. Tasks are chosen by the scheduler according to a **scheduling algorithm,** discussed in Section 7.3. While in the *running* state, a task can be put in the ready state by the scheduler (if it is time to given up the CPU), or it can be put in the *blocked* state if it requests an I/O operation that will take a while. The aforementioned task state change is illustrated in Figure 7.1.

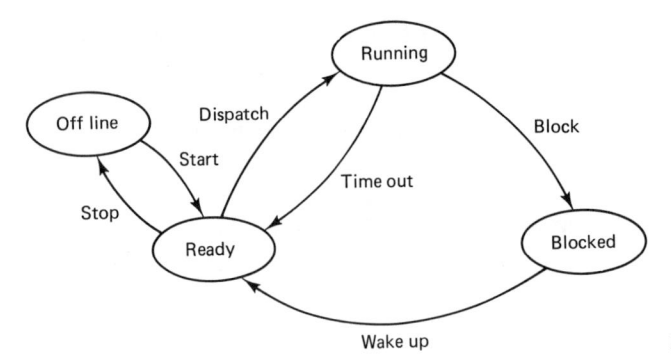

Figure 7.1 Process state transitions.

Process attributes and the process control block. In order to manage processes, an operating system needs certain attributes that, together with the process states, completely characterize the process. The number and name of the attributes generally change from computer manufacturer to manufacturer, but most include the following: process name, priority, pointer to a memory area where the process resides, pointer to allocated resources, a register save area, whether it is an interrupt process, etc.

A data structure that contains the process attributes (including the process state) is known as the **process control block** (PCB). Just as one needs information about the state of the process, one needs information about the state of the processor (i.e., the CPU). Processor information is given by the *processor context*, which is defined as the contents of all the processor registers (program counter, status register, scratch pad registers, etc.). Together, the *processor context* and the PCB define the **task (processor) context.** Any time processes go from the ready state to any other state, a **task context switch** is involved. The context of the outgoing task is saved in memory, and the OS uses the context of the incoming task to proceed with its execution.

7.2.2 Operations on Processes

Operating systems perform the following operations on processes:

>   create a process,
>   destroy a process,
>   suspend a process,
>   resume a process,
>   change a process's priority,
>   block a process,
>   wake up a process, and
>   dispatch a process.

Creating a process includes many operations such as:

>   naming the process,
>   inserting it in the system's list of known processes,
>   determining the process's initial priority,

creating the PCB, and
allocating the process's initial resources.

A process may spawn a new process, called a *child process*, with the creating process called the *parent process*. Only one parent is needed to create a child process. Such creation yields a *hierarchical process structure*, similar to the hierarchical file structure of some operating systems.

For some applications, it is convenient to *suspend* a process temporarily and have another process resume it some time later. An example of the use of suspension is in response to short-term fluctuations in system load. In this case, some processes may be suspended and resumed later when the load settles back to normal levels. The process state transition diagram can be modified, as shown in Figure 7.2, in order to include suspended states. The *blocked* state is also referred to as the *sleep* state, thus the need to wake up a process (i.e., to unblock it).

7.2.3 Critical Sections and Mutual Exclusion

As noted earlier, sharing data among concurrent asynchronous processes can cause problems. More specifically, a major problem with asynchronous concurrent processes is that while one process is modifying a variable(s), other processes have access to the same variable(s). This problem is also referred to as the *simultaneous access to the database*. This should be avoided at all cost. Preventing other processes from accessing shared data while one process is doing so is called **mutual exclusion.** The code that references a set of shared variables is called a **critical section.** We illustrate the simultaneous access to the database problem by means of the following example.

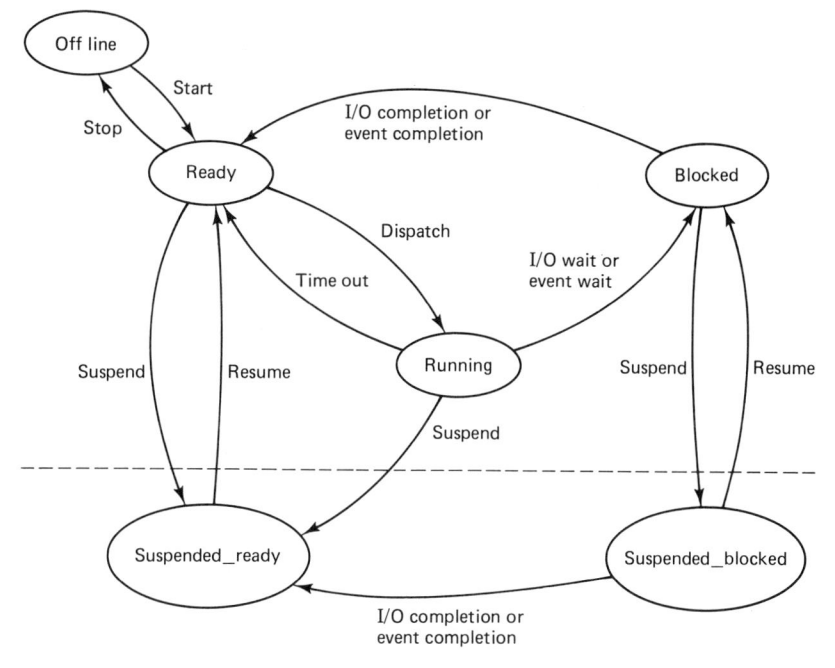

Figure 7.2 Process state transitions incorporating suspend states.

Example

Consider a warehouse for storing widgets, where the problem involves the design of an *on-line, real-time* inventory control system for keeping track of the widgets in the warehouse. It is suggested that an interrupt driven computer system, with a real-time, multitasking operating system is used to solve the problem. Two switches S_a and S_b are configured as shown in Figure 7.3(a), so that when a widget enters the warehouse, S_a closes, causing the operating system to schedule task A for execution. Likewise, when a widget leaves the warehouse, S_b closes, causing the operating system to schedule task B for execution. The code for tasks A and B is organized as in Figure 7.3(b).

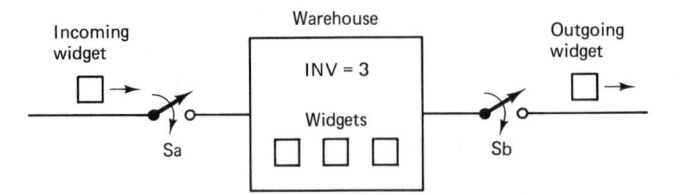

When Sa closes task A is scheduled.
When Sb closes task B is scheduled.

Figure 7.3(a) The simultaneous access to the database problem.

Task A	Task B
Begin	**Begin**
.	.
.	.
.	.
{housekeeping code}	{housekeeping code}
INV = INV + 1;	INV = INV − 1;
.	.
.	.
end;	**end;**

Figure 7.3(b) Organization for task A and task B.

Let us assume that there are 3 widgets in the inventory when S_a closes, thus causing task A to run. Let us assume further that after task A has read the variable INV = 3 and while it is performing some housekeeping functions, S_b closes and the operating system preempts task A and runs task B until completed.[2] Under these circumstances, when task B finishes execution, INV = 2. The operating system then allows task A to complete execution, which updates the variable INV = 4, since it uses the INV value before the interruption. The final value for INV is obviously incorrect. Since one widget entered the warehouse and another one left, the value of INV should remain at 3 rather than 4, as shown in this example.

Since INV is shared by tasks A and B, the statement INV = INV + 1; constitutes the critical section for task A. Likewise, the statement INV = INV − 1; constitutes the critical section for task

---

[2] This is possible if task B has higher priority than task A, or the operating system decides that it is time to switch the CPU to task B. These issues are related to scheduling techniques discused in Section 7.3.

B. The problem in the previous example happens because there is no mechanism (mutual exclusion) for preventing task B to access INV *while* task A is executing INV = INV + 1.

Thus, processes need to have *mutually exclusive access* to the critical sections they reference. There are several solutions to the critical section problem. We present two solutions and discuss the latter, which is based on semaphores, in detail. Before discussing the semaphore solution, it is convenient to define a construct useful for expressing mutually exclusive access to critical sections. We refer to these constructs as MUT_EX_BEGIN (for mutual exclusion begin) and its bracket MUT_EX_END (for mutual exclusion end). When a process wants to access a critical section, it executes MUT_EX_BEGIN; when it no longer needs access to the critical section, it executes MUT_EX_END. Two processes A and B requiring mutual exclusion might be coded as follows:

```
Process A:

                perform calculations outside critical section;
    MUT_EX_BEGIN;
                execute critical section;
    MUT_EX_END;
                perform more calculations outside critical section;
    END;

Process B:

                perform calculations outside critical section;
    MUT_EX_BEGIN;
                execute critical section;
    MUT_EX_END;
                perform more calculations outside critical section;
    END;
```

IMPLEMENTING MUT_EX_BEGIN AND MUT_EX_END

Solution 1. This solution is based on a global boolean variable, INSIDE, initialized to FALSE, indicating that neither process is in its critical section. The code for MUT_EX_BEGIN an MUT_EX_END is

```
            MUT_EX_BEGIN:
                DO WHILE (INSIDE);
                END;
                INSIDE = TRUE;
                    {critical section}
            MUT_EX_END:
                INSIDE = FALSE;
```

Unfortunately, this solution does not work satisfactorily in all situations. Because of the asynchronous nature of concurrent processes, it is possible that one process can gain entrance to its critical section when another process is already in its critical section. We present next a solution that always works.

Solution 2: Semaphores. A semaphore is an integer *system variable*, s, that can be accessed only through the following two standard *atomic* operations, P(s) and V(s), defined as follows:

```
P(s):      If s > 0
              then s := s − 1;
              else (wait on s)
V(s):         s := s + 1;
```

The previous operations are atomic in that once the operations P(s) or V(s) are initiated, they *cannot* be interrupted or divided into several execution stages. The variable *s* is a *system variable* in that it is accessed only through the operating system rather than by the application process directly. The operating system executes P(s) or V(s) either completely or not at all.

When a process attempts to execute P(s), the operating system checks whether the system variable $s > 0$; if it is, the process is allowed to continue execution. Otherwise, the process is *blocked*. When other processes cause that $s > 0$, the operating system allows only one process that may be waiting for the condition $s > 0$ to continue execution. Likewise, when a process executes the operation V(s), the operating system increments the variable s by one and lets that process to continue with its execution.

The implementation of MUT_EX_BEGIN and MUT_EX_END using semaphores is straightforward:

```
MUT_EX_BEGIN:
                   P(s);
MUT_EX_END:
                   V(s);
```

Thus, the MUT_EX_BEGIN and MUT_EX_END operations simply consist of the P(s) and V(s) operations, respectively.

Solution to the n-process Critical Section. Semaphores can be used in dealing with the n-process critical section. The n-processes share a common semaphore s, initialized to 1. Each process P_i is then organized as follows:

```
              Process Pi
Begin
    P(s);
    — {critical section}
    V(s);
    — {noncritical section}
End;
```

7.3 SCHEDULING TECHNIQUES

Transition changes between the running and ready states in Figure 7.1 are controlled by the *scheduler*.[3] The **scheduler** is part of the operating system which determines when and how the CPU is assigned to a different process (other than the one the CPU is currently executing).

The following list contains several objectives that a scheduler might fulfill:

Fair—All processes are treated the same.
Maximize throughput—Service the largest number of processes per unit time.

---
[3] In some books the *scheduler* is also referred to as the *dispatcher*.

Maximize the number of user interactions.

Be predictable—A given program should run in about the same amount of time and at about the same cost every time it is submitted to the system.

Minimize overhead.

Balance resource use—The scheduling mechanisms should keep the resources of the system busy.

Achieve a balance between response time and utilization.

Avoid indefinite postponement.

Enforce priorities.

Give preference to processes holding key resources

Give better service to processes exhibiting desirable behavior.

Degrade gracefully under heavy loads.

Many of these goals are in conflict with one another, thus making scheduling a complex problem.

7.3.1 Scheduling Criteria

To meet scheduling objectives, a scheduling mechanism should consider:

the I/O boundness of a process,
the CPU boundness of a process,
whether the process is batch or interactive,
real-time requirements,
process priority,
how frequently a process has been preempted by a higher priority process,
how much execution time the process has received, and
how much more time the process needs to complete execution.

Preemptive vs. nonpreemptive scheduling. A scheduling discipline is **nonpreemptive** if once a process has been given the CPU, the CPU cannot be taken away from that process. A scheduling discipline is **preemptive** if the CPU can be taken away. Preemptive scheduling is useful in systems in which high-priority processes required rapid attention. In real-time systems, for example, the consequences of missing an interrupt could be devastating. In interactive time-sharing systems, preemptive scheduling is important to guarantee acceptable response times.

The interval timer or interrupting clock. To prevent users from monopolizing the system (either maliciously or accidentally), the operating system has mechanisms for taking the CPU away from the user. The operating system sets an *interrupting clock* or interval timer to generate an interrupt at some specific future time. The scheduler then chooses the next process that should get the CPU. The process retains control of the CPU until it voluntarily releases the CPU, the clock interrupts, or some other interrupt diverts the attention of the CPU.

The period of the interval timer is referred to as the *quantum* size q. Determining quantum size values is critical to the effective operation of a computer system. Should q be large or small?

Should it be fixed or variable? Should it be the same for all users, or should it be determined separately for each user?

7.3.2 Priorities

Priorities may be assigned automatically by the operating system, or they may be assigned externally by end users. They may be earned or they may be bought; or they may be static or dynamic. Although *static priorities* do not change with time, they are easy to implement and have relatively low overhead. They are not, however, responsive to changes in the environment. On the other hand, *dynamic priority* mechanisms are responsive to change. In dynamic priorities, the initial priority assigned to a process may have only a short duration, after which it is adjusted to a better value.

Scheduling techniques. Many scheduling techniques are currently in use in computer systems. We discuss only three scheduling techniques which are used in applications involving computer networks and manufacturing systems: Highest Priority First, Round Robin, and Feedback Queues. The reader is referred to other texts on operating systems for additional scheduling disciplines.

1. Highest Priority First (HPF)—Under this scheme, the scheduler selects the task with highest priority to run next. There are two versions: nonpreemptive and preemptive. A *nonpreemptive HPF* scheduler runs the task until completion. Once the task is running, no other task can use the CPU. This scheduler is mostly used in data processing applications which do not involve time critical requirements. Thus, it is not suitable for real-time applications. A *preemptive HPF* scheduler assigns the CPU to the HPF task for q seconds. The task leaves the running state if one of the following situations arises:

q expires,

the task finishes execution,

the task blocks itself (goes to sleep) (e.g., some I/O device required by the task is busy), or

an operator stops the task.

When q expires, the scheduler assigns the CPU to another ready task with higher priority, otherwise the running task gets the CPU again. This process is repeated indefinitely.

Another version of a preemptive HPF scheduling algorithm involves the scheduler picking up another task to run when an event occurs. The event may be caused by an arrival of a task with higher priority, or when a task with higher priority makes a transition from the blocked to the ready state.

2. Round Robin (RR)—We distinguish three versions of Round Robin scheduling algorithms:

a. Simple RR—The scheduler uses no priorities. As depicted in Figure 7.4(a), tasks are served on a first-in first-out (FIFO) manner. A process gets the CPU for q seconds, after which it releases the CPU because one of the following possibilities arises:

The quantum expires. The process is put at the back of the queue.

The process blocks itself. It goes to the blocked state.

The process finishes execution within q seconds.

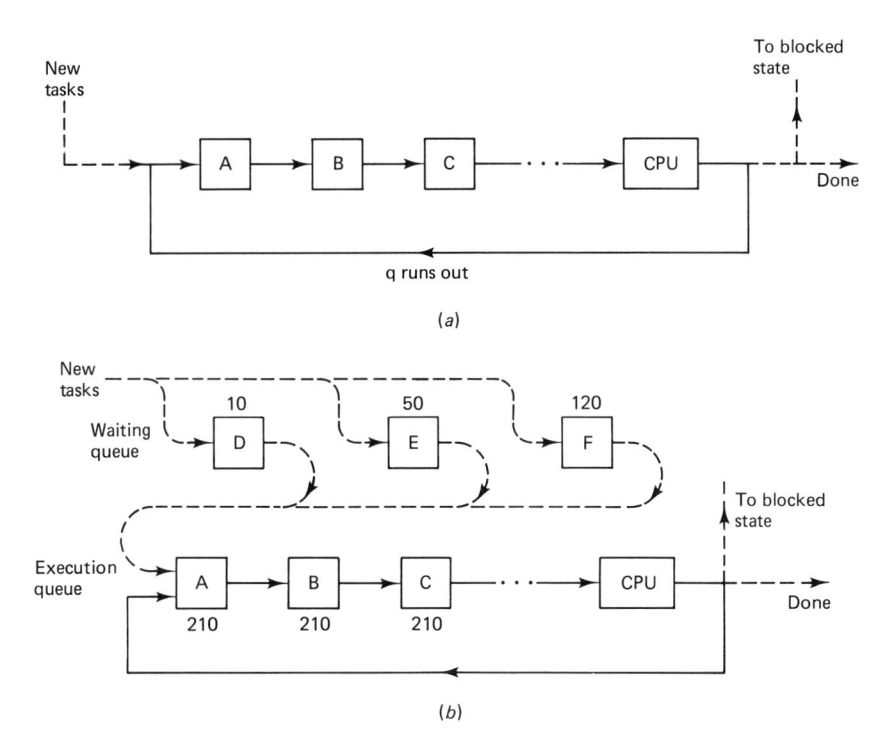

Figure 7.4 (a) Simple Round Robin (RR) scheduling algorithm. (b) Selfish Round Robin scheduling algorithm.

b. Biased RR—This is a priority-based algorithm where the quantum time q is based on priorities. As the priority increases, so does q. In all other aspects it is similar to simple RR. Thus, a task with higher priority executes longer than a task with lower priority.

c. Selfish RR—This is also a priority-based algorithm. Tasks are assigned an initial priority upon entering the system, as shown in Figure 7.4(b). While in the *waiting queue*, the task's priorities increase linearly with time until they reach a maximum priority. Upon reaching the maximum priority, tasks drop to the execution queue, where they execute in a simple RR fashion. In Figure 7.4(b), tasks D, E, and F arrive to the system with initial priorities of 10, 50, and 120, respectively. While they wait in the waiting queue, their priorities increase. When their priority reaches 210, each task drops to the execution queue.

3. Feedback Queues (FQ)—These schedulers use multiple queues arranged in several levels, 1, 2, . . . , N, as depicted in Figure 7.5. Associated with level n, the nth queue is served in a FIFO manner with a quantum q_n. At each queue, three possibilities exist:

a. The task finishes.
b. The task blocks itself.
c. Its quantum q_n expires.

When a task's quantum expires, the task drops to the next queue (from the $(n)^{th}$ to the $(n+1)^{th}$ queue). The only exception to this rule is the last queue (N^{th} queue) where tasks run in a simple

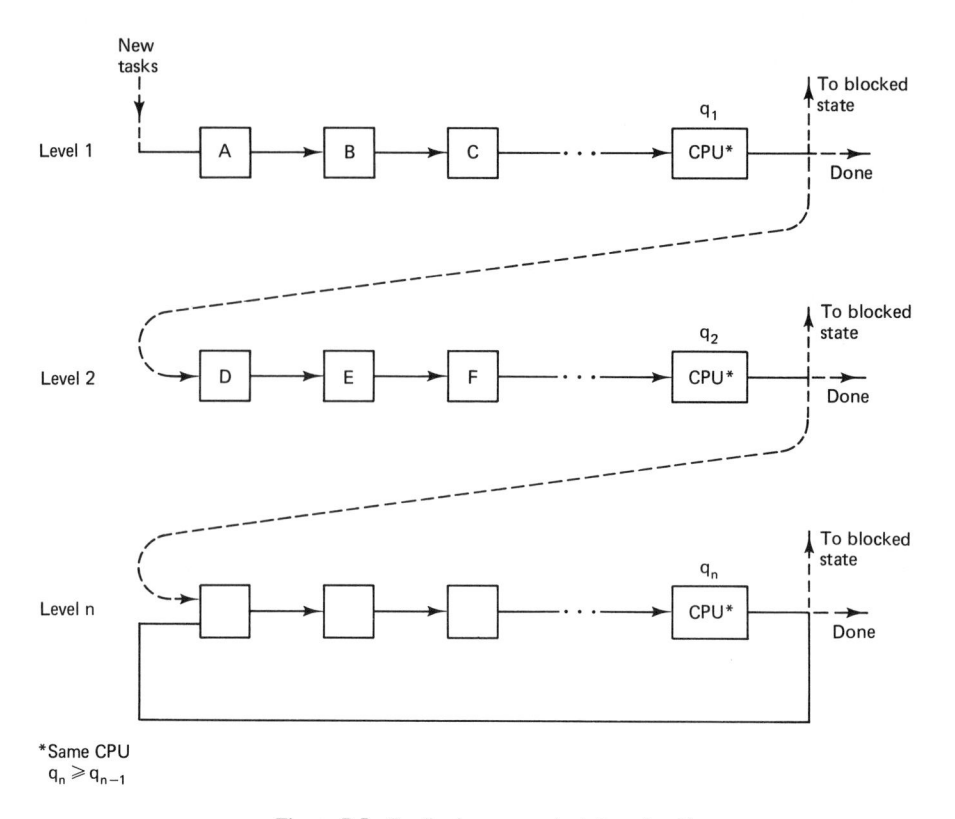

Figure 7.5 Feedback queues scheduling algorithm.

RR fashion. Lower queues are serviced only if the upper queues are empty. Typically, as tasks move down in levels, their quantum of time increases (i.e., $q_n > q_{n-1}$).

7.4 INTRODUCTION TO DISTRIBUTED SYSTEMS

One of the main advantages of computer networks is that they make distributed systems feasible. However, distributed systems are more than just computer networks. There are many definitions of distributed systems available in the literature. The definition we use is adapted from a similar definition given by Sloman and Kramer (1987). A **distributed system** is one composed of several autonomous intelligent devices which cooperate in achieving an overall goal. The intelligent devices are capable of supporting processes which coordinate their activities and exchange information by means of a communication network.

From the previous definition, it is clear that distributed systems cannot exist without communication networks. Examples of intelligent devices include microcomputers, minicomputers, mainframes, workstations, robots, vision systes, etc. The requirements of intelligent devices are that they include a) some kind of a processor or CPU so that they could support the execution of

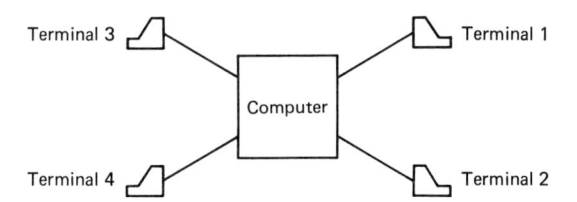

Figure 7.6 A time-sharing system with dumb terminals.

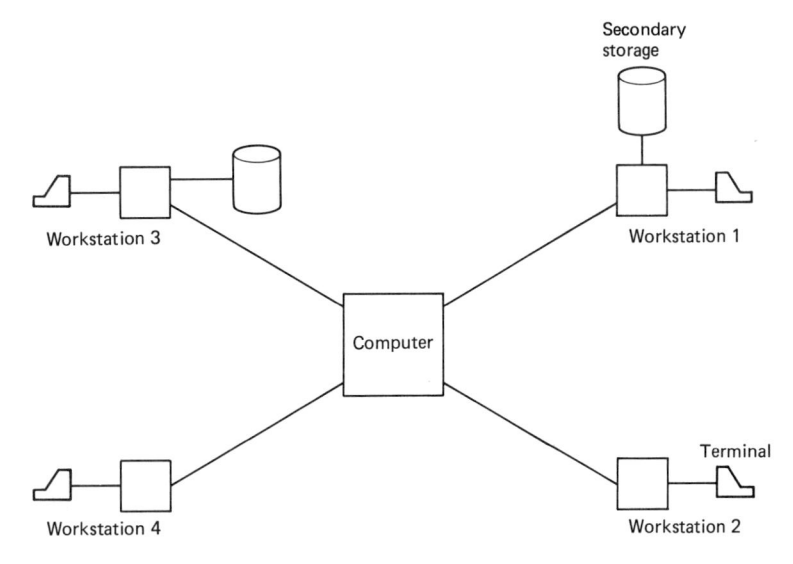

Figure 7.7 A time-sharing system with intelligent workstations interconnected by a point-to-point network.

processes, and b) sufficient memory so that they store information to be exchanged with other programmable devices.

We next present several examples of systems that are distributed, and others that are not.

Example

Consider the system depicted in Figure 7.6, in which several *dumb terminals* are connected to a computer in a time-sharing fashion. The term *dumb terminal* is used to indicate that the terminal has no processing capability and works in a master/slave configuration with the computer, thus the system configuration is not even a network. Since the devices (i.e., dumb terminals) are not autonomous, the system is not distributed.

Example

The system depicted in Figure 7.7 is similar to the one used in the previous example, except that the terminals are replaced with workstations with processing capability.[4] The workstations are assumed to be able to send and receive information from the computer autonomously. Thus, the system qualifies to be a computer network. Although the workstations are capable of supporting processes and exchange information using the computer network, the system is not considered a distributed system, because it is not stated that the devices cooperate in achieving a common goal (i.e., a common application).

[4] Also referred to as intelligent workstations.

Sec. 7.4   Introduction to Distributed Systems   295

An application can be thought of as the cooperation of processes to achieve a common goal. Applications which are completely executed within a single intelligent device are referred to as **local applications.** In contrast, applications involving the cooperation of several remote intelligent devices are called **global applications.** The ability of the system to execute global applications is an important requirement of a distributed system.

Example

Consider the system shown in Figure 7.8, which represents a bank with several branches at different locations. At each branch, a computer controls the teller terminals of the branch and the account database of that branch. The computers are interconnected by a communication network. It is assumed that there is an application which requires updating the databases at two different branches. The application involves transfering funds from an account in one branch to another account in a different branch. Since the application requires the cooperation of two remote intelligent devices, it is a global application and thus the system is distributed.

7.4.1 Closely Coupled and Loosely Coupled Distributed Systems

Depending upon the type of communication network used by the distributed system, one can distinguish two types of distributed systems: closely coupled and loosely coupled. A **closely coupled** distributed system is one in which the constituent communication network is a multiprocessor network. A fundamental characteristic of multiprocessor networks is that they generally share main memory and a clock. If the underlying communication network is a local area network, metropolitan area network, wide area network, or long haul network, the corresponding system is a **loosely coupled** distributed system.

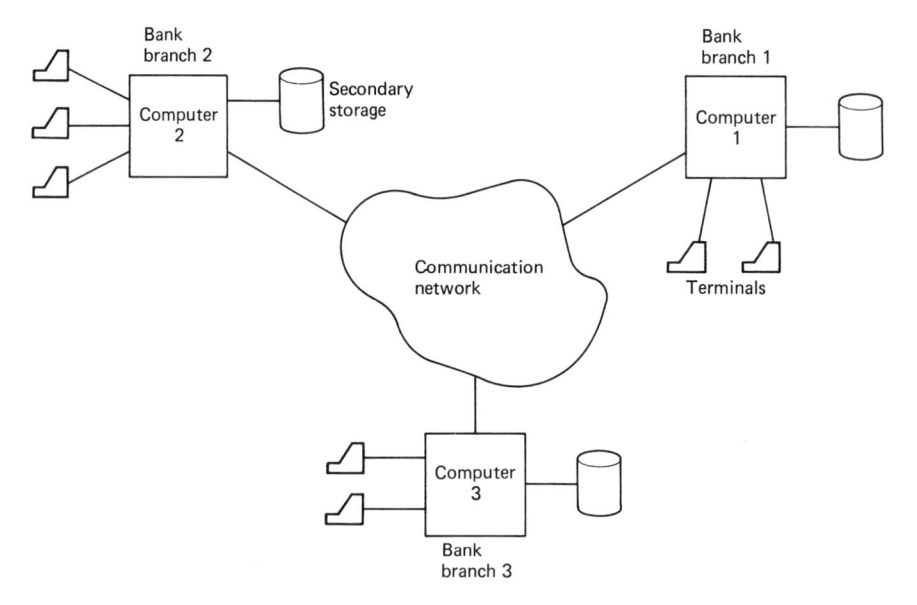

Figure 7.8 A distributed system representing a bank with several branches executing a global application.

In this book, we are interested primarily in local area networks; thus we will study only loosely coupled distributed systems. From now on we will drop the qualifier *loosely coupled* and just refer to them as distributed systems. Chapter 12 contains several examples of closely coupled distributed systems in the context of protocol implementation.

Although distributed systems can exist in the context of any layer of the OSI reference model, in this book we are primarily interested in distributed systems as perceived by the end user. In other words, the overall goal of distributed systems involves an end user application, such as a distributed algorithm, for production planning and control in automated manufacturing. One can identify distributed systems at any OSI layer.[5]

Example

> The token bus protocol discussed in Chapter 4 is a good illustration of a distributed system at the data link layer. Recall that the token bus protocol involves several autonomous network stations, which cooperate in accessing a shared channel. Thus, the overall goal is the successful acquisition of the channel. The network stations coordinate their activities and exchange frames (e.g., a token frame) by means of the network. Thus, the token bus protocol is a distributed system.

Distributed systems, as perceived by the end user, require functionality provided by the upper layers of the OSI reference mdel (i.e., Session, Presentation, and Application). Details of the lower layers are transparent to distributed systems. We make the following assumptions regarding the services required by distributed systems (Verjus, 1983):

A. Reliable message communication: Messages sent from sender to receiver are neither altered nor lost.

B. Sequenced message delivery: The order in which a source station sends messages to a destination station is identical to the order in which the destination receives them from the source.

C. Failure detection: A failure[6] in the transmission system portion associated with one station is detected and signaled to all other stations that attempt to communicate with that station.

D. Communication architecture independence: Whether subnetworks are used, the subnetworks are transparent to the communication between sender and receiver. Thus, the sender need not be concerned about issues such as naming, addressing, routing, and shared channel access.

The previous assumptions are met by sophisticated protocols such as the ISO Class 4 Transport Protocol. Assumptions A and B are met by connection-oriented data link protocols, such as the IEEE 802.2 class 2.

7.4.2 Synchronization

Synchronization is a major requirement for distributed systems. There are two main advantages offered by synchronization:

> Concurrency: Processes executing concurrently need to access shared resources (e.g., a file server) or just access shared data. Synchronization provides appropriate mechanisms so that concurrent processes can access shared resources or shared data successfully.

---

[5] Perhaps with the exception of the physical layer.

[6] The failure may be caused by the withdrawal of a station from the network.

Cooperation: Synchronization provides appropriate mechanisms for concurrent processes to cooperate in achieving an overall goal.

Consider a distributed system made up of several concurrent processes. We view the processes as proceeding in discrete steps, with each step producing an *event*. Events can be local or global. Local events are imperceptible to processes other than the one generating the event. We are primarily interested in global events; thus we discuss synchronization in this context. By definition, global events generate *observable events*, also referred to as **synchronization points.** We now give a definition of synchronization similar to one given by Verjus (1983). **Synchronization** is the regulation of the evolution of concurrent processes. The regulation involves the generation and use of *observable events* (i.e., synchronization points) throughout the lifetime of the processes.

For synchronization purposes, each process can be represented by a succession of events. The time between successive occurences of events is random.[7] The logical synchronization of a set of processes consists of regulating the evolution of the processes according to the rules of the overall system. Logical synchronization occurs at synchronization points. The term *logical synchronization* is used to distinguish it from *real-time synchronization*, such as the bit synchronization performed at the physical layer. Since we are only concerned with synchronization at the upper layers, we are interested in *logical synchronization*. In the remainder of this book we drop the qualifier *logical* and use just the term *synchronization*.

The synchronization monitor. The following example is adapted from Verjus (1983).

Example

Consider the following system based on the actions at a parking lot: Cars are analogous to processes that compete to occupy parking spaces (resources). Each of the processes can be represented by the following sequence of events:

e: Entry—A car is admitted into the lot.
p: Parking—A car parks in an empty space.
d: Departure—A car leaves the lot.

From the viewpoint of an attendant at the entrance of the lot, only *e* and *d* are externally observable events. If the parking lot has a total of N spaces (i.e., available plus occupied spaces), a *legal event trance* is a sequence of events (i.e., entries or departures) such that any prefix of the sequence satisfies the following two constraints.:

1. Since cars are neither created nor destroyed in the lot, the number of entries is greater than the number of departures. That is,

$$E \geq D \qquad (7.1)$$

2. Since the lot cannot be overfilled, the number of entries must be less or equal to the number of departures plus N:

$$E \leq D + N \qquad (7.2)$$

where E and D are the number of entries and departures, respectively.

[7] See Stark and Woods (1986) for a brief review of random phenomena.

Example

Assume a parking lot with N = 3. In this case, the event trace *eedeed* is legal, whereas the event trace *eeeed* is illegal.

The **synchronization monitor** observes the events and regulates the evolution of the processes so that the system constraints are satisfied. The monitor can stop and restart processes when they reach synchronization points to guarantee that an event trace remains legal. For example, in the parking lot case, if the monitor has allowed the legal event trace *eee*, then it must block any process which attempts to cross synchronization point *e*. The monitor continues to block the synchronization request until one of the three processes which has crossed point *e* requests to cross synchronization point *d* (i.e., a car leaves the lot).

Three classes of actions are performed by the synchronization monitor:

1. Handles synchronization requests: Processes requiring synchronization with other processes issue requests to the monitor. The monitor stores the requests and handles them according to the system constraints.

2. Authorization: The monitor authorizes blocked processes to continue execution. Processes are allowed to cross synchronization points only when authorized by the monitor.

3. Bookkeeping: For management purposes, the monitor keeps information such as event traces, process requests, and so on.

Thus, the event trace maintains a history of authorization actions performed by the monitor.

Problem of perceiving and scheduling events. Arrival of requests to the monitor and arrival of authorizations to the processes can be delayed from the actual occurrence of the observable events. The delays are caused by transmission delays in the communication network. In particular, variable delays which may be caused by routing delays through subnetworks can lead to problems in perceiving and scheduling events.

In the parking lot example, assume that there is only one outlet and one attendant. A problem arises when the attendant thinks that the lot is full and refuses entry to waiting cars, when in reality there may be some cars that have left their spaces but have not yet reached the outlet. Thus, the attendant has only partial knowledge of the state of the system. Furthermore, there is a delay from when events occur to when the events are actually perceived by the system.

Example

Consider the parking lot example, with two outlets each with one attendant. Further assume a third person for carrying information about actions in the lot from one attendant to the other. In this case, each attendant becomes aware of the actions of the other only after some delay. An attendant may think that no more spaces are available, when the other attendant has just logged the departure of a car but has not yet notified the other attendant about the availability of the space. Worse yet, the person carrying the information about the availability of the space may go for lunch or take unusually longer to convey the message.

The problem which arises in the last example involves the uncertainty about the actual state of the system when there is a multiplicity of decision-making centers. The uncertainty is caused by the delays in the communication system. Delays experienced by messages exchanged by distributed system processes have the following characteristics:

1. The delay is greater than the interval separating two observable events of the same process.
2. The delay is variable, depending upon the instant the messages are submitted to the communication network. For example, when the network is congested, messages take longer to reach their destination.
3. The delay is variable from one pair of machines to another. A pair of machines consists of a sender and a receiver.

Example

Consider a computer network with four sites, with site two generating event e_1 and site three generating event e_2, as shown in Figure 7.9. Both events are perceived by sites one and four. Because of variable delays, site one perceives the event trace $e_2\ e_1$, whereas site four perceives the event trace $e_1\ e_2$. Thus, the event traces perceived by sites one and four are inconsistent. This example also shows that the delay is variable from one pair of machines to another.

The previous example illustrates two important problems associated with distributed systems:

1. At any given time, a process at one site can have only approximate knowledge of the state of another process residing at any other site.
2. Even when messages are delivered in sequence, any two observable events in a system can be perceived as occurring in a different order by different sites.

Criteria for solving the synchronization problem. Before discussing methods for solving the synchronization problem, we identify three solution objectives:

1. The system functions consistently. This criterion guarantees that a site perceives observable events as happening in the same order as any other site. It is also assumed that the system constraints are satisfied (e.g., no car is allowed into the lot if no space is available).

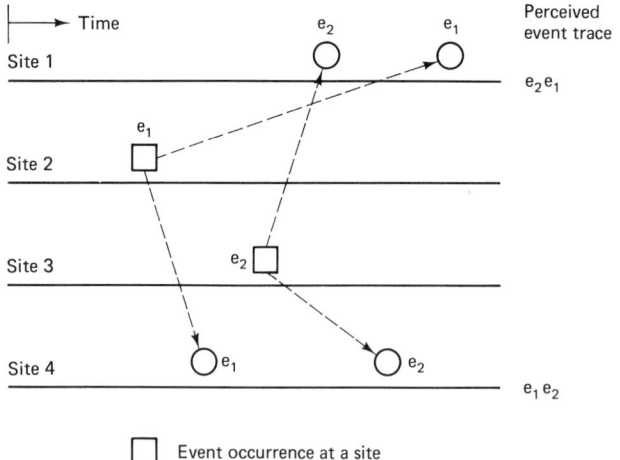

Figure 7.9 Problem of perceiving events. Site 1 perceives event trace $e_2 e_1$, whereas site 4 perceives event trace $e_1 e_2$.

2. The system prevents deadlock.

3. Depending upon actual applications, processes are treated with or without priority. When no priorities are used, all processes are treated equally and the system is fair. Priorities may allow, for example, higher priority vehicles entering the system regardless of the order of arrival at the inlets.

The synchronization monitor does not need to know the identity of the processes to achieve objectives 1 and 2. Objective 3, however, requires that the monitor know the identity of the processes (e.g., ordinary vs. high priority vehicle).

7.4.3 Solutions to the Synchronization Problem

Let us consider again the parking lot example, because it is a good analogy of a large number of problems arising in distributed systems. Using the nomenclature developed earlier, the system constraint to be met by the synchronization is

$$E - D \leq N \tag{7.3}$$

Furthermore, recall that the following expression is always true:

$$E \geq D \tag{7.4}$$

In order to satisfy the synchronization constraint, the monitor must execute the sequence S_1 or S_2 when a process reaches synchronization point e or d respectively, where

S_1: **if** $E - D < N$ **then**
  $E := E + 1$;
 else
  wait;   — the process is blocked

S_2: $D := D + 1$;

If several processes arrive simultaneously at d, the monitor must guarantee the consistency of operations S_2 by executing each operation S_2 in *mutual exclusion*. Operations executed in mutual exclusion are said to be **serialized.** Likewise, S_1 must be serialized when reaching synchronization point e. However, the operations S_1 and S_2 are independent and need not be mutually exclusive (i.e., serialized) with respect to one another.

Before discussing solutions to the synchronization problem, let us consider another formulation of the problem. For the parking lot example, let Y represent the number of available spaces, that is[8]

$$Y = N - E + D \tag{7.5}$$

Then both monitor operations update the same variable Y (i.e., Y is a *shared variable*):

S_3: **if** $Y = 0$ **then**
  $Y := Y - 1$;
 else
  wait;   — the process is blocked

S_4: $Y := Y + 1$;

---

[8] We assume here that the initial number of available spaces is N.

where S_3 is equivalent to S_1, and S_4 is equivalent to S_2. In this case, the monitor operations S_3 and S_4 must be *serialized*, since both operations access the same variable.

We now discuss general solutions to the synchronization problem. We summarize the main features of the solutions, and the reader is referred to more specialized works in the area for additional details, such as the book by Sloman and Kramer (1983). The book edited by Parker and Verjus (1983) contains a good discussion of the solutions to the synchronization problem. An interesting distributed control algorithm for solving the synchronization problem is proposed by Natarajan (1986).

Solutions to the synchronization problem can be discussed in the context of the following major system classes:

1. Centralized system
2. Distributed system.

Centralized system. Although we are not interested in centralized systems in this book, we nevertheless discuss this solution approach to distinguish it from the solution for distributed systems. A **centralized system** does not involve a network. This corresponds to a single outlet in the parking lot example. Since there are no other outlets, no communications are involved, and thus a network is not required.

The synchronization monitor can be represented by a single process, which is invoked by automobile processes reaching synchronization points e and d, one event at a time. As noted earlier, events e and d can be represented separately in variables E and D, or together in a single variable Y. The monitor must then employ a mutual exclusion mechanism for dealing with the corresponding critical section (i.e., one for E and one for D or else just one for Y). The semaphore concept discussed in subsection 7.2.3 is very effective for implementing the mutual exclusion mechanism.

Distributed system. By definition, a distributed system involves a computer network. In the context of the parking lot example, this corresponds to having several outlets. The outlets cooperate in handling entries and departures of automobiles in such a way that the system constraints are satisfied. The events e and d are not necessarily observable on the same sites. Depending upon the place where the synchronization monitor executes its *authorization action*, we distinguish two types of distributed systems:

Centralized control
Distributed control.

If the authorization action is performed by a single process at one site, the system is referred to as a *distributed system with centralized control*. On the other hand, if the authorization action is distributed among p processes each located in a different site, the system is a *distributed system with distributed control*.

Distributed system with centralized control. The solution in this case is fairly straightforward, consisting of grouping on a single site the variables and instructions necessary for synchronization. The coordination of the several concurrent processes is done by a single synchronization monitor process. The situation is very similar to the centralized system case. In the distributed system with centralized control, however, processes reaching synchronization points e

and *d* communicate the corresponding events to the monitor process using the communication network. The monitor then performs the authorization action, just as in the centralized system case.

Distributed system with distributed control. Distributed control involves several monitors performing the authorization action. Obviously, the monitors must coordinate their actions in order to achieve the overall goal. We assume that the authorization action is distributed into *p* monitors. Depending upon how the synchronization constraint variables are handled, we consider three techniques:

Variable distribution
Variable splitting
Variable duplication.

Variable Distribution. To illustrate this solution technique, assume in the parking lot example that there is one inlet and one outlet. Further assume that a monitor process keeps a record of the number of entries E at site 1, and another monitor keeps a record of the number of departures D at site 2. The monitor at site 1 knows precisely the value of E, and the monitor at site 2 knows precisely the value of D. Both sites can exchange values of E and D using the network.

A car is permitted to enter into the lot by the monitor at site 1 if the following condition holds

$$(E - D) < N \tag{7.6}$$

Since the monitor at site 1 knows the value of E, it only needs to obtain the value of D from the monitor at site 2. Because of transmission delays, the monitor at site 1 perceives the value D', which lags behind the actual value D. Thus,

$$D' \leq D \tag{7.7}$$

Because of the previous condition, the synchronization constraint applied by the monitor process at site 1,

$$(E - D') < N \tag{7.8}$$

implies the condition given by Equation 7.6. Thus, the two monitors cooperate in ensuring that the system synchronization constraints are met.

Variable Splitting. This scheme consists in distributing the parking spaces among the *p* monitors. Initially, each monitor *i* is given control of Y_i free parking places. After the initial distribution of places, some monitors may refuse entry to their outlets even though other monitors have free spaces under their control. Thus, for efficiency reasons, the distribution of places must be dynamic, allowing some monitors to obtain *credits* from other monitors. The credits indicate additional free spaces allocated to the monitor. Thus, the problem involves modifying the initial distribution of places by the use of credits. Initially, the total number of free spaces is N, that is

$$Y = \sum_{i=0}^{p-1} Y_i = N \tag{7.9}$$

We assume that credits are passed from monitor to monitor in a cyclic manner (i.e., the monitors are configured in a logical ring). Let R_i represent the number of credits which attendant *i* passes to its successor in the ring. The number of free spaces at any given time is given by

$$Y = N + D - E + \sum_{i=0}^{p-1} (Y_i + R_i) \qquad (7.10)$$

A monitor j receiving R_i credits from monitor i, modifies is variable representing free spaces in the following way:

$$Y_j := Y_j + R_i \qquad (7.11)$$

Likewise, when monitor i sends R_i credits to its successor monitor, it updates the number of free spaces as

$$Y_i := Y_i - R_i \qquad (7.12)$$

When a car attempts to enter outlet i, the monitor allows it to pass if $Y_i > 0$; otherwise the attendant blocks the car and waits for either of the following two events to happen:

the departure of a car from its outlet, resulting in $Y_i := Y_i + 1$, or

the arrival of a message carrying some credit R_j from monitor j, resulting in $Y_i := Y_i + R_j$.

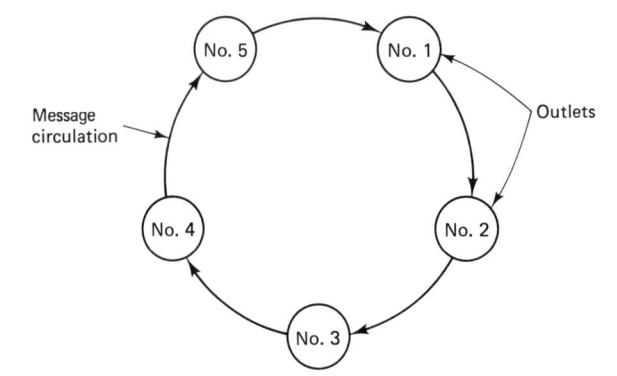

Figure 7.10 Message passing using a virtual ring in the variable duplication scheme of a distributed system with distributed control.

Variable Duplication. In this case, we assume that there are p monitors, each on a different site, which cooperate in making exclusive use of the shared variable Y (i.e., the number of free spaces). As in the case of variable splitting, we assume that the monitor processes are organized in a logical ring, as shown in Figure 7.10 for the purpose of communicating the value of Y. Our solution involves having a *traffic director*, which moves from monitor to monitor maintaining the value of Y. The traffic director is similar to the token concept discussed in Chapter 4 but at a higher layer. When the traffic director arrives at a monitor process where a car is waiting, and the value of $Y > 0$, the car is authorized to enter and $Y := Y - 1$.

Notice that only one outlet[9] allows entrance at any given moment. This is similar to the token passing protocol where there is only one token for providing access to a shared channel. A disadvantage of using a traffic director is that the rate at which cars enter the parking lot is given by the rate at which the traffic director moves around the ring, regardless of the actual rate at which cars arrive to the system.

---

[9] The one where the traffic director currently resides.

SUMMARY

This chapter has provided sufficient background in operating systems, tasks, scheduling techniques, distributed systems, and synchronization for understanding the upper layers.

The upper layers basically deal with the communication aspects for the appropriate support of *distributed systems*. An **operating system** is a system that manages the resources of a computer for efficient and user friendly use. Programs are classified into (operating) *system programs* and *application programs*. A **system program** is a subset of an operating system. Programs other than *system programs* are called **application programs.**

A **task** (or process) is an *application program* used by the operating system as a unit of management and control. The minimum information required to characterize a task is referred to as the task state. The following states are generally used to characterize tasks: undefined, ready, running, and blocked.

When an operating system allows more than one partially completed task to be processed concurrently, the system is referred to as a **multiprogramming system.** A special class of *multiprogramming systems*, where the tasks dealt with by the operating system handle requests from several users, is known as a **multiuser system.** A highly flexible multiprogramming system in which tasks can control each other is referred to as a **multitasking system.** A **multitasking operating system** is one that supports multitasking systems.

A system that responds sufficiently quickly, to affect its environment within a pre-specified time is referred to as a **real-time system.** *Real-time systems* are further classified into **hard real-time systems** and **soft real-time systems,** with the former having more stringent response time requirements than the latter. *Multitasking operating systems* able to meet real-time system requirements are known as **real-time multitasking operating systems.**

The scheduler basically chooses one task to be **run** from all tasks which are ready. Tasks to be run next are chosen by the scheduler according to a **scheduling algorithm.** Many scheduling algorithms exist. Some examples are Highest Priority First (HPF), Round Robin (RR), and Feedback Queues (FQ).

Sharing data among asynchronous concurrent processes can cause problems, such as the *simultaneous access to the database* problem, which can be solved if processes have *mutually exclusive access* to the *critical sections* they reference. There are several solutions to the critical section problem, with perhaps the most important one based on semaphores. A **semaphore** is an integer *system variable*, s, that can be accessed only through the two standard *atomic* operations P(s) and V(s).

A **distributed system** is one composed of several autonomous intelligent devices which cooperate in achieving an overall goal. The intelligent devices are capable of supporting processes which coordinate their activities and exchange information by means of a communication network. Two types of distributed systems can be distinguished: *closely coupled* and *loosely coupled*.

Distributed systems, as perceived by the end user, require functionality provided by the upper layers of the OSI reference model. Details of the lower layers are transparent to distributed systems. Synchronization is a major requirement for distributed systems. **Synchronization** is the regulation of the evolution of concurrent processes. The regulation involves the gneration and use of *observable events* (i.e., synchronization points) throughout the lifetime of the processes.

The **synchronization monitor** observes the events and regulates the evolution of the processes so that the system constraints are satisfied. The synchronization monitor performs three classes of actions: it handles synchronization requests, authorization, and bookkeeping. Variable delays through the network can lead to problems in perceiving and scheduling events.

Solutions to the synchronization problem can be discussed in the context of centralized or distributed systems. Two types of distributed systems exist: centralized control and distributed control. Three synchronization methods with distributed control can be distinguished: variable distribution, variable splitting, and variable duplication.

Bibliographic Notes

The following books address distributed systems: Bochmann (1983), Booth (1981), Chambers (1984), Duce (1984), Lientz (1981), Parker and Verjus (1983), and Sloman and Kramer (1987). Operating systems are treated by Deitel (1984), and Peterson and Silberschatz (1985). The article by Kleinrock (1985) provides a good introduction to distributed systems whereas Liu and Li (1980) discuss interprocess communication in a distributed environment.

PROBLEMS

1. What are the fundamental differences among multiprogramming, multitasking, and multiprocessing systems?
2. Describe few applications that you are familiar with and classify them as hard real time or soft real time systems.
3. Determining the quantum time q is a critical design step. Assume that the average context switching time between processes is s and that an input/output bound process takes, on the average, an amount t before generating an interrupt where $t \gg s$. Discuss the effect of each of the following quantum settings.
   (a) $q = $ infinity   (b) q slightly greater than zero
   (c) $q = s$ (d) $s < q < t$
   (e) $q = t$ (f) $q > t$
4. Consider the scheduling techniques discussed in section 7.3. Which scheduling technique is the most appropriate for time critical applications encountered in automated manufacturing?
5. Equation 7.5 assumes that the initial number of available spaces is N. Derive a recursive equation for the number of available spaces Y_n in terms of Y_{n-1}, E_n, and D_n, where n is the nth event which could be an entry or a departure.
6. One characteristic of a real time system is the granularity of its response time. The granularity may constitute the precision of the real time system. List five real time systems with which you are familiar and specify its real time precision. State the reasons for choosing the values.
7. Three processes with characteristics shown in the table below are scheduled using the method of feedback queues with four queues. Calculate the total execution times for these processes including the time during which the processes are blocked. Assume that the CPU quantum time is 50 msec and is the same for all queues. Further assume that the context switch is negligible and that the order of process arrival for execution is almost simultaneous with process A arriving first and process C arriving last. For each process, the I/O occurs the indicated interval after the corresponding process starts execution.

Process	CPU execution time required	Number of I/O requests	I/O occurrence	I/O duration
A	40 msec	0	—	—
B	150 msec	1	110 msec	10 sec
C	300 msec	1	90 msec	1 sec

8. A multiple robot assembly system (MRAS) is an important component of modern manufacturing systems. A MRAS is a system composed of two or more robots that cooperate in performing an assembly function. The two most important requirements for designing an MRAS are task synchronization and communication. An effective design of an MRAS can be done using a real-time, multitasking operating system.

   Basically, the operation of the MRAS shown in Figure 10.10 is as follows. Robot 1 picks parts (one a a time) from conveyor 1 and puts them on the working table. Robot 2 works on a part and when finished puts the part on conveyor 2. Conveyor 2 is continuously moving whereas converyor 1 needs to be controlled. Assume the existence of a limit switch to indicate when a part reaches the end of conveyor 1. Also assume that the robots can be controlled using operations for initiating an operation (e.g., pick up part), blocking, and resuming the operation.

   The constraints on the design of the MRAS are:
   - When the number of parts on the table reaches 2, robot 1 should be stopped.
   - When there is no parts on the table, robot 2 should be stopped.
   - When there are not parts on conveyor 1, robot 1 should be stopped.

   (a) For the MRAS shown in Figure 10.10, decompose the overall application into several tasks. For each task carefully specify its function, its inputs, and outputs.
   (b) Specify the synchronization operations among the taks that you defined previously.
   (c) Assume an operating system with the semaphore operations P(s) and V(s). Write the code for your tasks previously defined to achieve task synchronization.

9. Repeat the previous problem with the additional constraint that the robots should not collide while handling parts on the table.

10. Explain why solution 1 of section 7.2.3 does not work.

11. Consider a multiprocessor network for a vision system as shown in Figure P7.1. The graphics controller passes processing requests to 4 graphic processors (GP) on a (video) line by line basis. The graphics controller performs a simple round robin scheduling algorithm for passing processing requests to the graphics processors and for relaying processed lines to the display generator (DG) in the order GP_1, GP_2, GP_3, GP_4, and DG. The quantum interval for the round robin scheme is equal to one clock cycle assumed to be 1 usec. It is assumed that the display can always use available information on the next clock. Assume the processing of 5 lines L_1

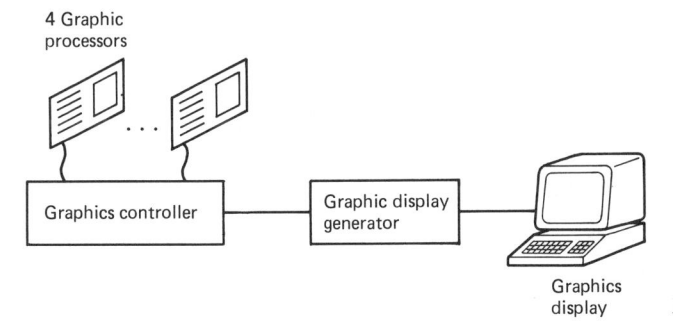

Figure P7.1

through L_5, with required processing times of 4, 8, 2, 7, and 2 msec respectively. After the lines are processed consecutively, starting with GP_1, what is the order of displayed lines on the graphics display?

12. Explain why the scheduling technique of feedback queues is considered to be fair for short jobs and for input/output bound jobs.

13. One of the assumptions regarding the services required by a distributed system is that of sequenced message delivered. Assume the existence of a catanet using the ISO connectionless network layer protocol. In this scenario, explain how can the sequenced message delivered requirement be met.

14. Consider the parking lot example of section 7.4.2 with three total spaces ($N=3$). Given the following three situations, with initial number of free spaces N_o, and the sequences shown, find the number of free spaces at the end of the sequences and indicate whether the sequences form a legal event trace.

Situation	N_o	Sequence
A	2	edeedded
B	1	edeedded
C	3	ededeepd

15. Consider the following version of a distributed system with centralized control based on connection oriented network services and which does not require mutual exclusion mechanisms. A single synchronization monitor process is attached to a unique service access point (SAP) used only for synchronization purposes. All processes reaching synchronization points *e* and *d* attempt to establish a connection with the synchronization monitor through the unique SAP. If some other connection already exists, the requesting process waits and tries again at a later time. Will this solution work? If so discuss its advantages and disadvantages.

8

The Session Layer

Having studied the OSI layers that deal with transmission issues (i.e., physical through transport) it is now time to start looking at the layers associated with communication issues (i.e., session, presentation, and application). As we move from the physical to the application layer the session layer is the first layer which provides functions for supporting communication management and synchronization between end user application processes. The presentation layer merely provides encoding and data transformation functions without any concern of communication and syncronization issues. Finally, the application layer adds communication and synchronization functions, which are specific for certain applications. Thus, whereas the functions of the session layer are generic in nature, the functions of the application layer are specific to the application in question. The purpose of the session layer is to provide the necessary means so that cooperating processes can organize and synchronize their dialog and to manage their data exchange.

In this chapter, we address the main functions of the session layer, different techniques for providing session layer functionality, and the ISO session layer standard. The chapter concludes with an overview of the MAP and TOP session layer features.

8.1 SESSION LAYER FUNCTIONS

Currently, protocol designers do not fully agree on the detailed functions of the session layer. This is understandable since, as noted, the degree of support which the session layer provides to application processes varies depending upon the type of application. Indeed, in some applications such as *file transfer* involving small files, the advantages of a session layer is questionable. However, in distributed processing applications requiring close cooperation and synchronization of application processes, a session layer can be advantageous.

One issue in which there is no total agreement regards the kind of applications that should be supported. For example, some proponents suggest providing facilities for distributing computing, such as remote procedure calls (RPC) at the session layer (Natarajan, 1986), while others do not support this idea. For example, the view of the session layer functions maintained by the ISO and the Department of Defense (DOD) is not the same (Stallings, 1985). The ISO view tends to support file management applications. New session layer functions being contemplated by protocol developers include remote procedure calls (TOP, 1986).

The session and presentation layers can be considered as direct servants of the application layer. Whereas the presentation layer deals with data representation issues, the session layer deals with data transfer and the means for end user application processes to manage and synchronize their *dialog*. Typically, end users do not use the services of the session layer directly. Rather, they use the services of the application layer, which in turn use the services of the session layer. The functions and services of the session and application layers are complementary in nature. Often, distributed system functionality not provided by the session layer must be added by the application layer.

The concept of a *dialog* is similar to that used by humans. A **dialog** can be defined as the exchange of information between two or more application processes. Just as signals in a transmission link can travel in one direction only (simplex), both directions in an alternating way (half duplex), or both directions simultaneously (full duplex), dialogs can also be in one direction, *two-way (direction) alternating* (TWA), and *two-way simultaneous* (TWS). A two-way alternating dialog is analogous to a CB (citizens band) radio, where the person can only talk but not listen simultaneously, or vice versa. A two-way simultaneous dialog is analogous to a telephone conversation, where the person can talk and listen at the same time.

Telephone System Analogy

An analogy would be useful here to explain the functions of the session layer. Session layer users can be compared to executives at office A who want to communicate with executives at office B indirectly through the use of secretaries at both offices. Suppose that Fred and Jim at office A want to communicate with John and Peter at office B, respectively. Further assume that there is only one secretary with only one telephone extension at each office. Fred starts by establishing a *connection* with John by asking the secretary to call John. The secretary proceeds to dial John's extension, perhaps trying several times if the line is busy and eventually contacting the secretary at office B. If John is there, the secretary at B will inquire if he is willing to communicate with Fred. If John agrees, his secretary conveys the information to the secretary at A, who in turn responds affirmatively to Fred. From there, Fred has a *session* with John.

The services provided by the telephone system are analogous to the services provided by the transport layer; namely, it allows users (i.e., the secretaries) to establish a connection with another station regardless of the number of processes (i.e., persons) in that station. The services provided by the secretaries are analogous to those of the session layer, in that they can be considered as *value added* functions on top of the services provided by the telephone system. The secretaries can be thought of session layer peer entities responsible for providing the executives (i.e., session users) with services by making use of the services provided by the transport layer (i.e., the telephone system). Finally, executives such as Fred and John can be compared to session layer users.

In our telephone analogy, examples of value added services include the following: Fred could request that he has three topics or *activities* to discuss with John during the duration of the *session* and that he could switch at will among them with the secretary identifying and keeping track of what messages belong to what topic. Fred could also stop normal information transfer and transmit urgent messages, such as *bring our proposal for the 11:00 meeting*. Fred could also request the secretary to transmit special messages outside the context of the topics identified at the beginning, such as *by the way, I saw your friend Charlie yesterday and he wants you to call him today*. Fred and his secretary could agree on message identifiers to go back in case some of the information is lost, for synchronization purposes. Their company could also own a summer apartment to which only Fred and John have access. Fred and John could negotiate the right to use the shared facility.

In addition to communicating with John, Fred could also communicate simultaneously with Peter by means of another *session*. The Fred-John and Fred-Peter sessions can each have a unique identifier that Fred can use to switch sessions at will. This is an example of multiplexing, with Fred switching his attention between John and Peter. All the options available to Fred could also be made available to Jim. Thus *sessions* could be on a one-to-one, many-to-one, one-to-many, or many-to-many basis.

The preceding analogy helps illustrate how the session layer provides value added functions on top of the transport layer functions. Session functions involve providing means for data transfer, process synchronization, negotiating certain characteristics about the dialog, such as half duplex or full duplex, agreements as to who will terminate the dialog, identifying shared resources, and so on, the ability to send normal, control, urgent, and out of context data, providing special message identifiers or marks for easier management and added reliability, and the management of the overall services. The data transfer could be connection-oriented or connectionless.

Session Layer Functions

Session layer functions can be grouped into three major categories: *data transfer*, *dialog management*, and *dialog synchronization*. Data transfer functions of the session layer involve the mechanisms for exchanging user data as bidirectional flows in a reliable and transparent fashion. Data exchange should also support *expedited* or *urgent data*.

As far as *dialog management* is concerned, the session layer provides the following general functions:

1. Increasing the confidence of a user by performing some error control functions: One aspect of error control involves the session users performing some transactions reliably without concern of loss of data. For example, in a connection-oriented dialog one user may terminate the dialog when the transport layer may still be sending data corresponding to the dialog. In this case, the session protocol waits until the transport layer finishes the transfer, and only then it terminates the dialog on behalf of the session service user.

2. Sectioning the data exchange into dialog units of user significance: Recall that the data link, network, and transport layers are also involved with message segmentation. However, unlike the session layer, these lower layers segment a message based on message length and other transmission system constraints rather than a user dependent criterion. A user dependent criterion may involve end-of-file marks, end-of-message marks, or end-of-transaction marks.

3. Identifying dialog units to the user: The dialog units must not only be provided by the session layer, but must also be made available to the session user by appropriate services.

4. Allowing references to former dialog points through the use of unit identifiers.

5. Reporting exceptional (i.e., errors) conditions: For example, when there is a failure in the underlying layers (i.e., a modem failure) the session layer must be able to pass along the failure information detected by the session layer or the layers below.

Functions associated with *dialog synchronization* include:

1. Supporting a user process in determining the current state of its peer user process: As noted in subsection 7.4.2, because of variable message delays there is uncertainty about the actual state of processes in a distributed system.

2. Regaining user synchronization after an error or loss of cooperation: This often involves reintializing or restarting the dialog.

3. Managing, where required, the turn to transmit (i.e., two-way alternate or two-way simultaneous): One way to achieve process synchronization involves a two-way alternate dialog. This is a special case of the token passing approach for synchronization, to be discussed in subsection 8.8.3.

4. Synchronizing the use of shared resources: This kind of synchronization involves a more generic class of synchronization.

5. Ensuring mutual agreement for some connection control actions, such as connection establishment, connection release, and changes of synchronization.

8.2 DISTRIBUTED SYSTEMS ISSUES

As discussed in Chapter 7, a **distributed system** involves a network of stations, each of which has its own memory which is not shared with any other station. Distributed systems are classified as closely coupled systems or loosely coupled systems. In this book, we are primarily concerned with *loosely coupled systems*.

If a computer network is to support distributed systems, as we move from the physical layer to the application layer, the session layer is the first layer where significant functionality must be provided for directly supporting distributed application processes. Although end users may access services of the session layer, the services are generally used by the presentation and application layers, which may add additional functionality for supporting distributed applications. The view that the transport layer presents to the session layer (or any layer above the session layer) is one of a virtual point-to-point link, regardless of the methods used for actual information transfer and regardless of the network's physical topology. This view is represented schematically in Figure 8.1, where the dotted lines represent a virtual link between processes.

As already noted in Section 7.4, a primary characteristic that distinguishes a *distributed system* with central control from one with distributed control is that in the latter there is no central controller directing all the activities in the system. A program or application that executes in a distributed system environment is called a distributed program or **distributed application.** Accordingly, we

Figure 8.1 Session layer model. Transport layer provides a reliable virtual point-to-point link to processes located at the session layer or above.

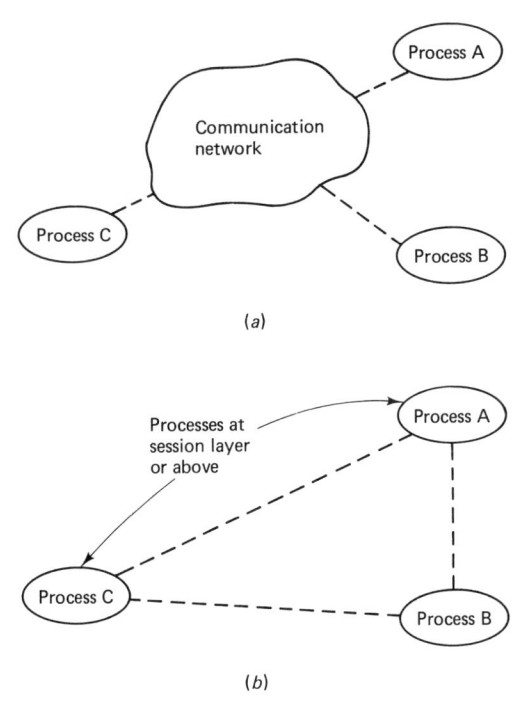

– – – – – Virtual link between processes

distinguish two types of distributed applications, one with centralized control and another one with distributed control.

A distributed application is typically composed of several processes or tasks with each process cooperating with other processes to reach a common goal. The various processes of a distributed application may execute in different stations of a distributed system. Since there is no shared memory between stations in a loosely coupled system, processes executing in different stations can cooperate only by communicating messages. Thus, interprocess communication is crucial to distributed systems. Furthermore, if communicating processes are to cooperate in the execution of a distributed application, they must be able to synchronize their activities to provide for both resource sharing and mutual exclusion. A classical example is the *producer* and *consumer* processes, in which the *producer* and *consumer* must be synchronized so that the *consumer* does not try to consume items which have not been yet produced. In this case, the *consumer* must wait until an item is produced (Peterson and Siberschatz, 1985).

Synchronization of Distributed Systems

Synchronizing processes in a distributed system with centralized control is fairly straightforward, as discussed in subsection 7.4.3. On the other hand, synchronizing processes in a distributed system with distributed control becomes rather involved. This is because in a distributed system with distributed control, the synchronization decisions are made independently of each process, and the decisions may be incompatible with one another. For example, process A may decide to synchronize with a candidate, but then discover that the chosen candidate has already synchronized with some other process. This would require A to backtrack an try to synchronize with some other candidate, if possible.

The design and implementation of various algorithms for accomplishing the synchronization require that communication processes be able to achieve an identical knowledge of the system-wide state. In a loosely coupled distributed system, it is not easy for all processes to share a common notion of global time and hence precise knowledge of the state of all other processes in the system, because of propagation delays which could be of variable length. Although the message traffic between any pair of processes is totally ordered, all of the message traffic viewed by a process is only partially ordered. However, there are some techniques that enable communicating processes to cooperate by achieving only a partial knowledge of the global system state (Feldman and Nigan, 1980).

A distinction exists between process synchronization and dialog synchronization. **Process synchronization** is a well-known concept in operating systems and distributed systems, and involves some processes waiting for signals or events from other processes before continuing execution. In a distributed environment, processes communicate only by exchanging messages, that is, engaging in a dialog with other processes. Thus, dialog synchronization is just one aspect of process synchronization. Furthermore, process synchronization can be provided only if appropriate dialog synchronization mechanisms are available.

8.3 SESSION PROTOCOL ISSUES

In this section, we discuss some techniques for providing the session layer with the functions identified in Section 8.1. Some of the techniques are used by standard session layer protocols, such as the ISO session layer standard. As noted, the session protocol issues center around data transfer, dialog management, and process synchronization.

8.3.1 Data Transfer

The data transfer functions are similar to that of the transport layer, with three major distinctions: First, data transfer at the session layer supports application processes, whereas data transfer at the transport layer supports network stations, regardless of who is performing the data transfer within the station. In our analogy, this is similar to a telephone extension (analogous to the transport layer) in an office supporting anyone that knows how to dial and talk. On the other hand, the secretary (analogous to the session layer) supports only specific people for which he or she is trained. Second, session layer data transfer offers an additional level of process-oriented reliability not traditionally encountered in the transport data transfer.[1] For example, when a session user wants to end a converstation, it can be sure that no data will be lost in the process. Third, session data transfer support dialogs transparently from the underlying communication mechanisms. For example, the transport connection could break at different points in a dialog, with the application process being unaware that this is happening. This is analogous to the secretary redialing the number several times to convey a message,with the secretary's boss being unaware that this is happening.

---

[1] The transport layer provides reliable end-to-end communications between two stations rather than between two processes.

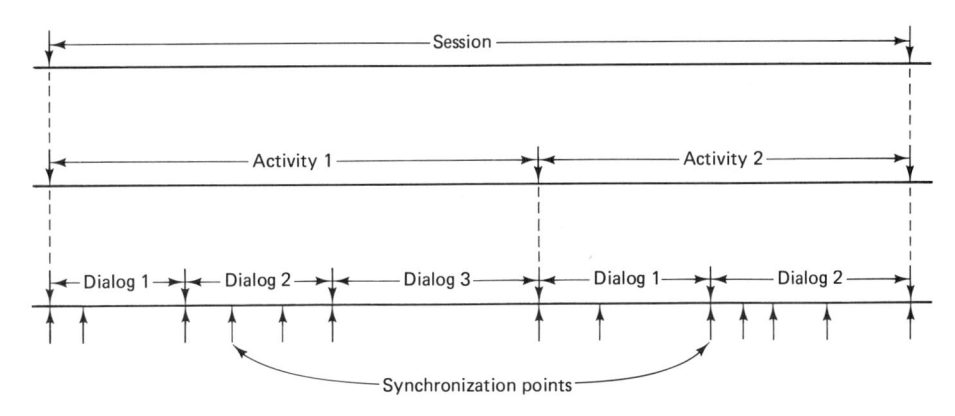

Figure 8.2 Sessions, activities, dialogs, and synchronization points.

Thus, assuming connection-oriented communications, supporting session layer functions basically involves providing session user processes,[2] with the ability of opening and closing connections and for transferring data on an already established connection. Session data transfer can be made more reliable by providing a mechanism for closing connections in a graceful (i.e., without the loss of data) manner. Transparency can be achieved by monitoring the status of the underlying connections and recovering from broken connections automatically. If the communication is connectionless, data transfer functions involve transferring data without the need of connections.

8.3.2 Dialog Management

Dialog management can be accomplished by subdividing dialog units into subunits for additional reliability reasons. Subunit boundaries are known as *synchronization points*. Dialog units can also be combined into larger units, called **activities.** Likewise, activities can be combined into still larger units called **sessions.** Boundaries between subunits for dialogs, activities, and sessions can be identified through the use of **synchronization points,** as depicted in Figure 8.2.

8.8.3 Process Synchronization

Process synchronization in a distributed environment is considerabe more difficult than process synchronization in a centralized environment. In a centralized system, processes can share a clock and memory. One technique that is often used for synchronizing processes in a centralized environment with shared memory is through the use of semaphores. Having the same clock reference or sharing memory can aid in determining the status of the communicating entity. In this subsection, we discuss techniques for performing process synchronization in a distributed environment. Recall from subsection 7.4.3 that distributed systems exhibit centralized control or distributed control.

Distributed systems with centralized control. Centralized control was introduced in subsection 7.4.3 and is discussed next in a more general context. In the centralized control approach, one of the processes in the distributed systems is designated as the **coordinator,** and coordinates the synchronization of all other processes. Each process requesting synchronization

---

[2] The processes could be end user application processes, application layer processes, or presentation layer processes.

sends a *request* message to the coordinator. When the process receives a *reply* message from the coordinator, it can proceed to perform the synchronization operation. When done, the process sends a *release* message to the coordinator and proceeds with its execution. Upon receiving a request message, the coordinator performs the desired synchronization with appropriate processes. If the synchronization is granted, the coordinator immediately sends back a reply message. Otherwise, the request is queued. All variables involved in the synchronization operation are handled by the *coordinator*.

The main advantage of centralized control is its simplicity. However, its main disadvantage is that it constitutes a single point of failure. If the coordinator fails, appropriate steps must be taken so that a new process can take its place.

Distributed control. Several techniques have been proposed in this category. Because of their relevance to the session layer we consider only two: a token passing, and a fully distributed approach. Additional material can be found in Peterson and Silberschatz (1985).

The Token Passing Approach. The token passing approach is similar to the one used by the token passing protocol for medium access control, in that a right to use certain resources is circulated among processes. In the case of the medium access control, the token enables access to a broadcast transmission channel. The session layer token enables processes to access data processing resources, such as critical sections in a program or shared files in a distributed database. If there is only one token per resource in the system, then exclusive access to shared resources can be guaranteed. Depending upon how the token is passed from process to process, we distinguish two types of token passing systems: ring structured and nonring structured.

Ring Structured System. Under this scheme, all processes that require synchronization are configured in a logical ring, which determines a sequence for passing the resource token. Processes perform synchronization operations only if they have the token. If processes do not use the token, they immediately pass it to the next process in logical sequence.

Since there is only one token per resource, only one process can access that shared resource at a time. In addition, if the ring is undirectional, freedom from starvation is ensured. One disadvantage of this technique is the performance degradation incurred while waiting for the single token available in the system. Another disadvantage is the maintenance that is required to handle contingencies such as lost tokens, duplicated tokens, ring initialization, and so on. However, similar distributed algorithms, such as the ones used by the token bus protocol, can be used.

Nonring Structured Systems. Unlike the ring structured approach, the token passing mechanism does not follow a ring pattern. Instead, the token can be passed to any other process. The token need not be passed around if no process wishes to perform synchronization functions.

The following algorithm ensures that each process requesting to perform a synchronization operation will receive the token within a finite time after the initial request (Chandy, 1982). Assume that there are n processes in the system $p_1, p_2, \ldots, p_n$. The token maintains a vector $T = (T_1, T_2, \ldots, T_n)$, where T_i indicates the number of times process p_i has performed a synchronization operation.

When a process p_i wishes to synchronize for the $(m_i)^{th}$ time, it sends a message *request* (p_i, m_i) to all other processes in the system and waits until it receives the token. When the token arrives, it sets $T_i = m_i$ in the token vector T, and proceeds with the synchronization. When the synchronization operation is done, p_i examines the incoming request queue. If the queue is empty, the process keeps the token and continues with its execution until it receives a token request message from other processes. If the queue is not empty, process p_i removes the first request, say (p_j, m_j) where $j \neq i$, from the queue. If $m_j > T_j$, then p_i sends the token to p_j. Otherwise, the process discards this request, since it is an old request that has already been satisfied. The queue is then examined for additional requests until the queue is empty, at which point the token is passed to another process.

Fully Distributed Approach. This approach requires a way to order events in a distributed system. We describe a method for event ordering suggested by Lamport (1978). Associated with each process p_i, there is a *logical clock* CL_i. The *time stamp* (TS) for an event is the value of the logical clock for the process that produces the event. The logical clock can be a counter which is incremented between any two successive events corresponding to the same process. If event A occurs before event B in the same process, then $LC_i(A) < LC_i(B)$. Thus, for any two events in the same process, the global ordering requirement is met. To ensure that the global ordering requirement is met across processes, we require that a process advance its logical clock when it receives a message whose time stamp is greater than the current value of its logical clock. More specifically, let event B correspond to process p_i receiving a message with time stamp t. If $LC_i(B) < t$, then it should advance its clock so that $LC_i(B) = t + 1$.

The fully distributed approach works as follows: When a process p_i wants to perform a synchronization operation, it generates a new time stamp, TS, and sends the message request (p_i, TS) to all other processes in the system (including itself). After receiving a *request* message, a process p_j may reply immediately by sending a reply message to p_i, or it may defer sending the reply. For example, a process p_j may defer sending a reply when it is in its critical section. A process that has received the reply message from all other processes can proceed with its synchronization. After the synchronization is completed, the process sends *reply* messages to all of its deferred requests. Thus, a reply message simply indicates that the process sending the reply does not intend to enter its *critical section* at the time it received the request message.

Upon receiving the request message (p_i, TS), a process p_j proceeds in the following way:

a. If process p_j is in its *critical section*, then it defers its reply to p_i.

b. If process p_j does not desire to enter its *critical section*, then a reply is immediately sent to p_i.

c. If process p_j desires to enter its *critical section* but has not yet entered yet, it compares the time stamp $TS(p_j)$ of its own request with the time stamp $TS(p_i)$ of the incoming request made by process to p_i since it asked first. Otherwise, the reply is deferred.

This algorithm has the following advantages:

a. Mutual exclusion is obtained.

b. Freedom from deadlock is ensured.

c. Since entry to the *critical section* is scheduled according to the time stamp ordering, freedom from starvation is ensured. Because of the time stamp ordering, processes are served on a first-come first-served (FCFS) basis.

d. The number of messages required to achieve synchronization is $2(n-1)$, where n is the number of processes to achieve synchronization. This is the minimum number of messages per critical section entry, when processes act independently and concurrently.

Example

Consider three processes A, B, and C, as shown in Figure 8.3, where processes A and C desire to enter their critical sections. According to the algorithm, process C sends the request message (C, 9) to processes A and B. Likewise, process A sends the message (A, 25) to processes B and C. Since process B does not desire to enter its critical section, it sends replies to both A and C. When process A receives the request messages (C, 9) and (A, 25), it replies to process C, since the time stamp 9 is less than its own time stamp (i.e., 25). When process C receives the request messages (C, 9) and (A, 25), it defers the reply, since its own time stamp is less than that of process A (i.e., 25). Upon receiving reply messages from processes A and B, process C can enter its critical section.

From the preceding example we see that the scheme requires the participation of all of the processes that desire synchronization. This approach has the following disadvantages:

1. The process need to know the identity of all other processes in the system. A process joining the group of processes desiring synchronization must not only receive the names of all other processes in the group, but also distribute its name to all other processes.

2. The system constitutes a single point of failure. If one of the processes fail, the scheme collapses. Thus, appropriate recovery algorithms are required.

8.4 THE ISO SESSION LAYER

The International Organization for Standardization (ISO) has developed a session layer protocol. The protocol is published in two sections: the service definition (IS 8326) and the protocol definition (ISO 8327). In this section, we provide an overview of the ISO session layer standard, concentrating on the *functional units* in subsection 8.4.1 and the *services* associated with the functional units in subsection 8.4.2. Before we discuss the details of the functional units and associated services, we discuss the general features of the ISO session layer protocol.

The ISO session layer protocol provides the means for achieving dialog and process synchronization. Dialog synchronization can be achieved by the use of *synchronization points*, as illustrated in Figure 8.2. Service users are allowed to distinguish between different logical pieces of information, referred to as **activities**. In order to provide good dialog management flexibility, *activities* are further divided into *dialog units*. Synchronization points are classified as *major synchronization points* or *minor synchronization points*, as shown in Figure 8.4. The former are used

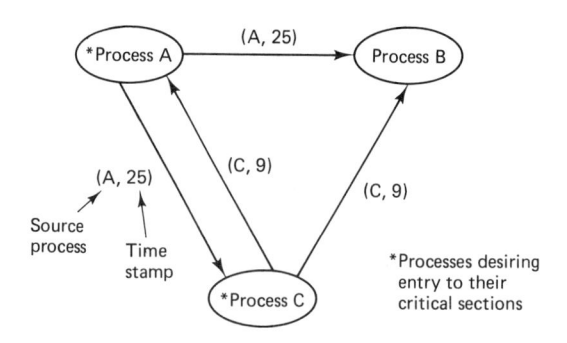

Figure 8.3 Three processes exchanging messages for synchronization purposes in the fully distributed approach.

Figure 8.4 Major and minor synchronization points.

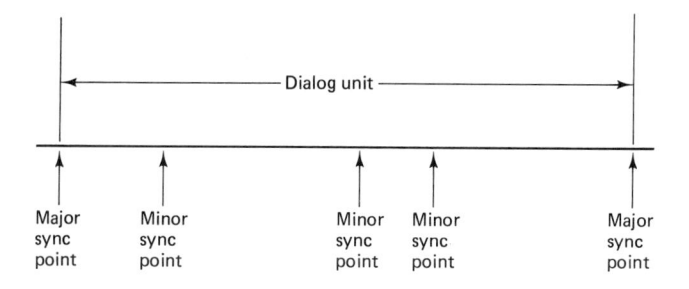

Sync: synchronization

for structuring the exchange of data into a series of dialog units, whereas the latter are used for structuring the exchange of data within a dialog unit.

Process synchronization is supported using a token passing approach, as discussed in subsection 8.3.3. The ISO session layer standard defines a **token** as an attribute on a session connection which is dynamically assigned to one session service user at a time to permit certain services to be invoked. A process having a token has the right to the exclusive use of a service. Hence, one of the token functions is to ensure mutual exclusion of service requests. Associated with a certain process, a token can be *available* or *not available*. If the token is available, it could be *assigned* or *not assigned*. The token can be passed from process to process either in a ring-structured or non-ring-structured approach. Four tokens are defined:

data token,

release token,

minor synchronization token, and

major sync/activity token.

The *data token* is primarily used for regulating a process's turn to transmit, and it may or may not be defined on a certain connection. If it is defined, only its owner can send data and request other synchronization services. This mode of operation is called *two-way alternate* (TWA). If the data token is not defined, the dialog is *two-way simultaneous* (TWS). However, the synchronization is still alternate. The *release*, *minor synchronization*, and *major sync/activity* tokens serve similar purposes associated with the release of session connections, minor synchronization points, and major synchronization points, respectively. The use of the various tokens is detailed in subsection 8.4.2, dealing with session services.

8.4.1 ISO Session Layer Functional Units

The purpose of the service definition of the OSI session layer protocol is to define the services provided to session users at the session-presentation boundary. Since the presentation layer can be bypassed in some instances, the services provided can be used directly by the application layer. The standard service definition defines the actions and events associated with the services, the options (through the use of parameters) associated with each service, and the sequence and relationships of actions and events.

Functional units are groupings of related services which are defined for ease of reference as well as for negotiation during session connection establishment. The ISO session protocol is a connection-oriented service protocol which provides twelve functional units as listed in Table 8.1. The 12 functional units are summarized next.

The *Kernel functional unit* constitutes the minimal set of services. This basic unit permits connection establishment, normal data transfer, and connection release. Connection termination may be initiated by either user, unless the *negotiated release functional unit* is also selected. This allows the communicating session users to dynamically negotiate which of the two users may request the connection termination.

Although the transport layer provides a full duplex data service to the session layer, the session layer users may view their connection as either half-duplex or full-duplex. The *half duplex functional unit* permits the two session users to communicate in a half-duplex environment, whereas the *duplex functional unit* allows the users to communicate in a full duplex environment. Permission to use the half-duplex data path is negotiated dynamically. Data transfer over a session connection is either half-duplex or full-duplex, but never both.

As depicted in Figure 8.5, two forms of special data are allowed over a session connection: expedited and typed data. The *expedited data functional unit* permits priority data to be sent independent of other data transfer that may be in progress. This allows application processes to communicate emergency (i.e., urgent) data on an escape path. The *typed data functional unit* allows the transfer of user data over what may be viewed as a secondary full duplex data channel, regardless of the kind of *data functional unit* that is selected. Typed data can be used for exchanging control information rather than bulk data exchange.

The *activity management functional unit* permits the two session users to communicate within a number of activities or contexts. While only one activity may be active at a time, users may

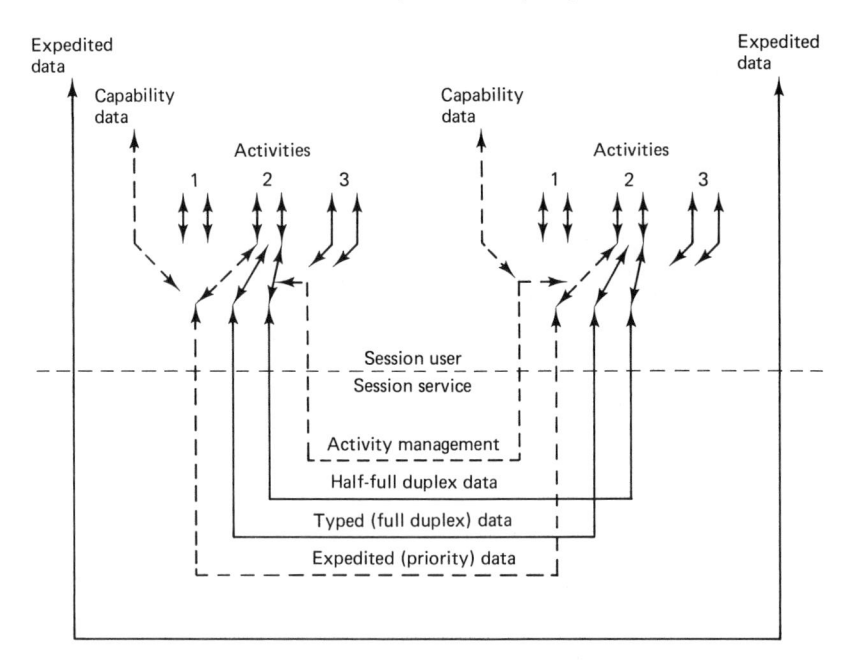

Figure 8.5 Session layer data flow in the ISO session protocol.

switch among several activities dynamically. Furthermore, an activity may be inactive under one connection and resumed under another. The *capability data exchange functional unit* permits the two session users to communicate a limited amount of data outside the context of an activity.

A mechanism to monitor the progress of a long data stream for detecting errors and performance error recovery is useful. The session layer provides such a mechanism by means of the major, minor, and synchronize functional units. The *major synchronize functional unit* permits the placement of major synchronization (sync) points in the normal data flow. Major sync points are acknowledged, and during the placing of a major sync point, no data is transferred. The *minor synchronize functional unit* permits the placement of minor synchronization pints in the normal data flow. Acknowledgment of minor sync points is optional and occurs in the course of normal data flow. Thus, a minor synchronization point may not be assured if a network failure occurs during or soon after its placement. The *resynchronize functional unit* permits the user to resynchronize the data flow based on previously set synchronization points.

The *exceptions functional unit* permits the reporting of errors when operating in half-duplex. Without this unit, errors during half-duplex data transfer result in termination of the session connection.

Normally, session functions are not made available directly to an application process. Rather, these functions represent services available to the presentation and application layers, which will use them to provide end user services. For example, session functions may be required on certain manufacturing applications, depending upon the nature of the end user application processes. For complex file transfer or when database access is required, a large number of these function units will be needed. Where messages are small and flow control is implied by the operation of the application, only a small subset of the session functionality is required.

8.4.2 ISO Session Services

We discuss the ISO session services in the context of the 12 functional units as listed in Tables 8.1 and 8.2.

1. Kernel functional unit. The *kernel functional unit* is composed of the following services: session connection, normal data transfer, orderly release, U_Abort, and P_Abort.

Service users can establish a connection between themselves by means of the *session connection service*. If two service users attempt to establish a connection simultaneously, two session connections may result. The session connection service is a *confirmed* type of service, which means that there are four primitives: request, indication, response, and confirm. The establishment of a session connection follows the following steps:

1. A requestor issues a S_CONNECT.req, indicating its willingness to establish a connection with its peer. The request carries several parameters to be negotiated by the service users.

2. The request is delivered as a S_CONNECT.ind to the corresponding service user at the receiver side.

3. Although a service user may reject an unwanted connection, the user is forced to respond with S_CONNECT.resp, indicating its acceptance or rejection.

4. Finally, the service provider at the requestor side issues a S_CONNECT.conf to the user to convey the final outcome of the request.

If the responding user accepts the connection request, by the end of step 4, both users have agreed on a set of parameters values concerning the session connection. There is no restriction on the number of connections that may exist at any instant between correspondent users.

After a connection is established, users are now in a position to transfer *normal data* over the connection using the *normal data transfer service*. Although the communication can be on a half-duplex or duplex basis, the *normal data transfer service* consists of just one nonconfirmed primitive: S_DATA. The only difference in the use of the S_DATA for the half-duplex or duplex cases is that for the half-duplex case, a *data token* is available and assigned to the user who initiated the service call, whereas a *data token* is not available for the duplex case. In either case, the service is initiated by a user at the sender side by means of the S_DATA.req primitive, which in turn is delivered to the corresponding user as a S_DATA.ind.

When no more data is to be exchanged, users may want to release the session connection in an orderly manner through the use of the *orderly release service*. This is done cooperatively by both service users without the loss of any data after all in-transit data have been delivered and accepted by both users. Regardless of the token availability, the *orderly release service* has just one confirmed primitive type; S_RELEASE. However, if the *release token* is available, the acceptor may refuse the connection release and continue the session connection without loss of data. On the other hand, if the release token is not available, the acceptor cannot refuse the release.

Whereas the *orderly release service* allows either user to release the session connection without the loss of data, the use of U_Abort and P_Abort services will cause loss of undelivered data. Either user can release the session connection and inform the corresponding user accordingly by means of the U_Abort Service. Likewise, a service provider may indicate the release of the session connection by means of the P_Abort Service. A service provider obviously must have its own reason(s) for releasing the session connection (i.e., no response from the corresponding session service provider). Whatever the reason may be however, the provider must include a code intended for its user which indicates the reason for the connection release. The U_Abort Service is made up of the nonconfirmed primitive S_U_ABORT, whereas the P_Abort service is made up of a service provider initiated S_P_ABORT primitive.

2. Negotiated release functional unit. The *negotiated release functional unit* is composed of the following services: *orderly release, give tokens*, and *please tokens*. The *give tokens* and *please tokens* services are equivalent to the V and P semaphore operations, respectively, as defined in subsection 7.2.3. Semaphore mechanisms generally provide four basic operations: semaphore creation, add units (i.e., the V operation), request units (i.e., the P operation), and semaphore deletion.

While establishing a session connection, the ISO session layer protocol allows semaphore creation. In ISO Session layer terms, a *token* represents a semaphore unit. In addition to creating a semaphore, establishing a session connection also allows the user to specify the initial assignment of tokens. The *give tokens service* allows the user to add units to the semaphore, whereas the *please tokens service* allows the user to request units from the semaphore. The semaphore is deleted when releasing the connection. The *give token* and *please token* services have each a nonconfirmed primitive, referred to as S_TOKEN_GIVE and S_TOKEN_PLEASE, respectively.

Three rules must be obeyed when using the S_TOKEN_GIVE and S_TOKEN_PLEASE primitives. First, a primitive for *adding* or *requesting* a certain token say, a data token to or from the system, has no effect or restriction on the other tokens (i.e., sync_minor, major/activity, and release tokens). Second, when a user is adding tokens, the tokens must be available and furthermore owned by the requestor. Third, when a user is requesting tokens, the tokens must be available and not assigned to the requestor. It does not make sense for a requestor to request tokens it already has.

3, 4. Half-duplex and duplex functional units. The *half duplex functional unit* contains two services, *give tokens* and *please tokens*, which were just discussed. The *duplex functional unit* requires no additional services other than the ones provided by the kernel functional unit.

5. Expedited data functional unit. When end applications communicate urgent messages, all layers must be able to handle urgent data. The *expedited data functional unit* involves just one service, referred to as the *expedited data transfer service*, which allows users to transfer expedited or urgent data of limited size over a session connection. The transfer of expedited data is free from token and flow control constraints of *normal*, *type*, and *capability* data. The service provider guarantees that expedited data will be delivered prior to any subsequently submitted normal or typed data on that session connection. The *expedited data transfer service* is provided by the nonconfirmed S_EXPEDITED_DATA primitive.

6. Typed data functional unit. The *typed data transfer service* is the only service available in the *typed data functional unit*. This service permits users to transfer *typed data* over the session connection. Typed data transfers are analogous to normal data transfers, with the exception that typed data transfers are not subject to token restrictions. The nonconfirmed primitive S_TYPED_DATA is associated with the *typed data transfer service*.

7. Capability data exchange functonal unit. The *capability data exchange functional unit* is provided by the *capability data exchange service*, which in turn is defined by the confirmed primitive S_CAPABILITY_DATA. The service is available only if the *activity management functional unit* has been selected. The *capability data exchange service* allows users to exchange a limited amount of user data while not within an activity. A user must have a *major/activity token* in order to issue a S_CAPABILITY_DATA.req, regardless of the existence of release tokens. Data and sync_minor tokens may or may not be available, but in case they are available, they must be assigned (i.e., owned) by the requestor of the primitive.

8. Minor synchronize functional unit. Three services, *minor synchronization point*, *give tokens*, and *please tokens* make up the *minor synchronize functional unit*. The *minor synchronization point service* allows users to define special marks, known as minor synchronization points, in the flow of normal and typed data. The *sync_minor token* must be available and assigned to the requestor of the service regardless of the availability of the major/activity and release tokens. If a data token is available, it must be owned by the requestor. If the activity management functional unit has been selected, the *minor synchronization point* service can only be initiated within an activity. A requestor may request explicit confirmation of a minor synchronization point request.

9. Major synchronize functional unit. The *major synchronize functional unit* is made up of three services: *major synchronization point*, *give tokens*, and *please tokens*. The *major* *synchronization point service* allows the requestor to define special marks, known as major synchronization points, in the flow of normal, typed, and exception data to completely separate the flow before and after the major synchronization point. The user initiating the service must possess the *major/activity token*. The *data token* and *sync minor token* may or may not exist, but in case they do, they must also be assigned to the user initiating the service. In order to avoid potential complications such as deadlocks in the handshaking between requestor and acceptor, there are certain restrictions to be met by the requestor after the issuance of a S_SYNC_MAJOR.req and before receiving the corresponding S_SYNC_MAJOR.confirm. For example, issuing a S_DATA.req will cause that the data just sent do not belong to any dialog unit; thus, the only primitives allowed to send by the requestor after the S_SYNC_MAJOR.req is issued and before the S_SYNC_MAJOR.conf is received are: S_TOKEN_GIVE.req, S_ACTIVITY_INTERRUPT.req, S_ACTIVITY_DISCARD.req, S_U_ABORT.req, and S_RESYNCRONIZE.req. Likewise, there are certain restrictions on the acceptor side after receiving a S_SYNC_MAJOR.ind and before issuing a S_SYNC_MAJOR.resp, and the reader is referred to the ISO standard service specification for details.

10. Resynchronize functional unit. The *resynchronize functional unit* involves just one service by the same name, which provides orderly reestablishment of communication within the current session connection, typically following an error or lack of response by either service user or service provider, or disagreement between users. The resynchronization service is used when things appear to go bad and no other cure is in sight. A reasonable alternative at this point is to set the session connection to an agreed defined state, including the assignment of all available tokens and start all over. Thus, this service is similar to the reset button in many computer systems.

11. Exceptions functional unit. When unexpected situations occur, such as trying to send data before establishing a session connection, the *exceptions functional unit* provides ways for indicating those situations by means of two services. Exceptions detected by the user are indicated by the *user exception reporting service*, whereas the exceptions detected by the provider are indicated by the *provider exception reporting service*.

12. Activity management functional unit. Users can define *contexts*, or *activities* within which certain actions can take place. For example, an activity may involve a file transfer, while another activity may involve data queries to database xyz. An *activity* is characterized by a set of *attributes* such as assigned tokens, sender and receiver states, etc. The main advantage of having activities is that users are allowed to change activities dynamically and thus change attributes and states automatically. An *activity switch* is similar to the *context switch* of operating systems, in that the old activity is saved and a new one is brought in. Along with the new activity, a new set of agreements is also brought that the communicating users understand. Users should be allowed to create, resume, interrupt, and end activities which are performed by the *activity start, activity resume, activity interrupt, activity discard,* and *activity end* services, respectively. Since an activity involves the use of the *major/activity token*, the *give tokens* and *please tokens* services are also part of the *activity management functional unit*. Finally, a *give control service* is also provided, which allows a user to surrender the entire set of available tokens. Table 8.1 contains a summary of the services associated with each functional unit, and Table 8.2 identifies the primitive and its type for each service.

TABLE 8.1 SERVICES ASSOCIATED WITH EACH FUNCTIONAL UNIT

Functional unit	Services(s)
1. Kernel (nonnegotiable)	Session Connection Normal Data Transfer Orderly Release U_Abort P_Abort
2. Negotiated Release	Orderly Release Give Tokens Please Tokens
3. Half-Duplex	Give Tokens Please Tokens
4. Duplex	(No Additional service)
5. Expedited Data	Expedited Data Transfer
6. Typed Data	Typed Data Transfer
7. Capability Data Exchange	Capability Data Exchange
8. Minor Synchronize	Minor Synchronization Point Give Tokens Please Tokens
9. Major Synchronize	Major Synchronization Point Give Tokens Please Tokens
10. Resynchronize	Resynchronize
11. Exceptions	Provider Exception Reporting User Exception Reporting
12. Actvity Management	Activity start Activity resume Activity interrupt Activity discard Activity end Give Tokens Please Tokens Give Control

8.5 MAP SESSION LAYER

The MAP 3.0 session layer is a subset of the ISO 8327 Session protocol standard. Specifically, the MAP architecture requires that its session layer support the minimum subset of the ISO standard, which is composed of the *kernel functional unit* and the *duplex functional unit*, where the options which are available are not required. In addition, the *resynchronize functional unit* is also specified. The following are additional characteristics of the MAP session layer.

In order to support the communication of messages with priority, a MAP implementation of the session layer must utilize the *transport expedited service*. Sending urgent data using T_DATA is considered a protocol error. Transport connections are not reused (i.e., multiplexed). To avoid incompatibilities with default values, the *user requirements parameter* in a session connection request

TABLE 8.2 SUMMARY OF SESSION LAYER PRIMITIVES

Service	Primitive	Type
CONNECTION ESTABLISHMENT PHASE		
Session Connection	S_CONNECT	Confirmed
DATA TRANSFER PHASE		
Normal Data Transfer	S_DATA	nonconfirmed
Expedited Data Transfer	S_EXPEDITED_DATA	nonconfirmed
Typed Data Transfer	S_TYPED_DATA	nonconfirmed
Capability Data Exchange	S_CAPABILITY_DATA	confirmed
Give Tokens	S_TOKEN_GIVE	nonconfirmed
Please tokens	S_TOKEN_PLEASE	nonconfirmed
Give Control	S_CONTROL_GIVE	nonconfirmed
Minor Synchronization	S_SYNC_MINOR	confirmed
Major Synchronization	S_SYNC_MAJOR	confirmed
Resynchronize	S_RESYNCHRONIZE	confirmed
P_Exception Report	S_P_EXCEPTION_REPORT	Provider Init.
U_Exception Reporting	S_U_EXCEPTION_REPORT	nonconfirmed
Activity Start	S_ACTIVITY_START	nonconfirmed
Activity Resume	S_ACTIVITY_RESUME	nonconfirmed
Activity Interrupt	S_ACTIVITY_INTERRUPT	confirmed
Activity Discard	S_ACTIVITY_DISCARD	confirmed
Activity End	A_ACTIVITY_END	confirmed
CONNECTION RELEASE PHASE		
Orderly Release	S_RELEASE	confirmed
U_Abort	S_U_ABORT	nonconfirmed
P_Abort	S_P_ABORT	provider init.

is required. Likewise, to avoid potential collision problems with the session *release* service, it is recommended that only the initiating application may request the release of the connection.

8.5.1 TOP Session Layer

The TOP 3.0 specification is also a subset of ISO 8327. The initial implementation of the ISO session layer includes the *kernel* and *duplex functional units*, which are required for TOP connectivity. None of the available options or tokens are required. The kernel functional unit is the minimum set of session services that must be provided to the session user. Additional functionality includes the following functional units:

typed data,
expedited data,
exceptions,
activity management,
half-duplex, and
minor synchronize.

SUMMARY

In this chapter, we have addressed the main functions of the session layer, different techniques for providing session layer functionality, the ISO session layer standard, and features of session layers in the MAP and TOP architectures.

As we move from the physical to the application layer, the session layer is the first layer that provides functions for supporting communication management and synchronization between end user application processes. The purpose of the session layer is to provide the necessary means so that cooperating processes can organize and synchronize their dialog, and to manage their data exchange.

A **dialog** can be defined as the exchange of information between two or more application processes. Session layer functions can be grouped into three major categories: *data transfer*, *dialog management*, and *dialog synchronization*. Data transfer functions of the session layer involve the mechanisms for exchanging user data as bidirectional flows in a reliable and transparent fashion.

A **distributed system** involves a network of stations, each of which has its own memory which is not shared with any other station. If a computer network is to support distributed systems, as we move from the physical layer to the application layer, the session layer is the first layer where significant functionality must be provided for supporting distributed application processes.

Process synchronization in a distributed environment is considerably more difficult than process synchronization in a centralized environment. In the centralized control approach, one of the processes in the distributed systems is designated as the **coordinator** and coordinates the synchronization of all other processes.

There are two major approaches for achieving process synchronization with decentralized control: token passing and fully distributed. In the fully distributed approach, all processes cooperate in synchronizing their activities. This approach requires a way to order events in a distributed system.

The International Organization for Standardization (ISO) has developed a session layer protocol. The ISO session layer protocol provides the means for achieving dialog and process synchronization. Dialog synchronization can be achieved by the use of *synchronization points*. Service users are allowed to distinguish between different logical pieces of information, referred to as **activities.** In order to provide good dialog management flexibility, *activities* are further divided into *dialog units*. Synchronization points are classified as *major synchronization points*, or *minor synchronizaton points*. Process synchronization is supported using a token passing approach. Four tokens are defined: data token, release token, minor synchronization token, and major sync/activity token.

Functional units are groupings of related services which are defined for easy of reference as well as for negotiation during session connection establishment. The ISO session layer standard defines the following 12 functional units: kernel, negotiated release, half-duplex, duplex, expedited data, typed data, capability data exchange, minor synchronize, major synchronize, resynchronize, exceptions, and activity management. The MAP and TOP session layers are subsets of the ISO session layer standard.

Bibliographic Notes

Very few sources provide session layer material. This is understandable, since some network designers believe that a session layer should not exist in the first place. The book by Stallings (1985) include some session layer material. The concept of synchronization which is important for the session layer is discussed by Nataragan (1986), Fedlman and Nigan (1980), Chandy (1982), and in the book by Peterson and Silberschatz (1985). The service definition and protocol specification of the ISO standard are published in ISO 8326 and ISO 8327 respectively.

PROBLEMS

1. In the past, several network architectures did not distinguish between the transport and session layer functions. What are the fundamental functional differences between the session and transport layers?
2. Define the term *dialog* and the three ways in which information associated with a dialog can flow.
3. What characterizes the *data transfer functions* offered by the session layer?
4. (a) Which of the following two systems generally share the same clock and main memory : closely coupled or loosely coupled systems?
   (b) State few reasons to support your answer on part a).
5. Explain the meaning of the term *synchronization points* in the context of the ISO Session layer Protocol.
6. What is the difference between ring structured systems and nonring structured systems.
7. Which functional unit permits priority data to be sent independent of other data transfer that may be in progress. It also allows application processes to communicate emergency data or an escape path.
8. In the fully distributed approach of process synchronization, develop a scheme useful for situations when a process fails.
9. Explain why the global ordering is met for events which are generated within the same process.
10. Describe one application where the functionality of the ISO session layer standard is advantageous and another one where it is not.
11. Consider the application described in problem 8 of Chapter 7. Can the synchronization problem be solved using the synchronization facilities of the ISO session layer protocol? If so, write the programs to achieve process synchronization.
12. Consider the variable duplication scheme for the synchronization of distributed systems. Can this scheme be implemented using the data tokens of the ISO session layer standard? If so, detail the implementation.

9

The Presentation Layer

The primary objective of this chapter is to discuss the functions of the presentation layer, including message compression and data encryption, which are treated in sections 9.2 and 9.3, respectively. The ISO presentation layer protocol is then discussed in Section 9.4. The chapter concludes with an overview of the presentation layer of the MAP and TOP architectures in Section 9.5. Most manufacturing networks will not probably use data encryption, but rather message compression for transferring large files. The section on encryption is included primarily for purposes of completeness.

9.1 PRESENTATION LAYER FUNCTIONS

The purpose of the presentation layer is the resolution and management of syntax differences of the data being passed between presentation layer users. For example, the ISO presentation layer standard accomplishes this by providing the means for negotiating a *transfer syntax* mutually understandable by the presentation layer service providers. Appropriate mechanisms exist for negotiating the transfer syntax and the required transformations to map the *local (data) syntax* to the *transfer syntax*. The concepts of local and transfer syntax are discussed in Section 9.4, dealing with the ISO standard for the presentation layer.

As noted, the presentation layer deals with transformations of the data as it moves from the application layer to the session layer, or vice versa. Three fundamental reasons make data transformations desirable:

message security,
message compression, and
data compatibility.

Message security involves the protection of data against accidental or intentional access by unauthorized users. When channel bandwidth is scarce, **message compression** techniques can be used to reduce the bandwidth required for data transmission. Depending upon the type of data to be transmitted, message compression can take the form of voice compression, image compression, or text compression. Another reason for performing message compression is that it reduces the amount of memory needed to store the message, thus saving computer resources. Computer systems sometimes use different codes to represent information. **Data compatibility** refers to the capability of exchanging information across the network even if the local data representations are different. For example, some computers use the ASCII code representation, whereas others use the EBCDIC[1] code. Thus, some form of translation between codes is necessary. When many codes are used, some form of management is also necessary.

In computer networks, an important issue that has not been completely resolved is whether the data transformations just referred to really belong to the presentation layer. For example, some authors consider encryption to be a transport layer function (Martin, 1981). Since *data compatibility* mostly involves data processing issues, should it be done at the higher layers rather than at the lower layers? As discussed in Chapter 3, dealing with the physical layer, the modulation scheme for the token bus protocol is used in conjunction with a scrambler, which is a special case of data transformation. Should this function really be a presentation layer function? The key to answering this important question lies in the intended purpose of data transformation.

9.1.1 Data Transformation Purposes

This section discusses the different types of data transformation often used in computer communications, and identifies the location within the OSI model where data transformation functions should be performed. Let us consider again the scrambler used in conjunction with some modulation schemes at the physical layer. As noted in Chapter 3, since unscrambled data produces additional frequency components in the signal spectrum, the main purpose of such scrambler is to improve the bandwidth efficiency of the modulator at the physical layer. An additional advantage of having a scrambler is that bit synchronization mechanisms perform better with scrambled data. Thus, the data transformation function performed by the scrambler directly supports physical layer functions and hence it should be located at the physical layer.

As a related example consider a digital communication system for the transmission of voice. In order to use less transmission bandwidth, the data could be encoded using codes suitable for voice. In *Pulse Code Modulation* (PCM) encoders, because voice signals have amplitudes that are not uniform, some codes assign fewer bits to voice amplitudes that are larger. In general, encoding techniques performed on the source data for the purpose of reducing the amount of bandwidth required for transmission are referred to as **source encoding**.

It is now well-established that some kind of data encryption techniques should be used for assuring the integrity of data carried by some computer networks. Data encryption techniques are available which can provide protection against passive or active intrusion. When deciding the layer

---

[1] Extended Binary Coded Decimal Interchange Code, an eight-bit code used primarily by IBM equipment.

at which data encryption functions should be supported within the OSI reference model, it is useful to determine the desired level of protection and the kind of attack that may be expected. Perhaps the simplest solution is to provide protection for each individual data link, which suggests providing encryption functions at the data link layer. The advantage of this approach is that the management of *keys*[2] can be handled easily on a local basis at each link, and the impact on the design of the communication protocols is minimized. However, although the intruder can learn very little by tapping the medium, he or she need only transfer his or her attention to the network layer (available at an exchange or node) where the data are in clear form.

Maximum security is achieved only if encryption is implemented on a source to destination basis with clear data unavailable at intermediate points. Thus, to fully protect data in a network environment, encryption should be performed at more than one layer in the OSI reference model. Whereas data encryption at the presentation layer is intended to provide an end-to-end protection, encryption at other layers provides a different kind of protection. For example, data encryption at the data link layer provides protection against a *traffic analysis* attack, in which the observer makes deductions about the traffic passing on the medium based on the traffic load and source and destination addresses.

9.2 MESSAGE COMPRESSION

When the bandwidth offered by a communication channel is scarce, an interesting question arises: Can the source message be encoded in such a way as to minimize the channel bandwidth required for its transmission? The same question arises when trying to reduce the number of bits used for representing different sources, so that they need the least amount of memory for storage. Fortunately, the general answer to this question is yes. Unfortunately, it is very difficult to sort out all the different techniques available and their relationships to the OSI reference model. Many encoding techniques for reducing the channel bandwidth are available, whose function from the communication standpoint could be in different layers of the OSI reference model. Regardless of how the encoding process is performed, the main advantage of encoding is based on the principle that the cost of processing is less than the cost of transmission. Performing certain message compression algorithms can lower the number of bits to be transmitted.

One can distinguish three main classes of data encoders referred to as *end user encoder*, *source encoder*, and *channel encoder* as depicted in Figure 9.1. **End user encoders** can be thought of being performed within the source, that is, before the message is given to the communication network. In the context of the ISO reference model, *end user encoders* lie outside the seven layers and are totally independent of any network services or protocols. Depending upon the particular message to be transmitted, end users can perform certain operations such as *dialog compression*, *editing*, and *substitution*. These operations are not generic, so their inclusion in the OSI reference model is not warranted.

The purpose of the **source encoder** involves performing data transformations on the source symbols, whereas the purpose of the **channel encoder** involves performing data transformations to allow the bit frames to be sent on a specific channel and be reliably reproduced at the output of the channel decoder. The distinction between *end user encoders* and *source encoders* is very subtle. Source encoders perform data transformation after the message is delivered to the communication

---

[2] We are refering to *key based encryption*, which is discussed in subsection 9.3.2.

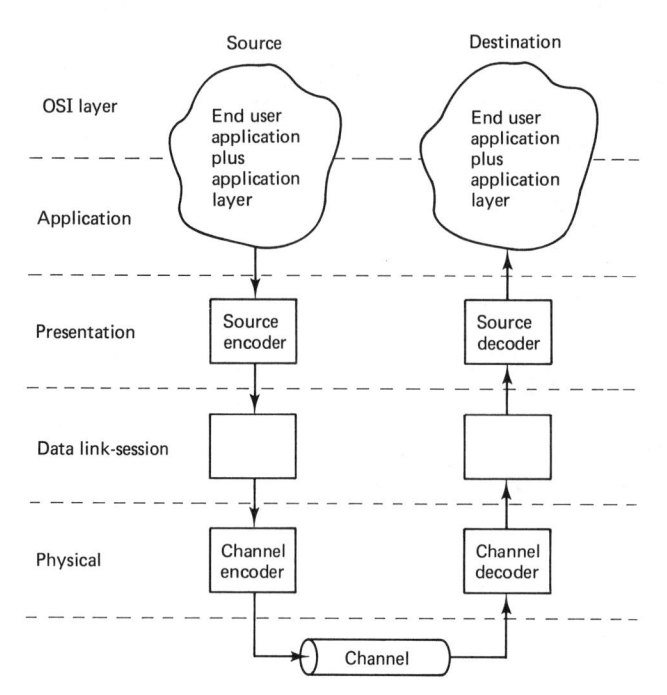

Figure 9.1 Location of source encoder/decoder and channel encoder/decoder functions in the context of the OSI reference model.

system. Although actual data transformations for source encoders can be performed inside or outside the seven layer model, encoder management and encoder negotiation aspects are performed by appropriate network services and protocols. In this chapter, we briefly discuss *end user* encoders, and *source* encoders. *Channel* encoders were discussed in Chapter 3.

9.2.1 End User Encoding

Many techniques can be considered as end user encoding, with perhaps the most important being *dialog compression*, *editing*, and *substitution*.

Dialog compression. Many applications involve several *end users* (possible persons) interacting with a network through the use of intelligent workstations or intelligent terminals with some processing power. *Dialog compression* simply involves users performing some preprocessing on the data and only sending summarized data through the network.

Example

Consider an accounting system running on a personal computer network. Let the file server be station A and the remaining workstations be stations B, C, etc. Further assume that it is only necessary for the file server to store balances for all the accounts rather than the detailed transactions associated with each account. Under this situation, the workstations can perform dialog compression by doing some preprocessing on the accounts and send only the balances associated with each account.

Editing. Message compression can be achieved by using a software system containing a variety of editing facilities for reducing the number of bits transmitted. For example, the editor can perform a function similar to that of differential encoding in which only the data that change are emitted from the source.

Example

Consider a questionaire which is sent to many users using an electronic mail facility. The questionaire is designed as a *form*, with most users having similar information to be filled in the forms (i.e., same department, same boss, etc). In this case, message compression can be achieved by sending the information that is not common (i.e., information which changes from transmission to transmission).

Substitution. The substitution technique sends identifiers for *long phrases* such as error codes and typical network messages such as *login please*, *enter password*, and others. For the English language, the 200 most used words can be encoded using just one byte.

Example

Suppose that a technique is proposed to encode the most used words in the English language using either one or two bytes, as given by the following rule. The encoder uses 16 possible bits, denoted as 1, 2, . . . , 16; the meaning of bit 1 is as follows:

$$\text{bit } 1 = \begin{cases} 0 \text{ ; the encoder uses the next 7 bits.} \\ 1 \text{ ; the encoder uses the next 15 bits.} \end{cases}$$

The frequently used word *food* might be encoded as 0110 0101, whereas the word *yuletide* might be encoded as 1100 1010 0011 0110. Calculate the total number of words that can be encoded with this scheme.

Solution If bit 1 is a 0, then the next 7 bits can be used to encode up to $2^7 = 128$ different words. If bit 1 is a 1, then the next 15 bits can be used to encode up to $2^{15} = 32768$ different words. Thus, the total number of words that can be encoded with this scheme is 32896.

The substitution technique works well for applications having small vocabularies. Programming languages are good examples of applications having small vocabularies. For example, a **C** compiler currently marketed by Microsoft has just 32 *keywords*.

9.2.2 Source Encoding

Whereas channel encoders are channel dependent, source encoders are channel independent. Another important difference between source and channel encoders is that source encoding is performed as close as possible to the end users (i.e., the source or destination), whereas channel encoding is performed as close as possible to the physical transmission medium.

In addition to making the design of the channel encoder and decoder virtually independent of the design of the source encoder and decoder, another advantage is that splitting the encoding and decoding functions fits nicely into the OSI reference model; namely, source encoding and decoding can be considered as a presentation layer function, whereas channel encoding and decoding is a physical layer function.

Example

We describe a simple source encoding algorithm which gets rid of spaces in a text which might be appropriately termed a *space buster*. Text used in most messages is composed of characters encoded using any of the 128, 7-bit ASCII code. An interesting message compression scheme can be obtained by realizing that the ASCII character that happens the most in any document is the space with an ASCII representation of 20 (Hex). Although the characters we are referring to only use 7 bits, computers routinely use 8 bits for their representation. The data transformation scheme works as follows:

Characters other than a *space* are encoded using the normal ASCII code, unless the character precedes a space. Since all 128 ASCII codes start with a **0,** the character preceding a *space* is modified so that it begins with a **1,** with the remaining bits unchanged. This technique in effect does not represent the space separately; rather its presence is indicated by the first bit position in the character preceding it. Since there is roughly 1 space per 7 characters (including the space), we expect to compress a message by 100/7 = 14.28 percent.

One of the major questions of concern when designing source encoders and decoders is determining how many bits are required to represent the output of any given source. The answer to this question is well known from a branch of communication systems known as **information theory.** A key to solving this problem is to realize that a source emits source letters with different probabilities. This fact was recognized about 100 years ago by Samuel F. B. Morse. He discovered that for the English language, the letter **E** occurs with the highest probability and thus assigned a simple code to it, a *dot*. For **Y,** which occurs with lesser probability, he assigned a more complex code, a *dash dot dash dash*. The corresponding code is known as the **Morse code.**

Example

Suppose that we have a document made of just 4 symbols (A, B, C, and D) representing the indicated English letters with probability of occurrence 0.6, 0.25, 0.1, and 0.05 respectively. It is desired to encode each of the symbols using a binary code for transmission on a communication system. Devise several codes to perform the encoding process.

Solution There are many codes that can be used for this example. Let us consider the following three codes, where n_k represents the number of bits per encoded symbol.

Code I. One of the most straightforward ways to perform the encoding process is to use codes which are widespread in computer systems such as ASCII or EBCDIC. These codes generally use 8 bits per symbol (i.e., $n_k = 8$). Thus, code I encodes each symbol (i.e., letter) by its ASCII (or EBCDIC) equivalent. For this code, the average number of bits per encoded symbol is

$$E[n_k] = 8 \text{ bit/symbol}$$

Code II. Since we are only dealing with four symbols, we can use two bits to represent each symbol, as shown in Table 9.1.

TABLE 9.1

Source symbol (a_k)	Code word
A	00
B	01
C	10
D	11

Clearly, for this code,

$$E[n_k] = 2 \text{ bit/symbol}$$

Code III. In an attempt to further reduce the average number of bits per encoded symbol, we assign the smallest code word to the most probable symbol (i.e., the A) as shown in Table 9.2.

TABLE 9.2

Source symbol (a_k)	Code word
A	0
B	10
C	110
D	111

For this code,

$$E[a_k] = 1.55 \text{ bit/symbol}$$

In the previous example, code II performs better than code I, and code III performs better than code II. Two natural questions naturally arise from this example: 1) Can we do better than code III? and 2) What is the fundamental limit for the average number of bits per encoded symbol.

TABLE 9.3

Letters		Digrams		Trigams		Words	
E	13.05	TH	3.16	THE	4.72	THE	6.42
T	9.02	IN	1.54	ING	1.42	OF	4.02
O	8.21	ER	1.33	AND	1.13	AND	3.15
A	7.81	RE	1.30	ION	1.00	TO	2.36
N	7.28	AN	1.08	ENT	0.98	A	2.09
I	6.77	HE	1.08	FOR	0.76	IN	1.77
R	6.64	AR	1.02	TIO	0.75	THAT	1.25
S	6.46	EN	1.02	ERE	0.69	IS	1.03
H	5.85	TI	1.02	HER	0.68	I	0.94
D	4.11	TE	0.98	ATE	0.66	IT	0.93
L	3.60	AT	0.88	VER	0.63	FOR	0.77
C	2.93	ON	0.84	TER	0.62	AS	0.76
F	2.88	HA	0.84	THA	0.62	WITH	0.76
U	2.77	OU	0.72	ATI	0.59	WAS	0.72
M	2.62	IT	0.71	HAT	0.55	HIS	0.71
P	2.15	ES	0.69	ERS	0.54	HE	0.71
Y	1.51	ST	0.68	HIS	0.52	BE	0.63
W	1.49	OR	0.68	RES	0.50	NOT	0.61
G	1.39	NT	0.67	ILL	0.47	BY	0.57
B	1.28	HI	0.66	ARE	0.46	BUT	0.56
V	1.00	EA	0.64	CON	0.45	HAVE	0.55
K	0.42	VE	0.64	NCE	0.45	YOU	0.55
X	0.30	CO	0.59	ALL	0.44	WHICH	0.53
J	0.23	DE	0.55	EVE	0.44	ARE	0.50
Q	0.14	RA	0.55	ITH	0.44	ON	0.47
Z	0.09	RO	0.55	TED	0.44	OR	0.45

The answer to the first question is yes and the answer to the second question involves the important concept of *entropy* from *information theory*, which we discuss next.

When encoding symbols originating from a source, one can consider each symbol individually or as a sequence of a fixed number of L consecutive symbols. For L = 2 and 3, the corresponding sequence is referred to as **digrams** and **trigrams,** respectively. Still another possibility is to encode a variable number of symbols, referred to as **words,** each time the encoding procedure is applied. Table 9.3 (Tanenbaum, 1988) gives the letters (i.e., symbols) with their associated probabilities and the most common digrams, trigrams, and words for the English language.

Example

Two devices agree to *talk with one another* by using just the English letters E, T, Q, and Z. Someone suggests two codes for encoding such letters, as given in Table 9.4. Evaluate the relative merits of each code.

TABLE 9.4

Letter	Prob.	Code I	Code II
E	0.7	00	0
T	0.2	01	10
Q	0.09	10	110
Z	0.01	11	111

Solution In code I, two bits are required to represent each source letter, whereas in code II, a variable number is required. Since **E** occurs with the highest probability, then code II will allow messages to be represented with fewer bits than code I. Thus, code II is more efficient than code I.

From the previous example, it is clear that the relative effectiveness of the two codes depends critically upon the frequency of occurrence of the different symbols.

In this section, we are mostly interested in encoding the output of a *discrete information source* into a sequence of letters from a given alphabet. Since we are interested in reducing the bandwidth of the different sources, we wish to choose the encoding rules in such a way that the number of code letters required per source symbol is as small as possible. Before going into the details on how to choose and quantitatively analyze codes, several definitions and nomenclature are required.

Assume that the source produces letters from a finite **source alphabet** $a_1, a_2, \ldots, a_K$ with probabilities $P(a_1), P(a_2), \ldots, P(a_K)$. For example, assuming that the source produces only English letters as given in Table 9.3, K = 26, a_4 = A, and $P(a_4)$ = 0.0781. Associated with each source letter a_K, a measure of the information it conveys is given by its **self-information** defined as

$$I(a_k) = -\log_2 P(a_k) \tag{9.1}$$

Just as the information per source letter a_k is given by the letter's self-information; the information of an **alphabet** $U = (a_1, a_2, \ldots, a_K)$ is given by the average value of self-information over the letters of the alphabet referred to as the **entropy** $H(U)$; thus

$$H(U) = E[I(a_k)] \tag{9.2}$$

$$= \sum_{k=1}^{K} P(a_k) I(a_k) = - \sum_{k=1}^{K} P(a_k) \log_2 P(a_k)$$

where $E[x]$ is the expected value or average value of x.

Example

Two robots engaged in a dialog agree to send programs to one another using only the *symbols*: MOVE, OPEN, CLOSE, and STOP. It is found that for most programs exchanged, the MOVE, OPEN, CLOSE and STOP symbols occur with 0.5, 0.2, 0.2 and 0.1 probabilities, respectively. For this case, the entropy of the source alphabet U = (MOVE, OPEN, CLOSE, STOP) is given by

$$H(U) = - \sum_{k=1}^{4} P(a_k) \log_2 P(a_k)$$

$$= - [0.5 \log_2 0.5 + 0.2 \log_2 0.2 + 0.2 \log_2 0.2 + 0.1 \log_2 0.1]$$

$$= 1.761 \text{ bit/symbol.}$$

9.2.3 Fixed Length Encoding

If the source symbols are encoded into code words of the same length, the corresponding encoder is referred to as a **fixed length encoder.** Let $U_L = (u_1, u_2, \ldots, u_L)$ be a sequence of L consecutive symbols from a discrete source where each symbol is a selection of the source alphabet $U = (a_1, a_2, \ldots, a_K)$. Although in most cases the encoder encodes one symbol at a time, we assume that the encoder can encode L symbols at a time. Thus, a codeword is assigned to U_L rather than to each symbol u_i. For Table 9.3, trigrams are denoted by U_3 and digrams as U_2, where a_k is any English alphabet letter A through Z. In Table 9.3, only 26 trigrams are tabulated. In general, there are K^L different sequences of length L that might be emitted from the source.

We are interested in encoding the source sequence into fixed length code words. Let us suppose that there are D code letters available in the **code alphabet** $V = (b_1, b_2, \ldots, b_D)$. Let each U_L be represented by a code word $V_N = (v_1, v_2, \ldots, v_N)$ of fixed length N. Each u_i, $1 \leq i \leq L$ can be a_1, or a_2, or . . . , or a_K. Likewise, each v_i, $1 \leq i \leq N$ can be b_1, or b_2, or . . . , or b_D. The fixed length encoding process is depicted in Figure 9.2. Clearly, for fixed length encoders, $E[n_k] = N$.

An important relationship between N,L,K, and D can be obtained by realizing that in order to uniquely decode each sequence of source symbols, the number of code words available must be greater or equal than the number of different source sequences. Thus,

$$D^N \geq K^L \tag{9.3}$$

from which

$$N/L \geq \log K / \log D \tag{9.4}$$

Example

In teletype transmission, the source has an alphabet of K = 32 symbols (26 English letters plus 6 special symbols). Calculate the minimum number N of binary code letters (i.e., D = 2) to encode single source symbols.

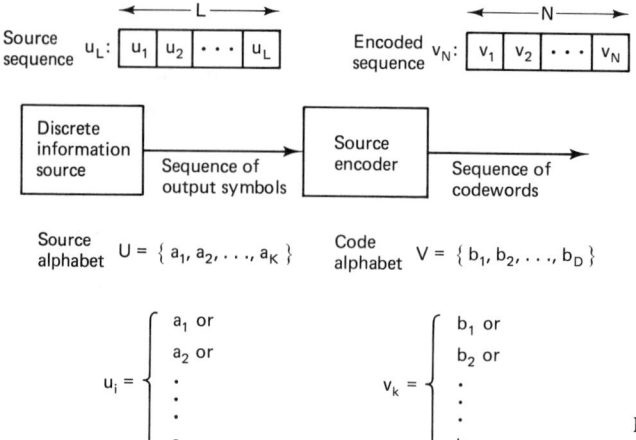

Figure 9.2 Message compression through fixed length encoding.

Solution For single source symbols, L = 1 using Equation 9.4,

$$N \geq L \log K / \log D$$

$$\geq 5 \text{ bits}$$

Thus, at least 5 bits are required to transmit each teletype character.

It is possible to use a smaller number N of code letters than the one given by Equation 9.4, provided we are willing to take the chance that there are not enough code words for all symbols. The following *source coding theorem* for fixed length codes specifies the best one can do. If only one source sequence can be assigned to each code sequence, and N is chosen so that

$$N/L > H(U) / \log D \tag{9.5}$$

then the probability that a source sequence is not assigned a code sequence can be made negligible by making L sufficiently large.

Example

For the English alphabet as listed in Table 9.3, if single (L = 1) letters are binary encoded (i.e., D = 2), calculates the minimum number of bits required to encode each letter.

Solution Using Equation 9.5 directly, N ≥ H(U), where H(U) is calculated using Table 9.3, yielding H(U) = 4.065. Thus N ≥ 4.065 bits/letter.

Example

This example is similar to the previous example, with the exception that we assume that all letters have equal probability; i.e., $P(a_k) = 1/26$ for all k. In this case, H(U) is given by

$$H(U) = -\sum_{k=1}^{26} P(a_k) \log_2 P(a_k) = -\log_2(1/26)$$

$$= 4.76 \text{ bits/letter}$$

Thus, N ≥ 4.76 bits/letter.

Therefore, if all the letters of the English alphabet were equiprobable, the number of bits required to encode a single letter increases from 4.065 to 4.76 bits.

Efficiency and redundancy. Some performance measures can be defined regardless of whether an encoder is fixed length or variable length. The ratio Eff = H(U)/N is referred to as the **efficiency** of the encoder, whereas the quantity R = (1 − Eff) is the **redundancy** of the encoder.

9.2.4 Variable Length Encoding

As the name implies, a **variable name encoder** encodes each source symbol a_k as a variable length code word n_k from a prescribed code alphabet. Again, let each symbol alphabet a_k occur with probability $P(a_k)$ and D denote the number of different symbols in the code alphabet. Since the number of code letters in n_k is variable, it has a mean value given by

$$N = E[n_k] = \sum_{k=1}^{K} P(a_k)\, n_k \tag{9.6}$$

The main objective of this section is to find encoders that minimize $E[n_k]$.

Example

Consider Table 9.5, which shows four (K = 4) source symbols, their occurrence probability, and four possible codes that might be used for encoding them.

An important question is whether there are any restrictions in configuring code letters which make up the *code words*. The obvious criterion to be used in configuring code letters is that the source symbols must be uniquely decoded from its corresponding *code word*. Using this criterion, code I from Table 9.5 has the misfortune that symbols H and C are both coded into the same code word 0. Thus, H cannot be uniquely decoded from 0. For this reason, codes such as code I are not considered for variable length encoders. Code II suffers from the same defect as code I, although in a slightly different way. If HH leaves the source, it will be encoded into 00, which is precisely the codeword for Y. If no spacing is used to separate codewords, this leads to problems, in that decoding 00 could lead to HH or Y.

In order to restrict codes such as II from further consideration, we use the following definition. A code is **uniquely decodable** if for each *source sequence*, its corresponding sequence of code letters is different from the sequence of code letters corresponding to any other source sequence. However, decoding *uniquely decodable* codes is not always straightforward. To simplify the process

TABLE 9.5

k	Source Symbols a^k	$P(a^k)$	Code I	Code II	Code III	Code IV
1	H	0.5	0	0	0	0
2	C	0.25	0	1	10	01
3	Y	0.125	1	00	110	011
4	W	0.125	10	11	111	0111

The mean number of code letters for code II is $E[n_k] = 0.5 \times 1 + 0.25 \times 1 + 0.125 \times 2 + 0.125 \times 2 = 1.25$.

of decoding code words into source symbols, we must restrict our attention to codes which are a subset of uniquely decodable codes and referred to as *prefix codes*. A **prefix condition code** is one in which no code word is the prefix of any other code word.

Example

Code I from Table 9.5 is not a *prefix condition* code, since the code for Y (i.e., 1) is a prefix of 1, a code word for W.

The main advantage of using *prefix condition codes* is the simplicity by which a sequence of code words is uniquely decoded into a sequence of source symbols. We simply start at the beginning and decode one word at a time. When we get to the end of a code word, we know it is the end since that code word is not the prefix of any other code word.

Example

Using code III of Table 9.5, suppose that the sequence 0111100 is to be decoded into a sequence of source symbols. Since 0 is the code word for H and is not the initial part of any other sequence, we decode 0 as H. The only other possibility is to take the next three code words, since a fewer number of code words does not correspond to any symbol. Thus, we assign W to 111. Likewise, the only other possibility is to take 10 and decode it into C, and finally 0 into H. Thus, the corresponding sequence of source symbols is HWCH.

We now go back to the problem of choosing a prefix condition code to minimize $E[n_k]$. The following theorem, referred to as the **source coding theorem** for variable length encoders, is useful for placing bounds on $E[n_k]$. Given a source U with entropy $H(U)$ and a code alphabet of D symbols, then, for every uniquely decodable set of code words

$$E[n_k] > H(U) / \log D \tag{9.7}$$

In addition, it is possible to assign code words to the source letters in such a way that the prefix condition is satisfied and

$$E[n_k] < H(U) / \log D + 1 \tag{9.8}$$

Huffman encoding. It is very difficult in practice to obtain the bounds given by the source coding theorems, because it requires that we encode source words having a long sequence of symbols (i.e., L is large). Huffman has discovered a scheme that allows the encoding of source words which removes the restriction of encoding long sequences of source symbols. One advantage of Huffman encoding is that the resulting code is a *prefix code*, which makes it easy to decode.

The procedure suggested by Huffman is illustrated here for a binary encoder (i.e., D = 2).

1. Arrange the source words in order of descending probability, as shown in Table 9.6.

2. Combine the last two words into one word. The combined word is assigned a probability equal to the sum of the probabilities of the constituent words.

3. Repeat steps 1 and 2 by treating newly combined words as source words until the number of words is reduced to 2.

4. The two remaining words are now assigned **0** and **1** as their first symbols in the code sequence.

TABLE 9.6

Code	Original source Source	Prob.	S1		S2		S3		S4	
00	w1	0.30	0.30	00	0.30	00	→0.43	1	→0.57	0
10	w2	0.25	0.25	10	→0.27	01	0.30	00⏋	0.43	1
010	w3	0.15	→0.18	11	0.25	10⏋	0.27	01⏌		
011	w4	0.12	0.15	010⏋	0.18	11⏌				
110	w5	0.10⏋	0.12	011⏌						
11	w6	0.08⏌								

5. Go back and assign the symbols **0** and **1** as the second symbol for the two words that were combined the previous step.

6. Repeat step 5 until the first column is reached.

7. The codes for the source words are obtained by backtracking the intermediate codes, starting with the two words obtained in step 3. The final code is shown in the first column of Table 9.6.

9.3 DATA ENCRYPTION

Security of computers and computer networks has been an important concern since these technologies were first developed. One security aspect deals with user authorization for accessing certain computers or networks. In this case, we need security against counterfeiting, forgery, or fraud of user identification. For document protection, we have been using fingerprints, handprints, and signatures for centuries. Other biometric identifiers such as retinal patterns and voice prints can also be used for providing document protection.

When documents are stored in a computer memory or sent to another computer through a network, the problem of document security increases in difficulty. For example, by monitoring the medium with appropriate devices, it is possible to obtain the correct ID code for later accessing, altering, or destroying confidential information such as computer programs, criminal records, medical records, bank accounts, and others.

The basis for providing security in computer networks consists of converting the data into nonsense at the sender and then back into its original form at the receiver. The principles and techniques used for rendering an original message unintelligible and for converting the transformed message back into an intelligent form is referred to as **cryptography. Data encryption** refers to the process of data transformation using cryptographic techniques.

Data encryption basically uses *codes* and *ciphers* for turning the data unintelligible. A **cipher** operates on blocks of source data of fixed length, whereas a **code** operates on blocks of variable length. Both techniques replace the source data blocks by other blocks using an *encryption algorithm*.

One of the oldest ciphers which was used for military purposes is known as the *Caesar cipher*. The Caesar cipher simply replaces each alphabet letter by another located three letters forward when the letters are arranged from A to Z. For example, A becomes D, B becomes E, and so on. Thus, the message ATTACK TOMORROW becomes DWWDFN WRPRUURZ. Another cypher version is one based on a *secret list*, such as the one shown in Table 9.7. Using Table 9.7, the same message can be encoded into WHITE HORSE.

TABLE 9.7 SECRET LIST

Symbol	Code	Symbol	Code
yesterday	head	tomorrow	horse
war	hell	Rome	sad
horse	monkey	surrender	dog
soldier	black	attack	white
space	$	money	fire

9.3.1 Uses of Encryption

In the context of computer networks, encryption can be used for

> preventing unauthorized access to transmitted or stored data,
> preventing the analysis of data traffic as data goes from a source to its destination,
> detecting any data modifications including data destruction,
> detecting denial of transmission service, and
> detecting unauthorized data access.

Because of their widespread use, we concentrate on cipher-based data transformations. Figure 9.3 depicts the stages that the message goes through on its way from the source to the destination. The message as emitted from the source is referred to as the **plaintext** or **cleartext.** After the encipherment stage, the message is referred to as **cyphertext.** At the receiver side, the ciphertext must be deciphered to obtain the original message. The terms *encipherment* and *encryption* are used interchangeably in the literature, and we use the latter from now on.

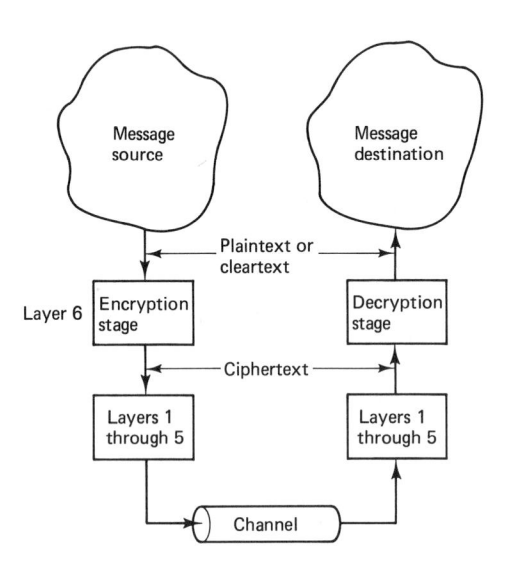

Figure 9.3 Encrypted message transformations and the OSI reference model.

342 The Presentation Layer Chap. 9

9.3.2 Key-Based Encryption

Early encryption schemes were very simple, and their security mostly depended on the secrecy of the data transformation method or algorithm. In contrast, modern encryption schemes are based on mathematical transformations controlled by a *key*. Unlike the early encryption schemes, modern encryption schemes do not keep the transformation or algorithm secret. Instead, the *key* is kept secret. A *key* is chosen so that it changes the nature of the algorithm drastically. From the viewpoint of decoding encrypted messages, changing keys has the effect of changing algorithms.

A *key*-base data encryption system is depicted in Figure 9.4. The ciphertext is obtained by applying a known encryption algorithm on the cleartext. At the receiver, the cleartext is recovered by applying a decryption algorithm on the ciphertext. The encryption and decryption algorithms are both controlled by a single secret key. Of course, this technique assumes that there is a safe way to share secret keys between a sender and a receiver.

Before discussing a standard for data encryption, let us examine a cipher classification. Ciphers can be classified as *stream* or *block* ciphers. **Stream ciphers** use a key, which is a random ordered stream of bits, equal in length to the message to be encrypted. These ciphers are the only class of ciphers that can be proven to be totally unbreakable (Wood and Cotton, 1983). However, their main disadvantage is that they are not practical because they require extremely long keys. **Block ciphers** encrypt fixed-size message blocks of data under the control of a key. The length of ciphertext is greater or equal than the length of the cleartext.

9.3.3 Data Encryption Standard (DES)

The National Bureau of Standards (NBS) has developed a *block cipher* encryption algorithm for use in the Federal Government. The standard is known as FPS 46 (Federal Information Processing Standard No 46.). As depicted in Figure 9.5, the input message block goes through an initial permutation and then is partitioned into a left and right block. The *key* dependent operation f operates on the right block R to produce an intermediate block $g = f(R,K)$, which is combined with the left block L to produce the intermediate block $R' = L + g = L + f(R,K)$. The corresponding intermediate block L' is obtained from the right block R, as indicated in the figure. Both intermediate blocks are fed back 16 times to the initial blocks L and R. After the feedback process, the intermediate blocks are combined into a single block, where the inverse of the initial permutation is performed to produce the output message.

9.3.4 Public Key Encryption

Whereas the data encryption standard requires that the single encryption key be secret, public key encryption uses two keys: a *public encryption key* and a *secret decryption key*, as shown in Figure

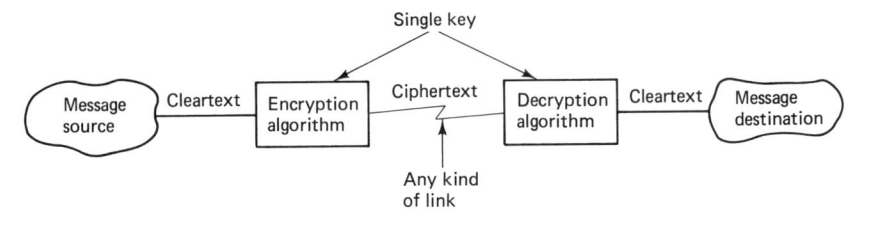

Figure 9.4 A key-based encryption system.

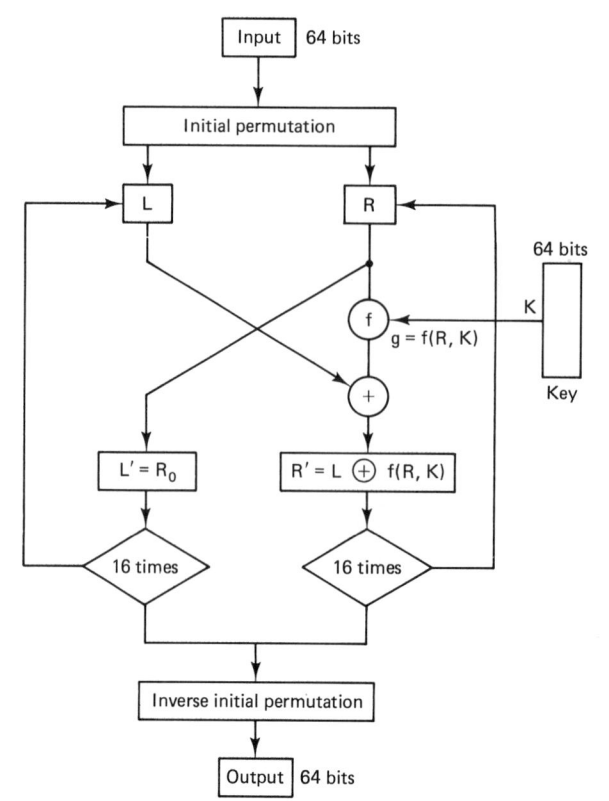

Figure 9.5 Signal processing involved in the data encryption standard (DES).

9.6. For example, assume that user B wants to send message M to user A. At the sender side, B encrypts the message M using A's public key P_a to yield ciphertext $C = E(M) = P_a(M)$. At the receiver side, A decrypts the ciphertext C using A's secret key S_a to yield $M = D(C) = D(E(M)) = S_a(P_a(M))$. The operators for the secret key S_a and public key P_a when user A is the receiver must meet the following constraint, which can be obtained if we switch the roles of A and B. If A is now the sender and B the receiver, then the following must be true: $M = P_a(S_a(M))$. We next consider a public key encryption scheme known as RSA.

Rivert-Shamir-Adleman (RSA) scheme. The RSA scheme is based on three integer numbers n, d, and e, where the number n is public but d and e are secret. The numbers n, d, and e can be chosen in the following way: First, n is factored into two prime numbers p and q

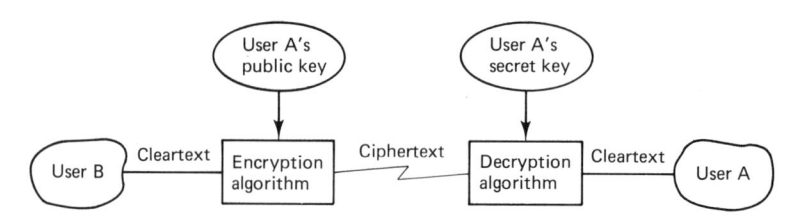

Figure 9.6 A public key encryption system.

344   The Presentation Layer   Chap. 9

(i.e., n = pq). Second, d is chosen as a large number relatively prime to $z = (p-1)(a-1)$. That is, the greatest common divisor of d and z is 1.

Finally, e is found as the *multiplicative inverse of d* using arithmetic module z. That is,

$$de = 1 \text{ Mod } z$$

To encrypt a message M, it is simply raised to the eth power module n. That is,

$$C = E(M) = M^e \text{ Mod } n$$

To decrypt the receiver ciphertext, C is raised to the dth power module n. That is,

$$D(E(M)) = D(C) = C^d \text{ Mod } n$$

As an example, let $p = 3$, $q = 5$, thus $n = 15$ and $z = 8$. Let us choose $d = 11$ since it is relatively prime with 8. We next find e from $de = 1$ Mod z, that is, $11e = 1$ mod 8, which yields $e = 3$. Let us now assume that the message to be encoded is $M = 8$. The ciphertext $C = E(M)$ is obtained as $C = (M^e \text{ Mod } n) = (8^3 \text{ Mod } 15) = 2$. The original message can be recovered by the following computation, $M = (C^d \text{ Mod } n) = (2^{11} \text{ mod } 15) = 8$, which is the message to be expected.

9.4 ISO PRESENTATION LAYER PROTOCOL

In this section, we discuss a specific presentation layer protocol developed by the International Organization for Standardization (ISO). The ISO presentation layer standard is a connection-oriented communication protocol and is published in two documents, with the service definition document published as ISO 8822 and the protocol specification document published as ISO 8823. We begin with an explanation of the terminology and definitions used in the standard, followed by an overview of the services provided.

Before application processes exchange information, the variables, their values, and corresponding, *data types*[3] of the information to be exchanged must be defined. The requirement for the *data type* definition results primarily from the use of modern structured programming languages such as C, Pascal, or ADA, which require type definitions for all variables at the beginning of all programs. In addition to variables, values, and data types, application processes also need to define the functions of application layer services (for example, read, write, send mail, get mail, etc.). Furthermore, the variables, values, data types, service attributes (for example, request, indication, etc.) must be arranged in a mutually understandable manner to both application processes. Together, the variables, values, data types, application layer service functions, service attributes, and their collective arrangement constitute the **abstract syntax** of the information to be communicated. In order for two application processes located in two different stations to communicate, the processes must share the same *abstract syntax*. For example, abstract syntax X might involve character strings, whereas abstract syntax Y might involve integer numbers.

---

[3] Data types are used here in the context of programming languages. See Appendix A for a definition and examples of data types in the context of the ADA language.

Example

Process A issues a service request to *write* the value TRUE into a *boolean* variable named bool_var located in a remote process. For this case, the information to be communicated by process A is given by the following abstract syntax:

$$\text{data type} = \text{(boolean)}$$
$$\text{variable} = \text{(bool\_var)}$$
$$\text{value} = \text{(TRUE)}$$
$$\text{service function} = \text{(write)}$$
$$\text{service attribute} = \text{(request)}$$
$$\text{arrangement} = \text{(request/write/boolean/bool\_var/TRUE)}$$

The way an *abstract syntax* is actually represented by the computer constitutes the **concrete syntax** of the data. There are two aspects of a concrete syntax. The first aspect regards how the computer actually represents the abstract syntax locally, without regard to whether communication will take place. The local representation of an abstract syntax, regardless of its intended use, is referred to as the **local syntax** of the data. Clearly, the local syntax depends only on the particular computer used. For example, computer A may represent integers using 16 bits of precision, whereas computer B may represent integers using 32 bits of precision.

The second aspect of the concrete syntax regards how a computer represents the abstract syntax for communication purposes. The concrete syntax for representing the information in a way that two communicating entities can understand one another is referred to as the **transfer syntax** of the data. Obviously the transfer syntax must be understood by the application processes involved in communications. Furthermore, some form of *transfer syntax* negotiation should be provided for effective communication management. For example, two communicating application processes P and Q may propose that the transfer syntaxes to be used involve, respectively, *binary* and *BCD* integer representations. Since the two proposed transfer syntaxes are not the same, P and Q cannot communicate.

A simple relationship between an *abstract syntax* and a corresponding *transfer syntax* is given by the **presentation context** (P_context). A *presentation context* does not contain the rules as to how a transfer syntax is obtained from an abstract syntax. Rather, is simply indicates that there is a relationship between a transfer syntax and an abstract syntax. How a transfer syntax is obtained from an abstract syntax is defined by an *encoder*, perhaps involving, for example, the data encryption standard (DES), Huffman source encoding, or data compression. Figure 9.7 depicts a data flow example when there are several presentation contexts and only one is selected. Appendix D contains a specific example of an *abstract syntax* and *transfer syntax* corresponding to an MMS message using the ASN.1 standard.

The essence of the ISO presentation layer protocol standard regards the provision of mechanisms for enabling presentation users to define and select the *transfer syntax* for their communications. There may be several transfer syntaxes to choose from and consequently several *presentation contexts* to choose from. It is up to the presentation users to negotiate appropriate *presentation contexts* by using the services of the presentation layer.

It is possible that presentation users are not able to agree on a mutually understandable *transfer*

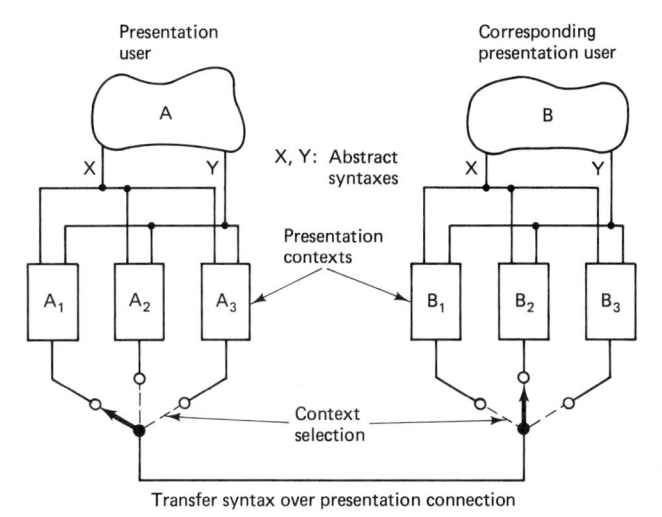

Figure 9.7 Data flow in a multiple presentation context environment.

syntax, and thus they are not able to communicate. The ISO presentation layer protocol assumes that there exist appropriate algorithms or other mechanisms for performing the required data transformation from the abstract syntax (or concrete syntax) to the transfer syntax. Examples of data transformation algorithms include message compression or data encryption, as discussed in sections 9.2 and 9.3. Furthermore, the ISO standard does not provide the means for managing data transformation mechanisms.

When selecting an appropriate transfer syntax, presentation users can identify the transfer syntax by:

a) *A priori agreement*: Whenever presentation users want to use a presentation context, they simply indicate so. There is a predefined *transfer syntax* which is always used. Under this scheme, application processes always communicate.

b) *Explicit naming*: It is assumed that there is a list containing the names of several transfer syntaxes to choose from at the sender and receiver sides (although not necessarily the same ones). Under this scheme, application processes may not always be able to communicate, because a transfer syntax proposed by one presentation user may not be acceptable by the corresponding presentation user.

c) *Transferring a description of the transfer syntax*: This is the most general and also the most complex of the three schemes considered. The two communicating presentation users do not have a single transfer syntax agreed upon a priori as in scheme a), nor do they contain a predefined list of transfer syntaxes to choose from as in scheme b). Rather, the initiator sends a description of the transfer syntax in an appropriate language. The responder then decodes the description and determines if it could be supported. Thus, under this scheme, presentation users may not always be able to communicate. Although not specified in the presentation standard, we use the following notation for denoting a *presentation context*:

$$\text{Presentation context} = \{a, (b,c)\}$$

where

a = abstract syntax

b = transformation to go from a to c

c = transfer syntax

Example

Assume that two presentation users A and B want to communicate using abstract syntax X and Y, where X involves *character strings* and Y involves *integer numbers*. User A proposes the use of DES and Huffman encoding for data transformation and *ASCII, EBCDIC, BCD* and *binary* for transfer syntaxes, as indicated in the following presentation contexts:

Context_A1 := {X,(DES, ASCII)}[4]

context_A2 := {X, (DES, EBCDIC)}

context_A3 := {X, (Huffman, ASCII)}

context_A4 := {Y, (DES, BCD)}

context_A5 := {Y, (Huffman, Binary)}

On the other hand, User B can support the following set of presentation contexts:

context_B1 := {X, (DES, ASCII)}

context_B2 := {X, (Huffman, EBCDIC)}

context_B3 := {Y, (Huffman, Binary)}

For this example, it is clear that applications A and B can communicate using presentation contexts {X, (DES, ASCII)} and {Y, (Huffman, Binary)}.

9.4.1 Overview of the ISO Presentation Services

There are two major functions associated with the ISO presentation layer: negotiation of transfer syntax and transformation to/from the transfer syntax. The ISO presentation layer standard only deals with the first function, since it is assumed that data transformations (e.g., DES, Huffman encoding etc.) have no effect on the presentation protocol design. Indeed, other standardization efforts are applicable for data transformations (e.g., FIPS 46 for encryption, ANSI/CCITT G.721 for voice compression, and ASN.1 for data compression).

Transfer syntaxes must be negotiated prior to message exchange. Negotiation of transfer syntax occurs when a user of the presentation service provides a specification of an abstract syntax for which a transfer syntax is required. The outcome of the negotiation process is a set of *presentation contexts* that both users can support, and it is referred to as the **context set.** If the presentation layer users cannot support common presentation contexts, then the *context set* is empty. An important

---

[4] As noted earlier, the ISO presentation layer standard does not actually deal with the data transformation rules. Rather, it simply indicates what rules are used to obtain the transfer syntax.

aspect of the protocol service has to do with managing the *context set* by allowing for example contexts to be defined and/or deleted from the set.

The services of the presentation and session layers are complementary rather than interdependent. The presentation layer does not make use of the session services to provide presentation services. Thus, the session services must be made available to the presentation user in a *pass through* manner. Because of this mode of operation, the service *functional units* associated with the presentation layer are divided into two major categories: session functional units and presentation functional units. The session functional units correspond to the services which are *passed through* from the session layer directly to the presentation users. The *session functional units* are:

1. Negotiated Release
2. Half Duplex
3. Duplex (i.e., full duplex)
4. Expedited Data
5. Typed Data
6. Capability Data Exchange
7. Minor Synchronize
8. Major Synchronize
9. Resynchronize
10. Exceptions
11. Activity Management.

Which were discussed in Chapter 8. On the other hand, the Presentation Functional Unit corresponds to the actual services provided by the presentation layer in addition to the *pass through* services. The presentation functional units are:

1. Presentation Kernel Functional Unit
2. Context Management Functional Unit
3. Context Restoration Functional Unit.

Whereas the *Presentation Kernel* is always available, the use of the *context management* or *context restoration* functional unit is optional.

The *presentation kernel functional unit* basically supports the essential connection-oriented mechanisms of the presentation layer, which are connection establishment, data transfer, and connection termination. As the name implies, the *context management* and *context restoration* functional units allow for the management of the *context set*. If the context management functional unit is selected, the defined context set may change during the connection. If the context restoration functional unit is selected, the presentation services will remember the defined context set at specified points during the connection. This is useful, for example, when the presentation user requests the return to one of these points. The defined *context set* will be restored to the one active at that point. The specific points during a connection which are remembered are:

- major synchronization points,
- minor synchronization points,

- activity interrupt, and
- start of presentation connection.

In addition to grouping presentation services into functional units, the service standard also groups presentation services into *facilities*. The following facilities are available:

1. Connection Establishment Facility
2. Connection Termination Facility
3. Context Management Facility
4. Information Transfer Facility
5. Dialog Control Facility.

Table 9.8 shows the services associated with each facility.

Service primitives. This section briefly describes one of the most important service primitives supported by the ISO presentation layer standard.

P_CONNECT. Since the P_CONNECT service is a confirmed one, it consists of four primitives: P_CONNECT.req, P_CONNECT.ind, P_CONNECT.resp, and P_CONNECT.conf. The P_CONNECT service is the most important and the most complex service offered by the presentation layer. In addition to establishing a presentation layer connection, the P_CONNECT service can be also used for defining and modifying the *context set*, for requesting a desired *quality of service*, for selecting optional presentation functional units, for managing certain parameters associated with the session layer (i.e., initial assignment of tokens), and even for transferring some user data. In order to provide the wide variety of functions listed previously, the P_CONNECT service uses many parameters, as described by the following.[5]

```
P_CONNECT.req (cg_p_addr, cd_p_addr, mult_def_ctxt,
P_ctxt_def_lst, dft_ctxt_nam, qos, P_req, s_req,
i_sync_pnt_ser_n, i_assgn_tok, s_conn_id, data)

P_CONNECT.ind (cg_p_addr, cd_p_addr, mult_def_ctx,
p_ctxt_def_lst, p_ctxt_lst, dft_ctxt_nam, dft_ctxt, res, qos, p_req,
s_req, i_sync_pnt_ser_n, i_assgn_tok, s_conn_id, data)

P_CONNECT.resp (r_p_addr, mult_def_ctxt, p_ctxt_res_lst,
dft_ctxt_res, qos, p_req, s_req, i_sync_pnt_ser_n, i_assgn_tok,
s_conn_id, data, res)

P_CONNECT.conf (r_p_addr, mult_def_ctxt, p_ctxt_res_lst,
dft_ctxt_res, qos, p_req, s_req, i_sync_pnt_ser_n, i_assgn_tok,
s_conn_id, data, res)
```

whereas the parameters cg_p_addr and cd_p_addr identify, respectively, the *calling presentation address*, and *called presentation address*, the parameter r_p_addr identifies an alternate *responding presentation address* to be used for reestablishing communication after a failure. The next five

---

[5] This description is only an example of the manner in which the primitives can be called by service user programs.

TABLE 9.8 SUMMARY OF PRESENTATION FACILITIES, THEIR SERVICES AND PURPOSES

Name of service primitive	Type of service	Purpose
Connection establishment facilities		
P_CONNECT	Confirmed	Connection establishment
Connection termination facility		
P_RELEASE	Confirmed	Connection release
P_U_ABORT	Nonconfirmed	User initiated abort
P_P_ABORT	Nonconfirmed	Provider initiated abort
Context management facility		
P_ALTER_CONTEXT	Confirmed	Connection definition and deletion
Information transfer facility		
P_TYPED_DATA	Nonconfirmed	Information transfer not subject to token control
P_DATA	Nonconfirmed	Information transfer which may be subject to token control
P_EXPEDITED_DATA	Nonconfirmed	
Dialogue control facility		
P_U_EXCEPTION_REPORT	Nonconfirmed	
P_P_EXCEPTION_REPORT	Provider-initiated	
P_TOKEN_GIVE	Nonconfirmed	
P_TOKEN_PLEASE	Nonconfirmed	
P_CONTROL_GIVE	Nonconfirmed	
P_SYNC_MINOR	Optionally confirmed	
P_SYNC_MAJOR	Confirmed	
P_RESYNCHRONIZE	Confirmed	
P_ACTIVITY_START	Nonconfirmed	
P_ACTIVITY_RESUME	Nonconfirmed	
P_ACTIVITY_END	Confirmed	
P_ACTIVITY_INTERRUPT	Confirmed	
P_ACTIVITY_DISCARD	Confirmed	

parameters following the cd_p_addr parameter in the P_CONNECT.ind primitive allow the management of *context sets*. If more than one element is desired in the *defined context set*, then the mult_def_ctxt must be present; otherwise, the *defined context set* should not have more than one member.

Sometimes it is desired to add a few presentation contexts to an already defined *context set* when establishing a presentation connection. When this is desired, the p_ctxt_def_lst parameter contains a list of elements (i.e., presentation contexts) to be added to the *defined context set*. The acceptance or rejection of each of the presentation contexts proposed by p_ctxt_def_lst is indicated by the parameter p_ctxt_res_lst.

When a presentation user requires to identify explicitly the *abstract syntax* supported by the default context, the parameter dft_ctxt_nam must be used. The corresponding presentation entity can either accept or reject the explicit abtract syntax using the dft_ctxt_res parameter. When optional functional units for the presentation service are required, the p_req parameter must be used. The parameters qos, s_req, i_sync_pnt_ser_n, i_assgn_tok and s_conn_id provide the presentation user with access to the *quality of service, session requirements, initial synchronization point serial number, initial assignment of tokens,* and *session connection identifier* parameters, respectively, of the ISO session layer service. It is also possible to send an initial amount of data during connection establishment using the *data* parameter. Finally, *res* is used to indicate the overall result of using the P_CONNECT service. There are four possible values for *res*: acceptance, rejection by user, transient rejection by provider, and permanent rejection by provider. Appendix D describes ASN.1, an ISO standard for defining the *abstract syntax* and *transfer syntax* associated with application layer protocols.

9.5 MAP PRESENTATION LAYER

The MAP 2.1 and 2.2 specifications do not require a presentation layer. However, MAP 3.0 specifies a subset of the ISO presentation layer standard which involves basically the functionality of the *Presentation Kernel Functional Unit*.

9.5.1 TOP Presentation Layer

The TOP 3.0 version is identical to that of MAP 3.0.

SUMMARY

The presentation layer deals with transformations of the data as it moves from the application layer to the session layer, or vice versa. The purpose of the presentation layer is the resolution and management of syntax differences of the data being passed between presentation layer users. The ISO presentation layer standard accomplishes this by providing the means for negotiating a *transfer syntax*, mutually understandable by the presentation layer service providers. There are three reasons why data transformations are desirable:

> message security,
> message compression, and
> data compatibility.

Message security involves the protection of data against accidental or intentional access by unauthorized users. When channel bandwidth is scarce, **message compression** techniques can be used to reduce the bandwidth required for data transmission. **Data compatibility** refers to the capability of exchanging information across the network, even if the local data representations are different.

There are three main classes of data encoders: *end user encoder, source encoder,* and *channel encoder*. **End user encoders** are performed within the source (i.e., before the message is given to the communication system). The purpose of the **source encoder** involves performing data transformations on the source symbols, whereas the purpose of the **channel encoder** is to allow the bit frames to be sent on a specific channel and be reliably reproduced at the output of the channel decoder. Depending upon the number of bits per code word, source encoding techniques are classified into *fixed length encoding* and *variable length encoding*.

The basis for providing security in computer networks consists of converting the data into nonsense at the sender and then back into its original form at the receiver. The principles and techniques used for rendering an original message unintelligible and for converting the transformed message back into an intelligent form are referred to as **cryptography. Data encryption** refers to the process of data transformation using cryptographic techniques.

Data encryption basically uses *codes* and *ciphers* for turning the data unintelligible. A **cipher** operates on blocks of source data of fixed length, whereas a **code** operates on blocks of variable length. Both techniques replace the source data blocks by other blocks using an *encryption algorithm*.

In simple terms, an *abstract syntax* is a specific representation of the information to be communicated by application processes. A computer representation of an abstract syntax has two components: noncommunication related and communication related. The latter representation constitutes the **transfer syntax** of the information. The ISO presentation layer standard is a connection-oriented communication protocol which basically provides appropriate mechanisms for enabling presentation users to define and select the *transfer syntax* for their communications. The transfer syntax is basically the actual representation of information in a way that two communicating entities can understand one another. There may be several transfer syntaxes to choose from. When selecting an appropriate transfer syntax, presentation users can identify the transfer syntax by: a) a priori agreement, b) explicit naming, and c) transferring a description of the transfer syntax.

There are two major functions associated with the presentation layer: negotiation of transfer syntax and transformation to/from the transfer syntax. The ISO presentation layer standard only deals with the first function. Transfer syntaxes must be negotiated prior to message exchange. Negotiation of transfer syntax occurs when a user of the presentation service provides a specification of an *abstract syntax* for which a *transfer syntax* is required. The outcome of the negotiation process is a set of *presentation contexts* that both users can support, and it is referred to as the **context set.**

Bibliographic Notes

Some data transformation issues are discussed by Martin (1981) with source encoding including the Huffman encoder being treated in the books by Lathi (1983) and Das and others (1986). The book by Tanenbaum (1988) and the article by Wood and Cotton in (Chou, 1983) discuss key based encryption. The ISO presentation layer standard is detailed in ISO 8822 and ISO 8823 covering the service definition and protocol specification respectively.

PROBLEMS

1. (a) List some applications of source encoding.
   (b) Explain in detail one of the applications chosen from your list of part a).
2. Explain the main difference between source encoding and channel encoding.
3. Write a program to perform message compression based on the space buster example of section 9.2.2.
4. (a) For the symbols shown in Table 9.5 and their probability of occurrence, find another *prefix condition code*.

(b) If the message to be encoded is HWCH, find the corresponding codeword.
5. A source emits six symbols with probabilities $\frac{1}{2}$, $\frac{1}{4}$, $\frac{1}{8}$, $\frac{1}{16}$, $\frac{1}{32}$, and $\frac{1}{32}$ respectively.
   (a) Find the entropy of the source.
   (b) Using Huffman encoding find codewords for the source symbols.
   (c) Find the average length of the codewords.
   (d) Determine the efficiency and redundancy of the code.
6. Consider the Huffman code assigned to the following symbols A, B, C, D, E, F, G, and H with respective probabilities 0.22, 0.20, 0.18, 0.15, 0.10, 0.08, 0.05, and 0.02. Suppose that you play *receiver* and receive the codeword 10101001011110110110100.
   (a) What was the message sent?
   (b) Is your answer unique? Why?
7. **(a)** Calculate the entropy of a binary source with alphabet U = {0,1} and respective probabilities {p, 1-p} where p is in the interval [0,1].
   (b) Plot H(U) versus p.
   (c) Find the value of p for which H(U) is maximum.
   (d) Note that when p = 0 or p = 1, H(U) = 0. Provide a physical interpretation of H(U) being 0.
8. What is the entropy of the following source alphabet A = (left, right, straight) with probabilities equal to 0.25, 0.25, and 0.5 respectively? Also, find the self-information of each source letter in A.
9. Write a program to perform message compression based on the Huffman encoding algorithm.
10. Extend Huffman encoding rules for D = 3.
11. Define *prefix codes* and explain why they are important.
12. How do *stream ciphers* differ from *block ciphers*?
13. For the RSA algorithm, let p = 5 and q = 7.
    (a) Find suitable values for d and e.
    (b) For the message M = 3, find the ciphertext C = E(M) and the corresponding decrypted ciphertext M1 = D(C).
14. Actual messages using the English language, such as CAB, are first represented as a block of numbers with values 0 to 32 (26 letters plus 6 punctuation symbols) before using data encryption. Assume that the representation is A = 1, B = 2, C = 3, . . . etc, so the numeric representation of the message CAB is 312. Use an RSA scheme with n = 33, d = 3, and e = 7. The message is encrypted by raising the value of every number in the block to the power 7 module 33. Configure a table showing the intermediate calculations of the encrypted mesage as well as the decrypted message.
15. Indicate whether the following statement is true or false: In the ISO presentation layer protocol standard, a presentation context does not indicate how the abstract and transfer syntaxes are related.
16. What constitutes the presentation functional units?
17. A positive response to the MMS primitive write.resp is shown next:

Encoded message (ASN.1)	MMS write.resp message
A1	confirmed-Response {
0A	10
02	Invoke ID, INTEGER,
04	4
0005	5
A5	Write {CHOICE}
02	2
81	SUCCESS NULL} ,
00	0

where the code on the left side corresponds to the ASN.1 encoder. Define the *relative efficiency* of the code as

$$R_{eff} = M/P$$

where M is the total number of bits in the encoded message and P is the total number of bits in the MMS write.resp message. Ignore spaces and CR-LF (carriage-return, line-feed) characters. Assume that each character in the MMS message is represented by an 8-bit ASCII code and each character in the ASN.1 code represents a hexadecimal digit (i.e., 4 bits).

Calculate the relative efficiency of the ASN.1 encoder for this particular situation.

10

The Application Layer

Our primary purpose in this chapter is to discuss the functions of the application layer of the OSI reference model while emphasizing the concepts used in the ISO application layer protocol standards. After an introductory section, the main concepts behind some ISO application layer standards are presented in Section 10.2, with Section 10.3 dealing with the Association Control Service Element (ACSE). Section 10.4 discusses the Manufacturing Message Specification (MMS), which is expected to play a major role in automated manufacturing applications. Section 10.5 discusses the ISO standard dealing with file systems known as the File Transfer, Access, and Management (FTAM) protocol. Since distributed databases are also expected to play a major role in future manufacturing networks (e.g., MAP and TOP), they are discussed in Section 10.6. Finally, Section 10.7 deals with the characteristics of the MAP and TOP application layer.

Because of space limitations, several topics which are relevant to the application layer for manufacturing networks have been omitted. Most notably among them are the Remote Operations Service Element (ROSE) and the Commitment, Concurrency, and Recovery (CCR) element. Another topic not discussed is the forerunner of MMS known as the Manufacturing Message Format Standard (MMFS). Other MAP/TOP application layer related standards omitted include the Message Handling Service (MHS), Network Management (NM), Virtual Terminal (VT), Product Definition Interchange Format (PDIF), Computer Graphics Metafile Interchange Format (CGMIF), Office Document Interchange Format (ODIF), and Computer Graphics Applications Interface (GKS INTF). Still another important topic left out is the *application layer interface* with end user application programs. However, the material in this chapter will enable the reader to pursue the topics not covered herein with no difficulty.

10.1 APPLICATION LAYER FUNCTIONS

For end users, the application layer is the most important layer because it provides the window for accessing the overall network functions. Although it is possible for an end user to directly access services of the presentation, session, or other layers of the OSI reference model without using the application layer, networks are designed so that end users obtain full benefits of the network only if access is made at the application layer. For example, in the context of ISO protocols, closing a connection at the transport layer may cause loss of data if the service provider receives the request in the midst of a data transfer. In contrast, closing a connection at any layer above the transport layer (i.e., session, presentation, or application) is safe since the service provider will wait until completion of any data transfer that might be in progress before closing the connection.

In Chapter 8, which dealt with the session layer, several concepts regarding distributed systems and distributed applications were introduced. Processes cooperating with other processes to reach a common goal are referred to as **application processes.** The application is related to the common goal, and the processes could reside in the same network station or in different stations. The latter case involves **distributed application processes.**

Example

Let's consider a LAN *file server* station with three additional stations s_1, s_2, and s_3. We wish to identify the common goal and appropriate application processes.

The file server station contains files and manage their access on behalf of the other stations. Thus, the common goal is the storage of files in the file server's secondary memory and the orderly access of information by the other stations. The number and nature of application processes depend on the characteristics of the overall system (e.g., operating system, application requirements, system complexity, etc.). The following is a typical arrangement of *application processes* with processes A, B, and C located in the file server station, and processes 1, 2, and 3 located at the s_1, s_2, and s_3, stations respectively.

Process A: Handle file server requests from processes located in the other stations.

Process B: Perform file input/output operations (e.g., open file, read record, write record, etc.).

Process C: Provides a human (i.e., operator) interface.

Process 1: Handle file server customer at station 1.

Process 2: Handle file server customer at station 2.

Process 3: Handle file server customer at station 3.

From the preceding example, we distinguish two types of process interactions: local and remote. Whereas *local process interactions* involve processes located in the same station, *remote process interactions* involve processes located in different stations. Thus, interactions among pro-

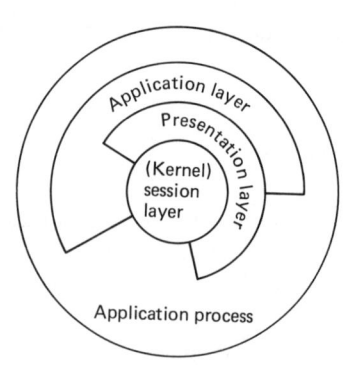

Figure 10.1 Functions provided by the application, session, and presentation layers are similar to a layered configuration of a distributed operating system.

cesses A, B, and C are local, whereas interactions between processes A and processes 1, 2, or 3 are remote. The behavior of cooperating application processes is truly dynamic, in that they initiate and terminate their interactions at any time. Processes can interact by exchanging messages. Thus, in this sense interprocess interaction is synonymous with *interprocess communication*.

Although *application processes* can reside within the same station in a computer network, communication protocols for the application layer deal only with *application processes* residing in different network stations. The main function of the application layer of the OSI reference model is to provide and manage the communications between *distributed application processes*. The communications could be connection-oriented or connectionless. The services provided by the application layer can be considered as the overall network services, because they include the services of all other layers. For example, end users accessing application layer services need not worry about their messages finding a path to a destination station or signals corresponding to their messages colliding at the physical medium with signals from other stations, because those functions are performed by the network and data link layers, respectively.

Together, the session, presentation, and application layers can be thought of as providing the functionality of the communication services component of a *distributed operating system*. The session layer, with functions such as *dialog management* and *synchronization control*, constitutes the kernel of the distributed operating system. The presentation layer, with functions such as data transformations and their management, constitutes an *operating system layer* that surrounds the kernel, as depicted in Figure 10.1. As the outmost *operating system layer*, the application layer provides the necessary functions so that application processes can effectively support distributed applications. Thus, whereas the functions of the session layer are fairly generic, the functions of the application layer are specific to certain applications. Note that end users cannot access the session, presentation, or application layers by means other than an application process. Distributed operating systems have other important components, such as processor management, memory management, and so on, that have no counterpart in the services provided by the session, presentation, and application layers. These other distributed operating system components fall outside the OSI reference model and thus they are not discussed.

10.2 APPLICATION LAYER CONCEPTS

Application layer protocols are not fully developed yet; in particular, the application layer model used by the ISO is still evolving. However, since manufacturing networks such as MAP and TOP are based on ISO protocols, we discuss ISO concepts as they currently stand. Since the emphasis of this book is not to provide a detailed description of current ISO protocols but rather to illustrate major concepts used in the protocols, our discussion is still relevant. Accordingly, this section presents current ISO concepts regarding the application layer.

Communication Between Application Processes

In order for application processes to communicate with one another, each must have information which is meaningful to the other. For example, a jet pilot and a horse rider have very little to talk about except perhaps the weather. All of the information associated with an application process is known as the **universe of discourse** of that application. Thus, communicating application processes must have their universes of discourse overlapping one another.

Formally, a *universe of discourse* is described by a **conceptual schema,** which is simply a data structure defining the information that makes up the universe of discourse. Typically, a *conceptual schema* is a portion of a process that contains *type* and *variable definitions*. Thus, the conceptual schema does not involve the code that is related to message transfer. Figure 10.2 shows a section of an ADA program which represents the *conceptual schema* of an application process associated with machine monitoring in a cell controller.

Two application processes are said to **interwork** if they are able to communicate with one another. Thus, two application processes are able to interwork only if their *conceptual schemas* overlap. The overlapped portion of a conceptual schema is referred to as the **shared conceptual schema,** or simply **shared schema.** Determining whether conceptual schemas overlap involves identifying the same *logical information* in both conceptual schemas. For example, conceptual schema A may use a variable, ss#, to represent an individual's social security number, and conceptual schema B may use the variable social_n to also represent a social security number. Thus, we can

```
declare
    type machine_state is (disconnect, halt, off, error, standby,
                    cycling, unload, busy, load);
    type part is
        record
            name : string(1..80);
            number : string(1..80);
            supplier : string(1..30);
            daily_use : integer;
            amount : integer;
        end record;

    m_number : string(1..9);      — machine identification
    m_name : string(1..80);       — name and function of machine
    m_type : string(1..15);       — type of machine
    m_location : string(1..80);   — location within a plant
    cyc_done : integer;           — number of completed cycles to date
    m_status : machine_state;     — state of machine
    m_part : part;                — part needed to supply machine
    on_hand : integer;            — actual number of parts on hand
```

Figure 10.2 Section of ADA program showing the conceptual schema for a machine monitoring application process.

```
                m_number : string(1..9);
                m_name : string(1..80);
                m_type : string(1..15);
                m_location : string(1..80);
                m_cost : float;
                supplier_name : string(1..80);
                supplier_phone : string(1..10);
```

Figure 10.3 Conceptual schema for the process *inventory*.

identify that ss# and social_n both represent the same logical information; thus, the corresponding conceptual schemas overlap.

Interworking simply involves the conditions under which application processes can communicate, and it does not indicate how the communication is to take place. Obviously, some portions of application processes involving some statements in a programming language must be responsible for message communication. However, how those portions are defined fall outside of the OSI reference model.

Example

Consider another application process for inventory control applications called *inventory*. Figure 10.3 is a possible conceptual schema associated with the *inventory* application process.

Example

Consider still another application process for performing machine maintenance, called *maintenance*, with its conceptual schema shown in Figure 10.4:

Example

Find the shared schema for the application processes *machine monitoring* and *inventory*, as described previously.

Solution Since the shared schema is simply the intersection of the conceptual schemas that correspond to the application processes, it can be obtained by inspection from Figs. 10.2 and 10.3. The answer is

```
        shared_schema = {m-number, m_name, m_type, m_location}
```

In our discussion, the location of the *shared schema* is irrelevant on a computer network, in that it could be located in its entirety in either process, or partitioned in both processes, or it could be located in a third location remote from either process. Obviously, depending upon where portions of the shared schema are actually located, application processes must access them accordingly.

In order for distributed application processes to do their job, (i.e., perform a global application) they need to communicate information regarding their corresponding *shared schema*. The information associated with a shared schema basically consists of object definitions (e.g., type and variable

```
        m_name : string(1..9);
        m_location : string(1..80);
        last_maint : string(1..6);  — date of last maintenance
        next_maint : string(1..6);  — date of next maintenance
```

Figure 10.4 Conceptual schema of the process *maintenance*.

definitions), object values (e.g., 94KJ4, Grinder #5, off, etc) and operations on the objects (e.g., read four variables associated with the *maintenance* process, send this variable to the *inventory* process).

Application layer protocols are rules and formats concerned with communicating object definitions, object values, and operations on the objects. The *shared schema* can be viewed as being made up of objects and it could correspond to two or more application processes.

Sometimes, the *shared conceptual schema* is large enough that it is advantageous to decompose it into groups referred to as **application contexts,** which are depicted in Figure 10.5. For example, one application context may involve file transfer, while another may involve process management, and still another may involve electronic mail. The criterion for decomposing a shared schema into *application contexts* depends on the specific end user application (hence the name). The idea is to have application contexts contain information that is specific to certain applications. Thus, when interpreting an application context one must not only pay attention to the information that it contains, but also the framework in which the information is used (i.e., the context).

Example

For the applications discussed previously, find the application contexts that correspond to communications between a) the *maintenance* and *inventory* application processes, and b) the *inventory* and *machine monitoring* application processes.

Solution Since an application context is a subset of the shared schema of the corresponding processes, there are many application contexts that can be defined, depending upon how the shared schema is partitioned. The solution presented is just one of many other possibilities.

a) context_1 (maintenance, inventory) = {m_name}

b) context_2 (inventory, machine monitoring) = {m_number, m_type, m_location}

End user application processes basically perform two types of functions; those that are communications related and those that are not. Those aspects of application processes dealing with communication-related functions are referred to as **application entities.** Thus, communication be-

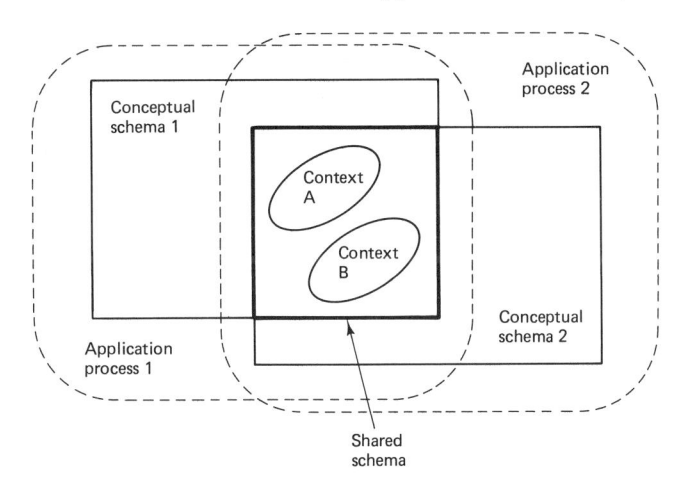

Figure 10.5 Decomposition of conceptual schemas into application contexts.

tween application processes can be modeled as communication between *application entities*, as depicted in Figure 10.6. One advantage of partitioning application processes into two major components is that application layer protocols can now deal with just application entities rather than entire *application processes*, which are much more general. Furthermore, the noncommunication aspects of *application processes* may cause some confusion if communication protocols were to deal directly with *application processes*.

Application entities are actually part of the application layer. Thus, as shown in Figure 10.6, our model of an application process is rather peculiar in that its communication component (i.e., application entity) resides in the application layer, and its noncommunication component (i.e., the rest of the application process) resides outside the seven layer OSI reference model. The model just described separates application process functions solely from a logical standpoint, to make it easier to discuss those aspects that are network-related from those that are not. Actual implementations, which may or may not reflect this decomposition in an explicit fashion, are not discussed here.

Unlike the session and presentation layers, which provide generic network services, the application layer must support a wide variety of end user distributed applications, such as: message service, distributed databases, virtual terminal, file transfer, manufacturing applications, graphics, and others. Thus, there is a potentially large list of application layer protocols with relatively few protocols for the presentation, session, transport, and network layers. From the discussion in the physical and data link chapters, there is also a potentially large list of physical and data link layer standards, giving a structure shown in Figure 10.7 and known as the *wineglass structure*.

Because of the wide variety of end user applications to be supported by the application layer, an *application entity* is further decomposed into a set of **application service elements** (ASEs), with each *service element* supporting a specific application, such as file transfer or electronic mail. *Application service elements* are a coherent set of integrated functions useful for providing interwork capabilities to *application entities*. It can be envisioned that there is a separate *application service element* per specific application protocol. Currently, ISO is developing *application service elements* for file transfer, virtual terminal, job transfer, distributed databases, document transfer, and others. *Application service elements* are also depicted in Figure 10.6.

As noted, in order for the two application processes to communicate with one another, there must be some kind of cooperation between the application processes and hence between the corresponding application entities. The cooperative relationship between two *application entities* is referred to as the **application association** (AA). An *application association* is formed by exchanging control information by making use of the services offered by the presentation layer. The management

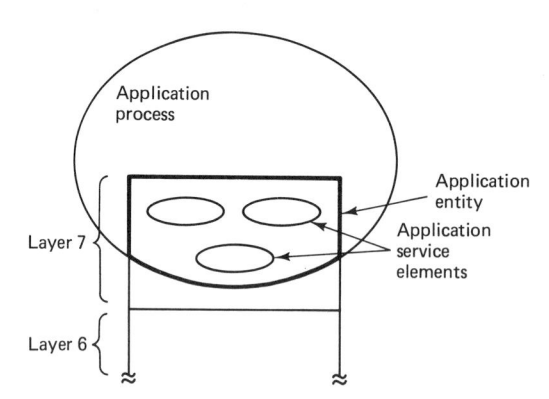

Figure 10.6 Decomposition of end user application processes into communication-related functions (application entity) and non-communication-related functions.

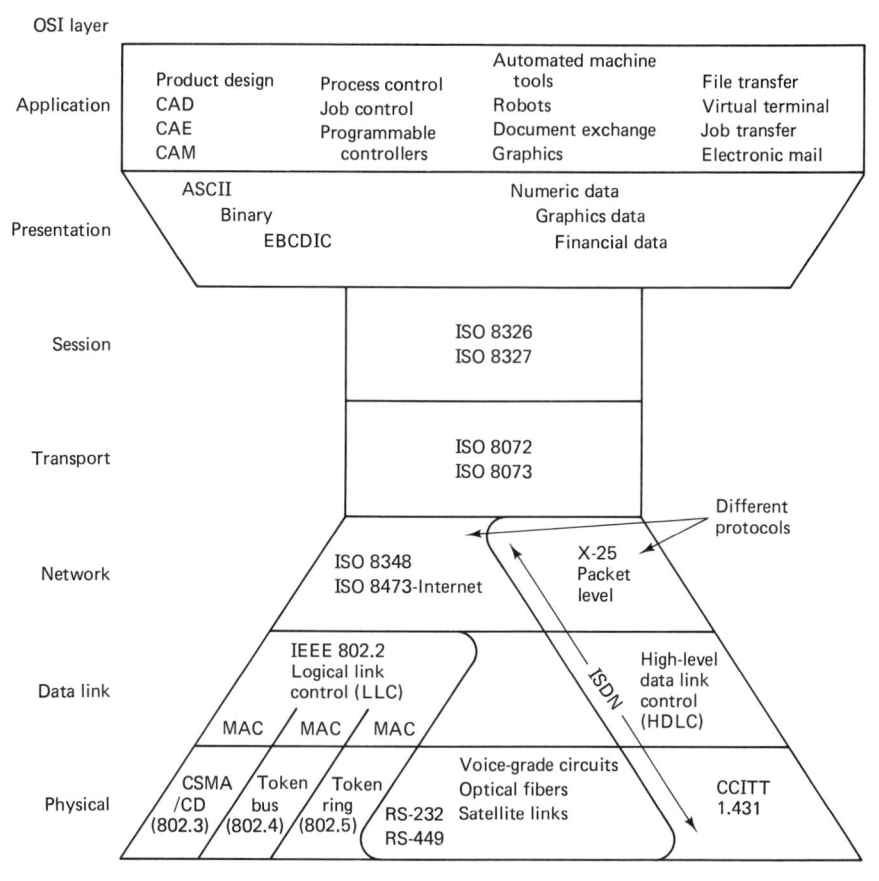

Figure 10.7 Standardized Protocol choices at different OSI layers appear as a "wineglass" structure.

of *application associations* is performed by an **association control service element** (ACSE), which includes the establishment of an *application context*. An association control service element is used to provide a single *association control* function, that is, a relationship between only two application entities. Providing multiple *association control* functions requires other means in addition to the ones discussed thus far, and is not discussed in this book.

10.3 ASSOCIATION CONTROL SERVICE ELEMENT (ACSE)

In the early days of telephony, telephone users communicated with one another with the help of telephone operators, who actually set up a circuit connection between the two communicating parties. In those days, you simply lifted up the telephone sets, which were directly connected to the branch offices where operators were located. You supplied the number of the party you wished to communicate with, and the operator attempted to perform the connection. If lines were busy, you were cordially asked to wait or try again later. ACSE is a component of the application layer that provides

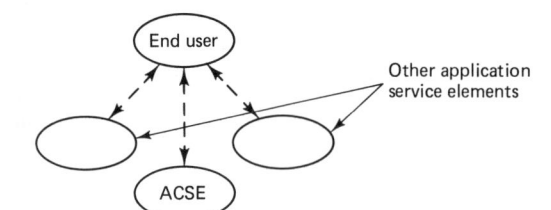

Figure 10.8 Services provided by ACSE are complemented by other application service elements.

similar services of telephone operators of the past, namely establishing a connection so that application processes can communicate with one another successfully.

Application processes may wish to communicate with one another for a variety of reasons. Regardless of the reasons for communications, certain services must always be provided. For example, if a connection-oriented service is provided, it is always necessary to establish the connection first, then use the connection for data transfer and at the appropriate time release the connection.

Like most OSI layers, application layer protocols can be connection-oriented or connectionless. If the protocol is connection-oriented, application layer protocols must establish an application layer connection between application entities before communicating the object definitions, object values, and operations on the objects that make up the *shared schema*. Thus, an *application association* can be thought of as an application layer connection between two application entities.

The **association control service element** (ACSE) is a major constituent element of an application layer protocol, which provides facilities for the establishment and release of *application associations*. Since ACSE has no mechanisms for communicating user information,[1] it is up to other constituent elements of an application layer protocol to include mechanisms for communicating information. It is intended that the functions provided by ACSE (i.e., management of application associations) must be complemented by other application service elements in order to provide a complete set of communication functions to an end user. Thus, whereas the services provided by ACSE are generic in nature, the services provided by other application service elements are more specific to the application in question. This situation is depicted in Figure 10.8.

The minimum functionality that the *association control service element* requires from the presentation layer is that of the presentation *kernel functional unit*. Other application service elements are required to coordinate their use of presentation layer services with the association control service element.

While establishing an association, the requestor has control over certain options in using the presentation and session services. Examples of options available to the association requestor include single or multiple *presentation context facility* and *session functional units*. Of course, the association requestor must obey all the rules of the underlying presentation and session layers. For example, if half-duplex communication is used at the session layer, then *data tokens* are required. In this case, the association requestor must define the data token that will regulate the half-duplex communication.

Thus, since other application service elements normally use ACSE to establish an application association prior to other communication activities, it is up to the application service element to coordinate the use of the presentation and session layer services by means of ACSE. As an example, the FTAM protocol can negotiate the *presentation context* to be used in their communication when requesting the establishment of an application association.

---

[1] Actually, the user has the option of sending a limited amount of information while establishing or releasing the connection.

10.3.1 Overview of the Service Definition

Four services make up the *association control service element*: A_ASSOCIATE, A_RELEASE, A_ABORT, and A_P_ABORT. The first two establish and release (with no loss of data) an *application association*, whereas the last two abort services release the application association with possible loss of data. A_ABORT is initiated by the service *user*, whereas A_P_ABORT is initiated by the service *provider*. Following established nomenclature, the first letter in the preceding service names (i.e., the A) indicates that the service is offered by the application layer. The remaining portion of the service name is chosen to give an indication as to the kind of service offered.

The A_ASSOCIATE is a confirmed service used for establishing an application association between two *application entities* under a specified *application context*. The application context is useful for identifying options, parameters, and the framework within which application processes communicate. Thus, the three most important parameters of the A_ASSOCIATE service are the name of the application entity making the service request, the name of the application entity containing the intended responder, and the name of the proposed *application context*, denoted respectively by cg_ae_title, cd_ae_title, and a_ctxt_nam.

Other useful parameters of the A_ASSOCIATE service include the name of the application entity which actually responds to the service request in case of failures, optional information transferred during the association establishment, and the status of the service call, denoted respectively by r_ae_title, *info*, and *res*. The parameter names used in this section are intended for illustration purposes only. However, the names correspond to the actual agreed parameter names as used in the standard. For example, *r_ae_title* stands for *responding application entity title*, as defined in the standard. Since the objective of this section is to give an overview of the nature of the services offered by ACSE, the service primitives are illustrated via examples similar to procedure calls. The examples give an idea of the parameters used in the primitive, and an indication on the nature of the parameters. However, the examples do not give a precise service definition as far as optional parameters and detailed actions are concerned, for which the reader is referred to the appropriate ISO standard (ISO 8649/2).

Since A_ASSOCIATE is a confirmed service, it consists of the following four primitives:

```
A_ASSOCIATE.req (cg_ae_title, cd_ae_title, a_ctxt_nam, info, cg_p_addr, cd_p_
                addr, sing_p_ctxt, p_ctxt_def_lst, dft_p_ctxt_nam, qos, p_req,
                s_req, i_sync_pnt_ser_n, i_assgn_tok, s_conn_id)

A_ASSOCIATE.ind (cg_ae_title, cd_ae_title, a_ctxt_nam, info, cg_p_addr,
                cd_p_addr, sing_p_ctxt, p_ctxt_def_lst, p_ctxt_def_res,
                dft_p_ctxt_nam, dft_p_ctxt_res, qos, p_req, s_req,
                i_sync_pnt_ser_n, i_assgn_tok, s_conn_id)

A_ASSOCIATE.resp (r_ae_title, a_ctxt_nam, info, res, r_p_addr,
                 p_ctxt_def_res, dft_p_ctxt_res, qos, p_req, s_req,
                 i_sync_pnt_ser_n, i_assgn_tok, s_conn_id)

A_ASSOCIATE.ind (r_ae_title, a_ctxt_nam, info, res, r_p_addr,
                p_ctxt_def_res, dft_p_ctxt_res, qos, p_req, s_req,
                i_sync_pnt_ser_n, i_assgn_tok, s_conn_id)
```

where:

cg_p_addr, cd_p_addr, and r_p_addr identify, respectively, the *calling presentation address*, the *called presentation address*, and the actual *responding presentation address* (in case of failure). The optional parameter sing_p_ctxt identifies a defined single or default *presentation context*. If this parameter is absent, the *multiple defined context facility* is used. The remaining parameters p_ctxt_def_lst, p_ctxt_def_res, dft_p_ctxt_nam, qos, p_req, s_req, i_sync_pnt_ser_n, i_assgn_ tok, and s_conn_id correspond to the same parameters defined in the ISO presentation service standard, and stand for *presentation context definition list, presentation context definition result, default presentation context name, quality of service, presentation requirement, session requirement, initial synchronization point serial number, initial assignment of tokens*, and *session connection identifier*, respectively.

The A_RELEASE is a confirmed service used for releasing an application association that exists between two *application entities*. Since an application association can only exist between two unique *application entities*, there is no need to identify the *application entities* explicitly in the A_RELEASE, A_ABORT, and A_P_ABORT services. This is similar to an office environment where the president of company A is communicating with the president of company B using an application association, with each office having just one telephone (no conference call is assumed). The association at office A is probably set up by an office assistant or secretary. When the president of company A requests that the connection be released, it is not necessary to identify the connection by name, since there is just one; nor is it necessary that the president of company A identifies the connection by naming the name of the president of company B, since it is understood who the communicating parties are.

Because the A_RELEASE is a confirmed service, it consists of the following four primitives:

$$A\_RELEASE.req\ (reason,\ user\_info)$$

$$A\_RELEASE.ind\ (reason,\ user\_info)$$

$$A\_RELEASE.resp\ (reason,\ user\_info,\ res)$$

$$A\_RELEASE.con\ (reason,\ user\_info,\ res)$$

the request primitive or the values *normal, not finished*, or *undefined* when it is used on the response primitive. The meaning of the *user_info* parameter depends on the *application context* that is in effect. The *res* parameter can take the values *affirmative* or *negative*.

The A_ABORT and A_P_ABORT services are used for abnormally terminating an *application association* by the service user and service provider, respectively. Whereas the A_ABORT service is unconfirmed, the A_P_ABORT is neither confirmed nor unconfirmed. The A_P_ABORT consists of just an indication primitive which originates at the service provider and is directed towards the service user. An example of an abnormal termination of an application association occurs when an application process is involved in a long transaction with another application process and is not willing to wait until the transaction is complete in order to release the connection.

The A_P_ABORT service is useful when there is a failure in the underlying layers (e.g., a modem failure) and the service provider abruptly terminates the connection and informs the user

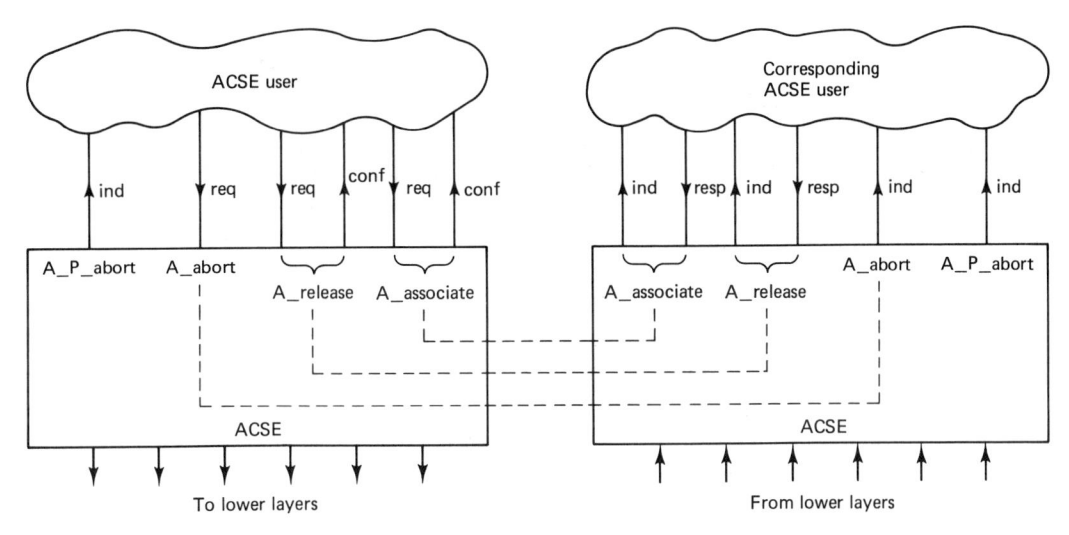

Figure 10.9 ACSE services as generated by a user and directed to a corresponding user.

accordingly. In our previous example, this is analogous to the secretary at company A after realizing that the line is down, gives up (i.e., terminates the connection), and simply informs president A that its connection has been terminated temporarily. Meanwhile, at company B, the secretary after many unsuccessful attempts in using the connection with president A also gives up, terminates the connection, and informs president B accordingly.

Since the A_ABORT is an unconfirmed service, it consists of the following two primitives:

A_ABORT.req (user_info)

A_ABORT.ind (abort_source, user_info)

where the abort_source parameter identifies the source initiating the abort, which can be an ACSE *service provider* or a *requestor*. The meaning of the user_info parameter depends on the *application context* that is in effect. The A_P_ABORT parameters are mapped directly from those in the presentation P_P_ABORT service.

Figure 10.9 illustrates all the primitives supported by ACSE as requested by an ACSE user and directed to a corresponding ACSE user. Notice that whereas the services for A_ABORT, A_RELEASE, and A_ASSOCIATE are paired, the A_P_ABORT service is self-contained.

10.4 THE MANUFACTURING MESSAGE SPECIFICATION

The **Manufacturing Message Specification** (MMS)[2] is a specific application layer protocol (formally, an application service element) which enables communication among intelligent devices found in manufacturing applications. Examples of intelligent devices include vision systems, robots, programmable logic controllers (PLC's),[3] numerically controlled (NC) machines, coordinate mea-

---

[2] The version of MMS discussed in this chapter corresponds to draft 7 which is current the ISO 9605 (DIS).

[3] The International Electrotechnical Committee (IEC) refers to the PLC as just *Programmable Controller* (*PC*).

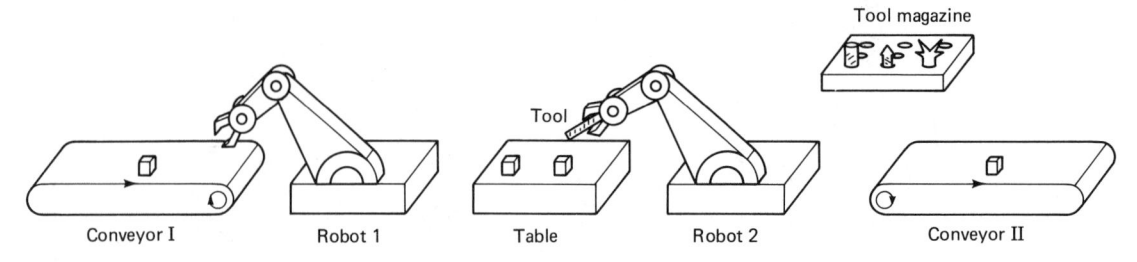

Figure 10.10 A multiple robot assembly system (MRAS).

surement machines (CMM's) and others. Thus, the services provided by MMS are specific to automated manufacturing applications.

MMS is part of the MAP 3.0 specification and it is also being reviewed by the (Electronics Industry Association) EIA for release as the RS-511 standard. Previous MAP specifications (e.g., 2.1 and 2.2) referenced a predecessor of MMS known as the Manufacturing Message Format Standard (MMFS). MMS contains additional functionality as compared with MMFS. However, the major distinction between the two protocols is the way in which the PDUs are described and encoded with the MMS protocol being more generic and more powerful. The description of MMS protocol data units is done using the ASN.1 syntax notation, and the encoding is performed using the ASN.1 encoding rules. Appendix D contains an example of how a specific MMS protocol data unit is described and encoded. As with other chapters in this book, in this chapter we concentrate on MMS services and their semantics rather than syntax.

A *client-server* model is used by MMS to describe its services with the *client* issuing requests for services to be performed by the *server*. In one message, the client issues one service request and the server responds with the disposition or outcome of the request in a different message.

In order to understand the environment in which MMS is used, the following section presents an example of a simple manufacturing facility.

10.4.1 A Multiple Robot Assembly System

A **multiple robot assembly system** (MRAS) is an important component of modern manufacturing systems. A MRAS is a system composed of two or more robots that cooperate in performing an assembly function. Typically, the robots of a MRAS are configured in a *manufacturing cell*. The manufacturing cell may incorporate other components such as conveyors, automated guided vehicles, tool magazines, computers, etc.

An example of a manufacturing cell which incorporates an MRAS is depicted in Figure 10.10. Robot 1 picks up parts from conveyor I and put the parts on the table, which has only room for two parts. Robot 2 performs some operation on the parts located on the table such as inserting four screws in each part. When finished, robot 2 puts the parts on conveyor II which is assumed to be continuously moving. We further assume that the manufacturing cell[4] operates under the following constraints:

---

[4] A more generic term for a MRAS such as the one described here is a *manufacturing cell* which is discussed in chapter 11.

- When the number of parts on the table reaches 2, both robot 1 and conveyor 1 should stop.
- When there are no parts on the table, robot 2 should stop.
- When there are no parts ready to pick up from conveyor I, robot 1 should stop.

Cell controller. Since we are interested in automated manufacturing, the operations involved in the manufacturing cell should take place in an automated fashion. Functions responsible for the automated execution of operations in the manufacturing cell is referred to as the **cell control functions.**

Although *cell control functions* in a network environment can be implemented in a *centralized* or *distributed* fashion, we consider a distributed implementation with the cell controller functions distributed in the *device controller*, *robot 1* and *robot 2*. A centralized implementation of the cell control functions have all functions located in one device commonly known as the **cell controller.** As shown in Figure 10.11, the manufacturing cell is configured around three network stations: device controller, robot 1 and robot 2. In addition, Figure 10.11 also includes an additional station called the *supervisory controller*, which although not part of the manufacturing cell, serves as the interface between the cell and the rest of the manufacturing facility. It is assumed that all stations have appropriate interfaces with the network.

Some devices which are not considered intelligent are not connected directly to the network. Rather, they interface with particular stations which in turn are connected with the network. In Figure 10.11, conveyors I and II, the table, the tool magazine, and the *operator terminal* interface directly with the device controller. The interface involves appropriate sensors that indicate whether the conveyor is running or whether there are parts on the table, and actuators used to perform some actions such as stop or restart conveyor I.

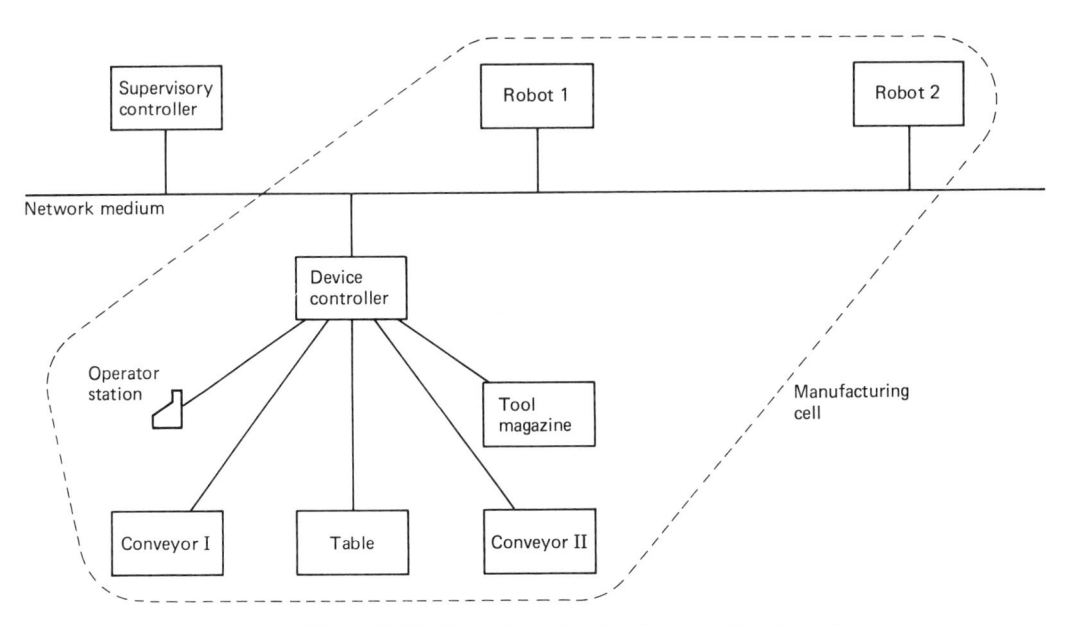

Figure 10.11 Network configuration for a manufacturing cell.

Sec. 10.4   The Manufacturing Message Specification

10.4.2 Application Layer Functionality

This section briefly addresses the application layer functionality which is required by the manufacturing cell. In other words, what service functionality should the network provide so that the manufacturing cell can perform its functions in an effective and simple way. Network requirements are further discussed in Chapter 14. Obviously, some software is responsible for controlling robots 1 and 2. Likewise, software is responsible for performing the device controller functions and supervisory controller functions as it relates to the manufacturing cell. Let the software processes which control robots 1 and 2 be referred to as *robot_1* and *robot_2* respectively. From the software standpoint, the situation is depicted in Figure 10.12 where the software components at each station are configured as *processes*. Since all processes in Figure 10.12 collectively cooperate towards a common goal (i.e., control of the manufacturing cell), they share some information. Obviously, information shared by processes needs to flow from process to process. The dotted lines in Figure 10.12 indicate communication links where shared information can flow.

When a process references a variable defined within itself or defined within other processes residing at the same network station, the variable is known as a **local variable.** When the variable referenced by the process is defined within a process residing at a different network station, the variable is known as a **remote variable.** Accessing *local variables* does not require a computer network. Local variables are referenced through the *programming language* in which the process is written or through the *operating system* residing at the local network station.

In order for application processes such as those of Figure 10.12, to collectively perform distributed application functions we require the following functionality:

- Variable access
- Message passing
- Resource sharing (synchronization)
- Program management
- Event management
- Other functions

10.4.3 Variable Access

Variable access is one of the most fundamental requirements in a distributed environment. An example of variable access for the processes in Figure 10.12 involves accessing the number of parts (*num_part_table1*) on the table which we assume to be defined by the robot_1 process. The robot_2 process needs to access *num_part_table1* since it must stop robot 2 when the table is empty.

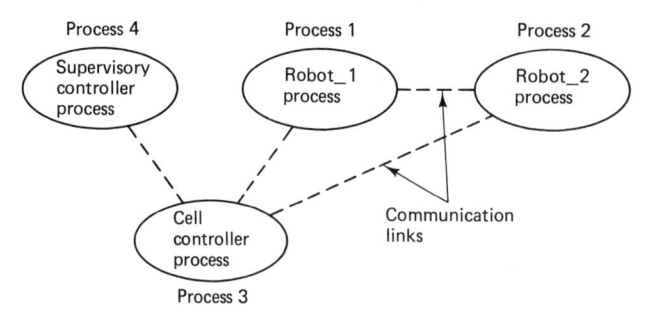

Figure 10.12 Process interaction in the manufacturing cell.

Robot 1 process

type t_nparts **is** integer **range** 0..2;
num_part_table1 : t_nparts;

.
.
.

if num_part_table1 = 2 **then**
    stop_robot1_proc;
else
.
.

Robot 2 process

type t_nparts **is** integer **range** 0..2;
num_part_table2 : t_nparts;

.
.

if num_part_table2 = 0 **then**
    stop_robot2_proc;
else
.
.

Figure 10.13 Processes for controlling robots 1 and 2.

Likewise, the robot_1 process needs to access *num_part_table1* since it must stop robot 1 when there are two parts on the table. A typical program organization for the robot_1 and robot_2 processes is shown in Figure 10.13, where stop_robot1_proc and stop_robot2_proc are appropriate procedures that stop robots 1 and 2 respectively and the dots indicate that the process have other program portions which are irrelevant for our discussion. Notice that the robot_1 and robot_2 processes use different names for the same logical information representing the number of parts on the table. Whereas num_part_table1 is a remote variable for the robot_2 process, it is a local variable for the robot_1 process. Since the num_part_table1 variable is defined within the robot_1 process, it is also a local variable for any other process residing in the same station as the robot_1 process.

The processes of Figure 10.13 both access the variable representing the number of parts on the table, which is referenced as *num_part_table1* by the robot_1 process and *num_part_table2* by the robot_2 process. Since the processes reside in different network stations, some mechanisms are needed so that *data types* and *variable values* can be remotely accessed. In addition, some management operations associated with the variables, such as creating or deleting variables, and creating or deleting data types are also needed.

MMS provides the following variable access services for allowing processes to access remote variables.[5]

- Define Named Type: Allows a client to define data types on a server. For example, the robot1 process can use this service to define the type *t_nparts on the robot_2 process*.

---

[5] When describing MMS services, because of space considerations, we describe only the most significant services. Likewise, we do not include the associated service parameters.

Robot 1 process

type t_nparts **is** integer **range** 0..2;   — local type definition
Define_Named_Type (t_nparts **is** integer range 0..2;);   — remote type definition
num_part_table1: t_parts;   — local variable definition
Define_Named_Variable (num_part_table2 : t_parts;);   — remote
                                                                    — variable definition[6]

.
.
if num_part_table1 = 0 **then**
    stop_robot1_proc;
else
.
.

Robot 2 process

:
If num_part_table2 = 2 **then**
    stop_robot2_proc;
else
.
.

Figure 10.14 Remote type and variable definitions.

- Delete Named Type: Erases a type name (e.g., *t_nparts*) previously defined at a server.

- Get Named Type Attributes: Allows a client to obtain data type attributes associated with symbolic names at a server. For example, the robot_2 process can use this service to obtain the type attributes of the *num_part_table1* variable which is remotely defined.

- Define Named Variable: Allows a client to define variables on a server. For example, the robot_1 process can use this service to define the name *num_part_table2* on the robot_2 process. As noted earlier, local variables can be defined using the programming language in which the process is coded.

- Delete Variable Access: Erases variable names (e.g., *num_part_table1*) previously defined at a server.

- Read: Allows a client to read the values of one or more remote variables defined at a server.

- Write: Allows a client to change the values of one or more remote variables defined at a server.

- Information Report: Allows a client to send some information to a peer process without being queried. The information sent is quite restricted in that it takes the form of a set consisting of one or more variables names and their associated values.

Using appropriate *MMS remote variable access services* the program layout for the robot_1 and robot_2 processes is shown in Figure 10.14.

[6] It is assumed that the data type and variable name are defined at the process having an *application association* with the process using the MMS service.

Notice that the robot_2 process does not need to provide definitions for the data type, nor variable since they are defined remotely by the robot_1 process using MMS services.

10.4.4 Message Passing

One can think of the *Read*, *Write*, and *Information Report* services of MMS as being examples of message passing in which the message takes the form of a set of variable names and their corresponding values. There are situations when it is desirable to send more generic information that involve more than just variables. For example, the message could include data for a program, actual program code, variable attributes such as *limit switch 7*, *conveyor number 12*, or an operator message such as *please order more widgets, current amount about to be depleted*.

Basically messages can be passed between two processes or between one process and specialized devices such as an operator's console. Depending upon the nature and size of the message to be passed, process to process message passing can take the form of file transfer or domain transfer.

As the name implies, message passing through *file transfer* means that the message is read from a file and transferred to another file located on a different station. On the other hand, *domain transfer* assumes that the message resides as segments in main memory. Process A uses a service that can transfer the message from main memory on the source station to main memory on the destination station where it could be used by process B. Both approaches have advantages and disadvantages. The advantage of *domain transfer* is that it is very efficient since there is no overhead in opening, closing and reading files. An advantage of message passing through file transfer is that large messages could be handled easily.

MMS provides services for message passing using the *domain transfer* method and a specialized message transfer method between an application process and an operator's console referred to as **operator communications.** MMS does not standardize message passing through *file transfer* although a set of file management services is provided as an appendix to the MMS standard.

The MMS domain management services include:

Initiate Download Sequence: This service is requested by a client process to instruct a server process to create a domain and to begin its loading.

Download Segment: A server process can use this service to request that a segment of information be transferred by a client process.

Terminate Download Sequence: Once the domain transfer operation is complete, the server process can use the *Terminate Download Sequence* service to indicate to a client process that the download sequence is completed.

The following three services have semantics similar to the preceding ones except that they deal with a domain upload rather than a domain download: *Initiate Upload Sequence*, *Upload Segment*, and *Terminate Upload Sequence*.

10.4.5 Resource Sharing

In the manufacturing cell of Figure 10.10, the working table is considered to be a *shared resource* since it can be used simultaneously by robot 1 and robot 2. In order for the cell to operate correctly, robots 1 and 2 must synchronize (coordinate) their use of the shared resource (i.e., the table).

Example

Consider a manufacturing cell similar to the one in Figure 10.10 except that a third robot is added which shares some tools with robot 2. Therefore, the tools in the tool magazine shared by robots 2 and 3 are considered to be *shared resources*.

The shared resource access problem. Great care must be exercised when using a *shared resource*. In a loosely coupled distributed system, variables are used to represent the status of a shared resource thus care must be taken when accessing the *shared variable*. The problems that could arise can be explained with reference to Figure 10.12. Suppose that we configure our software system as several processes with some of them running at different stations in the network. Since robot 1 should be stopped when the number of parts on the table reaches 2, the program layout for the robot_1 process is configured as shown in Figure 10.15(a). Likewise, since robot 2 should be stopped when there are no parts on the table, the program layout for the robot_2 process is configured as shown in Figure 10.15(b).

The statement n_part_table2 = Read(n_part_table1), uses the MMS primitive *Read* to obtain a copy of the value of the remote variable *n_part_table1* and assign it to the local variable *n_part_table2*. Likewise, the statement Write(n_part_table1) = n_part_table2, assigns the value of the local variable n_part_table2 to the remote variable n_part_table1.

To illustrate the specific problems that could arise when the software is configured as in Figure 10.15(a) and (b) let us make a few assumptions about the general environment in which the overall system operates. The assumptions are listed following.

- The Robot_2 process runs much faster than the robot_1 process. This assumption also implies that robot_2 is much faster than robot_1.

- Since the robot_1 and robot_2 processes run on different network stations, they proceed at their own pace, independent of one another, and make no assumptions whatsoever about the speed of the other process. Thus they are examples of *asynchronous concurrent processes*.

The first problem that can arise is that both robots can collide because there are no checks performed before each process can issue the corresponding procedure involving the shared resource (i.e., put_part_proc or get_part_proc). The reader may think that the solution of this problem is very straightforward, simply involving the use of appropriate variables to let the other process know if one robot is in the area where they could collide. However, as discussed in subsection 7.2.3 by just testing a variable to see if it is safe to perform an *action* is not enough.

The second problem that can arise is that if things happen at the wrong time, the system will not work correctly. Let us assume that robot 1 puts one part on the table and simultaneously, robot 2 takes one part from the table. Let us further assume that robot_1 just finished putting the part on the table and now the robot_1 process is executing the instruction n_part_table1 + 1. This instruction is a high level instruction which must be compiled (or translated) into a machine level instruction before the computer can actually execute it. Let us suppose that the compiler generates code which is organized in the following manner:

(a) Read current value of n_part_table1 from memory and put it into a CPU register.
(b) Increment the contents of the CPU register by 1. By now, the CPU register contents is (n_part_table1 + 1).
(c) Store the contents of the register in the location for the variable n_part_table1.

Robot_1 Process

```
task body robot_1 is
    .
    .
    .
    while n_part_table1 = 2 loop      — n_part_table1 is a local
                                      — variable for the robot_1 process
        wait_proc;                    — wait_proc is a procedure that
                                      — waits a short time.
    end loop;
    put_part_proc;          — procedure for instructing robot 1 to
                            — to put a part on the table.
                            — Procedure ends by stopping robot 1.
    n_part_table1 := n_part_table1 + 1;
    .
    .
    .
    end robot_1;
```

(a)

Robot_2 Process

```
task body robot_2 is
    .
    .
    .
    n_part_table2 := Read(n_part_table1);   — MMS primitive
    while n_part_table2 = 0 loop
        n_part_table2 := Read(n_part_table1);
        wait proc;
    end loop ;
    get_part_proc;          — procedure for instructing robot 2 to get
                            — a part from table and put it on conveyor II
                            — Procedure ends by stopping robot 2.
    n_part_table2 := Read(n_part_table1);   — MMS primitive
    n_part_table2 := n_part_table2 - 1;
    Write(n_part_table1) := n_part_table;   — MMS primitive
    .
    .
    .
    end robot_2;
```

(b)

Figure 10.15 Process configuration for robots 1 and 2 showing the use of MMS services.

Since we are dealing with asynchronous concurrent processes, the robot_2 process can run at the most inopportune time. Let's suppose that currently n_part_table1 = 1 and that robot_2 just finished getting the part from the table to put on conveyor II, and now the robot_2 process is about to update the n_part_table2 variable. The worst thing that could happen is for the robot_2 process to execute its Read(n_part_table1) statement right after step (a) and before step (b) above. Since we are assuming that the robot2 process is much faster than the robot_1 process, robot_2 process could execute its Write(n_part_table1); statement before step (c) of the statement n_part_table1 = n_part_table1 + 1; being executed by process 1.

Under these circumstances, the value of n_part_table1 read by the robot_2 process through the MMS Read service is 1, and thus the value written by the MMS Write service in the robot_2 process is n_part_table1 = 0. After the robot_2 process is finished with the *Write* operation, the robot_1 process executes step (c) which stores the value 2 as the new value for n_part_table1, which is the wrong value. Since at this point, robot 1 has put one part on the table, and robot 2 took one part from the table, the number of parts on the table should remain the same, that is *n_part_table1* should be 1 rather than 2 as the program would calculate.

The reason that the software configuration of Fig. 10.15 leads to errors is that the variable *n_part_table1* is allowed to be accessed by the robot_2 process *before* the robot_1 process is done updating it. What is needed is a way for the robot_1 process to prevent other processes from accessing shared variables while they are being manipulated. MMS provides such a way by supporting uninterruptible, atomic operations for preventing some processes to enter their *critical sections* while other processes are in their critical sections.

The key for solving the preceding problems consists of having special *global variables* which are manipulated by special *system instructions* in an uninterrupted and *atomic* fashion. The term *global* means that all processes in the network have access to the variable whereas the term *system instruction* means that an *operating system* rather than the end user is responsible for providing uninterrupted and atomic features of the instructions.

In MMS, depending upon the scope of the variable definition, three options exist for defining global variables. When the scope is a single *application association* (AA), a domain, or a virtual manufacturing device (VMD, discussed in section 10.4.9), the variable is said to have an *application association specific*, *a domain-specific*, *or a VMD-specific* scope respectively. Under the AA-specific option the variable has a scope only in one application association, and thus the variable can only be used by two processes. Under the domain-specific option, the variable has a scope in one domain, and thus the variable can be used only by processes related to that domain.

MMS uses a *binary semaphore* for solving the simultaneous access to the critical section problem. A semaphore can be thought of a *global* variable with several uninterruptible and atomic operations defined on the variables. MMS provides several operations for *defining* and *deleting* a semaphore variable, for *gaining control* and *relinquishing control* of a semaphore variable, for reporting the *status* (i.e., available or unavailable) of a semaphore variable, for *conditioning* other services by the availability of semaphore variables, and other purposes.

The MMS semaphore management services include:

Define Semaphore: Defines a semaphore variable on a server.

Delete Semaphore: Deletes a previously defined remote semaphore variable.

Take Control: Gains control of a semaphore variable. Processes attempting to gain control of an unavailable semaphore variable are forced to wait[7] before continuing execution.

Relinquish Control: Releases a semaphore variable. Only one of the processes waiting on the just released semaphore variable can gain control of it.

---

[7] Other nomenclature used instead of wait is *suspend*, *block*, or *sleep*.

Report Semaphore Status: Used to obtain the status (i.e., availabiity) of an already defined semaphore variable.

Since a semaphore variable is a system variable, several actions happen automatically whenever an event associated with the semaphore happens. For example, if a process releases a semaphore variable, only one of the waiting processes is given control of the semaphore automatically.

Using the semaphore services provided by MMS, Figure 10.16 shows the program structure of the robot_1 and robot_2 processes that avoid the problems that existed with the previous version of these processes. An important relationship exists between semaphores and the variables that it controls. In Figure 10.16, it is assumed that the semaphore named *table_semaph* is used to control access to the shared variable *n_part_table1* which in turn allows access to use the *shared resource* (i.e., the table). Since the variables n_part_table1 and n_part_table2 are controlled by the table_semaph semaphore, every time either variable is accessed, the corresponding process must perform a *Take Control* operation. Likewise, when another process is done using the variables n_part_table1 or n_part_table2, it must perform a *Relinquish Control* so that other processes can access the variable.

Robot_1 Process

task body robot_1 **is**
 .
 .
 .
Define Semaphore (table_semaph);   — It is assumed that the
                                         — semaphore table_semaph is defined on
                                         — process that has an application
                                         — association with robot_1
                                         — (i.e., the robot_2 process).
Take Control (table_semaph, prio1); — Robot_1 requests control
                                         — of the table_semaph semaphore with a priority
                                         — specified with *prio1*.
while n_part_table1 = 2 **loop**
    Relinquish Control(table_semaph);   — releases the table_semaph
                                            — so that other processes can use it.
    wait_proc;
    Take Control (table_semaph, prio1);
end loop ;
Relinquish Control (table_semaph);
put_part_proc;   — procedure to put parts on table
Take Control (table_semaph, prio1);
n_part_table1 := n_part_table1 + 1;
Relinquish Control(table_semaph);
 .
 .
 .
end robot_1;

Figure 10.16 Processes for robot_1 and robot_2 using semaphore services.

Robot_2 Process

task body Robot_2 **is**

.
.
.

Take Control(table_semaph, prio2);   — assumes that Take Control
                                          — checks if semaphore variable is local or remote
n_part_table2 := **Read**(n_part_table1);
while n_part_table2 = 0 **loop**
    Relinquish Control(table_semaph);
    wait proc;
    Take Control(table_semaph, prio2);
    n_part_table2 := **Read**(n_part_table1);
end loop ;
Relinquish Control(table_semaph);
get_part_proc;
Take Control(table_semaph,prio2);
n_part_table2 := **Read**(n_part_table1);
n_part_table2 := n_part_table2 − 1;
Write(n_part_table1) := n_part_table2;
Relinquish Control(table_semaph);

.
.
.

end robot_2;

(b)

Figure 10.16 (*continued*)

10.4.6 Program Management

As noted in Chapter 7, some manufacturing applications can benefit from a system which is capable of handling several *processes* (or *tasks*) concurrently, that is, a *multitasking system*. Also recall that the basic feature of a multitasking system is the ability of *processes* to control one another. The MMS program management services basically support a multitasking system by providing operations which permit to *create*, *start*, *stop*, *resume*, and *manage* programs (i.e., processes).

Figure 10.17 shows a simplified program *state transition diagram* which is used to explain the following MMS program invocation management services:

Create Program Invocation: In general, programs need data to work with, where the data can be configured in domains. The *create program invocation* service allows the definition of domains with which a specific program is to work. As depicted in Figure 10.17, this service causes a transition from the *non-existent* state to the *idle* state.

Start: An MMS client can use this service to request the execution of a program. In terms of Figure 10.17, the start service will cause a transition from the *idle* state to the *running* state.

Stop: This service allows an MMS client to stop the execution of a program. The stop service causes a transition from the *running* state to the *stopped* state.

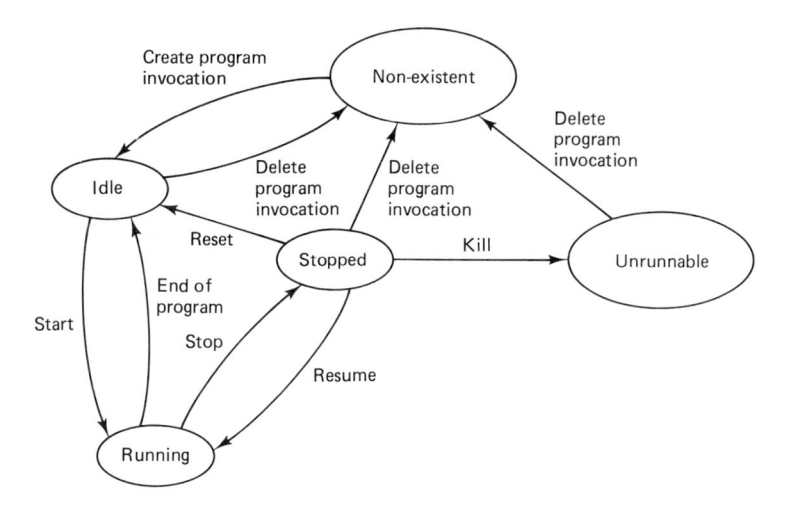

Figure 10.17 Simplified program invocation state diagram for the manufacturing message specification (MMS).

Resume: A stopped program can continue to execute, which can be accomplished using the *resume* service.

Example

Assume that process 3 in Figure 10.12 acts as the cell controller and thus the process needs to perform typical cell controller functions, such as starting a program which controls robot 1, resuming a program that controls robot 2, and stopping a currently running program named *monitor*. Process 3 can perform the preceding operations using the following:

start *robot_1*;
resume *robot_2*;
stop *monitor*;

10.4.7 Event Management

Successful operation of automated systems such as the one depicted in Figure 10.10 requires the monitoring of certain variables for the occurrence of certain events. Examples of event include the following:

- tool wear to the point where the tool is unusable
- conveyor failure
- out of limit condition on variables
- robot failure
- an alarm

An **event** can be defined as the occurrence of something noteworthy or significant for the normal operation of an application process. Events can represent deviations from safe operating limits.

Sec. 10.4   The Manufacturing Message Specification   379

Events need not only be detected but also dealt with in an appropriate fashion. Furthermore, the time to detect and the time to deal with events must be bounded. This introduces a requirement involving *real time response* for the communication system.

Associated with an event there are two additional concepts: *event condition* and *event action*. An **event condition** involves a set of rules for determining whether an event has occurred. After an event has occurred, a set of MMS operations referred to as **event actions** can be performed. Appropriate *event actions* corresponding to the events listed above are:

- change tool
- use a backup conveyor or fix failed conveyor
- report the out of limit condition
- use a backup robot or fix failed robot
- request specific alarm handling procedure

Since an event could either happen or not happen, it can be considered as a *boolean* variable.

MMS classifies event conditions as being either *monitored* or *network-triggered* events. An **monitored event condition** is used to define an event which occurs as a result of an application process performing its own monitoring without the intervention of other processes. A **network-triggered event** is used to define an event which occurs because of an explicit request of a client process using the *Trigger Event service*.

MMS defines many services for dealing with events, event conditions, event actions, and alarms in the **event management services** as summarized below:

Define Event Condition: This service does much more than what it implies (i.e., defining an event condition). In addition, it defines the *class* of the event condition (i.e., monitored or network-triggered), and further specifies the event condition by defining parameters such as the *severity*, a *priority* of this event relative to other events, an *evaluation interval*, and others.

Alter Event Condition Monitoring: Requests that a server alters the following event condition attributes: *enabled*, *priority*, and *alarm summary reports*.

Delete Event Condition: Erases an already defined event condition.

Report Event Condition Status: Obtains the status of an event condition from a server.

Define Event Action: Defines an event action at a server.

Delete Event Action: Deletes an already defined event action.

Event Notification: The *Event Notification service* is an *unconfirmed service* used by a user to notify a peer user of the occurrence of an event.

Acknowledge Event Notification: An MMS user can use this service to acknowledge a remote process the receipt of an event notification.

Trigger Event Service: Allows a client to request that a server trigger an event associated with a *network-triggered* event condition.

Get Alarm Summary: Once an alarm has occurred at the client and notified to a server, the client can use this service to request additional summary information about the current status of some event conditions.

10.4.8 Other Services

MMS also provides additional services involving *environment and general management*, *virtual manufacturing device* support, *operator communications*, and *journal management*. Since MMS is a connection oriented protocol, the *initiate* service allows to negotiate and establish a connection (i.e., an application association). Actually, in MMS terms, the environment created after the successful execution of the MMS *initiate* service by two MMS users is referred to as the **MMS environment.** In addition to the *initiate* service, the *environment and general management services* contains the *conclude*, *abort*, *cancel*, and *reject* services. Readers are referred to the Manufacturing Message Specification standard ISO 9506 parts 1 (service) and 2 (protocol), for additional details.

10.4.9 An Object Oriented View of MMS

So far, we have presented an end user view of MMS where the emphasis has been on describing the semantics of user operations which are supported by MMS. From the communication network (i.e., services and protocols) point of view, MMS basically consists of *objects* and *operations* defined on these objects. An **abstract object** can be thought of as the generalization of the concept of a variable to include programs, events, domains, and others. Each object has a *type* which is characterized by a number of *attributes*. It is the set of operations on these objects that constitutes the MMS services modifying the characteristics of an instance of an object. Some objects contain attributes which are conditional in that they are relevant to the object if and only if certain conditions (i.e., constraint) hold true.

Likewise, the MMS protocol can be thought of as the rules for exchanging object attributes. Objects defined by MMS along the several functional areas supported by the standard are listed in Table 10.1

Example

The following is a description of the MMS *program invocation* object. The description is done using a special notation similar to a record structure in ADA but with some conditional structural elements.

    Object: Program Invocation
      Key Attribute: Program Invocation Name
      Attribute: State (IDLE, STARTING, RUNNING, STOPPING,
                  STOPPED, RESUMING, RESETTING, UNRUNNABLE)
      Attribute: List of Domain References
      Attribute: MMS Deletable (TRUE, FALSE)
      Attribute: Reusable (TRUE, FALSE)
      Attribute: Monitor (TRUE, FALSE)
      Constraint: Monitor = TRUE
         Attribute: Event Condition
         Attribute: Event Action
         Attribute: Event Enrollment
      Attribute: Start Argument (initially empty)
      Attribute: Additional Detail

TABLE 10.1 MMS FUNCTIONAL AREAS AND ASSOCIATED OBJECTS

Functional area	Objects	Number of services
Environment and General Management	—	5
VMD Support	VMD	All MMS services
	Transaction	All confirmed services
Domain Management	Domain	13
Program Invocation Management	Program Invocation	8
Variable Access	Unnamed Variable	14 (Total)
	Named Variable	
	Scattered Access	
	Named Variable List	
	Named Type	
Semaphore Management	Semaphore	7 (Total)
	Semaphore Entry	
Operator Communication	Operator Communication	2
Event Management	Event Condition	19 (Total)
	Event Action	
	Event Enrollment	
Journal Management	Journal	6

The *List of Domain References* attribute contains pointers to domain objects. When the *Reusable* attribute is TRUE, a program invocation returns to the IDLE state after the program executes. The *Monitor* attribute indicates whether program monitoring is in effect for this program invocation. A program may need arguments containing initial conditions. This may be accomplished using the *Start* attribute which holds a character string to be passed to the program when started.

As noted, MMS services and protocol are based on a model of the manufacturing environment based on abstract objects. Of particular importance in MMS is the *virtual manufacturing device* (VMD) object. A VMD exists within the MMS server application process and constitutes that portion of an information processing task which makes available for control and/or monitoring a set of communication resources. Thus, a VMD is only concerned with communication issues. If an application process does not involve a VMD, it may not act as an MMS server. The VMD is an abstract representation of a specific set of resources and functionality at a real manufacturing device and a mapping of this abstract representation to the physical and functional aspects of the real manufacturing device is not defined by the standard. The VMD object is listed as follows:

```
Object: VMD
   Key Attribute : Executive Function
   Attribute     : Vendor Name
   Attribute     : Model Name
   Attribute     : Revision
   Attribute     : Logical Status (STATE-CHANGES-ALLOWED,
                   NO-STATE-CHANGES-ALLOWED,
                   LIMITED-SERVICES-SUPPORTED)
   Attribute     : List of Capabilities
```

Attribute	: Physical Status (OPERATIONAL, PARTIALLY OPERATIONAL, INOPERABLE, NEEDS COMMISSIONING)
Attribute	: List of Program Invocations
Attribute	: List of Domains
Attribute	: List of Transaction Objects
Attribute	: List of Upload State Machines
Attribute	: List of Other VMD-specific Objects

CONNECTION ESTABLISHMENT

Example

This example illustrates how an MMS application association is established between two end users located at stations A and B. We assume that a transport connection has already been established, that all protocols servers and users are willing to establish connections, and that everything is without error conditions. As noted, the MMS service *Initiate* is used to establish an application association and it is mapped to the A_ASSOCIATE, P_CONNECT, and S_CONNECT of ACSE, and the presentation and session layers respectively. Thus, as soon as the MMS Initiate.request service primitive is issued, internal mappings cause an A_ASSOCIATE.req, P_CONNECT.req, and S_CONNECT.req to be also issued as the data travels on its way down to the physical layer. Since a transport connection is available, the session layer uses normal transport data transfer services to convey a connection request to the peer session protocol entity at station B. Although both transport protocols engage in a dialog (i.e., using acknowledgments for the reliable transfer of session layer data, for the sake of simplicity we do not show the detailed dialog that occurs at the lower layers in this example.

Upon receipt of the T_DATA.ind containing a session connection request, the session protocol at station B passes the request as S_CONNECT.ind to the presentation layer which is eventually delivered to the end user at station B as an MMS Initiate.ind. At this point, we assume that the end user at station B wants to communicte with its peer and responds affirmatively with the MMS Initiate.resp primitive which is eventually delivered to the end user at station A as an MMS Initiate.conf primitive. Whenever they are issued at appropriate layers at station A, the primitives S_CONNECT.conf, A_ASSOCIATE.conf, and Initiate.conf establish the session connection, the presentation connection, the ACSE association, and the MMS environment respectively.

10.5 FILE TRANSFER ACCESS AND MANAGEMENT

Transferring, manipulating, and managing files are ubiquitous in many applications. Thus, it is advantageous to have standard protocols that deal specifically with operations involving the transfer, manipulation, and management of files between two network stations. The ISO has developed one such protocol referred to as the File Transfer Access and Management (FTAM) protocol. In this section, we discuss the main concepts associated with FTAM, with subsection 10.5.1 providing a review of file systems. Crucial to the understanding of FTAM is the *filestore concept*, explained in subsection 10.5.2. Finally, subsection 10.5.3 provides an overview of FTAM services.

10.5.1 File Systems

Before studying the ISO standard protocol dealing with files, it is important to review the main concepts associated with file systems.

Some programs get their data directly from the keyboard, perform some calculations, and output the results to a screen or printer. An example of this kind of program is an algebraic equation solver, in which the user enters the coefficients of the equation and the programs output the corresponding roots. In this case, all of the data is kept in main memory (e.g., RAM). This technique is fine when programs deal with small quantities of data. When programs deal with large quantities of data, the computer may run out of main memory or the user may take a few weeks just entering data every time the program is used. Thus, memory devices, other than main memory, capable of storing large (e.g., in the M bytes range) amounts of data are very useful and they are also referred to as **secondary storage devices.**

A named collection of data normally residing on a secondary storage device is called a **file.** Examples of secondary storage devices include magnetic tape, paper tape, bubble memory, floppy diskette, hard disk, etc.). Files may be manipulated as complete units by operations such as (Deitel, 1984):

open : Prepare a file to be referenced.

close : Prevent further reference to a file until it is open again.

create : Define a new file.

delete : Remove a file.

copy : Create an identical file with a new name.

rename : Change the name of a file.

list : Print or display the contents of a file.

Files in turn are made up of constituent data items, which can be manipulated by operations such as

read : Retrieve a data item from a file.

write : Store a new data item into a file.

update : Modify an existing data item.

insert : Add a new data item.

delete : Remove a data item from a file.

A storage system primarily responsible for accessing and managing files on secondary memory is referred to as a **file system.** The most important function that a *file system* provides to a user is one of user-friendliness. Since the actual storage devices can be rather complicated if used directly by the user, the file system acts as an interface between the physical devices containing the files and the file users. File systems give users a **logical view** of the data and the functions to be performed upon it rather than a **physical view.** The file system hides from the user the details on how data is actually stored, the characteristics of actual devices where the data resides, or the physical means for transferring data to and from these devices. For example, a user may perform read and write operations on a file in exactly the same way regardless of whether the secondary device is a floppy

```
type t_book is
    record
        publisher : string (1..30);
        title : string (1..40);
        author : string (1..30);
        cost : float;
    end record;
```

Figure 10.18(a) Record type declaration corresponding to book information.

disk, hard disk, or magnetic tape. Thus, users need not be aware of the kinds of storage devices being used.

In addition to performing the file operations and data items operations just listed, the *file system* provides mechanisms for sharing files among several users with various levels of access such as read access, execute access, write access, delete access, or some combinations of these.

A file exists as a group of related **records** with each record made up of several related **fields.** The example of Figure 10.18(a) shows an ADA declaration for a record type representing book information kept by a publishing company, where *publisher, title, author,* and *cost* are the record fields.

Let us now assume that we wish to construct a file made of records, as defined previously. Since a file is simply a collection of records, the simplest way to construct the file is by writing the records into the file in sequence as the records are being created. Figure 10.18(b) shows a section of an ADA program that creates a book file, inputs record components (i.e., fields) from an operator, writes the information into the file, and closes the file. Most of the statements in the preceding program section are self-explanatory, with the exception of the file operations *create, write,* and *close*.

We next explain the parameters associated with the *create* statement. The *my_file* parameter is a logical name used by the ADA program for subsequent file references. The *out_file* parameter

```
        book_record : t_book;
    begin
        put ("program to create a textbook file"); new_line;
        create (my_file, out_file, "textbook.dat");
                -- out_file is a file mode indicating a write only file.
        while not end_of_file loop
            put ("enter publisher name : "); new_line;
            get (book_record.publisher); new_line;
            put ("enter textbook title : "); new_line;
            get (book_record.title); new_line;
            put ("enter textbook author : "); new_line;
            get (book_record.author); new_line;
            put ("enter textbook cost : "); new_line;
            get (book_record.cost); new_line;
            write (my_file, book_record);
        end loop;
        close (my_file);
```

Figure 10.18(b) Program to enter records into a file.

indicates the mode in which the file is used relative to the program. If the file is a sequential file, the possible modes are input or output referred to as *in_file* (i.e., read only) and *out_file* (i.e., write only), respectively. For random files, a third mode called *inout_file* is available, meaning that one can read or write from or to the file. The third parameter (i.e., *textbook.dat*) is the name of the file as it exists in the computer system. For example, in a tree structured directory, one may have the following parameter *c:\data\textbook.dat*.

File organization. File transfer protocols such as FTAM must deal with different file organizations as they exist in actual computer systems. We next review how data is organized in files. Files such as the one shown in the previous example, in which records are placed one after the previous one in sequence, are called **sequential files.** It is not possible to directly access a specific record in a sequential file, because there is no identifier that uniquely identifies the record. Rather, records are accessed by content. If a specific record is needed, the program should read records from the beginning of the file in sequence, examining the record contents until the desired record is found.

When record identifiers for accessing individual records are supplied, the corresponding files are referred to as **random files.** For example, in a *random file* it is possible to read record number 362 without reading all previous records (i.e., 361, 360, etc.) as is the case with sequential files. Clearly, random files are a major improvement over sequential files. For some applications, however, even random files are not adequate. For example, a program may need to access data associated with *paint robot No 36*. If the program does not know the record number associated with *paint robot No 36*, then the only way to proceed is to read all records sequentially, which is very inefficient if there are a large number of records. What is needed is a way for programs to retrieve information without knowing the record number.

The solution consists in identifying each record uniquely by using an application dependent mnemonic referred to as the **key.** An appropriate *key* for retrieving information corresponding to *paint robot No 36* is, for example, *paint_rob_36*. In this way, the program needs only to supply the *key*, and the desired information to the file system which is responsible for finding the corresponding record and returning the desired information to the program. File systems that work on a *key* basis are referred to as **key indexed files.**

Example

Arpanet File Transfer Protocol

In the Arpanet network, each site maintains its own local file system. A user at site A cannot directly access a file at another site. Rather, the file must be transferred into the user directory at site A; then the file can be accessed. The file transfer is done using a program which is based on the Arpanet's *File Transfer Protocol* (FTP).

Suppose that a user at site A wants to transfer (i.e., copy) file Employee_1 residing at site B into a local file Employee_2, and transfer file Employee_3 residing at his site to file Employee_4 at site B. The user must first invoke the FTP program which requests the following information:

a. The site name acting as the source or destination for the file transfer (i.e., site B).

b. Access information to verify that the user has appropriate access privileges at site B.

Assuming that the user has appropriate privileges, file Employee_1 can be transferred by executing

get Employee_1 to Employee_2

Likewise, the user can transfer Employee_3 to Employee_4 by executing:

```
send Employee_3 to Employee_4
```

Since the user must know exactly where the file to be transferred is, the file location is not transparent to the user. Furthermore, there is no actual file sharing, because the user can only transfer a file from one site to another. Thus, several copies of the same file may exist, resulting in a waste of storage. Finally, if these copies are modified, they may become inconsistent.

10.5.2 The Filestore Concept

Different computers usually have different file representations and implementations. For example, computer A may contain the file *employee* in a tape as a *sequential file*, whereas computer B may contain the same file in a disk as a *random file*. Clearly, a method for file transfer is needed that is independent of how the file is actually represented and implemented. The method used by FTAM for providing independence from file representation and implementation consists of using a specific model for the file representation, known as the **virtual filestore** (VFS), or simply **filestore.** It is assumed that conversions from the filestore and the actual implementation referred to as the **local file system** (LFS) are performed by the protocol user. The *filestore* concept is very important to FTAM, since the FTAM service and protocol are defined in terms of the *filestore*.

The following steps are involved when an application process performs a file operation (i.e., transfer, access, or management) on a file which is located in a remote location. The steps are explained with reference to Figure 10.19.

1. The initiator application process makes a request for a file operation in terms of its *local file system (LFS)*.

2. The initiator system translates the file operation request into VFS terms.

3. The local system sends the request (in terms of FTAM services) to the local FTAM entity.

4. The local FTAM protocol entity communicates with the remote FTAM entity, using the FTAM protocol.

5. The remote FTAM entity delivers the request to the corresponding remote system.

6. The remote system performs the indicated file operations.

Model of the file service: the filestore concept. The concept of a *filestore* is important because it provides a model for the OSI file service. Describing FTAM services in terms of the *filestore* allows interconnection of a wide range of systems of different complexity.

The virtual filestore model is based on the **object-oriented** model, which is used in many branches of science and engineering. Basically, the object-oriented model consists of characterizing the system to be modeled as a set of **objects** and a set of **operations** that can be performed on the objects. Perhaps the best example of the object-oriented model is the one used by mathematicians when defining the system of *real numbers*. Since the real number system constitutes the foundations

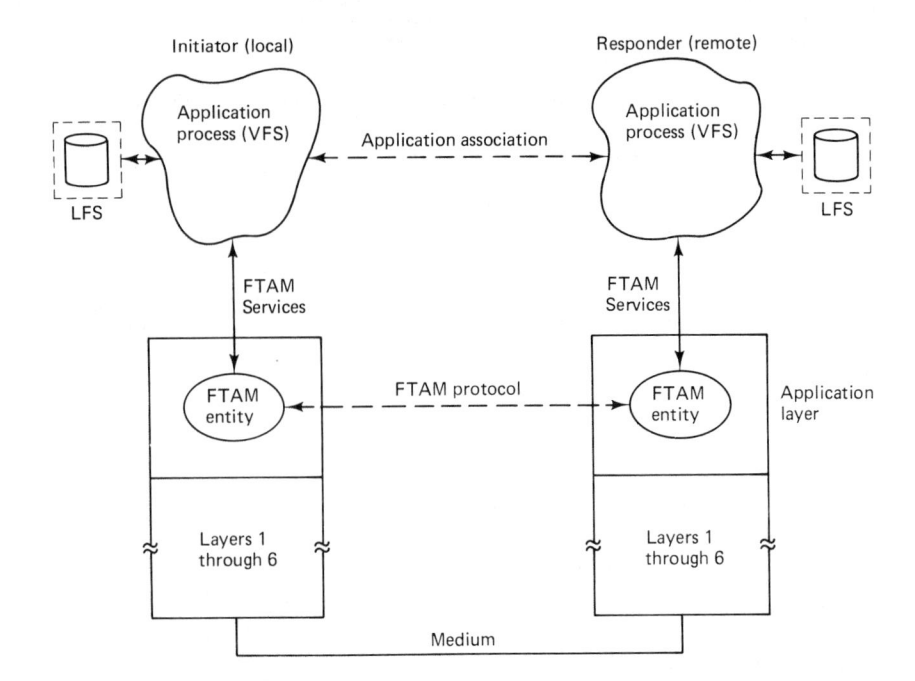

Figure 10.19 FTAM structure and sequence of file operations. The responder involves an application providing the function of the VFS. The initiator does not involve a VFS.

VFS: Virtual filestore
LFS: Local file system

of mathematics and hence engineering, it is interesting to understand how it is defined. Based on the object-oriented approach, the system R of real numbers is defined as a **set** of elements or *objects* (a, b, c, . . .) with two operations "+" and "." denoting, respectively, the sum and the product satisfying the following properties:

1. a + b   and   a.b   are numbers
2. a + b = b + a   and   a.b = b.a
3. a + (b + c) = (a + b) + c   and   a.(b.c) = (a.b).c
4. a.(b + c) = a.b + a.c
5. There exist particular elements in R denoted by **0** and **1**, such that

$$x + 0 = 0 \quad \text{and} \quad x.1 = x$$

6. There exist two numbers which are, respectively, the solution of the following two equations and called the inverse sum and inverse multiplicative of a.

   a) a + x = 0

   b) a.x = 1

At this point, the reader may have a number of observations and/or questions, such as: a) I learned this stuff in elementary school. b) What does this has to do with the virtual filestore model? and c) I thought we were learning about the filestore model and not elementary algebra.

The reasons for presenting the preceding definition (with the risk of boring some readers) is because the definition of a filestore model follows precisely the same approach. Just as the preceding definition of a number system is based upon defining objects and their basic operations, a filestore can also be characterized by defining a set of objects and a certain number of operations that can be performed on those objects. Whereas in the preceding definition the objects were very simple (i.e., just numbers), the objects in the filestore model are more complex which can include *fields*, *records*, *files*, and others.

Another difference between the definition of the real number system and that of the filestore model is that the six properties of the real number system are very elementary, and are also referred to as the **axioms** of the number system. In contrast, the operations defined on filestore objects are more complex.

The significance of the elementary operations in the real number system definition is twofold: First, they are absolutely required, and second, any other operation (e.g., algebra formulas, derivatives, and integrals) can be defined in terms of the two elementary operations and their properties. The disadvantage of defining only elementary operations is that it is not practical, because whoever is manipulating numbers is mostly interested in operations which are more involved than the axioms and with significance to the user. Hence, in the context of file operations, in order for file operations to be useful, they must be relatively complex (i.e., involved) and with significance to the user of the model. Examples of operations that can be performed on the filestore objects include: open a file, read a record, select a file, write a record, and others.

Virtual filestore objects. As noted, objects for the virtual filestore are quite complex. There are two major aspects of filestore objects: those that are associated with *file transfer and access* and those that are associated with *file management*. Objects for file management in turn have two aspects: those that deal with communication and those that do not (i.e., they deal with local processing only). Objects for *file transfer* and *access* are defined in the **file structure** component of the virtual filestore. Examples of objects defined in the *file structure* include fields, records, and files which are referred in a more generic way as **file access data unit** (FADU). The objects of file management which are independent of communications are described in the *file attributes* component of the filestore model and include the filename, time and date of creation, etc. The (file) **activity attributes** component of the filestore model deals with the object's communication aspects of file management and includes objects such as the identity of the initiator, communication passwords, and others. Finally, the operations defined on the filestore objects are referred to as **actions,** and include operations such as create a file, read a record, close a file, and others.

Thus, there are three important aspects to FTAM services. The first aspect involves the *objects* for file management operations, such as the identity of creator or current initiator identity. These objects are referred to as **attributes.** The second aspect involves the *objects* for file transfer and access operations, such as create a file or read a record. These objects are referred to as **file structures.** The final aspect involves the actual file transfer and access operations, which are also called **actions.**

File Attributes and Activity Attributes

As noted earlier, *attributes* can be divided into those that are independent of communications, known as **file attributes,** and those attributes that are communication-related, known as **activity attributes.**

File attributes then define attributes that are necessary to characterize a file, regardless of whether the file needs to be transferred or manipulated to/from another location. The most important *file attributes* include the *filename, actions* permitted on the file (e.g., read, write, replace, etc.), *date* and *time* of creation, *identity* of creator, and others.

In order for a file to get involved in FTAM operations, additional *activity attributes* are required. The activity attributes reflect the state of a file transfer or access already in progress. The most important *activity attributes* include *identity* of the service initiator, allowed *operations* to be performed under the file transfer or access (e.g., read, insert, replace, etc.), account for charges, and others.

File Structures

As already noted, the *file structure* defines the objects for file transfer and access. In addition, in order to simplify the file access and transfer operations, the filestore's *file structure* defines additional mechanisms:

> file access structure,
> file transfer structure,
> presentation structure,
> access context,
> identification structure, and
> constraint sets.

File access structure. The file access structure describes the organization of data contained within a file as it affects the access of the data. The data units (DU) contained in a file are related in some logical fashion. The relationships between data units may be sequential, hierarchical, random, or relational. The virtual filestore uses a hierarchical tree structure for representing the relationship of data units for access purposes. This structure is referred to as the **access structure.**

Objects defined in the *file access structure* are referred to as **file access data unit** (FADU). As depicted in Figure 10.20, FADUs are configured as subtrees of the hierarchical tree structure. Each node of the tree has two components: an identifier and an optional data unit. Two special cases of hierarchical access structures which are widely used are the *unstructured* and *flat* cases, respectively. The *unstructured* case is useful for situations in which the data unit consists of an indefinite number of data elements with no clear logical separation between them from the viewpoint of file operations. Examples of files in this category include binary and text files. Thus, the access structure for the *unstructured* case consists only of the root mode and one data unit of indefinite length, as shown in Figure 10.21(a).

The *flat* case is useful for situations in which the data unit consists of a number of logically related elements (e.g., records). Examples of file with a *flat* structure include sequential, random access, keyed, etc. Thus, the tree structure for the *flat* case consists of two levels, with data units only at the leaf nodes, as shown in Figure 10.21(b). A special case of a flat structured file is one where all data units are instances of the same record type.

File transfer structure. Obviously, information about the structure of a file must be communicated. This information is called the **file transfer structure,** and identifies entities such as access structure, node names, and abstract syntax for the transfer of file contents.

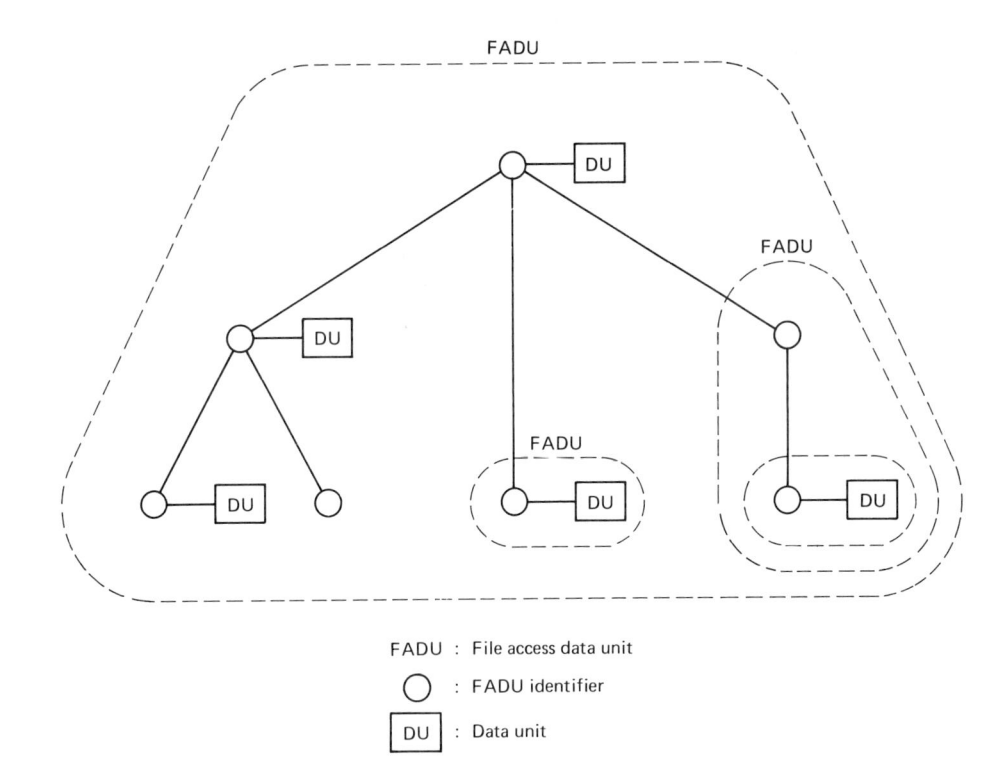

Figure 10.20 Hierarchical access structure of the FTAM virtual filestore.

Presentation structure. The *presentation structure* has nothing to do with the presentation layer. Instead, the presentation structure simply specifies the *abstract syntax* of the access structure. The data elements within a FADU are logically related by an abstract syntax, referred to as the **presentation structure.** An example of the presentation structure of FADUs could represent records in a COBOL index sequential file. Since, in general, an *abstract syntax* is related to application processes which are generic in nature, the abstract syntax of the presentation structure should not

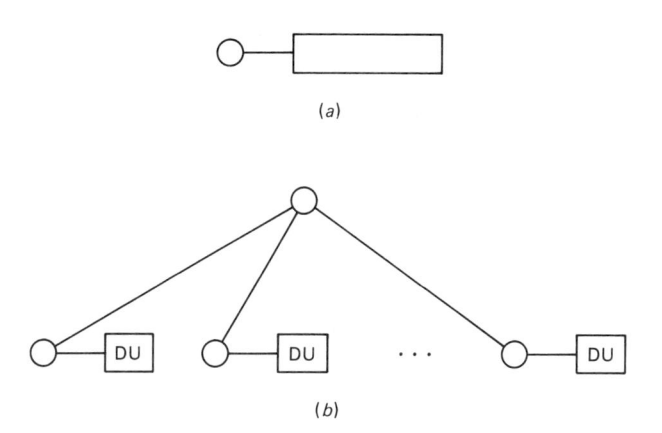

Figure 10.21 (a) Unstructured file access data unit (FADU); (b) Flat structured FADU.

Sec. 10.5   File Transfer Access and Management

be confused with the abstract syntax of an application process as dealt with by the presentation layer.

Access context. The **access context** determines what information is transferred when an FADU is accessed. Obviously, the access context must be defined in terms of the hierarchical tree file structure. In order to describe the different access contexts let's consider the three-level subtree shown in Figure 10.22. When it is desired to transfer all structuring information along with all FADUs in a tree such as the one shown in Figure 10.22, the following access context can be used:

$$\text{Context\_1} := (A, du1, /, B, /, D, du3, \backslash, \backslash, /, C, du2, /, E, du4, \backslash, /,$$
$$F, du5, \backslash, \backslash)$$

where the symbol / indicates entering a subtree and the symbol \ indicates leaving the subtree. If only structuring information is to be transferred, the following access context can be used:

$$\text{Context\_2} := (A, /, B, /, D, \backslash, \backslash, /, C, /, F, \backslash, \backslash)$$

Access contexts such as context_1 and context_2 are referred to as *hierarchical all data units* (HA) and *hierarchical no data units* (HN), respectively. The preceding format used for defining access contexts is not specified in the ISO standard. The format used in Context_1 and Context_2 above is arbitrary and is used only as an example. Other access structures can be defined, and the reader is referred to the Virtual Filestone definition of the ISO FTAM standard for additional details.

Identification structure. Information for uniquely referencing a particular FADU is referred to as the **identification structure.** There are several methods that can be used to define the structure. For example, the identification structure for referencing FADU_3 in Figure 10.22 is

$$\text{id\_struct\_3} := A/C/F$$

Constraint sets. Because of implementation reasons, filestore objects and actions sometimes need to be constrained. The constraint could apply to valid node names, valid file access

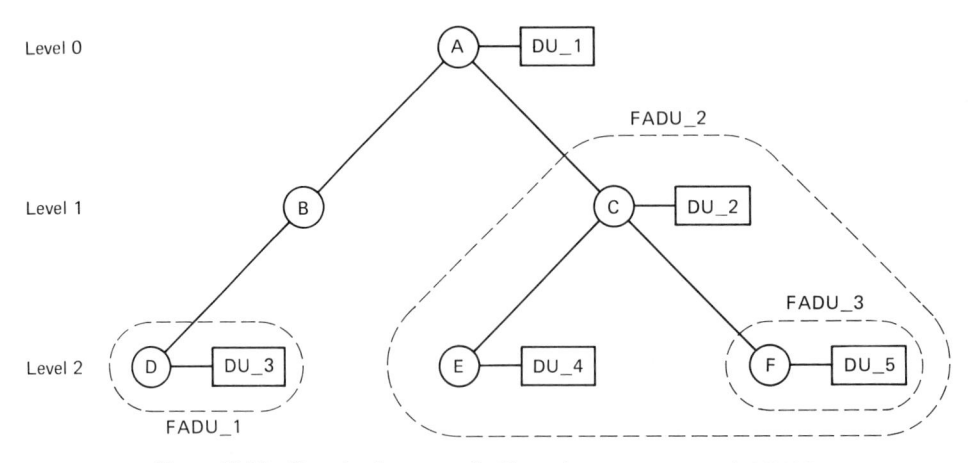

Figure 10.22 Three-level structure for illustrating access contexts in FTAM.

actions, and so on. The definition of all constraints applicable to the objects and actions of a filestore is given by the **constraint set.** Many constraints are defined by ISO in the *constraints set*, and the reader is referred to the appropriate standard for details.

Actions on Files

The different operations that can be performed on filestore objects (e.g., records and files) are called **actions on files.** File actions are invoked by FTAM service primitives. Depending upon whether the objects for file transfer, access, and management are entire files or FADUs, the actions are called **actions on complete files** or **actions for file access,** respectively.

The *action on complete files* set includes operations such as creating, selecting, opening, closing, deselecting, and deleting files. On the other hand, the *actions for file access* include operations such as locating, reading, inserting, replacing, appending, and erasing FADUs.

10.5.3 Overview of the FTAM Services

From the description of the virtual filestore concept, it is clear that in order to perform FTAM operations, users must proceed in the following order:

1. An *application association* must be established to use FTAM rather than any other application service element (e.g., MMS).

2. A particular file is selected.

3. The file is made ready for access. This is accomplished by opening the file and checking for appropriate security parameters.

4. The data transfer takes place.

5. The file is closed.

6. The file is deselected.

7. When all required file actions are completed, the application association is released.

Some of the preceding steps signal the beginning and end of a **regime,** with the **FTAM regime** beginning with step 1 and ending with step 7. Likewise the **file selection regime** begins with step 2 and ends with step 6; the **file open regime** begins with step 3 and ends with step 5; and the **data transfer regime** consists of step 4. Thus, one can view the FTAM services as being divided into a set of *regimes*, with each regime completely contained within another, as shown in Figure 10.23.

An **activity** is defined as an *FTAM regime* in progress. The FTAM service describes a single activity between the initiating and responding FTAM service users. However, as depicted in Figure 10.24, a user can establish an *activity* with other service users. The configuration of Figure 10.24 constitutes the basis for the *server model* used in many local area network installations. Within an FTAM context, a file **server model** is simply an FTAM service user referred to as the *file server*, having activities with other FTAM service users referred to as **file serve users.** Usually, the server users reside in personal computers or workstations with little or no secondary memory (e.g., disk). The *file server*, on the other hand, is usually equipped with large amounts of secondary memory

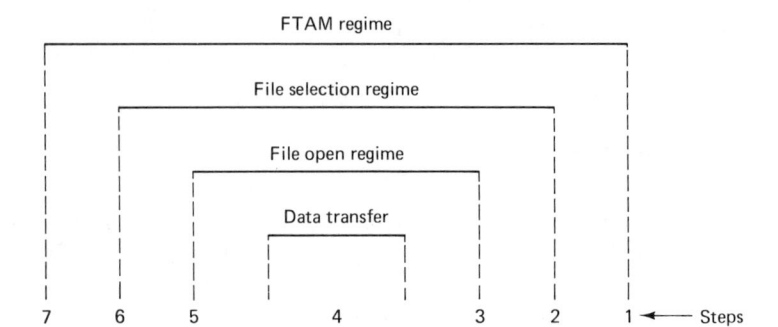

Figure 10.23 FTAM regimes.

to serve the needs of many users with typical values in the hundred of M bytes. Addresses for factory LAN stations remain fairly static during normal operation; thus, file servers on a cluster basis are more efficient and reliable than a single central server. An example of a cluster file server appropriate for a MAP network is illustrated in Figure 10.25.

File actions involve the following steps, which can be performed using FTAM services (ISO 357/1):

1. Allow the initiator and the responder to identify one another.
2. Identify which file is needed.
3. Establish file attributes and the data transfer which is to take place in an activity.
4. Engage in file management.
5. Locate the FADUs to be accessed.
6. Transfer, replace, or delete one or more FADUs.

Functional units, service classes, and service levels. FTAM services are organized into groups of related services called functional units. From the FTAM services standpoint,

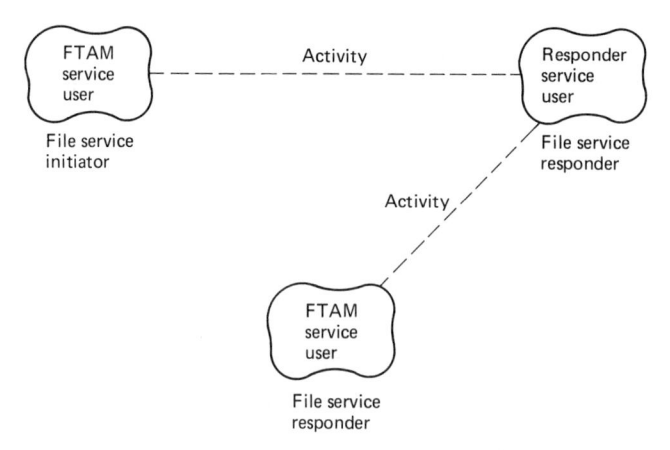

Figure 10.24 FTAM users and activities.

394 The Application Layer   Chap. 10

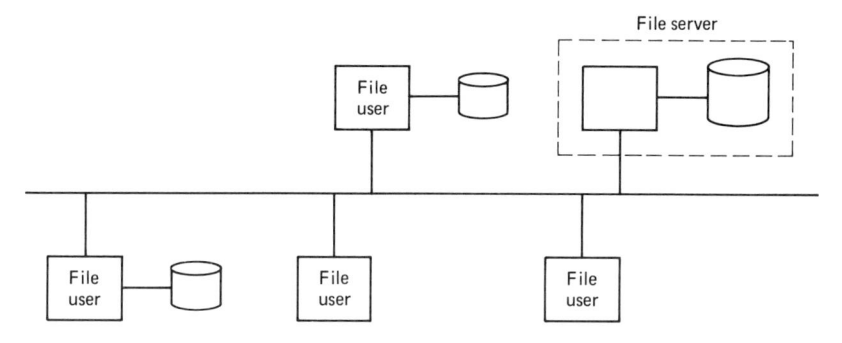

Figure 10.25 File server in a MAP network.

a **functional unit** is the smallest negotiable service unit. A **service class** is a grouping of functional units which provide a particular kind of service. Thus, whereas a *functional unit* is defined as helping the negotiation aspects of the services, a *service class* is defined as those functional units that have some meaning relative to a user.

The quality of FTAM services is determined by the **service levels.** When the FTAM protocol machine corrects errors which might occur in the file operations, the service level is called *reliable file service* (RFS). However, RFS does not imply that the FTAM protocol machine must invoke error control procedures if required. When the service user controls any attempt to recover from errors, the corresponding service level is called the *user correctable file service* (UCFS). On a given network, *reliable file service* may be less reliable than using *user correctable file service*. Using the reliable file service level simply determines that the service users will not invoke error recovery services. Using the user correctable file service level simply means that the FTAM machine will not invoke any error control procedures on behalf of the service user.

Nine functional units are defined, which are listed in Table 10.2 along with the services that they provide. Likewise, Table 10.3 lists the five *service classes* defined in the standard, along with the *functional units* that each service class provide, and an indication as to whether the respective functional unit is mandatory or can be negotiated.

10.6 DISTRIBUTED DATABASES

It is expected that distributed databases will play a crucial role in integrating the elements of *automated manufacturing*, and thus achieve what is called *computer integrating manufacturing* (CIM). The development of standards for distributed databases lags behind that of standards for file systems (e.g., FTAM). The ISO is currently working on standards for the support of distributed databases which include *Remote Database Access* (RDA), *Remote Operation Services Element* (ROSE) and *Commitment, Concurrency, and Recovery* (CCR).

Because the ISO standards for distributed databases are not currently well-developed, the approach taken in this section is different from that taken when discussing other layers. Our main objective is to discuss the fundamental concepts associated with distributed databases, making little reference to existing protocols or standards. It is expected that after reading the background in this section, readers will have no difficulty in understanding the appropriate protocols and standards when they are fully developed.

TABLE 10.2 FTAM FUNCTIONAL UNITS

Functional unit	Services
1. Kernel	FTAM regime establishment FTAM regime termination Regime termination (abort) File selection File deselection File open File close
2. Read	Request data read Data transfer End transfer End data transfer regime Cancel data transfer
3. Write	Request data write Data transfer End transfer End data transfer regime Cancel data transfer
4. File access	Locate FADU (record) Erase FADU (record)
5. Limited File Management	File creation File deletion Read file attributes
6. Enhanced File Management	Change file attributes
7. Grouping	Begin Group End Group
8. Recovery	Regime Recovery Checkpoint data transfer Cancel data transfer
9. Restart Data Transfer	Restart data transfer Checkpoint data transfer Cancel data transfer

Why Distributed Databases?

A collection of data involved in at least one *global application* is referred to as a **distributed database.** The global application is distributed over different stations of a computer communication network, and thus requires accessing data via the network. Of course, each station has autonomous processing capability and can perform local applications as well. Conventional databases (i.e., which are not distributed) are also known as **centralized databases.** The collection of data typically resides in secondary memory such as disks, types, etc.

TABLE 10.3 FTAM SERVICE CLASSES

Service class	Functional unit	Use
1. File transfer	Kernel	Mandatory
	Grouping	Mandatory
	Read	Negotiated
	Write	Negotiated
	Limited File Management	Negotiated
	Enhanced File Management	Negotiated
	Recovery	Negotiated
	Restart Data Transfer	Negotiated
2. File Access	Kernel	Mandatory
	Read	Mandatory
	Write	Mandatory
	File Access	Mandatory
	Grouping	Negotiated
	Limited File Management	Negotiated
	Enhanced File Management	Negotiated
	Recovery	Negotiated
	Restart Data Transfer	Negotiated
3. File Management	Kernel	Mandatory
	Limited File Management	Mandatory
	Enhanced File Management	Mandatory
	Grouping	Mandatory
4. File Transfer and Management	Kernel	Mandatory
	Limited File Management	Mandatory
	Enhanced File Management	Mandatory
	Grouping	Mandatory
	Read	Negotiated
	Write	Negotiated
	Recovery	Negotiated
	Restart Data Transfer	Negotiated
5. Unconstrained	Kernel	Mandatory
	Read	Negotiated
	Write	Negotiated
	File Access	Negotiated
	Limited File Management	Negotiated
	Enhanced File Management	Negotiated
	Grouping	Negotiated
	Recovery	Negotiated
	Restart Data Transfer	Negotiated

The reasons for the importance of distributed databases are numerous. The first reason deals with *organization* and *economics*. Many applications are decentralized, having components located in different physical locations. In addition, integrating the decentralized components by means of a communication system can result in economic benefits. Thus, organizing the data in the same way that the application is organized is a natural thing to do. Perhaps the best example that illustrates, the organizational and economic reason for distributed databases is an automated manufacturing system, or a computer integrated manufacturing system (CIM). As will be discussed in Chapter 11, the organization of a CIM system is truly distributed. Furthermore, one of the main driving forces in CIM technology is to remain competitive in worldwide markets (i.e., an economic one).

The second reason regards *performance*. It is well-established that a properly designed distributed database does its job better than an equivalent centralized database. Judging whether a distributed database does its job better than a centralized one can be done by looking at *performance measures* such as *response time*, *throughput* and *reliability*.

Another reason for the importance of distributed databases has to do with the interconnection of existing databases. Many organizations (or applications) already have centralized databases in different locations. If these organizations need to share data located in the different databases, then a distributed database that integrates the various centralized databases can provide an effective solution.

Still another reason deals with the possibility of a reduced communication overhead as compared with a centralized database.[8] In a centralized database, all transactions have to go to the only database available, thus increasing overhead in the communications. In distributed databases, much[9] of the transactions are processed locally instead of being processed at remote locations, thus reducing communication overhead.

A final reason for the importance of distributed databases is the possibility of increasing *reliability* and *availability* in the overall system. Since data in a distributed database is distributed across the network, failure of one network station does not mean a failure of the overall system. In fact, with proper database design, failure of one station could have no effect whatsoever on the performance of the distributed system. In general, after a failure of one component of a distributed system, the entire system does not fail; rather, the system continues to operate in a degraded level of service. Systems that are able to operate in degraded levels of service are said to exhibit **graceful degradation.**

Having looked at the reasons for studying distributed databases, and before we present distributed database organization and design, let us briefly review some general concepts associated with databases.

10.6.1 Review of Databases

This subsection presents the fundamental concepts associated with nondistributed (i.e., centralized) databases. Much of the methodology for designing distributed databases is based on centralized databases concepts, hence the importance of these concepts.

Database models. Conceptually it is important to distinguish different ways of organizing data. Consider a database involving *customers*, *orders*, and *parts*. Just as in a standard file cabinet, data can be organized hierarchically, with the cabinet at the top of the hierarchy and the files and orders located below, as depicted in Figure 10.26. In a **hierarchical database,** data is organized hierarchically (i.e., like an inverted tree). Data which is related to a specific branch of the tree is located beneath it. For example, in Figure 10.26, orders placed by customer number 2 are located directly beneath the node associated with customer number 2. The number of branches per node need not be the same for all nodes, and some nodes may not have branches at all.

One of the main advantages of the hierarchical organization is that it can be used to answer questions such as *what parts were ordered by customer 1 on order 3?* without difficulty. All that

---

[8] In centralized databases, we are refering to terminal to host communication overhead.

[9] Applications involving distributed queries and distributed commitment require remote processing.

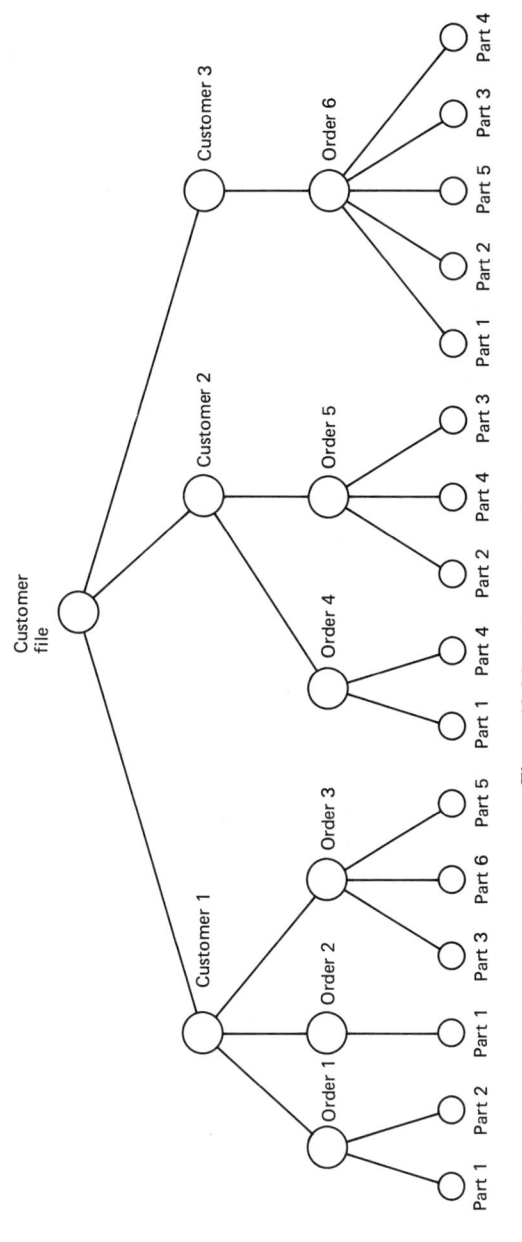

Figure 10.26 A hierarchical database.

is required is to look at the branches connected to order 3 beneath customer 1. The hierarchical database is not without disadvantages, however. What if one tries to answer questions such as *How many of part 6 were ordered in the previous month*? To answer this question, one would have to examine all possible branches to see if one reaches a node corresponding to part 6. If the tree is small, this is a trivial operation. Where one runs into trouble is when the tree is large, because it would involve going down on a node sequence until reaching the bottom, backtracking to the top, and repeating the operation on a different node sequence. Performing backtracking on the entire tree can take a considerable amount of time.

What is needed for effectively answering questions such as the latter one is a data organization where one can look at the various pieces of data in numerous ways. A **network database** allows accessing data in different ways without having to duplicate or reorganize the data. A *network database* has nothing to do with computer networks; a better name that could be used is *linked database*, to emphasize its linked structure. Figure 10.27 depicts a network database corresponding to Figure 10.26, where orders from customer 2 have been eliminated to keep the figure simple. As depicted in Figure 10.27, each *order* points to the parts contained in it. Unlike the hierarchical database, each part also points to the order in which they are contained.

Answering questions such as *how many of part 1 were ordered in the previous month*? is easy now. All that is required is to look at the orders pointed to by part 1. The main disadvantage of network databases is their complexity. To maintain all the relationships, the pointers must be maintained with care so that none of the links is lost. While maintaining the database is complex, user access of the data is more simple, as shown in the previous example.

A third database model, referred to as the **relational database,** views the data as being organized in tables, with rows representing records and columns representing fields of traditional file systems. Figure 10.28 depicts a relational database organization for a personnel file containing four fields: *name*, *ss number* (for social security), *position*, and *balance*. The relational database model is often used as a model for distributed databases; thus, we concentrate on this model in the remaining of this section.

The relational database model. In relational databases, data is organized in tables, called **relations,** with each relation having a number of columns, called **attributes,** and a number of rows, called **tuples.** *Relations*, *attributes*, and *tuples* correspond to files, fields, and records of traditional file organization. The number of attributes of a relation is called its **grade,** whereas the number of tuples is called its **cardinality.**

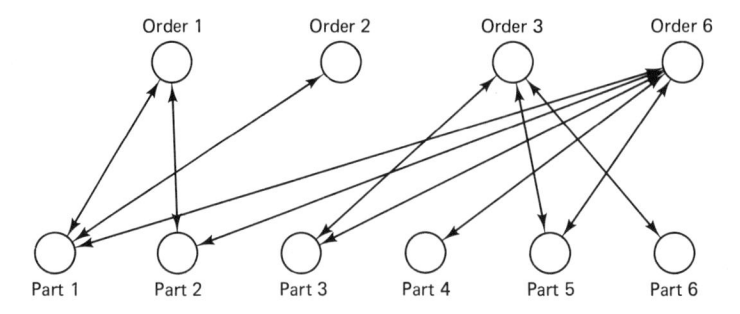

Figure 10.27 Linked (network) database.

Personnel file

Name	SS number	Position	Balance
John White	111-11-1111	Salesman	200.00
Steven Thompson	222-22-2222	Accountant	300.00
Jack Atkins	333-33-3333	Engineer	500.00
...			.

Figure 10.28 Relational database organization for a personnel file.

For example, Figure 10.29 shows a relation EMP1 (for employee1) having four attributes: *EmpNum* (for employee number), *Name*, *Age*, and *DeptNum* for departmental number, and five tuples. Likewise, the relation EMP2 also has four attributes and five tuples. Thus, one can say that the tuple (6, Doe, 33, 12000) is a tuple of the EMP1 relation, whereas the tuple (19, 19, 14000, Baker) is a tuple of the EMP2 relation. In what follows, we will not distinguish the order of attributes in a relation; thus, EMP1 is considered the same as EMP2, since they both have the same attributes but are organized in a different order.

The relation name and the names of the attributes contained in the relation is referred to as the **relation schema.** The following relation scheme is used to characterize the EMP1 relation:

EMP1(*EmpNum, Name, Age, DeptNum*)

The set of possible values for a given attribute is called its **domain.** For example, the *Age* attribute takes its values from the *domain* of numbers representing ages for human beings (e.g., from 0 to about 150 years). Although the values for *EmpNum* are also numbers, they cannot be intermixed

Tuple number	Emp Num	Name	Age	Dept Num
1	6	Doe	33	12000
2	19	Baker	19	14000
3	9	Brown	45	13000
4	13	Jones	25	12000
5	15	Miller	31	10000

(a)

Tuple number	Emp Num	Age	Dept Num	Name
1	6	33	12000	Doe
2	19	19	14000	Baker
3	9	45	13000	Brown
4	13	25	12000	Jones
5	15	31	10000	Miller

Emp Num: employee number
Dept Num: department number

(b)

Figure 10.29 Relation examples: (a) Relation EMP1; (b) Relation EMP2. Relation EMP1 is considered equivalent to relation EMP2.

with the values for *Age*, since they belong to different domains. It would make little sense to add two numbers representing age and employee numbers, respectively.

Relational algebra. Relational databases can be viewed as **sets** of tuples. An important consequence of this view is that one can derive important properties from the mathematical branch of **set theory.** Specifically, two important consequences of viewing relations as sets of tuples is that there cannot be two identical tuples in the same relation and that there is no defined order of the tuples in a relation.

While viewing relations as pure sets helps in modeling and analysing databases, practical implementations allow replicated tuples. However, in distributed databases, the modeling and analysis phases are performed separately from the implementation phase; thus, the set theory model for a database is a useful one.

Just as there are certain operations which are defined on sets (e.g., union, intersection, etc.) we also have several operations that can be defined on relations. Collectively, the operations that can be performed on relations define a **relational algebra.** Relational algebra **operators** take one or two *relations* as operands and produce a relation as the result. Although different versions of operators have appeared in the literature, we consider operators in two categories: basic and derived. **Basic operators** are independent from one another and are considered the simplest operators from which others can be derived. **Derived operators** are those operators that can be defined in terms of the basic ones. Five basic relational operators have been identified (Ceri and Pelagatti, 1984): selection, projection, union, difference, and cartesian product.

The *selection* and *projection* operators are referred to as **unary** operators because they take just one relation as the operand to produce another relation as the result. On the other hand, operators such as the *union*, *difference*, and *cartesian product* are called **binary** operators, since they take two relations as operands and produce another relation as a result. Relations R_1, R_2, and R_3 in Figure 10.30(a) will be used as examples when discussing relational operators.

The **selection** operator **SL** takes one relation as the operand and produces another relation as a result, with the same relation schema as the operand relation, and containing a subset of the tuples of the operand which satisfy a predicate F. The notation

$$R = SL_F(R_1)$$

indicates that the relation R is the result obtained by selecting tuples from relation R_1 according to predicate F. An example of a predicate for a relation scheme R_1 (A,B,C) is the following: F := (A < 4 **OR** C > 9).

Example

Find the result of applying the operator **SL** with predicate F := (A = a) to relation R_1.

Solution The solution is shown in Figurre 10.30(b).

The **projection** operator **PJ** also takes one relation as the operand and produces another relation as a result having selected attributes of the operand. Replicated tuples that might appear in the result relation are eliminated; thus, the cardinality of the result can be less than the cardinality of the operand. The notation

$$R = PJ_{Attr}(R_1)$$

R1

A	B	C
a	1	a
b	1	b
a	1	d
b	2	f

R2

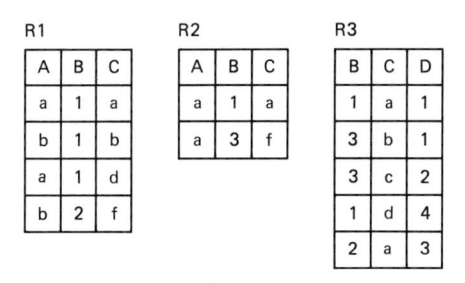

A	B	C
a	1	a
a	3	f

R3

B	C	D
1	a	1
3	b	1
3	c	2
1	d	4
2	a	3

(a) Relations for examples

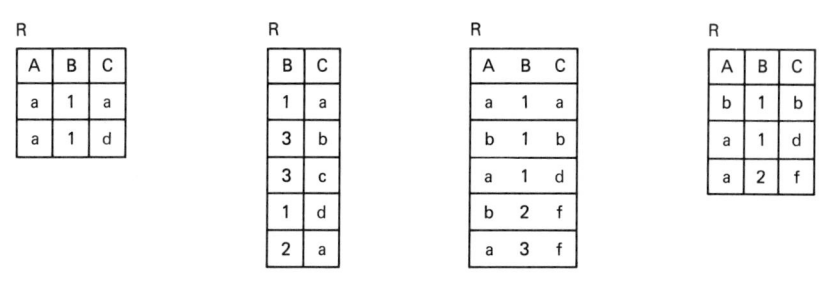

R

A	B	C
a	1	a
a	1	d

(b) Selection $SL_{A=a}$ R1

R

B	C
1	a
3	b
3	c
1	d
2	a

(c) Projection $PJ_{B,C}$ R3

R

A	B	C
a	1	a
b	1	b
a	1	d
b	2	f
a	3	f

(d) Union R1 **UN** R2

R

A	B	C
b	1	b
a	1	d
a	2	f

(e) Difference R1 **DF** R2

R1.A	R1.B	R1.C	R2.A	R2.B	R2.C
a	1	a	a	1	a
b	1	b	a	1	a
a	1	d	a	1	a
b	2	f	a	1	a
a	1	a	a	3	f
b	1	b	a	3	f
a	1	d	a	3	f
b	2	f	a	3	f

(f) Cartesian product R1 **CP** R2

A	R1.B	R1.C	R3.B	R3.C	D
a	1	a	1	a	1
a	1	a	2	a	3
b	1	b	3	b	1
a	1	d	1	d	4

(g) Join R1 $JN_{R1.C=R3.C}$ R3

A	B	C	D
a	1	a	1
a	1	d	4

(h) Natural joint R1 **NJN** R3

A	B	C
a	1	a
b	1	b
a	1	d

(i) Semijoin R1 $SJ_{R1.C=R3.C}$ R3

A	B	C
a	1	a
a	1	d

(j) Natural semijoin R1 **NSJ** R3

Figure 10.30 Relational database examples.

is used to indicate that R is obtained from R_1 by retaining only those attributes contained in *Attr*. For example, Figure 10.30(c) shows the result of the operation $R = \mathbf{PJ}_{B,C}(R_3)$.

The **union** operator **UN** takes two relations as operands and produces a relation result which contains the union of the tuples of the two operand relations. The following equation denotes the union operation where R contains all the tuples appearing in R_1 or R_2:

$$R = R_1 \text{ UN } R_2$$

An example is shown in Fig. 5(d).

The **difference** operator **DF** is similar to the union operator, except that the relation result contains the difference of the tuples of the two operand relations. The notation

$$R = R_1 \text{ DF } R_2$$

indicates that R contains all the tuples appearing in F_1 but not in R_2, as depicted in Figure 5(e).

The final basic operator is the **cartesian product, CP,** which produces a relation whose relation schema includes all the attributes of R_1 and R_2. Every tuple of R_1 is combined with every tuple of R_2 to form one tuple of the result. If two attributes having the same name appear in R_1 and R_2, they are nevertheless considered different attributes; to avoid ambiguity, the name of each attribute is prefixed with the name of its *original* relation. The result of the cartesian product operator is denoted by

$$R = R_1 \text{ CP } R_2$$

and an example is shown in Figure 10.30(f).

So far, we have discussed the *basic* relational operators; any other operators can be defined in terms of these *basic* operators. In what follows we consider four *derived operators*: join, natural join, semijoin, and natural semijoin.

The **join** operator **JN** takes two relations as operands and produces a relation result that includes all the attributes of the two operands, and all their tuples which satisfy a *join predicate*. The join operator can be derived from the selection and cartesian product operators, as indicated by the following equation:

$$R = R_1 \text{ JN}_F R_2 = \mathbf{SL}_F (R_1 \text{ CP } R_2)$$

For example, if we consider the relations $R_1(A,B)$ and $R_2(C,D)$ a valid formula for F is $F := (A > C \text{ OR } B = D)$. If only equality appears in the definition for F, then the operation is referred to as an **equijoin.** Thus, for the previous relations R_1 and R_2, a valid formula for F which denotes an equijoin is $F := (A = C \text{ OR } B = D)$. An example is shown in Figure 10.30(g).

The **natural join** operator is an equijoin in which all attributes with the same names in the two relations are compared. Since these attributes have both the same name and the same values in all the tuples of the result, one of the two attributes is omitted from the result. Thus, the *selection predicate* is implied for the natural join operation. For example, consider the relations $R_1(A,B,C)$ and $R_2(A,D,C)$. Then the corresponding selection predicate F for the natural join is $F := (R_1.A = R_2.A \text{ AND } R_1.C = R_2.C)$. The result of the natural join operation is denoted by

$$R = R_1 \text{ NJN}_F R_2 = R_1 \text{ NJN } R_2$$

since F is implied for the natural join operation. For an example, see Figure 10.30(h)

The **semijoin** operator takes two relations as operands and produces a result relation R given by

$$R = R_1 \; SJ_F \; R_2 = PJ_F \; (R_1 \; JN_F \; R_2)$$

where $F = \text{Attr}(R_1)$ denotes the set of all attributes of R_1. Thus, the result of the semijoin is a subset of the tuples of R_1, which contributes to the join of R_1 with R_2 under join predicate F. For an example, see Figure 10.30(i).

The **natural semijoin** of two relations R_1 and R_2 is another relation R denoted by

$$R = R_1 \; NSJ \; R_2$$

The result relation R is obtained by performing a semijoin with the same join predicate as in the natural join. Thus, the natural semijoin relates to the natural join, just as the semijoin relates to the join operator. Fig 10.30(j) shows one example.

Transactions and queries. Before leaving this section on the fundamentals of centralized databases, let us define the following important concepts: transaction and query. A **transaction** is an atomic unit of database access which is either completely executed or not executed at all. Atomicity in a transaction is required because of concurrent execution or because of failures. Concurrent execution and failures can cause incorrect data, which atomicity is supposed to prevent.

A **query** is an expression in a suitable language for defining a portion of the data contained in the database. Queries can be used for defining the semantics of an application or for designing programs which access the database. In systems supporting a **query interface,** end users can write a query and request its execution. By using the semantics specified by the query, the system can automatically generate the programs for accessing the database. Examples of query expressions include **select, from,** and **where,** as shown in the next query segment:

select < attribute list >
from < relation name >
where < predicates >

The preceding query segment indicates that tuples specified by the *predicates* parameters are chosen from the relation specified by the *relation name* parameter, and only those attributes specified by the *attribute list* parameters are displayed. Thus, *predicates* indicates the selection attribute F for a *selection* operation to be performed on the relation indicated by *relation name*, and the result relation is *projected* using the *attribute list* as the selected attributes.

An emerging standard for a query language being developed by ANSI and ISO is the *Structured Query Language* (SQL). SQL actually contains two languages, referred to as the *schema (data) definition language* (SQL–DDL), for declaring the structures and integrity constraints of an SQL database, and a *data manipulation language* (DML) for declaring procedures and statements of a specific database application.

Example

Write an expression for the relation that results for the following query segment. Assume that the relation schema for R_1 is $R_1(A,B,C)$.

select < B,C >
from < R_1 >
where < A = a >

Solution The selected attributes for the projection operation is given by Attr := (B,C), and the selection predicate F for the selection operation is given by F := (A = a). The result relation is given by

$$R = PJ_{Attr}(SL_F R_1)$$

Having discussed centralized database, we next discuss distributed databases.

10.6.2 Distributed Database Organization

Reference architecture. The reference architecture for distributed databases is intended to provide a conceptual understanding of distributed database organization. The architecture does not indicate how distributed databases should be implemented. As depicted in Figure 10.31, the reference architecture is composed of a global schema, a fragmentation schema, an allocation schema, local mapping schemas, optional *database management systems* (DBMS), and the local databases. The first three schemas are referred to as **station independent schemas,** because the schemas are independent of the station where data is ultimately located.

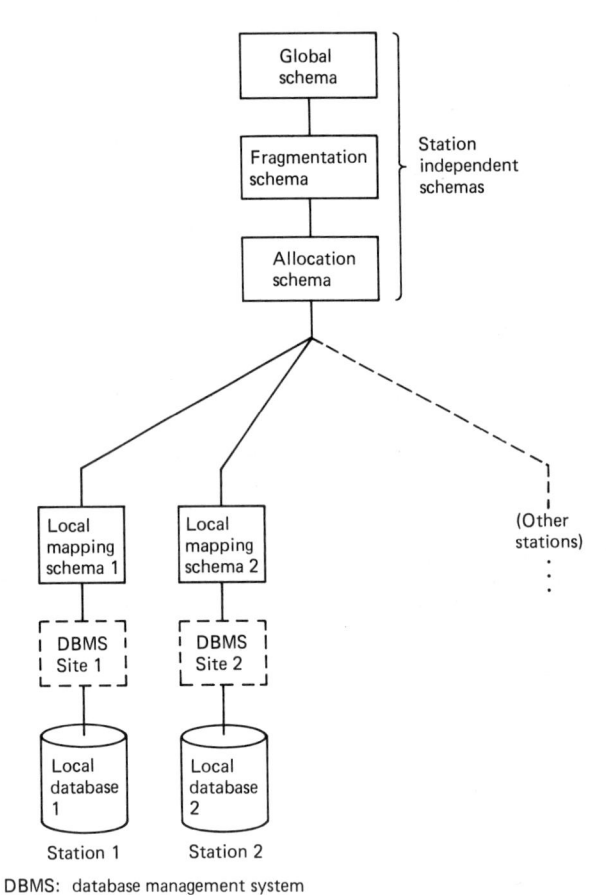

Figure 10.31 (a) A reference architecture for modeling distributed databases.

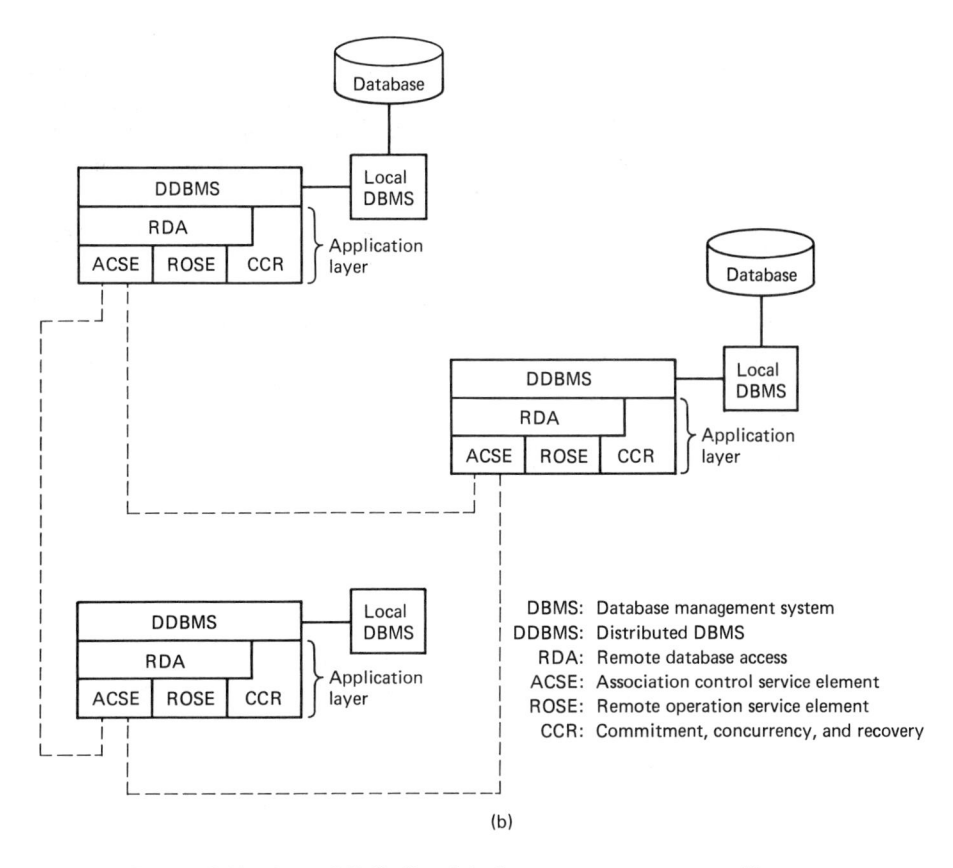

Figure 10.31 (b) An OSI distributed database management system architecture.

The **global schema** defines all the data contained in the distributed database, as if the database were not distributed at all. For the relational model, specifying a global schema involves defining all the relation schemas without regard for where the relations are located. The next step in the distributed database design process consists of splitting the global schema for suitable allocation to the different network stations. Splitting each global relation into several portions is referred to as **fragmentation.** Each portion of the global relation is also called a **fragment.** The location of fragments within the network is given by the **allocation schema.** Fragments corresponding to the same global relation R and which are located at the same station J constitute the **physical image** of global relation R at station J. The mapping of physical images to the objects which are manipulated by the local DBMS is contained in the **local mapping schema.**

Data Fragmentation

Data fragmentation is the decomposition of global relations into *fragments* for later allocation on network stations. Before discussing the techniques used for data fragmentation, let us state three rules that must be followed when defining fragments. The first rule, the **completeness condition,** states that all the data in the global relation must be mapped into the fragments. Thus, a data item belonging to a global relation must not be left out from being assigned to a fragment. The second rule, the **reconstruction condition,** states that it must be possible to reconstruct each global relation from its fragments. Consequently, in order for a fragmentation scheme to satisfy the reconstruction condition, there must exist relational operators that when applied to the relation fragments, can yield the global relation. The third rule, called the **disjointness condition,** states that fragments be disjoint, so that the replication of data can be controlled explicitly at the allocation level. However, this condition is useful mainly with horizontal fragmentation, whereas for vertical fragmentation this condition is sometimes violated.

Horizontal fragmentation. Since a relation can be viewed as a set of tuples, one way of partitioning the relations is simply by splitting the set of tuples into subsets. This particular way of splitting the relation is referred to as **horizontal fragmentation,** because fragments are obtained by making horizontal slices in the relation. Horizontal fragmentation is useful in situations where each fragment contains data which have common geographical properties. Fragments $Frag_1$, $Frag_2$, . . . obtained from horizontal fragmentation can be expressed as a *select* operation on the global relation, that is,

$$Frag_1 = \mathbf{SL}_{F1}(GlobRel)$$

$$Frag_2 = \mathbf{SL}_{F2}(GlobRel)$$

where $F_1, F_2, \ldots$ are selection predicates and *GlobRel* denotes the global relation. The preceding fragmentation satisfy the completeness condition if $F_1, F_2, \ldots$ together specify every tuple of the global relation. The reconstruction condition is verified, because it is always possible to reconstruct the global relation through the following operation:

$$GlobRel = Frag_1 \text{ UN } Frag_2 \text{ UN } Frag_3 \ldots$$

The disjointness condition holds as long as $F_1, F_2, \ldots$ are disjoint.

The selection predicates $F_1, F_2, \ldots$ are also called the **qualifications** of the global relation.

Vertical fragmentation. Whereas horizontal fragmentation produces fragments by slicing the global relation horizontally, **vertical fragmentation** produces fragments by slicing the global relation vertically (i.e., by attributes). Attributes are divided into groups, and fragments are obtained by projecting the global relation into each group. In order for the fragmentation to be complete, each attribute must be mapped into at least one attribute of the fragments. In addition, it must be possible to reconstruct the original relation by suitable operations on the fragments. A vertical fragmentation of the following relation GlobRel ($Attr_1, Attr_2, \ldots, Attr_n$) can be obtained as follows:

$$Frag_1 = \mathbf{PJ}_{F1} (GlobRel)$$

$$Frag_2 = \mathbf{PJ}_{F2} (GlobRel)$$

where F_1 and F_2 are subsets of the attributes of GlobRel. For example, $F_1 = (Attr_1, Attr_2, \ldots, Attr_j)$ and $F_2 = (Attr_1, Attr_{j+1}, \ldots, Attr_n)$ where $Attr_1$ is a *key* of GlobRel and $j < n$ are appropriate choices for F_1 and F_2.

The global relation GlobRel can be reconstructed from its fragments as

$$\text{GlobRel} = \text{Frag}_1 \, \mathbf{NJN}_F \, \text{Frag}_2$$

where the selection predicate $F := \text{Frag}_1.\text{Attr}_1 = \text{Frag}_2.\text{Attr}_1$.

10.6.3 Distributed Database Design

Clearly, designing a distributed database is more complicated than designing a centralized database. In addition to the steps that are normally required when designing centralized databases (i.e., design of relation schemas and queries), the design of distributed databases introduces three new problems. First, the stations must be interconnected by means of a network. This problem has two aspects, depending on whether the network is available or not. If the network is not available, the problem of course is to design one. If the network is available, the problem is interfacing with the network at the appropriate layer. Some networks (e.g., MAP) are expected to have a distributed database component as part of its application layer; thus, the interface will be fairly straightforward. In networks that do not provide a distributed database component, the interface is usually done at the transport, session, or application layers. Of course, interfacing with a network that does not provide a distributed database component is more difficult when compared to a network that does.

The second problem introduced when designing distributed databases regards the optimal distribution of data for meeting application requirements. Optimality in the distribution of data depends on the location of stations, from which applications are issued, the frequency of activation of the applications, and the number, type, and statistical distributions of database accesses made by applications.

The last, but certainly not least problem is the optimization of the performance of database accesses. Performance is usually measured in terms of response time and throughput. Performance is a complex problem that depends on many variables, such as database access technique, underling network structure, and station computer characteristics (e.g., operating system, buffer space, and so on).

As noted earlier, the design of distributed databases involves the design of the global schema (just as in the centralized database) and the design of fragmentation and allocation of data. Collectively, fragmentation and allocation are also referred to as **data distribution.** The objectives of the design of *data distribution* involve processing locality, availability and reliability of distributed data, workload distribution, and storage costs and availability. **Processing locality** requires that data should be distributed in such a way that an application should access local data more often than data located in other stations. **Availability of distributed data** refers to the ability of the system to switch to an alternative copy of the data when the one that is accessed under normal conditions is not available.

Reliability of distributed data refers to the ability of the system to recover from failures of some of the stations by using copies of data located somewhere else. Availability and reliability of distributed data can be usually achieved by storing multiple copies of the same information. **Workload distribution** allows parallelism to be used in situations where applications require a great deal of processing. Storage devices vary in cost and capacity. Costs can be further classified as initial costs and maintenance costs. **Costs and availability** of storage devices should be taken into account when designing data distribution.

The Design of Database Fragmentation

The purpose of designing a database fragmentation is to determine fragments which are *logical units* of allocation. Defining *tuples* or *attributes* as units of allocation is not a good idea, because the problems associated with accessing individual *tuples* or *attributes* would be unmanageable. A better approach consists of designing fragments as groups of tuples or attributes and defining a fragment as the unit of allocation.

Horizontal fragmentation. Determining the **horizontal fragmentation** of a global relation involves determining a set of disjoint and complete *selection predicates*. Each fragment's elements must be referenced homogeneously by all the applications. Let $P = (p_1\ p_2, \ldots, p_n)$ be a set of predicates of the form $p_j := (Attribute\ relation\ value)$, where relation can be $=, >, <, >=$, etc.

Minterm predicates are of the form

$$y_j = \wedge\, p_i^*$$

where $p_i^* = p_i$ or $p_i^* = \overline{p_i}$ where the bar over p_i indicates the logical complement operator and the $\wedge$ symbol stand for the logical AND operation involving several terms. A database fragment $Frag_j$ is the set of all tuples for which a minterm predicate holds. Thus, fragments are uniquely defined by y_j. A predicate p_j is **nonrelevant** if corresponding fragments are referenced in the same way by at least one application.

A method for producing horizontal fragmentation consists of the following steps:

1. Find a predicate p_1 which partitions the tuples of R into two parts, which are referenced differently by at least one application. Let $P = (p_1)$.

2. Find another predicate p_2 which partitions at least one fragment of P into two parts, which are referenced in a different way by at least one application. Let $P \leftarrow P\ U\ (p_2)$. Eliminate *nonrelevant* predicates from P. Repeat step 2 for $p_3, p_4, \ldots$ until the set of fragments of P is complete. P is complete if, and only if, any two tuples belonging to the same fragment are referenced with the same probability by any application.

Vertical fragmentation. Grouping global relation attributes which are referenced *in the same way* by applications is referred to as **vertical fragmentation.** The grouping of attributes results in sets called **fragments.** Depending upon whether sets can overlap each other, one can distinguish two types of fragmentation: in **vertical partitioning** the sets are disjoint, whereas in **vertical clustering** the sets can overlap. In order for the completeness condition to be satisfied, each attribute of R must belong to at least one set and each set must include either a *key* of R or a **tuple identifier.** Vertical fragmentation involves identifying fragments R_i such that most applications use the least number of fragments. If most applications reference all fragments, then vertical fragmentation is not beneficial.

Designing a vertical fragmentation is not simple, except in situations where the global relation has few attributes. For relations with a large number of attributes, *heuristic* approaches are often used.

10.6.4 A Remote Database Access Standard

Although standardization efforts in distributed databases and remote database access are in the early stages, in this subsection we describe current ideas behind the eventual standard. Basically, the remote database access (RDA) standardization is currently somewhat similar to that of MMS in that it is based on a client-server model and makes extensive use of abstrac objects. Some of the objects being defined include the virtual database server object (analogous to a VMD), association object, and data resource object. However, because the applications supported by MMS and RDA are very different, their service functionality also differs. Perhaps the two most distinguishing features of RDA are the support of the execution of *data manipulation language* (DML) statements and the support of the concept of *database transaction* as defined in subsection 10.6.1.

RDA defines a generic data manipulation language statement having both input arguments and results specified by formal parameters. For example, a client can request the execution of a DML statement by the server using the R_Execute DML operation. By invoking this operation, a DML statement (e.g., a query) is sent to the remote server for execution. The server parses and executes the DML statement, returning the resulting data or a completion indication. In an error is detected such as illegal access by the client, an error message is returned and the DML operation is rejected.

Transaction Management

As noted earlier, a transaction is an atomic unit of database access, consisting of one or more related DML operations, which is either completely executed or not executed at all. Grouping data manipulation operations into transactions facilitates preservation of database integrity by causing the server to treat all DML statements within the transaction as a single atomic unit. Updates made within a transaction are monitored as the transaction progresses, but are only committed (i.e., made permanent) and made available to other database users when the transaction is complete.

Depending upon the degree of commitment offered by a server and the number of servers supported, RDA supports three levels of commitment:

    Level-0: With this level, server and client use no commitment.

    Level-1: A commitment level used in situations involving a single server supporting multiple clients.

    Level-2: This level supports distributed environments involving multiple servers and clients.

Whereas level-0 is the most simple, level-2 is the most complex and could handle situations where identical copies of the same information are stored at two or more remote database systems. No commitment implies that, for example, the same read request issued at different times may return different values.

Designing a remote database access system offering level-0 commitment is straightforward since the data integrity problem is simply ignored as it is assumed that other means exist to ensure that only one client accesses the server at a time. Designing a system offering level-1 commitment is fairly straightforward requiring the server to serialize data manipulation statements issued by the client. Some solutions to this problem were discussed in section 7.4.3. Designing a system offering level-2 commitment is a bit more involved requiring a special handshake such as the following 2-phase commitment protocol.

Two-Phase Commitment Protocol

As noted, a two-phase commitment protocol is needed to support distributed environments involving multiple servers and clients (i.e., a level-2 commitment in RDA). A *client* issues a transaction which may involve multiple *servers*. In the context of the two-phase commitment protocol, one server can be designated as the **coordinator** with all remaining servers designed as **slaves.** We wish to preserve *data integrity* even when the following problems arise:

1. A slave can fail
2. A slave can deadlock
3. A transaction can self abort
4. A coordinator can fail
5. The communication network can fail

The two-phase commitment protocol helps solve the first three preceeding problems. The last two problems are solved by other means. Before discussing the two-phase commitment protocol, we make the following assumptions:

• Each database transaction involves a *coordinator* at one site and a number of *slaves* at several other sites.

• Locally, each transaction can **commit** or **roll back** (i.e., abort) depending upon the slave's local resources.

• As is the case with centralized databases, each slave has a recovery manager.

• Each slave can leave a transaction intact until a failure is repaired.

• No slave has to wait for a failed slave to continue. This is also referred to as the nonblocking assumption.

As the name implies, the two-phase commitment protocol involves the following two phases:

Phase 1: The coordinator requests all slaves to proceed until they get into a state in which they can go either way on the transaction (i.e., *commit* or *roll back*). If a slave succeeds in reaching this state, it replies with a *commit* message to the coordinator, otherwise it replies with a *roll back* message. Thus, each slave is responsible to commit or roll back and send a message to the coordinator accordingly.

Phase 2: If the coordinator receives all commit messages, it broadcasts a message to commit to all slaves; all slaves then complete their local commit processing. Otherwise, the coordinator broadcasts a roll back message to all slaves; all slaves then undo all local effects of the transaction. Thus, the net effect is that either all slaves commit the transaction or all roll it back; the transaction cannot be committed by some slaves and rolled back by others. The coordinator can also use a timeout mechanism to decide whether to broadcast a roll back message in case the slave fails or deadlocks.

A Distributed Database Management System (DDBMS) Architecture

As depicted in Figure 10.31, RDA in conjunction with ACSE, ROSE (Remote Operations Service Element), and CCR (Commitment, Concurrency, and Recovery) can support a DDBMS architecture. Whereas ACSE supports the establishment of an RDA application association, ROSE supports the execution of remote operations and the return of results from those operations, and CCR[10] supports a specific 2-phase commitment protocol for transaction management.

10.7 MAP APPLICATION LAYER

Although MAP 3.0 and TOP 3.0 both use FTAM, ACSE, directory services, and network management, their application layers differ significantly in the other protocols supported. Since MAP is primarily intended to support manufacturing environments, its application layer must have all the functionality required by manufacturing applications. Because the ISO did not have an appropriate application layer protocol for manufacturing at the time the MAP architecture was under development, the MAP task force at General Motors developed one called the **manufacturing message format standard** (MMFS). The MAP 2.1 and 2.2 architectures specify MMFS. Currently, MMFS has evolved into a more sophisticated protocol called **manufacturing message specification** (MMS), which is part of MAP 3.0. MMS was discussed in detail in Section 10.4.

The incorporation of FTAM services into the MAP 2.2 architecture is done in two phases. Phase 1 includes the file transfer kernel, read, write, and limited file management functional units and the kernel group of the *virtual filestore* attributes. In addition, phase 1 supports the transfer of both binary and ASCII text file formats and the remote creation and deletion of files. Not supported by phase 1 is the concatenation function and the F_BEGIN_GROUP and the F_END_GROUP services. Phase 2 supports file access capabilities and an enriched set of file formats.

The following are additional details of FTAM and its implementation for MAP 2.2. The *access structure type* is of the unstructured type only (i.e., no flat and hierarchical types are used). The FTAM implementation is mapped directly into session services without incorporating the use of the common application service element (CASE), where the F_INITIALIZE service corresponds to the S_CONNECT service and the F_TERMINATE service corresponds to the S_RELEASE service. No concurrency on file operations is provided, since the file attributes governing them are not supported. Thus, it is up to each implementation to support the degree of concurrency desired for local files. However, in order to avoid potential problems, two rules are recommended: First, a file may be involved in several transfers simultaneously only if accessed in read mode; and second, for a file involved in a transfer in a write mode, any request for access (i.e. a read or write) to the file should be rejected regardless of whether the request is local or remote.

---

[10] Actually, ACSE corresponds to the Common Application Service Elements (CASE) part 2 and CCR corresponds to case part 3.

10.7.1 TOP Application Layer

In addition to the protocols in common with MAP 3.0, the TOP 3.0 specification includes protocols for message handling system (MHS), and virtual terminal.

SUMMARY

For end users, the application layer is the most important layer because it provides the window for accessing the overall network. Although it is possible for an end user to directly access services of the presentation, session, or other layers of the OSI reference model without using the application layer, networks are designed so that end users obtain full benefits of the network only if access is made at the application layer.

Communication protocols for the application layer only deal with *application processes* residing in different network stations. The main function of the application layer of the OSI reference model is to provide and manage the communcations between *application processes*. The communications could be connection-oriented or connectionless. The services provided by the application layer can be considered as the overall network services, because they include the services of all other layers.

Unlike the session and presentation layers, which provide generic network services, the application layer must support a wide variety of specific end user distributed applications, such as message service, distributed databases, virtual terminal, file transfer, manufacturing applications, graphics, and others.

In order for application processes to communicate, each must possess information which is meaningful to the other. All of the information associated with an application process is known as the **universe of discourse** of that application. Thus, communicating application processes must have their universes of discourse overlapping each other.

Formally, a *universe of discourse* is described by a **conceptual schema.** Two application processes are said to **interwork** if they are able to communicate with each other. Thus, two application processes are able to interwork only if their conceptual schemas overlap. The overlapped portion of a conceptual schema is referred to as the **shared conceptual schema,** or simply **shared schema.**

End user application processes basically perform two types of functions: those that are communication-related and those that are not. Those aspects of application processes dealing with communication-related functions are referred to as **application entities.** The cooperative relationship between two *application entities* is referred to as the **application association.** An *application association* is formed by exchanging control information by making use of the services offered by the presentation layer.

The **association control service element** (ACSE) is a major constituent element of an application layer protocol which provides facilities for the establishment and release of *application associations*. The manufacturing message service (MMS) is another application layer *service element* which enables communication among intelligent devices found in manufacturing applications. MMS has a rich set of services, involving variable access, message passing, resource sharing, (synchronization) program management, event management, and other services.

Transfering, manipulating, and managing files are ubiquitous in many applications. The ISO has developed one such protocol, referred to as *file transfer access and management* (FTAM).

Different computers usually have different file representations and implementations. The method used by FTAM for providing independence from file representation and implementation consists in using a specific model for the file representation known as the **virtual filestore** (VFS).

It is expected that distributed databases will play a crucial role in the integrating aspect of *automated manufacturing*, and thus achieve what is called *computer integrating manufacturing* (CIM). A collection of data involved in at least one *global application* which is distributed over different stations of a communication network is referred to as a **distributed database.** The three most used models of databases are: hierarchical, network, and relational.

In relational databases, data is organized in tables, called **relations,** with each relation having a number of columns, called **attributes,** and a number of rows, called **tuples.** Relations, attributes, and tuples correspond to files, fields, and records of traditional file organizations. A **transaction** is an atomic unit of database access which is either completely executed or not executed at all. A **query** is an expression in a suitable language for defining a portion of the data contained in a suitable language for defining a portion of the data contained in the database.

The MAP 3.0 architecture currently specifies the following for its application layer: directory services, FTAM, MMS, and ACSE. The TOP architecture currently specifies directory services, FTAM, and ACSE.

Bibliographic Notes

Although there is a fair amount of material on distributed systems, that is not the case for the ISO application layer since many of the concepts are new. Thus, currently the best references are the appropriate standards. The article by Tanenbaum and Van Renesse (1985) provides a good discussion on distributed operating systems. Object oriented programming is treated in the book by Cox (1986). Whereas Summers (1987) discusses resource sharing in a LAN environment, interprocess communication in a manufacturing cell environment is addressed by Nagata (1986) and Shin and Epstein (1987). The book by Ceri and Pelagatti (1984) provides an extensive treatment of distributed databases and Pimentel (1986) discusses a MAP/TOP compatible distributed database in a manufacturing environment.The ISO application layer structure is detailed in ISO 9545, the ACSE in ISO 8649/2, MMS service and protocol in ISO 9506/1 and ISO 9506/2 respectively, and FTAM in ISO 8471/3 and ISO 8571/4 respectively.

PROBLEMS

1. What OSI layers provide the communication service component of a distributed operating system?
2. (a) Explain the term interworking.
   (b) State the main requirement for two application processes to interwork.
3. Briefly explain the ISO model for the application layer including the role played by the following:
   a) Application process
   b) Application entity
   c) Application service element
   d) Application association
4. Using the ADA language, define a conceptual schema for a process performing machine monitoring in a manufacturing application. The process collects cycle data corresponding to each

machine. During each cycle, certain cycle information is stored followed by the values of 300 variables. The information to be stored is shown next:

Information	Description
Time	Date on time of cycle occurrence
Cycle-No	Cycle number from start of machine life
Err	Error, set if cycle data does not meet specification
Run-time	Time spent processing part
Next_time	Time spent waiting for next machine
Data1	Variable No 1
Data2	Variable No 2
.	.
.	.
.	.
Data300	Variable No 300

5. Draw a timing diagram showing all primitives of the A_Associate service of ACSE.
6. Explain the similarities and differences of the A_ABORT and A_P_ABORT services.
7. Classify the four ACSE services as confirmed, unconfirmed, or neither.
8. Indicate which of the following ACSE services can result in the loss of data being transmitted.
   (a) A_Abort
   (b) A_P_Abort
9. When using ACSE services, how are the names of the initiating application entity, responding application entity, application context, and other options typically specified?
10. A computer integrated manufacturing (CIM) system integrates every aspect of manufacturing, from customer orders all the way until final production. Suppose you are designing an ADA program that processes car orders. The program is supposed to be integrated with other CIM programs by means of a computer network. You are only concerned with the following information:

Category	Information
customer	name, address, phone
car	manufacturer, year, model, serial No, color, cost
accessories	air, stereo, sun-roof

   a) Make variable type definitions suitable for the variables involved in this application.
   b) Make suitable variable declarations.
11. What role does the *virtual manufacturing device* (VMD) play in the client-server model used by MMS?
12. In MMS, what is the difference between a *monitored event* and a *network-triggered event*?
13. Solve problems 8 and 9 of Chapter 7 using the MMS program management services.
14. What are the advantages and disadvantages of using *file transfer* instead of *message transfer* for communications?
15. What is the key to solving the simultaneous access to a critical region problem that arises in asynchronous concurrent processes?
16. a) List the MMS services that allow remote processes to share variables.
    b) Indicate how local processes can share variables.
17. a) What is the object oriented model?
    b) How is the object oriented model useful in describing FTAM services and protocol?
18. Process A at a computer station is to write a record to an employee file located at a different station using FTAM services. List and explain the detailed steps that takes place in this record writing operation. The steps should involve the LFS, VFS, and the FTAM protocol.
19. Assume a LAN with a file server and a number of stations. Use FTAM services to rewrite the program in Figure 10.18(b) to write file records from a station into the file server.
20. Produce a sketch showing how an FTAM connection is established in the following two situations:

(a) a transport connection is already established.
(b) a transport connection is not available.

21. Write an expression for the relation that results from the following query

    select (A, E)
    from (R_1, R_2)
    where ($R_1.A = R_2.A$)

    assuming that the relation schemas are $R_1(A,B,C)$ and $R_2(A,D,E)$.

22. Given the relations in Figure P10.1, draw the relation for R where

    $$R = R_1 \, \mathbf{DF}(\mathbf{PJ}_{Attr} \, (\mathbf{SL_F} \, R_2))$$

    and Attr := (A,B), F := (C ≥ 2)

R_1

A	B
a	f
e	d
b	i
d	g

R_2

A	B	C
a	f	1
g	b	2
e	a	0
b	f	9
g	b	8
d	a	1
b	i	4

Figure P10.1

23. Consider the following global relations:
    EXTERNAL_TOOL (Name, Id, LowLim, HighLim, ExtChar, Feat)
    TOOL_CHARACT (Name, ToolId, PlanID, SurfFin)
    INTERNAL_TOOL (Name, Id, LowLim, HighLim, Intchar)
    where:
    Id = identification, LowLim = lower limit, ExtChar = external characteristic, Feat = feature, ToolId = Tool identification, PlanId = plan identification, SurfFin = surface finish, IntChar = internal characteristic.
    and the following application
    (a) An NC machine using tools with a surface finish <0.02 inches.
    (b) One robot of a cell controller requires Name, ExtChar, and Feat while the remaining robots require Name, LowLim, and HighLim of the EXTERNAL_TOOL relation.
    (c) A cell controller requires Id, IntChar while other cell controllers require Name, LowLim, and HighLim of the INTERNAL_TOOL relation.
    Design a fragmentation scheme for this application.

24. Consider the global relation DEPARTMENT (Dept, Location, Director). Using basic or derived relational operators,
    (a) Write expressions for the fragments of the following fragmentation:
        DEPARTMENT is fragmented horizontally by location, with two locations: local and remote; each location is headed by the same director.
    (b) Indicate how the global relation is reconstructed from its fragments

25. Can the two-phase commitment scheme recover when the communication network fails after phase 1 and before phase 2 is executed?

PART 3

11

Introduction to Automated Manufacturing

The manufacturing environment has changed dramatically in the last few years. Two major driving forces behind the changes are the stiff worldwide competition among manufacturing companies and the development and utilization of new technology which includes microprocessors, robots, databases, local area networks, artificial intelligence and others. The manufacturing environment has evolved from manual operation, where workers operated individual machines, to semiautomatic operation, where the machines were able to perform a few steps in automatic sequence, to a high degree of automation making extensive use of computers and other automated equipment.

We use the term *automated manufacturing* when referring to a manufacturing facility with a high degree of automation. Other terms used in the literature for describing the same or similar concept are *flexible manufacturing systems* (FMS), *computer integrated manufacturing* (CIM), and *Factory of the Future* (FOF). Unfortunately, there are no agreements on suitable definitions for these terms. We prefer not to use the term CIM, since it generally involves not only the production activities but also marketing, sales, engineering, materials, finance, and personnel (Kochan and Cowan, 1986).

In this chapter we provide an introduction to the main concepts behind automated manufacturing systems, with emphasis on a definition, a model, the elements, characteristics, and the organization of automated manufacturing facilities. Since automated manufacturing can be approached from many different perspectives, we approach it from the viewpoint of *Production Planning and Control*. This chapter complements Chapter 14, which discusses networks which are appropriate for automated manufacturing systems.

11.1 WHAT IS AUTOMATED MANUFACTURING?

As noted earlier, several definitions have been given in the literature. The following definition is adapted from similar definitions given by O'Grady (1986) and Ranky (1983). An **automated manufacturing system** is an interconnected system of material processing stations capable of automatically processing a wide variety of part types simultaneously and under computer control. The system is not only interconnected by a *material transport system*, but also by a *communication network* for integrating all aspects of manufacturing. The system exhibits flexibility in routing parts, part processing operations (e.g., drill), coordination and control of part handling, and in using appropriate tooling.

The preceding definition highlights the central role of the computer and the communication network in integrating the various aspects of the automated manufacturing system. The communication network not only transfers information, such as part programs, between processing stations, but also supports the coordination, monitoring, control, and management of the entire system. The required flexibility in virtually every aspect of the manufacturing process requires careful coordination of different components of the manufacturing system. Furthermore, planning and controlling the movement of parts through the system can be a complex problem.

An automated manufacturing system exhibits the following characteristics:

high degree of automation,
high degree of integration,
high degree of flexibility. Flexibility can take a number of forms, including:

a. Volume flexibility: The ability to handle changes in the production volume of a part or finished good.
b. Routing flexibility: The ability to route parts through the system in a dynamic fashion taking into account machine breakdowns, required tooling, and so on.
c. Product flexibility: The ability to handle requests for a wide variety of products, including the ability to reconfigure the system to handle the production of different products.

Part programs can be transferred from computers to manufacturing devices.

When compared with traditional manufacturing, numerous advantages have been identified with automated manufacturing systems, including (Koren, 1985):

increased productivity,
lead times can be reduced. When product requirements change, it often involves reconfiguring part of the system. With automated manufacturing the reconfiguration time can be reduced.
reduction of parts inventory,
reduction of work in progress,
reduction of labor costs,
equipment can be used more efficiently, and
improved product quality.

An automated manufacturing system is of an interdisciplinary nature, involving many technical areas, also known as *enabling technologies*, including (Kochan and Cowan, 1986):

computer aided design (CAD),
computer aided manufacturing (CAM) including flexible assembly and
flexible manufacturing
computer aided test (CAT),
production planning and control,
process technologies,
robotics, and
automated materials handling,

which are linked together by means of the communication network.

11.2 PRODUCTION PLANNING AND CONTROL

As noted earlier, an automated manufacturing facility involves many aspects, including financial and marketing systems. Since we are only providing an introduction to the subject, we need to narrow our scope and concentrate on one area of the overall system. One area that will benefit extensively from communication networks is that of *production planning and control*. As the name implies, **production planning and control** is the careful preparation of schedules, schemes, algorithms, and so on for the control of the automated manufacturing system so that the objectives are met.

Production planning and control is important for automated manufacturing systems for two major reasons (O'Grady, 1986): First, because of the shorter lead times as compared with traditional manufacturing, the overall activities of the system must be scheduled and controlled more closely. The second reason is related to the high cost of manufacturing system components, and thus the need to use them efficiently. Typical automated manufacturing systems have an average device utilization between 85 and 95 percent, whereas typical manufacturing utilization ranges between 40 and 60 percent. Because of the complexities involved, achieving effective production planning and control is very difficult. Currently, a great deal of research and development is being performed for developing methodologies and techniques for production planning and control.

Manufacturing Cell

The concept of the manufacturing cell is described next. Manufacturing operations are broken down into cells, with each cell responsible for the manufacturing of a specific part family, namely parts with similar features, determined by *group technology* principles (Koren, 1983). The cells are interconnected by a transport system for materials and finished parts. Two such examples of transport systems are automated guided vehicles (AGV) and conveyors. Figure 11.1 illustrates the manufacturing cell concept. The robot functions include part handling, machine loading and unloading, assembly, and others. Unworked parts that reach the cell are handled by the robot and routed to designated machines (e.g., lathe, mill, and drill) depending upon the type of part processing desired. The worked pieces are then routed to other manufacturing cells for subsequent processing.

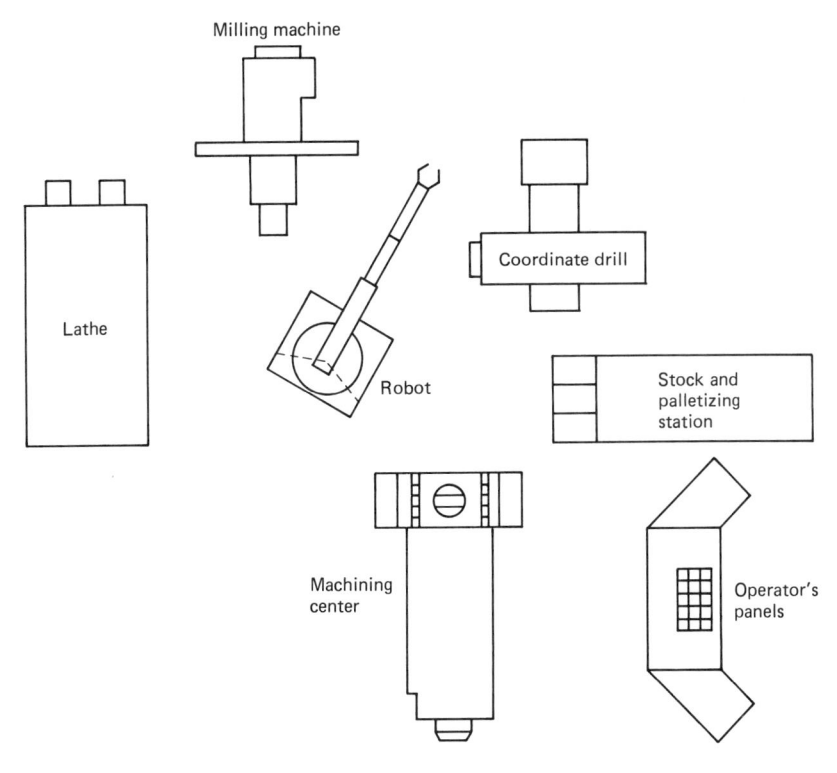

Figure 11.1 The core of a manufacturing cell.

Example

This example describes an automated car manufacturing facility. An automobile manufacturing plant manufactures automobile A for three days, automobile B for two days, and automobile C for one day. The production process is repeated cyclically with automobile A again. Changing production from automobile A and to C is a complex operation involving the use of a communication network to download new program for robots and other material processing stations, and new programs for overall coordination and control. In addition, the use of different tooling, and different sets of parts and material transport systems is also required. In a highly flexible system, automobile volume options and models can be dynamically changed on a day, shift, or quantity basis.

11.3 ELEMENTS OF AUTOMATED MANUFACTURING SYSTEMS

This section lists the constituent devices which make up an automated manufacturing system. The intent is not to consider every single device present in the system. Rather, the intent is to consider those devices that play a role in the *production planning and control* of the manufacturing facility and which generate information that will be transported using the communication network. For example, a *tachometer* for measuring the speed of motors used in robot control generates important information used in controlling the movements of the robot. However, this signal is usually not needed in places outside the robot; hence, it will not utilize the communication network. On the other hand, consider a limit switch that senses parts going through a conveyor. Several subsystems such as robots and automatic storage systems need to known the status of these switches. Thus, it is necessary to send this type of information through the network.

The elements of a manufacturing facility are:

Sensors. Sensors convert a physical signal into another signal (usually electrical) which is easier to manipulate than the original signal. Many sensors give an output signal in the form of a voltage, which is very easy to interface with a digital computer. In most cases, sensors are an integral part of other machines (such as robots). The reason that sensors are considered an element of a manufacturing facility is that sometimes they perform a function independently. For example, a position sensor (e.g., a limit switch) in a conveyor system will indicate the presence or absence of a certain part in a specified location of the conveyor. This information can be used for the other subsystems to perform further actions. Examples of variables obtained from sensors include pressure, temperature, position, torque, and so on.

Actuators. After *sensors* convert physical signals into electrical signals for easier processing, and once the processing is completed, the electrical signals need to be converted back into their original form. This is done using actuators. An **actuator** is a component or assembly of components that directly controls the motive power of actuated equipment. The major difference between *sensors* and *actuators* is that the latter convert signals to a form that is compatible with the process. The criteria used for sensors also apply to actuators for deciding when actuators should be considered elements of a manufacturing system. An example of an actuator is a *motor* used to convert electrical signals generated by a computer to actual movement of a conveyor system. Other actuators examples include *relays*, and *valves*.

Industrial robots. Robots are particularly useful in a wide variety of manufacturing applications such as material handling, spray painting, spot welding, arc welding, and inspection and assembly. There are several definitions of robots. The following one seems appropriate for manufacturing applications. The **industrial robot** is a programmable mechanical manipulator, capable of moving along several directions, equipped at its end with a device called the *end-effector*, and performing factory work ordinarily done by human beings. The term robot is used to identify a manipulator that has a built-in control system and is capable of stand alone operation (Koren, 1983). In an automated manufacturing facility, several robots are typically configured as an integrated multirobot system (IMRS). An IMRS consists of two or more robots, machines, and sensors and is capable of executing many industrial processes with efficiency, flexibility, and reliability (Shin, 1987).

Computerized Numerical Control (CNC). Computerized numerical control is the logical extension of numerical control (NC). Numerical control is the control of a machine tool by means of a prepared program. The Electronic Industries Association (EIA) defines NC equipment as a system in which actions are controlled by the direct insertion of numerical data at some point. The system must automatically interpret at least some portion of this data.

The main types of CNC machines are drilling, milling, and lathe. A highly flexible NC machine under computer control is sometimes referred to as a *direct numerical control* (DNC). The term DNC was originally used to describe systems in which a number of CNC machines were connected with a computer, which sent programs to the machines via serial communications using an interface connected to their paper tape reader ports.

Programmable logic controllers. A **programmable logic controller** is a solid-state device used to control the operation of machines or processes by means of a stored program and feedback from input/output devices (Jones and Bryan, 1983). Programmable logic controllers are intended to be used by automation specialists for the purpose of controlling machines and other sequential processes within an industrial environment. Two main features of PLCs are: First, they are typically programmed in a special language called **ladder diagram;**[1] and second, they are designed for harsh environments. A *ladder diagram*[2] program is composed of statements in a relay format, which makes it easy to write new programs and easy to comprehend existing programs. A *programmable controller* basically reads many input signals, performs logical operations based on the inputs, and delivers output signals, with this sequence repeated periodicaly. Input signals may be generated by limit switches, sensors, or push buttons. Output signals may drive communicators, actuators, and other devices. During program execution, the PLC reads all the inputs, and according to the control logic, energizes or deenergizes the outputs, thus solving the ladder network. The process of reading the inputs, executing the program, and updating the outputs is known as a *scan*, with typical values ranging from 1 to 100 msec.

Factors which influence the selection of a PLC for a given application include scan time, number of digital and analog I/O, remote I/O, special I/O (e.g., high-speed pulse counter), LAN interface, processor capability, memory size, power supply, environmental, and language support.

Example

The following is a PLC application in paint spraying, where the PLC is used to control the painting sequences in an automobile plant. Style and color information is entered by an operator or downloaded from a host computer. The PLC automatically tracks parts through the conveyors until they reach the spray booth. The PLC then decodes the part information and controls the spray guns to paint the automobile. The spray gun movement may be actually controlled by a robot, in which case the PLC sequences the robot operation through several stages corresponding to the automobile areas to be painted (e.g., doors, roof, etc.).

Material transport systems (transfer systems). Materials need to be transported between manufacturing cells, assembly stations, testing, and other stations. Robots are not used to perform this type of material handling because of the distances involved. Instead, the following devices are typically used:

Automated Guided Vehicles (AGV). An AGV is a system in which identical vehicles load, unload, and transport materials, under computer control, without human intervention. Directional control is provided by some type of guide path; usually built into the floor, or by transmitted radio messages. The carts are controlled by plant floor computers, on-board computers, and local traffic control devices which also communicate with the overall FMS control system.

An AGV system is composed of three functional units: a guidepath, the guided vehicles (carts), and the control system.

The *guidepath* consists of multiple media, such as wire, that a vehicle follows. These wires

---

[1] Other PLC languages include functional blocks, and Petri Net-like languages.

[2] Also called a ladder network.

are usually buried from one to three inches beneath the surface of the floor. A signal is sent along the wire, and the electronics of the vehicle detect these signals, which are used to control the vehicle.

The various wires used carry information about the physical path, intersection control, and vehicle status. The physical path is the trajectory that the vehicle follows. This is the primary path a vehicle uses for straight travel, and it is uninterrupted by other vehicles or intersections. The intersection control wire is used by the vehicle in places where guidewires intersect and multiple physical paths are present. The vehicle status is used by the vehicle to communicate status information about itself to the control system. The status information which is communicated includes battery charge level, operation status of hydraulic or mechanical components, and nonpath related commands.

The cart is a driverless *guided* vehicle equipped with electromagnetic guidance components. The vehicle uses the various wires for guidance and status communication. Most vehicles are equipped with collision avoidance devices.

The *control system* is based on a microcomputer or minicomputer. The microcomputers directly interface with the various guidewires and perform the following functions: driving signals into the wires, performing overall vehicle movement scheduling and monitoring, and communicating with upper level computers.

Towline System. In this system, pallet fixtures or platforms are carried on carts that are towed by a chain located beneath the floor. Workpieces are accurately located in the pallet fixtures. The latter can move and be clamped at successive machines in manufacturing cells.

Roller Conveyor Systems. Workpieces lay on top of rotating rollers which run through the factory. When a workpiece approaches the required cell, it can be picked up by a robot or routed to other cells via a cross-roller conveyor.

Belt Conveyor System. In the belt conveyor system, either a belt or a chain is used to transport the parts. Three different modes of operation can be noted: *continuous transfer*, *synchronous transfer*, and *power and free*; depending on whether the belts move continuously, in a synchronized fashion, or in a master slave mode.

Automated warehouses. Automated warehouses control the movement of materials and report information on such movements to appropriate computers in the factory. Another name that is used for such systems is automated storage/retrieval systems (AS/RS). The main functions of AS/RS are (Ranky, 1983):

1. computer control of material, which provides the status and location of materials for all subsystems within the manufacturing control architecture,

2. reducing inventory by the use of appropriate algorithms,

3. improving security and reducing product losses by handling damaged parts or components and locating errors, and

4. eliminating unnecessary handling and data management of material.

Bar code readers. Bar code readers consist of a set of symbols used for ensuring correct build while providing the ability to track an assembly or component through the manufacturing and assembly process. Thus, the main function of bar code readers is one of identification. Their main advantage is that they are easy to install, and the electronics involved to read the code are inexpensive and easily interfaced with a computer.

Vision systems. Vision systems are useful for testing or inspecting parts where they are used for object location, object identification, and other operations. For example, one current application of these systems is to locate missing components (e.g., distributors and EGR[3] valves) in an automobile engine. Another important vision application is *dimensional gaging*, where the vision system is used to verify dimensions of parts, holes, patterns, and so on. There are two types of information generated by vision systems which need to be transported over the network. The first one is logical information (e.g., a distributor is missing from engine NJS52197). The second type of information is video (e.g., a two-dimensional array containing all pixels that correspond to an image). The latter type of information finds application in security systems. Other intermediate forms are also possible, for example, a pixel map representing object edges.

Microprocessor based controllers. The function of this class of controllers is similar to that of PLCs discussed previously. The main advantage that microprocessor-based controllers have over PLCs are faster speed and better data handling capability. Even these distinctions are fading, as many PLCs now support high-speed coprocessors as well as a variety of languages. Other differences exist between microprocessor based controllers and PLCs. One difference has to do with the way they are realized (e.g., designed and manufactured). Computer-based controllers have, in general, a smaller number of input/output ports than PLCs. Another difference is that microprocessor based controllers have generally more capabilities than a PLC. For example, computer-based controllers can be programmed in a variety of high-level languages, and hence can be easily interfaced with other application programs written in the same language. PLCs, on the other hand, are generally more restricted in the use of programming languages.

Microcomputers and minicomputers. Production planning and control in automated manufacturing systems has been made possible by the availability of high performance microcomputers and minicomputers. These computers are either embedded into the manufacturing devices (e.g., several microcomputers usually control the movements of a robot), or they work as standalone units performing other types of monitoring and control functions (e.g., a CAD/CAM station or a cell controller).

Microcomputers and minicomputers are listed together because for many applications their functional and operational characteristics are similar. They are needed because they provide the means for automatic control of the other elements of the manufacturing facility. Much has been written on microcomputers and minicomputers, and the reader is referred to the excellent books on the subject.

Mainframe computers. The function of a mainframe computer is similar to that of microcomputers and minicomputers, one of control. However, unlike the microcomputers and minicomputers, the control performed by a mainframe computer is one of high level (to be discussed later in this chapter). One additional function of mainframe computers is that they will manage the databases for an entire manufacturing facility.

[3] Exhaust Gas Recirculation.

11.4 ORGANIZATION OF MANUFACTURING SYSTEMS

Having seen the elements of a manufacturing system, let us now turn our attention to the way in which these elements are grouped together to perform automated manufacturing functions. Figure 11.2 depicts one organization of an automated manufacturing system. One can clearly distinguish five subsystems interconnected by two types of transport systems, one for materials and the other for information. The five subsystems are computer aided design/computer aided manufacturing (CAD/CAM), flexible manufacturing systems (FMS), automatic assembly, automatic inspection, and the common database. The material transport system can be a conveyor or an AGV. The information transport system involves a computer network.

A Database Manufacturing Model

Several perspectives are useful for developing manufacturing models. We discuss next a manufacturing model based on a data-base perspective. The use of a wide variety of databases is pervasive in manufacturing systems. For example, a database file containing tooling data can be used by the following subsystems:

a) production planning,

b) process control,

c) part programming (that is, CAM),

d) tool preset and tool maintenance,

e) robots for tool assembly, and

f) stock control and materials storage.

The model basically shows the interactions of the databases located in the different manufacturing subsystems and the common database, as depicted in Figure 11.3.

Attributes of Production Planning and Control

As noted, since the subject of automated manufacturing is too broad, we concentrate on production planning and control. The two main attributes of a production planning and control system are *monitoring* and *control*. In the remaining of this section we discuss these concepts.

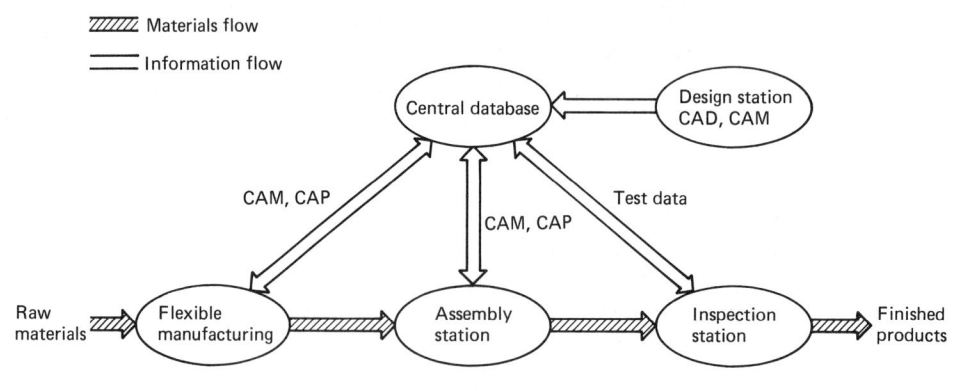

Figure 11.2 A computer integrated manufacturing system.

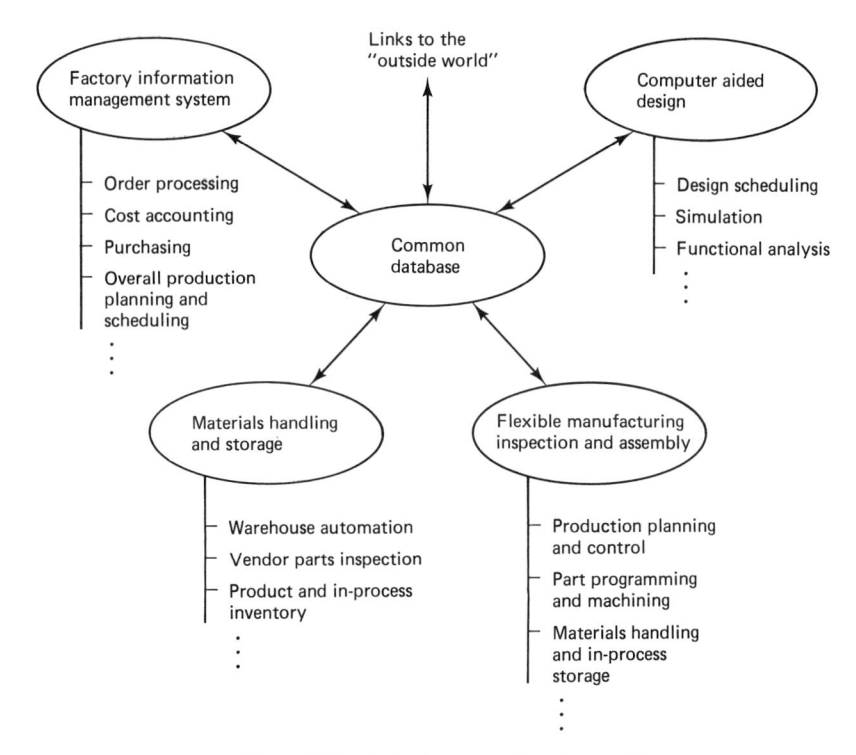

Figure 11.3 A database manufacturing model.

Monitoring. Monitoring is the gathering of data or information about a certain system for various purposes. Data gathered can be from sensor readings (e.g., motor velocity, temperature), machine status (e.g., ready, off), and so on. Some examples of systems to be monitored are NC machine tools, robot systems, conveyors, and automated guided vehicles. Monitoring can be used for control, data trend recording, maintenance dispatch, and other purposes.

Control. Control is the methodology that is used to alter the behavior or performance of a system according to a predetermined objective. Two examples of control systems encountered in a manufacturing facility are the control of the joint angles of a robot to follow a predetermined trajectory in a paint operation, and the control system that schedules the operation of several DNC machines which work together performing part processing operations. The basic configuration of most control systems involves the principle of **feedback,** as depicted in Figure 11.4. The output of the system is compared with the reference (i.e., objective) in order to drive the system in a way that the objective is met. The corresponding system is referred to as a **feedback control system.** The system's output is basically obtained by *monitoring* the variable of interest. Some control systems use a **feedforward** path in addition to the feedback path for improving the performance of the control system, as shown in the **feedforward control system** of Figure 11.5.

An automated manufacturing facility is computer controlled. Manufacturing systems are composed of discrete event and continuous processes. Discrete event processes typically generate digital signals which are readily incorporated into computer systems. Continuous processes, on the other hand, involve continuous signals which must be sampled at periodic intervals and converted to digital format for computer control. The corresponding system is referred to as a **sampled data**

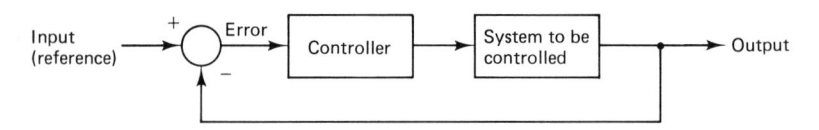

Figure 11.4 A feedback control system.

system, and is illustrated in Figure 11.6. Although the control functions of a production planning and control, and a robot control systems are similar, they differ in that they exist at different levels of abstraction.

Thus, several types of control systems can be distinguished. The following is a classification which is suitable for manufacturing applications. From a level of abstraction point of view the classification is done in a hierarchical way as follows:

1. Dynamic Control:

Dynamic control is the lowest level of control in the hierarchy. Control functions are performed by the **controller.** In this case, the controller is used to implement algorithms for generating the control signals that will *directly* control the process variables. An example of dynamic control is the controller used in robots for generating the voltage signals that control the motors that drive a robot arm to reach a desired position. Many control algorithms of this type are configured in the standard PID (proportional, integral, and derivative) form. For automated manufacturing, computer implementation for these controllers is essential. Dynamic controllers which are implemented on computers are also called *direct digital control* (*DDC*). An example of this type of control is the linear servamechanism, (servo) shown in Figure 11.7.

2. Sequence Control:

Under this control approach, a process is automatically *sequenced* through a number of stages during its operation. Each stage could be a simple binary actuation (e.g., sensing a limit switch) or the initiation of a DDC operation. Figure 11.8 shows a sequence type of control encountered in manufacturing applications, that of spray painting of small parts. For this example, the controller goes through the following sequence (stages) of operations:

a) Once the part is loaded into the carrier, move carrier to the work position where the part will be painted.

b) Signal the clamping device to clamp part.

c) Signal motor controller to start moving motor at a constant speed counterclockwise (cww).

d) When the upper limit switch (LS) senses that the sprayer is in the upper position, signal the motor controller to reverse the sprayer motion.

e) When the lower limit switch (LS) senses that the sprayer has reached the lower position, rotate the part.

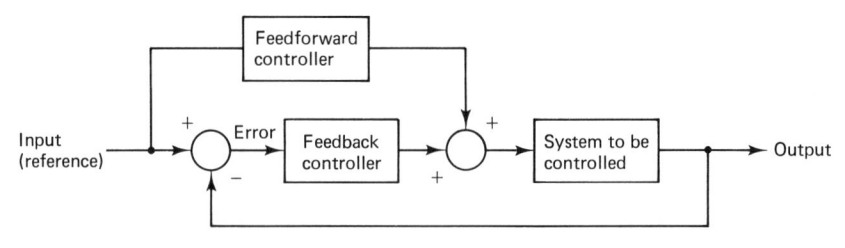

Figure 11.5 A feedforward control system.

Introduction to Automated Manufacturing   Chap. 11

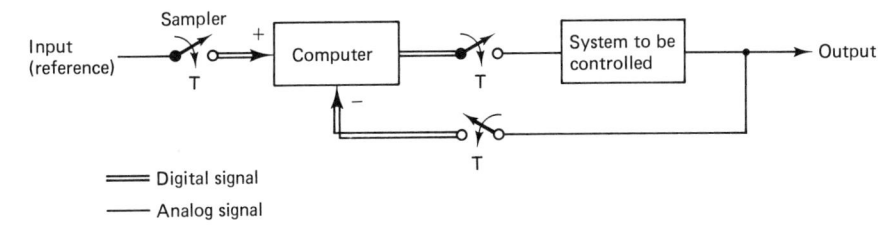

Figure 11.6 A sampled data (digital) control system. Switch closes every T seconds.

    f) Repeat steps b) through e) until the entire part is painted.
    g) Unclamp part.
    h) Signal carrier to move the part away.

Although any general purpose microcomputer or minicomputer can perform *sequence control* functions, a programmable logic controller is typically used as a sequence controller.

    3. Supervisory Control:

Supervisory control systems are used to specify or optimize the operation of a set of DDC or sequence control systems. For example, the objective of a supervisory system might be to schedule part processing or part production in a manufacturing cell or to maximize the cell production.

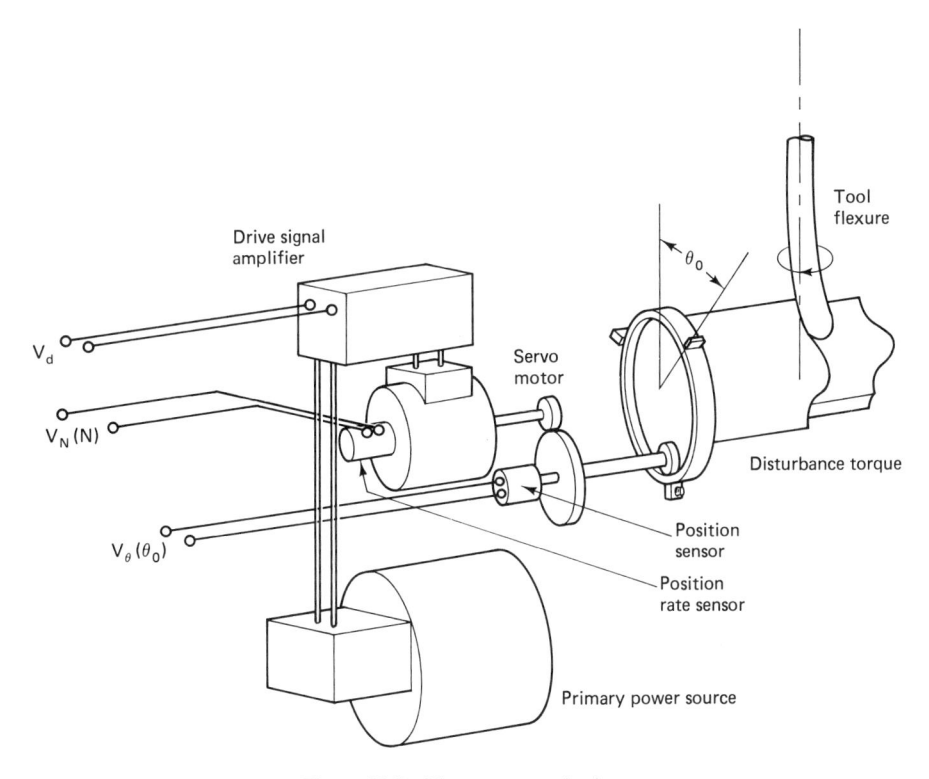

Figure 11.7 Linear servomechanism.

Sec. 11.4 Organization of Manufacturing Systems

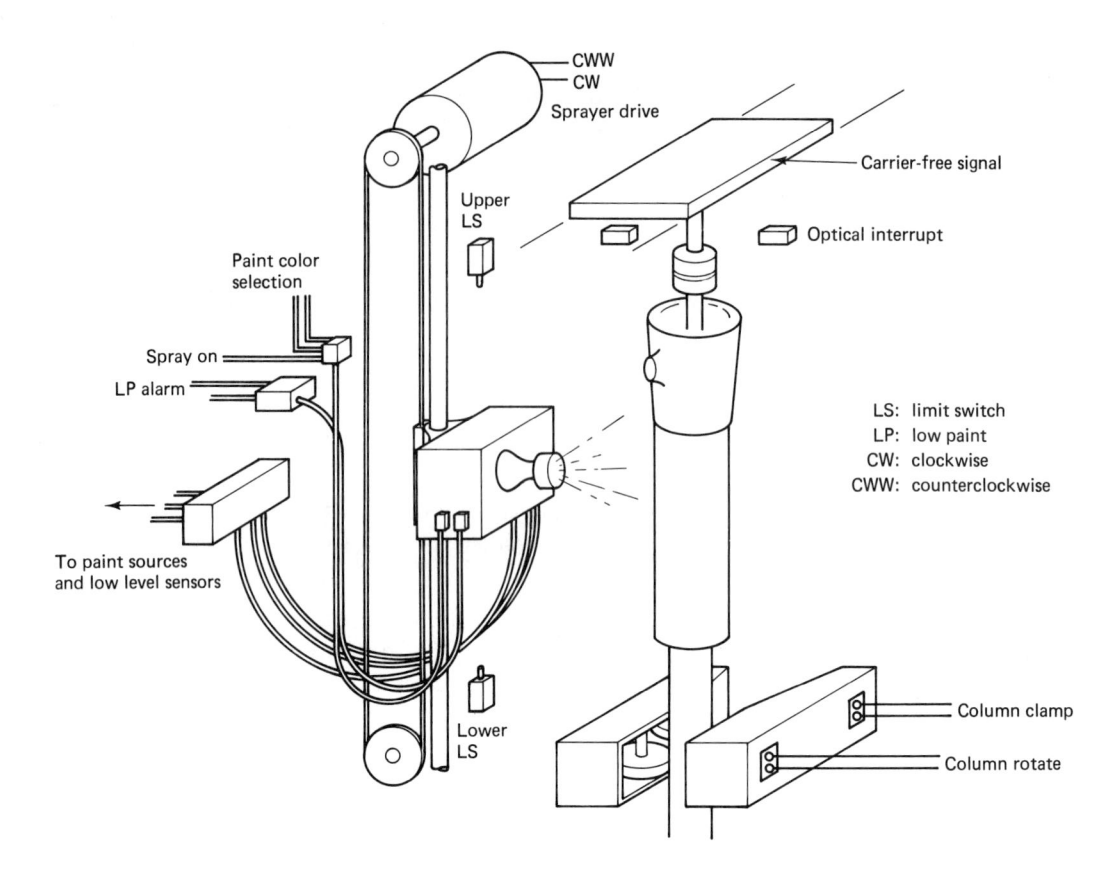

Figure 11.8 Sequencing control.

The following is a set of functions of a supervisory control system in a manufacturing environment, one of *dynamic part scheduling*. Scheduling finds applications when the machines involved in an FMS are idle and resources are wasted. A dynamic scheduling system allows an FMS to combine the benefits of a highly productive but inflexible transfer line and the flexible job shop type of production. Scheduling involves changing the order of activities of a system (e.g., the order in which parts are manufactured, order of tools delivered to processing stations, or order of parts mounted on pallets) in order to meet a specific objective.

The functions of a dynamic scheduling system are:

> Monitoring actual production by reading system status data via the network: Monitoring constitutes the sensory function of the scheduling system. The measurements collected are compared with the reference (objectives) production, and the deviations are used to perform actual control functions.
>
> Reading current data provided by the system dispatcher: The system dispatcher is in charge of part production.
>
> Evaluating tooling conditions (i.e., availability and requirements) and part processing requests.

Determining the sequence of part processing tasks.

Allowing the rearrangement of components.

Allowing cancellation and/or reassignment of resources.

4. System-wide Control:
This is the highest level of control. The control system function is to generate the necessary commands to ensure that the overall system objectives are met in a timely fashion. An example of a system-wide control system is one used in a manufacturing facility which schedules the flexible production of m units of product A, n units of product B, and so on, with enough flexibility to define the product type and their desired volume production.

11.5 MODELS FOR AUTOMATED MANUFACTURING SYSTEMS

In this section, we discuss two CIM models which will help analyze the role of networks in manufacturing. The first one is a model developed by SME, and the second one is a hierarchical control model.

SME CIM Model

The Society of Manufacturing Engineers (SME) has developed a CIM model, which is based on the realization that manufacturing productivity can be increased by the judicious use of computer technology, human factors, and education/professional development in the following four key areas:

factory automation,

manufacturing control,

manufacturing planning, and

engineering design.

The preceding areas are highly integrated by an appropriate architecture and a common database, as depicted in Figure 11.9. However, the model does not provide the system architecture for integrating the manufacturing subareas such as design, shopfloor control, and materials handling, nor the architecture for supporting the database component.

Hierarchical CIM Model

Although the SME CIM model takes into account the major CIM areas and their interactions, it does not take into account the levels of control and their time granularity, which are responsible for achieving a completely automated manufacturing facility. Furthermore, the SME CIM model depicts a flat system's organization with no consideration of the hierarchical organization structure of most manufacturing facilities. A hierarchical CIM model shows the different level of control encountered in a CIM system, ranging from the real-time *dynamic control*, involving sensors and actuators, to the *system-wide control* at the highest level of manufacturing operations, as discussed in the previous section.

Several hierarchical control models have been suggested in the literature. Two examples of

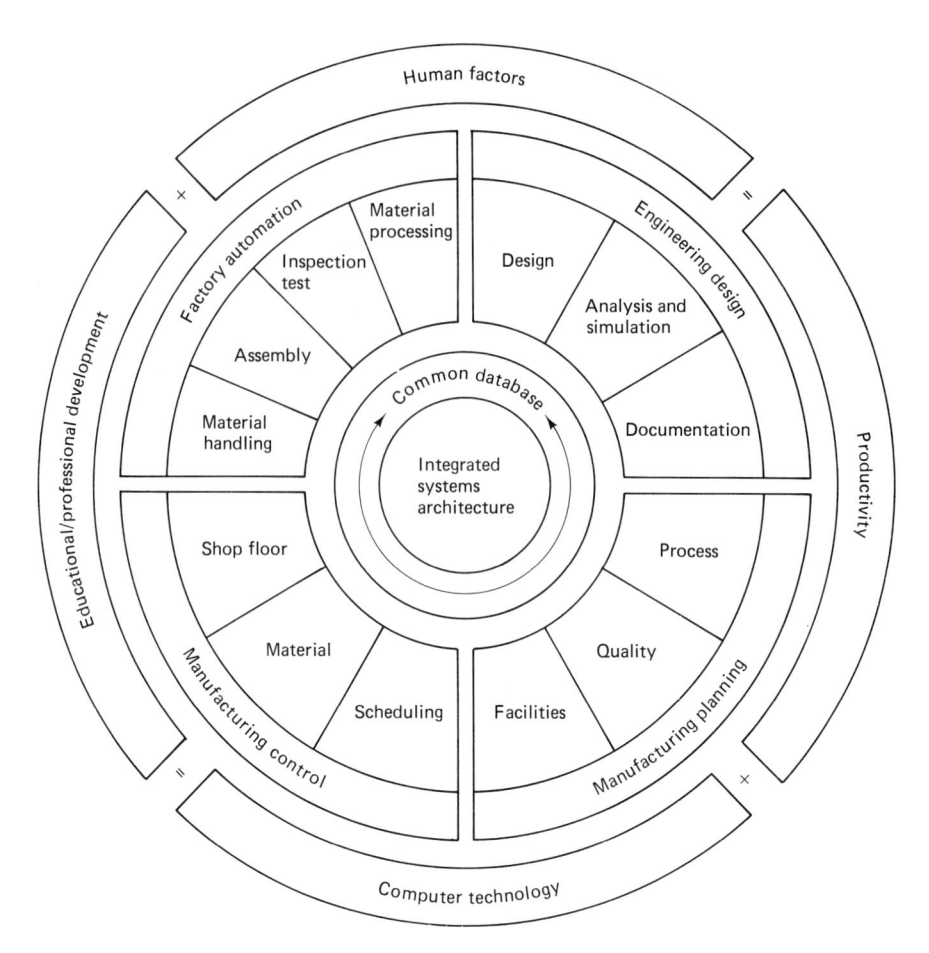

Figure 11.9 SME model of a CIM system showing the four major areas and subareas of manufactured automation.

hierarchical control models are the Advanced Factory Management System (AFMS) developed by Computer Aided Manufacturing Inc., and the Advanced Manufacturing Research Facility (AMRF) of the National Bureau of Standards (NBS) (O'Grady, 1986).

The advanced factory management system. The Advanced Factory Management System is a control hierarchy intended to break down the complex problem of planning and controlling shop floor activities into a series of smaller modules. The hierarchy consists of four levels.

1. Factory control system: This level considers such aspects as determining end-product requirements, product structure definitions (e.g., product planning), and individual shop capacities and capabilities.

2. Job shop level: This level takes commands from the level above (i.e., the factory control system) to generate commands for the work center levels. Functions included in this level include taking end-product productions and exploding the productions into processing operations and scheduling events associated with shop orders.

3. Work center level: The functions of this level include taking commands from the job shop level and generating detailed task requirements. The task events are then scheduled and commands for these tasks are passed to the next lower level (i.e., the unit/resource level).

4. Unit/resource level: In this level, the tasks from the work center level are broken down into subtasks which are in turn carried out.

Some functions are generic enough so that they can be performed at different hierarchical levels. The functions performed at each level are of the following types:

- resource monitoring,
- planning information update,
- requirements generation,
- scheduling of part production,
- resource planning (e.g., tool allocation),
- event generation,
- status monitoring,
- event prediction, and
- performance evaluation.

For example, *resource monitoring* includes checking the status and conditions (e.g., broken, not ready, available, worn, etc.) of the various resources at each level of the automation hierarchy. A *resource monitoring* system could keep track of the number of tools available in a tool magazine, whether they need maintenance, or replacement, their time history and some tool statistics.

The Automated Manufacturing Research Facility (AMRF). The automated manufacturing research facility is somewhat similar to the AFMS, in that the complex planning and control functions in an automated manufacturing facility are broken down into a series of levels in a planning and control hierarchy, as shown in Figure 11.10. The hierarchical levels in the AMRF are:

1. facility level,
2. shop level,
3. cell level,
4. workstation level, and
5. equipment level.

The *facility level*, the highest level, includes process planning, production management (including long-term schedules), and information management, with links to financial and other administrative functions.

Below the facility level is the *shop level*, which manages the coordination of resources and jobs on the shop floor. The functions involved at this level include the grouping of parts belonging

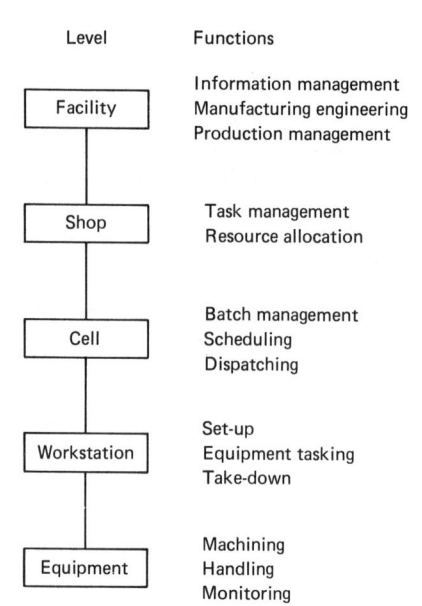

Level	Functions
Facility	Information management Manufacturing engineering Production management
Shop	Task management Resource allocation
Cell	Batch management Scheduling Dispatching
Workstation	Set-up Equipment tasking Take-down
Equipment	Machining Handling Monitoring

Figure 11.10 Hierarchical organization of the AMRF model.

to certain jobs into batches using a *group technology* (GT) classification scheme. A feature of the AMRF model is the introduction of the concept of a *virtual manufacturing cell*. A **virtual manufacturing cell** comprises machines which are interconnected in a truly dynamic fashion, that is; the configuration and number of virtual manufacturing cells can vary with time. In addition to configuring job groups and virtual manufacturing cells, the functions at this level include allocating tooling, jigs/fixtures, and materials to specific workstation/job combinations. The activities at the shop level are reevaluated based on feedback from the cell level and commands from the facility level.

The next level below is the *cell level*, which contains the cell control systems for scheduling and controlling the jobs. The jobs have already been divided into groups and allocated to each cell based on job similarities. Additional functions involve the scheduling of material handling and tooling within the cell.

Unlike the AFMS system, the next level below involves coordinating the activities of a workstation and is referred to as the *workstation level*. In AMRF terms, a **workstation** consists of a robot, a machine tool, a material storage buffer, and a control computer. Thus, the workstation controller is involved with the arrangement of the sequence of operations to complete the jobs allocated to the cell control system.

The lowest level of the planning and control hierarchy is the *equipment level*, consisting of the controller for individual resources such as machine tools, robots, or material handling systems and associated sensors and actuators.

Comparison of AFMS and AMRF. When comparing the Advanced Factory Management System with the Automated Manufacturing Research Facility, we notice that they both use a hierarchical approach for the planning and control of manufacturing systems. The advantages of decomposing the overall system into a series of levels are the same as those of decomposing the communication functions into the seven layer model developed by the International Organization for Standardization (ISO). The two hierarchies have levels with similar functionality, as indicated below:

AFMS	AMRF
Factory control	Facility
Job shop	$\begin{cases} \text{Shop} \\ \text{Cell} \end{cases}$
Work center	Workstation
Unit/resource	Equipment

The inclusion of an extra layer in the AMRF hierarchy is partly accounted for by the inclusion of the *virtual manufacturing cell* concept in the AMRF. Both the AFMS and the AMRF assume the existence of distributed databases or remote databases with some duplication of data, instead of relying on centralized databases.

In the remainder of this chapter we concentrate on the control of the AMRF cell level.

The AMRF cell level control. As any control system, the cell level control system must receive control references and objectives in order to generate control actions which may involve more detail references and objectives. The *cell control system* receives control objectives from the *shop control system* and generates specific commands for devices located at the *workstation* and *equipment* levels. The nature of the commands received from the shop level, and the degree of interaction with the shop level, determines the required functions of the cell level control system. For example, if the shop level control system generates very specific commands requiring frequent communication with the cell control system to oversee the entire operation, then the cell control system does not require extensive funcionality. On the other hand, if the shop level control system just gives general goals and objectives to the cell level control system, then the latter must generate its own schedules, commands, and so on. In this case, extensive functionality from the cell control system is required.

Determining whether a cell control system has the required functionality can be very complex, because it depends on the capabilities of the computer system and the communication network used in the cell. The kind of operating system (e.g., multitasking or non-multitasking), the type of high level (e.g., Pascal, C, or ADA) and application level programming languages (e.g., Grafcet, expert systems), the type of communication network (e.g., random or deterministic channel access schemes) and other factors influence the capabilities of a cell control system. Rather than going into the details involving these issues, we take a very simplistic view of a computer system by identifying two basic attributes: decision-making ability and local memory.

Decision-making ability simply means that devices in the cell have a microprocessor or any other type of processor with appropriate programming languages so that the capability exists for making decisions. Local memory involves primary or main memory (i.e., RAM memory) and secondary memory such as disk drives, tapes, and so on. Both the decision-making ability and the memory available in the cell determines the degree of interaction between the shop level and the cell level control systems. For example, a cell level with limited decision-making ability and limited memory, requires detailed commands and close supervision from the shop level control system.

Depending upon the decision-making ability and memory attributes, we distinguish four classes of cell control systems (O'Grady, 1986):

1. High memory, high intelligent systems: This is the most complex cell control system, having the capability of storing programs associated with the cell operation. The cell computer system is highly sophisticated, perhaps involving a *real-time, multitasking operating system*.

2. Low memory, high intelligent systems: The cell control system requires that programs or data for cell devices be transferred from shop level computers.

3. High memory, low intelligent systems: Although this class of systems is capable of local storage of programs, it still requires detailed commands from the shop level system.

4. Low memory, low intelligent systems: This is the simplest cell control system requiring detailed commands and the transfer of programs or data from the shop level system. Any additional functionality flexibility is provided by the shop level control system.

Thus, the degree of independence of the *cell control system* from the *shop control system* depends on the decision-making abilities and local memory attributes of the cell control system.

Cell configurations. The manufacturing cell as defined in Section 11.2 is responsible for the manufacturing of a specific part family determined by *group technology* principles. This section discusses typical arrangements of manufacturing cells.[4]

Although cell configurations vary tremendously, typical cells incorporate some of the following:

computer systems,

part processing devices such as CNCs or DNCs,

material transport systems,

part testing devices, such as vision systems, and

part storage systems.

The main constituent element of the manufacturing cell is a computer system for planning and controlling the production process in the cell, with the other elements being added based on the specific manufacturing requirements. Depending upon the decision making ability and the local memory, computer systems may range from small, microprocessor-based systems to highly sophisticated minicomputers with powerful operating systems and programming languages.

Cells requiring extensive part processing include a wide variety of NC machines, incorporating lathes, mills, and drills, and material transport systems such as conveyors, robots, automated guided vehicles, etc. Sometimes it is advantageous to perform part (or product) testing as the part is being manufactured rather than performing the testing after a batch of parts has been manufactured. Testing involves specialized devices such as vision systems, coordinate measurement machines (CMM), robots, optics, and other devices. Part storage devices range from buffer areas for tools and parts to automated warehouses for storing large quantities of finished goods. Thus, part storage devices may or may not be part of a cell.

---

[4] In actual implementations, the term cell has often different meanings. In the project Vanguard of GM for example, a cell is equivalent to an AMRF workstation, whereas the AMRF cell is referred to as a *cell pool*.

Cell sizes vary markedly, with small cells having very simple control systems incorporating just a few components. As already noted, one of the largest manufacturing cells proposed is that of the *automated manufacturing research facility* (AMRF) of the National Bureau of Standards (NBS). The AMRF concept views an entire manufacturing facility being a dynamic arrangement of *virtual manufacturing cells*. The virtual manufacturing cells are assumed to be highly automated and flexible.

11.5.1 Cell Control System Types

Depending upon the structure, configuration, and requirements of the manufacturing cell, the functions the cell's control system vary considerably. Consider the control of a group of manufacturing cells. Several possibilities exist for the control of the cells, ranging from a highly centralized system to a decentralized one. Accordingly, we distinguish the following cell control system types (O'Grady, 1986):

>centralized,
>loading,
>itemized, and
>decentralized.

In the centralized control system, the control of the group of manufacturing cells is centralized in one place. Basically, the *loading*, *itemized*, and *decentralized* types are all somewhat decentralized schemes with varying degrees of decentralization. The *loading* scheme is the least decentralized system. Note that the criterion for classifying cell control systems is based not only on the ability to control each cell individually, but also on the ability of controlling an integrated group of cells.

Manufacturing cell with centralized control. The control of the group of manufacturing cells is centralized in the shop level system. The group of cells is controlled from a different level (i.e., the shop level) with little or no control capabilities at the cell level. A communication network linking the shop level control system and the different cells is crucial in this type of control. If the communication network fails for any reason, all cell activities stop.

Example

This example illustrates a possible dialog between the shop level and cell level control systems.

SHOP LEVEL CONTROL SYSTEM	INFORMATION PASSED	CELL LEVEL CONTROL SYSTEM
	AGV number 65 arrived at input station 6.	←
	Load robot R2D3 with program *slow-motion*.	→
	R2D3 robot loaded OK.	←
	Execute program on robot R2D3. (Robot moves part fromf AGV 65 to DNC 32.)	→
	Starting execution of program at robot R2D3.	←

SHOP LEVEL CONTROL SYSTEM	INFORMATION PASSED	CELL LEVEL CONTROL SYSTEM
	← Execution completed. (DNC 32 is now loaded with part.)	
	Load DNC 32 with program *engine*. →	
	← DNC 32 loaded OK.	
	Execute program on DNC 32. →	
	← Executing program on DNC 32. (Part is being machined.)	
	← Program at DNC 32 completed OK.	
	etc.	

Manufacturing cell with loading control. As noted, this control system, as well as the remaining ones, is somewhat decentralized. The *loading* and *itemized* types of the cell control system are very similar, differing only by the degree of dependence from the shop level control system. The cell control system of the loading type receives a quantity of work to be done by the cell during a specified period of time. The quantity of work is called a **work lump** and typically involves several jobs. The shop level control system has already performed some planning and control functions for arranging the jobs in the *work lump*.

The following sequence of activities illustrates the interaction between the shop level control system and a cell level with a *loading* control system.

1. The cell control system receives a request from the shop level control system for executing a series of jobs contained in the *work lump*. The request also includes a *deadline* for completion of the *work lump*.

2. After receiving the request to execute the work lump, the cell control system evaluates the cell resources (i.e., machines, tools, fixtures, etc.) required to complete the work lump in the specified time. Any problems identified by the cell control system are notified to the shop control system, which must determine appropriate actions.

3. Assuming that the manufacturing cell can execute the *work lump* satisfactorily, the cell control system receives the work lump from the shop control system.

4. The cell control system carries out the detailed schedules worked out by the shop control system and contained in the *work lump*.

5. When the *work lump* is completed, the cell control system notifies the shop control system accordingly.

Manufacturing cell with itemized control. Whereas cell control systems with loading control receive several jobs at a time from the shop level system, control systems with itemized control receive one job at a time. This has two implications on the cell control system. First, the itemized control system must have better decision-making ability than the loading control system. The additional decision-making ability is necessary for performing planning and control functions associated with the execution of the jobs. The second implication is that the itemized control system work under tighter time constraints than the loading control system. The tighter time constraints in turn translate into bounded response time requirements for the computer system and communication network used in the cell.

The sequence of activities of the cell with itemized control is similar to that of loading control, as listed below.

1. The cell control system receives a request from the shop level control system for executing a single job. The request also includes a *deadline* for the completion of the job. Although each job is executed independently by the cell control system, there is a provision that job requests can be queued.

2. After receiving the request to execute a job, the cell control system not only evaluates the cell resources required to complete the job in the specified time, but also produces a detailed schedule of job related activities to be completed within the cell. Any problems identified by the cell control system are notified to the shop control system, which must determine appropriate actions.

3. Assuming that the manufacturing cell can execute the jobs satisfactorily, the cell control system receives the work lump from the shop control system.

4. The cell control system carries out the detailed schedules developed in step 2.

5. When jobs are completed, the cell control system notifies the shop control system accordingly.

Manufacturing cell with decentralized control. This is the most decentralized type of cell control system. The control of the group of manufacturing cells is decentralized into the cell control system and the shop level control system. There are many possibilities for arranging the overall control system. One possibility is that one of cell control systems receives job information from the shop level control system and generates enough information for the other manufacturing cells to complete the job. Thus, the involvement of the shop level control system is minimal. Likewise, communication between the shop and cell levels is minimal, with most of the communication flow passed across manufacturing cells.

Assuming that the shop level control system requests the manufacture of 20 parts involving four cells in the following order (i.e., the part route) 12, 24, 65, and 89. The communication messages among the various control systems might take the following form:

Shop control system to first cell in the route (i.e., cell 12).

Job and Part Information.

Job number 948393, part id ER3187, lot size 20, routing 12, 24, 65, 89.

Individual Cell Information.

Cell number 12, operation id drill342, program id R234, estimated arrival time 12:23:45, estimated finish time 12:29:10.
Cell number 24, . . .
.
.
.

As the first cell in the route, cell number 12 evaluates the resources and schedules activities in order to complete the job. Any deviation from the deadlines suggested by the shop control system must be notified to the shop level control system. Assuming that everything is proceding normally, when cell number 12 finishes its processing, it requests a material transport system to carry the part to the next cell in the route (i.e., cell number 24). To accomplish this, cell number 12 sends the transport system the following information.

Material Transport Information.

Job number 948393, part id ER3187, lot size 20, source cell 12, estimated finish time 12:29:10, destination cell 24, estimated arrival time 12:31:00.

After sending the previous message to the transport system, cell number 12 sends the following message to cell number 24.

Next Cell Message.

Job and Part Information.

Job number 948393, part id ER3187, lot size 20, routing 24, 65, 89.

Individual Cell Information.

Cell number 24, operation id lathe727, program id N894, estimated arrival time 12:31:00, estimated finish time 12:32:40.

Cell number 65, . . .
.
.
.

Likewise, the remaining cells process the parts and communicate with the other cells for completing the job.

11.6 CHARACTERISTICS OF AUTOMATED MANUFACTURING SYSTEMS

In this book, we are interested in discussing local area networks suitable for automated manufacturing. However, before discussing networking aspects, certain elements of automated manufacturing systems should be noted. In particular, the following can be noted from the models for automated manufacturing systems discussed in the previous section:

1. An automated manufacturing system is composed of many elements.
This is a characteristic of most large and complex systems, which are simply an interconnection of smaller constituent systems (subsystems). In particular, a CIM system can be viewed as being composed of the following subsystems: CAD, CAM, CAP, manufacturing cells, materials handling,

flexible assembly, testing and others. The different levels in the AMRF can be also viewed as manufacturing subsystems.

2. A subsystem is composed of many devices.

This is also a characteristic of most large systems. The constituent subsystems are themselves large. For example, a manufacturing cell subsystem is usually composed of the following elements: robots, conveyors, materials storage and retrieval systems, DNC machines, CAD/CAM stations, programmable controllers, and other minicomputers and microcomputers.

3. Intersubsystem communication traffic.

Intersubsystem communication traffic is the amount of information transferred between subsystems. For example, how much information do the flexible manufacturing and flexible assembly subsystems exchange? The amount of information depends on two variales, the rate (r) of information exchange and the length (l) of the messages exchanged. A low intersystem communication traffic means a low value for the product (rl). For example, the flexible manufacturing subsystem needs to send the following to the assembly subsystem: the number of parts manufactured, storage location, parts inventory, etc. As previously discussed, intersubsystem traffic depend on the control schemes used for the different levels of the manufacturing system hierarchy.

4. Intrasubsystem communication traffic.

Intrasubsystem communication traffic is the amount of information transferred within subsystems. Intrasubsystems traffic can be higher or lower than intersystem communication traffic. For example, tooling data is typically contained in very large files, sometimes up to several M bytes. Tooling data is generated by a CAD/CAM station and sent to various other elements such as robots for tool assembly, DNC machines, or process control. However, tooling data is rarely needed in other subsystems such as testing unless it is used for actual tool testing.

5. On-line system.

An on-line system is one that accepts inputs directly from the area where they are created and returns the outputs directly where they are needed. The physical location of the system elements is determined by the application requiring that the elements are placed where they are needed. Since the size of some subsystem elements (e.g., a DNC machine) is usually large, it is difficult to move them easily. Thus, if a communication network is to support manufacturing applications, the network topology must be designed so that the overall system is *on-line*.

11.7 DESIGN CONSIDERATIONS FOR COMPUTER CONTROLLED SYSTEMS

Design issues for network based control systems are discussed in detail in Chapter 14. However, in this section we discuss general considerations of computer based control systems which will set the context for Chapter 14. Basically, we discuss the two major approaches for designing computer systems for production planning and control in manufacturing: centralized and distributed. The degree of centralization is a function of the number and location of the computers responsible for the control and monitor functions. The centralized system approach, which involves no computer network, is briefly described here. Since we are mostly interested in manufacturing applications of distributed systems, they are discussed in more detail in Chapter 14.

Centralized System

Many of the systems currently in operation belong to this category. Under this approach, either a single computer of a few computers are located close to one another in a central location (control room). This approach does not generally involve a local computer network.[5] The computer system reads the signals from the process to be controlled through long, dedicated cables and, likewise, it routes the appropriate output signals to the locations where they are needed using a different set of long cables. Thus, the centralized system is not *on-line*.

The advantages of the centralized approach are:

a) It is effective as long as the system is neither large nor complex.
b) It is easy to maintain since only one or a few computers which are located in a single place are involved.
c) Application programs are generally easier to develop, since the computers are usually provided by the same vendor thus involving a single family of operating systems and programming languages.

The disadvantages of this approach are:

a) The computer system has a limited capacity for handling monitoring and control applications, such as the ones found in production planning and control of automated manufacturing systems.
b) It constitutes a single point of failure. If the computer fails, unless there is a redundant computer, the entire system fails.
c) It is unsuitable for supporting automated manufacturing[6] applications. An automated manufacturing system is large, complex, on-line, and therefore cannot be efficiently handled by centralized systems.

Distributed Systems

The monitoring and control functions are distributed in several nodes of a computer network, thus constituting a *distributed system*. The nodes are scattered throughout the entire plant, perhaps involving subnetworks. The computer network must, of course, have the means to allow communication between any two nodes belonging to the network. If one node fails, this should not affect the operation of the other nodes. However, in some cases, depending on the communication system, a node failure may have an effect on the communication capability of the remaining nodes. In automated manufacturing systems, communication networks are used to carry information about parts traveling on conveyors, part design and manufacturing data, robot programs, DNC programs, etc.

Network stations are not restricted to minicomputers and microcomputers, but can also be any kind of *intelligent devices*, such as programmable controllers, DNC machines, or robots. It is

---

[5] If several computers are used in the control room, they typically communicate using specialized high-speed channels rather than LAN technology.

[6] We refer to automated manufacturing as it was defined in Section 11.1. Certainly, centralized systems have been used to support many somewhat automated manufacturing systems.

understood that microcomputers can be embedded in these elements; thus, when they are not standalone units, they are not referenced separately.

Before continuing, we clarify some nomenclature. In manufacturing systems, the term *station* is sometimes used to denote a set of devices which together perform a manufacturing function. For example, a *testing station* is composed of robots, materials handling systems, vision systems, and other elements which together may perform automated testing of finished goods. On the other hand, recall that in communication networks the term, *station* is used to denote any device capable of sending and receiving information through the network.

Distributed systems have the following advantages:

a) The overall capabilities of the distributed system are much larger than those of a centralized system. This advantage occurs because multiple network stations (i.e., computers, robots, etc.) are working simultaneously or concurrently, thus increasing the capability of the system.

b) The distributed approach can support the design of large, complex, and *on-line* systems. A computer network can have its constituent stations located where they are needed (e.g., close to robots, DNCs, in a manufacturing cell, in a testing station).

c) A distributed system supports the high degree of automation, integration, and flexibility, which were identified in section 11.1 as major characteristics for automated manufacturing systems.

d) It is easier to debug new applications without affecting existing ones on other stations. This is because each station is fairly independent of one another.

e) A distributed system allows a gradual system expansion. Instead of acquiring all the capabilities at once, they can be acquired incrementally, as the need arises.

Thus, it clear from the previous advantages that the distributed approach can support automated manufacturing applications. However, distributed system have the following disadvantages:

a) Harsh environment: On-line systems in manufacturing environments imply that the network stations are located where they are needed. Some areas in a plant are subject to dust, noise, vibration, dirt, and so on, which must be considered when placing manufacturing devices.

b) Communications: Since a manufacturing system is large and complex, it typically incorporates devices from different manufacturers. Multivendor communication is a difficult problem, since each vendor typically has its own communication protocols. The successful development of automated manufacturing requires not only computer networks, but also standard communication protocols. It is expected that network architectures (e.g., MAP) based on international standard protocols will provide an effective solution to this problem. Although much progress has been made in the MAP community, many problems associated with an effective communication systems are still unsolved.

c) Interoperability: Because of implementation details, even if computer stations use the same communication protocols they are not guaranteed to communicate with one another.

Computer Hardware Requirements

Although a detailed discussion of computer hardware requirements is outside the scope of this book, we nevertheless discuss them briefly. As noted in Section 11.5, the capabilities of computer systems have an effect on the type of control system used at different levels of the control hierarchy. Features of the computer hardware also have an effect on the computer interface with the network and with the process. We assume that the computer hardware can be stand alone or embedded in a manufacturing device.

Depending upon the complexity of the control systems used in the manufacturing hierarchy, computer hardware generally has the following requirements:

1. Enough buffer space.

Computer systems acting as controllers need sometimes to store programs for manufacturing devices, such as robots.

2. Direct memory access (DMA).

DMA improves system performance.[7] Communication networks are usually very fast, with transmission rates in the order of 10 M bps (bits per second) and higher. DMA techniques allow the transmission of messages directly from memory onto the transmission medium without involving the computer's processor (CPU). Thus, the CPU is free to perform other useful tasks, thus increasing system performance.

3. I/O interface.

Computers embedded in *intelligent devices* must provide the required interface to the device itself. The interface is usually configured as a set of I/O in the form of *digital*, *binary*, or *analog* channels. *Digital* channels can be a multiple of eight bits wide and are useful to interface with bar code readers and other similar devices. *Binary* channels are digital channels in which every single bit is treated independently and could represent machine status, conveyor status, on/off type of commands, etc. Analog channels are used to deal with signals that vary continuously between a lower and an upper limit. Analog channels used to monitor or control devices that have analog signals, such as servomotors.

4. Real-time environment.

A real-time[8] environment indicates that the computer system must react sufficiently quickly to affect its environment within a specified time interval. The response time suitable for real-time operation is relative and depends on the application. Some systems require a response time of 1 msec, while others might require a response time of 100 msec. Usually, this is met by having a real-time, multitasking, operating system in charge of the computer.

5. Time structure.

The previous requirement had to do with relative time. However, the computer system must also have knowledge of absolute time (i.e., the time of day). For example, a facilities monitoring and control system may need to know the time of day to run a program that does maintenance dispatching at the end of every shift (i.e., 07:00, 15:00, and 23:00 hours). This requirement is met by having an absolute time clock (time of day clock).

6. Multiprocessor structure.

High performance applications may require two or more processors in their implementation. For example, two processors may be used for performing application-related and communication-related functions, respectively. In multiprocessors, the use of dual-port memories is advantageous. Basically, a dual-port memory provides two ports with separate controls, addresses, and input/output

---

[7] Performance is discussed in detail in Chapter 13.

[8] A *real-time* system is also known as a *time-critical* system.

lines that permit independent access for reads or writes to any memory location. Thus, two processors accessing a dual-port memory need not synchronize their memory access.

SUMMARY

An automated manufacturing system is an interconnected system of material processing stations capable of automatically processing a wide variety of part types simultaneously and under computer control. The system is interconnected by a material transport system and by a communication network. The system exhibits flexibility in routing parts, part processing operations, coordination and control of part handling, and in using appropriate tooling.

An automated manufacturing system exhibits the following characteristics:

High degree of automation,
High degree of integration,
High degree of flexibility, and
Part programs can be transferred from computers to manufacturing devices

Production planning and control is the careful preparation of schedules, schemes, algorithms, and so on for the control of an automated manufacturing system so that the objectives are met. Manufacturing operations are broken down into cells, with each cell responsible for the manufacturing of a specific part family. Cells are interconnected by a transport system for material and finished parts.

The elements of a manufacturing facility include sensors, actuators, robots, computerized numerical controllers, programmable logic controllers, material transport systems, automated warehouses, bar code readers, vision systems, microprocessor based controllers, microcomputers and minicomputers, and mainframe computers. A manufacturing communication network is intended to interconnect the preceding elements. An automated manufacturing system typically consists of the following five subsystems: computer aided design/computer aided manufacturing (CAD/CAM), flexible manufacturing systems (FMS), automatic assembly, automatic inspection, and a common database.

Since the subject of automated manufacturing is too broad, we concentrate on production planning and control whose main attributes are monitoring and control. Several types of control can be distinguished with the following classification being appropriate for automated manufacturing: dynamic, sequence, supervisory, and system-wide.

Two major models exist for analyzing the role of networks in manufacturing: the SME model and the hierarchical model as represented by the automated manufacturing research facility (AMRF). The hierarchical levels in the AMRF model are: facility, shop, cell, workstation, and equipment.

We distinguish the following cell control system types: centralized, loading, itemized, and decentralized. In the centralized control system, the control of a group of manufacturing cells is centralized in one place. Basically, the loading, itemized, and decentralized types are all somewhat decentralized.

From the viewpoint of manufacturing networks, automated manufacturing systems have the following characteristics:

An automated manufacturing system is composed of many elements.

A subsystem is composed of many devices.

Intersystem communication traffic.

Intrasystem communication traffic.

On-line system

The basic approaches for designing computer controlled systems are centralized and distributed. The latter involves a computer network and it is advantageous for supporting automated manufacturing systems.

Bibliographic Notes

Many books are appearing which deal with various aspects of manufacturing systems. Ranky (1986), and Rembold and others (1985) give a comprehensive treatment of computer integrated manufacturing systems. The books by Asfahl (1985) and Koren (1985) discuss robots in a manufacturing environment whereas Jones and Bryan concentrate on programmable controllers. The AMRF is detailed in Jones and McLean (1986). The book edited by Stecke and Suri (1986) contain a good collection of articles dealing with flexible manufacturing systems.

PROBLEMS

1. Describe the role of the communication network in automated manufacturing systems.
2. List some of the advantages of automated manufacturing systems over traditional manufacturing.
3. Why is production planning and control an important area of automated manufacturing systems?
4. What is a manufacturing cell?
5. List the major elements of a manufacturing facility and give an example of each element.
6. Describe the organization of an automated manufacturing system.
7. Explain the different types of controls available for manufacturing applications from a hierarchical point of view.
8. Compare and contrast the Advanced Factory Management System (AFMS) model for automated manufacturing systems and the Advanced Manufacturing Research Facility (AMRF) model.
9. Discuss the attributes that should be considered when categorizing cell control functionality. What are the different classes of cell control systems?
10. Distinguish between the different types of cell control systems based on their ability to control an integrated group of cells.
11. What are the key characteristics that describe a CIM (Computer Integrated Manufacturing) system?
12. What is an on-line system? And how does it affect the design of a communication network?
13. Compare and contrast the centralized approach for designing computer systems with the distributed approach, listing the advantages and the disadvantages of each.
14. Extend the concepts of centralized, loading, itemized, and decentralized control system types to the ARMF workstation level control system.

12

Network and Protocol Implementation

Communication network protocols are not useful if they only exist as concepts. To be useful, protocols need to be realized in some physical fashion. **Protocol implementation** is the realization of a protocol specification in some tangible form so that they can be used in a variety of applications. In OSI networks, a protocol specification is given by a standard. However, protocol standards are not a complete specification since their general nature implies that they must be somewhat independent from the specific machine, operating system, memory management policy, and so on used in the implementation. Furthermore standard specifications are generally written in a language such as English and thus they may be ambiguous.

Protocols are implemented in a combination of hardware and software components. Examples of hardware components include integrated circuits (ICs), circuit boards, and special hardware devices. Examples of software components include operating systems, computer languages, procedures, functions, and so on. Once individual protocols are implemented, they need to be combined appropriately in order to implement a network station. Figure 12.1 depicts a typical station hardware configuration showing its major components. In this chapter we discuss design considerations for protocol implementation, as well as how the protocol implementations are combined to produce a network station implementation. Several examples of significant protocol and network station implementations are also presented at the latter portion of the chapter.

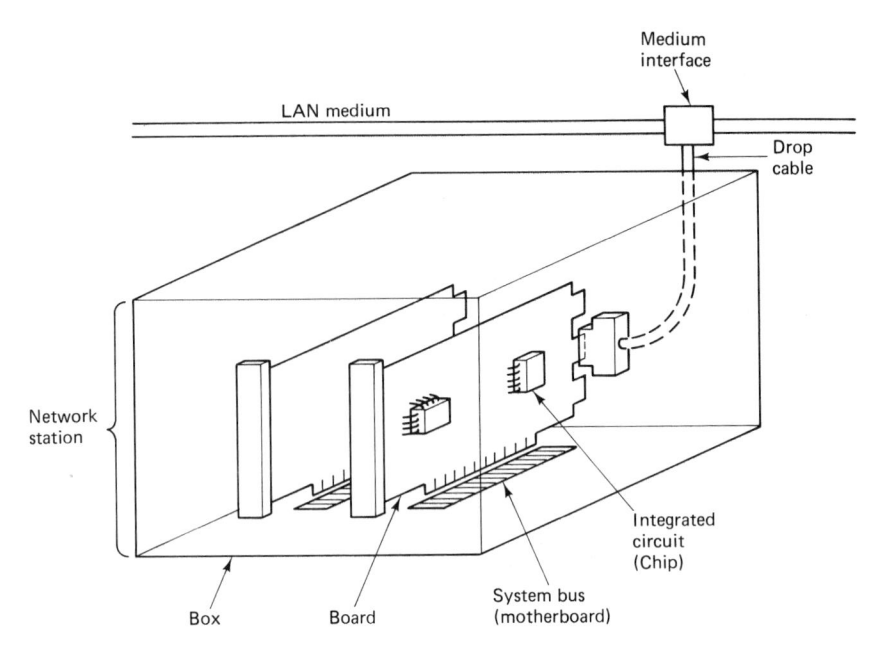

Figure 12.1 Hardware configuration for a typical network station.

12.1 CHARACTERISTICS OF HARDWARE AND SOFTWARE IMPLEMENTATIONS

Some protocol functions are more amenable to their implementation in hardware rather than software. For example, although a cyclic redundancy check (CRC) used for error detection can be implemented in software, it is generally implemented in hardware because a) the CRC algorithm is fixed for a large portion of the system's lifetime, thus, there is no need for flexibility in the implementation; b) a hardware implementation works faster than the corresponding software implementation; and c) most likely, the software implementation would run on a processor which is used for performing other tasks, thus tying up processor resources which could be used by the other tasks.

Some communication functions, such as the medium interface, can only be implemented in hardware. Indeed, it is impossible to implement a signaling technique without using hardware, since the medium itself is hardware. Thus the medium interface portion must be implemented in hardware.

In summary, hardware implementations of communication protocols and associated functions have the following characeristics:

fast (i.e., they can achieve real-time processing),
most efficient for the OSI lower layers,
relatively inflexible, and
limited intelligence.

Other protocol functions are advantageous when implemented in software. When implementing upper layer protocols, processing requests coming from adjacent layers require a great deal of flexibility. This is because there are several types of requests (i.e., establish a connection, open a file, read a variable, etc.) with many options for the parameters in each request (addresses, names, data, connection number, etc.). Since hardware implementations do not generally provide the required flexibility, the upper layers are more likely to be implemented in software. Actually, there is also a third way to implement protocols, referred to as **firmware,** which consists in a mixture of hardware and software. Since firmware is just a combination of hardware and software, we will concentrate only on hardware and software issues.

On the other hand, software implementations have the following characterstics:

very flexible,

advantageous for higher layers, and

share the same processor with implementations of other layers and perhaps with applications (depending upon performance requirements).

12.2 DESIGN CONSIDERATIONS

Since we are interested in implementing communication network and protocols using computer hardware and/or software, the design considerations center around protocols, hardware and software, and architectural issues. The design issues facing network and protocol implementors include the following:

application requirements,

implementation architecture, protocol standards and algorithms,

processors, operating systems, and programming languages,

higher layer implementations,

implementation interfaces,

implementation options,

implementation technology, and

system bus types.

Some of the preceding issues are applicable to either, a station implementation or a protocol implementation. For example, an Ethernet-like protocol (i.e., a data link layer) implementation is irrelevant of whether the network will be used for file transfer or graphics exchange applications. In contrast, a station implementation involving all layers depends on how applications are to be supported by the network. In some cases there are some design constraints which limit the choices available. For example, if one has to implement a protocol on a specific computer, then one cannot use any operating systems or bus other than those provided with the computer.

Application Requirements

This is the most important consideration, since it will determine the major options open to a network designer. The end user application determines the number and type of protocols needed to support the functionality required by the application. For some applications, end to end response time is more important, whereas for others, end to end throughput is more important. For example, an application involving *electronic mail* typically requires high throughput so that the mail system delivers as many bytes/sec as possible. On the other hand, applications involving interactive voice and data require stringent response time requirements.

Implementation Architecture, Protocol Standards and Algorithms

Before we begin a network implementation, we need to know what specific protocols will make up the network. An **implementation architecture** specifies the number, name, configuration, functions, protocols, and protocol options of all implemented layers. The implementation architecture should also specify how the functions of each layer relate to one another, and also their relationship to the OSI reference model. Other terms used to denote implementation architecture is *layer profile*, and *protocol stack*.

At each layer the protocol under implementation could be a well-established de facto standard protocol, such as Ethernet, SDLC, or it could be a *de jure* standard such as the token bus protocol as used in MAP, or it could be a brand new proprietary protocol. In the latter case, the exact protocol algorithm must be known prior to the implementation. A design could implement an entire protocol standard or algorithm or a subset of it. Implementations should spell out what portions of the standard are implemented and what portions are not. For example, the MAP 3.0 specification requires only a subset of the ISO session protocol standard. Likewise, the TOP specification requires a different subset of the ISO session standard.

The following issues, which may or may not be specified by the protocol being implemented, need to be addressed by the designer: message priority, recovery mechanism, and initialization mechanism. If user requirements dictate the need of some kind of priority, then conventional random access techniques are automatically discarded, since they do not support priority.[1] The system should recover successfully from special failures. Likewise, the system should provide a way to initialize the network.

Processors, Operating Systems, and Programming Languages

The power and flexibility of processors, operating systems, and programming languages generally affects the performance of network implementations. Most current processors are able to handle data ranging from 8 to 32 bits at a time, with clock speeds ranging from 1 to 20 M Hz. When available, a real-time, multitasking operating system can be advantageous because of its power and flexibility. Examples of multitasking operating systems include RSX-11M (PDP11), RMX (Intel), VRTX (Hunter Ready), Versados (Motorola), and VAX/VMS (Davis, 1987). An operating system that is not multitasking, but nevertheless is enjoying widespread acceptance in some network environments, is DOS from IBM.

Because of the complexity of some protocols, any programming language that supports structured programming and complex object definition is appropriate. Programming languages often used for protocol implementations include Assembler, Pascal, C, and PLM. When more efficient,

---

[1] There are, however, some modified random access schemes which take priority into account. One such scheme was discussed in subsection 4.9.5.

inexpensive, and powerful compilers become available, ADA is likely to become an excellent language for protocol implementation, because of its good support of abstract data types and multitasking.

Higher Layer Implementations

Whereas lower layer implementations are mostly done in hardware, upper layer implementations are currently done in software.[2] Design issues for higher layer implementations include configuration of software processes, multiplexing connections, connection management, interprocess communication, buffer management, processor management, and the provision of services.

Implementation Interfaces

Implementations for protocols which are located at adjacent layers in the OSI reference model need to interface with one another. A protocol implementation for layer N sends and receives data to or from a protocol implementation for layer (N − 1). For example, if the implementation under consideration corresponds to the physical layer, a medium interface must be provided. Likewise, when implementing the application layer protocol, appropriate interfaces to the end users must be provided. Since protocols are implemented in a combination of processors, memory, subsets of operating systems, programming languages, software utilities, and so on, protocol interfaces are described in terms of appropriate hardware and/or software components. For example, the MAP architecture has defined a very specific interface between the MAP application layer and the end users. The interface is known as the *MAP application layer interface*.

Use of timers in implementations. From the protocol description at the various layers of the ISO reference model, we can see that the use of timers is pervasive. However, protocol standard specifications do not give timers an adequate treatment and regard them as *local matter*, or *left to the implementor*. To make matters worse, the performance of an implementation is related to the actual timer implementations. Mumprecht and others (1988) suggest that in addition to the normal communication services, an implementation ought to support the following set of timer services:

Timer_Create_Request(*ur*),
Timer_Create_Confirm(*ur*, *pr*),
Timer_Delete_Request(*pr*),
Timer_Restart(*pr*, *value*),
Timer_Cancel(*pr*), and
Timer_Indication(*ur*).

where *ur* (user reference) is the identification of the timer in the context of the user, *pr* (provider reference) identifies the timer instance in the context of the timer facility, and *value* is the time duration of the specified timer. Whereas the Timer_Create creates and initiates the operation of a

---

[2] Another reason for the upper layer software implementations is the potential changes in protocol specifications.

single timer or a set of timers, the Timer_Delete destroys the timer(s), and the Timer_Cancel terminates the timer operation. The Timer_Restart basically rewinds the timer regardless of whether it is running and the Timer_Indication is the notification of the actual timeout, and is passed to the service provider as an interface event.

Implementation Options

In addition to implementing a subset of an entire standard protocol, a designer may implement additional options which, while not required by the standard, help with performance, diagnostics, management of resources, additional flexibility, or even implementing subsets of other standards. For example, the *Token Bus Controller* chip from Motorola implements a real-time option and diagnostics in addition to the functions specified by the token bus protocol. Likewise, the *82586* chip from Intel has a priority option not specified by the IEEE 802.3 standard.

Implementation Technology

Depending upon the number and complexity of the protocols which are required by a LAN architecture, some implementation options available to a designer include: integrated circuits, circuit boards, station boxes, and entire network systems on the hardware side, and operating systems, programming languages, and special utilities on the software side. We do not discuss details of IC technology (e.g., HCMOS, ECL) since it involves microelectronics, which is outside the scope of this book. Although we do not provide a generic discussion on the remaining options just identified, we give examples of integrated circuits, boards, boxes, and entire network systems.

System Bus Types

Another option open to a designer regards the size and configuration of the system bus. A **system bus** is a collection of data, addresses, and control lines used by host computers. The processor communicates with memory and peripherals using the system bus. Typically the *processor board,* (memory board, *LAN* interface board), and *input/output boards* plug into the system bus. The system bus should not be confused with the serial bus used as the communication medium by computer networks such as Ethernet and MAP.

In principle, one can use a special purpose bus for each design. In practice, however, there are few buses that have achieved widespread acceptance. Some of the most popular ones are Multibus from Intel, VME from Motorola, the IBM PC bus, and the Q bus from DEC. Typically, a bus is chosen based on multiprocessor support, flexibility, and the ability to support high data rates.

12.3 DETAILED EXAMPLE: AN ISO SESSION LAYER IMPLEMENTATION

The following example illustrates the concepts discussed in this section and corresponds to the design and implementation of a subset of the ISO session layer protocol standard, with an additional datagram service on a multiprocessor-based LAN known as MODIAC (Ciminiera et al., 1987). Thus, some understanding of the ISO session protocol is required in order to follow the example. Section 8.4 contains enough information to obtain the necessary understanding.

With this example, we do not intend to discuss the best method of implementing protocols. Rather, the intent is to illustrate how protocols can be implemented. Indeed, because of performance considerations, this particular implementation may not be optimal. Although an important topic, efficient protocol implementation is outside the scope of this book.

Application Requirements and Implementation Options

The design process begins by considering an end user application which is to be supported. The application is one typically found in industrial automation environments characterized by the following set of message profiles:

>Message_1: short message delivery.
>Message_2: file and job transfer.
>Message_3: inquire and response message profile.
>Message_4: cyclic message.
>Message_5: complex dialogs.

The Message_1 profile identifies short warning and alarm information units which are messages generally representing a small fraction of the overall network traffic. A guaranteed short delivery delay for this type of dialog constitutes the main communication requirement. In the MODIAC network, this problem is solved by introducing a *datagram* service accessible to a session user which allows to by-pass message processing performed by both the session and the transport layers. In this way, the application process can invoke directly lower layers communication functions, with reduced protocol overhead.

The Message_2 profile identifies transfer operations between remote stations which involve large amounts of data. Typically, file and job transfers are carried out without stringent response time and memory constraints. Since high throughput is often required, on-line recovery procedures play an important role for implementing low-cost file and job transfer protocols, while making appropriate use of resources.

The *inquire and response* profile (i.e., Message_3) introduces a message exchange mechanism between two application processes which alternate in the communication process. Unlike the *inquire and response* message profile, the *cyclic* message dialogue (Message_4) involves a master/slave process configuration, where the master generates a request message forcing the slave task to respond with a sequence of messages every predefined unit interval. Generally, even if one or more messages of the sequence get lost, information consistency is not affected. The fifth class (i.e., *complex dialogs*) refers to more complex structures, involving a combination of previous profiles.

Because of protocol overhead, a connection-oriented service is not appropriate for the message_1 profile. For the other dialogue types, the implementation of a connection-oriented service protocol is appropriate.

In addition to the *expedited data flow* service, the *data transfer* service of the ISO session layer protocol can also be used for short messaage transfer (i.e., Message_1) if the datagram service is unavailable. The datagram service, however, is preferable for requirements involving short response time and message priority. All other dialogue types, except for Message_1, base their normal data transfer operations on the availability of the *data transfer* function of the ISO session layer protocol.

Expedited messages have higher priorities than normal ones; thus they should be delivered before other normal messages. Expedited messages are not required for Message_2, Message_3, and Message_4 profiles, since the messages involve a considerable amount of data without critical response time or priority requirements. In contrast, the expedited service plays an important role for Message_5. To clarify this, let us consider an application involving two processes, the first dealing with data acquisition, and the second one dealing with data collection and statistical analysis. The sampled data taken by the first process are processed, compared to predefined thresholds, and a summary is sent to the second process. If the first process detects an out of range condition for a variable, it should immediately send a warning message to the second process, which can be done if a second prioritized data flow between the two processes is provided. Thus, for this case the expedited data service satisfies all the requirements for solving the problem.

The negotiated *disconnect* service of the session layer is needed when the connection must be closed in a graceful way. In the case of Message_1 and Message_4, the disconnect service is often useless, since the dialogue is based on a master-slave configuration and the disconnection initiative is taken unilaterally by the master process. On the other hand, since Message_2, Message_3 and Message_5 involve a symmetric communication between user processes, the negotiated disconnect service can be used for a negotiated release of the connection.

The nonnegotiated disconnect service (i.e., abort services, as discussed below), guarantees the immediate release of the connection by the user processes involved in the communication; it can be used successfully for all dialogue types and particularly when the processes are configured in a master-slave fashion for implementation reasons.

The (service) *provider abort* and *user abort* services play an important role in all types of dialogue. When a protocol error arises, the connection is immediately destroyed by the server itself, and the user is notified of the failure by a *provider abort indication* primitive; on the other hand, if the application program detects an error, it may activate the abort function and the remote user is notified with an *user abort indication* primitive. Recall that the provider abort service is strictly a local operation, which does not involve the remote protocol service provider. The *user abort*, on the other hand, involves both protocol service providers.

The *major synchronization function*, while unnecessary for Message_1, is of great importance for Message_2 when used together with the resynchronization service to solve data transfer failure. A typical example arises in a file transfer operation, in which the session user can request a major synchronizaton point after every N records sent to the corresponding user. If one or more records get lost during the transfer process, it is possible to resynchronize the transfer activity referring to the last major synchronization point inserted by the sender and acknowledged by the receiver. In the case of Message_3 profiles, this service is unnecessary, since the synchronization points are virtually represented by the sequence of inquiries, each one defining disjoint communication units.

In most application dialogs, Message_4 and Message_5 may also be organized into communication units, so that, if necessary, a recovery procedure can be designed using the *major synchronization* service. Similarly, the *minor synchronization* service may be useful for the Message_2 dialog, where further recovery procedures may be required other than those provided by the major synchronization service.

The resynchronization service allows the implementation of recovery procedures when used together with the major synchronization service for improving the reliability of Message_2, Message_4 and Message_5 profiles.

The *exception reporting function* is required by all profiles, since this mechanism informs the user when the required service cannot be terminated because of protocol errors, or for other reasons. Since both user processes are informed, a resynchronization procedure may be started.

Implementation Architecture and Implementaton Interfaces

Having discussed session layer implementation options according to application requirements, let us now discuss how the ISO session layer protocol can be actually implemented. Since the session layer is a higher layer, its implementation is mostly concerned with software issues, such as process organization, interprocess management, service access points, connections, and connection multiplexing.

The session layer implementation software is organized in four cooperating processes, each one devoted to a specific function: The first acts as a logical interface with the user processes, handling *user service* requests. The second process implements the protocol rules according to the ISO session *protocol specification* while the third one acts as a logical interface with the transport layer. Finally, the fourth process implements the management functions of the session layer, allowing direct control and monitoring of the local and remote layer communication resources, as shown in Figure 12.2.

The user interfaces directly with the session layer and with the management service. Let us consider the mechanisms which allow the application process to exchange information with the

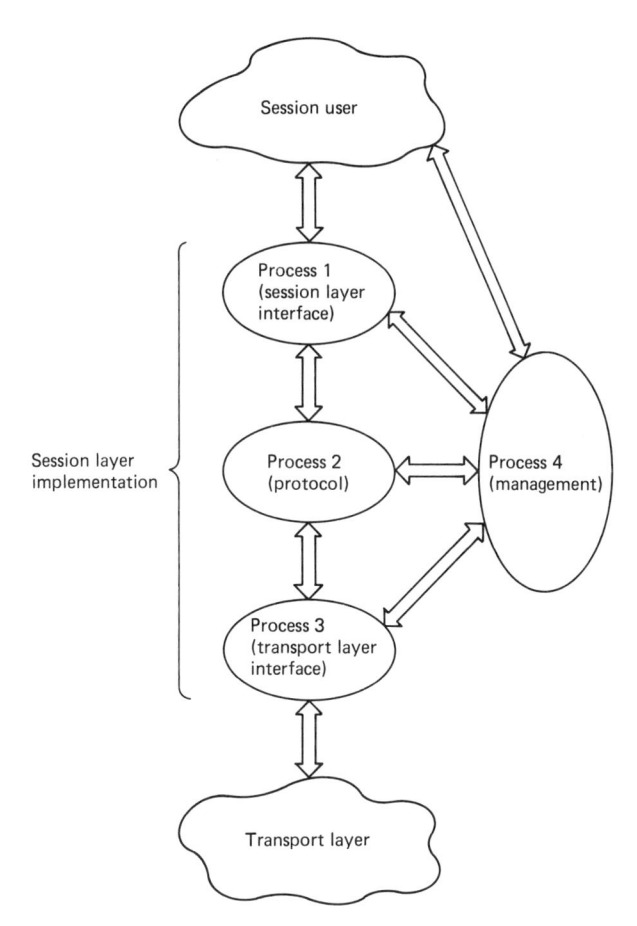

Figure 12.2 Software organization for a session layer implementation.

session layer. The software environment of the communication system is based on the MODOSK (Faro et al., 1984) operating system, which provides efficient message exchange primitives based on mailbox mechanisms. Hence, user processes can access session services through service access points (SAPs) consisting of specialized mailboxes associated with three different data paths: normal data, expedited data, and datagrams.

SAPs can be dynamically created, and the communication management server controls the maximum number of SAPs which can be simultaneously activated at a given time, depending upon available resources. Each user process may gain access to the session layer by sending a request message to its *service access point*, which specifies the service required. Communication inside the layer is implemented using the mailbox mechanism as well, and data exchanges with the transport layer are performed via a transport service access point in a similar manner. Each service request by the user process involves the following:

1. A memory buffer is allocated containing user data and parameters which are related to the service to be activated.
2. A message is constructed using data and parameters specified by the user, in accordance with the format requirements of the session layer protocol.
3. A pointer to the message is passed to the session server through a service access point.

If the user process requires a service which cannot be performed by the layer, the service provider returns the message to the user, after having appended the failure reason code in an appropriate message field. Messages can be rejected because the total number of active virtual channels exceeds the maximum allowed, and because of insufficient memory, parameter inconsistency, and other situations.

The communication resource manager interfaces with all the session layer components and can affect, for instance, the number of active channels and SAPs at any time; thus, it is able to effectively manage the layer resources. The following classes of management functions are introduced for this purpose:

1. status information collection and monitoring;
2. parameter modification; and
3. service access point and virtual channels creation/destruction.

Specifically, the MODIAC session management handles information related to the service access points, channel identifiers, and session protocol handlers. For instance, the current number of active SAPs is monitored and controlled by the management server, while other SAPs needed by additional users are created dynamically if enough system memory is available. Since each SAP can be connected to multiple session channels, the management service allows the monitoring and control of the number of virtual channels associated to each active SAP in the network. Since the opening of a virtual channel involves the creation of two interacting protocol handlers on different stations, the management service also controls the total number of protocol handlers activated on each station, in order to avoid deadlock situations caused by lack of memory resources. Management functions are supported by a specific module which may access the session layer database on each network station. Requests are sent to the layer management through SAP number 0, which differs

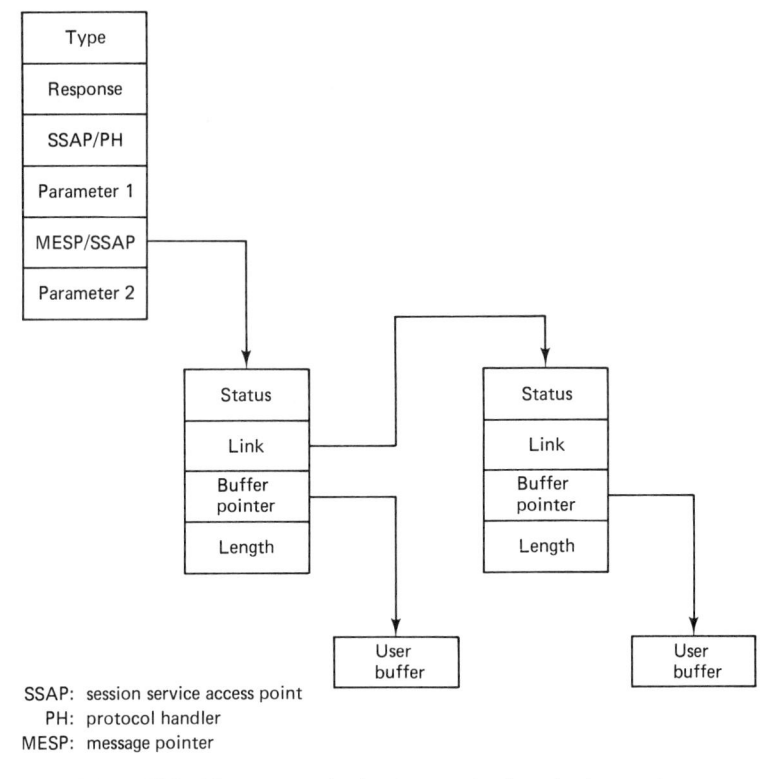

Figure 12.3 Message organization for a session layer implementation.

from other SAPs because it has a single message path, allowing only *management* messages to be exchanged. The organization of this kind of message is depicted in Figure 12.3.

The *type* field classifies the management primitive, while *response* reports the operation result returned to the user by the management server; *SSAP/PH* indicates the session service access point or the protocol handler identifier involved in the request, while *MESP/SSAP* contains the connection status descriptor pointer; the *parameter* fields specify parameter codes depending on the primitive types.

12.4 DESIGN OPTIMIZATION

The performance of protocol implementations is important for everyone involved with computer networks. Performance is important for protocol implementors, because if the performance is poor their products will not sell. Likewise, bad performance will not allow end users to meet their application requirements. Accurate performance evaluation of an entire network is very difficult because it not only depends on the protocols wich are implemented, but also on the intricacies of the implementations as well.[3]

Overall network performance is often a misunderstood issue. Many people associated with

---
[3] Performance is treated in more detail in Chapter 13.

networks tend to disregard performance; the end users because they think it has been optimized by the implementors, and the implementors because they think it will be tuned by the end users. However, there are certain factors that a designer can take into account while implementing networks and protocols that will help improve performance. The factors are:

> implementation architecture,
> network data rate,
> multiprocessors,
> channel access control schemes,
> protocols at all OSI layers,
> speed of NIU to host transfer, and
> buffer management.

Implementation architecture. The protocol implementation of OSI systems can be a very complex endeavor depending upon the complexity of the implementation architecture, and the actual protocols used. The implementation must not only conform to the standard but must also have high performance and be flexible enough to be supported by a wide variety of hardware and software. For example, is it better to use a multitasking operating system kennel or an ad hoc operating system as the basis for the architecture implementations?

Network data rate. In general, network performance improves with higher data rates. Because of overheads in the protocols and their implementation, the data rate is not a true indication of network performance. The network data rate simply indicates the potential of the network to provide good performance. For example, a network with a data rate of 10 M bps may achieve an end user throughput of only 500 K bps.

Multiprocessors. Performance can be improved when dedicated processors are used for implementing communication protocol functions, thus relieving host processors from performing communication functions. Many current implementations feature multiprocessor implementations for network stations.

Channel access control schemes. Algorithms for medium access control are usually tailored to support special classes of applications. For example, token passing algorithms are preferred if deterministic access to the medium is desired. Many books and other literature on LANs put too much emphasis on channel access control schemes when discussing network performance. As discussed throughout this book, computer networks are much more than channel access schemes.

Other protocols. Overall network performance not only depends on the medium access control scheme, but also on the protocols for all other layers. A potential problem to be avoided is the implementation of functionality that is not needed by the applications to be supported, because it will degrade performance with no real advantages. For example, simple devices with no file capabilities cannot benefit from a file transfer capability.

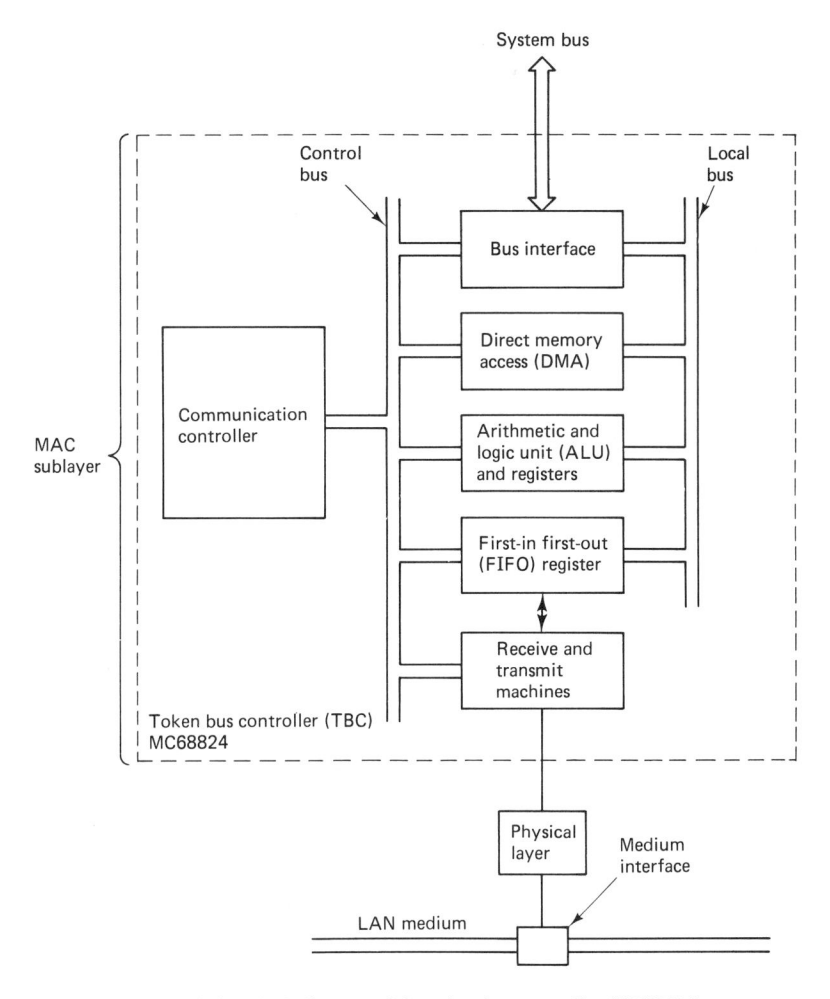

Figure 12.4 Block diagram of the token bus controller (MC68824).

Speed of NIU to host transfer. An effective way to improve the performance of message transfer between the NIU and a host is using a *local bus* in addition to the *system bus*, and direct memory access (DMA) links. A local bus can improve performance by allowing data transmission or reception to or from the physical medium, while the system bus is used for other tasks as shown in Figure 12.4.

Buffer management. Memory is a resource which must be carefully managed for its efficient use. Protocol implementations need memory for the receiver portion, the transmitter portion, and for control purposes. Having enough memory buffers can improve performance, since messages arriving to a system with no buffers available are rejected. Another aspect of buffer management aims at providing as many connections (i.e., virtual circuits) as possible, because every time a connection is established, a certain amount of memory is reserved for storing connection parameters.

12.5 INTEGRATED CIRCUIT COMPONENTS

Hardware Components

By hardware components, we mean the typical components found in computer systems, such as integrated circuits (ICs), boards, boxes, and complete systems which include ICs, boards, boxes, cables, and associated software.

In terms of the OSI reference model, there is a boundary below which most protocol implementations are done in hardware, and above which protocol implementations are done in software. Currently (1988), the boundary is between the data link layer and the transport layer, and it is expected to move upwards toward the application layer as time goes on. Since hardware implementations do not provide much flexibility or intelligence, it is not expected that all seven layers will be implemented in hardware.

Approaches for implementing protocols. There are two major approaches for implementing protocols. The first approach consists of designing the appropriate hardware and/or software for each layer of the OSI reference model, and putting the implementation for each layer in a separate hardware device or software package. To construct a network station, one simply puts together seven pieces, one for each layer. The disadvantage of this approach is that, while trying to keep each protocol implementation separate from one another, the station implementation is not efficient. For example, additional symbol or connection tables and additional management overhead may be required. Furthermore, an IC or a board may have additional space which could be utilized.

The second approach consists of maximizing resource utilization in the protocol implementation. However, in trying to maximize resources, the hardware or software components may not correspond exactly with each OSI layer. For example, an integrated circuit may correspond to a portion of one layer or several layers. Because of economic justification, the second approach is preferred by protocol implementors, and thus we will concentrate on it.

An **integrated circuit** contains thousands of transistors in one small package, also called a *chip*. With current technology, it is possible to have over 100,000 transistors per chip. The design process begins with a constraint on the size of the chip. This constitutes the available real state. The idea is to put as much protocol functionality in the real state as possible. Following, we discuss some chips used in LAN implementations for the physical and data link layers of the OSI reference model.

Token Bus Controller (Motorola 68824)

The Token Bus Controller (TBC) is a Very Large Scale Integration (VLSI) chip using HCMOS technology that implements the IEEE 802.4 MAC sublayer. The chip is designed to interface with the physical layer circuitry at the data rate of 10 M bps. Because of the complexity of the token bus MAC sublayer and the relative high speed of operation, a local bus architecture is used which incorporates a communication controller, direct memory access (DMA) circuitry, a 40 byte first-in first-out (FIFO) memory, and other circuitry, as shown in Figure 12.4. The main advantage of the local bus architecture is that the communication controller gets quick access to the local memory. The TBC chip has been designed so that it can interface with different versions of the physical layer, such as those using PSK or FSK modulation. Thus, its serial interface with the physical layer sends and receives generic *data symbols*, with each symbol representing the unit of data transmitted or received within one bit time. In this way, the chip fits into any IEEE 802.4 token bus station and matches any physical layer implementation (i.e., those requiring PSK or FSK modulators) required by the application (Alexis-Dirvin and Miller, 1985).

Chip operation. The chip interfaces with the logical link sublayer (LLC) and station management through shared memory, and with the physical layer, or modem through a serial interface recommended by IEEE 802.4. In general, when data are passed from sublayer to sublayer, or from layer to layer, it is very inefficient to rewrite the data at each layer or sublayer. A better scheme is to have the data residing in just one place, and exchange pointers indicating where the data is located. The TBC chip uses a double-linked data structure containing *frame descriptors*, *buffer descriptors*, and *data buffers*, as depicted in Figure 12.5. Since a double-linked data structure is

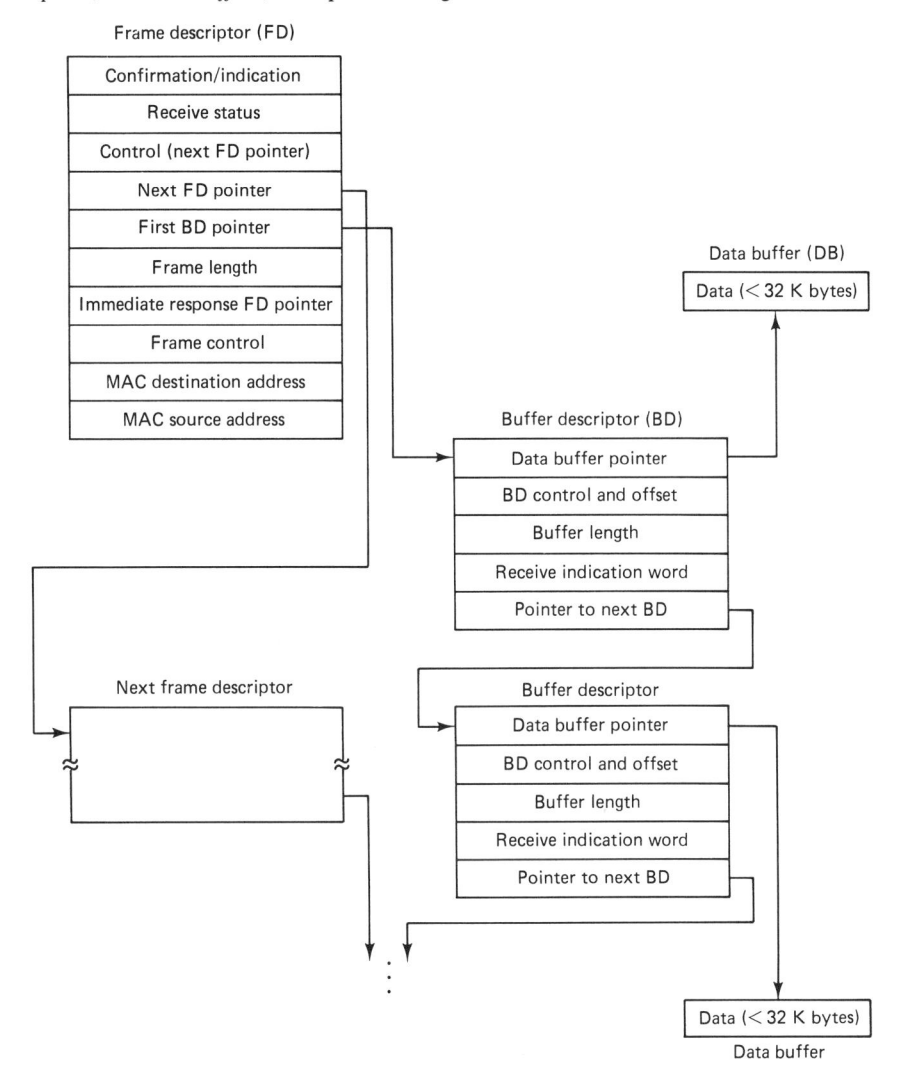

Figure 12.5 Double linked data structures used in the token bus controller (TBC).

used, the first link of the frame descriptor points to buffer descriptors, and the second link points to the next frame descriptor in the queue. Likewise, the first link of the buffer descriptor points to a data buffer, and the second link points to the next buffer descriptor in the frame. For efficient memory management, the user can choose a data buffer size that most efficiently matches the expected frame length. For example, a frame length of 1024 bytes would require four data buffers of 256 bytes each.

The buffer descriptor maintains an offset count of 1 byte that marks the beginning of specified data in the buffer. As frames pass through the OSI layers, some overhead information (e.g., addresses and control) are appended to the front of each frame. The offset count takes into account the size of the overhead information.

The TBC performs the following steps when transmitting a frame.

1. The controller gets a frame descriptor from a pointer stored in the previous frame descriptor located in the same priority queue.

2. Using its own internal memory, as well as DMA links to the system memory, the chip stores the MAC destination and source addresses, and the frame control bits.

3. Using the appropriate links, the chip fetches data to be transmitted from the appropriate data buffer.

4. If the frame has more than one data buffer, the controller follows another pointer to the next buffer descriptor and then to the subsequent data buffer.

5. Step 4 is repeated until the last data buffer is transmitted.

6. When the transmission of a frame is completed, confirmation is written onto the frame descriptor, indicating success or failure of the transmission and the number of retries that occurred.

7. If the *token hold timer* has not expired, the controller follows a pointer to the next frame descriptor on the queue for transmission. Otherwise, the process is terminated.

Additional capabilities. In addition to implementing all functions required by the IEEE token bus protocol, the TBC chip provides two major capabilities: real-time extension, and *network management* support.

The real-time extension is intended to work with the IEEE 802.2 LLC sublayer type 3, which calls for an immediate acknowledgment (i.e., response). This is useful, for example, in a real-time version of MAP referred to as *enhanced performance architecture* (EPA). Under this extension, the TBC gives each station on the network the opportunity to transmit within a time window in the order of tens of milliseconds. Each station on the network is also enabled to maintain a list of active transmitting stations, and to issue acknowledgments immediately without the need to possess the token.

Intel 82586 LAN Coprocessor

The 82586 is Intel's VLSI chip implementation of the medium access control (MAC) sublayer for the IEEE 802.3 and other Ethernet-like protocols. The chip performs the following functions associated with data transfer between memory and the medium: framing, medium access control,

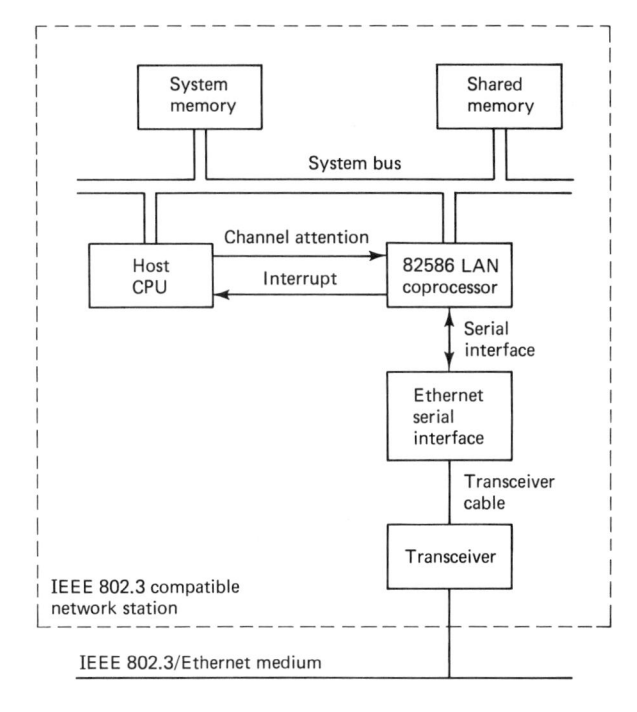

Figure 12.6 Hardware configuration for an IEEE 802.3 compatible station featuring the 82586 LAN coprocessor.

address recognition, error detection, data encoding, network management, direct memory access (DMA), buffer chaining, and interpretation of special commands from the user. Because the 82586 includes a microprogrammed controller for relieving the host CPU of most tasks associated with controlling access to the medium, the chip is called a LAN coprocessor.

In addition to meeting the requirements of the 802.3 standard, the 82586 supports DMA transfer at 4 Mbps; it tolerates local bus latency of over 10 microseconds without losing data and also supports configurable parameters, such as slot time, interframe spacing, and framing parameters (for example, address length, frame delimiters, and padding data). Built-in diagnostic aids such as time domain reflectometer, external and internal register dump, and a self-test procedure enhance network and station reliability. Figure 12.6 depicts a typical station hardware configuration consisting of a host CPU, shared main memory, the 82586 controller, serial interface unit, transceiver, and the medium.

One of the major responsibilities of the 82586 involves transfering data between shared memory and a channel on the medium, in a way that resolves contention that might exist due to the existence of other stations using the same channel. The 82586 has two interfaces: the first one with a local or system bus, and the second one with the network medium. On the bus side, the 82586 acts as the master station and communicates directly with the CPU by means of two signals known as the *channel attention* and *interrupt* signals. On the network medium side, the 82586 is connected to an Ethernet serial interface that provides clocks for transmission and reception, data, *collision detect*, *carrier sense*, *request to send*, and *clear to send* signals.

28586 transmit functions. This section describes one of the major functions performed by the 82586, that of transmitting data from memory to the serial network interface. The other major function performed by the 82586, which consists of receiving data from the interface and placing it into memory, is not discussed, because it is performed similarly.

The transmission process is initiated by the host CPU, which prepares a sequence of frames located in shared memory and instructs the 82586 to start transmission. The chip is responsible for accessing and resolving bus contention on the channel. After the channel has been acquired, frames are transmitted one at a time.

Framing is performed in accordance to the IEEE 802.3 MAC protocol and consists of the fields shown in Figure 4.28. The preamble is used for performing frame synchronization for correct frame decoding. Frames are delimited by two alternative methods provided by the 82586 and referred to as **end of carrier** and **bitstuffing,** which are discussed next.

In the *end of carrier* method, the 82586 transmits (depending on the configuration) 8,24,56, or 120 preamble bits of alternating ones and zeros, followed by a start of frame delimiter field (10101011). The end of frame is indicated by the carrier going inactive immediately after the Frame Check Sequence field. This frame boundary delineation method is compatible with IEEE 802.3.

The *bitstuffing* method implements the HDLC[4] zero bit insertion/deletion mechanism. The 82586 transmits a preamble of 8, 24, 56, or 120 alternating ones and zeros, followed by an HDLC flag (01111110). End of frame is also indicated by an HDLC flag. To achieve data transparency, the 82586 performs HDLC *zero bit insertion* (inserts a 0 after five consecutive 1s) on the fields between flags (i.e., not including the flags). The chip can be configured to pad the data with additional flags so that the total frame length becomes longer than the slot time, as required by Equation 4.5.

Regardless of the frame boundary delineation method, the two fields following the SFD field are the destination address and source address. The former is fetched from memory, and the latter is usually inserted from the internal individual address, which can be configured to a value from zero to six bytes. The destination address can be one of three types: individual address (least significant bit is zero), multicast address (least significant bit in one), or broadcast (all ones).

The length field and data field are fetched by the 82586 from memory and transmitted after the source address. The length field is 2 bytes long. The 82586 itself poses on limit on the data field length. The chip can be configured to one of two CRC algorithms: the CCITT V.41 16-bit polynomial, or the Autodin II (IEEE 802.3) 32-bit polynomial.

Medium access control. The 82586 handles the medium access control algorithm according to the IEEE 802.3 standard. The medium access control algorithms are adaptable to a variety of network topologies via programmable configuration parameters. In addition, station priorities are also programmable. The 82586 constantly monitors channel activity, and whenever it senses the carrier (i.e., data transitions), the 82586 defers by delaying any pending transmission. After the carrier goes inactive, the 82586 continues to defer for an interval equal to the interframe spacing time.

After transmission has started, the 82586 attempts to transmit the entire frame. In the normal case, frame transmission is completed, and the host notified. Otherwise, one or more of the following events causes a transmission to terminate prematurely: the clear-to-send signal goes inactive during transmission; the data transfer rate from memory to the chip did not keep up with transmission (DMA underrum); carrier sense goes inactive (in case the chip is configured to expect the return of carrier sense signal); a collision is detected via a *collision detect* signal, or the *collision retry* counter exceeded the maximum specified value.

---

[4] High-level Data Link Control, an ISO protocol standard for the data link layer.

When the 82586 has finished deferring and has started transmission, it is still possible to experience channel contention. This situation is called a *collision*, and it is generally detected by the transceiver. The 82586 enforces a collision by transmitting a Jam pattern of 32 **1**s. If a collision is detected during the preamble, transmission of the preamble is completed before jamming starts.

The dynamics of collision handling are largely determined by the slot time. Slot time is the maximum end to end round trip delay of the network plus *jam time*. Slot time is important because it represents the time to detect a collision in a worst-case situation.

After waiting the *backoff time*, the 82586 attempts to retransmit the frame, unless the number of retransmissions has exceeded the maximum allowed. The 82586 calculates the backoff algorithm according to the IEEE 802.3 standard. *Backoff* is an integral number of slot times. It is a random number, from 0 to a maximum given by $(2^R - 1)$, where R is the minimum between 10 and the number of retransmission attempts. This range can be extended using the *accelerated contention resolution* mechanism (see the section on priority mechanisms). The beginning of backoff time is configurable to one of two methods. If configured according to the IEEE 802.3 standard, it starts immediately after the end of jamming; if configured as an alternate backoff method (designed for lower bit rates and/or shorter topologies), backoff starts after the deferring period following collision.

The 82586 maintains a retry counter that is incremented after each retransmission attempt. If retransmission is successful, the user is notified. If the number of retries exceeds the maximum, an error is reported. The only difference between transmission and retransmission, is that transmission clears the retry counter, whereas retransmission increments it. On completion of transmission or retransmission, the 82586 reports the number of collisions that occurred, and whether it exceeded the maximum. The 82586 also indicates if the chip had to defer to passing traffic on its first transmission attempt.

The user may attempt to abort a transmission by issuing an abort command. Upon receipt of the abort command, the 82586 transmits a jam pattern to cause a CRC mismatch. The chip reports to the host either that the abort succeeded or that the frame transmission completed before the abort was accepted.

Priority mechanism. One of the goals for the IEEE 802.3 standard is to ensure fairness among stations trying to access the medium. However, there are applications (e.g., periodic traffic) where station priority is necessary for uninterrupted service. The 82586 implements two priority mechanisms: linear and accelerated contention resolution. Simulation studies show that both priority mechanisms provide lower network delays for a subset of stations at the expense of others (Chlamtac, 1986).

Linear priority determines the number of *slot times* the 82586 waits after deferring, or after the end of *backoff* (whichever comes last), before transmitting. If the channel becomes busy during the wait period, the process of deferring and waiting starts again.

Accelerated contention resolution extends the range from which the random number for backoff is drawn. It is configurable from zero to seven. Zero provides the highest priority and is IEEE 802.3 compatible.

The station's programmable parameters. As noted, the 82586 has several configurable parameters which enable the user to tailor, and thus, optimize system operation for different network configurations and applications. The configurable parameters are (Chlamtac, 1986):

1. Slot_Time:
The Slot_Time is a period slightly longer than the maximum round trip propagation delay in the network. The slot time is used to calculate the backoff time during which a station is forced to wait following a collision. The slot time is also the maximum delay any station is required to wait in order to establish the true state (i.e., busy or idle) of the channel, and is therefore used in implementing the 82586 priority mechanisms discussed below. The slot time takes values between 0–2048 bit times (0.1microsecs on the 10 Mbp channel).

2. Interframe_Spacing:
This specifies the time period expressed in bit times that the station waits before transmitting following the loss of carrier. Its values are between 32–255, thus allowing for turnaround times which may be shorter or longer than the standard 96-bit times.

3. Min_Packet_Length:
This gives the size in bytes of the shortest frame accepted for transmission. Values between 6 and 256 bytes are accepted, as long as Equation 4.5 is satisfied.

4. Preamble Length and Address Length:
The preamble can be set to 2, 4, 8, or 16 bytes, and the addresss length can be between 2 and 8 bytes.

5. Cyclic Redundancy Check (CRC):
The length of the cyclic redundancy check can be configured as 32-bit Autodin-II, 32-bit CRC, or 16-bit CCITT.

6. No_CRC_Insertion:
This allows for use of one of the preceding CRC generation (inserted at the end of the frame) or total detection of the CRC field. It is assumed that a ligher layer protocol is responsible for the error detection and correction mechanisms.

7. Number_of_Retries:
This specifies the number of times a station retransmits a frame following a collision and before aborting it. The 82586 controller can be programmed to any number between 0–15 retransmissions.

8. Exponential_Backoff_Method:
Its purpose is to efficiently implement the backoff mechanism for nonstandard *Ethernet* network configurations. In the IEEE 802.3 standard, the enforced *backoff delay* period starts at the station which detected a collision immediately following the jam transmission, and concurrently with the Interframe_Spacing delay. However, the random backoff values, obtained from the algorithm, multiplied by the short slot times, may cause the station to time out within the Interface_Spacing period. Consequently, all such stations will transmit simultaneously at the moment of the Interframe_Spacing delay expiration, defeating the purpose of the backoff mechanism. By setting the Exponential_Backoff_Method parameter, the backoff timeout will be started only after the Interframe_Spacing expiration, enabling the backoff algorithm to work efficiently.

9. Linear Priority:

This parameter, configurable to values between 0–7, determines the station's priority, as follows: A station ready to transmit following the backoff delay or following deference to ongoing transmission, computes an additional delay which is equal to its Linear_Priority*Slot_Time value. At that time, (and not before the Interframing_Spacing expiration following loss of carrier) the station assumes that a higher priority station has acquired the channel and backs off. Otherwise, the station transmits the queued frame immediately. All stations configured to zero Linear Priority (being in effect the highest priority) also execute the standard Ethernet (i.e., no carrier sensing is done following the Interframe_Spacing expiration).

10. Exponential Priority:

This parameter provides a prioritization mechanism by manipulating the contention resolution (backoff) process, rather than altering the channel access mechanisn, as in the case of linear priority. The setting of the Exponential_Priority parameter (values 0–7) alters the average backoff delay. A station involved in N collisions so far will compute a random backoff value r from the interval

$$r = [0, 2 * \exp(N + \text{Exponential\_Priority})]$$

Thus, when Exponential_Priority is set to 0, the standard Ethernet backoff algorithm is obtained and value greater than 0 will decrease the station's priority in the network.

12.6 BOARD LEVEL

Integrated circuits alone are not sufficient to implement protocols. They need power, additional memory, interfaces, and other circuitry. The aforementioned elements are combined into a larger device called a *circuit board*. The criteria for designing circuit boards is similar to that of the design of chips. One starts with a board real state which is constrained by the size of the product enclosure. Each major manufacturer has a number of computer systems, each with its unique motherboard. Again, the idea is to put as much circuitry as possible in a given board. Thus, a board has the capability of implementing several OSI protocol layers.

The intel iSXM 554 board. The iSXM 554 board implements the IEEE 802.4 standard and consists of an 80186 processor, a token bus handler chip set, a token bus modem, memory, and interface circuitry, as shown in Figure 12.7. The 80186 processor is responsible for providing an intelligent interface between the iSXM 554 board and a host processor, and also for running the software implementations of the transport layer and portions of the data link layer corresponding to the Intel's MAP 2.1 implementation.[5]

The 80186 processor is capabe of addressing 1 M byte of address space, which is divided into four quadrants, as shown in Figure 12.8. Whereas the first quadrant (0 − 256 K byte) is local RAM memory, the second quadrant contains memory mapped token bus handler addresses, and the third quadrant (512 − 768 K byte) maps into two Multibus windows of 128 K bytes each. These windows allow the board to access the total 16 M byte of Multibus memory in 128 K byte

---

[5] It is expected that MAP 2.2 and MAP 3.0 implementations will use the iSXM 554 board.

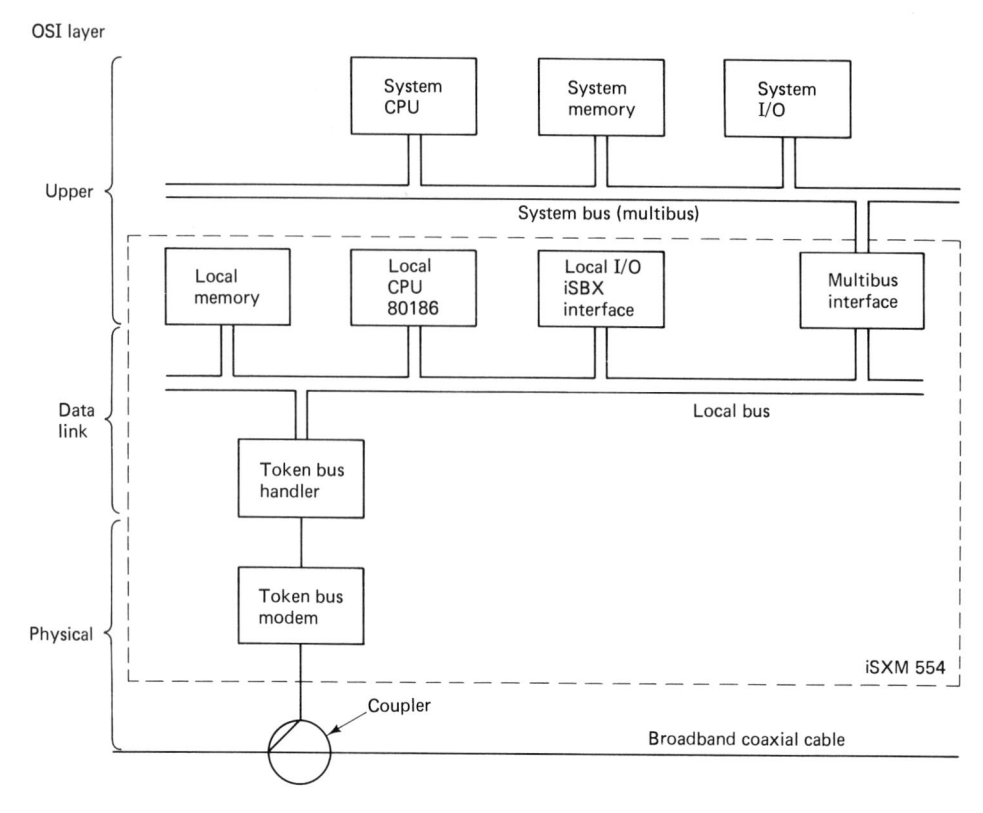

Figure 12.7 Architectural blocks of the iSXM 554 board showing the multibus interface and the medium interface.

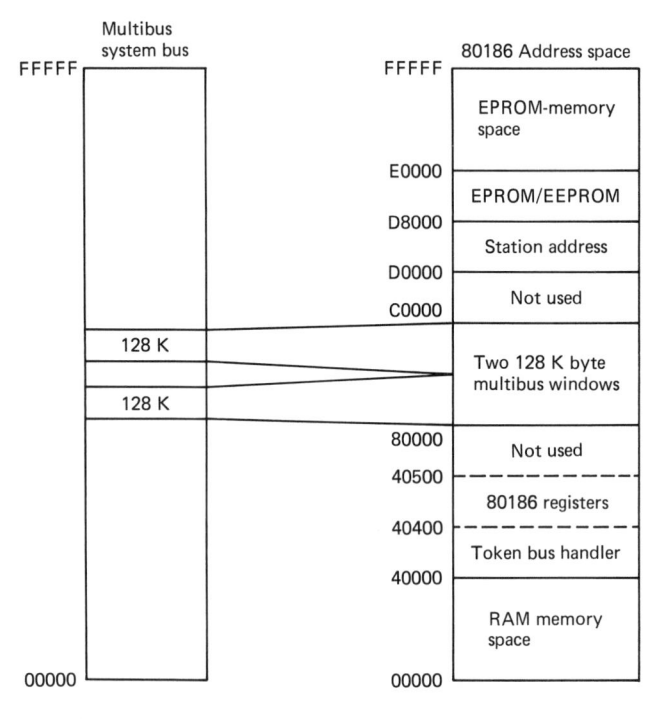

Figure 12.8 iSXM 554 memory configuration showing the mapping of 80186 address space onto the multibus system bus.

segments. Finally, the fourth quadrant (768 K − 1 M byte) is local ROM, which contains the 80186 firmware, the token bus station address, and relocated 80186 internal registers.

12.7 BOX LEVEL: INTEL'S 310 DEVELOPMENT STATION

Whereas different chip level and board level implementations are very few, box level implementations are numerous. The reason is that manufacturers can readily incorporate already available chips and boards in a broad range of products, thus leading to many dfferent box implementations. Box level implementations are typically configured as shown in Figures 12.9 and 12.10.

The Intel *system 310* is a Multibus based box that can support several operating systems, such as Xenix, MS-DOS and RMX, and several programming languages, such as Assembler, Fortran, Basic, Pascal, C, and PLM. Multibus enjoys the privilege of being supported by many companies with a wide variety of products, including LAN products. One can configure the *system 310* to be an Ethernet station, a MAP station, or virtually any other LAN station, provided a Multibus compatible NIU is available.

From the viewpoint of an end user, the *system 310* can perform a wide variety of roles ranging

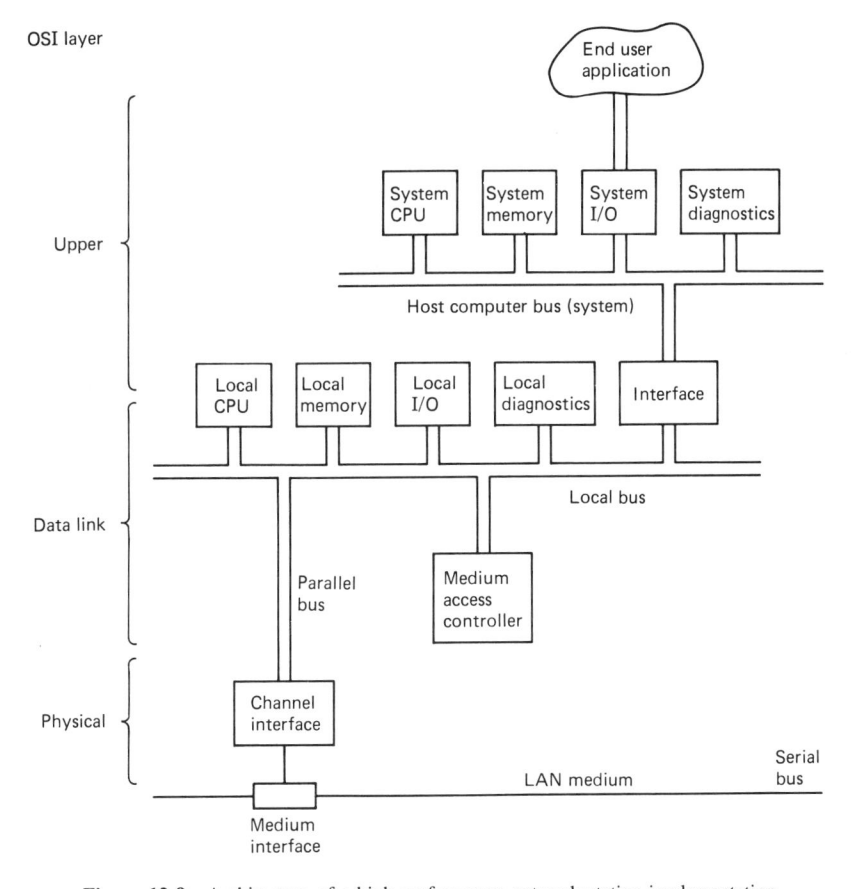

Figure 12.9 Architecture of a high-performance network station implementation.

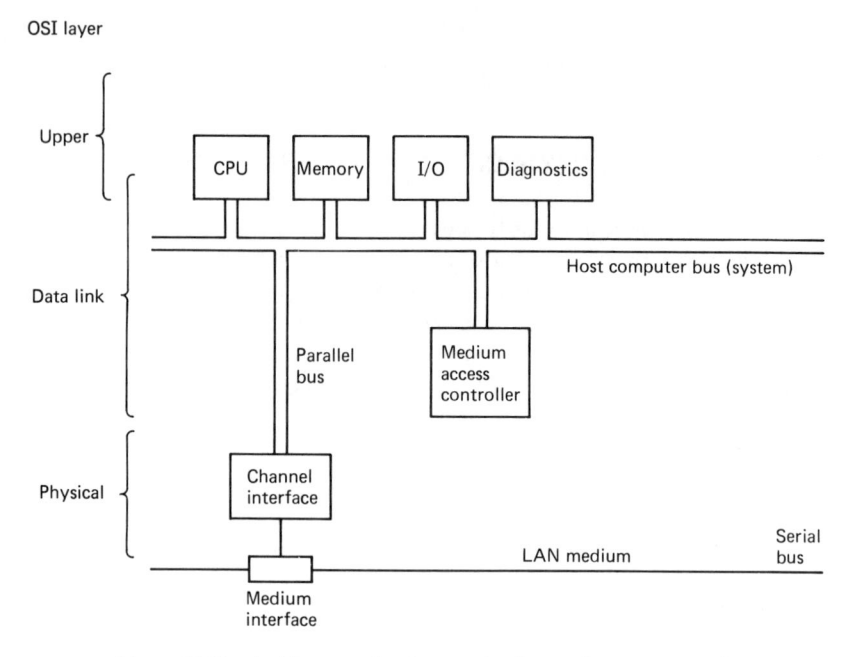

Figure 12.10 Architecture of an inexpensive low-performance network station implementation.

from a *file server*, to a *cell controller* in a manufacturing environment. Naturally, depending upon the intended application, an appropriate operating system and programming language must be selected. For applications such as the design of a cell controller, system 310 enjoys the support of RMX, which is a powerful real-time, multitasking operating system.

12.8 SOFTWARE COMPONENTS

iNA960. The iNA960 is Intel's software implementation of the ISO protocol standards for the logical link control (LLC) sublayer, the network, and transport layers. In addition, some aspects of network management are also supported. The software package runs on top of the iSXM552 board (i.e., Ethernet) or on top of the iSXM554 board (i.e., token bus).

The transport layer protocol is the class 4 option of the ISO 8073 specification. Both virtual circuits and datagrams are provided. In addition to providing reliable end to end message delivery, virtual circuits provide mechanisms for flow control, multiple simultaneous connection support, variable message support, and expedited data delivery support. The datagram option provides a *best effort* delivery service for noncritical messages.

The iNA960 support 2 types of network environments:

1. Single network environments consisting of a single **subnetwork** or **subnet** implementing the same protocols at the physical and data link layers. An example is a network where all stations have IEEE 802.4 interfaces.

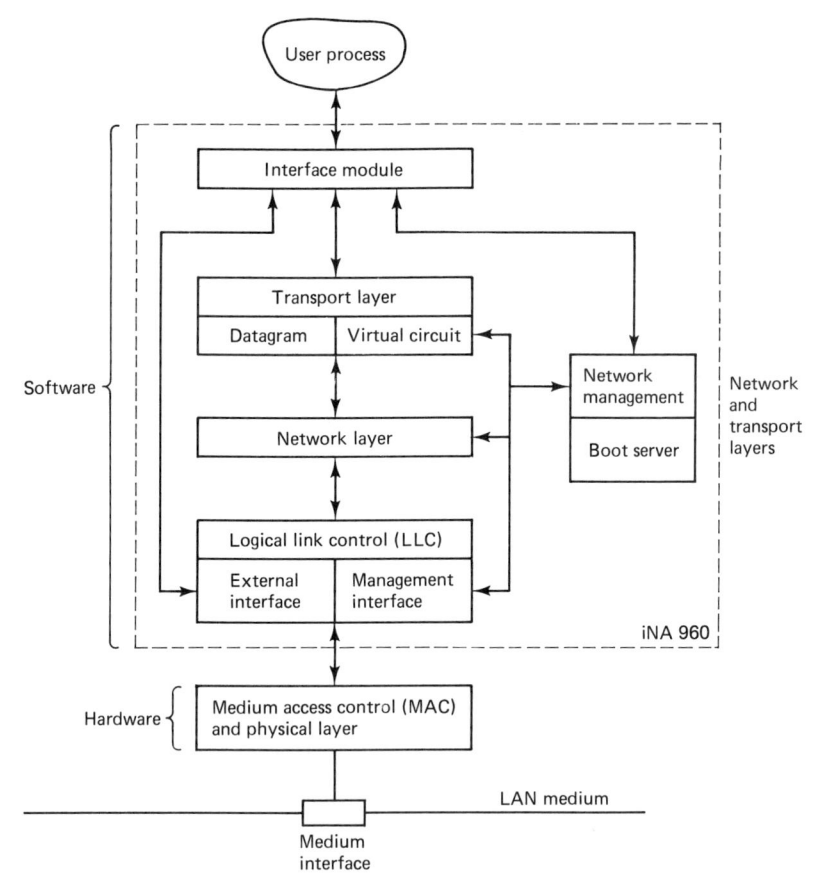

Figure 12.11 Constituent software elements of the iNA960 protocol implementation.

2. An **internetwork** or **internet** composed of two or more individual subnetworks interconnected together. An example is an IEEE 802.3 LAN interconnected with an IEEE 802.4 LAN. The *internet* protocol supported is the ISO 8473 protocol standard.

The *logical link control* (LLC) sublayer supported is the class I option of the IEEE 802.2 standard. The LLC sublayer supports both the *subnet* and *internet* environments referred to earlier. The *network management* service family supports the users of the network in planning, operating, and maintaining the network by providing network usage statistics, and by allowing the monitoring of network services. Furthermore, it also supports uploading and downloading of files to or from a system without secondary storage. The latter functionality can be used for configuring a *boot server*. The different constituent elements of the iNA960 software implementation is depicted in Figure 12.11, where the *user process* can be either the software for the remaining OSI layers (i.e., session, presentation, and application), or an *end user application process*. Because of the importance played by the transport layer in LANs such as MAP and TOP, the transport layer supported by iNA960 is discussed in more detail next.

Sec. 12.8 Software Components

```
type iNA960_request_block is
    record
        reserved : bit_string (1..16);
        length : bit_string (1..8);
        user_id : bit_string (1..16);
        response_port : bit_string (1..8);
        return_mailbox_token : bit_string (1..16);
        segment_token : bit_string (1..8);
        subsystem : bit_string (1..8);
        opcode : bit_string (1..8);
        response_code : bit_string (1..16);
        arguments : bit_string (1..N); -- N depends on the specific command.
    end record;
```

Figure 12.12 iNA960 request block organization.

iNA960 transport layer. Regardless of the actual hardware configuration supporting the iNA960 software package, the iNA960 user software interface is based on exchanging memory segments between the user and the protocol implementation. Request blocks are memory segments containing the data to be passed. The format and contents of the *request blocks* are shown in Figure 12.12.

Issuing an iNA960 command consists of filling in the *request block* fields and transferring the block to the iNA960 implementation for execution. After processing the command, iNA960 returns the request block with one of the predefined response codes placed in the *response code* field of the request block. The response code indicates whether the command was executed successfully or an error has occurred. By examining the response code, the user can take appropriate action for that command.

Hardware configurations. The iNA960 protocol implementation supports the execution of communications software as a job under the host operating system or a dedicated processor, as shown in Figure 12.13 (a) and (b). The advantage of the former method is its simplicity. However, its disadvantage is a degradation in performance because the communication software shares host processor resources with other user tasks.

In the latter method, also called the **communication front end processor,** the communication software runs separately from the host and other user programs. The main advantages of this method are improved performance, good flexibility, and easy software upgrades. Figure 12.13 (b) further illustrates how the dedicated processor protocol implementation is done using dedicated 8086, 8088, or 80186 microprocessors.

12.9 MAPNET

MAPNET is Intel's implementation of the MAP 2.1 specification, including their version of directory services, and network management. MAPNET includes the iNA960 software implementation as a constituent element and runs on the iSXM554 board implementing the token bus protocol.

As depicted in Figure 12.14, the MAPNET implementation supports protocols for the application, session, transport, network, data link, and physical layers. The following summarizes

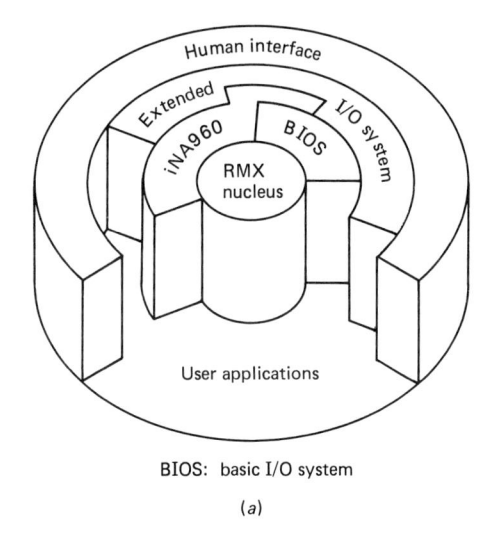

Figure 12.13 (a) iNA960 software implemented as an RMX job.

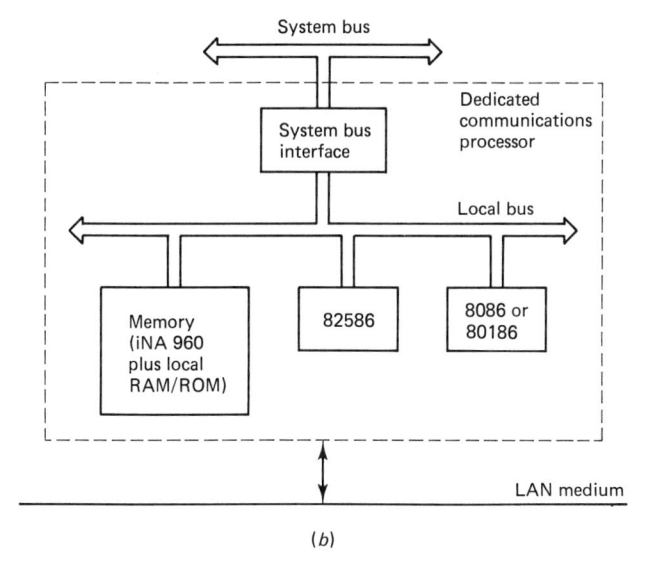

Figure 12.13 (b) iNA960 software implemented under a dedicated communications processor.

the main features of the implementation for each layer. The section concludes with a detailed discussion of the FTAM portion of MAPNET.

Application layer. The MAPNET application layer implementation of MAP 2.1 supports FTAM, CASE (Common Application Service Element), and directory services. CASE is the frontrunner of ACSE (Association Control Service Element). FTAM is an application layer protocol for performing file-oriented operations such as file creation, file reading, file writing, file deletion and getting file attributes.

The *directory services* portion of MAPNET has two configurations, server and client. A client

Sec. 12.9   MAPNET   473

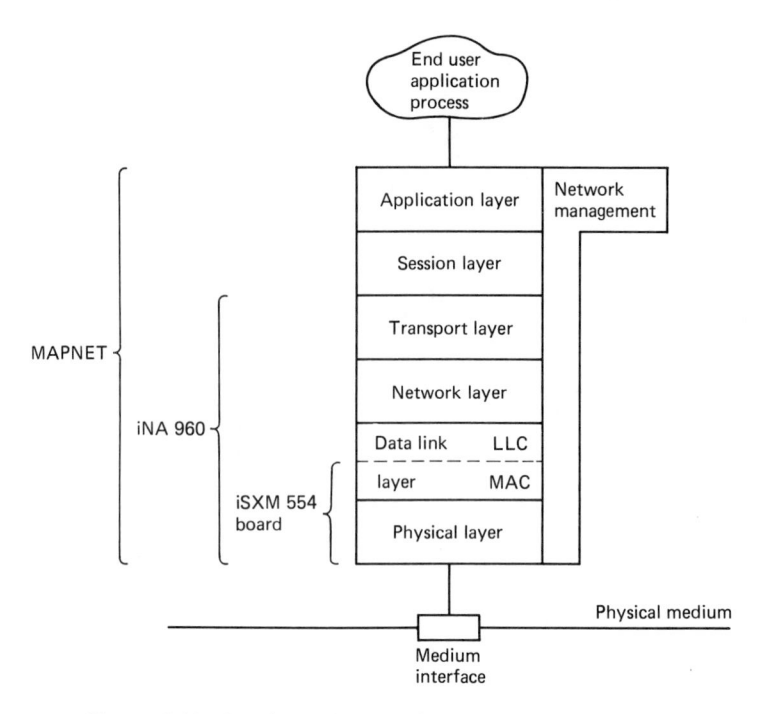

Figure 12.14 Constituent elements of the MAPNET implementation.

station requests name/address information from the server in order to update its local name/address data with the latest information. Name/address information requests are first handled by the local client. If no match occurs in its local directory, the directory server's directory is examined. MAPNET comes with the server and client version of *directory services*. Thus, it is possible that every station can be its own server (i.e., none of the stations are client). In this case, a distributed algorithm is required so that all server stations update their directory when a network station is added or deleted.

The CASE implementation of MAPNET allows remote processes to establish a connection in a transparent fashion. Transparency is achieved by providing a physical address to a logical name translation, which CASE handles by accessing and managing *directory services* to provide the logical name conversion.

Session layer. The session layer provides the required functionality for cooperating session users to organize and synchronize their dialogue and manage their exchange of data. The session layer services are available regardless of whether the underlying layers provide virtual circuits or datagram services. One of the primary functions of the session layer is to provide orderly management of transport layer connections. One aspect of this is allowing graceful close of a connection to an aborted virtual circuit. Graceful close in this case means that the queued requests are handled appropriately without loss of data. The session layer makes use of the name server of network management to maintain and translate the *process name* to *transport address* bindings.

Transport layer. The transport layer provides transparent transfer of data on behalf of transport users. Therefore, the transport layer relieves the transport users from any concern with the detailed way in which reliable and cost-effective transfer of data is achieved.

The transport layer is designed primarily for supporting the transfer of moderate to large amounts of data over the network. Some examples might be file transfers, block data moves, or file sharing applications.

The transport layer is designed to provide a commonly used error free service that does not depend on the particular characteristics of any specific lower layer. In addition, the transport layer supports multiple connections to one or more network layer entities, thus supporting internetworking capabilities of the network layer.

Network layer. The network layer provides the means to establish, maintain, and terminate network connections between systems containing communication application entities, and the functional and procedural means to exchange network service data units between transport entities over network connections.

This layer also provides independence to transport entities from routing and relay considerations associated with the establishment and operation of a network connection. The network layer of iNA960 offers a datagram service to higher layer users.

In a multiple network environment where network routers are used to interconnect several incompatible networks, the network layer has the responsibility of routing data between networks. The routing of data between networks is accomplished through a routing table that is maintained and updated at the Network layer level.

Data link layer. The data link layer provides functional and procedural mechanisms to establish, maintain, and release data link connections among network layer entities. A data link connection is built upon one or several physical connections. The data link layer is responsible for framing, addressing, error detection, and link management.

Physical layer. The physical layer provides functional and procedural means to activate, maintain, and deactivate physical connections for bit transmission between two network stations. This layer is directly related with the actual transmission medium (i.e., wire, optical fibers, radio), data encoding into voltage or current signals, data rate and mechanical specifications. As previously discussed, the physical communication between MAP nodes is based on the IEEE 802.4 (i.e., token passing bus) standard.

Network management. Network management provides a network with planning, operation, and maintenance facilities. The planning capability gathers network usage information, such as peak activity, total packets sent, and CRC errors. This allows the system manager to make adjustments for day-to-day usage of the network. Normal day-to-day operation deals with network functions, such as initialization, shut down, monitoring, and performance optimization. Maintenance deals with detection, isolation, location, and repair of network faults. Many functions can be performed both on local and remote nodes.

iNA960 includes some network management support for initialization, address conversions, operation, and maintenance. Network management is a distributed function that is built into every layer on every network station; its activities are being performed continuously to ensure the proper operation of the network. Since a *network control center* does not exist as in traditional network management implementations, inquiries about the state of the network can be made from any station on the network. Thus, network management is the responsibility of every station.

MAPNET File Transfer and Access Management (FTAM). The FTAM implementation of MAPNET has two parts: file servers and file consumers. **File consumers** are stations that access files which are located on other stations. File consumers may or may not have local mass storage capability. If local mass storage is not available, the file consumers must rely on other stations for all storage related operations. **File servers** are stations that permit file consumers to access files on their local disks, and to queue printer request to be printed locally. Since the application layer supports a number of simultaneous transactions, a station could be both a *file consumer* and a *file server*. Thus, the server portion of FTAM allows remote access of its local files by a remote FTAM consumer. The consumer is the part of FTAM that uses remote files offered by the server. MAPNET comes preconfigured to serve as a consumer, and as a server. Since the FTAM specification for MAP 2.1 does not recognize *hierarchical file structures* but rather a *flat structure*, a default FTAM server directory must be used. MAPNET only supports file transfer functions. Future versions are expected to support additional functionality such as remote file access. Currently, FTAM is implemented on top of the session layer and interfaces with directory services to get physical addresses.

The MAPNET FTAM implementation provides the capability to remotely read or write an entire unstructured file of any size, to create or delete a remote file, and to read certain attributes of a remote file. FTAM contains file *consumers* driven by applications software, which requests services from a remote FTAM implementation. As listed in Table 12.1, the services include reading, writing, creating, and deleting files as well as reading file attributes. The *FTAM server* responds

TABLE 12.1 COMMANDS AVAILABLE TO A CONSUMER FOR PERFORMING FILE OPERATIONS ON A REMOTE SERVER

FTAM consumer commands	
Command name	Description
1. Connect	Establish an FTAM connection with remote FTAM server
2. Release	Gracefully terminates the FTAM connection with the remote server
3. Abort	Abruptly terminates the FTAM connection with the remote server
4. Create	Creates new file at the remote server's *virtual filestore*
5. Delete	Deletes an existing file at the remote server's *virtual filestore*
6. Select	Selects an existing file at the remote server's *virtual filestore*
7. Detach	Detaches a previously *selected* or *created* file at the remote server's *virtual filestore*
8. Get_Attributes	Reads and returns file attributes of a previously *selected* or *created* file at the remote server's *virtual filestore*
9. Open	Opens a previously *selected* or *created* file at the remote server's *virtual filestore*
10. Close	Closes a previously *opened* file at the remote server's virtual filestore
11. Read	Reads and returns file data from a previously *opened* file at the remote server's virtual filestore
12. Write	Writes file data to a previously *opened* file at the remote server's *virtual filestore*
13. Write_end	Indicates that the user has finished the file *read* or write and returns to the *opened* file state
14. Cancel	Abruptly ends a file *read* or *write* and returns to the *opened* file state.

to remote consumer requests for operation on its local files. After an FTAM connection is established, the FTAM user requests that a dialogue be established with the server.

FTAM consumer protocol. The MAPNET FTAM implementation assumes a flat directory structure with files transferred completely, and no provision for partial file access or hierarchical file structure.

Users interface with MAPNET via *request blocks* which are operating system memory segments allocated from the user's memory pool. Figure 12.15 shows the different components (i.e., fields) of the request block user_rb_str. Fields can be either general or command specific. *General* fields contain data relevant to the user and the target layer. Examples include the length, owner, and *reg_id* fields. *Command specific* fields, on the other hand, are determined by the actual command

```
Type user_rb_str_part1 is
record

      apex_p              : bit_string (1..16); -- address pointer
      length              : bit_string (1..8 );
      user_id             : bit_string (1..32);
      response_port       : bit_string (1..8 );
      ret_entity          : bit_string (1..16); -- actually an
                                                -- array of 2 elements
      subsystem           : bit_string (1..8 );
      opcode              : bit_string (1..8 );
      response            : bit_string (1..16);
      reference           : bit_string (1..16);
      link                : bit_string (1..16); -- address pointer
end record;

type user_rb_str_part2 is
record
      user_data_ptr       : bit_string (1..32);
      user_data_len       : bit_string (1..16);
      filled_len          : bit_string (1..16);
      diag_data_ptr       : bit_string (1..32);
      diag_data_len       : bit_string (1..16);
      name_ptr            : bit_string (1..32);
      file_control        : bit_string (1..8 );
      file_context        : bit_string (1..8 );
      file_size           : bit_string (1..16);
end record

type user_rb_str is
record
      user_rb_str_part1;
      user_rb_str_part2;
end record;
```

Figure 12.15 MAPNET FTAM request block.

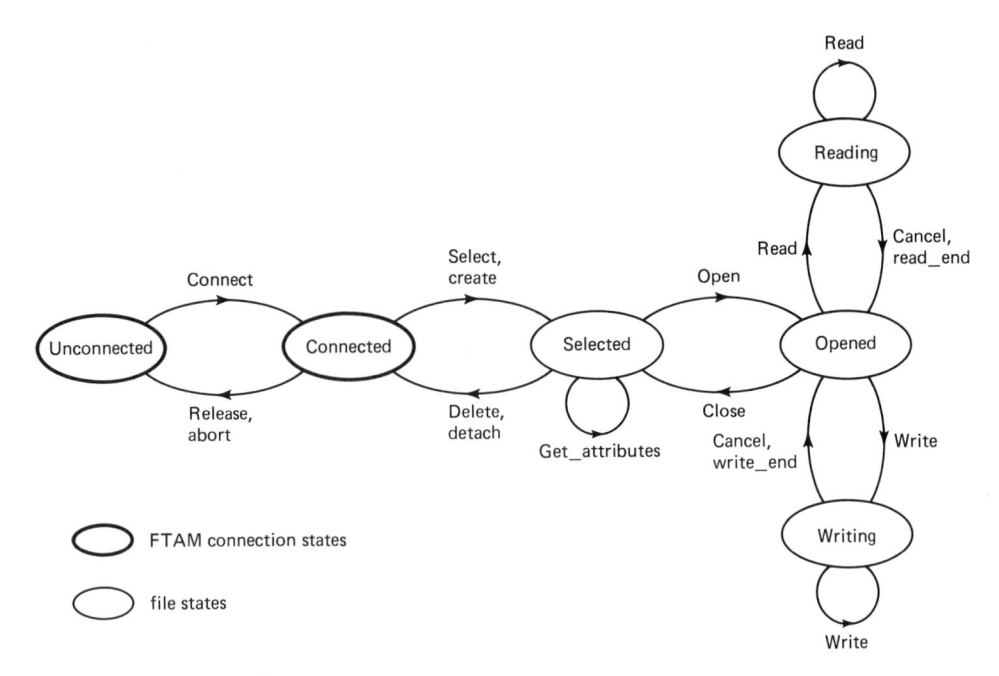

Figure 12.16 FTAM consumer state transition diagram.

being executed. These fields will have different meanings depending on the command indicated in the *opcode* field.

The user is responsible for filling each field of the request block. The user then calls a special routine that delivers the request block to the iNA 960 software for execution. Upon completion, the request block is delivered to the destination specified by the *response* field of the request block.

The first part of the request block of Figure 12.15 is a generic record structure, whereas the second part is the specific FTAM request block structure. The state transition diagram for the FTAM consumer is depicted in Figure 12.16. The FTAM user is responsible to follow the transitions of Figure 12.16. Failure to do so results in a protocol error which the user can determine by examining the variable response. Possible values of *response* include error conditions such as bad file name, unavailable resources, unknown connection, and context error. The *opcode* parameter indicates which of the 14 FTAM operations is in current use. The *reference* parameter uniquely identifies the connection which has been established. The *user_data_len* and *user_data_ptr* parameters indicate the size and address pointer, respectively, of the data buffer involved in file operations. A response buffer is also available, which is filled out after the command is executed and whose length is given by *filled_len*. When some error occurs, diagnostic error information is pointed to by *diag_data_ptr* whose length is given by *diag_data_len*. The *name_ptr* parameter contains the name of the remote server. File access attributes, such as read permission and write permission, are contained in *file_control*. The presentation layer context is indicated by *file_contex*, whereas the size of the file to be created is indicated by *file_size*.

SUMMARY

Protocol implementation is the realization of a protocol specification in some tangible form so that they can be used in a variety of applications. Protocols are implemented in a combination of hardware, software, or firmware. Some protocol functions are more amenable to their implementation in hardware while others are advantageous when implemented in software.

Hardware implementations have the following characteristics:

fast (they can achieve real-time processing),
most efficient for the OSI lower layers,
relatively inflexible, and
limited intelligence.

Software implementations have the following characteristics:

very flexible,
advantageous for higher layers,
share processor with implementations of other layers and perhaps with applications depending upon performance.

The design issues facing network and protocol implementors include the following:

application requirements,
implementation architectures, protocol standards,
processors, operating systems, and programming languages,
higher layer implementations,
implementation interfaces,
implementation options,
implementation technology, and
system bus types.

Performance of protocol implementations is important for everyone involved with computer networks. A designer should consider the following factors when implementing protocols in order to improve performance:

implementation architecture,
network data rate,
multiprocessors,
channel access control schemes,
protocols at all OSI layers,

speed of NIU to host transfer, and
buffer management.

Implementation hardware consists of integrated circuits (chips), boards, boxes (computer systems), and entire network systems. Implementation software involves procedures and modules which implement one or several OSI layers.

The medium access sublayers for the IEEE 802.4 and IEEE 802.3 are implemented in VLSI by the token bus controller (Motorola 68824), and Intel 82586 respectively. The former has a real-time extension capability and network management support whereas the latter has a priority mechanism and allows several parameters to be programmed. At the board level, the Intel iSXM 554 implements the complete IEEE 802.4 standard and includes an 80186 processor, a token bus handler chip set, a token bus modem, memory, and interface circuitry. Intels 310' system is a box level system which can be configured to be a MAP station, a TOP station, or virtually any other network station.

On the software side, the iNA960 module is Intel's implementation of the LLC sublayer, the network, and transport layers; whereas MAPNET is Intel's implementation of the MAP 2.1 specification including FTAM, directory services, and network management.

Bibliographic Notes

Unfortunately, there is not much material on OSI implementations probably because much of this material is kept confidential by the implementors. Information on hardware and software components are available from the appropriate manufacturers. Alexis-Dirvin and Miller (1985) and Erickson (1986) discuss VLSI for implementing the IEEE 802.4 standard, whereas Chlamtac (1986) discusses an implementation of the IEEE 802.3 standard. Interprocess communication in a common bus system is discussed by Rosemberg (1986). The general design of a network system is treated in the book by Hooper and others (1986), whereas a programmer's interface is discussed by Spenke (1985). Details of the ISO session layer implementation of section 12.3 can be found in Ciminiera and others (1987). Several software issues associated with local area networks are discussed by Tripathi and others (1987). Janssens and others (1987) suggest an end user approach for LAN implementation.

PROBLEMS

1. Explain the advantages of using a local bus in the implementation of network protocols.
2. Consider the use of a computer network exclusively for an application involving the transfer and manipulation of large files. State the required functionality of the ISO session layer standard to meet the requirements of this application. List all service primitives which are necessary for this application,
3. Consider the use of a computer network for distributed database management systems (DDBMS). Identify the functionality needed by this application which is not provided by the ISO session layer standard.
4. In section 12.3, a specific implementation of the ISO session layer standard is described which is based on a multitasking system involving four asynchronous concurrent processes. Discuss the advantages and disadvantages of this implementation.

5. Provide an implementation architecture different from the one given in section 12.3. List the advantages of your design.
6. Consider the Motorola token bus controller (TBC) implementation with a token hold timer of 800 msec, R = 10 Mbps, and a frame length of 1024 octets. What is the minimum buffer area required by the TBC implementation including the data buffers? Assume that the implementation uses the minimum number of data buffers and all fields of Figure 12.5 are 32 bits of length.
7. Why is the configurable parameter padding data necessary in the Intel 82586 LAN coprocessor?
8. Assume an IEEE 802.3 network implementation with length L = 1 Km.
   (a) What is the minimum slot time?
   (b) to how many transmit clock units is the slot time equivalent?
   (c) for the slot time value found in a), what is the maximum backoff?
9. What is the difference between the term slot_time as used in the token bus and CSMA/CD protocols?
10. For a network with L = 1 Km, R = 10 M bps, what is the minimum value of the MIN_PACKET_LENGTH configurable parameter of the 82586 integrated circuit.
11. Summarize the priority options of the Intel 82586 implementation. Are these options suitable for time critical applications?
12. Why are timers needed in protocol implementations?
13. Timers can be implemented in hardware and software. What are the advantages of each method of implementation?
14. Although CRC calculations are typically done in hardware, write two programs to implement the CRC algorithms using the CRC–16 and IEEE 802.4 polynomials discussed in Chapter 4.
15. Rewrite the example corresponding to Figure 10.18 using MAPNET FTAM commands.

13

LAN Design and Performance

The performance of local area networks is an important topic, since it allows choices to be made in terms of the many factors affecting performance. In this chapter, we provide a discussion of performance issues, how performance results can be used, and analyze the performance of a token bus protocol network as well as a CSMA/CD network. We begin by providing a classification of network users in Section 13.2, followed by a classification of performance models in Section 13.3. The applications of LAN performance evaluation, along with a definition of relevant performance metrics, are addressed in sections 13.4 and 13.5. Section 13.5 contains a brief discussion of queueing theory necessary to understand the development of performance results of the token bus, and CSMA/CD networks which are presented in sections 13.7, 13.8, and 13.9. The last 4 sections of this chapter assume that the reader has a working knowledge of probabilities including random variables. The book by Stark and Woods (1986) is recommended for reviewing some concepts.

Designing a local area network involves allocating network resources to accommodate user demands while meeting cost and performance requirements. The network design process is depicted in Figure 13.1, which shows the major factors involving the design process. The factors are *network resources*, *end user application requirements*, and *performance requirements*.

Network resources include all elements used in the network implementation. For example, a list of MAP network resources include data rate (i.e., 10 or 5 M bps), token bus timers, network architecture (i.e., full MAP or EPA), buffer sizes at different OSI layers, implementation characteristics (i.e., type of operating system), and specific hardware (ICs, boards, boxes, etc.). All network resources affect performance either directly or indirectly.

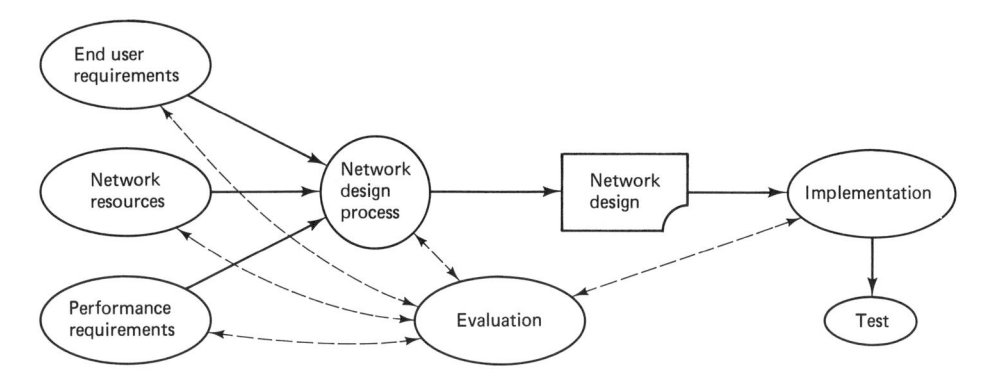

Figure 13.1 Network design process.

End user applications are varied and may include distributed databases, intelligent devices, file transfer, multiple robot assembly system (MRAS), receiving inspection system, body shop, tool room, etc. Collectively, the applications present some load to the network which can be characterized by a certain average rate of message arrivals (e.g., 75 message/sec) and average message size (e.g., 200 byte/message).

Network performance addresses the issue of how well the overall network system is doing its job. Performance can be characterized in many different ways. The following is a partial list of variables which are indicators of performance:

   message delay
   transaction response time,
   queue lengths,
   information throughput,
   connection time,
   residual error,
   number of rejects before establishing a virtual circuit,
   packet or message delay,
   congestion,
   percent of packets discarded,
   token rotation time,
   protocol (channel) efficiency, and
   application functionality.

13.1 PERFORMANCE-BASED NETWORK DESIGN

An effective way for designing networks consists of using models for evaluating the performance of the overall network. Performance models usually belong to three major categories: *analytical*, *simulation*, and *measurement*.

Network performance evaluation allows assessing the different alternatives available in a local area network in order to optimize certain potential benefits, while minimizing their associated costs. For example, a MAP network allows certain options such as setting various timers and buffer sizes at the different layers of the OSI reference model. Examples of potential benefits (e.g., performance) include improved response time, better serviceability, etc.

Network performance evaluation is useful because it provides users with estimates of feasible regions of operations, ways to optimize network operation, and the ability to tune network parameters for specific applications.

Optimizing certain LAN performance variables results in some trade-offs. For example, increasing throughput results in increased message delay (Tanenbaum, 1988). Fortunately, not all possible benefits are important for a given application, because if this were true, optimum values could not be found. Some performance variables which are appropriate for some applications could be disregarded for others. For example, *serviceability* is very important in automated production applications where the penalty paid when the network is down is measured in terms of hundreds of thousands of dollars per hour (Campbell and Pimentel, 1986). For office automation, however, serviceability has a much lesser effect as compared to its factory automation counterpart. Thus, it is important to specify the type of user before doing any kind of performance evaluation study.

Several user classifications have been made for performance evaluation purposes. Ilyas and Mouftah (1985) classify users in three categories: user, manager, and designer of networks. Their classification does not consider network implementors (i.e., vendors) and provides a narrow definition for network designers. Following, we provide a more comprehensive user classification.

13.2 USER CLASSIFICATION

As noted, network performance evaluation is user-dependent. In order to provide more flexibility for characterizing, and for studying the benefits of performance, we classify users in the following categories (Pimentel, 1985):

> protocol development users,
> protocol implementor (vendor) users,
> value added (application) users, and
> end users.

Organizations involved with networks may belong to one or several of these user categories. **Protocol development users** are concerned with the design, analysis, and specification of communication protocols for one or more layers of the OSI reference model. These users are typically concerned with protocol issues such as protocol stability, protocol performance, and protocol deadlock. Examples of users belonging to this category include protocol designers and standards groups such as the IEEE project 802, and the ISO.

Protocol implementor (vendor) users are comprised of organizations that take already developed protocols or networks and design and build products according to the protocol specifications. These users typically assume that the protocols are stable and have no deadlocks and, furthermore, that the protocols or networks are efficient for the market aimed at by their products. Some issues that *vendor users* are typically concerned with include the effect of processor types on protocol delay and the effect of buffer sizes, and interfaces on throughput (Woodside, 1983).

Companies like Motorola and Honeywell are examples of users belonging to this user category.

Value added (application) users assume that the network has already been developed and installed in an end user premise. Application users concentrate on adding value to the network intended for specific applications. For example, an application user may develop software that uses the network to perform monitoring and control functions for production machines in a manufacturing environment. Some issues of interest to this category of users are the functionality of the network's application layer, how services from the application layer are made available, the interface with the application layer, and other network implementor issues (e.g., simple access to files).

End users are those organizations or people that have problems to solve and believe that networks are important components of the overall problem solution. End users are not usually interested in the details of the underlying network characteristics. For example, an end user does not usually look at the efficiency of a certain protocol at a certain layer. Rather, end users are interested in the overall effect of all protocols and all layers on their applications. Issues of interest to end users are typically directly related to the end application (i.e., cell and FMS control). Some examples of issues of concern to end users are cycle time, response time, cost, and expandability.

Several observations can be made regarding the preceding user classification. First, all user types are involved in some kind of design. *Protocol development* users are involved with protocol design, *vendor users* design architectures, interfaces, network stations, and sometimes entire networks (i.e., network design). *Value added users* design software systems to support architectures and applications. *End users* design the overall system from a top level viewpoint by selecting network options available to fit a given application. Second, it is important to note that what is of interest to one user is of little or no interest to another user. For example, *protocol deadlocks* are crucial for protocol development users, but are of little interest for end users. This observation suggests a user-performance variable chart for indicating what performance variables are of interest to each user.

Tables 13.1 through 13.4 give a potential list of performance variables and the factors influencing them for each user category just identified. From the tables, one can notice two types of performance variables. The first type is made up by variables that are traditionally easy to evaluate quantitatively, such as response time and throughput. The second type is made up by variables that are not so straightforward to evaluate quantitatively, but are nevertheless important for certain applications (Kleinrock, 1982). Examples of the second type of performance variables include

TABLE 13.1 PERFORMANCE VARIABLES AND RELATED PARAMETERS FOR PROTOCOL DEVELOPMENT USERS

Performance variables	Parameters
Protocol efficiency	Sliding window size
Protocol stability	Data rate
Resource starvation	Medium length/spacing
Services at the interface	Address length
Protocol security/privacy	Acknowledgments
Congestion	PDU discard
Effect of protocol on throughput	PDU lifetime
Fairness	Channel access scheme
Number of rejects before establishing a virtual circuit	Maximum packet size
	Padding
Number of discarded PDUs	Network layer segment length

TABLE 13.2 PERFORMANCE VARIABLES AND RELATED PARAMETERS FOR PROTOCOL IMPLEMENTOR USERS

Performance variables	Parameters
Transparency	Fault recovery
Fairness	Data rate
Throughput	Topology
Buffer utilization	Operating system
Protocol compliance	Channel access scheme
Hardware/software cost	Standards
Response time	Protocol Interface
System flexibility	Channel characteristic
Diagnosis	Processor clock rate
Product reliablity	Architecture
	Hardware interface
	Implementation parameters

TABLE 13.3 PERFORMANCE VARIABLES AND RELATED PARAMETERS FOR VALUE ADDED USERS

Performance variables	Parameters
Throughput	Programming languages
Response time	Operating system
User friendliness	Application layer interface
Software cost	Topology
Expandability	Standards
Transparency	Channel characteristics
Debug capability	Security/privacy
Software effectiveness	Architecture
Software development capability	Hardware components

TABLE 13.4 PERFORMANCE VARIABLES AND RELATED PARAMETERS FOR END USERS

Performance variables	Parameters
Application functionality	Number of stations
Response time	Station delay
Token rotation (cycle) time	Fault recovery
Throughput	Network topology
Installation/operational cost	Channel access
Reliablity	Hardware delays
Expandability	Standards
Physical topology	Buffer size
Transparency	Protocol interface
Problem diagnostics/isolation	Channel characteristics
Noise immunity	Timer values
User friendliness	Message/packet/address sizes
Network utilization	Data rate
Queue length/delay	Redundancy
Bus utilization	Vendor product
	Load characteristics

reliability, expandability, problem isolation, diagnosis, and costs (installation and operational) (Campbell and Pimentel, 1986). The list of performance variables in the tables is not exhaustive; however, the tables include performance variables of interest for most users in each user category.

13.3 NETWORK PERFORMANCE EVALUATION

As noted, models for evaluating the performance of local area networks typically fall into the following categories: analytical, simulation, and measurements.

13.3.1 Analytical Models

Analytical methods are based on mathematical models that characterize the system under study. The models are usually queueing models, although other model types have been used (Franta and Chlamtac, 1981).

A queueing model is a mathematical model used to represent a physical system in which there is contention for resources. The evolution of the system over time is described by using probability functions. To fully describe a queueing model, it is necessary to describe the following:

customer arrival,

service demand for each customer,

service rate of each server,

order in which customers are served, and

flow of customers through the system.

As an example, when modeling the lower two layers of a MAP network, customers are the frames to be transmitted over the communication channel. The server is one channel of a broadband coaxial cable. A service center is composed of one queue and the shared resource. As discussed in Section 4.8, the access control machine (ACM) determines the order in which frames are transmitted (i.e., served). The service demand is the amount of service required by a frame at a MAC-physical layer interface (i.e., frame length). The service rate is the speed at which the physical layer sends data into the medium (i.e., data rate).

Depending upon the complexity of the models, the choice of performance variables, and the type of solution desired, analytical models can be classified as: approximate, stochastic, and extended.

Approximate models. Approximate models attempt to estimate *maximum* or *worst case* values by making assumptions on load, speed, protocols, interfaces, etc. (Stuck and Arthurs, 1985). Let us assume that one is interested in calculating *upper bounds* for the frame delay T_{fd}, throughput T_h, and token rotation time T_c. The desired values for the performance variables can be found by assuming that all stations are active (i.e., all stations have frames to send). As soon as one station sends a frame, the station generates another frame. This assumption was also used by Stuck and Arthurs for the evaluation of upper bounds for other variables. Based on the previous assumption, and the token bus protocol discussed in Chapter 4, one has the following:

$$E[T_{fd}] = N \left[\frac{E[X] + X_t}{R} + T_{prop} + T_{int} + T_{st} \right] \qquad (13.1)$$

$$E[T_h] = \frac{E[X]}{\frac{E[X]+X_t}{R} + T_{prop} + T_{int} + T_{st}} \quad (13.2)$$

$$E[T_c] = E[T_{fd}] \quad (13.3)$$

where T_{prop}, T_{int}, and T_{st} are the medium propagation delay, interface delay, and station delay, respectively. X and X_t denote respectively the frame length and token frame length. The notation $E[X]$ stands for the expected value of X. We next provide similar results for the token bus protocol and token ring protocol for two load situations. The first load situation is when one station is active and all the remaining ones are listeners. The second load situation is the one considered earlier, with all stations being active.

Token bus protocol. In this section, we calculate worst case values for some performance measures based on approximate models.

One Station Active. Since there are no queueing delays, the worst scenario is for a frame to arrive just after the corresponding station has sent the token to the next station. Thus, the frame has to wait $N(T_{prop} + T_{int})$ before the station can send the frame. The term $\omega = (T_{prop} + T_{int})$ is also called the **walk time**. It takes an additional interval of $(X_{max} + X_t)/R$ to send the data frame including overhead where X_{max} is the maximum frame length. Thus the maximum value for the station to station frame delay is

$$T_{fd} = (X_{max} + X_t)/R + N\omega \quad (13.4)$$

and the maximum user throughput is

$$T_h = X_{max} / T_{fd} \quad (13.5)$$

All Stations Active. Since all stations have frames to send on a token rotation cycle, the interval $N(X_{max} + X_t)/R$ sec is spent sending frames and the interval $N\omega$ spent passing the token. Again, the worst scenario is for a frame to arrive to the head of the queue just after the corresponding station has sent the token to the next station. Thus, the maximum value for the station frame delay is

$$T_{fd} = N[X_{max} + X_t)/R + \omega] \quad (13.6)$$

and the maximum user throughput is

$$T_h = N X_{max} / T_{fd} \quad (13.7)$$

Token ring protocol

One Station Active. Like the token bus protocol, the time to send the data frame is $(X_{max} + X_t)/R$. Since the stations are physically configured as a ring, it takes T_{prop} for the token to circulate around the ring. Because of the nature of the ring interface processor (RIP), it only takes the equivalent of 1 bit delay to clock the bits into the station, where the header portion could be decoded on the fly to see if the message is intended for the particular station (Stuck, 1983). Thus, for the token ring, $T_{int} = 1/R$ (i.e., 1 bit delay). The maximum value for the station to station frame delay is then

$$T_{fd} = (X_{max} + X_t + N)/R + T_{prop} \tag{13.8}$$

and the corresponding user throughput is

$$T_h = X_{max} / T_{fd} \tag{13.9}$$

All Stations Active.   In this case, following the same reasoning as in the token bus protocol we obtain

$$T_{fd} = N(X_{max} + X_t + 1) / R + T_{prop} \tag{13.10}$$

and

$$T_h = N X_{max} / T_{fd} \tag{13.11}$$

Stochastic models.   Stochastic models take into account the stochastic nature of the system under study, and typically provide solutions in terms of *mean values* and *higher moments* of performance variables. For this reason, we also refer to these models as *mean value* models.

Mean value models allow a more detailed performance evaluation. Typical solutions desired are mean, variance, and higher moments of performance variables such as queue lengths, messages delay, response time, throughput, etc. Some of the simplifying assumptions made in the approximate model are dropped here. For example, network load is allowed to vary following some statistical distributions.

The following is a mean value model for token bus LANs developed by Menasce and Lerte (1984). The model gives the average values for the frame delay and token rotation time as well as exact[1] upper and lower bounds. The average frame delay is defined as the time interval between the arrival of a frame at the source station and the arrival of the last bit of the frame at the destination station.

A feature of the model is that it considers the influence of the immediate preceding cycle on the following one (i.e., the queues are not independent from one another). The results are:

$$E[T_{fd}] = E[w] + (E[X] + X_t) / R \tag{13.12}$$

$$E[T_h] = \lambda N E[X] / R \tag{13.13}$$

$$E[T_c] = C_o / (1 - E[T_h]) \tag{13.14}$$

where:

$$E[w] = \frac{E[C_1^2]}{2E[C_1]} + \frac{\lambda E[C_2^2]}{2(1 - \lambda E[C_2])} \tag{13.15}$$

$$E[C_1^2] = (N-1)\left[\lambda E[C_1]\frac{E[X^2]}{R^2} - \left(\lambda E[C_1]\frac{E[X]}{R}\right)^2\right] + (E[C_1])^2 \tag{13.16}$$

[1] The term *exact* is used in this context to indicate that the model solutions are exact, rather than approximations, with respect to the model. However, it does not indicate that the model solutions are exact with respect to the physical system being modeled.

$$E[C_2^2] = (N-1)\left[\lambda E[C_2]\frac{E[X^2]}{R^2} - \left(\lambda E[C_2]\frac{E[X]}{R}\right)^2\right]$$

$$+ \frac{E[X^2]}{R^2} - \left(\frac{E[X]}{R}\right)^2 + (E[C_2])^2 \tag{13.17}$$

$$E[C_1] = \frac{C_o}{1 - \lambda E[X](N-1)/R} \tag{13.18}$$

$$E[C_2] = \frac{(C_o + E[X]/R/)}{1 - \lambda E[X](N-1)/R} \tag{13.19}$$

$$C_o = N\, C_1/R + r + T_{prop} + T_{int} + T_{st} \tag{13.20}$$

where: w is the frame waiting time, r is the equivalent of a solicit successor interval in the token bus protocol, and λ is the fame arrival rate.

Extended models. Extended models attempt to provide solutions similar to mean value models. Extended models provide two types of extensions to mean value models. First, more involved solutions, such as probability density functions (pdf's), are provided, and second, other performance variables that are usually difficult to evaluate, such as reliability, are also taken into account. One example of an extended model is a performability (performance and reliability) model (Meyer, 1985). Queueing theory does not lend itself to model systems that exhibit the following properties: 1) concurrency, 2) timeliness, 3) fault tolerance, and 4) degradable performance. Extensions to Petri Net theory called Stochastic Activity Network (SAN) are currently being used to construct performability models used for modeling systems exhibiting the preceding properties.

An example of solutions that can be obtained using SAN methodology is the probability density function of response time (or token rotation time) under the presence of token losses in the token bus protocol (Muralidhar and Pimentel, 1987).

13.3.2 Simulation

Simulation models are somewhat similar to analytical models. Analytical and simulation models differ, in that simulation models include model extensions for obtaining the solution through the use of a computer program that behaves like the system under study. By studying the performance of the program, one can infer the performance of the simulated system.

There are several types of simulation models. They roughly correspond to the different user types discussed in Section 13.2. Simulation models that capture all variables and mechanisms defined in a protocol are useful for protocol development users (Rahimi and Jelatis, 1983). Simulation models that provide some interaction between the protocols and the hardware and software used to implement them are useful for vendors and application users (Kremien, 1985). Simulation models that consider performance variables suitable for specific applications are useful for end users. Pimentel (1985) presents a simulation model for factory automation, whereas Dahmen et. al. (1984) concentrate on models for office automation.

The following factors are important in simulation: programming languages (procedural versus high level language orientation), user interface, simulator view of the system (process versus discrete events), simulator stopping criteria, performance variables, user friendliness, etc.

13.3.3 Measurements

Performance can be evaluated through measurements, provided the network is under operation and available. One problem with this technique is how to obtain measurements without disrupting what is being measured. Another problem relates measuring traffic containing specific message types such as SDA (send data with acknowledgment) and SDN (send data with no acknowledgment), which were discussed in subsection 4.12.1. Thus, the measurement experiments must be designed with great care.

Most of the experimental studies have been performed with ethernet type LANs (Amer et. al., 1983). The National Bureau of Standards is currently working on an experimental program to study the performance of MAP-like networks through measurements. Problems involved with measurements include load generation, data acquisition, instrumentation, and test design.

13.4 APPLICATIONS OF LAN PERFORMANCE EVALUATION

Protocol development users are interested in such issues as deadlocks, protocol efficiency, fairness, and stability. The models should give relationships between these issues and factors that influence them.

Vendor users are interested in the effect of implementation strategies on network performance. Typical questions that should be answered by the model include the effect of buffer sizes and interfaces on throughput.

Application users are interested in the effects of the communication semantics on throughput or delay.

End users have a pragmatic view of performance. For real-time applications, token rotation times are important, because they are related to sampling rates of the variables under consideration.

13.4.1 Performance Evaluation of MAP's Physical and Data Link Layers

This section presents numerical values for the performance evaluation of the lower two layers of a MAP network. The performance variables are *frame delay* and *token rotation time* for the highest priority queue (access class 6) of the MAC sublayer. Results from this example should be used with caution. Full MAP architectures (that is, with all 7 layers) introduce delays at every layer which should be taken into account. However, numerical values from this section are accurate for networks that are mostly comprised by the physical and data link layers (e.g., the MAP enhanced performance architecture and the mini-MAP architecture).

We assume a 4-station MAP network with the IEEE 802.4 standard for the physical layer and the IEEE 802.2 class 1 for the data link layer. Since the IEEE 802.2 class 1 model is simple, its model is relatively straightforward.

For the MAP network, the token frame length is $X_t = 208$ bits. Let $R = 10$ M bit/sec, $N = 4$, and $X = 8192$ bits, $T_{prop} = 1.33$ μsec, $T_{int} = 10.5$ μsec, $T_{st} = 100$ μsec.

Mean Value Model. Let $\lambda = 10$ packets/sec, $r = 15$ μsec. Using Equations 13.12 through 13.20, one obtains $\overline{C}_o = 210.03$ μsec, $\overline{C}_1 = 211.76$ μsec, $\overline{C}_2 = 1037.73$ μsec, $\overline{w} = 107.93$

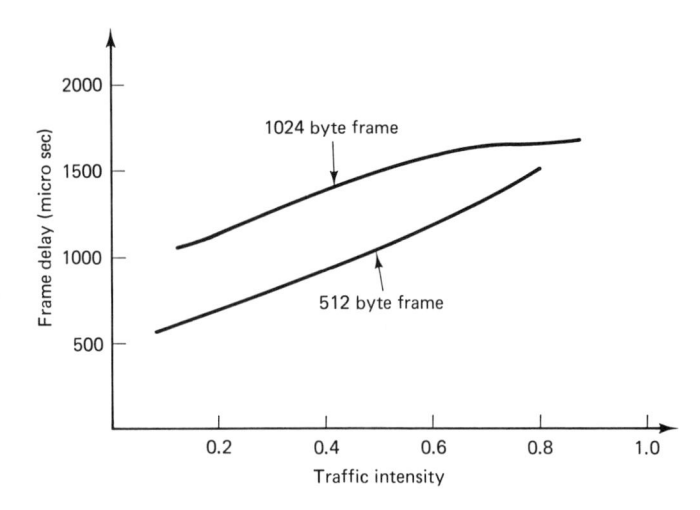

Figure 13.2 Simulation results for frame delay versus traffic intensity of the highest priority class queue of token bus protocol.

μsec. Using these values, the frame delay is T_{fd} = 0.97 msec, and the token rotation is T_c = 217.145 μsec.

Simulation Model. The simulation results from (Pimentel, 1985) was used with λ = 10 packets/sec, which corresponds to a traffic intensity ρ = 0.032 where:

$$\rho = N \lambda X / R \qquad (21)$$

The frame delay T_{fd} is shown in Figure 13.2, where T_{fd} is approximately equal to 1 msec, which agrees with the result provided by the mean value model and the upper bound given by the approximate model.

13.5 PERFORMANCE METRICS

Performance analysis is made by evaluating some functions or measures, referred to as **metrics**, which indicate the relative merits of the system under consideration. For computer communication networks, the *metrics* typically depend on *random variables*, such as the load on the network and the message length. Some typical *metrics* are the delay involved in a message transmission, the number of retransmissions needed to successfully send a message, the throughput, etc. An important aspect of performance analysis is the selection of a set of *metrics* that are appropriate and relevant for particular applications. Several criteria are available for selecting performance measures. For example, Goel and Amer (1983) developed performance metrics consisting of 40 functions which are primarily based on state transition diagrams for the protocols involved. Thus, the metrics that they developed are protocol dependent and they are primarily intended for protocol designers.

We are interested in a set of *performance metrics* that are independent of the protocols used, and the physical media. The main criterion used to developed *metrics* is that the *metrics* should be meaningful to the application (i.e., end users). Another criterion is that the number of *metrics* should not be excessive. Still another criterion is that the *metrics* should be consistent with similar *metrics*

TABLE 13.5 PERFORMANCE METRICS APPLICABLE FOR SOME MANUFACTURING APPLICATIONS

	Control services	Transmission services
RELIABILITY	Percent of packets retransmitted	Percent of lost messages Percent of messages with a deadline transmitted
DELAY THROUGHPUT	Response time Station to station packet delay Station to station prioritized packet delay Interface buffer occupancy Throughput	End to End response time Station to station message delay Message tardiness Station toleration time User throughput
AVAILABILITY	Utilization factor Number of interruptions	Effective utilization factor

that have been used elsewhere to evaluate the performance of computer networks for other applications, such as voice networks.

Depending upon the kind of performance aspect that they help measure, performance metrics can be decomposed into two major areas: control service metrics and transmission service metrics. **Control service metrics** are concerned with functions that measure the performance of the network, taking into account the control (including overhead) and operational aspects of the network such as transient situations, channel access schemes, etc. The **transmission service metrics** include functions that measure the performance of the network only in terms of user information messages. In other words, the overhead involved with the control bits, retransmissions, collisions, etc. is not included.

Another way to group the performance metrics is based on the degree with which they help quantify the reliability, delay-throughput, and the availability aspects of services offered by the communication network. Based on the preceding considerations, Table 13.5 shows a sample of performance metrics applicable for some manufacturing system applications.

The definition of the variables that characterize the performance metrics follows.

13.5.1 Control Service Metrics

1. Percent of messages retransmitted: The percentage of messages sent by a station which had to be retransmitted at least once. This metric can be used at any layer performing retransmission functions.

2. Station to station message delay: The time from when a message originates at one station until that message is received at the destination station. Queueing delays and channel access delays are components of the station to station message delay.

3. Station to station prioritized message delay: The time interval from when a prioritized message originates at one station until that message is received at the destination station.

4. Interface buffer occupancy: The fraction of total buffer capacity containing messages to be transmitted. The interface buffer is typically located in the network interface unit (NIU).

5. Throughput: The number of bits communicated by peer entities per unit time. The data rate can be thought of as the maximum throughput at the physical layer.

6. Utilization factor: The ratio of *mean message length/mean station interarrival time* × *data rate*. Mean message length is the average message length received at all stations. Mean station message interarrival time is the average of times that messages arrive at the stations. Data rate is the speed at which bits travel on the channel in bits per second (bps). The utilization factor depends on the transmission medium and the electronics at the transmitting/receiving ends. This definition only applies when the network is not saturated.

7. Number of interruptions: The number of times that the communication channel is unavailable for packet transmissions per unit time. A unit time could be 24 hours, 1 week, 1 month, etc. The number of interruptions is in turn a measure of network availability.

13.5.2 Transmission Service Metrics

1. Percent of lost messages: The percentage of messages sent by a source station that arrived corrupted or never arrived at their destination station.

2. Percent of messages with a deadline transmitted: The percentage of messages having a deadline that were successfully received by the destination station.

3. Station to station message delay: The time interval from when a message is sent by a station until the message is assembled *successfully* at the receiver station.

4. Message tardiness: The difference between actual *station to station message delay* and the *desired station to station delay*. The *desired delay* specified by the user is the time within which a user would like a message to be communicated.

5. Station toleration time: Period of time between the instant a *station overload* starts and the *breakdown* of the station. A **station overload** is the situation in which a station can no longer receive any more messages due to its finite interface buffer capacity. A *station breakdown* is a situation in which messages are sent to an overloaded station.

6. User throughput: The total number of information bits communicated from a station per second. Information bits are those data bits not including control and delimiter bits. Bits of redundant transmissions are not information bits.

7. Effective utilization factor: This is the utilization factor where the mean message length includes only information bits.

Determining whether communication requirements for certain applications are satisfied can be done by analysing the protocol used with such a network. For example, the IEEE 802.4 protocol has a limited capability for prioritized messages, in that message priority is in effect only when the station has the token. Otherwise, the station has to wait until all other stations are done transmitting before it can send an important message.

13.5.3 Applications

One use of the performance metrics involves the performance evaluation of subnetworks by means of analytical or simulation models. The simulation approach allows one to evaluate different protocols, different network architectures, or any new combination of parameter sets. However, another useful application of simulation is in the design area. In this case, one is simulating the performance of networks based on available protocols.

The preceding performance metrics can be used in a network design context. The following discusses several possible network design applications of performance metrics.

1. Initial Network Configuration: In this case, a network configuration and the associated protocols must be selected. The metrics that are appropriate for this step are the ones that deal with reliability, availability, and performance. For example, an application may require that the number of interruptions per month be less than two.

2. Application design: In this case, it is assumed that a network is already in place. The objective is to take into account performance metrics while designing application software. The metrics that are appropriate for this step are the ones under the delay-throughput category (station to station message delay, message tardiness, station tolerance time, user throughput, etc.). For example, a time critical control application cannot tolerate an excessive station to station message delay.

3. Network tuning: Performance metrics are used to tune the operation of the network.

4. Network management: Performance metrics can aid in the management of the network. In fact, network management systems such as the one specified by the MAP/TOP 3.0 specification has a functional facility dealing with *performance management*.

13.6 QUEUEING THEORY FUNDAMENTALS

In this section, we develop a detailed analytical model to be used in performance analysis of local area networks. In particular, the model is used for analyzing the performance of the token bus and CSMA/CD protocols. First, recall that the token bus protocol operates on a bus configuration, as depicted in Figure 13.3. Although the token bus protocol is capable of operating without a headend (e.g., in the MAP EPA architecture), the analysis in this section is for a single cable network with headend (HE). The model is also valid for networks without a headend with minor modifications. The **data rate** R is defined as the speed at which bits are sent and received through the physical medium.

Regarding Figure 13.3, assume that station D sends a message to station B. Because of the broadband nature of this network, D first sends the message to the headend, which remodulates it and send it to all other stations. Station B realizes that the message is addressed to it and therefore decodes and reads the message. Thus, the message flows in the following sequence: D → HE → B. The delay experienced by a single bit due to the length of the cable is maximum when stations are furthest away from the headend. The maximum propagation delay experienced by a single bit is referred to as the **end to end propagation delay** and is given by

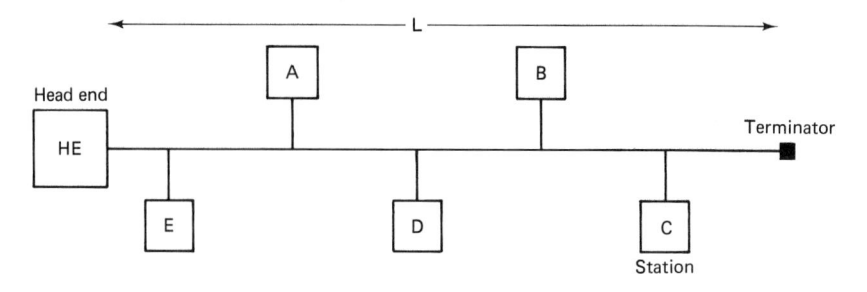

Figure 13.3 A MAP network configuration with head end.

$$\tau = 2L / 0.85 c, \text{ or} \tag{13.22}$$

$$\tau = 2L / c \tag{13.23}$$

where L is the cable length in meters and $c = 3 \times 10^8$ m / sec is the speed of light. Equation 13.22 applies for wires and coaxial cables, whereas Equation 13.23 applies for optical fibers.

Among other things, performance analysis of network protocols is influenced by the overhead (i.e., headers and trailers) in the protocol data units (PDUs). The overhead involved in the token bus protocol can be obtained from Figure 13.4, which shows the PDUs for the LLC and MAC sublayers. Let X_t represent the length of the token frame (a control frame) in bits, and E[X] represent the average length of a data frame including overhead. Assuming a preamble length of 2 bytes, a source and destination address of 6 bytes each (as used in the MAP network), and that the message length M in bits is a fixed number, then $X_t = 21 \times 8 = 168$ bits (i.e., LLC length = 0) and $E[X] = 8 \times (24 + M) = (192 + 8M)$ bits.

Example

Calculate the average time that it takes a station to transmit an entire data frame over the physical medium measured from when the first bit is put on the medium until the last bit is put on the medium by the transmitting station.

Solution Since the average length of a data frame is E[X] and bits are transmitted at a speed of R bit/sec, the average time to send an entire data frame is E[X]/R.

From the viewpoint of any station (e.g., station D), the elapsed time from consecutive receipts of the token is called the **cycle time** T_c. Thus, the cycle time includes the time used by station D while sending frames, and the time it takes the token to circulate through all other stations until it returns to station D. Since the time used by each station to send frames are different, T_c is different

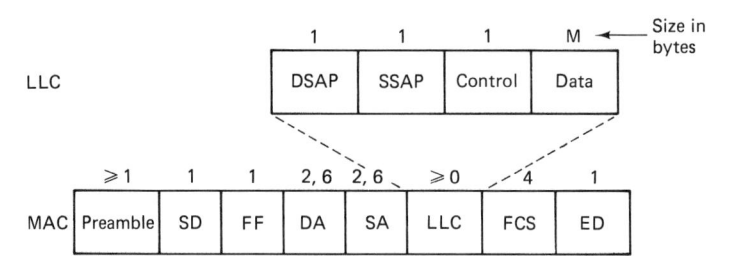

Figure 13.4 LLC and MAC frame format for the IEEE 802.4 standard.

for each station. Thus, $T_c = T_c(i)$, where i is a station index. In token bus protocol terms, T_c is also known as the **token rotation time** (TRT).

An important performance measure is the **frame delay** T, which is defined as the time it takes a frame to be transmitted, measured from the instant the frame arrives at the LLC sublayer at a source station until the frame arrives at the destination station. There are two major factors contributing to the *frame delay*. The first involves the delay in sending frames which arrived prior to the frame in question (i.e., a queueing delay). The second factor includes the delay in waiting for the token.

Frame delay is important because it measures the delay contribution of the lower two layers of the OSI reference model. Cycle time is particularly important for manufacturing and process control applications, because it can be used for calculations involving sampling times T_s for process signals and application specific cycle times. For periodic traffic, $T_s \geq T_c$. Since we do not know in advance when messages arrive for transmission, T_c and T are *random variables*. Thus, in order to calculate T_c and T, we need some elementary concepts from queueing theory.

13.6.1 Queueing Systems

How long will you spend waiting in lines next week? Exact answers to questions such as this are very difficult to obtain. For example, the next time you go to your favorite bank, can you say *in advance* the time that you will be spending in line? Although we cannot give an exact answer to this question, we can say something about the *statistics* of the time spent in line such as the average value (i.e., mean), its standard deviation, and so on. Queueing theory provides some powerful tools for analyzing systems that are random in nature.

Let us suppose that you go to your favorite bank where you find just one teller attending customers (it must be a Friday). You arrive at the bank and join the single queue, where you wait a random time W before you obtain service. After you are served, you depart happily from your bank (you just obtained some cash). The situation just described corresponds to a typical queueing system. The teller is referred to as a **server**. Persons going to a *server* are generally referred to as **customers**. Thus, a **queueing system** is one in which customers arrive at the system and join a queue in order to obtain service. Customers wait for their turn and eventually they receive service. After service completion, customers depart from the system. The diagram of Figure 13.5 is often used to represent a queueing system.

Question: a) Have you ever thought of calculating the time that tellers (i.e., servers) take in servicing customers?
b) How often do customers show up at a bank?

Answer: Again, we cannot answer these questions in a deterministic fashion. However, we can say something about the answers in a probabilistic fashion.

The previous question introduces two important concepts related to queueing systems. The time between successive arrivals of customers to a queueing system is called the **interarrival time**. The time that the server takes in serving one customer is referred to as the **service time**. Because

Figure 13.5 A schematic representation of a queueing system.

Customer generation — Queue (line) — Server (teller) — Customer sink of their random nature, *interarrival times* and *service times* are characterized in terms of **probability density functions** (pdf).

Example

Interarrival time X is usually assumed to follow an exponential probability density function (pdf). Thus,

$$f_X(t) = \begin{cases} \lambda e^{-\lambda t} &, \quad t > 0 \\ 0 &, \quad \text{otherwise} \end{cases}$$

where X is the *interarrival time* random variable and t represents time. The parameter λ is called the **interarrival rate,** or simply **arrival rate,** and it is a simple exercise to show that $\lambda = (E[X])^{-1}$ (i.e., the reciprocal of the mean of X).

Example

Service time Y is also usually assumed to follow an exponential pdf, that is

$$f_Y(t) = \begin{cases} \mu_T e^{-\mu_T t} &, \quad t > 0 \\ 0 &, \quad \text{otherwise} \end{cases}$$

where Y is the service time random variable and the **server rate** is given by

$$\mu_T = (E[Y])^{-1}$$

The ratio

$$\rho = \lambda/\mu_T = \text{arrival rate/service rate}$$

is an important measure of the load offered to a queueing system, and is referred to as the **traffic intensity.**

Let N represent the average number of customers in the system which consists of the queue and the server. Let T represent the average time a customer spends in the system. Likewise, the average number of customers in the queue is represented by N_q, whereas W represents the average time a customer spends in the queue. The meaning of the preceding variables is depicted in Figure 13.6. Clearly, $N \geq N_q$ and $T \geq W$.

13.6.2 Little's Law.

Little's Law, also known as Little's formula, is one of the simplest yet most important results in queueing systems. It establishes a powerful relationship for the variables N, T, and λ in the following way:

$$N = \lambda T \tag{13.24}$$

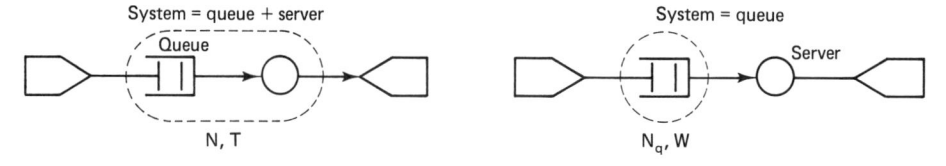

Figure 13.6 Relationship between queue and server in a queueing system.

TABLE 13.6 POSSIBLE DISTRIBUTIONS FOR INTERARRIVAL TIME AND SERVICE TIME FOR AN A/B/m QUEUEING SYSTEM

Distribution		Description
Symbol	Name	
M	Markovian	The probability distribution is exponentially distributed.
G	General	The probability distribution is of a general type. No special assumption is made as to the probability distribution.
D	Deterministic	The corresponding random variable is not really a random variable, i.e., it is a constant.

Thus, Little's law states that the average number of customers N in the systems is equal to the product of the average customer arrival rate λ to the system, and the average time T these customers spend in the system. Little's law can also be applied to the queue portion of Figure 13.6 (i.e., no server included) yielding

$$N_q = \lambda W \qquad (13.25)$$

The reader can prove that with reference to Figure 13.6. The expressions for T and N are:

$$T = W + 1/\mu_T \qquad (13.26)$$

$$N = N_q + \lambda/\mu_T = N_q + \rho \qquad (13.27)$$

Queueing theory specialists have developed a notation for representing queueing systems. The most important variables in a queueing system are the cusomter *interarrival time*, the server *service time*, and the number of servers. Accordingly, the notation A/B/m is used to represent a queueing system, with A indicating the probability distribution type for the *interarrival time*, B indicating the distribution type for the *service time*, and m indicating the number of servers. Since both A and B represent probability distributions, they could represent the same or different distributions. Table 13.6 shows some choices for these distributions.

Example

The notation M/M/1 represents a queueing system with one server and *service time* and *interarrival time* exponentially distributed.

13.6.3 Main Queueing Results (M/M/1 and M/G/1)

Let us assume that we have a queueing system with just one server, as shown in Figure 13.7. The objective of this subsection is to find expressions for the average number N of customers in the system and the average time T that a customer spends in the system. The results for the M/M/1 case are developed analytically, and the M/G/1 case is formulated to be solved as an exercise at the end of this chapter.

We begin our analysis by considering the M/M/1 case, which implies exponential distribution for the interarrival times and service time. Let λ be the arrival rate, μ_T the service rate, and k

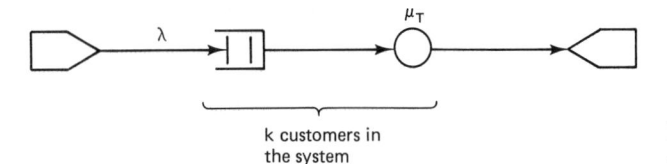

Figure 13.7 A queueing system with exponential interarrival and service times.

represent the number of customers in the system at a certain point in time. Thus, we are mainly interested in the expected value of the random variable k, that is, the average number of customers in the system $N = E[k]$. We further assume that at any instant only a single arrival or a single departure is permitted. We define the **state** of the system as the number k of customers in the system. Thus, if the system is at state k there are only two possible events: a customer may arrive, which will change the state of the system to state (k + 1); or a customer may depart, which will change the state of the system to state (k − 1). Because of the assumption that only one departure or arrival is permitted at any instant, the two events are disjoint. Furthermore, given that the system is at state k, the rate at which the state makes a transition into state (k + 1) is λ. Likewise, the rate at which state k makes a transition into state (k − 1) is μ_T. This process is depicted in Figure 13.8, and is referred to as a **birth-death** process.

Let p_k denote the probability that the system is at state k, thus

$$p_k = \text{Prob \{state} = k\} \tag{13.28}$$

We are mostly interested in an equilibrium condition, otherwise the number of customers in a certain state may grow without bound. Assuming that state k is in equilibrium, we have

$$\lambda p_{k-1} + \mu_T p_{k+1} = (\lambda + \mu_T) p_k \tag{13.29}$$

where except for a multiplying factor, the left side of the equation represents the probability that the system enters state k, and the right side represents the probability that the system leaves state k. Equation 13.29 is a **difference equation** for p_k, whose solution is fairly straightforward. To solve the difference equation we first need a boundary condition, which is given by

$$\lambda p_0 = \mu_T p_1 \tag{13.30}$$

From Equation 13.30 it appears that a general relationship is the following:

$$\lambda p_{k-1} = \mu_T p_k \tag{13.31}$$

which is compatible with Equation 13.29. Equation 13.31 is in fact true, and the mathematically inclined reader can prove it using mathematical induction.

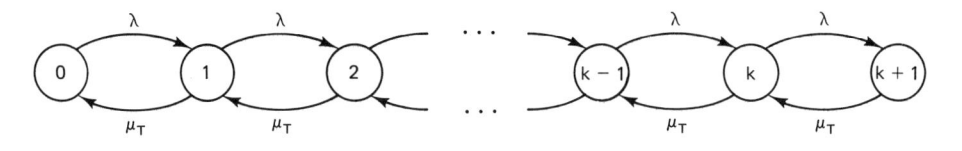

Figure 13.8 A birth-death process for modeling the number of customers in a queueing system.

From Equation 13.29,

$$p_k = (\lambda/\mu_T)p_{k-1} = \rho p_{k-1} \tag{13.32}$$

Thus,

$$p_1 = \rho p_0$$

$$p_2 = \rho p_1 = \rho^2 p_0$$

$$\cdot$$
$$\cdot$$
$$\cdot$$

In general,

$$p_k = \rho^k p_0 \tag{13.33}$$

which is a recursive solution giving the probability of having k customers in the system in terms of the probability of having no customers in the system. To find an explicit solution for p_k we realize that p_k are probabilities; thus, their sum equals 1. Therefore,

$$\sum_{k=0}^{\infty} p_k = 1 = p_0 \sum_{k=0}^{\infty} \rho^k = p_0/(1-\rho) \quad , \quad \text{for } \rho < 1$$

from which

$$p_k = \rho^k (1 - \rho) \tag{13.34}$$

Finally,

$$N = E[k] = \sum_{k=0}^{\infty} k\, p_k = (1 - \rho) \sum_{k=0}^{\infty} k\, \rho^k$$
$$N = \rho/(1 - \rho) \tag{13.35}$$

which is the result that we were looking for.

The corresponding result for the M/G/1, also known as the *Pollaczek-Khinchine* (P-K) equation is given by

$$N = \rho + \rho^2 (1 + C^2[Y])/2(1 - \rho) \tag{13.36}$$

where $C[Y] = (\text{var}[Y])^{1/2} / E[Y]$ is the coefficient of variation of the service time random variable Y and $\rho = \lambda E[Y]$.

Example

Using Little's law, calculate T for a) the M/M/1 case and b) the M/G/1 case.

Solution a) For the M/M/1 case,

$$T = N/\lambda = \rho/\lambda(1-\rho) = 1/\mu_T(1 - \rho) = 1/(\mu_T - \lambda) \tag{13.37}$$

b) For the M/G/1 case,

$$T = E[Y] + \rho^2(1 + C^2[Y])/2\lambda(1 - \rho) \tag{13.38a}$$

$$= 1/\mu_T + \rho^2(1 + C^2[Y]/2\lambda(1 - \rho) \tag{13.38b}$$

Likewise, we can derive expressions for N_q and W. The results are:

a) M/M/1 case

$$W = \lambda/\mu_T (\mu_T - \lambda) \qquad (13.39)$$

$$N_q = \rho^2 / (1-\rho) \qquad (13.40)$$

b) M/G/1 case

$$W = \rho^2(1 + C^2[Y]) / 2\lambda(1-\rho) \qquad (13.41)$$

$$N_q = \rho^2(1 + C^2[Y]) / 2(1-\rho) \qquad (13.42)$$

13.7 TOKEN BUS PERFORMANCE ANALYSIS

We are now in a position to calculate the delay experienced by a frame, measured from when the frame arrives to the data link layer at one station in a token bus network configuration, until the frame arrives at a destination station. The queueing system model is shown in Figure 13.9, which consists of one server (i.e., the shared bus) and many queues, each corresponding to one network station. The components of the frame delay are:

average delay due to the frame size $E[X]/R$,

average delay due to the length of the medium $\tau/3$,

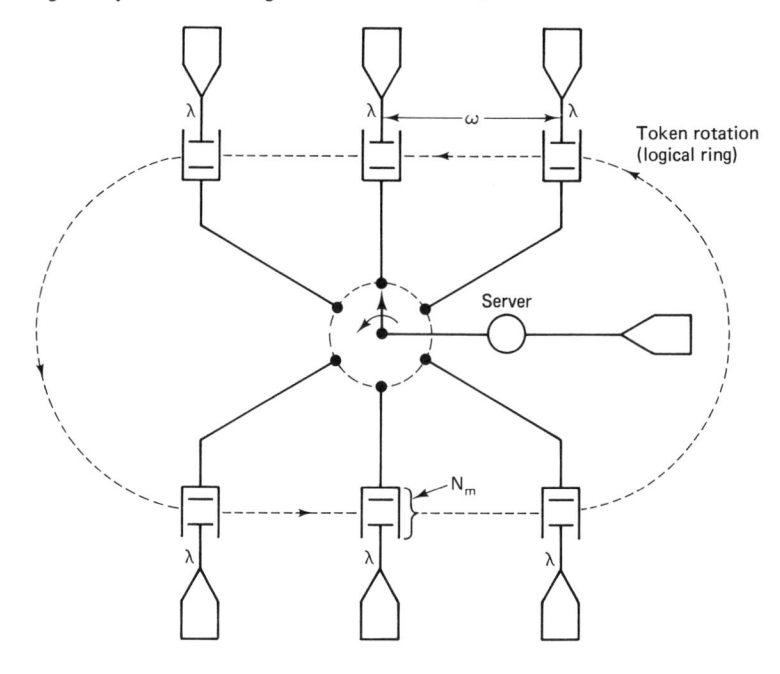

ω: walk time

Figure 13.9 Queueing model for a token bus network.

delay contributed by the physical layer (e.g., modem), and

delay involved in waiting for the token, and waiting at the queue.

Before proceeding with the frame delay calculation, we need to make a few assumptions. Frames arrive according to a *Poisson process* (i.e., exponentially distributed interarrival times) with arrival rate λ. The *service time* distribution is assumed to be deterministic, with service rate equal to R bits/sec. This assumption is accurate, since the data rate R does not change in the middle of a frame transmission. The service rate in units of frames/sec is

$$\mu_T = R / E[X] \qquad (13.43)$$

where X is a random variable representing the frame size in bits and E is the expected value operator. It is assumed that X follows a general distribution. We further assume that there are N stations in the logical ring, and that it takes ω seconds for the token to go from a station to its successor in the logical ring. The parameter ω is known as the **walk time** and is given by

$$\omega = X_t / R + \tau / 3 \qquad (13.44)$$

where X_t is the token frame size and τ is the end to end propagation delay. The factor 1/3 on the ω term accounts for the fact that the location of stations are uniformly distributed on a cable of length L.

Let N_m be the average number of frames, each with average length of E[X] bits, stored at a station when the token arrives. Each station waits for the token before transmitting its frames until the queue is emptied (exhaustive service). Frames are selected for transmission on a first come first serve basis (FCFS). Recall that in the token bus protocol, a queue is not served exhaustively, rather, a queue is served until the *token hold timer* THT associated with the queue expires, at which point the token must be sent to the next station in logical sequence. Although the queueing system with exhaustive service does not accurately reflect the token passing operation, it gives accurate results for the variables of interest. The last assumption regarding our token bus queueing model regards the use of only the priority queue in each network station.

Having stated the assumptions of our model, let us proceed with the calculation of the average frame delay T. We begin by calculating the average cycle time, which will be used in the calculation of the average waiting time W experienced by an arriving frame before reaching the end of the queue.

13.7.1 Average Cycle Time (T_c) Calculation

From the viewpoint of each station, the average time to empty its queue and send the token to the next station is $N_m E[X]/R + \omega$. Since there are N stations in the logical ring, the average cycle time T_c is

$$T_c = N [N_m E[X] / R + \omega] \qquad (13.45)$$

The average number of frames N_m that must be transmitted to empty a station buffer is determined from the arrival rate λ and the average cycle time T_c as

$$N_m = \lambda T_c \qquad (13.46)$$

Combining equations 13.45 and 13.46, we obtain

$$T_c = N\omega / (1 - N\lambda E[X] / R) = N\omega / (1 - N\rho) \qquad (13.47)$$

where

$$\rho = \lambda E[X] / R = \lambda / \mu_T \qquad (13.48)$$

is the traffic intensity and $\mu_T = R / E[X]$ is the server rate in frames/sec. The preceding formulas only hold for $N\rho < 1$.

Waiting time (W) calculation. Let W be the average time an arriving packet at a typical station must wait before reaching the head of the queue in the station buffer. As depicted in Figure 13.10, W has two components:

1. The waiting time W_1 in the station buffer while other stations are being served.
2. The waiting time W_2 in the station buffer while that particular station is being served.

Thus,

$$W = W_1 + W_2 \qquad (13.49)$$

It can be shown (Hammond and O'Reilly, 1986) that

$$W_1 = (1 - \rho)T_c / 2 \qquad (13.50)$$

Thus, from Equation 13.47,

$$W_1 = N\omega(1 - \rho) / 2(1 - N\rho) \qquad (13.51)$$

W_2 is a queueing delay which can be obtained using the (P−K) equation with a new equivalent arrival rate of $N\lambda$,

$$W_2 = S E[X^2] / 2 E[X] R(1 - S) \qquad (13.52)$$

where

$$S = N\rho \qquad (13.53)$$

represents the overall load presented to the system. Replacing equations 13.51 and 13.52 in Equation 13.49, we obtain

$$W = N\omega(1 - S/N / 2(1 - S) + S E[X^2] / 2 E[X] R(1 - S) \qquad (13.54)$$

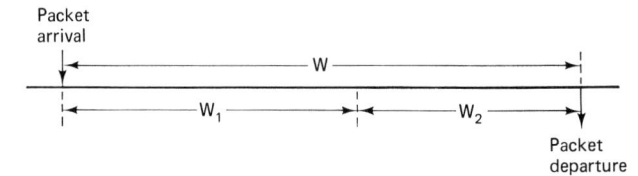

W_1: waiting time while other stations are being served.
W_2: waiting time while the station is being served.

Figure 13.10 Delays for a typical station.

and finally,

$$T = W + E[X]/R + \tau/3 \tag{13.55a}$$
$$T = N\omega(1 - S/N)/2(1-S) + S\,E[X\,]/2\,E^2[X]\,R(1-S) + E[X]/R + \tau/3 \tag{13.55b}$$

13.7.2 Exhaustive, Gated, and Limited Service Types

The waiting time W found in the previous section was obtained under the assumption that when a station receives the token, it continues to send frames until the station queue is empty. Such service type is called **exhaustive**. When the station sends only those frames found at the queue when the token is received, the corresponding service type is **gated**. In a **limited** service type, a station continues to send frames until either 1) the queue empties, or 2) the first fixed number L of frames are sent, whichever occurs first. The latter scheme models the token bus protocol standard more accurately. The corresponding expressions for the average waiting time for the gated and limited service types are (Takagi, 1985):

Exhaustive Service

$$W_E = N\omega(1 - S/N)/2(1-S) + SE[X^2]/2\,E[X]\,R(1-S) \tag{13.56}$$

Gated Service

$$W_G = N\omega(1 + S/N)/2(1-S) + SE[X^2]/2\,E[X]\,R(1-S) \tag{13.57}$$

Limited Service

$$W_L = N\omega(1 + S/N)/2(1-S-N\lambda\omega) + SE[X^2]/2\,E[X]\,R(1-S-N\lambda\omega) \tag{13.58}$$

From the corresponding average waiting time expressions, it can be shown that

$$W_E \leq W_G \leq W_L \tag{13.59}$$

Equations 13.56 through 13.58 assume that the rate of frame arrival to each station is the same (i.e., symmetric case). Similar results for the asynmmetric case are given by Boxma and Groenendijk (1986).

13.8 PERFORMANCE OF RANDOM ACCESS PROTOCOLS

As noted in Chapter 4, there is a large family of random channel access techniques, with perhaps the best known being ALOHA, CSMA, and CSMA/CD. Most access techniques used currently in local area networks are of the CSMA/CD type. In particular, the access technique used in the Technical and Office Protocol (TOP) is of the CSMA/CD type. The objective of this section is to analyze the performance of random access techniques, with emphasis on the CSMA/CD protocol. The approach taken in analyzing the performance of random access protocols is an intuitive one rather than a rigorous one. For a more rigorous treatment, the reader is referred to more specialized books such as Schwartz (1987), and Hammond and O'Reilly (1986).

Although not generally used with local networks, we begin our analysis with the ALOHA and Slotted ALOHA Protocols. The results of the analysis can be used for comparing the results for the CSMA, and CSMA/CD cases. In addition, the insight gained in analyzing ALOHA and

Slotted ALOHA is useful when analyzing more sophisticated algorithms, such as CSMA or CSMA/CD.

13.8.1 ALOHA

In this technique, also known as **pure ALOHA,** whenever stations have frames to transmit, they do so immediately regardless of whether other stations are transmitting (i.e., stations are not polite). As a result, two or more transmissions may overlap, causing a collision, as shown in Figure 13.11(a). Stations are assumed to be able to recognize collisions (e.g., by using positive acknowledgments), and attempt to retransmit the message after a random delay.

Let us assume a network composed of N identical stations. Each station generates frames of constant size X_m bits, according to a Poisson process with rate λ frames/sec. The variable S is commonly used to denote normalized throughput, which in this case is equal to the traffic intensity; thus,

$$S = N\lambda X_m/R \qquad (13.60)$$

where R is the data rate in bit/sec.

Because of collisions, the total traffic on the channel consists of new frames, as well as frames to be retransmitted. We also assume that the new and retransmitted frames follow a Poisson process with rate $\lambda' > \lambda$, as shown in Figure 13.11(b). Thus, the combined load to the system is

$$G = N\lambda' X_m / R \qquad (13.61)$$

After a frame is sent, it takes X_m/R seconds to be transmitted. The worst scenario is for a collision to occur when the entire message is almost transmitted (at point t_c in Figure 13.11(a)). Since in the ALOHA scheme, the entire frame is sent regardless of whether a collision occurs (i.e., no collision

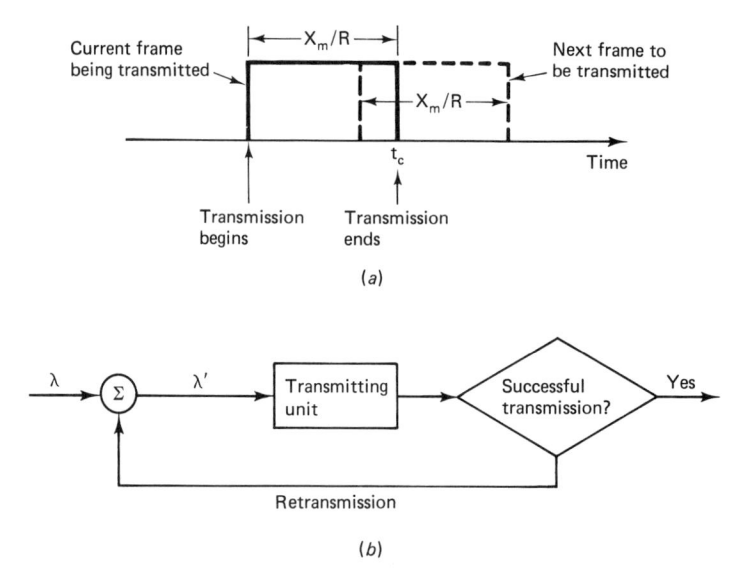

Figure 13.11 Collisions and retransmissions in the ALOHA scheme.

detection), the vulnerable period is actually $2 X_m/R$. Thus, from Figure 13.11(b), the normalized throughput is given by

$$S = G \, \text{Prob} \{ \text{no collision within } 2 X_m / R \text{ sec} \}$$

The probability of no collision is simply the probability of no message arrival during an interval of $2 X_m / R$ secs. Because of the Poisson process assumption,

$$\text{Prob \{no arrivals within } 2 X_m/R\} = \binom{N}{0} (N \lambda' X_m/R)^0 (e^{-2N\lambda'X_m/R})/0! \qquad (13.62)$$
$$= e^{-2G}$$

Thus,

$$S = G e^{-2G} \qquad (13.63)$$

whose maximum value is 0.18 (i.e., 18 percent of channel capacity).

To calculate the delay experienced by a frame, we calculate the elapsed time from when the frame arrives to the transmitter, until the station in question receives an acknowledgment indicating that the frame reached the receiver station. In the absence of retransmissions, the delay is $D = X_m / R + Q X_m / R$, where Q is the round trip propagation delay plus processing time involved in obtaining an acknowledgment. Q is normalized to X_m / R. In the presence of retransmissions, the delay is

$$D = (X_m / R) (1 + Q + Y (Q + Z)) \qquad (13.64)$$

where Y and Z are random variables representing the number of retransmission attempts per message transmitted, and the retransmission delay (also normalized to X_m / R), respectively. Thus,

$$E[D] = (X_m / R) (1 + Q + E[Y] (Q + E[Z])) \qquad (13.65)$$

Since Z is assumed to follow a discrete uniform distribution over 0 and K, $E[Z] = (K + 1) / 2$. To find E[Y] we realize that the total average traffic G is equal to the average incoming traffic S plus the average retransmitted traffic S E[Y]; thus,

$$G = S + S E[Y] \qquad (13.66)$$

Using Equation 13.63,

$$E[Y] = e^{2G} - 1 \qquad (13.67)$$

Finally,

$$E[D] = [1 + Q + (e^{2G} - 1)(Q + (K + 1)/2] X_m / R \qquad (13.68)$$

13.8.2 Slotted ALOHA

The analysis of the slotted ALOHA is similar to that of pure ALOHA. Slotted ALOHA improves the throughput of pure ALOHA to a maximum of about 38 percent (i.e., $S_{max} = 0.38$). The improvement is achieved by slotting time into *slots* each of length X_m/R and forcing users to attempt transmission only at the beginning of each slot time. In order for this scheme to work, all users need to be synchronized in time. Figure 13.12 depicts a situation where station 1 transmits without

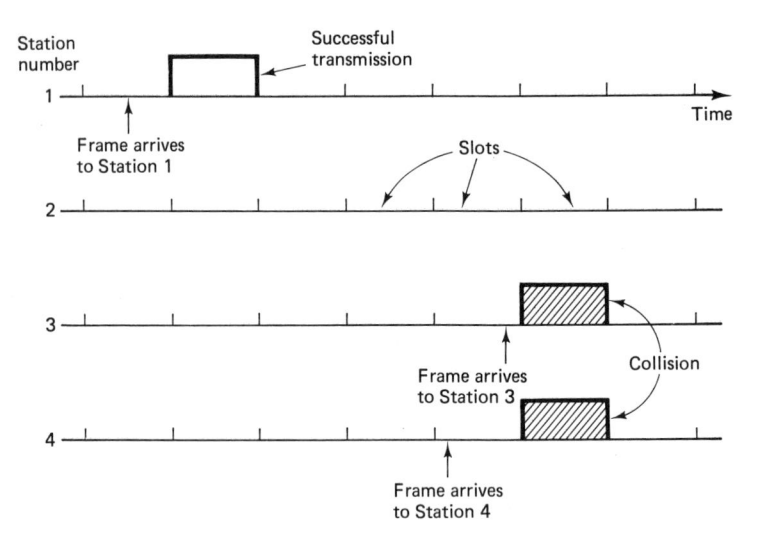

Figure 13.12 Successful and unsuccessful transmissions on a four-station slotted ALOHA network.

collision, whereas stations 3 and 4 are involved in a collision. The normalized throughput and delay are, respectively,

$$S = G e^{-G} \qquad (13.69)$$

$$D = (1.5 + Q + E[Y] (Q + 0.5 + (K + 1)/2)] X_m / R \qquad (13.70)$$

where

$$E[Y] = e^G - 1 \qquad (13.71)$$

Exact values for E[Y] depend on K, however, for K ≥ 5 the previous expressions are accurate. For more accurate calculations, see Hammond and O'Reilly (1986).

13.8.3 Carrier Sense Multiple Access (CSMA)

This subsection presents the analysis for the nonpersistent case using Figures 13.13(a) and 13.13(b). The normalized throughput can be expressed as

$$S = E[U] / (E[I] + E[B]) \qquad (13.72)$$

where U, I, and B are random variables denoting the time during a cycle during which the channel is used without collisions, the idle period, and the busy periods, respectively. Since each frame has a length of X_m bits, the average time in a cycle when the transmission is successful E[U] is

$$E[U] = m \text{ Prob \{First frame is successful\}} \qquad (13.73)$$

where m = X_m/R.

The probability that the first frame is successful is equal to the probability that no frames arrive in the vulnerable interval [t, t + τ]. Since arrivals follow a Poisson process,

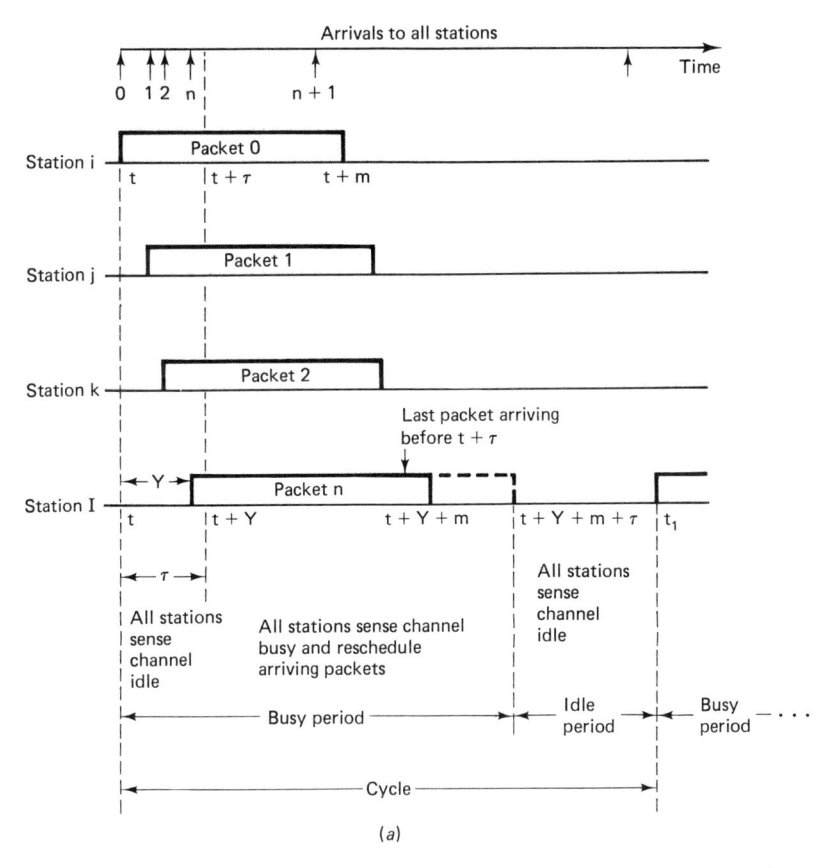

Figure 13.13 (a) Cycle components containing an unsuccessful busy period for nonpersistent CSMA. (Adapted from Figure 9.15 with permission from Hammond/O'Reilly, *Performance Analysis of Local Computer Networks*, © 1986, Addison-Wesley Publishing Co., Inc., Reading, Massachusetts. Reprinted with permission.)

$$\text{Prob \{no arrival in } \tau \text{ sec.\}} = e^{-N\lambda'\tau} \quad (13.74)$$
$$= e^{-G\tau/m}$$

Thus,

$$E[U] = m\, e^{-G\tau/m} \quad (13.75)$$

From Figure 13.13, the busy period is

$$B = Y + m + \tau \quad (13.76)$$

and

$$E[B] = E[Y] + m + \tau \quad (13.77)$$

To determine E[Y] we make use of the following result:

$$E[Y] = \int_{-\infty}^{\infty} [1 - F_Y(y)]\,dy \quad (13.78)$$

Sec. 13.6 Queueing Theory Fundamentals

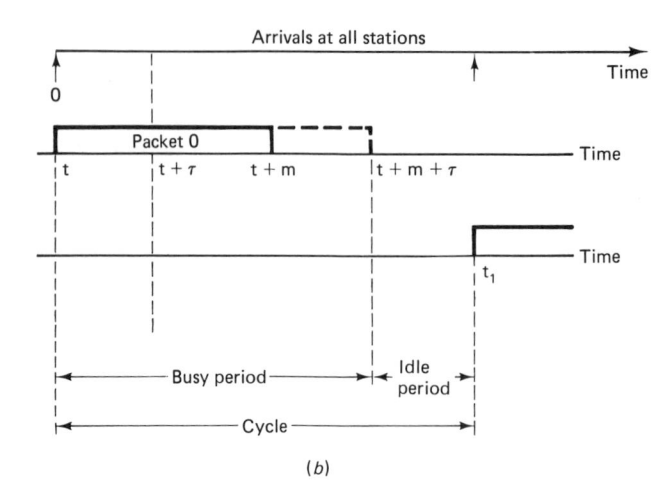

Figure 13.13 (b) Cycle components containing a successful busy period for nonpersistent CSMA. (Adapted from Figure 9.16 with permission from Hammond/O'Reilly, *Performance Analysis of Local Computer Networks*, © 1986, Addison-Wesley Publishing Co., Inc., Reading, Massachusetts. Reprinted with permission.)

where, by definition, the probability distribution function of Y is

$$F_Y(y) = \text{Prob}\{Y \leq y\} \tag{13.79}$$

The probability that the random variable $Y \leq y$ is the same as the probability that there are no arrivals in the interval $(\tau - y)$. Thus,

$$F_Y(y) = \text{Prob}\{\text{no arrivals in }(\tau - y)\} = e^{-G(\tau - y)/m}$$

Since $0 \leq y \leq \tau$,

$$E[Y] = \int_0^\tau \left[1 - F_Y(y)\right] dy = \tau - \frac{m}{G}\left(1 - e^{-G\tau/m}\right)$$

Thus,

$$E[B] = m + 2\tau - \left(1 - e^{-G\tau/m}\right) m/G \tag{13.80}$$

The *idle period* is the time interval between the end of a busy period and the next frame arrival. We are assuming that the new and retransmitted frames arrive according to a Poisson process, thus, the interarrival times are exponentially distributed with mean rate $N\lambda' = G/(X_m/R)$. Invoking the *memory less property* of the exponential distribution,

$$E[I] = (N\lambda')^{-1} = m/G, \quad m = X_m/R \tag{13.81}$$

Substituting equations 13.75, 13.80, and 13.81 in Equation 13.72 and simplifying, we obtain

$$S = \frac{G e^{-aG}}{G(1 + 2a) + e^{-aG}}, \quad a = \tau/m \tag{13.82}$$

We list next other results for the CSMA protocol which are obtained using a similar approach (Hammond and O'Reilly, 1986).

Slotted, Non persistent CSMA

$$S = \left(aG e^{-aG}\right) / \left(1 - e^{-aG} + a\right) \tag{13.83}$$

1 −Persistent CSMA

$$S = \frac{G[1 + G + aG(1 + G + aG/2)]\,e^{-G(1+2a)}}{G(1+2a) - (1 - e^{-aG}) + (1 + aG)\,e^{-G(1+a)}} \tag{13.84}$$

Slotted 1 −persistent CSMA

$$S = \frac{G\,e^{-G(1+a)}\,[1 + a - e^{-aG}]}{(1+a)(1 - e^{-aG}) + a e^{-G(1+a)}} \tag{13.85}$$

13.8.4 Carrier Sense Multiple Access with Collision Detection (CSMA/CD)

The analysis for the CSMA/CD case is similar to the CSMA case, with the major difference that after a station detects a collision, it transmits a *jamming signal* for J seconds. The normalized throughput can again be calculated with the help of Figure 13.13, as

$$S = E[U] / (E[B] + E[I]) \tag{13.86}$$

whose result for the nonpersistent case is (Hammond and O'Reilly, 1986)

$$S = \frac{G\,e^{-aG}}{G\,e^{-aG} + \gamma aG(1 - e^{-aG}) + 2aG(1 - e^{-aG}) + (2 - e^{-aG})} \tag{13.87}$$

where $\gamma = J/\tau$ and τ is the maximum end-to-end propagation delay.

13.9 NETWORK PERFORMANCE

The term *performance evaluation of computer networks* is often misused and misunderstood. In most of the literature, the term is used in a very narrow sense to indicate the performance of channel access schemes (i.e., protocol performance). Furthermore, network performance metrics often used include the access delay and the throughput at the data link layer. Such performance measures are appropriate for protocol designers but are of little interest for other users.

Computer networks are much more than channel access schemes. A computer network is composed of several layers, including the channel access protocol. For example, the real-time MAP/EPA architecture involves three layers: physical, data link, and application. More importantly, it is the application software which allows end applications to access the network. Since networks are tools which are used by end applications, network performance should be studied in the context of end applications. Accordingly, network performance evaluation should not only include *all* layers defined in the network architecture, but also communication aspects of end user applications.

Unfortunately, evaluating network performance in the context just described is a difficult task, because of the complexities involved in incorporating all layers. This is the major reason why there are few studies on network performance that take all relevant factors into account.

Following, we summarize a network performance evaluation study that takes into account all relevant factors of a specific network architecture (Murata and Takagi, 1987). The architecture consists of a LAN using the token ring protocol and incorporating the physical layer, the data link layer with connectionless LLC (logical link control), a connection-oriented transport layer, and an

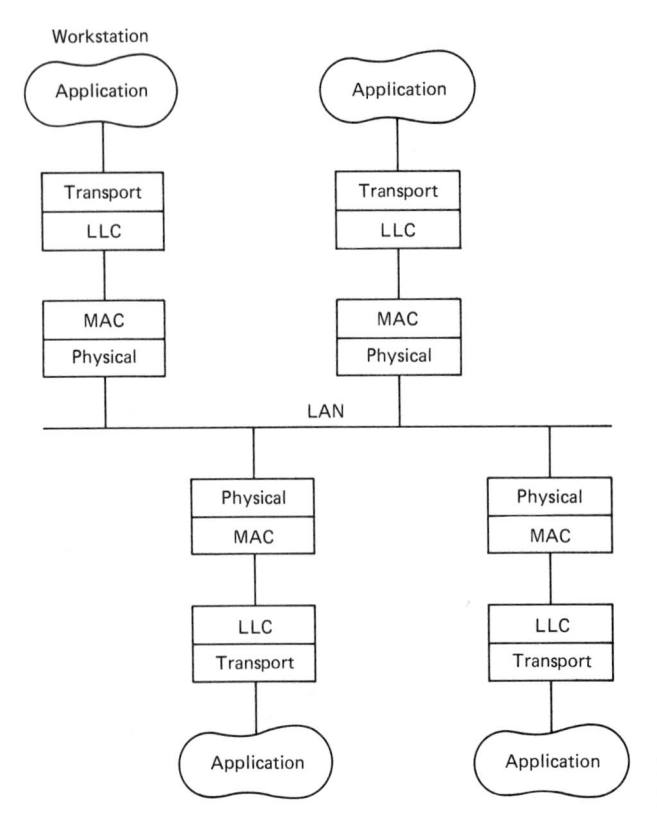

Figure 13.14 A model for LAN performance evaluation.

application process involving a client server model. Although the study presents results for the token ring protocol, the methodology is very general and could be applied to any other network architecture. Figure 13.14 depicts the model as it would be used with a bus topology. The following versions of the model have been studied:

- stations with symmetric load and transport layer with piggyback acknowledgments,
- stations with asymmetric load and transport layer with explicit acknowledgments,
- Full-duplex communication support for application processes, and
- Client / server model.

13.9.1 MAC Sublayer Modeling

The MAC sublayer can be modeled using the results from Section 13.6, where the channel access mechanisms is represented as a multiple queueing system with cyclic service. From the three possible service schemes (i.e., exhaustive, gated, and limited), the limited (i.e., nonexhaustive) service scheme has been used because it models the token ring protocol more accurately (Murata and Takagi, 1987). The following assumptions are made regarding the MAC sublayer model:

1. There are N stations in the ring.
2. Messages arrive at the MAC queue of station i according to a Poisson process with rate λ_i (i = 1, 2, . . . , N).

3. The service time T_i of messages at station i is independent and identically distributed random variable with $E[T_i] = b_i$ and $E[T_i^2] = b_i^{(2)}$. Recall that $T_i = X_i / R$, where X_i is the frame length at station i and R is the data rate.

4. The mean and variance of the *walk time* are r and δ^2, respectively. For the token ring case, the walk time represents the propagation delay between two adjacent stations plus the bit latency at each station.

5. Traffic intensity due to station i is given by

$$\rho_i = \lambda_i b_i \quad, \quad i = 1, \ldots, N \tag{13.88}$$

The overall traffic intensity is

$$\rho = \sum_{i=1}^{N} \rho_i \tag{13.89}$$

We are interested in the average frame waiting time w_i for station i. For the symmetric case in which arrival rates and service time are identical for all stations, an exact formula has been found which is given by

$$w_i = \frac{\delta^2}{2r} + \frac{N[\lambda b^{(2)} + r(1 + \lambda b) + \lambda \delta^2]}{2[1 - N\lambda(r + b)]} \tag{13.90}$$

$$i = 1, \ldots, N$$

where

$$\lambda = \lambda_1 = \lambda_2 = \lambda_3 = \ldots = \lambda_N, \quad b = b_1 = b_2 = \ldots = b_N$$

and

$$b^{(2)} = b_1^{(2)} = \ldots = b_N^{(2)}$$

For the asymmetric case, exact formulas have not been found; however, the following approximation has been shown to be in good agreement with simulation results.

$$w_i = \frac{1 - \rho - \rho_i}{1 - \rho - \lambda_i r} \frac{1 - \rho}{(1 - \rho)\rho + \sum_{j=1}^{N} \rho_j^2} \left[\frac{\rho}{2(1 - \rho)} \sum_{j=1}^{N} \lambda_j b_j^{(2)} \right.$$

$$\left. + \frac{N\rho\delta^2}{2r} + \frac{r}{2(1-\rho)} \sum_{j=1}^{N} \delta_j (1 + \delta_j) \right] \quad i = 1, \ldots, N \tag{13.91}$$

Finally, the total frame delay from when the frame arrives at the MAC sublayer until the frame reaches the destination station is

$$f_i = w_i + b_i + Nr/2 \tag{13.92}$$

where the Nr/2 term represents the mean propagation delay between sender i and a receiver station, which is assumed to be uniformly distributed over the ring.

Sec. 13.9   Network Performance

13.9.2 Transport Layer Modeling

The transport layer control message flows between the source and destination stations, such as sequencing and error and flow control. We assume a half duplex (i.e., unidirectional) connection-oriented transport service in which messages are individually acknowledged. The transport connection can be modeled as a **closed queueing network**[2] for connecting the two stations.

Each queueing network representing a transport connection is also referred to as a **chain.** The chain interacts with the MAC sublayer, as shown in Figure 13.15. Since the LLC sublayer is connectionless, its delay is considered constant. The effect of the MAC sublayer on the chain is taken into account by setting the service time of the MAC queue to f_i given by Equation 13.92, and assuming that the queue is unbounded, service times for the LLC queues correspond to datagram processing times, and are considered constant parameters.

Service times of a source application process correspond to the interarrival times of messages for the corresponding application process. The service time of a destination application process queue depends on whether piggybacked acknowledgments or explicit acknowledgments are used by the transport layer, as explained by the following:

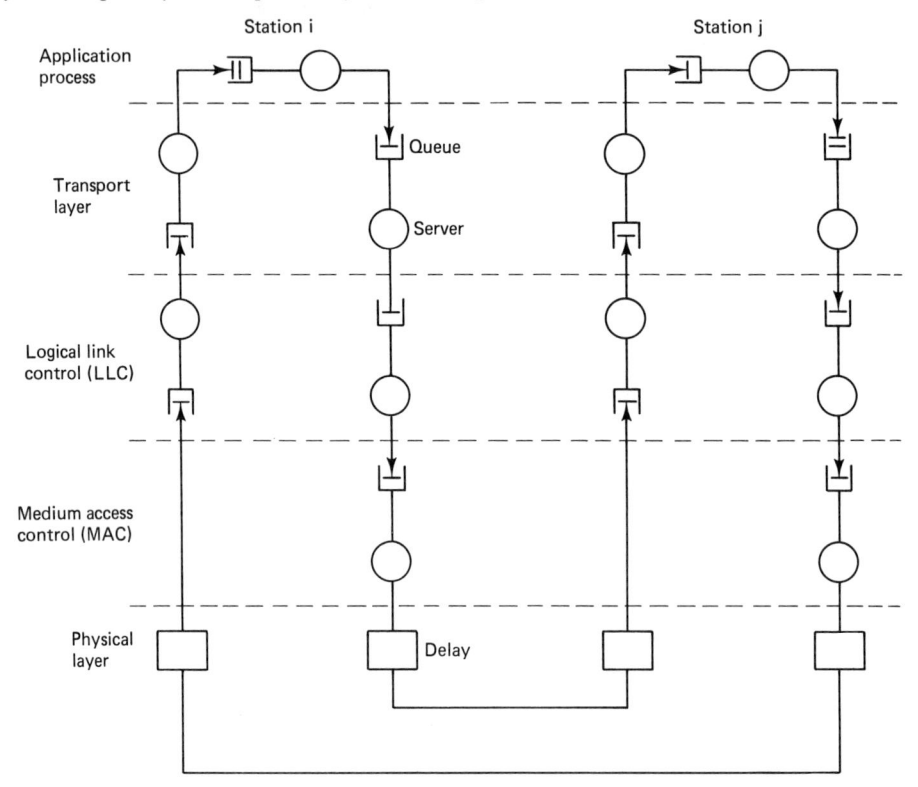

Figure 13.15 A queueing network submodel involving all layers and the application process.

---

[2] The term network used in this context has nothing to do with computer networks; rather, it simply means an interconnected system of queues.

514   LAN Design and Performance   Chap. 13

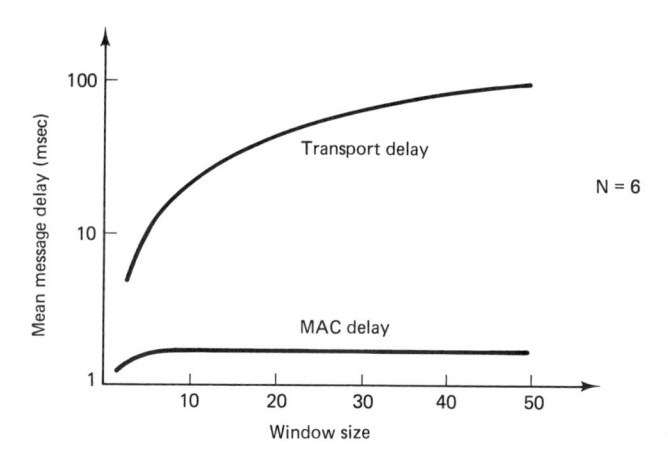

Figure 13.16 Mean message delays in the case of asymmetric load.

1. When piggyback acknowledgments are used, the service times at the destination application process queue correspond to the interarrival times of the messages generated by the application process at the destination station.

2. When acknowledgments are returned by themselves, service times at the destination queue correspond to the time to generate the acknowledgment at the transport queue in the destination. Messages are passed to the application process separately with explicit acknowledgments.

The solution to the model follows a technique developed for closed queueing networks known as **mean value analysis** (MVA), whose details are beyond the scope of this book. Interested readers are referred to the paper by Murata and Takagi, or consult (Lavenberg, 1983).

Figure 13.16 shows the performance results for the queueing network representing a six station LAN, in which one station is the server and the remaining ones are clients. Performance results are in terms of mean message delay at the transport and MAC layers of the chain. The window size of the chain is variable. The following additional assumptions are made: processing time of client stations and server stations are 5 msec and 10 msec respectively, processing times of transport queues are 4 msec.

The result of Figure 13.16 shows that the transport layer message delays are higher than MAC message delays. Similar results are obtained by (Meister et al, 1985). In general, performance results such as the ones shown in Figure 13.16 depend on where the bottleneck is as well as on other factors, as listed in Tables 13.1 through 13.4.

SUMMARY

The performance of local area networks is an important topic, since it allows choices to be made in terms of the many factors affecting performance. Designing a local area network involves allocating network resources to accommodate user demands while meeting cost and performance requirements. Major factors involving the design process are network resources, end user application requirements, and performance requirements.

Network performance addresses the issue of how well the overall network system is doing its job. A partial list of indicators of performance include:

message delay,

transaction response time,

queue lengths,

information throughput, and

congestion.

An effective way for designing networks consists of using models for evaluating the performance of the network. Performance models usually belong to three major categories: analytical, simulation, and measurement. Analytical models in turn are classified into approximate, stochastic, and extended models.

Network performance evaluation is user dependent with users classified in the following categories:

protocol development users,

protocol implementor (vendor) users,

value added (application) users,

end users.

Performance analysis is made by evaluating some functions or measures, referred to as metrics, which indicate the relative merits of the system under consideration. An important aspect of performance analysis is the selection of a set of metrics that are appropriate and relevant for particular applications. Metrics can be classified as control service metrics or transmission service metrics depending upon the performance aspect that they help measure. Functionally, metrics are classified into reliability, delay-throughput, and availability metrics. Performance analysis is useful for initial network configuration, application design, network tuning, and network management.

Because of its stochastic nature, network performance is analyzed with the help of queueing systems. A queueing system is one in which customers arrive to the system and join a queue in order to obtain service. Customers wait for their turn and eventually they receive service. After service completion, customers depart from the system. Little's law states that the average number of customers in the system is equal to the product of the average customer arrival rate, and the average time these customers spend in the system. The main queueing systems used in network performance analysis are $M/M/1$, and $M/G/1$. Section 13.7 contains the calculation of frame delay and token rotation time (TRT) for the token bus protocol using the exhaustive service model. Results are also presented for the gated and limited service models. Analysis of the ALOHA and CSMA schemes are included in section 13.8, along with results for the Slotted ALOHA and CSMA/CD schemes. Finally, section 13.9 presents the performance analysis of an entire network including several layers and an application process involving a client server model.

Bibliographic Notes

Whereas modeling and simulation are treated generically in the books by Law and Kelton (1982), and Cellier (1982), computer network performance modeling is treated in the books by Hammond and O'Reilly (1986), Stuck and Arthurs (1985), Hayes (1984), MacNair and Sauer (1985), and Sharma (1982). There are also many excellent articles that cover the subject of network performance, for example, Reiser (1982), Bux (1981), and Spaniol (1976). LeLann (1983) discusses performance requirements for some real-time systems. Performance measurements particularly for Ethernet type networks are reported in Shoch (1980), Toense (1983), and Murray and Enslow (1984). The design of computer networks are treated in the books by Ellis (1986), and Hooper (1986). Whereas Collela and others (1985) analyzes the performance of the ISO transport protocol in satellite environments, Kong (1987) discusses the performance of ISO transort protocol in a MAP environment. The articles by Pimentel (1985), Colvin and Weaver (1986), Janetzky and Watson (1986), DeTreville (1984), and Jayasumana (1987) provide various levels of discussion of MAP performance particularly the lower two layers.

PROBLEMS

1. Provide a list of resources which affect the performance of a TOP network.
2. Define the network design problem from the viewpoint of
   (a) protocol development users
   (b) protocol implementor users
   (c) value added users
   (d) end users
3. Consider the use of a computer network in a manufacturing cell application as defined in section 11.2. List several metrics that are appropriate for characterizing the performance of such application.
4. (a) Using Equations (13.1) and (13.2) plot delay versus throughput for the approximate model.
   (b) Verify the statement that increasing throughput increases message delay.
5. (a) Use an approximate model by making the same assumptions as those of subsection 13.3.1 to derive the throughput and message delay as a function of the data rate for the CSMA/CD protocol.
   (b) Plot the results.
6. Prove Equations (13.26) and (13.27).
7. Prove Equation (13.31) using mathematical induction. That is, prove that the equation is true for $k = 1$, then assuming that the equation is true for k, prove it is true for $(k + 1)$.
8. If X is the exponential random variable with rate λ, show that $E[X] = 1/\lambda$.
9. Consider a LAN medium with length L where two stations can be located at random. Let station 1 be located at X1 and station 2 be located at X2. Assume that X1 and X2 are uniformly distributed over [0, L] and define the distance between them as

$$Y = \max(X1, X2) - \min(X1, X2)$$

   where max and min select the larger and smaller of the two variables X1 and X2 respectively. Prove that the expected value of the distance between stations $E[Y] = L/3$.
10. Derive the formula for the expected value of the number of customers waiting in the queue for the M/G/1 system. Assume that customer arrivals and customer departures are statistically independent.
11. Calculate the frame delay T, waiting time W, and the average number of frames that must be transmitted to empty the station buffer N_m for the broadband IEEE 802.4 network using exhaustive service. Assume that the data component of a frame has 1024 octets, the frame arrival rate is 1 frame/sec, and there are 100 stations.
12. Plot the waiting time W versus traffic intensity for the exhaustive, gated, and limited service types. Assume a token bus network with head end, $R = 10$ Mbps, fixed frame size of 1024 octets, and medium length = 4 Km.

13. Plot the throughput S versus the combined load to the system G for the ALOHA, Slotted ALOHA, CSMA, and CSMA/CD. Assume a network with R = 10 Mbps, fixed frame size of 1024 octets, and medium length of 1 Km.
14. In addition to the medium access control, the number of stations, message size distributions, message arrival, and the medium length, what other network resources significantly affect end to end network performance?

14

Manufacturing Applications

Once protocols and networks are developed, an important question remains as to how can they be used effectively to solve problems in many application areas and more specifically, in automated manufacturing. In fact, networks must justify their existence by helping solve problems in specific areas. Thus, the view taken in this book is that networks are important tools for solving automated manufacturing problems. In this sense, networks are a means to an end rather than the end itself.

This chapter addresses the question of how networks can be used to solve communication problems in automated manufacturing. We focus our attention on one of the most important problems arising in automated manufacturing, that of control. Accordingly, we discuss the application of *production planning and control* in detail. The network role in the control of manufacturing systems is studied in the context of two models for automated manufactured systems developed by the Society of Manufacturing Engineers (SME), and a hierarchical CIM model. The material of this chapter is intimately related to that of Chapter 11.

14.1 NETWORKS IN MANUFACTURING

Networks can be used in virtually every aspect of manufacturing. The major manufacturing areas that can benefit from computer networks are: flexible manufacturing systems (FMS), manufacturing cells, flexible assembly, testing, design (CAD, CAM), quality control, inspection, etc. Because of the wide variety of applications found in manufacturing, it is expected that manufacturing will

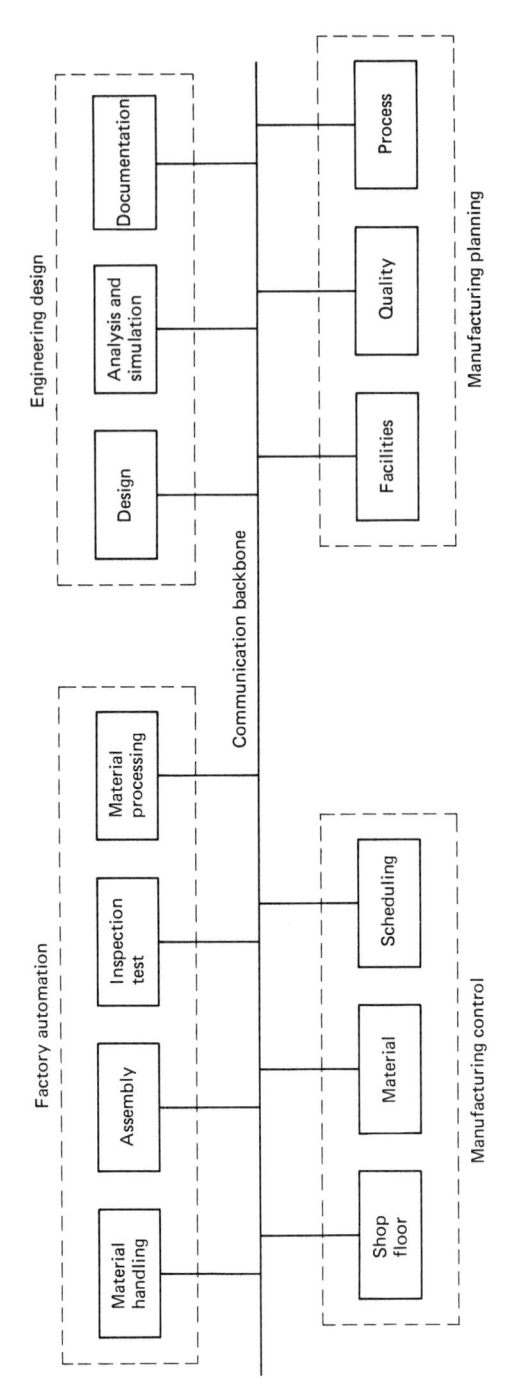

Figure 14.1 A computer network supporting the SME CIM model.

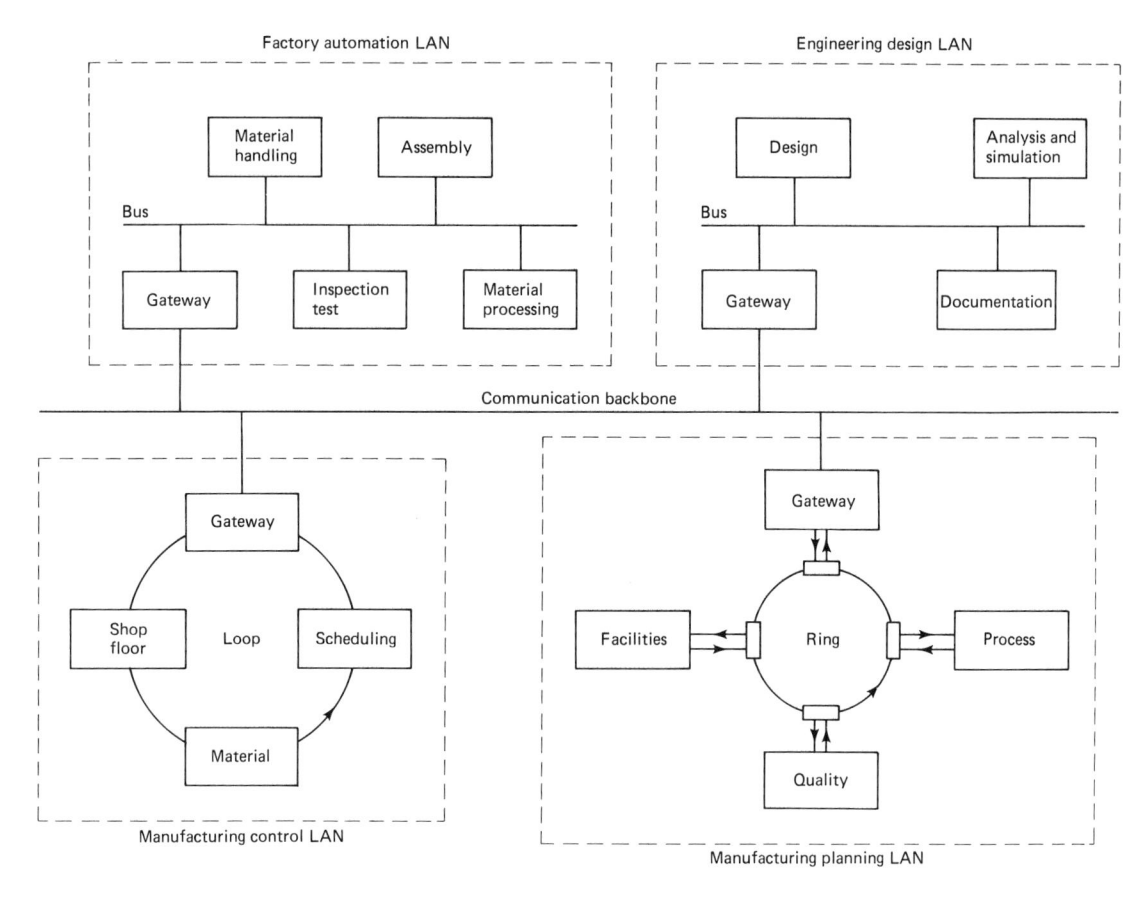

Figure 14.2 Subnetwork-based network supporting the SME CIM model.

benefit from different types of networks including MAP, TOP, other Ethernet-like networks (i.e., Decnet), SNA, and a wide variety of personal computer networks currently available.

It is precisely in the design of the system architecture and common database that computer networks will play a key role. More specifically, networks can allow communications between the elements of the system architecture, and also allow accessing common databases.

To begin with, we need a communication backbone to interconnect intelligent devices in each of the subareas shown in the CIM model of Figure 11.9. Depending upon the size of the overall manufacturing facility, network stations corresponding to the different subareas could be connected directly to the backbone, or indirectly through the use of subnetworks, as depicted in Figures 14.1 and 14.2, respectively. When subnetworks are used, the constituent LANs could be based on bus, loop, or ring architectures, as shown in Figure 14.2.

The advantages of the subnetwork approach are better reliability and performance. The subnetwork design is more reliable, since the constituent LANs continue to operate even when the communications backbone goes down. The performance advantage results from the lower message traffic on the communication backbone. The disadvantage of using subnetworks is that message delay increases for area-to-area communication. Furthermore, if the protocol/networks used in each

TABLE 14.1 A MANUFACTURING CONTROL HIERARCHY

Control level	Other names
System-wide control level	Factory level
	Facility level
Supervisory control level	Job shop level
	Shop level
Sequence control level	Cell level
	Workstation level
	Work center control level
Direct digital control	Equipment level
	Machine level

area are different, more sophisticated protocol translation mechanisms are needed, the network is more complex, and may be more expensive.

In this book, we use two generic hierarchical structures for characterizing an automated manufacturing facility. The first structure is a *control structure* similar to those used by the AFMS and AMRF. The second hierarchy is a *device hierarchy*, which considers the objects for control. The primary reason for using yet another hierarchical model is one of nomenclature. We envision the use of hierarchical control systems not only in automated manufacturing but also in the process control area; thus, a more generic nomenclature is needed. The principle advantage of considering two hierarchical structures (i.e., control and device) is that they help in analyzing the role of networks in manufacturing. A computer network basically interconnects *devices* at the same or different levels in the *device hierarchy*. Messages interchanged by the different devices involve the actions of *control systems* at various levels in the control hierarchy; hence, the importance of both hierarchical structures.

As noted, the control hierarchy is similar to that used by the AFMS and AMRF and has four levels, as described below. Table 14.1 lists other names given to the levels identified next.

1. System-wide control level: As the name implies, this level involves the control on a system wide-basis, including master production scheduling (MPS), material requirements planning (MRP), computer aided design (CAD), and process planning systems. The system-wide control level is the highest level in the control hierarchy.

2. Supervisory control level: The major function of the supervisory control level is the supervision and optimization of several controllers located beneath the supervisory level. This level contains a system (supervisory) controller, which is concerned with the overall coordination and control of a major section of the automated manufacturing system, perhaps comprising several cells. Thus, the supervisory control level is essential to the production planning and control function of manufacturing systems.

3. Sequence control level: The sequence control level is primarily concerned with the control of machines or other facilities in a *sequential* fashion. In manufacturing systems, a sequence controller may take the form of a cell controller. The functions of the cell control system (CCS) involve scheduling and controlling the individual elements of the cell to achieve the objectives set by the shop level controller.

4. Direct digital control level: The reason for the peculiar name of this control level is that it executes the commands received from the sequence control level directly without generating subcommands for other lower layers, since there are no other lower layers. Thus, this level of control is responsible for generating actual movements in robots, machine tools, or reading status information directly from where they are generated rather than obtaining the values from intermediate devices.

The relationship between the hierarchical control structure and some major automated manufacturing control functions is depicted in Figure 14.3. Not all control levels are required for a particular manufacturing application. Clearly, more sophisticated systems tend to require more levels than simpler systems. For example, if a manufacturing system contains only a small number of cells which do not interact to any appreciable degree, then the supervisory level (i.e., shop level) need not be included.

The controller at each level generates *commands* for the level below by processing commands received from the level above. Depending upon the nature of the controller functions, the controller can also carry out some commands directly, in order to produce some outputs at each particular level. For example, a controller may generate a listing of machine malfunctions at the end of the day. In this way, each level has control of the level immediately below. In order for a level to perform its control functions adequately, its controller requires *feedback* from the level below, as shown in Figure 14.4. The role of the communciation network is to provide the means for the effective communication of *feedback* and *commands* at different levels in the control hierarchy, and

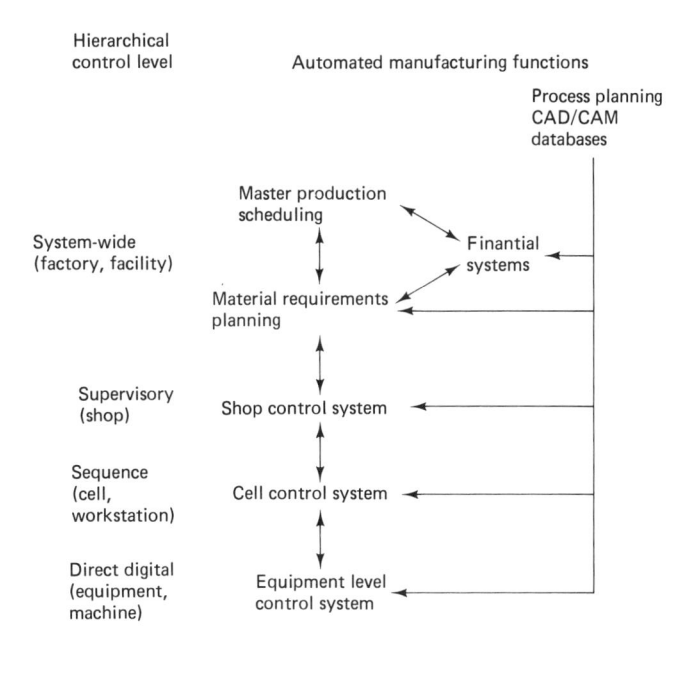

CAD: computer aided design
CAM: computer aided manufacturing

Figure 14.3 Relationship between hierarchical control levels and automated manufacturing functions.

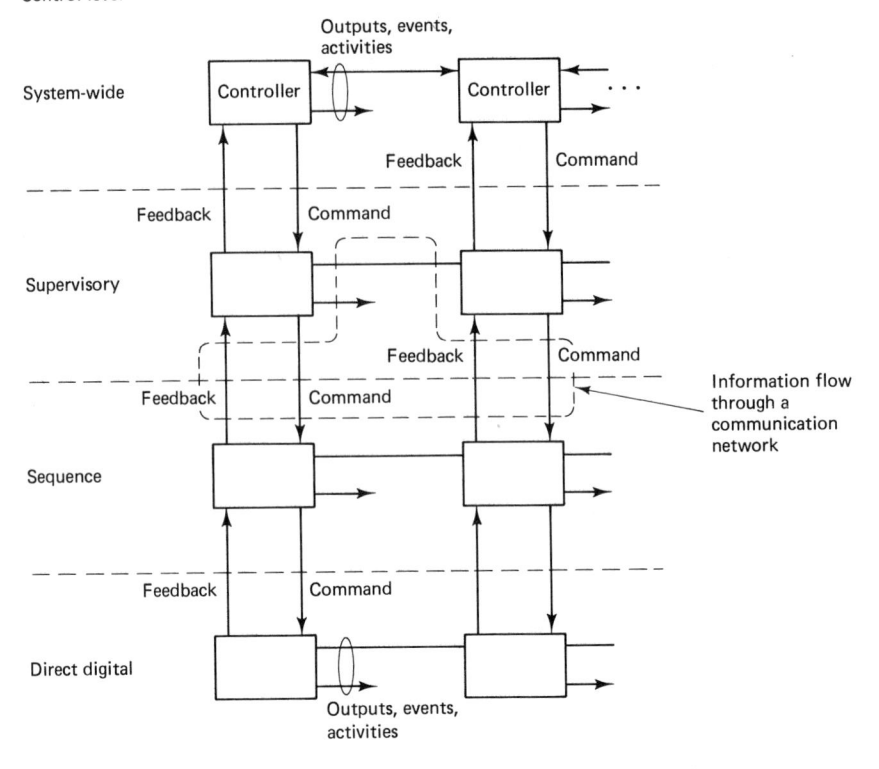

Figure 14.4 Role of computer networks in the context of hierarchical control of automated manufacturing systems.

events, *activities*, and *outputs* from controllers located at the same level in the control hierarchy.

Since control can be viewed as a set of actions performed on controlled devices, the following device hierarchy can be identified for an automated manufacturing facility:

1. factory level
2. shop
3. cell
4. machine
5. sensor.

In general, as discussed in Chapter 11, a control system operates in a closed loop fashion, as depicted in Figure 11.4. The control system accepts reference inputs, compares with feedback, and generates appropriate commands to control the device. Thus, whereas devices[1] are being controlled, a control system specifies the actions to be performed on devices.

---

[1] The term *device* as used in this chapter is equivalent to the *controlled system* in the nomenclature of Chapter 11.

524 Manufacturing Applications Chap. 14

14.2 COMPUTER NETWORKS AND HIERARCHICAL CONTROL

In the context of the hierarchical CIM model, one can envision the use of one or more networks at each layer of the control hierarchy. All devices located at the same level in the hierarchy are connected to one network or several networks with similar capabilities. Thus, from the hierarchical CIM model point of view, one can distinguish the following manufacturing network levels:

1. factory level network,
2. shop level network,
3. cell level network,
4. machine level network, and
5. sensor level network.

The relationship between the network level hierarchy, and the *control* and *device* level hierarchy discussed previously, is depicted in Figure 14.5. The topologies chosen for the networks at different levels, as shown in this figure, are completely arbitrary. Actual topologies to be used in particular applications depend on the requirements imposed by the applications. This subject is treated in more detail in sections 14.5, 14.6, and 14.7. When choosing a network for a certain level in the network hierarchy, the most important network characteristics are topology, medium access control, upper layer protocols, application layer services, performance characteristics, and available functionality. Table 14.2 lists some choices existing at each network level.

Distributed Applications in Automated Manufacturing

In each of the hierarchical control levels of an automated manufacturing system, as discussed in the previous section, one can find distributed applications. A distributed application is one that requires the cooperation of several stations (i.e., devices) interconnected by a computer network in order to perform a global function. To illustrate the concept of distributed applications in manufacturing, we use an example which corresponds to the sequence control level (e.g., a cell controller).

A cell controller distributed application. We assume that the cell controller operates in the decentralized mode; that is, the cell is relatively independent from supervisory controllers (e.g., a shop level control). The cell receives commands and objectives from the shop level controller containing enough information to start a job, and also to generate outputs, events, or activities for other cells if necessary. The cell schedules and/or reschedules its own activities by monitoring feedback information in order to meet its objectives. The cell reports to the shop level controller only when the job is completed, or when some insurmountable problems arise.

Once a cell controller receives objectives from the shop level controller, it performs the following distributed applications:

1. Distributed Monitoring: The cell monitors the state of all machines and devices belonging to the cell. Since some machines and devices can be located on different network stations, this application is a distributed application.

2. Distributed Control: The cell controls the operation of all machines and devices in the cell. Examples of control operations include start a machine, load a machine, run program *escape*

Figure 14.5 Relationship between the control and device level hierarchies and networks supporting them.

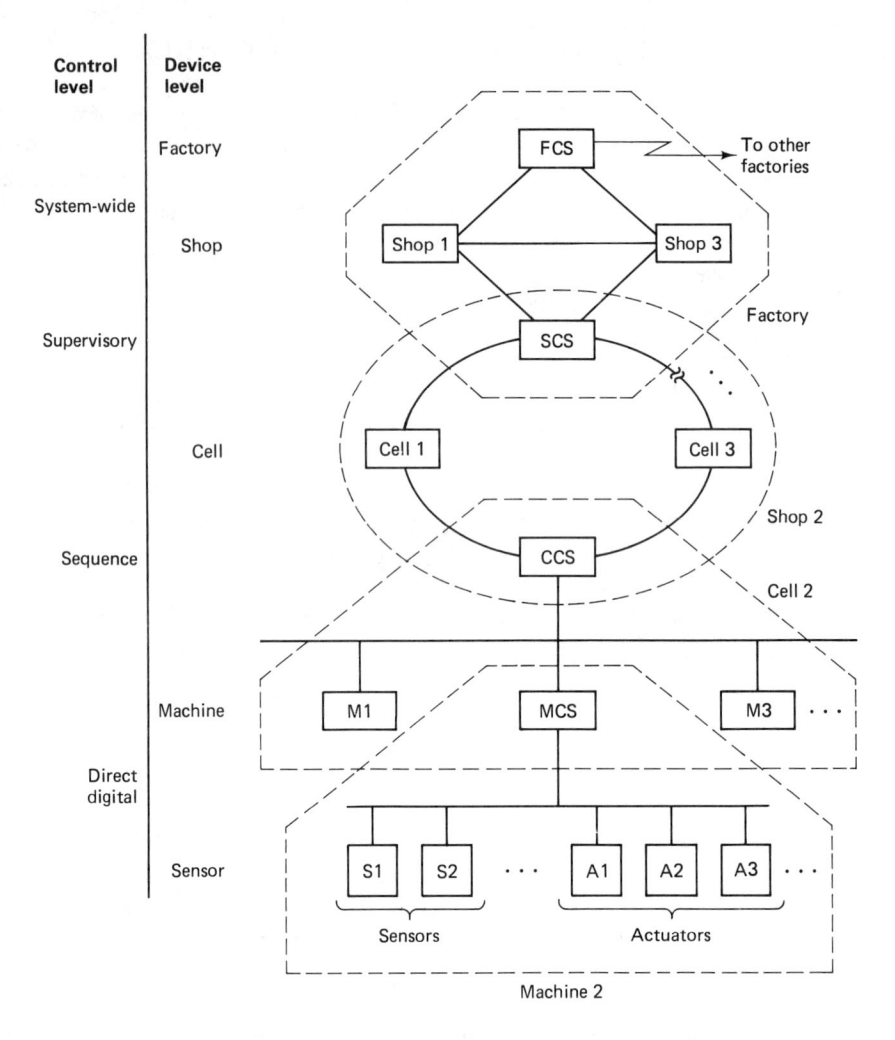

FCS: factory control system
SCS: shop control system
CCS: cell control system
MCS: machine control system

from danger on robot R2D2, etc. The control function is also a distributed application for the same reason just given.

3. Distributed Scheduling: Once the cell receives the commands and objectives from the shop level controller, it generates its own schedule in order to meet the objectives. The schedule is generated by taking into account the resources available and the predetermined objectives. The resources consist of both physical (i.e., parts available) and nonphysical (i.e., scheduling/timing

TABLE 14.2 SOME CHOICES EXISTENT AT EACH NETWORK LEVEL

Network level	Topology	Medium access control	Upper layers protocols	Performance variables of most interest	Overall functionality
Factory	Partial interconn.	*	MHS, FTAM, Databases	Throughput	High/Medium
Shop	Bus, ring, loop Partial interconn.	Token passing, Ethernet (CSMA/CD)	FTAM, Graphics, Databases	Throughput	High
Cell	Bus, ring, loop	Token passing, Ethernet	FTAM, MMS, Databases	Response time, throughput	High
Machine	Bus	Token passing	MMS	Response time	Medium
Sensor	Bus	Polling, token passing	MMS (subset)	Response time	Low

* Point to point communications.

requirements of machines, constraints, etc.). Since the resources can be located on different stations on the communication network, scheduling is also a distributed application.

Manufacturing-Related Functions of Communication Networks

In this section, we briefly state the main function of communication networks as they relate to automated manufacturing systems in the context of the OSI reference model, the SME CIM model, and the hierarchical control model.

OSI reference model. From the viewpoint of the OSI reference model, a network provides the functions of all layers in a transparent fashion. This is possible because of the organization of the OSI reference model, in which each layer provides services to the layer above by making use of the services of the layer below. Since end user applications interface with the network at the application layer, end user applications see the application layer services as the overall network services. Thus, the application layer of communication networks must be tailored to support manufacturing applications.

SME CIM model. As shown in figures 14.1 and 14.2, depending upon the size of the manufacturing facility, a single network backbone may link the four major areas of the model (i.e., factory automation, engineering design, manufacturing planning, and manufacturing control). Regardless of the actual network configuration, the major network function is the support of information sharing between the various areas and subareas of the SME CIM model. For example, once a product is designed in the design subarea, the design needs to be sent to the other areas to start production of the product. The communication network must then provide appropriate services so that the activity of sending design information can be performed in a simple and efficient manner.

Hierarchical control model. In the context of the hierarchical control model, a communication network basically is responsible for exchanging command and feedback information between adjacent levels in the control hierarchy as well as outputs, events, and activities to end users or other controllers located at the same level. This network function is illustrated in Figure 14.4. In some cases, it is possible to combine the exchange of command and feedback information corresponding to several control levels by using one single communication network.

14.3 THE NETWORK DESIGN PROBLEM

Not all manufacturing enterprises are alike. They vary in function, size, and type. Thus, it is natural to expect that they have different network requirements in terms of cost, functionality, and performance. The network design problem can be formulated as follows: Given a manufacturing application, specify a network architecture and associated protocols, and appropriate application software to support the given application while meeting cost and performance constraints.

Assumptions

Network Integration Role in CIM. It is now generally accepted that networks play an important role in the realization of the Computer Integrated Manufacturing (CIM) concept. The network role is one of integration. A network acts as the glue that ties together all aspects of CIM, from plant floor devices, all the way up to the management levels, including financial and accounting applications. It is also assumed that the network application designers are aware of this role played by networks and design their applications accordingly. Furthermore, it is assumed that the designers are already committed to the use of networks in manufacturing. Although the application designers may not know at this stage what specific network or protocols are to be used, they realize the advantages offered by networks.

Network and Protocol Components. If the protocols are standard protocols such as the ones used in MAP and TOP, then there is no protocol development work to be done, because it is assumed that they are already available commercially. If, however, one is using nonstandard protocols, then they must be developed fully first. The subject of protocol development was treated extensively in chapters 3 through 10, so it is not discussed in this chapter. Thus, in a network application design context, one can assume that protocol and network implementations are readily available as network components. The components may have been developed previously by the same designer, or be available from a third party. Thus, the problem of network design reduces to a selection problem rather than a network or protocol development problem.

Application Device Configuration. Every application involves a list of devices to be interconnected by the network. The list may include a wide variety of devices such as programmable logic controllers (PLC), digital numerically controlled (DNC) machines, robots, vision systems, coordinate measurement machines (CMM), personal computers, minicomputers, and mainframe computers.

It is not enough just to have a list of the aforementioned devices. Since the devices are used to perform a manufacturing application, they are physically located where they are needed by the application. Furthermore, the device location cannot be easily changed to satisfy network interconnection problems. Thus, in addition to the list we need a network topology for interconnecting all devices, taking into account devices that might be installed in the future.

Known Application. Obviously, before networks are brought in to help solve a problem, the end user application itself must be fully defined and understood by the network designers. Often, network designs do not work, because the applications themselves are poorly understood. Only if the applications are well understood, can appropriate network design goals and objectives be generated for both the network and the application software.

The problem (design considerations). As discussed in Chapter 13, depending upon the designer's user category, the design problems encountered are quite different. In this chapter, we assume that the designer belongs to the *end user* category. Most books on computer networks deal with design issues for the other user categories (i.e., application, vendor, or protocol). More specifically, this section discusses design considerations that should be addressed by the network designer. An end user *network designer* is faced with the following design issues:

Choose a Network Architecture. This includes choosing a channel access control mechanism, as well as all other protocols used in the network. Of particular importance is the functionality to be offered by the application layer. Additional options to be chosen include baseband or broadband communication, medium type (i.e., twisted pair, coaxial cable, optical fibers, etc), real-time support, and degree of network management supported.

Design a Specific Network Topology. The topology must connect all devices to be interconnected. Possible topologies include star, minimum spanning trees, ring, and others. In principle, topologies depend on specific applications; thus, when applications change, a new topology with enough room for future expansions may be needed (Campbell and Pimentel, 1986). In practice however, some networks rarely support single applications. Furthermore, once a network is physically in place, it is unlikely that its topology will change.

Choose Specific Implementations. Since there are many protocol and network implementations, network application designers must choose specific implementations so that they match the selected network architecture, provide adequate performance, and interface easily with the other devices used in the application. The interfaces may be constrained by system buses (i.e., Multibus, Q, VME, etc.), operating systems, programming languages, or already existing application software.

Develop a Set of Application Requirements. These requirements are those that can be expressed only in terms of the application itself rather than the network.

Application requirements can be in terms of the application themselves or the software associated with the application. Examples of application requirements include:

1. Time to verify engine information using specialized software = 3 sec.

2. Time to make a drawing change on a CAD/CAM station = 2 sec.

3. Vehicle production rate in a certain manufacturing area = 27 vehicles/hour.

4. Average size of messages going from a management database to a terminal = 689 bytes/message.

5. Programmable Logic Controller (PLC) cycle time = 500 m sec.

Translate Application Requirements into a Set of Network Requirements. The application requirements considered in the previous section imply certain *network requirements* that the designer must translate. There is no unique procedure to generate the specific network requirements, since it depends on the specific applications.

Examples of network requirements include: response time, information throughput, uniform medium type for all networks and subnetworks, no single point of failure, common software interface to all applications, common terminal access to applications, and specified level of network management (Williams, 1986).

Design the Applications Software. In addition to communication software, applications software is also needed to actually perform end user functions. Special consideration should be given to the interface with the application layer, choice of programming languages, and organization of end user application programs.

Evaluate the Overall Design. An effective way to evaluate the overall design is to evaluate the performance of the complete system using analytical models, simulation, or measured data.

The problem solution constraints. Typically, problem solutions have constraints in terms of cost and deadlines. Unfortunately, it is very difficult to quantify network communication costs in a highly integrated manufacturing environment. The reason is that computer networks provide many advantages in just about every aspect of manufacturing which are difficult to quantify (Kochan and Cowan, 1986). Because of these advantages, some companies are willing to pay a high price for integration. Thus, when quantifying network costs, it should be approached strategically, taking into account the long-term benefits of a fully integrated facility. Fortunately, the deadline constraint is simpler to evaluate because either it is met or not.

14.4 THE PROBLEM SOLUTION

Design procedure. Designing an application which incorporates networking is different from the application, which is not networked.

The following steps are intended to show how to proceed with a design. The design procedure does not consider all software aspects of the application; rather, it only considers those aspects that have a direct bearing on the communication network.

1. Characterize the application precisely.

In the context of the hierarchical CIM model, it is important to identify how many levels in the hierarchy will be included in the design. Also identify the functions to be supported at each layer of the hierarchy.

2. Develop a set of application requirements.

The application requirements can include desired functions, the expected performance, and constraints of costs and deadlines. Usually, the outcome of this step is a set of design specifications. A potential problem that often arises in this step is that, when the application project is large, the different groups working on the various aspects of the problem may come up with incompatible specifications. In other cases, some issues are ignored by the different groups. In order to solve this, it is *essential* that interface specifications also be developed and the functions to be performed at each level included.

3. Generate several proposed alternatives.

Based on an initial consideration of the network requirements and the constraints, one can generate several possible solutions to the network design problem. Some of these possible solutions may be discarded immediately, because it can be determined quickly that they fail to meet some requirements and/or constraints. Other possible solutions may need further evaluation, since it would not be obvious whether they meet the requirements. This is performed in the next step.

4. Evaluate the alternatives against the requirements.

Once the unsatisfactory possible solutions have been discarded, this step makes use of specialized tools to determine whether the remaining possible solutions meet the requirements and constraints. The tools available to a designer include analytical models and/or formulas, simulation models and/or packages, measured data, and other appropriate charts, plots, formulas, software packages, etc. that could be of assistance in evaluating some aspect of the overall network design.

5. Choose the best solution.

The simplest case of the overall design procedure is that step 4 generates a single solution to the problem. However, in some cases there are several solutions to the problem. In this case, additional considerations may be needed to select one of the possible solutions. Some of the additional considerations involve whether standard protocols are used, market considerations, vendor reputation, in-house expertise, and even politics, which are outside the scope of this book. If no satisfactory solution results, a redefinition of the problem and requirements may be needed.

General Network Requirements

Before looking at the specific network requirements of each one of the hierarchical network levels, we consider the general network requirements in this section. From previous discussions, it is clear that effective automated manufacturing systems require one or more networks for supporting the interconnection of all manufacturing devices. In general, networks for manufacturing have the following requirements:

1. Partial interconnection (cluster concept). The computer network must support the interconnection of devices which are located in clusters, possibly through internetworking. This follows from the observation that an automated manufacturing environment is itself configured in clusters.

2. Hierarchical organization. The control functions in automated manufacturing systems are organized hierarchically. Consequently, the computer network responsible for supporting these control functions must be organized accordingly.

3. Reliability. Manufacturing operations are very sensitive to system breakdowns (e.g., due to device, machine, or cell failures) since these stoppages typically are very costly to the manufacturer. Thus, communication networks, to be reliable, must insure a low probability of a communication failure causing a stop in the goods production of manufacturing systems.

14.5 SENSOR LEVEL NETWORK

The **sensor level network** is intended to support communications at the lowest level of the automated manufacturing control hierarchy; that is, the interconnection of intelligent devices with their sensors and actuators, as shown in Figure 14.6. Since these devices are typically located in the field, sensor level networks are also called **fieldbus networks.** For example, numerically controlled (NC) machines are typically wired to many actuators and sensors, which are located in close proximity (i.e., within 30 m). Two other areas that can benefit from fieldbus networks are the *process control* and *instrumentation* areas. Unlike manufacturing systems, which are mostly discrete event driven systems, *process control* is a continuous system. For example, the production of paper is a continuous system where the raw material (e.g., pulp) continually flows through several stages until it exits the system as a final product. Although networks for process control applications are outside the scope of this book, we discuss them briefly, because some process control systems are constituent elements of manufacturing systems (e.g., furnaces, forging), and because fieldbus networks are intended to support both continuous and discrete event systems.

Device and traffic characteristics. Devices interconnected by *fieldbus* networks are those that are connected to the first level in the control hierarchy of automated systems. Examples of intelligent devices[2] include robots, programmable logic controllers (PLCs), computerized numerical control (CNC) machines, and associated sensors, actuators, or other devices as listed below:

status indicators, such as contact closures,

on/off actuators for conveyors, pumps, power supplies, lamps, etc.,

---

[2] An intelligent device has an embedded microcomputer with enough memory and programming capabilities.

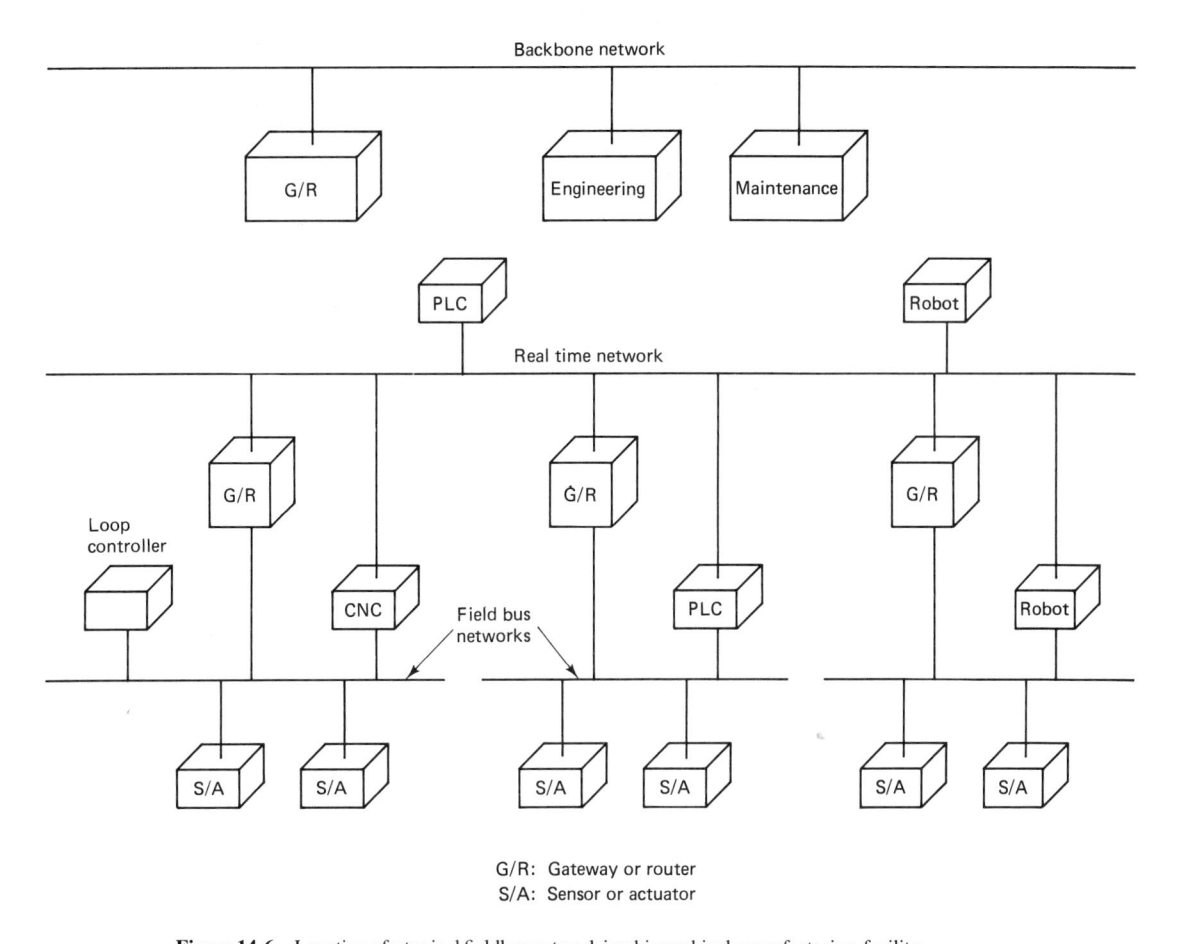

Figure 14.6 Location of a typical fieldbus network in a hierarchical manufacturing facility.

G/R: Gateway or router
S/A: Sensor or actuator

analog and discrete sensors, transmitters, or transducers for the measurement of physical parameters such as temperature, flow, pressure, levels, etc.,

counters or totalizators, and

intelligent devices such as motor controllers or heat flow computers.

Device traffic can be characterized by message length and message interarrival times. For the fieldbus level, some messages have interarrival times which are periodic. For periodic messages, a related traffic measure is *response time* defined as the time between a change in an input and the corresponding change at the output. Table 14.3 shows typical sensor and actuator characteristics (Decotignie, 1987).

From the previous discussion, it is clear that application requirements for fieldbus networks are different from application requirements for networks supporting other levels in the automated manufacturing control hierarchy. We can now begin to identify the communication characteristics

Sec. 14.5 Sensor Level Network

TABLE 14.3

Variable type	Number of bits	Response time	Approximate price
Rapidly varying analog values	12	1ms	$ 50
Slowly varying analog values	12	1s	$ 50
Event type logic inputs	1	1ms	$ 1 − 5
State logic inputs	1	20 − 100ms	$ 1 − 5
On/off actuators	1	20ms − 1s	variable
Counters/totalisators	16	1ms	$ 200

for devices at the first hierarchical control level (i.e., the machine level). The major communication characteristics are:

short messages,

some periodic traffic (refreshing period, validity time),

short response times,

good reliability and safety, and

low cost.

Fieldbus networks, having the previous characteristics, have the following advantages:

1. Overall costs can be drastically reduced. This is perhaps the single best advantage. As depicted in Figure 14.7, cost reduction can be obtained by replacing many wires by a single wire as the network medium (i.e., serial communications), and by using simpler network architectures and protocols than networks at other levels of the control hierarchy.

2. Easier installation and maintenance, since these operations involve the manipulation of a unique cable.

3. Easier detection and localization of cable faults.

4. Easier expansion because of the modular nature of the network.

In addition, replacing traditional wiring with a network brings new functionalities that were not previously available, such as:

1. Data consistency: All network stations are interconnected by a broadcast channel in a reliable fashion. Thus, it is very unlikely that one device will receive one set of data values while another device receives a different set of the same data values.

2. Better noise immunity: Since communication is digital, the signal to noise ratio can be improved by using more bits for representing an analog value.

3. Preprocessing capability: Typically, each network station has some processing capabilities that could be used to perform some signal conditioning or preprocessing operations before the samples are sent over the network.

Network requirements. The requirements imposed by the fieldbus applications dictate the design principles which must be used for designing fieldbus networks. Analyzing the

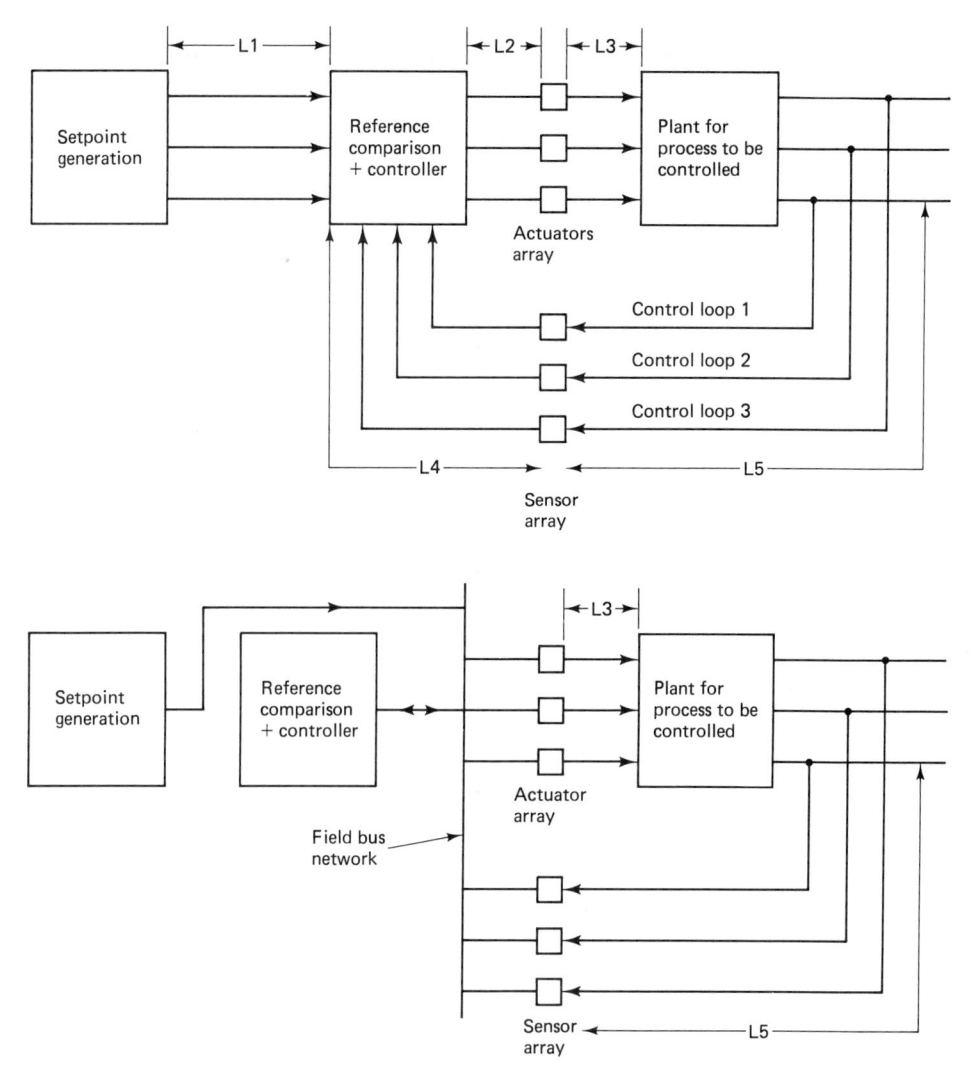

Figure 14.7 Fieldbus network in a multiloop controller application. The three wirings with lengths L_1, L_2, and L_4 have been replaced with two network connections.

application requirements discussed previously, we can now proceed to generate a list of network requirements, as follows:

1. Ability to handle very short messages in an efficient manner. Clearly, a network that adds 60 bytes of overhead to 2 bytes of information is not very efficient.

2. Ability to handle periodic and aperiodic traffic. Periodic traffic is due to sampled data, and aperiodic traffic is due to event conditions such as a conveyor failure.

3. Bounded and sometimes fixed response times. This is a consequence of the periodic traffic, and real time requirements of some event conditions such as alarm messages.

Sec. 14.5 Sensor Level Network

4. No single point of failure. The design should provide redundancy to cover failure of devices which may bring the network down (e.g., cables and master controllers).

5. Adequate error control mechanisms. Traditional error control mechanisms used in computer networks based on acknowledgment and retransmissions are not appropriate for *synchronous* traffic, since retransmissions alter the cycle time. Thus, communication errors should be detected but not corrected, since data consistency can be ensured by cyclic repetition (Decotignie, 1987).

6. Short geographical coverage and limited I/O. Sensors and actuators are located relatively close to intelligent machines. In addition, the number of sensors and actuators per machine is limited. Since fieldbus networks are intended to support a few machines relatively close to one another, they need only cover a small geographical area, and a limited number of input/output units.

7. Low network interface cost. All network protocol and implementation decisions must be made with the goal of minimizing the network interface cost. This requirement implies that communications be serial to save on cable costs, and virtually *all* features of protocols and their implementations must be significantly simpler than networks used at other levels in the automated manufacturing control hierarchy.

8. No bandwidth constraints. No attempt is made to use other channels on the communication medium, since this implies additional overhead, increased systems complexity, and reduced reliability.

9. Appropriate signaling with adequate timing content. This is necessary if we assume that no clock signal is transmitted between sender and receiver.

Architectures, protocols, and standards. Fieldbus architectures, protocols, and standards are just beginning to appear. The first ideas for a fieldbus emerged from the nuclear, military, and instrumentation applications giving birth to the following communications systems: CAMAC, MIL-STD 1553, and IEEE 488; however, only the MIL-STD 1553 is based on serial communications thus capable of meeting the requirements of a fieldbus. More recently, several proposals for standardization have appeared, such as FIP (Thomesse, 1987), Bitbus (Intel, 1987), Proway (1984), and Profibus (1988).

Since fieldbus is just another computer network, its architecture is best described in terms of the OSI reference model. However, because of the specialized requirements to be met, the use of a full seven layer architecture is precluded. Since transmission of states associated with sensors and actuators across subnetworks can be avoided, the network layer is not needed. An additional reason for not having a network layer is that it will contribute to a cost reduction of the network interface. The transport layer is not needed, because in the absence of a network layer, its most important functions (e.g., error control, and reliable data transfer with error recovery) can be performed by the data link and application layers, respectively. Likewise, the session layer is not needed, since its basic functions (e.g., process to process communications) can be performed by the application layer, and its more sophisticated functions (e.g., dialog synchronization) are not needed in the context of fieldbus applications.

Individual bits in a fieldbus message do not typically represent a character code such as ASCII or EBCDIC; rather, the bits represent conditions of sensors or actuators. For example, bit number 5 may indicate the condition of conveyor 2 in cell 68. Thus, data are not usually related to character codes as in most computers. In addition, fieldbus applications do not require the management of data encoding algorithms and transformation operations such as data compression or encryption, since they can be *preconfigured*. Thus, there is no need for the presentation layer. This leaves basically three layers in a fieldbus network architecture: the application, data link, and physical layers.

The Physical Layer. Most of the proposals for the physical layer have adopted the bus topology because of simplicity of implementation. Shielded twisted pair is the most commonly used transmission medium, with coaxial cable and optical fibers as options. Appropriate encoding techniques (i.e., signaling) include Manchester encoding for MIL STD 1553 and FIP, and Non-Return-to-Zero Inverted (NRZI) for Bitbus because of their good timing content properties. More sophisticated encoding techniques, such as *duobinary* with *pulse shaping*, are not required, because bandwidth efficiency is not an issue.

Data Link Layer. Sophisticated medium access control algorithms such as Ethernet or token passing (i.e., IEEE 802.4) work in a decentralized fashion. For fieldbus applications, complex decentralized algorithms are not advantageous because of complex (i.e., costly) interfaces, reduced performance due to extensive management functions, and because of the difficulty in achieving a constant cycle time which is required for periodic messages. The advantages of centralized channel access control techniques for fieldbus network are:

1. Minimum update time when all process variables change simultaneously.

2. High protections against loss of information by using cycle repetition.

3. Combination of real-time data acquisition and restitution of process data with real-time network management.

4. Ability to achieve quantified constant cycle time.

5. Support of broadcast or multicast messages with minimum address overhead.

6. Simple channel access protocol leading to inexpensive network interfaces. Typically, the channel access protocol is a variant of a polling scheme on a master slave configuration.

A major argument against centralized access control is reduced system availability, because the operation of the entire network depends on a master station which constitutes a single point of failure. However, this argument can be overcome by powerful redundant schemes for both network interfaces of master stations and the physical medium as shown in Figure 14.8, which is the FIP proposal for handling redundancy in a fieldbus network. An interesting alternative used by the Profibus proposal is the use of a combination of a simple decentralized scheme (simplified token bus protocol) involving master stations, with a centralized scheme involving slave stations.

Application Layer. The application layer for fieldbus networks is not yet well defined. Since fieldbus networks are expected to coexist with MAP networks, compatibility with a subset of the manufacturing message service (MMS) is under consideration. Specifically, the following MMS functionality is under study: variable access, event management, and program management. In addition, database refreshment services for pure cyclic operations, especially with nonintelligent field devices, are also being considered.

Having looked at generalities of fieldbus networks, we discuss next a specific example of a fieldbus network developed by Intel, even though this solution does not meet all requirements identified previously.

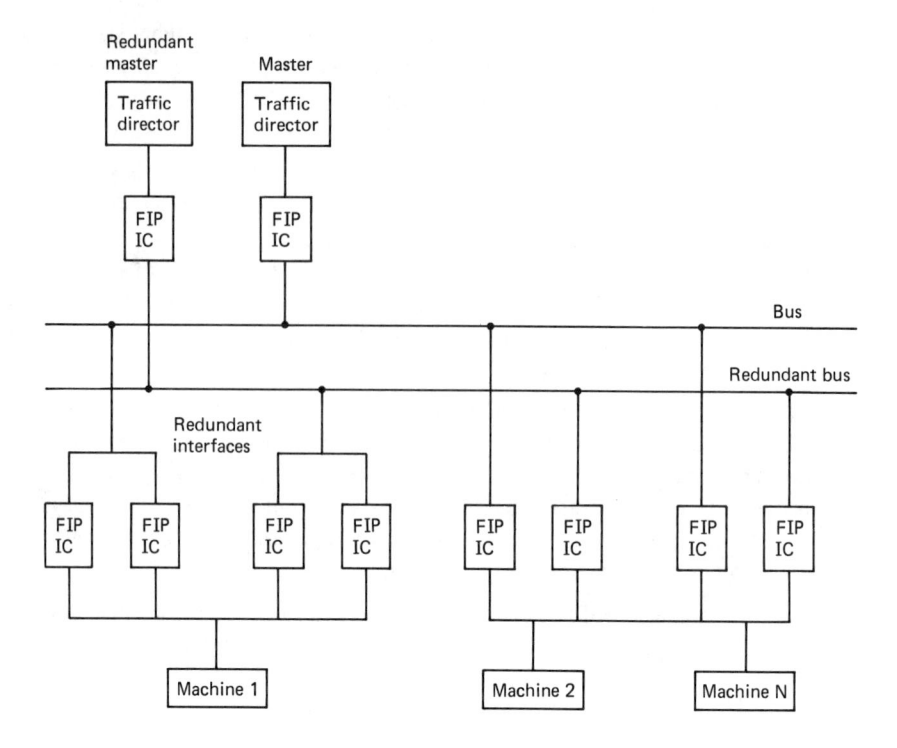

Figure 14.8 FIP proposal for a fieldbus network showing a redundant master, redundant bus, and redundant network interfaces.

FIP IC: network interface (factory instrumentation protocol integrated circuit)

Bitbus. Bitbus is Intel's proposal for a fieldbus standard. The architecture consists of three layers: physical, data link, and application. The proposal is detailed in the *Distributed Control Modules Databook* (Intel, 1987). The main features of the bitbus architecture are summarized next.

Physical Layer. The physical layer is based on a bus topology using twisted pair (RS485) as the physical medium. Because of the relative low bandwidth offered by twisted pair, no attempt is made to use other channels on the medium, and thus the communication type is baseband (i.e., one channel with no modulation). Bitbus defines two modes of operation, each with its own data encoding technique:

a) Synchronous mode: This mode is intended to be used for distances short enough that clock information is transmitted on a different pair of wires. Since actual clock information is transmitted along with the data, there is no problem in achieving bit synchronization, since bits are simply read (clocked) on the low to high transition of the clock signal, as illustrated in Figure 14.9. Data rates range from 500 Kbps to 2.4 Mbps.

b) Self-clocked mode: This mode allows one to extend the distance between network stations, since timing information and data are combined into one signal by using an appropriate encoding technique. The encoding technique used is a Non-Return-to-Zero Inverted (NRZI), which combines data and clock into a single signal. The NRZI encoding scheme works as follows: A logical zero

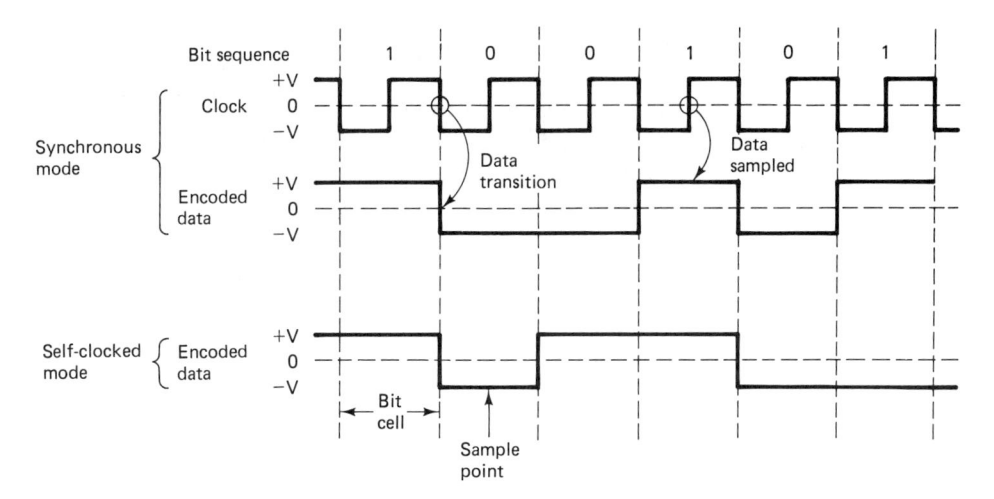

Figure 14.9 Data encoding techniques used in the synchronous and self-clocked modes of Bitbus.

is represented by a change in the polarity of the signal from the preceeding bit cell (i.e., a transition occurs on the bit cell boundary). A logical one is represented by no change in the polarity of the data signal from the preceeding bit cell. Signal waveforms obtained from the encoders in both modes of operation and corresponding to the bit sequence 100101 are shown in Figure 14.9.

In order for the receiver to recover timing information from the receive data, a digital phase lock loop (DPLL) is used which is synchronized with the transmitter clock before the transmission of a frame. The DPLL remains synchronized for the duration of a frame. Initial synchronization for the DPLL is guaranteed by the transmission of a preamble at the beginning of each frame. The preamble consists of a minimum of 8 zeros (i.e., transitions) that allows the DPLL to adjust its frequency until it is synchronized with the transmitter clock. Two data rates are supported in this mode: 375 Kbps with up to 2 repeaters, and 62.5 Kbps with up to 10 repeaters. Each repeater is able to handle up to 28 stations.

Data Link Layer. Since the physical medium is a shared bus, a medium access control mechanism is needed. Bitbus uses a polling scheme based on master-slave configuration, because of its simplicity and corresponding cost reduction. The data link protocol used is a subset of IBM's Synchronous Data Link Control (SDLC) protocol, because of its reliability and proven use. As discussed in Chapter 4, in performing its functions, the data link layer achieves *multiple access synchronization*, *frame synchronization*, *content synchronization*, and *dialog synchronization*. The following briefly describes how Bitbus performs these various levels of synchronization.

Multiple access synchronization is achieved by having the master station poll each slave station in turn to see if they have any data to send. In this way, there is no bus contention, because the master regulates the access to the shared medium by the polling mechanism.

Since *frame synchronization* involves identifying the beginning and end of frames, and also ensuring its error-free transmission, the synchronization is performed by having flag fields as frame delimiters in the frame format, as shown in Figure 14.10, along with the FCS field. The flag fields contain the unique bit pattern 01111110. A data link protocol should be transparent, in that it should

```
                        From application
                         \ layer
      ≥1    1    1      1  \   N  / 2    1      Bytes
    ┌────────┬────┬───────┬───────┬──────┬─────┬─────┐
    │Preamble│Flag│Address│Control│ Data │ FCS │Flag │
    └────────┴────┴───────┴───────┴──────┴─────┴─────┘
```

I-frame	0	N_s		1	N_r			
S-frame	1	0	S	0	1	N_r		
U-frame	1	1	M	M	1	M	M	M
	1	2	3	4	5	6	7	8	Bit number

(a)

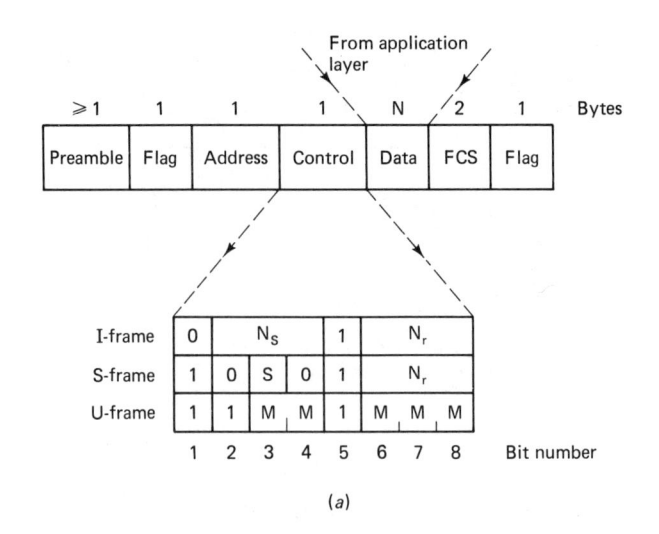

Slave state	Incoming frame	Frame type	Next state	Response
NDM	DISC	U	NDM	UA
NDM	SNRM	U	NRM	UA
NDM	Other	I, S, U	NDM	FRMR
NRM	Data	I	NRM	RR, RNR, I
NRM	RR	S	NRM	RR, RNR, I
NRM	RNR	S	NRM	RR, RNR
NRM	Data, RR, RNR with irrecoverable sequence error	I, S	NDM	FRMR
NRM	Other	I, S, U	NDM	FRMR

(b)

Figure 14.10 Frame format and specific frames used at the data link layer of the Bitbus network. NDM = normal disconnect mode; NRM = normal response mode.

allow the transmission of any bit pattern, including one that looks just like a flag. Let us suppose that the transmitter sends a data bit pattern that looks just like a flag. To avoid having the receiver interpret the data bit pattern as the end of the frame, the transmitter uses a technique called *zero bit insertion*. Specifically, the transmitter inserts a zero into the bit stream (not including the flag bits) any time it detects five consecutive 1s, regardless of the next bit value. In this way, a bit stream that would look like a flag is now something different. Obviously, the receiver must perform the inverse operation (i.e., a *zero bit deletion*) for the scheme to work.

Content synchronization is achieved by having the frame structure, as depicted in Figure 14.10, which allows for the distinction of control and data frames and the exchange of *I-frames* and *S-frames*. Since there are only two supervisory frames, receiver ready (RR) and receiver not ready (RNR), content synchronization is performed by exchanging RR and RNR commands, and I-frames. Content synchronization using I-frames involves checking the sequence numbers Nr and Ns, which are used to perform flow control purposes.

Dialog synchronization is achieved by exchanging U-frames. With the five modifier (M) bits in the U-frame format of Figure 14.10, it is possible to encode up to 32 types of frames (i.e., commands). Bitbus only specifies 4, which are known as set normal response mode (SNRM), disconnect (DISC), unnumbered acknowledge (UA), and frame reject (FRMR).

Example

>This example illustrates how *content synchronization* is achieved when the master station sends a message to a slave station. Content synchronization assumes that the two communicating stations are synchronized at the dialog level (i.e., dialog synchronization has been achieved). The *I-frame* carrying the message also contains the sequence numbers Ns = Nr = 0. Upon receipt of the message, the slave station verifies that the incoming Nr equals its Ns, and that the incoming Ns equals its Nr. The slave then increments its Nr to indicate the receipt of the information frame and returns an RR frame with sequence count Nr = 1 to acknowledge the frame. Upon receipt of the acknowledgment frame with the Nr sequence count, the master station assumes that its information frame has been received correctly, increments its Ns sequence count for the next message, and releases the transmit buffer to make room for additional messages.

Example

>This example illustrates how *dialog synchronization* is achieved. Dialog synchronization is used to set the slave device in the NRM state and Nr = Nr = 0. Dialog synchronization is required whenever the master or any slave detects an irrecoverable protocol error. The master station initiates the synchronization sequence by sending a DISC frame. If the slave device is in the NRM mode, it responds with a FRMR; otherwise (i.e., the slave is in the NDM) it responds with UA. The master station continues sending DISC commands until a UA is received, verifying that the slave station is in the NDM state. The master station then completes the synchronization sequence by sending an SNRM command. At this point, the slave device (which is in the NRM state) simply responds with a UA command. Finally, the master, upon receipt of the UA command, assumes that the slave station is properly synchronized. After the master and slave stations have performed the dialog synchronization procedure, they are ready to perform content synchronization.

Application Layer. The Bitbus application layer supports distributed applications at the lowest level of the network hierarchy of Figure 14.6. The key feature of Bitbus's application layer is the support of interprocess communication between a process on the master station and a process on a slave station. The interprocess communication is based on an order/reply structure, with the master issuing orders to slave stations which must respond with replies.[3]

The order/reply structure is depicted in Figure 14.11. With the exception of the *data* field, all other fields are required in all messages. Bitbus allows the existence of other processors in a node (i.e., multiprocessing) and referred to as master (or slave) extension processors. The *source*

---

[3] The order/reply is also known as a command/response.

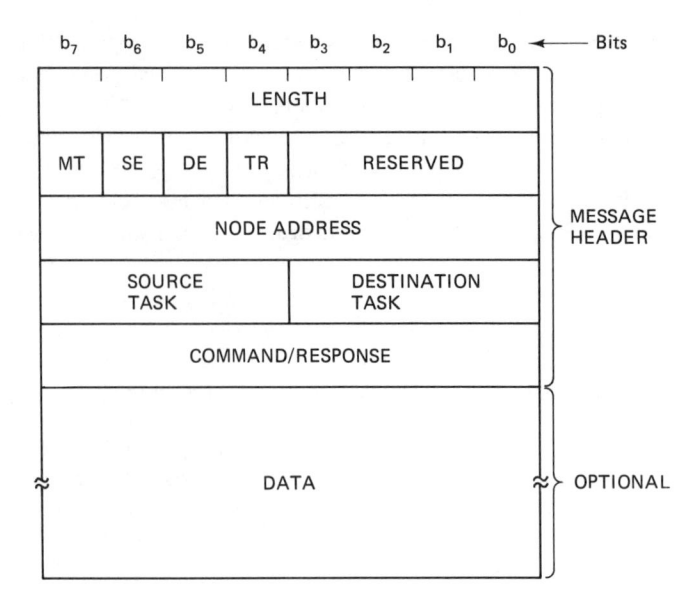

```
          b₇   b₆   b₅   b₄   b₃   b₂   b₁   b₀  ←── Bits
        ┌────┬────┬────┬────┬────┬────┬────┬────┐
        │               LENGTH                  │
        ├────┬────┬────┬────┬───────────────────┤
        │ MT │ SE │ DE │ TR │     RESERVED      │  ⎫
        ├────┴────┴────┴────┴───────────────────┤  ⎬ MESSAGE
        │            NODE ADDRESS               │  ⎭ HEADER
        ├────────────────────┬──────────────────┤
        │   SOURCE TASK      │ DESTINATION TASK │
        ├────────────────────┴──────────────────┤
        │         COMMAND/RESPONSE              │
        ├───────────────────────────────────────┤
        │                                       │  ⎫
        ≈              DATA                     ≈  ⎬ OPTIONAL
        │                                       │  ⎭
        └───────────────────────────────────────┘
```

LENGTH: Indicates total message length including overhead.
MESSAGE TYPE (MT): Indicates whether message is order or reply.
SOURCE EXTENSION (SE): Indicates whether message involves source extension.
DESTINATION EXTENSION (DE): Indicates whether message involves destination extension.
TRACK (TR): Indicates whether message received is local or remote.
NODE ADDRESS: Contains destination nodes for orders and source nodes for replies.
SOURCE TASK: Identifies the task that has generated an order or is to receive a reply.
DESTINATION TASK: Identifies the task that is to receive an order or has generated a reply.
COMMAND/RESPONSE: Used to identify the various RAC commands or responses.
DATA: Actual user message to be transmitted.

Figure 14.11 Bitbus message format for the application layer.

extension (SE) and *destination extension* (DE) bits indicate whether the message involves source or destination extension processors.

Since Bitbus relies on a multitasking operating system, a special task, called *task 0*, is given responsibility for distributed interprocess communication. Task 0 provides a special intertask communication interface called *remote access and control* (RAC). Therefore, Bitbus does not provide an OSI-like application layer interface, as discussed in Chapter 10. Rather, communication services are incorporated into a programmer user interface provided by RAC, which are summarized in Table 14.4. When service results are available, they are returned in a reply message.

14.6 MACHINE LEVEL NETWORK

The **machine level network** is intended to interconnect manufacturing devices operating in a *sequence control* mode such as controllers, robots, AVGs, vision systems, CNC machines, and PLCs. A typical example involves a machine level network interconnecting all devices located within a

TABLE 14.4

RAC Functions	Description
Create Task	Executes the iRMX[a] 51 RQ$CREATE$TASK system call.
Delete Task	Executes the iRMX 51 RQ$DELETE$TASK system call.
Download Memory or Code	Writes data (or code) into specified memory locations.
AND I/O	AND's values with specified I/O ports.
OR I/O	OR's values with contents of specified I/O ports.
Read I/O	Reads specified I/O ports.
Update I/O	Writes and then reads to (or from) specified ports.
Write I/O	Writes to specified I/O ports.
XOR I/O	Performs an exclusive-OR operation with contents of specified I/O ports.
Upload Memory	Reads data or code from specified memory locations.
Get Function ID	Executes the iRMX 51 RQGETFUNCTION$IDS system call.
Read Internal	Reads contents of internal memory.
Write Internal	Writes data into internal memory.
Node Information	Returns device related information.
RAC Protect	Suspends or resumes remote access services.
Offline	Sets a node off-line.
Reset	Performs a software reset.

[a] Intel's real time, multitasking operating system.

manufacturing cell. This section deals with the requirements and characteristics of the second level network hierarchy (i.e., the machine level network). Historically, networks for the higher levels (i.e., factory, shop, cell) were the first ones to be developed. A natural step was an attempt to use these higher level networks for applications involving lower levels in the control hierarchy. It was soon discovered that the high level networks were too cumbersome in meeting performance requirements for applications at the lower layers. The low performance is due mostly to the overhead introduced by all seven layers that networks at the higher levels normally have. Another aspect of the problem is the relatively high cost of network interfaces associated with complex architectures. The solution to this problem generally consists of simplifying the architecture by reducing the number of layers in the network; and also by either choosing simpler protocol options or simpler protocols. A good example of a network for this level is the time critical MAP architecture which is a network offering less functionality than the seven layer MAP architecture but with better performance for time critical applications. For this reason, a version of the real-time MAP architecture is called the MAP *Enhanced Performance Architecture* (MAP/EPA). Another version of the real-time MAP architecture is the so-called *mini-MAP*. All MAP architectures are summarized in appendix C.

Network Requirements

• Ability to handle fairly short messages in an efficient manner. Typical message sizes for *machine level networks* are in between those of *sensor level networks* and higher level networks with typical values ranging from 16 to 20 bytes.

• Ability to handle discrete event traffic. Depending upon the size of the messages, communication could be based on shared variables, memory to memory, or file transfers.

• Machine resource management. In controlling a manufacturing cell, the cell controller deals with many resources which are often shared by several machines. For example, a tool may be shared by two assembly robots. Thus, the machine level network should support the management of shared resources.

• Bounded response times. The communication network should not be the bottleneck for the distributed applications running at the machine level network level.

• No single point of failure. However, redundancy for single points of failure should be provided only when it is cost effective and reasonable. For example, broadband cable typically fails less frequently than a facility's power system; in this case, redundant cables may not be reasonable or cost effective.

• Good error control mechanisms. Unlike the sensor level network, communication errors should be detected and corrected through acknowledgments.

• Limited geographical coverage.

• Relatively low network interface cost. The cost of the interface should be less than the cost of the connected equipment and the interface costs of higher level networks.

• No bandwidth constraints. Like the fieldbus network, the communication medium is not a backbone used for other types of communication (e.g., voice and video) mostly because it would add to the cost of the system. Thus, no attempt is made to use other channels on the same communication medium.

• Adequate timing content. The encoding technique should be able to carry timing as well as data since no clock is shared between the sender and receiver.

• Prioritized messages.

• Message deadline. Some applications require that each message has an attribute indicating the latest time it should be delivered to the destination.

Network Architecture

In analyzing the requirements for machine level networks it is clear that the functionality of a seven layer architecture may not be needed. Since all machines and most of their controllers are located within a limited geographical area, it is not necessary that machines in one area communicate with machines in another area. Since machine controllers are interconnected to a *machine level* network and a *cell level* network, the machine controllers are responsible for internetworking. Thus, whereas the machine controllers are expected to have a network layer, the machines themselves do not.

The need for the transport, session, and presentation layers is a bit more complex to analyze. Although a limited functionality regarding each of these layers is required for some applications at the machine level, cost and performance requirements may dictate that these layers be null or very simple. For example, some functionality of the transport, session, and presentation layers would be desirable when downloading fairly long programs or data files to machines. However, when all machines are properly initialized, such functionality is not required.

Two major approaches can be used for solving this problem. The first one involves including some of the required functionality of the network, transport, session, and presentation layers into a new version of the application layer. The main advantage of this approach is its simplicity; however, its main disadvantage is that by doing so it may become necessary to deviate somewhat from the OSI reference model (i.e., an ISO incompatible architecture). The second approach consists of having a dual architecture using all seven layers for applications requiring increased functionality and using fewer layers for applications requiring good performance. The main advantage of this approach is that the station having the dual architecture remains compatible with the OSI reference model. Whereas the MAP/EPA architecture has followed the latter approach, the mini-MAP architecture, discussed in Appendix C has followed the former.

Real Time Map

A real-time version of the Manufacturing Automation Protocol (MAP) is a good example of a machine level network. The real-time MAP architecture as suggested by Chauhan (1987) was designed using the following criteria:

- Maximum medium access time   25 ms
- Maximum number of stations   32
- Maximum distance between stations   1 Km
- Typical message length   16 to 20 Bytes
- Maximum message length   1 K Byte
- Broadcast capability
- PROWAY and IEEE 802 compatibility
- Low cost

In order to reduce the access time to the shared channel, MAP provides a facility whereby a station can respond with an acknowledgment immediately after receiving a frame even though the station does not have the token at the time the frame is received. This mechanism is referred to as **immediate acknowledgement.** To reduce the response time even further, the real-time MAP network architecture consists of just three layers: physical, data link, and application. The major features of the real time MAP network is a physical layer based on the IEEE 802.4 specification using a phase-coherent, frequency shift keying (FSK) modulation scheme, a data link layer that includes PROWAY extensions, and an IEEE 802.2 type III protocol (which includes the *immediate acknowledgement* mechanism). This version of a real-time MAP architecture is very similar to the mini-MAP architecture described in Appendix C. We next discuss additional details of each of the layers of the real-time MAP network architecture.

Physical layer. The physical layer is based on a coaxial cable. However, unlike the full MAP architecture, the coaxial cable for real-time MAP need only be capable of supporting one channel instead of many. Since there is no attempt to use other channels on the medium, the encoder and modulator are chosen on the basis of *bit error rate* (BER) rather than *bandwidth efficiency*. The channel center frequency is relatively low (e.g., few tens of M Hz), thus the modems are relatively inexpensive to design, allowing reduction in the cost of the system. In addition, because of the relatively short geographical coverage, no *head end* is needed, which reduces the overall system cost even further.

Recall from section 3.9 that the performance of the FSK modulation scheme is the same as that of the PSK scheme. The main advantage of the FSK scheme is its simplicity when compared to PSK. A disadvantage of FSK is that it requires more channel bandwidth; however this is not an issue for machine level networks.

Data link layer. At the MAC sublayer, the real-time MAP architecture specifies the IEEE 802.4 standard with some extensions for implementing the *immediate acknowledgement* mechanisms. At the LLC sublayer, the IEEE 802.2 class III option is specified. The class III option provides an *acknowledged connectionless service*, thus requiring less functionality from the upper layers.

Application layer. MAP defines a specific application layer protocol known as manufacturing message specification (MMS) and its predecessor the Manufacturing Message Format Standard (MMFS). The application layer of the real time MAP architecture uses a subset of MMS.

As noted earlier, the real-time MAP architecture is able to enhance performance by reducing the network functionality as compared to a full MAP network. However, it should be clear that most of the additional functionality offered by the full MAP network is not required by applications using machine level networks. The functionality present in a full MAP network and not offered by the real-time network includes:

- High quality, guaranteed data delivery.
- Session layer services (e.g., data synchronization)
- Global message delivery (i.e., off segment)
- Unlimited message lengths
- Improved flow control
- Connection oriented communications.

14.7 CELL LEVEL NETWORK

A **cell level network** is intended to interconnect manufacturing devices involved in supervisory control functions such as cell controllers, AS/RS, material transport systems, automated warehouses, and other microcomputer and minicomputer controllers. A typical example involves a cell level network interconnecting several manufacturing cells and other elements which together constitute a flexible manufacturing system. In this section we consider the requirements and characteristics of the third level network hierarchy (i.e., the cell level network).

Network Requirements

- Ability to handle fairly short and long messages in an efficient manner. Typical message sizes for *cell level networks* range from a few bytes to several M bytes.

- Ability to handle discrete event traffic. Depending upon the size of the messages, communication could be based on shared variables, memory to memory, or file transfers.

- Cell resource management. While controlling a group of manufacturing cells, the cell control system deals with many resources which are often shared by several cells. Thus, the cell level network should support the management of shared resources.

- No single point of failure.

- Excellent error control mechanisms. Like the machine level network, communication errors should be detected and corrected through acknowledgements.

- Not so limited geographical coverage. A cell level network typically encompasses an entire manufacturing facility within a radius of few Km, thus still in the LAN domain.

- Bandwidth constraints. Unlike the machine and sensor level network, the communication medium can be used as a backbone for other types of communication (e.g., other networks, voice and video) mostly because its geographical coverage typically spans the entire plant. Thus, other channels on the same communication medium might be used. This means that the data encoders and modulators should be chosen using a *bandwidth constraint* criterion.

- Adequate timing content. The encoding technique should be able to carry timing as well as data since no clock is shared between the sender and receiver.

- Real-time environment. The different intelligent devices must exchange information in a timely fashion if high productivity is to be maintained in the manufacturing facility. This simply means that there should be an upper limit for the time to send a message between any two stations that need to communicate. Thus, the communication network should not be the bottleneck for the distributed applications running at the cell level network.

- Global time structure. This requirement is similar to the time structure requirement for the computer hardware discussed in section 11.6. The difference is that all stations must have the capability of determining time of day. Furthermore, they should be able to synchronize their clocks.

- Prioritized messages. Certain stations need to send, from time to time, important information as quickly as possible. The communication system must be able to accommodate this request. The communication system should be able to send messages with higher priority before sending messages with lower priority. The following is a prioritized classification of end user traffic: emergency, urgent, normal, and time available.

- Message deadline. In this case the communication system must, with high probability for success, be able to deliver messages before a certain *deadline*.

- Reliable message transfer. As noted in section 7.4, a distributed system assumes that messages sent from sender to receiver are neither altered nor lost.

Network architecture. In analyzing the requirements for cell level networks, it is clear that the functionality of most or all of the seven layers of the OSI reference model is required. The full MAP architecture (e.g., MAP 3.0) is an example of a cell level network. The full MAP architecture is not expanded here since it has been used as the main example while discussing the OSI layers in this book. Appendix C summarizes all MAP architectures.

14.8 CASE STUDY: GMT400 SYSTEM ARCHITECTURE

The purpose of this section is to present an example of an automated manufacturing system in an automotive environment. The project, referred to as the *GMT400 project*, is being developed by the Truck and Bus Group of the General Motors Corporation. It supports the production of 1987 C/K full-size pick-up trucks using state of the art technology. The program is intended to be a major step in achieving a computer integrated manufacturing (CIM) system. The project goals are:

> to achieve a near perfect quality index of 142 out of 145,
> to improve productivity by utilizing an economic balance of direct labor and automation, and
> to achieve a production rate of 60 trucks per hour per plant.

One specific feature of the project is the extensive use of several computer communication neworks, including one based on the manufacturing automation protocol (MAP) architecture. Currently, the two assembly plants located in Fort Wayne, Indiana and Pontiac, Michigan are using the system architecture to be discussed next for the production of full-size light duty trucks.

The system architecture consists of a hierarchical control structure having five control levels, which are referred to as the information processing center (IPC), plant host, area manager, cell controller, and plant floor devices. There have been two driving forces behind the development of the preceding hierarchical control structure. First, is the current availability of support needed by sophisticated factory automation equipment (i.e., computer networks, CAD/CAM), and second, the need to eliminate *islands of automation* through the application of CIM concepts. The major functions of each layer are summarized below.

Information processing center level. The IPC level is the highest level in the control hierarchy, supporting functions not directly associated with the plant floor production processes. The IPC functions involve keeping track of orders, ordering materials, processing customer orders, and financial calculations. These functions are supported by many (currently 38) **business systems** classified in the following categories:

> order processing systems,
> material control systems,
> logistic systems,
> industrial engineering systems, and
> financial systems.

Business systems support modern manufacturing requirements and concepts such as just-in-time (JIT) manufacturing. The IPC that supports Pontiac and Fort Wayne is located remotely in Dallas, Texas.

Plant host level. This level, which is located in each of the assembly plants, is used for supporting plantwide applications such as *flexible scheduling*, rescheduling, and *shipping control*. This level provides the intelligence and the means to allow flexibility in the way unfinished parts flow through the plant. In a highly flexible system, unfinished products can follow different paths in the production process, depending upon manufacturing requirements (e.g., paint, accessories, size, etc.) rather than the same path provided by inflexible systems. Each part may involve several serial production lines.

The systems provide the means to most effectively utilize the plant resources. Each vehicle can follow a different production path based on option content or necessary repairs. The system can make decisions regarding the sequence in which vehicles are moved from one area of the plant into the next (i.e., *Paint Shop* to *General Assembly*). These decisions are made so as to even out the downstream work loads.

Area manager level. The functions performed at this level are directly related to plant floor applications such as monitoring vehicle information, managing the movement of components throughout the plant, statistical process control, and others. The functions are performed by many **information systems** (currently 29) which support devices at this level as well as the levels below. The *information systems* are grouped into the following *plant floor systems*:

fabrication support systems,
cell control systems,
area management systems,
vehicle systems,
manufacturing systems,
test and control systems, and
plant support systems.

A feature of this level is the development of the *vehicle processing system* (a software application within the *vehicle system*), with the intelligence to perform the tracking of vehicles and components throughout the plant and the delivery of information regarding vehicle movement to other applications.

Plant floor level. The plant floor layer level is responsible for the monitoring, control, and dynamic configuration (i.e., setup) of automated equipment in a real-time basis. The plant floor level receives commands and additional information from the area manager level. Features of this control level include the introduction of decentralized databases and a more robust integration of test systems.

Programmable device level. This layer incorporates the use of robots, programmable logic controllers, automated guided vehicles, automated storage and retrieval systems (AS/RS), automated vehicle identification (AVI) systems, and weld controllers involved in the production of C/K trucks.

Table 14.5 shows some statistics regarding intelligent devices involved in the GMT400 automation project.

GMT400 Network Architecture

The purpose of this section is to present the communication network architecture for the support of the GMT 400 Project.

Since there is only one Information Processing Center (located in Texas) supporting many

TABLE 14.5

	Assembly Plants			Fabrication Plants	
	Fort Wayne	Pontiac	Oshawa	Flint	Indianapolis
LEVEL 1					
IPC					
LEVEL 2					
IBM 4381	2	2	2	—	—
LEVEL 3					
DEC VAX 8600	4	4	3	2	1
DEC VAX 785	—	—	—	—	1
DEC VAX 750	—	—	—	—	1
LEVEL 4					
IBM, DEC, HP CPUs	59	58	45	5	4
LEVEL 5					
Robots	135	136	127	5	0
PLC	199	208	278	63	156
AGV	100	—	424	—	—
AVI/Scanners	54	117	63	N/A	167
Weld controllers	134	153	124	226	251
Terminals	475	475	475	21	39
Printers	175	175	175	13	11
Storage/Retrieval	—	—	—	2	—
Monitor Points[4]	5000	5000	8000	2000	2000

plants and typically one Plant Host per assembly plant, the IPC level and the Plant Host level are interconnected by a *long haul network* with dial-up service. Currently, IBM's System Network Architecture (SNA) is used as the network architecture for communications between these levels (Williams, 1986).

Because of the few number of area manager controllers per area manager level, their interconnection is usually vendor-dependent. Area managers are interconnected by Decnet, an Ethernet-based local area network. The interconnection of the area manager level and the plant host level is achieved using an SNA gateway on a point to point basis. The SNA implementation provides the following functions:

    terminal and printer emulation,

    remote job entry,

    SNA application access, and

    SNA application to application support.

Network backbone. The GMT 400 project requires that each plant supports communications among a multitude of devices which are supplied by different vendors. The devices must communicate over a variety of dynamic logical connections involving simplex, half-duplex, and full-duplex modes. The information that may be transferred between devices consists of video, data, and audio forms. The communication backbone must not constitute a single point of failure

---

[4] Current estimates indicate that there will be 20000 monitors and control points in each of the assembly facilities.

and must be expandable. To meet these requirements, a coaxial cable capable of supporting broadband (i.e., many channels) communications is used. Some channels of the cable can be used for video, others for data, and still others for audio. Each logical channel provides a transparent path between devices, and coexists independently from the other channels on the same physical medium (i.e., coaxial cable). The logical channels are not dependent upon physical locations on the cable.

The requirement involving no single point of failure is met by having a redundant network topology (i.e., redundant cable plus headend), with each network serving the entire plant and serving as a backup for the other. Enhancing the redundant network, the design includes a *status monitoring system* for monitoring and controlling the cable system. The monitoring system constantly monitors each cable run and deals with both major failures and the prediction of failures.

Terminal access. A major requirement for communications below the area manager level involves the use of terminals for providing access to applications in the control hierarchy. This is accomplished by interconnecting the appropriate devices with the terminals by means of a local area network. The GMT 400 implementation uses a CSMA/CD based broadband network, because the same network medium is shared with two other local area networks, as discussed following. Devices interconnected by the CSMA/CD network include:

asynchronous terminals and printers,

plant floor devices which can only communicate through proprietary protocols,

IBM 3270 type devices,

other synchronous type devices, and

personal computers requiring file and printer sharing and multiple connections through multiple windows.

MAP 2.1 network. Communication among the area manager, the cell controllers, and certain robot controllers is supported by a MAP 2.1 broadband network with the following characteristics:

data rate of 10 M bps,

use of board level products wherever possible,

MAP standard protocols for layers 1 through 7 running on board level products,

CASE and MMFS implemented on MAP stations,

network management including directory services.

Three major types of devices are interconnected by the MAP network: area managers, cell controllers, and robots.[5] The MAP and the CSMA/CD networks use different headends but coexist on the same cable through frequency division multiplexing techniques. Thus, when the area manager downloads a file to a cell controller, the MAP network is used. When an operator at the cell controller uses a terminal for examining a file located at the area manager, the CSMA/CD network is used.

In addition to the CSMA/CD based and MAP networks, some devices (e.g., test systems) are interconnected using several channels of the broadband coaxial cable in a point to point con-

---

[5] Other devices include a diagnostic system and a network manager system.

figuration using the DDCMP[6] protocol. Thus, through the use of frequency division multiplexing, the coaxial cable supports three networks: CSMA/CD, MAP 2.1, and a DDCMP based network.

Communication between the plant floor level and the programmable device level is provided by a variety of networks. In most cases, the cell controllers supports proprietary networks (e.g., Allen Bradley's Data Highway or Pertron's Pernet), which in turn interconnects programmable devices. Currently, cell controllers support the Data Highway, Pertnet, and other proprietary networks. Robots and programmable logic controllers are connected to these proprietary networks. In addition, networks based on CSMA/CD, DDCMP, and MAP are also used for the communications between devices on the plant floor and programmable device levels.

Communication between the programmable devices and their sensor and actuators is provided by the specific vendors, consisting typically of hardwire interconnections.

14.9 CASE STUDY: THE FACTORY OF THE FUTURE PROJECT

One of the most advanced MAP testbeds within General Motors is the *Factory-of-the-Future* (FOF) project, being developed in a manufacturing plant at Saginaw, Michigan. The plant manufactures and assembles automobile transaxles, utilizing state-of-the-art techniques such as computer monitoring and control via MAP. The overall system is controlled by computer subsystems that coordinate machines, parts and resources. The objectives of the FOF project are:

1. To create a fully automated, integrated pilot manufacturing and assembly facility.

2. To have flexible machining of parts. The system should be easily reconfigured to manufacture different parts easily.

3. To produce products (i.e., automobile transaxles) of world class quality at competitive costs.

4. To develop and use a broad range of advanced technologies such as robots, computer vision, MAP communications, cell controllers, automatic guided vehicles, and coordinate measurement machines in an integrated fashion.

5. To document project experiences and results.

The purpose of this section is to examine the use of MAP at the Saginaw FOF. Connected via the MAP network are stations supporting a variety of control and manufacturing functions. Stations are grouped into the following five major systems:

1. Automated Guide Vehicle (AGV) System and Automated Storage and Retrieval (ASRS) System,
2. cell controllers,
3. factory control systems,
4. directory services, and
5. programmable device file server.

[6] Digital Data Communications Message Protocol.

We next describe the functions and interrelations of each system. The section concludes with a detailed example of file transfer between two stations using MAP.

The Automated Guided Vehicle System and the Automated Storage and Retrieval System

The AGVs and ASRS are used for transferring resources, materials, and production parts between the cell controllers. The AGV system consists of an AGV controller and the vehicles used to transport the materials throughout the plant. The AGV controller, after receiving requests via MAP for tooling, resources, and/or part transport from the cell controllers, determines vehicle destination and routing, and communicates with the ASRS concerning what to retrieve from the storage system. The AGV controller then determines a suitable vehicle to comply with the request and then directs it to its destination.

The AGV system and the ASRS system communicate with one another, while the factory control system communicates periodically with the ASRS system. Most frequently, however, the cell controllers communicate with the other systems for facilitating the production of parts. All communication is performed via MAP.

The ASRS system manages the plants' inventory using a *stacker crane* scheme, and is programmed to automatically find and retrieve materials upon receiving a request by the AGV system. The ASRS system also communicates with the factory control system about various aspects of inventory control such as low and high inventory levels, inventory turnover rate, etc.

Cell Controller

Each cell controller is connected to one or more independent device control systems such as programmable logic controllers (PLCs), numerically controlled (NC) machines, and coordinate measurement machines (CMM). Each device is self-supporting but relies on the cell controller to manage and coordinate its activities.

The main functions of the cell controller are *supervisory, control/monitoring, device coordination*, and *communications* (Morel, 1987).

Supervisory control/monitoring. There are several supervisory control/monitoring functions briefly described below:

1. Configuration Management. This function deals with configuring devices such as PLCs, robots, etc., so that the current manufacturing operation can be accomplished. Simply put, it makes sure the cell has proper tooling, programs, databases, and resources for the manufacturing of the current part.

2. Part Management. Controls delivery of parts to the cell and also keeps track of the status of part processing. The controller also sends part processing status to the factory control system periodically.

3. Performance Management. Monitors the length of time it takes each of the devices to complete their individual operations. It also keeps track of the total time it takes for the cell to complete its designated machining operation. It then sends this information to the *factory control system*.

4. Quality Management. Receives and analyzes part quality information from the *device coordination* module. The analysis information is then sent back to the *device coordination* module to improve the control of processes in the cell. Quality information includes tool compensation calculations, part acceptance or rejection, tool change analysis, and statistical process control (SPC) analysis. The SPC reports are sent to the factory control system.

5. Tool Management. Keeps track of tool life on all the various tools in the cell and sends the information to the factory control system.

Device coordination. The device coordination functions of the cell controller deal with power up control, cycle control, mode control, sequence control, alarm coordination, and error recovery. A brief description of each function follows.

1. Power-Up Control. Controls the initialization of variables within the device coordination application or module (DCA), the establishment of communication connections with the *supervisory control monitoring* application and the cell devices, and the initiation of execution of the DCA. Essentially, this sets up the DCA to coordinate the cells devices. This function is internal to the DCA.

2. Mode/Cycle Control. This function selects the following modes of device operation: maintenance, manual, or automatic. Depending upon the mode selected, this function also selects the cycle to be used. In the maintenance mode, the cell controller has no control over the devices. In the manual mode, the cycle control functions involve initializing devices, device calibration, and initiation of the gage cycle. In the automatic mode, the cycle control functions are select cycle, start cycle, stop cycle, and purge cycle.

3. Sequence Control. Controls the sequence of operations the devices undergo while performing a manufacturing task. That is, the sequence control takes into account all of the operations that the cell must perform to accomplish its task and then decides in which order these operations will be done. This is done by knowing the current state of each device in the cell and developing a command plan from this information.

4. Alarm Coordination. The controller receives alarms, determines the priority of alarms, and forwards the information to the Factory Control System.

5. Error Recovery. The controller is able to recover from certain types of device errors automatically. For example, a recoverable error might be one where a tool is broken and requires a subsequent tool change. The controller automatically changes the broken tool and resumes machining operations. The system corrects types of nonfatal errors, such as the one just described.

Communications. The cell controller also functions as a means for communication between MAP and the various devices connected with the cell. The cell controller sets up a gateway of communication for each device.

Factory Control System

The *factory control system* (FCS) coordinates the activities of the various cells. The main functions of the factory control system are scheduling of parts production, resource allocation, quality assurance, alarm annunciation, energy management, and maintaining the cell configuration database. A brief description of each function follows.

1. Scheduling. The FCS receives the master schedule for parts processing from Saginaw Steering Gear Division Headquarters. The master schedule indicates the FCS how many parts are required by a certain date. The FCS uses this information to form a work schedule so that the cell controllers can meet production plans. The FCS actually makes the decision for when the cells should start working and determines just what cells are necessary to meet the production level. It also decides when changeover to another part should take place based on the master schedule and on the information received from the cell controller on the status of part processing.

2. Resource Allocation. The FCS controls the allocation of resources such as people, programs, parts, and tooling to the cells. For example, whenever it is time for a part changeover, the FCS sends out a request to the AGVs to get the proper tooling sent to the cell in question, dispatches a job setter to the cell, and also sends the database for the job to the cell. This database contains current part information, the list of resources for the current part, quality, performance, and tooling information for the current part, tooling set-up for the current part, and previously logged alarms. The cell controller uses this information to determine such things as error location, so that it can inform the FCS exact nature of a cell's failure.

3. Quality Assurance. After receiving statistical process control information from the cell controller, the FCS issues a warning when there is a problem. Although not commonly used, the system has error correction capabilities.

4. Alarm Annunciation. The FCS receives alarm detection information from the various cell controllers and then relays the information to appropriate places.

5. Energy Management. Keeps track of energy usage in the various cells and notifies personnel when a potential problem is identified. This function is currently not being used.

6. Cell Configuration Database. Contains the databases of various cell configurations in case a specific cell requests information. The database information is the same as that described under resource allocation.

The factory control system controls most of the operations of the plant automatically without human intervention in the decision-making process.

Directory Services

The function of the directory services is to store a list of addresses of each system attached to the MAP network and to provide this information when requested. Since each station on the network has a copy of the master list found in the directory, the directory does not have to be accessed each time a communication link between two stations is set up. When new devices are attached to the network or old devices are deleted from the network, the change in address is put into the directory service. Because of these additions and deletions directory services need to be accessed. An example of each situation follows.

Suppose Station 1 has just been added to the network and Station 2 wants to establish a communication with it. The directory needs to be accessed by Station 2 so it can obtain Station 1's address. Station 2 obtains this information by making a new copy of the list of addresses. Now suppose Station 1 is deleted from the network and Station 2 tries to establish a communication with it. When Station 1 fails to respond, Station 2 contacts directory service to find out if Station 1 is still on the network.

From the preceding information, it is clear that the function of directory services is keeping track of whether a station is attached to the network and providing station addresses.

Program Device File Server (PDFS)

The function of the PDFS is to store the various programs and databases necessary for part processing within each cell. Whenever the FCS calls for a part or product changeover, it requests the PDFS to download the specific programs and resource information needed for the new part processing operation. Whenever necessary, individual cell controllers request the PDFS the transmission of programs or databases for one of its constituent devices. Essentially, the PDFS serves as a memory bank of programs and resource information that assists the operation of the plant. When called upon, it sends the required information to the appropriate stations.

Detailed MMFS Communications Dialog

This section presents a detailed example of communication between two devices in the MAP network. The devices are the programmable device file server and a cell controller. The Vanguard (FOF) MAP implementation uses the manufacturing message format standard (MMFS), as described in the MAP specification versions 2.0 and 2.1.

The communication example between the cell controller and file server involves the download of a file from the file server to the cell controller. This download is done in several stages and requires a dialog between the devices. The dialog contains commands, instructions, acknowledgments, and data arranged in standard MMFS fields. Each field and its purpose is explained as it is used as well as the actual encoding done before transmission. The dialog involves nine steps, as described below.

1. The PDFS first establishes a connection with the cell controller using CASE.

2. The file server reserves the device in the cell so that the device is not available for communication with stations other than the PDFS. It does this by requesting the cell controller to reserve the gateway for the device where the gateway is the interface between the device and the cell controller. The PDFS sends a MMFS request command having the following MMFS syntax:

⟨OC:A⟩ ⟨TN:0001⟩ ⟨CRQ⟩ ⟨USFF:01⟩

which is encoded as:

01 82 00 0A 1F 82 00 01 20 01 82 FF FF 01

where ⟨OC:A⟩ indicates a message length (octet count) of 10, not including the ⟨OC:A⟩ field. The ⟨TN:0001⟩ field specifies a transaction number. ⟨CRQ⟩ signifies that this is a command that requires a response, and ⟨USFF:01⟩ is a user specified field that has been defined at Saginaw as the command to reserve a device. The FF[7] is hexadecimal and signifies that this is US field number 255.

[7] In the encoded line, numerical values are in hexadecimal, while in the description following, the values are in decimals. We only provide the encoding for one of the steps.

3. In response, the cell controller acknowledges that the device is reserved. The cell controller sends:

⟨OC:A⟩ ⟨TN:0001⟩ ⟨FRS⟩ ⟨USFF:01⟩

The message length is again sent since it is required to proceed any message of data along with the same transaction number, as this is a response to the earlier command. The ⟨FRS⟩ stands for a final response to the command issued and, the ⟨USFF:01⟩ signifies that the device is indeed reserved to the PDFS.

4. The next action is taken by the PDFS, and it represents an instruction by the file server to the cell controller. Since the PDFS cannot just send a file on its own initiative, the cell controller must request the PDFS to download a file. This is to prevent a situation where the cell controller is not ready for such a transfer. Therefore, this instruction tells the controller to request a download. The PDFS sends:

⟨OC:11⟩ ⟨TN:0002⟩ ⟨UDI⟩ ⟨GET⟩ ⟨CH: "PROGRAM"⟩

In the preceding command, the transaction number has been incremented because this is a new command in the dialogue. ⟨UDI⟩ indicates an instruction for the device to do something. The ⟨GET⟩ ⟨CH:"PROGRAM"⟩ specifies the request to be a download of a file called PROGRAM.

5. Once the cell controller receives this command, assuming that the controller knows that the device is ready for a download, it requests the download from the file server. The cell controller sends:

⟨OC:11⟩ ⟨TN:0003⟩ ⟨CRQ⟩ ⟨GET⟩ ⟨CH: "PROGRAM"⟩

The transaction number is again incremented, as this message is seen as being unrelated to the message just sent by the PDFS. The response for ⟨TN:0002⟩ occurs after the download, as described next. The ⟨CRQ⟩ again indicates a command with a required response with the command being ⟨GET⟩ ⟨CH:"PROGRAM"⟩ (i.e., download a file with the filename PROGRAM).

6. Upon receiving this command, the file server will send the file to the cell controller in discrete segments of a certain length, specified by MAP parameters. Each segment is sent to the controller in the form:

⟨OC:C⟩ ⟨TN:0003⟩ ⟨DRS⟩ ⟨GET⟩ ⟨DS:XXXX⟩ ⟨DATA. . . .⟩

The transaction number remains the same, as this is a response to the request for a download. ⟨DRS⟩ indicates that this is a section of a file rather than the entire file. The ⟨GET⟩ indicates a data transfer, while the ⟨DS:XXXX⟩ specifies that a segment of the file of length XXXX (hex) is being sent. The PDFS continues to send this message with new data until the last segment of the file is transmitted. When the entire file is sent, the PDFS sends:

⟨OC:C⟩ ⟨TN:0003⟩ ⟨FRS⟩ ⟨GET⟩ ⟨DS:YYYY⟩ ⟨LAST DATA . . .⟩

The only difference between this command and the previous one is the field ⟨FRS⟩ indicating that this is the final file segment and ⟨DS:YYYY⟩ representing the size of that segment.

7. Upon receipt of the final segment, the cell controller informs the file server that the download is complete by sending:

⟨OC:A⟩ ⟨TN:0002⟩ ⟨CMD⟩ ⟨US00:00⟩

The transaction number corresponds to the PDFS's initial instruction for the cell controller to request a download. ⟨CMD⟩ means that this is a command without a response and the ⟨US00:00⟩ is another *user specified* field that is defined at Saginaw indicating the completion of a download. The 00 indicates that the download was successful. Had the download been unsuccessful for any reason, the controller would have sent ⟨OC:A⟩ ⟨TN:0002⟩ ⟨CMD⟩ ⟨US00:01⟩, with the ⟨US00:01⟩ field indicating that the download was completed but a fault was detected.

8. Since the PDFS is finished, it now releases the reserved device. It does this by requesting the cell controller to release the device gateway. The PDFS sends:

⟨OC:A⟩ ⟨TN:0001⟩ ⟨CRQ⟩ ⟨USFF:02⟩

where ⟨USFF:02⟩ represents the release command. The gateway is now free to communicate with devices other than the PDFS.

9. The PDFS again uses the CASE service to disconnect the communication link that it had established in step 1, and the download is complete.

SUMMARY

Once protocols and networks are developed, an important question remains as to how they can be used effectively to solve problems in automated manufacturing. Networks must justify their existence by helping solve problems in specific areas. Networks can be used in virtually every aspect of manufacturing. Major manufacturing areas that can benefit from computer networks are: flexible manufacturing systems (FMS), manufacturing cells, flexible assembly, testing, design (CAD, CAM), quality control, and inspection.

Typically, manufacturing networks are configured as a communication backbone, surrounded by several subnetworks which support communication in various manufacturing subareas. The advantages of the subnetwork approach are better reliability and performance. The subnetwork design is more reliable, since the constituent LANs continue to operate even when the backbone goes down. The performance advantage results from the lower message traffic on the communication backbone.

The role of the communication network is to provide the means for the effective communication of feedback and commands at different levels in the automation control hierarchy, and events, activities, and outputs from controllers located at the same level in the control hierarchy.

In the context of the hierarchical CIM model, one can envision the use of one or more networks at each level of the control hierarchy. All devices located at the same level in the hierarchy are connected to one or several networks with similar capabilities. From the hierarchical CIM model point of view, the following manufacturing networks can be distinguished:

1. factory level network,
2. shop level network,

3. cell level network,
4. machine level network, and
5. sensor level network.

The network design problem can be formulated as follows: Given a manufacturing application, specify a network architecture and associated protocols, and application software to support the given application while meeting cost and performance constraints. An end user network designer is faced with the following issues:

Choose a network architecture,

design a specific network topology,

choose specific network implementations,

develop a set of application requirements,

translate application requirements into network requirements,

design the application software, and

evaluate overall design.

The sensor level network (also called fieldbus network) is intended to interconnect devices at the lowest level of the manufacturing control hierarchy, that is, the interconnection of intelligent devices with their sensors and actuators. In addition to manufacturing, the areas of process control and instrumentation can also benefit from fieldbus networks. The station architecture of fieldbus networks generally consists of three layers: physical, data link, and application. A machine level network is intended to interconnect manufacturing devices operating in a sequence control mode such as controllers, robots, AGVs, vision systems, CNC machines, and PLCs. A typical example involves a machine level network interconnecting all devices located within a manufacturing cell. A cell level network is intended to interconnect manufacturing devices involved in supervisory control functions such as cell controllers, AS/RSs, material transport systems, automated warehouses, and other microcomputer and minicomputer controllers. A typical example involves a cell level network interconnecting several manufacturing cells and other elements which together constitute a flexible manufacturing system.

Bibliographic Notes

Keil (1986) and Schutz (1986) discuss the role of MAP in industrial networks, and Kaminsky (1986) outlines the protocol features used in MAP. The book by Holligum describes earlier MAP specifications. Architectures for process control and other industrial networks are discussed by Sloman and Prince (1980), and Senior and others (1987) respectively. Although not dealing with networks, the book edited by Mellichamp (1983) contains much material on monitoring and control in a real-time environment. The article by Shiobara and others (1987) proposes an interesting approach for achieving real-time using a MAP architecture different from the one described in section 14.6. Dytewsky (1986) discusses general considerations when implementing MAP networks, while Pelton (1986) concentrates on an application architecture and Laurance (1986) discusses the applications of MMS to CNC. Gomaa (1986) discusses software development in real-time environments, and Naylor and Volz (1987) propose a framework for designing software for automated manufacturing based on the ADA language. The performance of real-time MAP architectures including immediate acknowledgements are discussed by Janetzky and Watson (1987), and Ciminiera and Valenzano (1987).

PROBLEMS

1. What are subnetworks? What are the advantages and/or disadvantages of using the subnetwork approach in manufacturing?
2. Give reasons why two hierarchical models (i.e., control and network) are used to characterize the use of networks in automated manufacturing applications.
3. Describe the function of the communication network in the framework of the control hierarchy.
4. What are the network characteristics that should be considered when choosing a network for a certain level in the network hierarchy?
5. Describe the significance of the functionality offered by computer networks for distributed system applications in automated manufacturing systems.
6. What is the network design problem from an end user perspective?
7. What design considerations should be addressed by an end user network designer?
8. What are the steps that should be followed to obtain a solution to the network design problem?
9. What is a fieldbus network? Describe a specific example of a fieldbus network.
10. How is frame synchronization achieved in Bitbus?
11. List the network requirements for a machine level network.
12. What are the fundamental differences between the MAP 2.2, MAP 3.0, MAP/EPA, and mini-MAP architectures?
13. Rework the example of the Saginaw factory of the future case study using MMS.
14. The bitbus network does not provide functionality for process synchronization. If the bitbus network is used for interconnecting the devices of a MRAS as described in Chapter 10, how do you propose to solve the problem of process synchronization?

Appendix A

ADA

This appendix is intended to provide a brief overview of some aspects of the ADA language, emphasizing its main features as they are used throughout this book. Other important features (e.g., process synchronization) are not addressed and the reader is referred to Barnes (1984) and Price (1984). ADA was developed by Honeywell Bull from a set of language specifications set forth by the United States Department of Defense (DOD).

Prior to the development of ADA, the Department of Defense identified the following language related problems:

a proliferation of programming languages (over 450 in 1973),

the use of languages ill-suited for their applications,

the use of archaic languages and/or language style, and

the lack of useful software environments.

ADA is particularly well-suited for applications which the DOD calls embedded systems. An **embedded system** is one which exists as an integral component of a larger system. For example, the computers controlling the flight of an airplane can be considered an embedded system because the computers are part of a larger system (i.e., the airplane).

Software for embedded systems generally have the following characteristics:

large programs with thousands and millions of lines of code,

long lived programs with typical lifetimes from 10 to 15 years, frequent program changes due to changing system requirements,

rigid physical constraints involving hardware address space, processor speed, and weight, and

high reliability and fault tolerance.

In addition, software for embedded systems generally have stringent requirements such as parallel processing, real-time execution, exception handling, and unique input/output (I/O).

WHY ADA?

ADA is not just a programming language, it is an adventure in software engineering. It can be used for not only writing *pseudo-code* for describing a system generally, but also for writing the detailed implementation code. For example, ADA has been used for specifying a portion of the IEEE 802.4 Protocol (i.e., token bus). ADA's powerful features can be used in the following situations:

1. Data Abstraction. Computer network protocols, including the services they provide, require the use of sophisticated data structures for their implementation and description. ADA has powerful capabilities for defining new data types and operations based on the newly defined data types. In particular, ADA is particularly advantageous for describing *abstract objects*.

2. Description of Algorithms. ADA's structured programming constructs and data abstraction capabilities can be used to describe algorithms and detailed mechanisms of computer network protocols.

3. Specification Language. The previous two features enable ADA to be used as a language for specifying a design or system implementation. A good example is the specification and implementation of communication protocols (Castanet et al., 1986).

4. Distributed Systems. Since a computer network is an integral component of distributed systems, it is advantageous to use a language which is useful for network analysis and design, as well as distributed system design. Although ADA does not directly support distributed systems in a LAN context, it has powerful mechanisms for the design and analysis of closely coupled distributed systems. The mechanisms are: multitasking, communication, and synchronization between processes.

5. Process Control and Manufacturing Systems. The powerful ADA features mentioned thus far have contributed to its use in process control and manufacturing systems applications (Voltz, 1983).

LANGUAGE OVERVIEW

Data Types

Just as human languages such as English use nouns to describe things, ADA uses **types** to describe **objects** which are analogous to things in English. Data types can be *predefined* or *user defined*.

Predefined data types. Predefined data types are implicitly defined by the language. In ADA, there are several predefined data types which include **integer, character, boolean,** and **float.** The following are examples of variable declarations in terms of *predefined* data types.

> first_number : **integer;**
> first_letter : **character;**
> machine_busy : **boolean;**
> second_number : **float;**

Variables belonging to the *integer* type can assume values 0, ± 1, ± 2, . . . up to values specified by the particular computer. *Character* variables denote only one character such as *A*,*P*, or ≥. *Boolean* variables can assume only two values which are called TRUE and FALSE. Variables belonging to the *float* type are used to approximate real numbers, for example 3.14159, 2.3533, 1.0 and so on.

User defined data types. Unlike predefined data types, **user defined data types** are explicitly defined by the user. An example of a user defined data type is

> **type** week_day **is** (monday, tuesday, wednesday, thursday, friday, saturday, sunday);

A data type like the previous one is referred to as **enumerated data type,** because the type is defined by enumerating all possible values that a variable belonging to the data type can assume. It is also possible to define data types which are a subset of already defined data types through the use of the **subtype** identifier. For example, let us suppose that we need to represent a person's age in an ADA program. We can safely assume that a person's age is between 0 and 200 years (at least someone on this planet). Thus, the following is an appropriate data type definition suitable for representing ages:

> **Subtype** person_age **is integer range** 0..200;

Other appropriate subtype examples are:

> **subtype** work_day **is** week_day **range** monday..friday;
> **subtype** temperature **is** float **range** 0.0..500.0;
> **subtype** capital_letter **is** character **range** 'A'..'Z';

Notice that character variables are enclosed with single quotes.

So far, we have been dealing with *scalar objects*. ADA also supports *composite objects* such as strings, arrays, and records. Since any variable used in an ADA program must have a type, there must be data types for strings, arrays and records. Actually, the data type for strings is already defined (i.e., predefined) in ADA. Although not required in any program, the definition of the predefined **string** data type is repeated next for clarity

> **subtype** positive **is** integer **range** 1..integer'last;

> **type** string **is array**(positive range ⟨⟩) **of** character;

Language Overview

where integer'last in ADA refers to the highest integer number corresponding to the computer being used. The definition of the *string* data type indicates that it is an array of characters. The symbol ⟨⟩ in the index part of the string type definition indicates that the indices are to come later, and that the indices belong to the *positive* subtype. The following shows declarations for the name, city, and zipcode variables with sizes 10, 15, and 6 characters, respectively. The last declaration corresponds to the constant *home*.

>   name : string(1..10);
>   city : string(1..15);
>   zip_code : string(1..6);
>   home : **constant** string := Washington DC;

Like most computers, we assume that a character is represented using 8 bits. Thus, the variable *city* above is represented by 120 bits.

Arrays. The definition of array data types simply involves specifying the name and type of each array element and the type and range of each index of the array. For example, the array *data type* definition

>   **type** vector **is array** (integer **range** 1..20) of integer;

defines *vector* as a one-dimensional array *data type* with its index being of the *integer* type. The values of the array index go from 1 to 20, and the *of integer* portion of the declaration indicates that the array elements are of type *integer*. The following is a declaration of a two dimensional array data type whose array components are real numbers.

>   **type** matrix **is array** (integer range 1..4, integer **range** 1..6) of float;

The *integer* type in the preceding definition indicates that the indices for the row and columns of the array are integer numbers ranging from 1 to 4 and 1 to 6, respectively.

Once array *data types* are defined, variables belonging to the already defined data types can be defined as follows.

>   A,B: vector;
>
>   C,D: matrix;

Process control and manufacturing systems make extensive use of *boolean* variables, each requiring one bit for representation. Although boolean variables are typically grouped in groups of eight, they can be grouped in groups of any size. To aid in the definition of variables which are groups of boolean variables, we need a new variable type which we will call *bit string*, defined as follows:

>   **type** bit_string **is array** (positive **range** ⟨⟩) of boolean;

A variable bit_var representing nine boolean variables can be declared as

>   bit_var : bit_string(1..9);

Records. One limitation of arrays is that all elements are of the same data type. For example, all elements of the *matrix* data type defined previously are of type *float*. ADA overcomes the limitation of arrays by providing another composite object, called **record**, whose constituent elements can be of different data types. The following is a typical example of a record data type.

```
type employee is
    record
        first_name : string (1..25);
        last_name : string (1..30);
        social_sec_number : string (1..11);
        salary : float;
    end record;
```

The following shows an ADA example where sophisticated objects are defined.

Example

A computer integrated manufacturing (CIM) system integrates every aspect of manufacturing, from customer orders all the way until final production. Suppose you are designing an ADA program that processes car orders. The program is supposed to be integrated with other CIM programs by means of a computer network. You are only concerned with the following information:

CATEGORY	INFORMATION
Customer	name, address, phone
Car	manufacturer, year, model, serial number, color, cost.
Accessories	air-conditioner, stereo, sun-roof.

a) Make variable type definitions suitable for appropriate variables involved in this application.

b) Make suitable variable declarations.

Solution As in any programming exercise, there are several solutions to this problem. The following solution attempts to take advantage of ADA's powerful data abstraction capabilities.

a)
```
type t_customer is
    record
        name : string (1..25);
        address : string (1. 30);
        phone : string (1..10);
    end record;

type t_car is
    record
        manufacturer : string (1..30);
        year : integer (1900–3000);
        model : string (1..20);
        serial_num : string (1..30);
        color : string (1.15);
        cost : float;
    end record;
```

Language Overview 565

```
type t_accessories is (air_conditioner, stereo, sun_roof);

type t_order is
    record
        customer : t_customer;
        car : t_car;
        accessories : t_accessories;
    end record;
```

b) The following defines *order* as an array of records.

```
order : array (1..N) of t_order:
```

Notice that the index corresponding to the object *order* does not have a type. This is an example of an *anonymous data type*.

We can now initialize individual record components in the following way

```
order(7).car.model := "Pontiac Fiero";
```

Some notation. In ADA, we need to name both a type and an object belonging to the type. Some authors use *type employee is* . . . for the type definition and *empl:employee* for the object definition. Thus, it is very difficult to tell whether a name is a type or an object. Although ADA places no restrictions whatsoever on the names, in this book we prefix "t_" in front of all type declarations.

Like Pascal, ADA uses the *dot notation* when referring to record components. In the above example order(7).car.model the two dots are used to indicate the *model* component of the object *car* and the *car* component of the object *order(7)*.

Control structures. All programming languages have a certain number of statements which alter the normal execution flow in a program. ADA provides the following structures: if-then-else, case, loop, and goto.

The if-then-else structure is used for testing a boolean expression to see if it is TRUE or FALSE. If the expression is TRUE, the set of statements following the keyword **then** are executed. If the expression is FALSE, the set of statements following the keyword **else** are executed. For example, let us assume that a program just read the variable furnace_temperature and it is to be checked to see if it is within certain limits. The following program section prints the message *value within limits* if furnace_temperature is between 50 and 300; otherwise, the message *value out of limits* is printed.

```
furnace_temperature : positive;
if furnace_temperature >= 50 or furnace_temperature =< 300 then
    put("value within limits");
else
    put("value out of limits");
end if
```

Whereas the **if-then-else** structure allows one to execute a group of statements out of two possible groups, the *case* structure allows one to execute a group of statements out of several possible groups. Let us modify the previous example so that the message *temperature too high* is printed if furnace_ temperature is above 300 and the message *temperature too low* is printed if furnace_temperature is below 50. The new version of the example is:

```
furnace_temperature : positive;
case furnace_temperature is
    when 0..49   => put ("temperature too low");
    when 50..300 => put ("value within limits");
    when others  => put ("temperature too high");
end case;
```

The **case** structure cannot test Boolean conditions, but rather the discrete data values that the variable can assume, as shown in the previous example.

When a group of statements is to be executed a certain number of times, ADA provides the **loop** structure, which basically has three forms: infinite loops, finite loops, and logically controlled loops. Infinite loops are used to execute a group of statements contained in the loop forever. In practice, a means for exiting the loop is provided through the use of the **exit** statement. The following example shows a program section that prints the message *infinite loop* to an output device unless the device is off.

```
device_state : boolean;
loop
    put ("infinite loop");
    exit when device_state = FALSE; -- FALSE indicates
        -- that the device is off.
end loop;
```

Finite loops are used to execute a group of statements contained in the loop a fixed number of times. Let us modify the previous example to print the message *finite loop* exactly nine times.

```
for I in 1..9 loop;
    put ("finite loop");
end loop;
```

Sometimes, one desires to execute a group of statements contained in the loop a fixed number of times depending upon a logical condition. This can be done by using a logically controlled loop.

```
number := 100;
while number > 0 loop
    put ("variable is still positive");
    number := number - 1;
end loop;
```

ADA provides an additional control structure for transferring control to any statement that begins with a label. The following is an example of an infinite loop using the *goto* statement.

```
<<label_1>> put ("this is another infinite loop");
    goto label_1;
```

In the preceding example, notice that labels are enclosed in double angle brackets.

Language Overview

Appendix B

Who's Who in Standards

Keeping track of network standards is hard enough, not to mention the organizations developing them. This appendix is intended to help with this task. The article by Chapin (1983) provides an introduction to communication standards.

There are over 400 organizations involved with setting and adopting standards in the United States, and many more in other countries. We list next some of the most prominent US and international organizations organized alphabetically.

American National Standards Institute (ANSI)—This group, based in New York City, is the US member of the International Organization for Standardization (ISO). It coordinates the writing of many US domestic standards and approves them. It has recently changed its name to American Standards Committee (ASC).

Computer & Business Equipment Manufacturers Association (CBEMA)—This trade association of equipment manufacturers holds the Secretariat for the X3 Information System Committee.

Computer and Communications Industry Association (CCIA)—The CCIA is a leading US trade association of computer and communications equipment manufacturers.

Corporation for Open System (COS)—This consortium of vendors and users was formed in 1985 to accelerate the development and commercial availability of interoperable computer and communications equipment and services that conform to ISDN, the Open System Interconnection (OSI) model, and related international standards.

Electronics Industries Association (EIA)—This trade association represents manufacturers of electronic equipment and components, telecommunications equipment, radios, and televisions.

European Standards Coordinating Committee-European Committee for Electrotechnical Standardization (CEN-Cenelec)—Major equipment manufacturers join European standard-setting bodies and user groups in this organization for Common Market members. It has the main standardization role for computers in Europe.

European Communities (EC)—This key European administration and policy-making group—also known as the Common Market—seeks harmonization of telecommunications standards.

European Computer Manufacturers Association (ECMA)—Despite its name, this Geneva-based technical group does more work in setting international standards than other work as a trade organization for its equipment makers. ECMA standards often become the basis for ISO and IEC information processing standards.

European Conference of Postal and Telecommunications Administrations (CEPT)—All European telecommunications carriers belong to this group based in Bern, Switzerland. It has the main technical role in the European Community's efforts to standardize telecommunications standards.

Information Technology Steering Committee (ITSTC)—This newly formed group, based in Brussels, Belgium, has the aim of coordinating European efforts on standard functions for the OSI model. It incorporates the work of CEPT and CEN-Cenelec.

Institute of Electrical and Electronics Engineers (IEEE)—In its role as the technical and professional association for electrical engineers, the IEEE develops standards in many areas of electrotechnology. It acts internationally through the US National Committee for the IEC, and through ANSI (the US member-body) for ISO.

International Consultative Committee for Telephone and Telegraph (CCITT)—The national telecommunications companies of the world gather in this organization, chartered by the United Nations, to set telecommunications standards. CCITT has a great deal of input into ISO standards, and final standards issued by the two groups in areas of common interest are frequently identical. The US State Department heads the US delegation to CCITT.

International Electrotechnical Commission (IEC)—Founded in 1906. This international standards organization has a membership comprising 43 countries that produce over 95 percent of the world's electric energy. It develops standards covering the entire field of electrotechnology, including electric power apparatus, electronics, appliances, radio communications, and transportation equipment.

International Organization for Standardization (ISO)—This worldwide voluntary standards association, based in Geneva, is composed of 77 countries' standards-setting bodies. It has over 150 technical centers, writing standards in many areas. One task, for example, is to create OSI standards through Subcommittee 21 of its Technical Committee 97 for Information and Data Processing. An ISO draft proposal (DP) contains a specification which is submitted for a review process. Not all technical issues are fixed in a DP and thus they are likely to change. After a voting process, the DP may become a draft international standard (DIS) which means that all major technical issues are fixed and that potential changes to be made are minor. Finally, after appropriate changes and an approval process, the DIS becomes an IS (international standard).

International Telecommunications Union (ITU)—This is the international organization responsible for the adoption and assignment of international communications protocols and frequency allocations. It does its technical work through its two committees, the International Radio Consultative Committee (CCIR), and the CCITT.

Manufacturing Automation Protocol & Technical and Office Protocols (MAP/TOP) User Group—This group includes professionals and corporations involved with communication integration in the areas of engineering, office, and manufacturing automation. It became a technical group of the Society of Manufacturing Engineers (SME) in 1985. It works to develop existing and emerging international communications standards and accepted operating practices. It has groups in Canada, Australia, Japan, and Europe (EMUG).

National Bureau of Standards (NBS)—The NBS is the US government organization responsible for basic physical and measurement standards in the United States, and for research and development of scientific measuring methods. It also develops computer and information systems standards used by the US government, called Federal Information Processing Standards (FIPS). It has recently changed its name to National Institute of Science and Technology (NIST).

National Electric Manufacturers Association (NEMA)—This old and influential trade association of electrical equipment manufacturers develops standards for products produced by its members.

Standard Promotion and Application Group (SPAG)—This trade group is composed of computer makers in the European Community (EC). Under EC sponsorship, they provide technical recommendations to ITSTC.

Appendix C

MAP and TOP Architectures

This appendix is intended to provide an overview of the different architectures that have been developed for MAP and TOP. We only describe the latest architectures since earlier ones have been mostly used as stepping stones to produce more stable architectures. Furthermore, the architectures described in this appendix have been used for actual implementations. The architectures described are MAP 2.2, MAP 3.0, MAP-EPA, mini-MAP, and TOP 3.0. Earlier architectures include MAP 2.0, MAP 2.1, and TOP 1.0.

The term architecture, as used in this appendix, refers to a station architecture. A station architecture specifies the number, name, configuration, functions, protocols, and protocol options of all layers which taken together allow network stations to communicate with one another. The layer architecture should also specify how the functions of each layer relate to one another, and also the relationship to the OSI reference model. Other terms which are sometimes used to denote a station architecture are *node architecture*, *layer profile*, or *protocol stack*.

Historically, the initial MAP document was issued in October 1982, with major additions incorporated in 1984. MAP 2.0 was issued in February 1985, MAP 2.1 in March 1985, MAP 2.2 in August 1986, and MAP 3.0 in April 1987. TOP 1.0 was released in October 1985, and TOP 3.0 in May 1987.

MAP 2.2 ARCHITECTURE

The MAP 2.2 architecture is upward compatible and very similar to the MAP 2.1 specification and is depicted in Figure C.1 (a). Two options exist at the physical layer: an AM/PSK modulator at 10 M bps or an FSK phase coherent modulator at 5 M bps. The MAC sublayer uses the token bus protocol as described in the IEEE 802.4 standard, and the LLC sublayer specifies the use of the

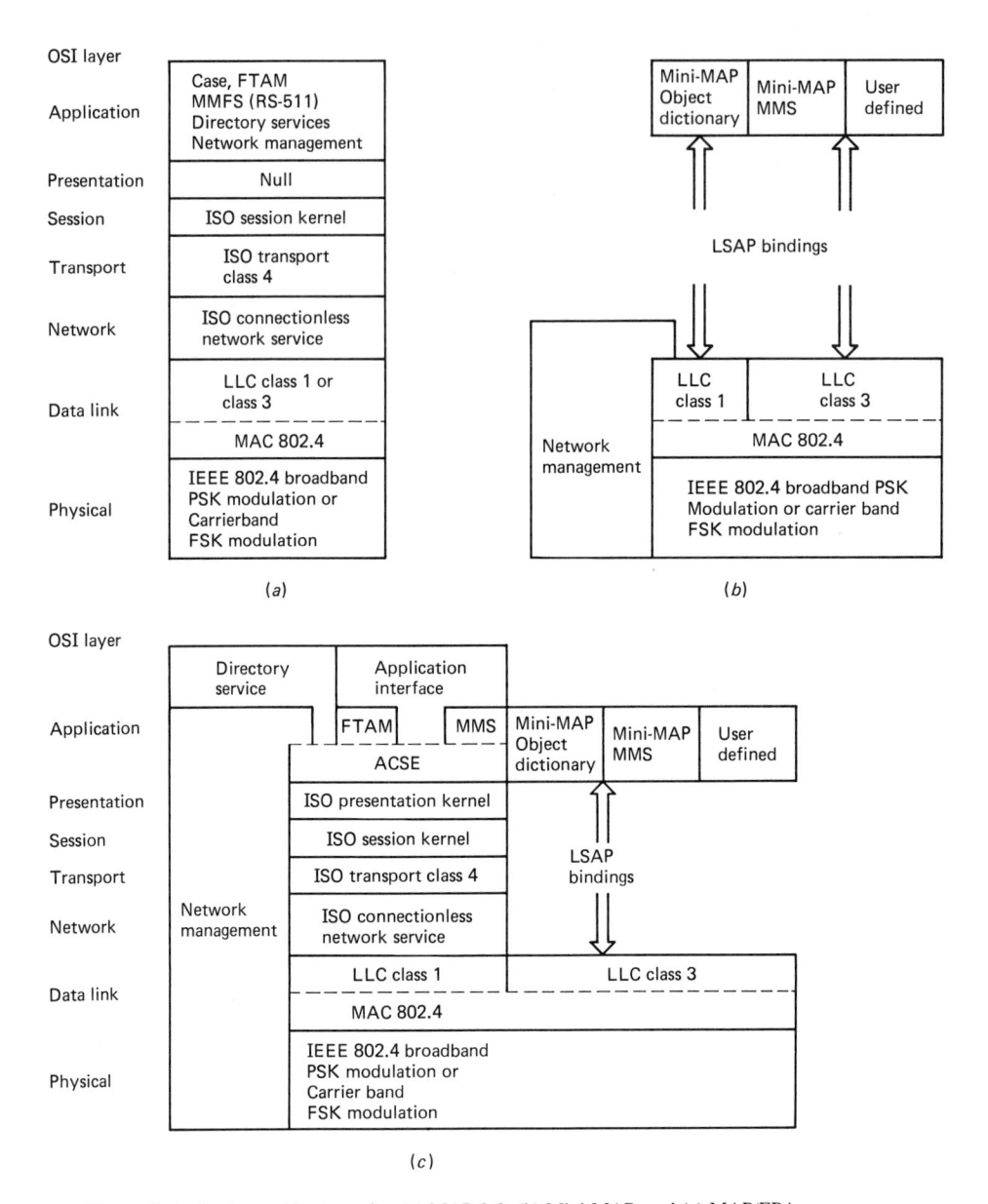

Figure C.1 Station architectures for: (a) MAP 2.2; (b) Mini-MAP; and (c) MAP/EPA.

IEEE 802.2 with class 1 or 3 options. The network layer corresponds to that of the ISO connectionless network standard. The connection oriented, ISO transport class 4 standard is used at the transport layer. The session layer uses the kernel functionality of the ISO session layer standard. Whereas the presentation layer is null (i.e., empty), the application layer specifies CASE, FTAM, MMFS, Directory Services, and Network Management. With the exception of directory services and network management, all other specified standards were discussed extensively in the book. Although we did not provide an extensive treatment, the case study in section 14.9 gives a practical use of MMFS.

MAP 3.0 ARCHITECTURE

Whereas MAP 2.2 and MAP 2.1 were very similar, MAP 3.0 provides significant enhancements and it is not upward compatible with MAP 2.2. In addition to enhancements in virtually all layers, perhaps the major enhancements over MAP 2.2 are the inclusion of the Manufacturing Message

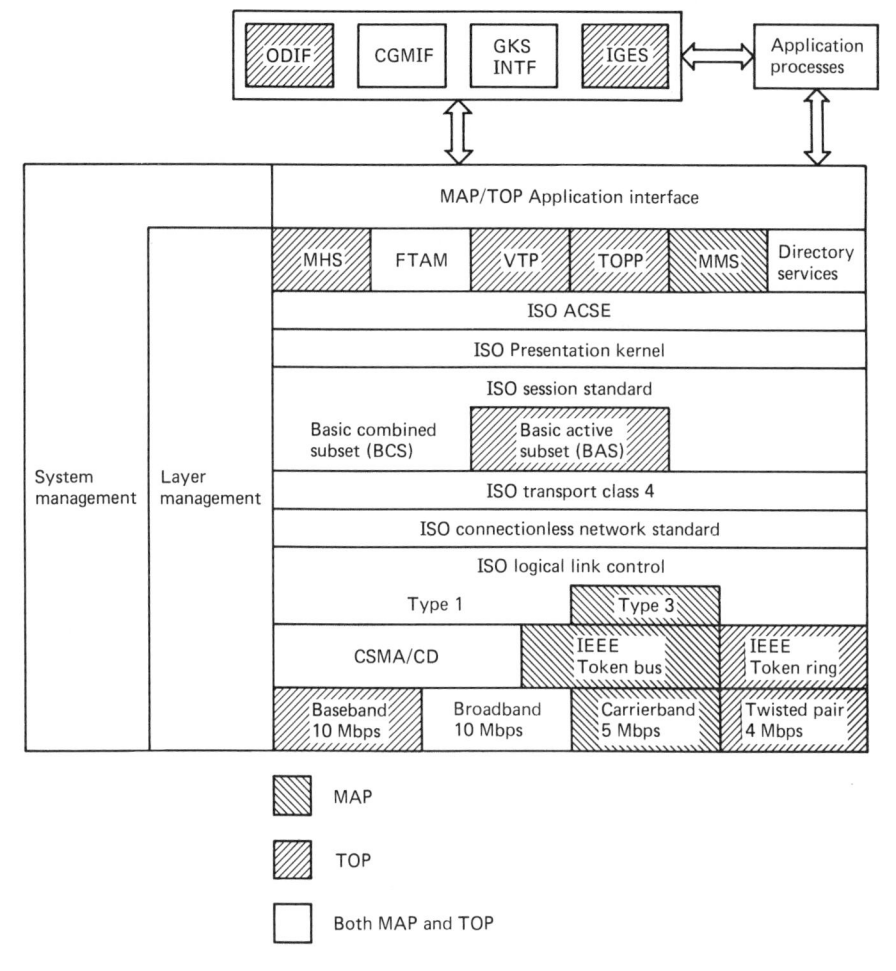

Figure C.2 MAP/TOP 3.0 station architecture.

Specification (MMS), the use of the Association Control Service Element (ACSE), the incorporation of the ISO presentation layer, and the specification of an application layer interface with application processes. With the exception of directory services, network management, and the application layer interface, all the standards have been treated in detail in this book. The MAP 3.0 architecture is depicted in Figure C.2.

In addition to the network management, directory service, and application layer interface specifications, the MAP 3.0 specification also contains a detail specification for broadband transmission systems including topology, coaxial cables, system design, performance, installation, test, and maintenance procedures. The broadband specification is also applicable for TOP 3.0. As depicted in Figure C.2, there are some application specific standards which interface with the application layer through the MAP/TOP application layer interface. The application specific standards include the computer graphics metafile interchange format (CGMIF) and computer graphics application interface (GKS INTF).

MAP/EPA ARCHITECTURE

As noted in chapter 14, one approach to having a simpler architecture (for performance reasons) while still maintaining ISO compatibility is to use a dual architecture. As depicted in Figure C.1 (c), the MAP/EPA architecture follows this approach. In addition to the dual architecture, perhaps the most significant feature of MAP/EPA is the use of an LLC class 3 sublayer. As discussed in section 4.12, class 3 operation allows a responder to issue an acknowledgment immediately without the need to wait for the token (immediate acknowledgment). Crucial to the operation of a MAP/EPA station is a version of MMS called mini-MAP MMS and its direct interface to the data link layer which is known as LSAP bindings. Optionally, a user may use a mini-MAP object dictionary or a user defined application layer protocol (instead of mini-MAP MMS).

Normally, a MAP/EPA station communicates with similar stations using the three layer path (i.e., application, data link, and physical). When the station communicates with an ISO node, the seven layer path is used. As noted, the dual architecture allows the MAP/EPA station to behave as an ISO station only when it is required.

MINI-MAP ARCHITECTURE

If it is not important to be ISO compatible but still have a simple architecture, then a mini-MAP architecture could be used. As depicted in Figure C.1 (b), the mini-MAP architecture is basically one of the portions of the dual architecture of MAP/EPA, thus the same observations made on the MAP/EPA architecture also apply here. One difference, however, is that network management in a mini-MAP environment (at least at the time being) works in an environment consisting only of the physical and data link layers.

MAP NETWORK ARCHITECTURE

In addition to the station architecture, one should also specify a network architecture. By network architecture we mean the topological configuration, transmission system devices, transmission media, and station configuration which taken together, allow end user applications to interwork even when the applications are on different physical segments.

Possible topologies for MAP include a bus, rooted tree, and a star. Transmission system devices include head ends, amplifiers, taps, bridges, routers, and gateways. The transmission medium is broadband and baseband (for carrierband) coaxial cable. Stations can be configured using the MAP 2.2, MAP 3.0, MAP/EPA or mini-MAP architectures.

TOP 3.0 ARCHITECTURE

Since the Technical and Office (TOP) protocol specification basically addresses different applications (i.e., design and office automation) from those of MAP, it is expected that their application layer protocols differ. Likewise, because of real time considerations, it is expected that the lower two layers also differ. Accordingly, as shown in Figure C.2, the TOP 3.0 specification basically shares the network, transport, session, and presentation layers with the MAP 3.0 specification. In addition, MAP 3.0 and TOP 3.0 also share the LLC class 1 sublayer, ACSE, FTAM, application layer interface, directory services, and network management.

Although not defined in the OSI station architecture, MAP and TOP architectures can also share a broadband coaxial cable as the medium since both networks can coexist on the same cable.

As depicted in Figure C.2 the TOP option for medium access control is the CSMA/CD based IEEE 802.3 specification on a baseband coaxial cable at 10 M bps (10 BASE 5). Other options of the TOP architecture at the MAC sublayer and physical layer include the IEEE 802.5 at 4 M bps on twisted pair wires, the IEEE 802.4 at 10 Mbps on a broadband coaxial cable, CSMA/CD at 10 M bps on a broadband coaxial cable (10 BROAD 36), and a TOP packet switching interface based on the X.21 standard.

At the application layer the TOP architecture specifies the message handling system (MHS), file transfer access and management (FTAM), virtual terminal (VT), directory services, and network management. Application specific standards defined on top of the TOP 3.0 architecture include the product definition interchange format (PDIF), office document interchange format (ODIF), computer graphics metafile interchange format (CGMIF), computer graphics application interface (GKS INTF), and remote file transfer application interface.

In addition, TOP 3.0 groups subsets of standards into the following building blocks:

CSMA/CD subnetwork access,
Token passing ring subnetwork access,
X.25 packet switching subnetwork access,
MAP token passing bus subnetwork access,
Remote terminal access,
Remote file access,
Electronic mail,
Network directory,
Network management,
Computer graphics Metafile Interchange format,
Product definition interchange format,
Office document interchange format,
Computer graphics application interface, and
Remote file transfer application interface.

Appendix D

ASN.1 with MMS Examples

In this appendix we provide a brief overview of the Abstract Syntax Notation One (ASN.1) and its application within the Manufacturing Message Specification (MMS). As noted in chapter 9, communication systems need to encode information to be transmitted for efficient transmission and to resolve different data representations at end systems. Encoding the information before it can be transmitted basically involves two major steps: describing how the information is to be communicated (i.e., the syntax) and performing the actual encoding operation. Accordingly, ASN.1 involves two standards for describing the syntax and for encoding the information to be communicated known as ISO 8824, and ISO 8825 respectively.

Encoding schemes involve the direct mapping of values from one type onto values of another, previously defined type. Programming languages usually attempt to conceal details of the representation of data in memory in order to encourage program portability. Communicating PDUs in computer communications however, must use an explicit encoding so that various dissimilar computer systems can exchange data using a mutually understood data representation.

D.1 ASN.1 OVERVIEW

Although the brief overview presented in this section contains the main ideas of ASN.1, it is incomplete. The reader is referred to the ASN.1 standard for additional details.

Syntax Notation

The ISO 8824 standard defines a notation (i.e., a language) for defining the *abstract syntax* of information to be communicated between application processes. The syntax notation language is somewhat similar to a programming language in that it defines character sets, keywords, simple types, complex (constructed) types, modules, and macros. Although the syntax notation provided by ASN.1 is generic in that it can be used for describing the syntax of specific applications, we are primarily interested in using ASN.1 for describing the syntax of protocol data units. Basically, protocol data units are composed of data organized in a specific fashion. Thus, we need to specify the data and its structure as it relates to a PDU. Accordingly, ASN.1 defines two classes of types for specifying data and its structure which are called *simple types* and *structured types* respectively. Whereas simple types include BOOLEAN, INTEGER, BITSTRING, OCTETSTRING, and NULL, structured types include:

Sequence. This is analogous to a record in ADA in that it consists of a fixed, ordered, list of elements which could be of different types. The SEQUENCE type is the most used when defining PDUs since a PDU is basically a sequence of components.

Sequence of. This is analogous to an array in ADA in that it consists of an ordered list of elements of the same type.

Set. This is a fixed, unordered list of elements which could be of different types.

Set of. This is an unordered list of elements of the same type.

Choice. This is a fixed, unordered, list of elements which could be of different types. It is used to specify that only one of several elements is present in a PDU.

Associated with every type, ASN.1 also defines a tag. Tags are useful for identifying elements within one PDU, for example whether an MMS Write or Read service is used can be determined by examining an appropriate tag. Likewise, the possible elements in a CHOICE construct are typically identified through tags. The following four classes of tags are specified:

1. UNIVERSAL. These tags are used with all types defined by ASN.1 (e.g., INTEGER, SEQUENCE, etc).

2. APPLICATION. These tags are common to a specific application. Examples include the tags defined in the so-called MMS Companion standards for process control, numerically controlled machines, robots, etc.

3. PRIVATE. These are user defined.

4. CONTEXT SPECIFIC. These tags are related to the specific situation in which they are used. For example, given that we know that data follows, a context specific tag is used to specify the data type.

In addition, ASN.1 also supports the definition of an element with an implied type by using the IMPLICIT keyword. For example, in the definition of Data in Figure D.1, the line bcd   [13] IMPLICIT INTEGER

means that the type (i.e., INTEGER) of the variable bcd is implied and that the tag [13] is used to identify one element of the CHOICE construct. In general, the use of IMPLICIT tagging results in a more compact code since the type of the variable can be implied from the tag field and thus no additional encoding is necessary for encoding the type. Likewise, the keyword OPTIONAL indicates that the corresponding element is optional.

In reference to Figure D.1, an MMSpdu is one of 14 possible choices with the confirmed-RequestPDU being a SEQUENCE of three fields: an invokeID, an optional listOfModifier, and a ConfirmedServiceRequest. The latter field indicates the actual MMS service (i.e., read, write, and so on). The Write-Request element consists of a variableAccessSpecification and one or more Data elements. All tags used in this example are context specific.

Encoder

Basically, the ASN.1 encoder is composed of three main fields referred to as the identification (ID), length, and contents fields. As the name implies, the ID field identifies the particular value to be encoded. For example, in the MMS protocol, the ID field is used for uniquely identifying the specific PDU used. The length field is used for indicating the length of the contents field. Finally, the content field contains the data referred to by the ID and length fields. A feature of the encoder is that it is

```
MMSpdu ::= CHOICE
    {
      confirmed-RequestPDU    [0] IMPLICIT Confirmed-RequestPDU
      confirmed-ResponsePDU   [1] IMPLICIT Confirmed-ResponsePDU
      .
      .
      conclude-ErrorPDU       [13] IMPLICIT Conclude-ErrorPDU
    }

confirmed-RequestPDU ::= SEQUENCE
    {
        invokeID      unsigned32,
        listOfModifier SEQUENCE OF Modifier OPTIONAL,
        ConfirmedServiceRequest
    }

ConfirmedServiceRequest ::= CHOICE {
    status              [0] IMPLICIT Status-Request,
    getNameList         [1] IMPLICIT GetNameList-Request,
    .
    .
    write               [5] IMPLICIT Write-Request,
    .
    .
```

Figure D.1 ASN.1 syntax definition of the MMS write service request.

```
Write-Request ::= SEQUENCE {
    variableAccessSpecification VariableAccessSpecification,
    listOfData      [0] IMPLICIT SEQUENCE OF Data
    }

VariableAccessSpecification ::= CHOICE {
        listOfVariable [0] IMPLICIT SEQUENCE OF SEQUENCE {
            variableSpecification VariableSpecification,
            alternateAccess    [5] IMPLICIT AlternateAccess OPTIONAL
            },
        variableListName [1] ObjectName
        }


VariableSpecification ::= CHOICE {
    name                    [0] ObjectName,
    address                 [1] Address,
    variableDescription     [2] IMPLICIT SEQUENCE {
        address                 Address
        typeSpecification       TypeSpecification
        },
    scatteredAccessDescription [3] IMPLICIT
                                    ScatteredAccessDescription,
    invalidated             [4] IMPLICIT NULL
    }

Data ::= CHOICE {
    array               [1] IMPLICIT SEQUENCE OF Data,
    structure           [2] IMPLICIT SEQUENCE OF Data,
    boolean             [3] IMPLICIT BOOLEAN,
    bit-string          [4] IMPLICIT BIT STRING,
    integer             [5] IMPLICIT INTEGER,
    unsigned            [6] IMPLICIT INTEGER,
    floating-point      [7] IMPLICIT FloatingPoint,
    octet-string        [9] IMPLICIT OCTET STRING,
    visible-string      [10] IMPLICIT VisibleString,
    generalized-time    [11] IMPLICIT GeneralizedTime,
    binary-time         [12] IMPLICIT TimeOfDay,
    bcd                 [13] IMPLICIT INTEGER,
    booleanArray        [14] IMPLICIT BIT STRING
    }

ObjectName ::= CHOICE {
    vmd-specific        [0] IMPLICIT Identifier,
    domain-specific     [1] IMPLICIT SEQUENCE {
        domainID    Identifier,
        itemID      Identifier,
        },
    aa-specific         [2] IMPLICIT Identifier
    }
```

Figure D.1 (Continued.)

Sec. D.1   ASN.1 Overview

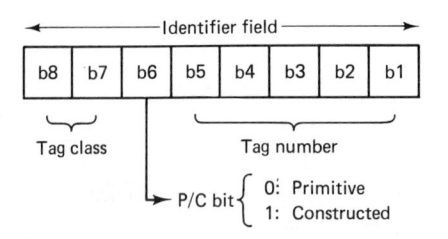

Figure D.2 Identifier field used in ASN.1 rules.

recursive, meaning that one should be careful in interpreting the contents field because it may contain additional ID, length, and contents. Each field is further detailed next.

1. Identifier Field

Three important pieces of information are contained in the identifier octets: the tag class, the tag number, and whether the encoded method is primitive or constructed. As depicted in Figure D.2, bits b8 and b7 are used to encode the four possible tag classes available: Universal, Application, Context-specific, and Private. If bit b6 = 1, the encoding is primitive, otherwise it is constructed. The remaining five bits are used to encode the tag number. A primitive encoding is one that does not use recursion, otherwise it is constructed.

2. Length Field

As the name implies, the length field indicates number of the octets in the contents field. Two formats are provided, the short form and the long form as shown in Figure D.3. The short form is used when the number of octets in the content field is less than 128, otherwise the long form is required.

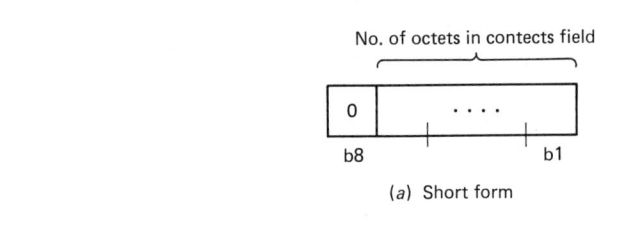

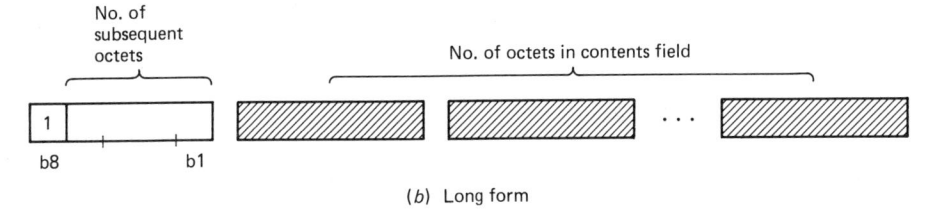

Figure D.3 Length field used in ASN.1 rules.

580 ASN.1 with MMS Examples

TABLE D.1

Data type	Encoding	Length (in octets)
Boolean	primitive	1
Integer	primitive	≥ 1
Bitstring	primitive or constructed	≥ 1
Octetstring	primitive or constructed	≥ 1
Sequence	constructed	≥ 1
Choice	primitive or constructed	≥ 1

3. Contents Field

The contents field depends primarily on the data type to be encoded. Table D.1 shows the major characteristics about the encoding of some data types. When encoding a Bitstring value, the first octet of the contents field indicates the number of unused bits in the last octet of the content field. We next present two examples to illustrate some encoding details. All numbers in the resulting code are expressed in the hexadecimal (Hex) notation.

Example

The value 0A 3B 5F 29 1C D (Hex) of type BIT STRING is to be encoded using the primitive and constructed encoding. The following illustrates each encoding. The constructed encoding shows the recursive nature of the encoder.

a. Primitive encoding

ID (bitstring)	Length	Contents
03	07	04 0A 3B 5F 29 1C D0

The encoded values correspond to a Bitstring of 7 octets with the first octet in the contents field (i.e. 04) indicating that the last four bits of the last octet (i.e. D0) are unused. Thus the actual encoded data is 0A 3B 5B 29 1C D.

b. Constructed encoding

ID (bitstring)	Length	Contents		
23	0C			
		ID (bitstring)	Length	Contents
		03	03	00 0A 3B
		03	05	04 5F 29 1C D0

The overall encoded value corresponds to two content component values with total length of 12 octets. The first component has a length of 3 octets with the first octet of the contents (i.e. 00) indicating that there are 0 bits unused in the contents portion. Thus the actual data in the first component is 0A 3B. The second content component has a length of 5 octets. The first octet of the contents field (i.e. 04) indicates that there are four bits unused in the last content octet. Thus the actual data corresponding to the last component is 5F 29 1C D

Example

Data corresponding to the following type definition is to be encoded.

connectPDU ::= SEQUENCE
[
myAddress NetworkAddress,
yourAddress NetworkAddress,
reverseCharging BOOLEAN,
userData [UNIVERSAL 6] IMPLICIT OCTET STRING
]
NetworkAddress ::= OCTET STRING

The data to be encoded is given by the following value definition

overture ConnectPDU ::=
[myAddress the White House ,
yourAddress the Kremlin ,
reverseCharging TRUE,
userData Let's talk
]

Since we are encoding a sequence, according to Table D.1, the encoding method is constructed. The ASN.1 encoded value is:

ID (sequence)	Length	Contents
30	2D	
		04 0F the White House
		04 0B the Kremlin
		01 01 FF
		06 08 Let's talk

which describes a SEQUENCE (30), encoded in 45 octets, containing a 15-octet Octet string (the White House), an 11-octet Octet string (the Kremlin), a Boolean TRUE, and a 10-octet Octet string (Let's talk).

A good feature of the ASN.1 encoding method is that it is independent from the syntax description language, and also independent from the semantics. Accordingly, this allows the PDU syntax specification to be separate from the encoding.

D.2 MMS EXAMPLE.

In the following example, we obtain the abstract syntax and transfer syntax corresponding to an MMS service primitive. Assume that an application process wants to write the value 2B39F1 into a remote variable named *vmdl* of type octet-string having a scope of a single virtual manufacturing device (i.e., vmd-specific).

In MMS, the WriteRequestPDU is a confirmed request PDU whose ASN.1 syntax definition is given in Figure D.1 where Address, TypeSpecification, ScatteredAccessDescription, and

```
TRANSFER SYNTAX           ABSTRACT SYNTAX

A0                        confirmed-RequestPDU
1A                        length

  02                        invokeID INTEGER
  04                        length
    05

  A5                        write
  15                        length

    A0                        variableAccessSpecification CHOICE
    0C                        length
      A0                        listOfVariable
      0A                        length

        A0                        variableSpecification CHOICE
        08                        length
          A0                        name
          06                        length
            80                        vmd-specific    VALUE
            04                        length
              vmd1                    value
        A0                        listOfData CHOICE
        05                        length
          88                        octet-string    VALUE
          03                        length
            2B 39 F1                value

PDU LENGTH (OVERHEAD) : 28
DATA OCTETS :   7
CODE EFFICIENCY :   7/28 = 25%
```

Figure D.4 Transfer syntax and abstract syntax corresponding to the MMS write service.

AlternateAccess are additional definitions which are not directly relevant to our example. For details, consult the MMS protocol reference.

Further assume that the Write PDU has an invokeID = 05, the VariableAccessSpecification CHOICE is listOfVariable, the VariableSpecification CHOICE is *name*, the ObjectName CHOICE is *vmd-specific*, and the listOfData CHOICE is *octet-string* with value 2B 39 F1. Based on the previous assumptions, the transfer syntax and abstract syntax corresponding to the write service is given in Figure D.4.

D.3 DETAILED MAP ENCODING EXAMPLE

Although the ASN.1 encoder is not used by all protocols in the MAP 3.0 specification, the following example shows the flow of actual encoded data corresponding to the MMS write operation between

(PR) (SD) 43 00 11 22 00 33 44	MAC-Header
FA 18 03	LLC-Header
00	Network-Header
07 F0 00 04 80 00 00 02	Transport-Header
01 00 01 00	Session-Header
61 26 30 24 02 01 01 A0 1F	Presentation-Header
A0 1A 02 01 05 A5 15 A0 0C A0 0A A0 08 A0 06 80 04 56 4D 44 31 A0 05 88 03 2B 39 F1	MMS-message
(FCS) (ED)	MAC-Trailer

Figure D.5 Encoded header, trailer, and information fields at each OSI layer.

two end systems. In our example, ASN.1 is used by MMS, ACSE, and the presentation layer. Other layers use specific encoding algorithms which were not discussed in this book.

Our example corresponds to a MAP 3.0 architecture with an inactive network layer protocol where an end user application wants to change the value of a remote variable using the MMS Write service as illustrated in the previous example. We assume that the appropriate connections at the MMS, presentation, and session layers have been established. We also assume that a connection already exists at the transmission system level, that is, at the transport layer with the support of the lower layers. Figure D.5 gives the encoded header, trailer, and information fields of each OSI layer.

The network layer header (i.e., 00) corresponds to that of the inactive network layer. The actual bit patterns for the preamble (PR), start delimiter (SD), and end delimiter (ED) are not shown because they do not actually exist in bit form since they are only used by the physical layer to achieve bit synchronization and frame synchronization as discussed in chapters 3 and 4. We leave as an exercise to the reader to calculate the frame check sequence (FCS) using the IEEE polynomial of section 4.11, on the bit pattern which starts on 43 (i.e., the frame control field) and ends with the last bit of the MMS message (i.e., F1).

References

ABRAMSON, N. The ALOHA System, in *Computer Communication Networks*. Abramson, N. and Kuo, F. F., Editors, Prentice-Hall, Englewood Cliffs, N.J., 1973.

AHUJA V. *Design and Analysis of Computer Communication Networks*, McGraw-Hill, 1982.

ALEXIS-DIRVIN, R., AND MILLER, A. The MC68824 Token Bus Controller, VLSI for the Factory LAN, *IEEE Micro*, pp. 15–25, June 1985.

AMMAR, M. H. Performance of a Two-Stage Manufacturing System with Control and Communication Overhead, *IEEE Trans. on Syst., Man, and Cybernetics*, vol. 17, July 1987.

ASFAHL C. R. *Robots and Manufacturing Automation*, John Wiley & Sons, 1985.

BACKES, F. Transparent Bridges for Interconnection of IEEE 802 LANs, *IEEE Network*, vol. 2, pp. 5–9, Jan. 1988.

BAKER, G. B. *Local-Area Networks with Fiber-Optic Applications*, Prentice-Hall, 1986.

BARNES, J. G. P. *Programming in Ada*, Addison-Wesley, 2nd Ed., 1984.

BERGMAN, E. E. Fiber Optics as a Physical Network Layer for MAP, *INFOCOM' 1987*, San Francisco, Ca., pp. 64–69, April 1987.

BERTSEKAS, D., GALLAGER, R. *Data Networks*, Prentice-Hall, 1987.

BOCHMANN, G. V. *Concepts for Distributed Systems Design*, Springer-Verlag, 1983.

BOOTH, G. M. *The Distributed System Environment*, McGraw-Hill, 1981.

BOUNDENANT, J., FEYDEL, B., AND ROLIN, P. LYNX: an IEEE 802.3 Compatible Deterministic Protocol, *INFOCOM'87*, pp. 173–579, San Francisco, Ca., April 1987.

BOXMA, O. J., AND GROENENDIJK. Pseudo-conservation Laws in Cyclic-Service Systems, *Internal Report, Center for Mathematics and Computer Science*, Amsterdam, The Netherlands, May 1986.

BUX, W. AND GRILLO, D. Flow Control in Local Area Networks of Interconnected Token Rings, *IEEE Trans. on Comm.*, pp. 1058–66, Oct. 1985.

BUX, W. Local Area Subnetworks: A Performance Comparison, *IEEE Transactions on Communications*, pp. 1465–73, Oct. 1981.

BYLANSKI, P., AND INGRAM, D. G. W. *Digital Transmission Systems*, Institution of Electrical Engineers, 1976.

CALLON, R. Internetwork Protocol, *Proc. IEEE*, vol. 71, pp. 1388–93, Dec, 1983.

CAMPBELL, G. F. AND PIMENTEL, J. R. Topological Aspects of MAP Network Design, *11th Conf. Local Computer Networks*, Minn., MN. pp. 34–43, Oct. 1986.

CAPETANAKIS, J. I. Generalized TDMA: The Multi-Accessing Tree Protocol, *IEEE Transactions on Communications*, pp. 1476–84, Oct, 1979.

CARLSON, A. B. *Communication Systems*, 2nd ed. McGraw-Hill, New York, 1975.

CASTANET, R., DUPEUX, A., AND GUITTON, P. ADA, A Well Suited Language for Specification and Implementation of Protocols, in *Protocol Specification, Testing, and Verification*, V. M. Diaz, editor, North-Holland, pp. 247–58, 1986.

CELLIER, F. E. *Progress in Modelling & Simulation*, Academic Press, 1982.

CERF, V. G. AND KAHN R. E. Protocol for Packet Network Intercommunications, *IEEE Transactions on Communications*, pp. 637–48, May, 1974.

CERF, V. G., AND KIRSTEIN. Issues in Packet-Network Intercommunications, *Proc. IEEE*, pp. 180–202, Nov. 1978.

CHANDY, K. M., AND MISRA, J. Distributed Computation on Graphs, *Communications of the ACM*, vol. 25, pp. 833–37, 1982.

CHAMBERS, F. B., DUCE, D. A., AND JONES, G. P. *Distributed Computing*, Academic Press, 1984.

CHAPIN, A. L. Computer Communication Standards, *ACM Computer Communication Review*, 1983.

CHAPIN, A. L. Connection and Connectionless Data Transmission, *Proc. IEEE*, vol. 71, pp. 1365–71, Dec. 1983.

CHAUHAN, V. Real-Time MAP: A Network Architecture Standard for Manufacturing Cells, *NBS Workshop on Factory Communications*, Robert Rosenthal, Editor, March, 1987.

CHLAMTAC, I. A Programmable VLSI Controller for Standard and Prioritized Ethernet Local Networks, in *Local Area & Multiple Access Networks*, R., Pickholtz, Editor, Computer Science Press, 1986.

CHORAFAS, D. N. *Designing and Implementing Local Area Networks*, McGraw-Hill, Inc., 1984.

CHOU, W., EDITOR. *Computer Communications*, vol. 1, Principles, Prentice-Hall, Englewood Cliffs, N.J., 1983.

CIMINIERA, L., DEMARTINI, C., NICOLA, E., SAMAROTTO, R., AND VALENZANO, A. Design and Implementation of an ISO/OSI Session Layer for a Microprocessor-based Lan, *Euromicro Journal*, 1987.

CIMINIERA, L., AND VALENZANO, A. Acknowledgment and Priority Mechanisms in the 802.4 Token-Bus, *IEEE Trans. on Industrial Electronics*, vol. 35, pp. 307–16, May 1988.

CLARK, D. D., POGRAN, K. T., AND REED, D. P. An Introduction to Local Area Networks, *Proc. IEEE*, vol. 66, pp. 1497–1517, Nov. 1978.

COLLELA, R., ARONOFF, R., AND MILLS, K. Performance Improvements for ISO Transport, *9th Data Communications Symposium*, Sept. 1985.

COLVIN, M. A., AND WEAVER, A. C. Performance of Single Access Classes on the IEEE 802.4 Token Bus, *IEEE Trans. Comm.*, vol. 34, pp. 1253–56, Dec. 1986.

COOPER, E. *Broadband Network Technology*, Sytek Press, Mountain View Ca. 1984.

COX, B. J. *Object Oriented Programming*, Addison Wesley, 1986.

CYPSER, R. J. *Communications Architecture for Distributed Systems*, Addison Wesley, 1978.

DAHMEN, N., KILLAT, U., AND STECKER, R. Performance Analysis of Token Bus and CSMA/CD

Protocols Derived from FORCASD Simulation Runs, *Proc. 2nd Int. Symp. on Perf. of Comp. Comm. Syst.*, Zurich, March 1984.

DAS, J., MULLICK, S. K., AND CHATTERJEE, P. K. *Principles of Digital Communication*, John Wiley & Sons, 1986.

DAVIES, B. *Communication Networks for Computers*, John Wiley & Sons, London 1973.

DAY, J. D. AND ZIMMERMANN H. The OSI Reference Model, *Proc. IEEE*, vol 71. pp. 1334–40, Dec., 1983.

DECOTIGNIE, J-D. Field Bus in the Hierarchy of Factory Communications: The Limits of a Classical Approach. *NBS, Workshop on Factory Communication*, Robert Rosenthal, editor, March, 1987.

DEITEL, H. *An Introduction to Operating Systems*, Addison Wesley, 1984.

DETREVILLE, J. D. A Simulation-Based Comparison of Voice Transmission on CSMA/CD Networks and on Token Buses, *Bell Sys. Tech. Journal*, vol. 63, pp. 33–55, Jan. 1984.

DIAZ, M., EDITOR. *Protocol Specification, Testing, and Verification, V*, IFIP, 1986.

DIXON, STROLE, AND MARKOV. A Token-Ring Network for Local Data, *IBM Systems Journal*, vol. 22, pp. 47–62, 1983.

DUCE, D. A. *Distributed Computing Systems Programme*, Peter Pergrinus, 1984.

DYTEWSKI, D. A. Considerations in Implementing a MAP Network, *Proc. Ultratech*, Long Beach, Ca., pp. 21–28, Sept. 1986.

ELLIS, R. L. *Designing Data Networks*, Prentice-Hall, 1986.

ENSLOW, P. H., JR. *Multiprocessor & Parallel Processing*, John Wiley & Sons, Inc., 1974.

ERICKSON, I. L. VLSI for a Carrierband Node, *IECON'86*, Milwaukee, Wi., pp. 601–6, Oct. 1986.

FARO, A., SERRA, A., VALENZANO, A., AND VITA, L. The MODIAC Communication Network for Process Control, *Proc. 1st Int. Conf. on Computer and Applications*, Beijing (Peking), pp. 669–676, June 1984.

FEHER, K. *Digital Communication Microwave Applications*, Prentice-Hall, 1981.

FEHER, K. *Digital Communication Satellite/Earth Station Engineering*, Prentice-Hall, 1983.

FELDMAN, J. A., AND NIGAM, A. A Model and Proof Technique for Message-Based Systems, *SIAM Journal*, vol. 9, pp. 768–84, Nov. 1980.

FRANTA, W. R. AND CHLAMTAC, I. *Local Networks*, Lexington Books, D.C. Heath and Co., 1981.

GARCIA-TOMAS, J., PAVON, J., AND PEREDA, O. OSI Service Specification: SAP and CEP Modeling, *ACM Computer Communication Review*, vol. 17, pp. 48–70, Jan/April 1987.

GERLA, M. AND KLEINROCK, L. Congestion Control in Interconnected LANs, *IEEE Network*, vol. 2, pp. 72–76, Jan. 1988.

GERLA, M. AND KLEINROCK, L. Flow Control: A Comparative Survey, *IEEE Transactions on Communications*, pp. 553–74, April 1980.

GIEN, M. AND ZIMMERMANN, H. Design Principles for Network Interconnection, *ACM-IEEE 6th Data Communications Symposium*, Ca., pp. 109–19, Nov. 1979.

GLAZIER, D. W., AND TROPPER, C. Congestion Based Dynamic Routing Algorithm, *Int. Conf. on Comm.*, Seattle, Washington, pp. 27.4.1–27.4.6, June 1987.

GOEL, A. K., AND AMER, P. D. Performance Metrics for Bus and Token-Ring Local Area Networks, *Journal of Telecommunication Networks*, vol. 2, pp. 187–209, Summer 1983.

GOMAA, H. Software Development of Real-time Systems, *Communications of the ACM*, vol. 29, pp. 657–68, July 1986.

HALSALL, F. *Introduction to Data Communications and Computer Networks*. Addison-Wesley, 1988.

HAMMOND, J. L. AND O'REILLY, J. P. *Performance Analysis of Local Computer Network*, Addison-Wesley, Reading, Mass., 1986.

HATFIELD, W. B., COOLEN, M. H., AND SCHOLL, F. W. Fiber Optic LANs for the Manufacturing Environment, *IEEE Network*, May 1988.

HAYES, J. F. *Modeling and Analysis of Computer Communications Networks*, Plenum Press, 1984.

HAWE, B., KIRBY, A. AND STEWART, B. Transparent Interconnection of Local Networks with Bridges, *Journal of Telecommunication Networks*, pp. 116–30, Summer 1984.

HEGER, D., WATSON, K. S., NIEMEGEERS, I. G., AND DAEMEN, J. Performance Analysis of Local Area Networks for Real-time Environments, in Informatik-Fachberichte No 111, *Kommunication in Verteilen Systemen II*, pp. 93–107, Springer-Verlag, 1985.

HINDEN, R., HAVERTY, J., AND SHELTZER, A. The DARPA Internet: Interconnecting Heterogeneous Computer Networks with Gateways, *IEEE Computer*, vol. 16, Sept. 1983.

HOLLINGUM, J. *Manufacturing Automation Protocol*, IFS and Springer-Verlag, 1986.

HOOPER, A. The Cambridge Ring—A Local Network, in *Advanced Techniques for Microprocessor Systems*, Hanna, F. K., Editor, Peter Pergrinus Ltd., Stevenage, U.K., pp. 67–71, 1980.

HOPPER, A., TEMPLE S., AND WILLIAMSON, R. *Local Area Network Design*, Addison-Wesley, 1986.

ILYAS, M. AND MOUFTAH, H. T. Performance Evaluation of Computer Communication Networks, *IEEE Communications*, vol. 23, pp. 18–29, April 1985.

Intel Corporation. *Distributed Control Modules Databook*, Literature Distribution, Santa Clara, CA., 1987.

JANETZKY, D. AND WATSON, K. S. Performance Evaluation of the MAP Token Bus in Real Time Applications, in *Advances in Local Area Networks*, Kummerle, Limb, and Tobagi, Editors, IEEE Press, NY, 1987.

JANETZKY, D. AND WATSON, K. S. Token Bus Performance in MAP and Proway, *IFAC Workshop on Distrib. Comp. Control Syst.*, Mayschoss, W. Germany, Oct. 1986.

JANSSENS, G. K., RAES, J. AND STAELENS, D. An Implementation Approach for Local Area Networks, *Computer Networks and ISDN Systems*, vol. 14, pp. 365–72, 1987.

JAYASUMANA, A. P. Performance Analysis of a Token Bus Priority Scheme, *INFOCOM' 1987*, San Francisco, Ca., April 1987.

JOHNSON, R. *Transmission Lines and Networks*, McGraw-Hill, 1950.

JONES, A. T. AND MCLEAN, C. R. A Proposed Hierarchical Control Model for Automated Manufacturing Systems, *Journal of Manufacturing Systems*, pp. 15–25, Jan. 1986.

JONES, C. T. AND BRYAN, L. A. *Programmable Controllers*, International Programmable Controls Inc., 1983.

KAMINSKY, M. A., Protocols for Communicating in the Factory, *IEEE Spectrum*, April, 1986.

KEIL, R. B. MAP in the Factory, *Compcon'86*, pp. 404–5, March 1986.

KEISER, G. *Optical Fiber Communications*, McGraw-Hill, 1983.

KLEINROCK, L. *Queueing Systems. Vol. II, Computer Applications*, John Wiley & Sons, New York, 1976.

KLEINROCK, L. A Decade of Network Development, *Journal of Telecommunication Networks*, pp. 1–11, Spring 1982.

KLEINROCK, L. Distributed Systems, *Communications of the ACM*, vol. 28, pp. 1200–13, Nov. 1985.

KLESSIG, R. W. Overview of Metropolitan Area Networks, *IEEE Communications*, vol. 24, Jan. 1986.

KOCHAN, A., AND COWAN, D. *Implementing CIM*, IFS, 1986.

KONG, T. L. A Simulation of the Transport, Logical Link Control, and Medium Access Control Layers of MAP, Master's thesis, Rensselaer Polytechnic Institute, Troy, N.Y., June 1987.

KOREN, Y. *Computer Control of Manufacturing Systems*, McGraw-Hill, Inc., 1983.

KOREN, Y. *Robotics for Engineers*, McGraw-Hill Inc., 1985.

LATHI, B. P. *Modern Digital and Analog Communication Systems*, CBS College, 1983.

LAURANCE, N. The Use of MMS for Remote CNC Control, *IECON'86*, Milwaukee, Wi., pp. 620–25, Oct. 1986.

LAVENBERG, S. S. *Computer Performance Modeling Handbook*, Academic Press, 1983.

LAW, A. M., AND KELTON, W. D. *Simulation Modeling and Analysis*, McGraw-Hill, Inc., 1982.

LE LANN, G. On Real-time Distributed Computing, *IFIP Congress 83*, Paris, Sept. 1983.

LESSARD, A., AND GERLA, M. Wireless Communications in the Automated Factory Environment, *IEEE Network*, May 1988.

LIENTZ, B. P. *An Introduction to Distributed Systems*, Addison-Wesley, 1981.

LININGTON, P. F. Fundamentals of the Layer Service Definitions and Protocol Specifications. *Proc. IEEE*, vol. 71, pp. 1341–45, Dec, 1983.

LIU, C. R., AND CHANG, T. C. *Integrated and Intelligent Manufacturing*, The American Society of Mechanical Engineers, 1986.

LIU, M. T. AND LI, C. M. Communicating Distributed Processes: A Language Concept for Distributed Programming, in *Local Area Networks*, Proc. IFIP Int. Work. on Local Nets., North-Holland, pp. 375–406, Aug. 1980.

MACNAIR, E. A. AND SAUER CH. H. *Elements of Practical Performance Modeling*, Prentice-Hall, 1985.

MARTIN, J. *Computer Networks and Distributed Processing*, Prentice-Hall, Inc., 1981.

MCNAMARA, J. E. *Technical Aspects of Data Communication*, 2nd Ed., Digital Equipment Corporation, 1982.

MEIJER, A., AND PEETERS, P. *Computer Network Architectures*, Computer Science Press, 1982.

MEISTER, B. W., JANSON, P. A., AND SVOBODOVA, L. Connection-Oriented Versus Connectionless Protocols: A Performance Study, *IEEE Trans. on Computers*, vol. 34, pp. 1164–73, Dec. 1985.

MELLICHAMP, D. A., EDITOR. *Real-Time Computing with Applications to Data Acquisition and Control*, Van Nostrand Reinhold, 1983.

METCALFE, R. M., AND BOGGS, D. R. Ethernet: Distributed Packet Switching for Local Computer Networks, *Communications of the ACM*, vol. 19, pp. 395–404, July 1976.

METZGER, G., AND VABRE, J. P. *Transmission Lines with Pulse Exitation*, Masson and Cie, 1969.

MEYER, J. F., MOVAGHAR, A., AND SANDERS, W. H. Stochastic Activity Networks: Structure, Behavior and Application, *International Workshop on Timed Petri Nets*, Torino, Italy, pp. 106–15, July 1985.

MOREL, L. J. JR. Cell Control Implementation in Discrete Parts Manufacturing, *International Programmable Controllers Conf.*, Detroit, Mi., April, 1987.

MUMPRECHT, E., GANTENBEIN, D., AND HAUSER, R. Timers in OSI Protocols: Specification versus Implementation, *Int. Zurich Seminar on Dig. Comm.*, pp. 93–8, Zurich, Switz., March 1988.

MURALIDHAR K. H., AND PIMENTEL, J. R. Performability Analysis of the Token Bus Protocol, *INFOCOM' 1987*, San Francisco, Ca., pp. 55–63, April 1987.

MURATA, M., AND TAKAGI, H. Two-Layer Modeling of Local Area Networks, *INFOCOM'87*, San Francisco, Ca., pp. 132–40, April 1987.

MURRAY, D. N., AND ENSLOW, P. H. JR. An Experimental Study of the Performance of a Local Area Network, *IEEE Communications*, vol. 22, pp. 48–53, Nov. 1984.

NAGATA, M. Interprocess Communication for Robot Control, *IECON'86*, Milwaukee, Wi., pp. 233–37, Oct. 1986.

NAKAGAMI, T. AND SAKURAI, T. Optical and Optoelectronic Devices for Optical Fiber Transmission Systems, *IEEE Communications*, vol. 26, pp. 28–33, Jan. 1988.

NATARAJAN, N. A Distributed Synchronization Scheme for Communicating Processes, *The Computer Journal*, vol. 29, pp. 109–17, 1986.

NAYLOR, A. W., AND VOLZ, R. A. Design of Integrated Manufacturing System Control Software, *IEEE Trans. on Syst., Man, and Cybernetics*, vol. 17, pp. 881–97, Dec. 1987.

O'GRADY P-J. *Controlling Automated Manufacturing Systems*, Kogan Page Ltd., 1986.

PAKER, Y., VERJUS J-P. *Distributed Computing Systems*, Academic Press, 1983.

PELTON, G. A. Application Architecture for Communications on the Manufacturing Floor, *IECON'86*, Milwaukee, WI., pp. 614–19, Oct. 1986.

PERLMAN, R., HARVEY, A., AND VARGHESE, G. Choosing the Appropriate ISO Layer for LAN Interconnection, *IEEE Network*, vol. 2, pp. 81–86, Jan. 1988.

PETERSON, J. L., AND SILBERSCHATZ. *Operating System Concepts*, 2nd Ed. Addison-Wesley, 1985.

PIMENTEL, J. R. A MAP/TOP Compatible Distributed Database for Manufacturing Applications, *Proc. 15th ISATA Conference, paper No 86027*, Flims, Switzerland, Oct. 1986.

PIMENTEL, J. R. Performance Evaluation of MAP Networks, *IECON'85*, San Frans., CA., pp. 619–30, Nov. 1985.

PITT, D. A., SY, K. K., AND DONNAN, R. Source Routing for Bridged Local Area Networks, *Proc. Globecom*, pp. 1019–23, Dec. 1985.

PRICE D. *Introduction to Ada*, Prentice-Hall, 1984.

PROAKIS, J. G. *Digital Communications*, McGraw-Hill, 1983.

PROFIBUS. PROFIBUS: Process Field Bus, German Standard DIN V 19245 Teil 1: Ubertragunstechnik, Buszugriffs, und ubertragunsprotokoll, Dienstschnittstelle zur Anwendung-Schnitt, Management, Jan. 1988.

RANKY, P. G. *Computer Integrated Manufacturing*, Prentice-Hall, 1986.

RANKY, P. G. *The Design and Operation of FMS*, North-Holland Publishing Company, 1983.

RAUBOLD, E., AND HAENLE, J. A Method of Deadlock-Free Resource Allocation and Flow Control in Packet Networks, *Proc. 3rd Int. Conference on Computer Communic.*, pp. 483–87, Toronto, 1976.

REISER, M. Performance Evaluation of Data Communication Systems, *Proc. IEEE*, vol. 70, pp. 171–96, Feb. 1982.

REMBOLD, U., BLUME C., AND DILLMAN R. *Computer Integrated Manufacturing Technology and Systems*, Marcel Dekker, Inc., New York, 1985, pp. 19–46.

ROBERTS, L. G. AND WESSLER, B. D. The ARPA Network, in *Computer Communication Networks*, Abramson, N. and Kuo, F. F., Editors, Prentice-Hall, Englewood Cliffs, N.J., 1973.

ROSEMBERG, F. An ADA Oriented Protocol for Intertask Communication in Real Time Common Bus Systems, in *Computer Networking and Performance Evaluation*, Hasegawa, T. and others, Editors, North Holland, 1986.

SCHUTZ, H. A. The Role of MAP in Factory Automation, *Proc. IECON'86*, Milwaukee, Wi., pp. 607–13, Oct. 1986.

SCHWARTZ, M. *Computer Communication Network Design and Analysis*, Prentice-Hall, 1977.

SCHWARTZ, M. *Telecommunication Networks*, Addison-Wesley, Reading, Mass. 1987.

SEIFERT, W. M. Bridges and Routers, *IEEE Network*, vol. 2, pp. 57–64, Jan. 1988.

SENIOR, J. M., WALKER, W. M., AND RYLEY, A. Topology and MAC Layer Access Protocol Investigation for Industrial Optical Fibre LANs, *Computer Networks and ISDN Systems*, vol. 13, pp. 275–89, 1987.

SHARMA, R. L., DE SOUSA, P. T., AND INGLE, A. D. *Network Systems, Modeling, Analysis and Design*, Van Nostrand Reinhold Co., 1982.

SHIN, K. G. AND EPSTEIN, M. E. Intertask Communications in an Integrated Multirobot System, *IEEE Journal of Robotics and Automation*, vol. 3, pp. 90–100, April, 1987.

SHIOBARA, Y., MATSUDAIRA, T., SASHIDA, Y., AND CHIKUMA, M. Advanced MAP for Real-Time Process Control, *Proc. IECON'87*, Cambridge, MA., pp. 883–91, Oct. 1987.

SHOCH, J. F. Inter-Network Naming, Addressing, and Routing, *Proc. COMPCON Fall'78 Conference*, pp. 72–79, Sept. 1978.

SHOCH, J. F., AND HUPP, J. A. Measured Performance of an Ethernet Local Network, *Communications of the ACM*, pp. 711–21, Dec. 1980.

SLOMAN M., AND KRAMER J. *Distributed Systems and Computer Networks*, Prentice-Hall International, 1987.

SLOMAN, M. S., AND PRINCE, S. Local Network Architectures for Process Control, North-Holland, pp. 407–28, *Proc. IFIP Int. Work. on Local Nets.*, Zurich, Aug. 1980.

SPANIOL, O. Modelling of Local Computer Networks, *Computer Networks*, vol. 3, pp. 315–26, 1976.

SPENKE, M. Programmer's Interface and Communication Protocol for Remote Procedure Calls, *Informatik-Fachberichte No. 111, Kommunikation in Verteilen Systemen II*, Springer-Verlag, pp. 103–23, March, 1985.

STALLINGS W. *Data and Computer Communications*, Macmillan Publishing, 1985.

STALLINGS, W. *Local Networks*, 2nd Ed., Macmillan Publishing Co., New York, 1987.

STARK, H., AND WOODS J. W. *Probability Random Processes, and Estimation Theory for Engineers*, Prentice-Hall, 1986.

STECKE, E. K., AND SURI, R., editors. *Flexible Manufacturing Systems*, Elsevier Science, 1986.

STUCK, B. W. AND ARTHURS E. *A Computer & Communications Network Performance Analysis Primer*, Prentice-Hall, 1985.

SUMMERS, R. C. A Resource Sharing System for Personal Computers in a LAN: Concepts, Design, and Experience, *IEEE Trans. on Soft. Eng.*, vol. 13, pp. 895–904, Aug. 1987.

SUNSHINE, C. A. Interconnection of Computer Networks, *Computer Networks*, pp. 175–95, 1977.

TAKAGI, H. Mean Message Waiting Times in Symmetric Multi-Queue Systems with Cyclic Service, in *Performance Evaluation*, North-Holland, pp. 271–77, 1985.

TANENBAUM, A. S. *Computer Networks*, Prentice-Hall, Englewood Cliffs, N.J., 1988.

TANENBAUM, A. S., AND VAN RENESSE, R. Distributed Operating Systems, *ACM Computer Surveys*, vol. 17, pp. 419–70, Dec. 1985.

TEMPLE, S. The Design of the Cambridge Ring, in Dallas, I. N., and Spratt, E. B. Editors, *Ring Technology Local Area Networks*, IFIP, Elsevier Science, pp. 79–88, 1984.

THOMPSON, G. O. Comparison of Methods of Implementing a Fiber Optic IEEE 802.3 Ethernet, *Proc. of the SPIE Conference on Fiber Optic Networks*, San Diego, CA, Aug. 1987.

TOENSE, R. E. Performance Analysis of NBSNET, *Journal of Telecommunication Networks*, vol. 2, pp. 177–86, 1983.

TRIPATHI, S. K., HUANG, Y., AND JAJODIA, S. Local Area Networks: Software and Related Issues, *IEEE Trans. on Soft. Eng.*, vol. 13, pp. 872–79, Aug. 1987.

VOLZ, R. A., MUDGE, T. N., AND GAL, D. A. Using ADA as a Robot System Programming Language, *13th Int. Symp., Ind. Robots & Robots 7*, vol. 2, April 1983, Chap. 12, pp. 42–57.

WARE, C. The OSI Network Layer: Standards to Cope with the Real World, *Proc. IEEE*, vol. 71, pp. 1384–87, Dec, 1983.

WILLIAMS, K. MAP Dependence in GMT 400, *Proc. Ultratech*, Long Beach, Ca., pp. 161–71, Sept. 1986.

ZIEMER, R. E., AND TRANTER W. H. *Principles of Communication Systems, Modulation, and Noise*, 2nd Ed. Houghton Mifflin, 1985.

STANDARDS INFORMATION

MAP and TOP material can be obtained from: North American MAP/TOP Users Group, ITRC, P.O. Box 1157, Ann Arbor, MI 48106.

IEEE standards can be obtained from: IEEE Sales Office, 445 Hoes Lane, Piscataway, NJ 08855-1331.

ISO standards can be obtained from: International Telecommunications Union, Place des Nations, 1211, Geneva, Switzerland.

Index

Abstract syntax, 345, 391
Abstract syntax notation one (ASN.1):
  encoder, 578–82
  MAP example, 583
  MMS example, 582
  overview, 576–82
  syntax notation, 577–78
ACSE, 365
Actuators, 422
ADA, 561, 567
  control structures, 566
  data types, 562
Address, 214
  flat, 215
  hierarchical, 215
Advanced factory management system, 432–33
ALOHA, 2, 172
  performance analysis, 506–8
Amplitude shift keying (ASK), 120–26
  power spectral density, 122
  probability of error, 126
Application:
  association (AA), 362, 376
  context, 361
  entity, 362
Application layer, 21, 75, 356–417
  association control service element (ACSE), 363
  distributed applications, 357
  distributed databases, 395
  file transfer, access and management (FTAM), 383
  functions, 357
  manufacturing message specification (MMS), 367
  MAP/TOP, 413
  remote database access, 411
Application processes, 285, 357–59
  conceptual schema, 359
  interworking, 359
  shared schema, 359
  universe of discourse, 359
Application program, 282
Application service element (ASE), 362
ARPANET, 1–4, 216

Association control service element (ACSE), 363
Asynchronous:
  protocols, 143
  transmission system, 143
Asynchronous protocols:
  echo checking, 143
  error control, 143
  flow control, 144
Attenuation, 43
Autocorrelation, 38
Automated manufacturing, 418–41
  characteristics, 440–41
  distributed applications, 525–28
  elements, 421–25
  models, 426
Automated manufacturing research facility (AMRF), 433, 522
Automated warehouses, 424
Automatic repeat request (ARQ), 154

Bandlimited signal, 40
Bandwith:
  channel, 52
  medium, 52
  signal, 43
Baseband communications:
  additive noise, 107
  carrierband, 106
  repeater systems, 107
Bit error probability (*see* Bit error rate)
Bit error rate (BER):
  ASK, 126
  FSK, 126
  PSK, 126
Bit-oriented protocols (*see* Synchronous protocols)
Board level components:
  Intel iSXM554, 467
Box level components:
  Intel 310, 469–70
Broadband communications:
  components:
    amplifiers, 115
    attenuators, 116
    couplers, 116–17
      insertion loss, 117
      tap loss, 117
    directional couplers, 117
    drop cable, 117
    head end, 118
    noise figure, 116
    splitters, 117
    taps, 117
    trunk cable, 117
  modulation, 109
  multiplexing:
    frequency division, 112
    time division, 109–12
      asynchronous, 112
      control bits, 112
      digit interleaving, 112
      pulse code modulation (PCM), 112
      synchronous, 111
      T1 carrier, 112
      word interleaving, 112
Broadcast network, 6
Bus:
  local, 459
  system, 452, 459
Bus interface unit (BIU), 6

Carrier sense multiple access (CSMA), 173–77
  performance analysis, 508–11
  persistent and nonpersistent, 175–77
Carrier sense multiple access with collision detection (CSMA/CD), 177–83
  backoff algorithm, 180
  Intel 82586 LAN coprocessor, 462–67
  jaming signal, 178
  performance analysis, 511
Cascading, 214
Catanet, 4, 233
Cell controller, 369, 525–28
Cell level, 435–40
Cell level network:
  architecture, 547
  requirements, 546–47
Centralized system, 302, 442
Channel access schemes:
  classification, 156
    channel assignment-based, 160
    communication phase-based, 156
      CPCC, 156
      DEDC, 157
      DEDD, 158
      DPDC, 156
Channel, 43–57
  attenuation, 43
  distortionless:
    group delay, 54
    effect on spectral densities, 54
  model, 52
Channel assignments:
  adaptive, 160

Channel assignments (*cont.*)
   attenuation, 43
   demand, 160
   distortionless, 53
   fixed, 160
   model, 52
   phase delay, 54
   random, 160
Channel slot time (CST), 175
Character-oriented protocols, 143
Circuit switching, 7
Cipher, 341
   block, 343
   stream, 343
Client-server model, 368
Closely coupled networks, 11
Coaxial cable, 16
   constants, 50
Coherent demodulation, 125
Collision, 154
Communication:
   devices, 5
   direct, 6
   front end processor, 472
   indirect, 6
Communication networks:
   manufacturing functions, 528
Communication networks for manufacturing applications (CNMA), 4
Computer control system, 442–45
Computer room networks, 17
Computer integrated manufacturing (CIM), 418
   hierarchical model, 431–32
   SME model, 431
Computerized numerical control (CNC), 422
Congestion, 216
Connectionless communications, 73–75
Connectionless mode network service (CLNS), 244
Connection-oriented (*see* Virtual circuits)
Contention, 151
Content synchronization, 142
Context set, 348, 349
Continuous RQ:
   Go-Back-N, 149
   selective retransmission, 147
Control, 427–31
   dynamic, 428
   feedback, 427
   feedforward, 427
   sequence, 428
   supervisory, 429
   system wide, 431
Convolution, 38
Credit, 261

Critical sections, 287
Crosscorrelation, 38
Cryptography, 341
CSMA (*see* Carrier sense multiple access)
CSMA/CD (*see* Carrier sense multiple access with collision detection)
Cycle time, 496
Cyclic codes:
   generator polynomials, 195
   properties, 192, 195
   systematic, 193
      cyclic redundancy check (CRC), 194
      frame check sequence (FCS), 194
Cyclic redundancy check (CRC), 142

Data:
   capability, 323
   compatibility, 330
   normal, 323
   type, 323
Databases:
   models, 398
      hierarchical, 398
      network, 400
      relational, 400
Datagrams (*see* Connectionless communications)
Data encoding:
   bipolar, 96
   design criteria, 92
   duobinary, 97
   encoding rules, 93
   frequency spectrum, 93
   manchester, 97
   on-off, 94
   polar, 95
   split-phase, 97
Data encryption:
   cipher, 341
   code, 341
   cyphertext, 342
   key-based, 343
   plaintext, 342
   public key encryption, 343
   Rivert-Shamir-Adleman (RSA) scheme, 344
Data encryption standard (DES), 343
Data manipulation language (DML), 411
Data transformation, 330
Data link layer, 22, 139–210
   Bitbus, 539–41
   error control, 140
   flow control, 140
   functions, 140
   ISO standards, 184–87, 196–204
   link management, 140

Data link layer (*cont.*)
  MAP/TOP, 204–7
  medium access control, 140
  synchronization, 140–42
    content, 142
    dialog, 142
    frame, 142
    multiple access, 141
Data rate, 10, 90
Deadlocks:
  buffer, 231
  protocol, 230
    store-and-forward lockup, 231
Delay:
  message transmission, 10
  propagation, 8
Deterministic CSMA/CD, 180–83
Dialog:
  management, 311
  synchronization, 311
  two-way alternating (TWA), 310
  two-way simultaneous (TWS), 310
Digital transmission:
  maximum data rate, 91
Dijkstra's algorithm, 218
Directory services, 473, 474
Disjoint process, 285
Distributed database management system (DDBMS), 413
Distributed databases, 395
  data fragmentation, 407
    horizontal, 408
    vertical, 408
  design, 409–10
  reference architecture, 406
  remote database access (RDA), 411
Distribution application, 312, 357
Distributed application process, 357
Distributed system, 280
  loosely coupled, 312
  synchronization, 313
  with centralized control, 315
Distributed system with distributed control:
  fully distributed approach, 317
  nonring structured system, 316
  ring structured system, 316
  token passing approach, 316
Domain, 376
Domain transfer, 373

Echo checking, 143
Encoder:
  channel, 331

  end user, 331, 332
  source, 331
End-to-end propagation delay, 495
End user encoding:
  dialog compression, 332
  editing, 332
  substitution, 332
Energy, 38
Energy signals, 42
Energy per bit, 57
Energy spectral density, 39
Entropy, 336
Error control, 140
Error detection and correction codes:
  block codes, 188
  conditions for detecting and correcting errors, 189
  convolutional codes, 188
  cyclic codes, 192
  systematic codes, 190
Ethernet, 180
Events:
  perceiving, 299
  scheduling, 299
Event management, 379–80
  event action, 380
  event condition, 380
  monitored, 380
  network-trigered, 380
  services, 380

Factory level network, 525
Factory of the future (FOF), 418
Factory of the future (FOF) project:
  automated guided vehicles (AGV), 553
  cell controller, 553–54
  directory services, 555–56
  factory control system, 554–55
  MMFS dialog, 556, 558
  programmable device file server (PDFS), 555
Fieldbus network (*see* Sensor level network)
File consumer, 476–78
File server, 476–78
File transfer, 373
File transfer, access and management (FTAM), 383–95
  activity attributes, 389
  actions on files, 393
  file structures, 390
  functional units, 394
  local file system (LFS), 387
  regimes, 393
  services, 393
  virtual filestore (VFS), 387

Fixed length encoding, 337
Flexible manufacturing system (FMS), 418, 426
Flow control:
  asynchronous protocols, 144
  data link layer, 140
  network layer, 213
  synchronous protocols, 150
    window mechanisms, 150
  Transport layer, 260
Fourier:
  series, 32
  transform, 32
Frame:
  delay, 497
  format, 186, 203, 204
  synchronization, 142
Frequency division multiplexing (FDM), 112–15
Frequency domain representation, 30
Frequency shift keying (FSK):
  phase coherent, 123
  phase continuous, 123
  power spectral density, 124
  probability of error, 126
Frequency spectrum:
  continuous, 37
  discrete, 37
Full conformance network layer protocol, 245
Functional units:
  FTAM, 394
  presentation layer, 349
  session layer, 321

GMT 400 project:
  network architecture, 549–52
  system architecture, 542–49
Go-Back-N (*see* Continuous RQ)

Huffman encoding, 340
Hamming distance, 189
Hierarchical data link model, 140
Hierarchical control, 525–28
Hierarchy:
  control, 522
  device, 572, 524
  network, 525

IEEE 802.4 physical layer:
  implementation, 460–64
  primitives, 128
  services, 128, 130

IEEE 802.3 physical layer:
  attachment unit interface (AUI), 131
  implementation, 462, 467
    accelerated contention resolution, 465
    priority mechanism, 465
    programmable parameters, 466
  medium attachment unit (MAU):
    jabber functions, 133
    monitor functions, 133
  medium dependents interface (MDI), 131
  physical medium attachment (PMA), 131
  physical signaling (PLS), 131–34
  services, 134
IEEE 802.4 protocol (*see* Token bus)
IEEE 802.5 token ring protocol:
  frame format, 187
  token frame, 185
Immediate acknowledgment, 545
Implementation architecture, 450
Implementation:
  application requirements, 449, 453
  architecture, 450, 455
  higher layer, 451
  interfaces, 451, 455
  operating systems, 450
  options, 452
  processors, 450
  programming languages, 450
  standards, 450
  technology, 452
  timers, 451–52
Inactive network layer protocol, 245
Information frames, 200
Initial connection protocol, 259
Intelligent device, 5
Integrated circuits components:
  Intel 82586 LAN coprocessor, 462–67
  token bus controller (TBC), 460–62
Intersymbol interference, 100
  Nyquist's first criterion, 101
  Nyquist's second criterion, 102
ISO network layer standard:
  OSI network service, 239
    connection-oriented, 239
    connectionless, 242
  network layer architecture, 242
    subnetwork access facility (SNACF), 243
    subnetwork dependent convergence facility (SNDCF), 243
    subnetwork independent convergence facility (SNICF), 243
    routing and relaying, 243
ISO presentation layer:
  abstract syntax, 345
  concrete syntax, 346

ISO presentation layer (cont.)
   context set, 348
   functional units, 349
   local syntax, 346
   service facilities, 350
   services, 348, 350
   presentation context, 346
   transfer syntax, 346
ISO session layer:
   activities, 318
   functional units, 319
   services, 321
   token, 319
ISO session layer functional units:
   activity management, 324
   capability data exchange, 323
   duplex, 323
   exceptions, 324
   expedited data, 323
   half duplex, 323
   kernel, 321
   major synchronize, 323
   minor synchronize, 323
   negotiated release, 322
   resynchronize, 324
ISO standards:
   application layer, 367–95, 411
   data link layer, 196–204
   network layer, 239–44
   physical layer, 128–34
   presentation layer, 345–52
   session layer, 318–25
   transport layer, 265–76
ISO transport layer:
   class 4, 268
      protocol, 271
      services, 268
   quality of service, 267
   three-way handshake, 273
   user requirements, 267

LAN (*see* **Local area networks**)
Layer profile (*see* Protocol stack)
Link management, 140
Link connection management, 150
Listen before transmitting (LBT), 174
Listen while transmitting (LWT), 177
Local area networks, 11–19
   applications, 16
   automated manufacturing applications, 18
   characteristics, 12
   topologies, 13
   transmission media, 15

Local syntax, 329
Logical link control (LLC):
   acknowledged connectionless, 197
   classes, 201
   connection-oriented, 197
   format, 201
   immediated response, 197
   protocol, 199
   services, 199
   unacknowledge connectionless, 197
Long haul network, 12
Looping, 223
Lower layers, 250

MAC sublayer:
   CSMA/CD, 203
   frame format, 186, 203, 204
   performance analysis, 512–13
   token bus, 202
   token ring, 184
Machine level network, 542–44
   architecture, 544
   requirements, 544
Manufacturing applications, 519
   case studies, 548–58
      factory of the future, 552–58
      GMT400, 548–52
   cell level network, 546–48
   hierarchical control, 525–28
   machine level network, 542, 546
   network design, 528–32
   sensor level network, 532–42
Manufacturing message specification (MMS):
   event management, 379
   message passing, 373
   object oriented view, 381
   program management, 378
   resource sharing, 373
   variable access, 370
Manufacturing cell, 369, 420
   configurations, 436–37
   control system types, 437–40
      centralized control, 437
      decentralized control, 439
      itemized control, 438
      loading control, 438
   virtual, 434
Manufacturing systems:
   models, 431–40
   organization, 426–31
MAN (*see* Metropolitan area networks)
Manufacturing automation protocol (MAP):
   application layer, 413

Manufacturing automation protocol (MAP)
(*cont.*)
  architectures, 571–75
  data link layer, 204
    LLC sublayer, 205
    MAC sublayer, 206
  directory services, 214
  network layer, 244
  mini-MAP, 545, 574
  physical layer, 134
  presentation layer, 352
  real time, 545–46
  session layer, 325
  transport layer, 276
MAP/EPA, 574
Material transport system, 423
Medium access control (MAC), 6, 140
  communication phases, 152
    attributes, 153
  multiplexing scheme, 152
  polling, 154
  protocols:
    CSMA/CD, 203–4
    token bus, 202–3
    token ring, 184–87
  random access techniques, 154
Medium bandwidth, 52
Message compression, 330
Message security, 330
Mini-MAP, 545, 574
MODIAC, 452
Modulation system:
  performance, 120–27
    bandwidth efficiency, 120
    bit error rate (BER), 125
  power spectral density, 120
Modulation:
  continuous wave, 120
  pulse wave, 119
Monitoring and control, 426–27
Multiplexing:
  frequency division (FDM), 27, 152
  time division (TDM), 27, 152
Multiprogramming system, 282
Multiprocessing system, 283
Multitasking operating system, 283, 378
Multiprocessors, 11
Multiuser system, 283
Mutual exclusion, 287

Network:
  broadcast, 6
  closely coupled, 11
  computer room, 17

  factory automation, 519
  local area, 11
  long haul, 12
  office automation, 17
  personal computer, 17
  point-to-point, 7
  relaying, 6
  switching, 7
Network architectures:
  cell level network, 547, 571–75
  machine level network, 544–46, 571–75
  MAP/TOP, 571–75
  mini-MAP, 574
  sensor level network, 536–42
Network congestion:
  flow control techniques, 224–29
    centralized, 225
    distributed, 228
    flow deviation, 225
  routing techniques, 229–30
Network design problem:
  assumptions, 528–29
  design procedure, 531–32
  problem statement, 529–30
  solution constraints, 530–31
Network interconnection, 233–39
  LAN-to-LAN, 238
  bridge, 235
  brouter, 239
  gateway, 235
  repeater, 235
  router, 235
Network interface unit (NIU), 6
Network layer, 22, 211–49
  addressing, 214
  congestion control, 212
  functions, 211
  internetworking, 212, 233–39
  naming, 214
  protocol, 239–44
  routing, 212
Network management, 475
Network performance:
  MAC sublayer, 512–13
  transport layer, 514–15
Network requirements:
  cell level network, 546
  machine level network, 544
  sensor level network, 434–36
Node architecture (*see* Protocol stack)
Noise:
  crosstalk, 55
  impulse, 55
  thermal, 55

Open system interconnection (OSI):
  architecture, 66–71
  end system, 243
  intermediate system, 243
  reference model, 19–23, 64–66, 75–76
  service conventions, 79–83
  services and protocols, 76, 83
  virtual circuits and datagrams, 71–74
Operating Systems, 280–94
  modules, 284
  multitasking, 283
  processes, 282, 283
  real-time, 283
  scheduling techniques, 290
Operator communications, 373
Optical fibers, 16, 57–64
  advantages, 57
  graded-index, 59
  intermodal dispersion, 60
  modulation index, 62
  photodetector noise, 62–64
  signal attenuation, 61
  step-index, 59, 60
  structure, 58
  transmission link, 58
OSI architecture:
  communication functions, 66, 69
  communication requirements, 66
  communication system, 66
  connection end point (CEP), 70
  connection establishment, 70
  elements, 66
  error control, 70
  flow control, 70
  layers, 67
  multiplexing, 70
  naming, 69
  protocols, 69
  service access points (SAP), 68
  services, 68
OSI model extensions, 83
OSI reference model, 64
  history, 64
  layered architecture, 65
    service specification, 65
    protocol specification, 65
    OSI environment, 65
OSI services and protocols:
  information unit, 79
  interface, 78
  layer, 77
  protocol, 77
  service, 76

OSI service conventions:
  confirmed service, 80
  unconfirmed service, 80
Overlapping processes, 285

Packet radio networks, 4
Path (*see* Route)
Performance analysis:
  ALOHA, 506–7
  CSMA, 508–11
  CSMA/CD, 511
  slotted ALOHA, 507–8
  token bus, 502–5
Performance evaluation:
  analytical models, 487
    approximate, 487
    extended, 490
    stochastic, 489
  applications, 491
  measurements, 491
  simulation, 490
Performance metrics:
  applications, 495
  control service, 493
  transmission service, 494
Performance variables, 485–86
Periodic signals, 32–35
Personal computer networks, 17
Phase shift keying (PSK), 120, 122, 126
  power spectral density, 122
  probability of error, 126
Physical layer, 22, 88–138
  CSMA/CD, 131–34
  functions, 88
  implementation, 460–67
  MAP/TOP, 134–35
  standards, 128–34
  token bus, 128–31
Point-to-point network, 7
Pollaczek-Khinchine (P-K), 501
Polling:
  hub, 155
  roll-call, 154
Power, 38
Power signals, 42
Power spectral density, 41
Presentation context, 346
Presentation layer, 21, 329–52
  data encryption, 341
  data transformation, 330
  functions, 329
  ISO protocol, 345

Presentation layer (*cont.*)
   MAP/TOP, 352
   message compression, 331
Presentation layer functional units:
   context management, 349
   context restoration, 349
   kernel, 349
Processes, 283–90
   application, 357
     distributed, 357
   attributes, 286
   critical sections, 287
   disjoint, 285
   operations, 286
   overlapping, 285
   states, 285
Production planning and control, 418, 420–21, 426–31
Programmable device, 5
Program invocation, 378
   object, 381
Propagation delay, 8
Protocols:
   character oriented, 143
   classification, 143
   implementation, 447
   specification, 455
   start-stop, 143
Protocol data unit (PDU), 79
Protocol implementation, 447–81
   design considerations, 449–52
   design optimization, 457–59
   detailed example, 452–57
   hardware, 448
   software, 448
   timers, 451
Protocol stack, 571
Public key encryption, 345

Query, 405
Queueing theory:
   Little's law, 498
   M/M/1, 499
   M/G/1, 501
   queueing systems, 497–98
     customer, 497
     interarrival time, 497
     server, 497
     service time, 497

Random access schemes:
   ALOHA, 172
   carrier sense multiple access (CSMA), 173
     nonpersistent, 175
     persistent, 175

   carrier sense multiple access with collision detection (CSMA/CD), 177
   slotted ALOHA, 172
Real-time system:
   hard, 283
   soft, 283
Relational databases:
   algebra, 402
   model, 400
   queries, 405
   transactions, 405
Relaying network, 6
Remote database access (RDA):
   transaction management, 411
   two-phase commitment protocol, 412
Ring interface processor (RIP), 7
Robots, 422
Routing:
   algorithm, 215
   table, 215
Routing algorithms:
   congestion based, 229
   dynamic routing, 221
     centralized, 221
     distributed, 222
     isolated, 221
   fixed routing, 219
     directory, 220
     flooding, 220
   incremental routing, 216
   shortest path, 218
   source routing, 216

Satellite networks, 4
Shared resource, 373
Scheduling techniques, 280, 285, 292
   criteria, 291
   feedback queues (FQ), 293
   highest priority first (HPF), 292
   priorities, 292
   round robin (RR), 292
Scrambling, 104
Selective retransmission (*see* Continuous RQ)
Semaphores, 289, 376
Sensors, 422
Sensor level network:
   architectures, protocols, and standards, 536–37
   Bitbus, 538–42
   device and traffic characteristics, 532–34
   requirements, 534–36
Service access point (SAP), 456
Service data unit (SDU), 79

Service primitives:
    confirmed, 80
    unconfirmed, 80
Service provider, 82
Service user, 82
Session layer, 22, 309–28
    data transfer, 311, 314
    dialog management, 311, 315
    dialog synchronization, 315
    functions, 309
    ISO standards, 318–25
    MAP/TOP, 325–26
    protocol issues, 314
Sequence numbers (*see* Synchronous protocols)
Shannon's equation, 91
Shop level network, 525
Shortest path first (SPF), 218
Signal:
    bandlimited, 40
    bandwidth, 29, 43
    distortion over a channel, 55
    nonperiodic, 36
    periodic, 32
    propagation, 30
    time-limited, 40
Signal to noise ratio, 38, 57
Signal transmission, 27–43
Signaling techniques (*see* Data encoding)
Sliding window flow control (SWFC), 260
Slotted ALOHA, 172
Software components:
    iNA960, 470–72
    MAPNET, 472–79
Source coding theorem, 340
Source encoding, 330, 333–41
    digrams, 336
    entropy, 336
    fixed length encoding, 337
    self-information, 336
    source alphabet, 336
    trigrams, 336
    variable length encoding, 339
    words, 336
Standards organizations, 568–70
Store-and-forward switching, 7
Stochastic models, 489–90
Structured query language (SQL), 405
Subnetwork service, 243
Start-stop protocols, 143
Supervisory frames, 201
Syntax:
    abstract, 345
    concrete, 346
    local, 329–46
    transfer, 329, 346

Synchronization:
    content, 142
    dialog, 142
    frame, 142
    monitor, 298
    multiple access, 141
    problem, 300
    process, 314
    resource sharing, 370, 373–78
Synchronization points:
    major, 318, 323
    minor, 318, 323
Synchronous protocols, 144–50
    automatic repeat request (ARQ), 145–46
        idle RQ, 145
        continuous RQ, 146
    continuous RQ:
        selective retransmission, 147
        Go-Back-N, 149
    error control, 144
    flow control, 150
    sequence numbers, 149
Synchronous transmission system, 143
System program, 282
Switching:
    network, 7
    nodes, 7
    store-and-forward, 7

Task (*see* process)
Task context switch, 286
TDM (*see* Time division multiplexing)
Technical and office protocol (TOP):
    application layer, 414
    architecture, 575
    data link layer, 207
    network layer, 246
    physical layer, 135
    presentation layer, 252
    session layer, 326
    transport layer, 277
Three-way handshake, 273
Time division-multiplexing (TDM), 109–12
    asynchronous, 112
    synchronous, 111
Time domain representation, 30
Time limited signal, 40
Timers, 451
Time sharing system, 283
Token:
    bus, 161–87
    data, 319
    major sync/activity, 319, 323

Token (*cont.*)
  minor synchronization, 319, 323
  passing, 153
  release, 319
  ring, 183–87
Token bus, 161–71, 460–62
  access control machine (ACM), 163
  access delay, 164
  dynamic ring maintenance, 165
  fairness, 163
    token hold timer, 164
  fault tolerant aspects, 165
  implementation, 460–62
  performance analysis, 502–5
    exhaustive service, 505
    gated service, 505
    limited service, 505
  priority mechanisms, 164
  symplified protocol, 166
Token rotation timer (TRT), 497
Traffic intensity, 492, 498
Transaction, 405
Transducer, 28
Transfer syntax, 329
Transmission facility, 6
Transport layer:
  connection management, 253
  functions, 250
  ISO standard, 265–75
    class 4 services, 268–71
    class 4 protocol, 271–76
    connection request PDU, 275
    quality of service, 267
  MAP/TOP, 276–77
  model, 254
  performance analysis, 514–15
  services, 252
  use of network services, 256
Transmission channel, 43
Transmission lines, 44–52
  CATV, 49
  characteristic impedance, 47
  coaxial cables, 46, 50
  correctly terminated, 48
  loss free, 47
  parallel-wires, 46, 50
  propagation velocity, 48

Transport protocol data unit (TPDU), 273–75
  connection request (CR), 275
  reincarnated, 274
Transport protocol issues:
  addressing, 258
  flow and error control, 260
  information units, 263
  multiplexing, 259
  protocol operation, 264
  protocol specification, 265
Transport service access point (TSAP), 275
Two phase commitment protocol, 412
Twisted pair wires, 15

Unnumbered frames, 201
Upper layers, 250, 280
User classification, 484–87
  end, 485
  protocol development, 484
  protocol implementor, 484
  value added, 485

Variable:
  access, 370
  local, 370
  remote, 370
Variable length encoding, 339
  Huffman encoding, 340
  source coding theorem, 340
  uniquely decodable, 339
Virtual circuits, 71–73
Virtual manufacturing device (VMD), 376, 382
  object, 382
Vision systems, 425

Wideband communications (*see* Broadband communications)
Window mechanisms, 150
Workstation level, 434

X-on/X-off (*see* Asynchronous protocols, flow control)